The Ciné Goes to Town

The Ciné

RICHARD ABEL

Goes to Town

French Cinema
1896-1914

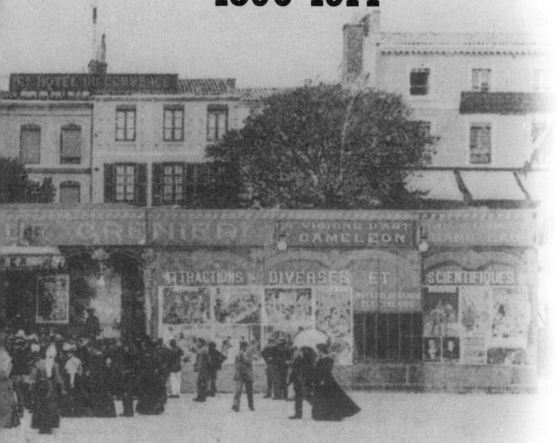

UNIVERSITY OF CALIFORNIA PRESS • BERKELEY LOS ANGELES LONDON

The publisher gratefully acknowledges the contribution
provided by the General Endowment Fund of the Associates of the
University of California Press

University of California Press
Berkeley and Los Angeles, California
University of California Press
London, England
Copyright © 1994
by The Regents of the University of California

Library of Congress Cataloging-in-Publication Data

Abel, Richard, 1941–
  The ciné goes to town : French cinema, 1896–1914 / Richard Abel.
  p.   cm.
Filmography: p.
Includes bibliographical references and index.
ISBN 0-520-07935-3 (alk. paper)
  1. Motion pictures—France—History.   2. Motion picture industry—
France—History.   3. Silent films—France—History and criticism.
I. Title.
PN1993.5.F7A63   1994
791.43′0944′09041—dc20   93-20640

Printed in the United States of America
1   2   3   4   5   6   7   8   9

This one is dedicated to those without whose prior mappings
I may not have been able to trace my own, those with names
like Coissac, Deslandes, Fescourt, Jasset, Jeanne et Ford, Lacassin,
Lapierre, Mitry, and Sadoul.

Piglet sidled up to Pooh from behind.

"Pooh," he whispered.

"Yes, Piglet?"

"Nothing," said Piglet, taking Pooh's paw.

"I just wanted to be sure of you."

A. A. Milne, Winnie-the-Pooh, 1926

Contents

Illustrations   *ix*

Preface   *xiii*

Acknowledgments   *xxi*

Note on Terms   *xxiii*

1 Turn-of-the-Century France   *1*

2 The French Cinema Industry, 1896–1914   *9*
The Big Four, 1896–1902   *10*
Pathé Comes to Power, 1902–1907   *19*
Strategies of Dominance, 1907–1911   *25*
Strategies of Survival, 1911–1914   *46*

3 The Cinema of Attractions, 1896–1904   *59*
Trick Films and *Féeries*   *61*
Comic Films   *87*
Diverging Paths: From *Actualités* to Historical
   and Realist Films   *91*

4 The Transition to a Narrative Cinema, 1904–1907   *102*
The *Bricolage* Model   *105*
The Comic Chase Film and Company   *109*
The Pleasure and Pain of Just Looking: Erotic Films
   and Others   *117*
The Dramatic and Realist Films   *121*
Dissemination and Difference   *136*
The Cinema of Attractions (continued)   *156*

5 The Pre-Feature, Single-Reel Story Film, 1907–1911   *179*
Contemporary Melodramas: Light and Dark Variants   *183*
Comics Come in Series   *215*
Film d'Art and Films d'Art: The Historical Film
   and the Literary Adaptation   *246*
Trick Films and *Féeries*   *278*

6 The Rise of the Feature Film, 1911–1914   *298*
The Historical Film Comes of Age   *302*
Life As It Is: In and Out of Fashion   *326*

Contents

Crime Pays: Detectives Versus Criminals *354*
The Comic Series in Full Swing *388*

Afterword *429*

Filmography *433*

Notes *463*

Bibliography *537*

Index *547*

Illustrations

1. Alice Guy   *12*

2. Méliès Montreuil studio (Georges Méliès, left)   *13*

3. Ferdinand Zecca and Charles Pathé   *15*

4. Cinématographe Grenier (c. 1900)   *16*

5. *Le Petit Journal* (16 May 1897): The fire at the Bazar de la Charité   *18*

6. Pathé's Vincennes studio   *21*

7. Pathé's film splicing lab   *22*

8. Cinématographe Pathé program (1905)   *26*

9. Cinéma Pathé poster (c. 1907)   *30*

10. Gaumont-Palace (renovated, 1911)   *32*

11. Omnia-Pathé exterior (remodeled, 1912)   *56*

12. Omnia-Pathé interior (remodeled, 1912)   *56*

13. *Rêve de Noël,* 1900 (production photo)   *68*

14. *Barbe-bleue,* 1901 (production photo)   *69*

15. *Le Voyage dans la lune,* 1902   *71*

16. *Le Voyage dans la lune,* 1902   *73*

17. *Le Royaume des fées,* 1903   *74*

18. *Le Royaume des fées,* 1903   *75*

19. *La Soubrette ingénieuse,* 1903   *79*

20. *Metamorphose du papillon,* 1904   *80*

21. *Le Cakewalk chez les nains,* 1903   *81*

22. *Don Quichotte,* 1903   *84*

23. *Le Chat botté,* 1903   *86*

24. *Ma Tante,* 1903 (Dranem)   *89*

25. *Un Drame au fond de la mer,* 1901   *97*

26. *Histoire d'un crime,* 1901   *98*

27. *Victimes de l'alcoolisme,* 1902 (poster)   *100*

28. *Victimes de l'alcoolisme,* 1902   *100*

29. *Dix Femmes pour un mari,* 1905 (production photo)   *110*

30. *Toto fait de la peinture,* 1907   *115*

31. *Les Petits Vagabonds,* 1905   *116*

32. *Les Petits Vagabonds,* 1905   *116*

33. *En Vacances,* 1906 (title frame)   *117*

34. *En Vacances,* 1906   *117*

35. *La Grève,* 1904 (poster)   *122*

36a, b. *Au pays noir,* 1905   *125*

37. *Au pays noir,* 1905   *126*

38. *Au pays noir,* 1905   *126*

39. *Honneur d'un père,* 1905   *129*

40. *La Loi du pardon,* 1906   *134*

41. *Le Matelas alcoolique,* 1906   *142*

42. *L'Homme animanté,* 1907 (production photo)   *143*

43. *Le Nihiliste,* 1906   *146*

44. *Le Nihiliste,* 1906   *146*

45. *L'Espionne,* 1907   *148*

46. *La Fille du Corse,* 1907   *149*

47. *La Fille du Corse,* 1907   *149*

48. *Les Quatre Cent Farces du diable,* 1906 (production photo)   *159*

49. *La Vie du Christ,* 1906   *165*

50. *La Vie du Christ,* 1906   *165*

51. *La Vie du Christ,* 1906   *165*

52. *La Vie du Christ,* 1906   *165*

53. *La Poule aux oeufs d'or,* 1905 (poster)   *172*

54. *La Poule aux oeufs d'or,* 1905   *174*

55. *Cendrillon,* 1907 (poster)   *177*

56a, b, c. *The Pirates,* 1907   *189*

57. *The Pirates,* 1907   *190*

58. *The Pirates,* 1907   *190*

59. *The Pirates,* 1907   *190*

60. *Le Contremaître incendiaire,* 1908   *191*

61. *Le Contremaître incendiaire,* 1908   *192*

62. *A Narrow Escape,* 1908   *194*

63. *A Narrow Escape*, 1908   *194*

64. *Nick Carter*, 1908 (poster)   *197*

65. *L'Homme aux gants blancs*, 1909   *200*

66. *L'Homme aux gants blancs*, 1909 (Jacques Grétillat)   *200*

67. *L'Homme aux gants blancs*, 1909   *200*

68. *Nuit de Noël*, 1908 (poster)   *203*

69. *Rembrandt de la rue Lepic*, 1911 (production photo)   *224*

70. *Tout est bien qui finit bien*, 1910   *239*

71. *Max hypnotise*, 1910 (Max Linder)   *242*

72. *Les Débuts de Max Linder au cinématographe*, 1910   *245*

73. *Le Fils prodigue*, 1907   *247*

74. *L'Assassinat du Duc de Guise*, 1908 (poster)   *250*

75. *L'Assassinat du Duc de Guise*, 1908 (Charles Le Bargy, left)   *251*

76. *L'Assassinat du Duc de Guise*, 1908   *251*

77. *L'Assassinat du Duc de Guise*, 1908   *251*

78. *L'Assassinat du Duc de Guise*, 1908 (Gabrielle Robinne, Albert Lambert)   *252*

79. *L'Assassinat du Duc de Guise*, 1908   *252*

80. *Cléopatre*, 1910 (Stacia Napierkowska, Madeleine Roch)   *259*

81. *L'Arrestation de la Duchesse de Berry*, 1910   *261*

82. *Werther*, 1910   *262*

83. *La Mort du Duc d'Enghien*, 1909 (Georges Grand, right)   *269*

84. *Christophe Colomb*, 1910   *273*

85. *Christophe Colomb*, 1910   *273*

86. *Christophe Colomb*, 1910   *273*

87. *Christophe Colomb*, 1910   *273*

88. *Cagliostro*, 1910 (Henry Krauss, Stacia Napierkowska)   *276*

89. *Tormented by His Mother-in-law*, 1908 (production photo: Max Linder)   *279*

90. *Les Chrysanthèmes*, 1907   *285*

91. *Fantasmagorie*, 1908   *287*

92. *Une Excursion incohérente*, 1910   *290*

93. *Notre Dame de Paris*, 1911 (Henry Krauss, left)   *306*

94. *Notre Dame de Paris*, 1911 (Claude Garry, Stacia Napierkowska)   *307*

95. *Le Siege de Calais*, 1911 (production photo)   *309*

96. *Le Siege de Calais*, 1911   *310*

97. *Madame Sans-Gêne*, 1911 (production photo: Gabrielle Réjane, Jacques Volnys, Georges Dorival)   *313*

98. *La Dame aux camélias*, 1912 (Sarah Bernhardt, Lou Tellegen)   *315*

99. *Queen Elizabeth*, 1912 (production photo: Sarah Bernhardt)   *317*

100. *Les Misérables*, 1912 (Marie Ventura, Henry Krauss)   *322*

101. *Les Misérables*, 1912 (production photo: Henry Krauss)   *324*

102. *Les Vipères*, 1911 (production photo)   *330*

103. *La Broyeuse des coeurs*, 1913 (production photo: Léontine Massart)   *337*

104. *Le Signalement*, 1912 (Jean Kemm, Marie Fromet)   *339*

105. *Sacrifice surhumain*, 1914 (production photo: Jean Dax, Suzanne Delve)   *349*

106. *Le Mystère des Roches de Kador*, 1912   *353*

107. *Nick Winter: Le Pickpocket mystifié*, 1911   *355*

108. *Nick Winter: Le Pickpocket mystifié*, 1911   *355*

109. *Nick Winter: Le Pickpocket mystifié*, 1911   *356*

110. *Zigomar contre Nick Carter*, 1912   *362*

111. *Zigomar contre Nick Carter*, 1912 (Josette Andriot, Alexandre Arquillière, Charles Krauss)   *362*

112. *Fantômas*, 1913 (René Navarre)   *372*

113. *Juve contre Fantômas*, 1913   *375*

114. *Juve contre Fantômas*, 1913 (René Navarre, Yvette Andreyor)   *375*

115. *Le Mort qui tue*, 1913 (Luitz-Morat)   *378*

116. *Le Faux Magistrat*, 1914 (René Navarre)   *380*

117. *L'Enfant de Paris*, 1913 (Jean-Marie Laurent, Suzanne Prévet, Emile Keppens)   *382*

Illustrations

118. *L'Enfant de Paris*, 1913 (Maurice Lagrenée) *383*

119. *Rosalie et sa phono*, 1911 (Sarah Duhamel) *392*

120. *Little Moritz aime Rosalie*, 1911 *394*

121. *Boireau cuirassier*, 1912 (André Deed) *401*

122. *Calino sourcier*, 1913 (poster) *403*

123. *Onésime horloger*, 1912 (Ernest Bourbon) *406*

124. *Max pédicure*, 1914 (Max Linder) *416*

125. *Léonce à la campagne*, 1913 (Léonce Perret) *422*

126. *Léonce à la campagne*, 1913 (Valentine Petit) *422*

127. *Léonce à la campagne*, 1913 (Léonce Perret, Valentine Petit) *422*

128. *Léonce à la campagne*, 1913 (Léonce Perret) *422*

129. *Léonce cinématographiste*, 1913 (production photo: Georges Specht, Léonce Perret, Bout-de-zan) *424*

130. *Champignol malgré lui*, 1914 (production photo) *426*

Preface

What one writes . . . is . . . the history of the situations of the texts,
and not some "history" of the texts themselves. . . .
FREDRIC JAMESON

The "eye" is a product of history reproduced by education.
PIERRE BOURDIEU

THIS BOOK IS CONCEIVED as an extension of my previous work on the silent cinema in France, but it also attempts to address a nagging sense of dissatisfaction. Soon after completing *French Cinema: The First Wave, 1915–1929* (1984), I realized that I had accepted far too many assumptions about the first two decades of film history, most specifically about how the French cinema industry was organized and operated, how it was positioned vis-à-vis the American cinema industry, and what principles of representation and narration governed its production. In the initial section of *French Film Theory and Criticism, 1907–1939* (1988), I took some steps to address that deficiency by uncovering and analyzing a broad spectrum of French discourse on the cinema prior to the Great War. Yet whatever success that book may have garnered as a portable archive and a revision of film theory history, certain writers and texts, I have since discovered, were either left out entirely—as is the case with Edmond Benoît-Lévy of *Phono-Ciné-Gazette* (1905–1908)—or else badly shortchanged—for instance, Victorin Jasset's early sketch of cinema history in *Ciné-Journal* (1911). This current book, however, is not just one more attempt to "get it right"; instead, it offers an extensive excavation and reassessment of the French cinema between 1896 and 1914, particularly during those years when Pathé-Frères led the world in film production and distribution, roughly from 1904 to 1911. Put simply, I mean to reinstate French films at the center of early cinema history and recover their contribution to the cinema's development as a major mass culture industry of the "moving image."

Such a study, of course, involves a fundamental assumption that cannot go unexamined—that the concept of a national cinema is a viable epistemological category for this period. Despite a certain "international" character to early cinema, such an assumption is not without justification. First of all, the French cinema can be situated economically within the historical context of imperialism—in the sense used by Eric Hobsbawm that the world economy of capitalism had become an aggregate of rival national economies engaged in colonial conquest—which defined Europe as well as the United States at the turn of the century. The space of colonial expansion, along with that constructed by the more direct trading rivalry between national economies, provided a field of exploitation for Pathé-Frères when it became the first film company to move into mass production in 1904–1905. Second, the French cinema can be situated

xiii

within the related historical context of nationalism, specifically in terms of the institutions and practices that defined the French Third Republic as a distinct nation-state. Although the new secular system of education served as the principal bonding agent of late nineteenth-century French society, a loose network of new mass culture practices proved increasingly crucial during the period. Within this network, the cinema quickly assumed a significant role, especially through the appropriation of a historically specific cultural tradition, so that certain film genres gained a privileged importance—the trick film and the *féerie*, the comic series, the biblical film, the historical film, and the *grand guignol* version of melodrama. Finally, the French cinema can be situated historically according to its definition under French law, for the courts consistently classed the cinema as a *spectacle de curiosité*, subjecting it to the control and censorship of local officials. In 1906, a state decision to end all censorship restrictions against the theater provoked efforts by the industry to upgrade the cinema's status. The consequences of this move to align the cinema with the theater were profound— the theater analogy, at the level of both commerical enterprise and critical discourse, became more deeply engrained in France than anywhere else. That these economic, cultural, and legal practices gave the French cinema a high degree of historical specificity makes all the more valid an interrogation of the early French cinema as a more or less distinct national cinema.

During the past fifteen years, several archaeological projects have stimulated renewed interest in the study of early cinema. The 1978 Congress of the International Federation of Film Archives (FIAF), held in Brighton, England, probably was most responsible for renewing this interest, in that it brought archivists and academics together for one full week to view nearly six hundred fiction films made between 1900 and 1906, many of them newly rediscovered and printed. The Brighton Project, as this collaborative endeavor soon came to be called, encouraged other retrospective screenings, many of them organized in terms of national cinemas, perhaps most significantly at the annual "Giornate del cinema muto" in Pordenone, Italy (launched in 1982), the annual film festival sponsored by the Institut Jean Vigo in Perpignan, France, and the biennial conference organized by the international association, Domitor.[1] In the wake of these screenings as well as further archive discoveries and restorations, historical scholarship has advanced primarily along two paths. One has followed the Brighton Project in reexamining the first ten years of the cinema's emergence worldwide, a period for which the term *primitive cinema* generally has been replaced by André Gaudreault and Tom Gunning's less pejorative and more accurate *cinema of attractions*. The second path has followed that opened up by Noël Burch and Barry Salt and has focused on the gradual formation of the so-called classical American cinema and its continuity system during the early 1910s—a path for which David Bordwell, Janet Staiger, and Kristin Thompson's *The Classical Hollywood Cinema* (1985) serves, at least for now, as a culmination. Until recently, the transition between these two kinds of cinema, however, has received scant attention, except when that transition has been read in terms of a teleological development whose inevitable end was the American model of a narrative cinema. And the hegemony of this American model has produced a singular lacuna—near silence, despite the well-documented prominence of Pathé-Frères at the time, on the French contribution to the emergence of early narrative cinema.[2]

If one posits the transition from a cinema of attractions to a narrative cinema as a kind of paradigm shift during these first two decades, and sees the French cinema as providing a crucial impetus to that shift, then one has to reconceptualize early cinema in terms of a new schema of periodization. In this schema, the cinema of attractions dominates much of the first decade, between 1896 and 1904, as *actualités*, trick films, féeries, and short comic acts become increasingly popular within the variety format of such spectacles as music halls, wax museums, and *fêtes foraines* or fairgrounds, where exhibitors could select and edit their own films. The transition to a narrative cinema gets underway between 1904 and 1907, as Pathé-Frères takes the lead in producing story films—in order to wrest authorial and editorial control from exhibitors—and constructs a synthetic model of representation and narration, particularly in what the company calls its "dramatic and realist" films. The single-reel, pre-feature story film then consolidates this model between 1907 and 1911, with variations emerging among both French and American production companies (the latter of which begin to challenge Pathé) as well as between various genres of film. Indeed, this consolidation occurs as one of several strategies to legitimize the cinema within the variety format of a growing number of permanent cinemas. Finally, between 1911 and 1914, the American model of continuity editing begins to emerge, in parallel with the development of the multiple-reel film into the feature-length film, which quickly begins to contest the dominance of the single-reel story film. And this move to features is supported by the construction of new "palace" cinemas in imitation of the legitimate theater. Although its rise was initially impelled by French producers who, in conjunction with their counterparts in Italy and Denmark, were seeking to market a new, distinctive product, the feature-length film would also be appropriated by American producers just before the outbreak of war. Consequently, it can be argued that the French cinema played a significant role throughout three more or less discrete stages in the transition to a narrative cinema, including the development of both the single-reel and the feature-length film.

Following the contours of this periodization schema, one of the major aims of this book is to reconstruct the emerging system of representation and narration which governed the production of early French fiction films. Such a reconstruction has to address a number of questions. How did the narrative cinema, for instance, constitute both a break with and a continuation of the cinema of attractions in its negotiation between spectacle or display and narration? As the narrative cinema developed, what were the initial parameters of its articulation as a system of spatial coherence and temporal linearity, especially in terms of mise-en-scène, framing, and editing? Also, what was the function within that system of such adjunct elements as intertitles and musical accompaniment? Were the characteristic features of that system distributed evenly or differently according to film production companies, and how did the popularity or strategic importance of particular film genres affect that distribution? Furthermore, what changes occurred in the shift from single-reel to feature-length films? More generally, how were the narrative cinema's parameters of articulation defined in relation to those of prior French cultural practices, especially other mass spectacles, and how did changes in those parameters correspond to those marking related cultural practices in the early twentieth century? Finally, given the emergence of an American continuity system in the early 1910s, did the French cinema depend on a partially overlapping, yet alternative model of representation and narration to that which ultimately would become dominant in the American cinema?

In reconstructing a textual system of representation and narration, however, one is also reconstructing the ideological mechanisms of that system, in which a body of films works on and is worked on by a body of spectators. The process of signification or "making of meaning" in any discourse is always framed according to culturally established categories of social experience. Given the ideological importance of the new mass cultural practices in Third Republic France, the cinema can be seen as an increasingly influential locus for the construction of social identity or subjectivity, especially at the point of reception. This, too, demands that one address certain key questions. In what ways are the representational strategies of the early French cinema, along with their sites of reading and interpretation, specifically mapped according to a referential body of Third Republic social relations? Do those relations tend to be determined by certain hierarchies of difference—for instance, class, gender, generation, race, or region—providing crucial axes of subject construction for the existing social order? How are specific film genres closely bound up with particular sets of social relations of difference, and do the constituent elements of that nexus shift from one period to another? Finally, how seriously can the cinema interrogate and even critique those relations when its principal function, much like other mass cultural practices, is to reproduce and legitimize the social order—particularly by constructing a space as well as providing models of identity and integration for the white-collar employees and civil servants so crucial to the *embourgeoisement* of turn-of-the-century French society? If, as a textual system of representation and narration, the French cinema existed in a continual state of renegotiation over time, then, as a cultural practice, it constituted an ideological site of constant struggle and conflict, in which the hegemony of the dominant French culture also was continually up for renegotiation.

Given the exigencies of time for research, access to materials, and the acumen of the researcher, any historical study is shaped, in part, by the sources it chooses or else is forced to privilege over others. Within the broad range of sources or documents from which one could construct a history of early French cinema, I rely extensively on two particular kinds of material. These include approximately seven hundred surviving film prints in various archives and private collections and the published discourse on the French cinema during the period—from advertisements to theoretical pieces—most of it appearing in trade journals and newspapers in France, England, and the United States. These have been supplemented by business correspondence, personal letters and memoirs, prior histories, and critical studies. Such a hierarchy of source material determines, to some extent, the tasks I have set myself. First of all, I have placed the films themselves at the center of my historical analysis and interpretation, generally framing them within the genre categories used by Pathé and others during the period—as "social contracts," to borrow Fredric Jameson's language, which provide guidelines for their "proper use" as "cultural artifacts."[3] Second, since all but a few film prints are unavailable for public screening, I have tried, through extensive description and reprinting of frame stills, to present or represent as many of those films as possible—almost as a kind of portable archive—in hopes of making them more accessible for teaching purposes as well as for further research. Third, for each film title described and analyzed, I have sought to provide precise, accurate documentation establishing the date of release (depending on the country), the personnel involved in production (where known), and some of the physical characteristics of the source print (for instance, length in meters or feet, the number and placement of intertitles, the "coloring" of the film stock). The textuality of a certain body of film prints, then, forms the basis of this history, even if the sense I make of the films is predicated on both their intertextual relation with other French cultural practices and their mapping of Third Republic social relations.

Doing history this way, of course, has its risks. The surviving prints available for viewing represent only a small fraction of the French films produced between 1896 and 1914. Although a good percentage of Georges Méliès's films has come down to us, partly because of Gaston Méliès's paperprint deposits (for copyright purposes) at the Library of Congress as well as the dedicated research of Les Amis de Georges Méliès, the survival rate for the output of other companies and filmmakers has been uneven. Almost nothing survives, for instance, of Alice Guy's work for Gaumont (1898–1906), only a few survive of the hundreds of films produced later by Eclipse and by Lux, slightly more than one hundred titles have come down to us from Eclair, and even more from Gaumont (that is, after 1909). If a greater percentage of Pathé-Frères films is still extant, chiefly because the number of prints distributed around the world was so large to begin with,[4] that is not the case with those produced by Pathé's subsidiaries—for instance, SCAGL (Société Cinématographique des Auteurs et Gens des Lettres), SAPF (Séries d'Art Pathé-Frères), and even Film d'Art—especially after 1909, when Charles Pathé took the draconian measure of recycling much of his company's (used) positive film stock in order to have the quantities of negative film stock required to continue operation. Furthermore, the "authenticity" of many surviving film prints is sometimes difficult to determine. For one thing, until at least 1906–1907, an exhibitor could make any kind of changes he might wish to the films he purchased, which promoted a wide range of textual variance in performance. For another, very few prints even from after that date now exist in the condition of their initial release—they have lost beginnings and endings, titles and intertitles, as well as whole shots or scenes, and some have been reedited at a later date. Matching a film print with the description originally published in a company catalogue or trade journal can sometimes establish a degree of certainty about a specific film title, yet release prints of the same film title could still differ greatly from country to country. Together, the dearth of surviving film prints and the questionable textual authenticity of those that have make the task of describing and analyzing early French films rather perilous.[5]

Perhaps the least examined area in this history, a space left open for further research, is that involving the historical reception of films—that is, the range of readings performed by groups of historical spectators in France before the Great War. The problems in exploring this space are legion: the relative scarcity of "evidence," the difficulty in recovering it from reviews, articles, government documents, and company records, and the need to theorize whatever is recovered as already mediated discourse. One of the most vivid descriptions of spectatorship before the war—Sartre's account in *Les Mots* (1964)—for instance, was written nearly fifty years after the experience. Yet, further work obviously has to be done in establishing more precisely, for France, the social constitution of its spectators, the social meaning of "going to the cinema" there, and the specific ways the cinema elicited and fulfilled expectations of pleasure. My own analysis of early French cinema, however, creates an additional problem, for to single out discrete film texts for discussion, of course, is to do violence to the way the cinema was experienced at the time, particularly by spectators in the music halls and fêtes foraines. It constructs a somewhat artificially defined, fixed object of study, one dependent on the conceptual framework of French film producers and distributors as well as the survival status of film prints. Despite these problems, interrogating individual films within the genre categories of the period does recognize, to paraphrase Raymond Williams, the conditions of their articulation and circulation as cultural forms.[6] And that, in turn, opens onto the reconstruction of the French "public sphere" and its range of possible "reading practices" or "reading positions,"[7] within the context of which individual films and groups of films—as historically specific forms of symbolic representation—might be interpreted and appropriated. If this history does not offer a full account of how films were seen and used and by whom in France—unlike the recent, finely detailed work on the early American cinema—it does go some way toward uncovering the textual and contextual determinants of those spectators' response.

This book is apportioned into five major sections, preceded by a short prologue. The prologue sketches the economic, political, and cultural institutions and forces structuring Third Republic France at the turn of the century and is offered not simply as background but as an initial exploration of how the early French cinema was actively embedded in a particular social formation. The first major section then writes a detailed history of the French cinema industry divided into stages generally predicated on changes in Pathé's organizational structure and strategy of operation. The following four sections more or less parallel that division—although the economic, political, and cultural lines of development are never perfectly aligned—and presents a sustained argument that French films played a crucial role in the transition to a narrative cinema. The first of these sections surveys the spectrum of genre films constituting the cinema of attractions, between 1896 and 1904, and distinguishes between those closely adhering to that paradigm and others already beginning to deviate from it. The second section tracks the shift, between 1904 and 1907, from the cinema of attractions to a narrative cinema through several models of transformation, culminating in their synthesis, mapped according to a specific referential body of social relations, in Pathé's "dramatic and realist" films. The third then traces their consolidation into a relatively coherent system of representation and narration governing the single-reel film, between 1907 and 1911, with local variations, including referential mapping, in such genres as the comic series, the contemporary story film, and the historical film. The fourth and final section focuses on the transition from single-reel to feature-length films, again tracking changes in the now-established narrative cinema paradigm across the historical film, the contemporary melodrama, the crime film, and its lesser corollary, the detective film. And in the ending of this last section lies another beginning. For the argument this book articulates extends beyond its boundaries into a story I have already once told before, in *French Cinema: The First Wave, 1915–1929*, but a story that may need to be retold again through a similar framework of re-vision.

Acknowledgments

A TIMELY AND MUCH appreciated grant from the American Council of Learned Societies (1986), together with a sabbatical leave from Drake University, allowed me to initiate this project with several research forays into a half-dozen film archives in Europe and the United States. For writing the first draft of the manuscript, I was fortunate to have the support of a one-year fellowship (1988–1989) at the National Humanities Center, whose splendid, efficient staff were more than a match for the sylvan surroundings. Throughout the past six years of research and writing, the Center for the Humanities at Drake University generously has provided funds for specific archive trips and research acquisitions (the most important being microfilm copies of a half-dozen early French film journals).

Particular archivists and archives have been extremely helpful, not only providing access to a wide range of research materials, but pointing me in new directions and correcting errors in documentation. In the United States and Canada, they include Paolo Cherchi Usai at the George Eastman House, Susan Dalton and Elias Savada at the National Center for Film and Video Preservation, Paul Spehr and Patrick and Katherine Loughney at the Library of Congress, Eileen Bowser and Charles Silver at the Museum of Modern Art, Robert Daudlin at the Cinémathèque Québécois, George Tselos at the Edison National Historical Site, and Murray Glass at Em Gee Film Library.

In Europe, they include Vincent Pinel, Renée Lichtig, Glenn Myrent, and others at the Cinémathèque Française, Michelle Aubert and her staff at the Archives du Film, Laure Forestier at the Cinémathèque Gaumont, Emmanuelle Toulet and her staff at the Bibliothèque de l'Arsenal, Elaine Burrows, Jackie Morris, and their staff at the National Film Archive, Hoos Blotkamp, Ivo Blom, Frank van der Maden, Peter Westervoorde, and others at the Nederlands Filmmuseum, the late Jacques Ledoux at the Royal Film Archive of Belgium; and the organizing committee (particularly Lorenzo Codelli and Paolo Cherchi Usai) for the annual Pordenone Silent Film Festival.

I am especially indebted to several colleagues in cinema studies for reading the manuscript at various stages. Donald Crafton and Alan Williams wrote thorough, knowledgeable reader's reports, with numerous emendations and suggestions for revision. Tom Gunning also read large sections of the manuscript and offered valuable ideas, from reconceptualizing analyses and arguments to correcting small points of documentation. Others who have provided help at one time or another include Dudley Andrew, Christian Belaygue, David Bordwell, Lenny Borger, Ben Brewster, Roland Cosandey, Bernard Eisenschitz, André Gaudreault, Charles Keil, Jacques Kermabon, Antonia Lant, Thierry Lefebvre, Eric Le Roy, Richard Maltby, Sara Maza, Charles Musser, Patricia O'Brien, Roberta Pearson, Doug Riblet, Barry Salt, Ben Singer, Kristin Thompson, William Uricchio, and Ginette Vincendeau.

At Drake University, I am pleased to have had the intellectual support of the Cultural Studies Reading Group, and I thank the staff of Educational Media Services who prepared many of the photograph illustrations as well as those running the Inter-Library Loan Services with such efficiency.

At the University of California Press, I am grateful to have had Edward Dimendberg's enthusiastic support for the manuscript as well as his useful suggestions and patience during its final revision. I also am pleased to have had Rebecca Frazier handle the book's production so graciously and efficiently and to have had Diane Mark-Walker perform such a meticulous job of copyediting. And I am indebted to Joanna Hitchcock who, despite overwhelming odds, gave unstinting encouragement to this project.

Finally, once again I speak of my deepest debt to the one who has most inspired, delighted, and pleased me during this long period of writing, who has read and commented incisively on every version of the manuscript—a superb writer and scholar in her own right—my best reader and collaborator, Barbara Hodgdon.

Permission has been granted to reprint portions of this book, which originally appeared in different formats in *Post Script* 7 (Fall 1987), *Screen* 30 (Summer 1989), *French Cultural Studies* 1 (1990), *iris* 11 (1990), *Griffithiana* 44/45 (1992), and *Griffithiana* 47 (1993).

Illustration Acknowledgments

George Eastman House: 31, 32, 33, 34, 46, 47, 56a-b-c, 57, 58, 59, 65, 66, 67, 70, 72, 90, 107, 108, 109, 120, 125, 126, 127, 128.

British Film Institute: 13, 20, 23, 25, 28, 39, 40, 41, 45, 98, 99.

Cinémathèque Française: 22, 82, 88, 94, 96, 97, 101, 103, 105.

Nederlands Filmmuseum: 53, 117, 119, 122, 130.

Paolo Cherchi Usai/David Turconi Collection: 17, 18, 30, 36a-b, 37, 38, 43, 44, 54, 60, 61, 71, 73, 80, 83, 84, 85, 86, 87.

Paolo Cherchi Usai: 49, 50, 51, 52, 81.

Donald Crafton: 10, 91.

Tom Gunning: 62, 63.

Note on Terms

IN THOSE SECTIONS of the book devoted to close textual analysis, my descriptions of specific shots rely (for reasons of space) on notational acronyms designating camera distance and angle that have become widely used in cinema studies. They include the following:

    ECU   extreme close up
    CU   close up (the shot of a face or object)
    MCU   mid close up (the shot of a person from the chest up)
    MS   mid shot (the shot of a person from the waist up)
    AS   "American shot" (the shot of a person from the knees up)
    FS   full shot (the shot of a person from the feet up)
    LS   long shot
    ELS   extreme long shot
    HA   high angle (a shot taken from above eye level, looking down)
    LA   low angle (a shot taken from below waist level, looking up)

When a film's mise-en-scène combines two or more planes of interest within the frame, I use a double acronym, such as MS/LS or even HA MS/LS. Only one other acronym appears frequently—POV, for point-of-view shot.

    In referring to specific films throughout the book, I use the French title circulated at the time of the film's release in France. When the French title is unknown or uncertain, I use the English title given for the film's release in the United States or England.

1

Turn-of-the-Century France

In societies where modern conditions of production prevail,
all of life presents itself as an immense accumulation of spectacles.
GUY DEBORD

THE PARIS "UNIVERSAL EXPOSITION," which opened on 15 April and ran
through 12 November 1900, was designed, according to one of its guidebooks,
to celebrate the world's progress over the course of the past hundred years and
to serve as a "dawning beacon for the twentieth century."[1] That progress was
defined globally in terms of European or, rather, French domination (and racial
superiority) over the rest of the world through what Maurice Talmeyr reported
as an "ornamental delirium" of colonial pavilions and native villages spilling over
the Trocadéro.[2] And it was positioned in time through Disneyland-like attractions
that nostalgically appealed to past ways of life—for instance, an "Old Paris" of
reconstructed medieval streets, and a complete Swiss peasant village surrounded
by artificial mountains, forests, and streams. As the principal sign of progress,
however, the Exposition's planners selected their exhibits and events to pay
homage, not as before to industrial machinery, but to "the magic of electricity."
The "spectacles of light" on and about the Champs du Mars ranged from Venetian celebrations using illuminated boats on the Seine to Salles des Fêtes projections of Lumière films and photographs on a giant sixty-by-seventy-foot screen.
But perhaps the most popular of these was "the sparkling Palace of Electricity
whose ornate white facade at night" Charles Rearick has aptly described "as a
starry backdrop for a rainbow-brilliant thirty-foot-wide sheet of water cascading ninety-five feet in a Château d'Eau."[3] Such a "fairyland of electricity"
seemed a perfectly planned environment to symbolize the "cultural revolution"—at least in the "First World" of advanced capitalist development—that
was ushering in a century increasingly devoted to leisure and mass consumption.

The 1900 Exposition that put Paris at "the center of the universe," however,
also masked certain fundamental economic conditions in France. The prolonged
economic depression that afflicted the agricultural sectors of the world economy
from 1873 to 1896, for instance, proved especially costly in France, with its still
largely rural population. According to French historians such as Jean-Marie
Mayeur and Madeleine Rebérioux,[4] the decline in agricultural productivity acted
as a brake on industrial productivity, and French agriculture continued to lag
behind industry as the latter's production rose rapidly after 1905. Furthermore,
the larger French banks tended not to invest in industrial enterprises, which all

1

too well complemented the French firms' own obsession with preserving their independence—outside bank financing, for instance, comprised only 29 percent of total industrial investment. Instead, a good deal of the capital amassed by the banks was exported as direct private investment in allied countries such as Russia, and the government tended to side with banking rather than industrial capital in such matters. In 1904, for instance, the symbol of French metallurgy (and weaponry), Le Creuset, was shut out of negotiations over the French annexation of Morocco.

Consequently, even though it could sustain its position as the second greatest financial power in the world, the French national economy actually slipped, in terms of industrial production, from second to a distant fourth place behind the United States, Germany, and Britain, accounting for only 11 percent of worldwide production just before the war. Large-scale industrialization and its attendant principles of economic concentration in "trusts" and scientific management—which governments throughout the Third Republic actively and consistently discouraged as a violation of the ideal of a "balanced economy"— thus came rather slowly to France. For innovative, high-quality, labor-intensive goods continued to be prized more than the sheer quantity that could result from mass production. In 1896, for instance, whereas 84 percent of industrial firms had just one to four employees, only slightly more than 1 percent had more than fifty. Saint-Gobin, which dominated the new chemical industry, was an exception, with 120,000 workers in twenty-four factories. More typically, whether in the older coal mining or the newer automobile industries, the dominant trend was toward middle-sized or even small-scale companies, none of which felt any compunction to corner a market and eliminate its competitors.[5] And, as late as 1906, the ready-made clothing trade even continued to rely on "the family as the basic unit of production," through a "contract system" of put-out work done in the home.[6]

An oppositional labor movement grew up no less slowly, partly because the French working-class population remained relatively small, except in concentrated areas in and around Paris, in the north (iron foundries and coal mining), and in Lyon (textiles). Moreover, the various trade unions that emerged in the 1890s—see especially the National Federation of French Miners—tended to maintain their independence as fiercely as did their industrial and commerical counterparts. This independent attitude rested on a long revolutionary tradition suspicious of any kind of mass organization as well as on the large number of small craftsmen still shoring up the French economy, but it also testified to the persistent influence of anarchism or revolutionary syndicalism. It was anarchists within the Fédération des Bourses du Travail and the Parti Ouvrier Socialiste Révolutionnaire, for instance, that launched the strategy of the general strike, which was then taken up by the CGT (Confédération Générale du Travail) when it assumed a position of dominance in the labor movement around 1902. The general strike strategy essentially refused to acknowledge the state: it attacked employers directly without attempting to go through the mediation of parliamentary political action. This tactic put some distance between the CGT and the SFIO (the newly renovated Socialist party led by Jean Jaurès), the latter of which was aligned more closely with the parliamentary model of the Social Democratic Party in Germany. Between 1904 and 1908, strikes proliferated throughout France, reaching a peak of more than 1,300 in 1906, which eventually led, despite their strategy, to violent confrontations between the striking workers and the state. Most of the 1906 strikes, for instance, broke out around 1 May and forced passage of a bill, on 13 July, which finally mandated a compulsory weekly day of rest. Four years later, however, the government retaliated with its own strategy—it broke up a general rail strike simply by conscripting 150,000 railway workers into the army.

The 1900 Paris Exposition also deflected attention from the political crises that continually threatened and yet never quite toppled the Third Republic. As the conservative opposition waned, through the defeat of the Bonapartists and Orleanists in 1877 and then the failure of Boulangerism in 1889, the republican locus of power gradually shifted, repeatedly reconstituting itself, from a moderate to a radical majority. Perhaps the most potentially disruptive of these crises was the Dreyfus affair of 1898–1899, in which the "two nations" of France came sharply into focus: once more the clash between the Enlightenment or Revolutionary tradition of justice and reason and the Absolutist or Royalist tradition of order and authority divided the country, this time into hostile Dreyfusard and anti-Dreyfusard camps. Sparked especially by Emile Zola's famous letter, "*J'Accuse*"—which was printed on the front page of 300,000 copies of the daily *L'Aurore* (13 January 1898)—the vehement debate between these camps quickly turned into what Emile Duclaux described as "two tragic choruses insulting one another." Finally, after nearly two years of vacillation, in September 1899, now that Dreyfus had been tried and not surprisingly condemned a second time (due to apparent collusion between army and court), the newly elected "Government of Republican Concentration" ordered him pardoned. This politically expedient compromise reasserted the Republic's uneasy balance of power, which soon led to the formation of the Radical and Radical-Socialist republican parties, whose coalition bloc won control of the government in the 1902 elections.

Behind the political crises throughout this period, the "real cement which kept the republican majority together," Mayeur and Rebérioux argue, "was the common desire to secularize the State and social life."[7] Whatever their differences, political parties of both the left and center shared an anticlericalism that fueled a steady de-Christianization of French society, which had begun as early as the French Revolution and eventually culminated in the legislated separation of church and state in December 1905. Most significantly, in a series of laws the republicans succeeded in wresting control of schooling from the Catholic Church and in establishing secular institutions of primary, secondary, and higher education. This even included the creation of secondary *lycées* and *collèges* for girls, although the education they received still tended to prepare them for "careers" as moral exemplars within the restricted domestic space of a good bourgeois marriage.[8] Moreover, these state institutions were paralleled, especially in the wake of the Dreyfus affair, by the *Ligue d'enseignement*'s network of *uni-*

versités populaires throughout the country, in which intellectuals established, by means of lecture series and educational fairs, a limited dialogue with local officials, shopkeepers, clerical workers, craftsmen, and laborers.[9] However, it was the state primary schools that were most crucial, particularly after attendance was made compulsory in 1882, for they would 1) ensure that a new generation—particularly those making up Gambetta's "new strata" of petit-bourgeoisie, white-collar workers, and civil servants—was taught how to be good subjects and citizens of the Republic and 2) strengthen *la patrie* by affirming a single, united conception of the national community, not least of all through an imposed common language.

This policy of secularization or laicization, however, also coincided with and was partly undermined by the imperialist policies of the Third Republic—through the shared goal of emancipating, enlightening, and civilizing the people. Initially, it was the political left and center that championed the drive for French colonies as a means of restoring national pride following the 1871 military defeat at the hands of Germany. Despite former Prime Minister Jules Ferry's argument, in 1890, that colonial policy was an offshoot of industrial policy, the French colonial empire never came to constitute a significant sector of the country's overall economy; rather, its chief function continued to be political and ideological. By the time of the Dreyfus affair, in fact, the policies of colonial expansion were giving the parties of the right as well as groups such as the Ligue des patriotes (revived and transformed by Paul Déroulade) and Action française (led by Charles Maurras) an opportunity to begin to redefine the very concept of French nationhood, particularly through the "cult of the army" as an instrument of unity and a rampart against foreigners (as well as "bad Frenchmen" such as striking workers), all of which would culminate in a "nationalist revival" just prior to the war. The myth of French superiority through its colonial empire not only disguised the country's real economic (and military) inferiority, vis-à-vis the other advanced capitalist powers, but also constructed a sense of collective identity which could compensate for the social inferiority of the new intermediate class of "little people" within France, particularly those for whom the Republic's educational system did not provide social mobility.

Although the Third Republic survived and prospered in part because its secular system of schools encouraged aspirations to "middle-class respectability," formal education also proved to be the principal sign of an individual's admission into or exclusion from social membership in the ruling class of bourgeoisie. Ideology (in the Marxist, post-Althusserian sense) just as much as economics determined one's class position within turn-of-the-century French society. Mayeur and Rebérioux put it bluntly: "The [free] primary school was the school of the people; the *lycées* and *collèges*, with their fee-paying elementary classes, were the schools of the bourgeoisie." Indeed, by 1910, less than 3 percent of French children attended the secondary lycées or collèges, and only one-third of those passed the *baccalauréat*, which then gave them access to university study. If education served as the key marker of class position, it was also strongly enforced by more or less distinctive forms of lifestyle, culture, and leisure activity. The French bourgeoisie was indeed becoming a "leisure class" devoted to consumption, with increasing numbers of *rentier* families living off their investments or land and more and more youth between adolescence and marriage with money to spend. French families rising socially set themselves off from their "inferiors" by engaging at least one domestic servant (usually female), which then allowed a further display of social exclusivity through the conspicuous idleness of the married woman. Generally, the bourgeoisie took over the traditional cultural pursuits of the aristocracy and its canons of official taste—for instance, in their preferences for horse racing, the most academic historical paintings at the Salons, and spectacular theatrical performances at the Opéra and Comédie-Française, such as Edmond Rostand's *L'Aiglon* (1900), starring Sarah Bernhardt.[10] But they also engaged in practices of their own more recent invention, such as automobile club tours and holiday excursions to the fast-developing spas and resorts—the latter of which became showcases for the new fashions in urban living, gradually reorienting interior decoration from heavy furniture and dark wallpaper to light colors (especially white) and more spacious rooms.

To some extent, a common "popular culture" still survived in the villages, *bourgs*, and small towns of the French provinces, whose fairs and cafés or bars brought together a community of peasants, craftsmen, shopkeepers, and local officials. A distinct working-class culture also had grown up in the cities, as evidenced in the annual May Day celebrations inaugurated in 1890, the participatory entertainment of *faubourg* café-concerts, spectator sports such as soccer and bicycle racing, and particular features of dress such as the worker's peaked cap. And a separate avant-garde culture began to flourish in Paris, more strikingly in painting (from the Post-Impressionists to the Cubists) and music (see, for instance, the scandals of Claude Debussy's *Pelléas et Mélisande* [1902] and Igor Stravinsky's *Le Sacre du printemps* [1913]) than in the literary arts where representational verisimilitude and the "classical" power of the word held sway. If the Paris avant-garde deliberately challenged and overturned the aesthetic conventions accepted by the Institutes and Salons of the bourgeoisie, however, it also had little in common with a leftist political or social "avant-garde." Many Socialists like Jaurès, for instance, actually shared the traditional artistic tastes of the bourgeoisie, but much of the avant-garde also tended to see itself as a kind of secular priesthood of independent creators, whose concept of art still often assumed a "metaphysics of subjectivity" based on the "data" of sense perception, which had been devalued and marginalized in industrialized society. Here, too, was testimony to the influence of anarchism, for a whole literary generation in the 1890s, wrote Léon Blum, "was affected or at least tinged by anarchist propaganda."[11] And that influence eventually would even lead writers such as the poet and art critic Guillaume Apollinaire—who wrote for *L'Intransigéant* and admired Action française—to associate with the neonationalism of the political right, in which the *culte du moi* was not inconsistent with the *culte de la patrie*.

None of these more or less separate cultures, of course, could match the development of a mass-produced culture that steadily penetrated French society and "colonized everyday life" during this period. Eric Hobsbawm suggests that the reinvention of tradition and ritual within a network of new mass cultural practices was almost as significant in "cementing" the Third Republic as was its reconstitution of education. Dependent on consumer price levels that closely coincided with wage levels (both of which, during a period of relative monetary stability, actually decreased slightly between 1899 and 1913), these practices took advantage of as well as spurred technological innovations in recording and printing and mass market dissemination. Perhaps foremost among them was the cheap daily newspaper, which, after an 1881 law freed the press from government control, quickly rose to mass circulation levels radiating out along the railway lines from Paris and other regional captials far into the provinces—the first to reach a circulation of one million was *Le Petit Journal* in 1887, which was then overtaken by *Le Petit Parisien*, the "Holy Scripture of the Countryside." Through these papers, illustrated magazines such as Lafitte's *L'Illustration* and Hachette's *Lectures pour tous*, large color posters, and postcards, advertising then spread through the countryside as a corollary to the catalogs issuing from the big city department stores (a major French innovation in the theatrical display and distribution of consumer goods). These, along with the serialized novels appearing weekly in the papers, were the principal components of the mass culture supplanting the older "popular culture," even among the working class by the century's end. And they were more than complemented by urban-oriented spectacle entertainments of all kinds, from fairgrounds, wax museums, and even the Paris morgue to automobile trade shows and world expositions, the latter of which constituted, to use Guy Debord's language, representations of "accumulated capital [condensed into a spectacular] image."[12] The most consistently popular of these spectacles were the melodrama theater and the café-concert—now transformed into what Jules Claretie called the "democratized theater" of the music hall, with its richly varied programs and showy interiors[13]—which, in turn, would give way to the cinema. That the use of electricity in private French homes was hampered by unreliable distribution and a high tax placed on electrical consumption only added to the allure of such dazzling "light show" entertainments, as the "magic of electricity" extended the hours of their public performance far into the night.

Although hardly centrally coordinated like the Third Republic's school system, mass culture functioned, in one sense, to construct a space as well as provide models of identity and integration for the "little people" within French society, especially white-collar employees who, according to Lenard Berlanstein, "were all too eager to build their lives around their leisurely pastimes."[14] This was even reflected in the choice of newspaper titles—*Le Petit Journal, Le Petit Parisien, La Petite Republique Française*. Yet, as a social site or "heterotopia," to invoke Michel Foucault's neologism,[15] mass culture also served—along with city parks, railway stations, and public transport (both street car and subway)—to break down or blur class, gender, and ethnic or regional distinctions as well as the resistance to homogenization which made France somewhat different from the United States.[16] This went well beyond the habit of mixing or "slumming" at popular spectacles, in which the well-to-do and socially prominent "men about town" indulged, for people of different classes, according to Rearick, "increasingly shared a common consciousness of amusements" on a regular basis, especially in Paris.[17] Astute observers such as Charles d'Avenal, who were enthusiastic about "the relative luxury" of the lower middle class, for instance, specifically praised the Paris metro (which opened in 1900), where "duchesses and millionaires [could now] rub shoulders with cooks and clerks."[18] Others, however, foresaw in this "era of various publics," all of which seemed so transitory and fluctuating, a disruption of stable hierarchical boundaries which was potentially dangerous.[19] Spectacles such as the music hall and cinema were perceived as particularly threatening, as Jean-Paul Sartre witnesses, in 1912:

> [The cinema] had popular ways that shocked serious people. It was an amusement for women and children. My mother and I loved it. . . . The social hierarchy of the theater had given my grandfather and late father, who were accustomed to second balconies a taste for ceremonial. When many people are together, they must be separated by rites. . . . The movies proved the opposite. . . . I developed a dislike for ceremonies, I loved crowds.[20]

Mass culture thus seemed, through the common consciousness and new ritual of festivity it created, to open up the possibility of unexpected, unwanted change. That ranged from inadvertently undermining the "woman by the hearth" ideal (shared by Catholic conservatives, anticlerical republicans, and working-class trade unionists alike) to encouraging the energetic, independent figure of the "new woman," which was sometimes linked with deviance— whether defined in terms of French "female criminality" or of American culture.[21] But such threats were also consistently overridden by the degree to which any standardized spectacle produced by the mass culture "image factories" tended to reinforce representations of entrenched behavior, to constitute the family (with the woman in charge of its domestic space) as the principal unit of recreation and leisure, and to encourage the desire of everyone, everywhere, to consume—and be consumed.

Into this structural matrix of interrelated economic, political, and cultural practices, in 1895, came the *cinématographe* or cinema. By 1902, short films were major attractions in the fairgrounds and on the café-concert or music hall programs throughout France. By 1907, permanent cinemas were being constructed, and not only in Paris, to project programs of a dozen or more films on an exclusive basis, and French films, particularly those produced by Pathé-Frères, were being exhibited around the world in numbers greater than those of any other country. By 1911, when the eleven-year cycle of Paris world expositions came to an end without a new world fair, the renovated Gaumont-Palace, as a kind of symbolic replacement, opened its doors to seat up to 3,400 spectators and quickly became the premier cinema in France. What place did the young French cinema industry occupy in the economic arena of the late Third Republic, and how did established economic forces shape the various stages of its development? How was the spectacle of the cinema defined in legal terms, and how did government policies of investment and censorship affect its circulation and consumption? How did earlier as well as concurrent cultural practices determine the development of specific film formats or genres, particular features of a system of representation and narration, and perhaps even hierarchies of film art? And what ideological function did the cinema's circulation of images have within the contradictory, contested site of French mass culture? The attempt to address such questions constitutes the principal subject of this book and largely determines its organizational framework.

The French Cinema Industry,
1896-1914

I may not have invented the cinema,
but I did industrialize it.
CHARLES PATHÉ

DURING ITS FIRST twenty years of development, the French cinema industry
was marked by rapid changes that continually redefined its structure and composition. In what is still the best overall history of the period, Georges Sadoul
sought to grasp those changes through a periodization scheme that designated
1897–1902 as the "Age of Méliès" and 1903–1909 as the "Age of Pathé," with
the next ten years characterized by attempts to elevate the cinema to the status
of art. My own understanding, while indebted to Sadoul, suggests a slightly
different periodization based more specifically on shifts in film production, distribution, and exhibition, spearheaded by Pathé, of course, as France's largest
and most powerful film company. In this sense, the period from 1896 to 1902
was one in which the technological novelty of the cinema apparatus held sway,
particularly for Lumière and Gaumont, one in which first Lumière and then
Méliès led the way in production and exhibition. Between 1902 and 1907,
Pathé surged to world dominance by marketing reliable cameras and projectors,
quickly tripling its film production and establishing film programs as a regular
spectacle attraction in the *fêtes foraines* or fairgrounds, café-concerts and nickelodeons. From 1907 to 1911, Pathé sought to consolidate and extend its position, through a strategy of monopolistic expansion, by moving to exert greater
control over distribution (renting rather than selling its films, through a half-
dozen regional subsidiaries) as well as exhibition (constructing a circuit of more
than two hundred permanent cinemas across France). But its dominance was
undermined in the United States, largely through the emergence of "independent" producer-distributors that confronted the Edison Trust (of which
Pathé was a member) and through Eastman Kodak's monopoly on film stock.
In France, other companies, led by Gaumont and Eclair, also began to challenge Pathé's position at home. From 1911 to 1914, then, while Pathé adjusted
to its loss of dominance (the company still contrived to increase its stockholder dividends), the French cinema industry overall assumed the structure of
a "cottage industry" of loosely related production firms, distribution companies, and exhibition circuits. In less than ten years, that industry, with Pathé

9

in the lead, had achieved a brief, tenuous hegemony throughout the world; and, despite Pathé's "dethronement," on the eve of the Great War, the French still remained a close second to the Americans.

The Big Four, 1896-1902

The origins of the four major French firms initially involved in the cinématographe business reveal the outlines of a framework for the cinema's early development. In 1893, the Société Antoine Lumière et fils, located in Lyon, was one of the largest manufacturers of photographic plates and film stock in France. One son, Louis Lumière, was well known as an inventor of visual recording processes and apparatuses—his work, for instance, had won a Grand Prix at the 1889 Paris Exposition. In 1895, Léon Gaumont, having served a dozen years of apprenticeship as an optical craftsman and business manager in Paris, received the financial backing of such entrepreneurs as Gustave Eiffel and assumed control of the Comptoir général de photographie, a reputable firm for whom he was then acting as managing director (its clients included the psychologist Jean Charcot, the politician René Waldeck-Rousseau, and the writer Emile Zola). Changing the company's name to L. Gaumont et cie, he set out to manufacture and market photographic and optical equipment on a larger scale. In very different circumstances, that same year, Charles Pathé was exhibiting counterfeit Edison phonographic cylinders and kinetoscope films to a fairground clientele, not only around Paris but in the provinces as well. Such was his success that, in less than a year, he and brother Emile were able to found their own store of phonographic merchandise, Pathé-Frères, in Vincennes, on the outskirts of the capital. Georges Méliès, by contrast, was the owner-manager of the Robert-Houdin Théâtre in the boulevard entertainment section of Paris, where he directed his own very popular magic acts and *féeries* or "fairy plays" such as *La Fée des fleurs* and *L'Auberge du diable*. As each of these four enterprises, between 1894 and 1896, came to see possible ways of exploiting this new mechanical wonder, their experience prepared them for producing and marketing apparatuses and material in parallel with those of photography and phonography as well as making and exhibiting films within already established institutions of popular spectacle attractions.

The principal interest of both Lumière and Gaumont, during this period, lay in the technological possibilities of the cinema. From 1894 to 1895, as Alan Williams and others have shown, much of Lumière's research capital (this was a very prosperous bourgeois family business dependent on self-financing) went into developing a camera-projector and film stock that then would be capable of quickly being manufactured and marketed throughout France and elsewhere.[1] After Louis Lumière had solved the problem of intermittent motion for registering an image on a 35mm celluloid filmstrip (through an analogy with the textile industry's sewing machine),[2] the company embarked on a promotional campaign for its *cinématographe* (the neologism meant "writing in movement"), using various forms of publicity and the "popular science" press of the day. Demonstrations of the Lumière apparatus were given at photography and learned society congresses (in Paris, Lyon, and Brussels), until enough interest had been generated to warrant a public screening in the elegant Salon Indien of the Grand Café in Paris, on 28 December 1895, and the commercial manufacture of some two hundred apparatuses by early 1896.[3] Over the next two years, Lumière cameramen such as Alexandre Promio, Felix Mesguisch, Francis Doublier, and Gabriel Veyre[4] toured the world (as many as twenty-one may have traversed the United States alone), producing nearly one thousand short films or *actualités*, primarily as a means of publicizing the company and its products—for instance, Lumière's very first film, *La Sortie des usines* (1895), was clearly a publicity film.[5] And Georges Hatot (a former crowd-scene manager at the Hippodrome Theater) directed a series of comic acts as well as one of the first multiple-shot films, *La Vie et la Passion de Jésus-Christ* (1897), in thirteen tableaux. Once the company had established a market for its camera-projector and film stock (and made a healthy profit of three million francs), it abandoned film production and turned to developing other apparatuses—for instance, a stereoscopic cinema and photographic panorama—as well as the giant-screen cinema for the 1900 Paris Exposition, which proved a huge success for nearly one and a half million spectators.[6] Although its cameramen resumed making actualité films between 1899 and 1901, in a second wave of publicity, the Lumière company took no interest in the commercial exhibition of films—even the giant-screen cinema was primarily a promotional venture—and, by 1905, abandoned film production altogether.[7]

Gaumont also showed an early interest in designing and marketing various cinematographic apparatuses. In 1896, Gaumont's chief engineer, L.-R. Decaux, constructed the company's first camera-projector based on the "chronophotographique" invention of Georges Demenÿ (a former assistant to Etienne-Jules Marey), for which Gaumont had acquired the commercial rights. A year later, Decaux designed an improved "Chronographe" model that could use 35mm film stock, and Léon Gaumont's young secretary, Alice Guy or "Mademoiselle Alice," was given the task of producing short films for its promotion. Recognizing the commercial value of the films themselves, Gaumont assigned Guy and her cameraman, Anatole Thiberville, to produce comic films (drawn, for instance, from illustrated postcards)[8] and ballet films as well as actualités on a regular basis. Then, in 1898, he contracted with A. C. Bromhead in London to market both cinema equipment and films (some of them actualités recorded there); and, four years later, Bromhead's agency was selling the company's films in the United States, principally through American Mutoscope and Biograph.[9] But technological development remained his chief concern, and Gaumont took advantage of the 1900 Paris Exposition to further exploit a new model of the "Chrono" projector—which won a Grand Prix and led to its widespread adoption in France and elsewhere. The success of the Chrono encouraged Gaumont's research in the areas of color cinematography and image-sound synchronization. An initial interest in color photography, for instance, impelled Gaumont to con-

1. Alice Guy

duct experiments with several color film processes, none of which would produce satisfactory results until just before the war. The company's work on syn-
chronizing a Chrono projector with a phonographic cylinder, however, was
somewhat more successful, especially in contrast to the relative failure of Paul
Decauville's Phono-Cinéma-Théâtre at the 1900 Exposition (which offered

2. Méliès Montreuil studio (Georges Méliès, left)

"talking films" of Sarah Bernhardt, Gabrielle Réjane, Ernest Coquelin, and Cléo de Mérode in brief theatrical scenes).[10] By November 1902, Gaumont was able to present his own speaking image to the Société française de photographie and then launch what proved to be a premature attempt to market this "Chronophone" system commercially.[11]

A witness to the first public screening of the Lumière cinématographe, Méliès saw a different, and ultimately more limited way to exploit the new technology—as a means of augmenting his own theatrical performances or magic shows. Within six months after that screening, he added Edison and Bioscope films to his programs, designed his own camera (his offer to purchase a cinématographe had been refused), and then began producing short films (most of them single shot-scene actualités of no more than twenty-five meters in length, in imitation of Lumière) which could be projected at the Robert-Houdin Théâtre as well as be sold in its lobby. In the spring of 1897, a "glass house" studio was constructed on some family property in Montreuil; and, on most evenings in the fall, the Robert-Houdin was turned into a cinema to display the spectacles bearing his new trademark, Star-Film. By 1898, Méliès was directing more and more "transformation views" or trick films such as *Illusions fantastiques* and *Le Diable au couvent*, and even screening publicity films (of his own making) in an open-air cinema in an adjacent street.[12] Within another year, Méliès's films were becoming fewer in number but longer—for instance, *Cendrillon* (20 tableaux, 120 meters), *L'Affaire Dreyfus* (12 tableaux, 240 meters), *Jeanne d'Arc* (12 tableaux, 250 meters)—and some were being sold in hand-colored prints; yet the annual negative film stock production consistently ran between 1,200 and 1,500 meters. Throughout this period, the Méliès business was a family operation that relied exclusively on self-financing through film print and ticket sales, and it remained so even after the phenomenal worldwide success of the féerie films, from *Cendrillon* (1899) to *Le Voyage dans la lune* (1902). The single exception to this practice was the historical reconstruction film, *The Coronation of Edward VII* (1902), which was financed (and perhaps codirected) by Méliès's British distributor, Charles Urban of Warwick Trading. In order to dissuade the Edison and Lubin companies from duping his films in the United States (where the trick films and féeries were unusually popular), Méliès finally sent his brother Gaston off to New York to open a distribution office for Star-Film, in March 1903.[13] And, at the Montreuil studio, as production began to increase, he initiated the practice of using two side-by-side cameras so as to produce a second negative that could be shipped to the United States for making positive prints there.

The growth of Pathé-Frères depended on a different kind of magic—the infusion of capital from outside the family business—as well as the ambition and persistence of Charles Pathé himself.[14] Pathé's first brief brush with the cinema came in 1895, in an attempt to sell counterfeit Edison kinetoscopes to the company's fairground clientele (Edison had not applied for patent protection in Europe). Soon after, he contracted with inventor Henri Joseph Joly to manufacture and market an apparatus much like the Lumière cinématographe. After a falling-out with Joly (although he himself probably perpetrated the separation, Joly's camera-projector did not sell well), Pathé had his first real break. He was approached by Claude Grivolas, the new owner of Continsouza and Bunzli's precision tool factory at Chatou, who had become fascinated by the cinema and wanted to invest in its development (he also happened to be an amateur magician). In December 1897, Pathé and Grivolas—along with financier Jean Neyret and the Crédit Lyonnais bank—reached an agreement that transformed Pathé-Frères into a joint-stock company (with one million francs of capital stock), officially known as the Compagnie générale des cinématographes, phonographes, et pellicules. The name clearly indicated Grivolas and Pathé's ultimate plans for the new firm, but for several years the phonograph branch of the business (run by brother Emile) contributed up to 90 percent of its revenue, while Charles supervised the work on perfection apparatuses and film stock. By 1900, when Pathé-Frères had become the Chatou factory's chief client, Grivolas and his partners had decided to merge the two into one company, and Charles was ready to begin full-scale exploitation. Although the Pathé camera and projector took several years to develop into marketable apparatuses, Charles quickly capitalized on the commercial value of films and set about mass producing them very much like clothing or canned goods. In 1900, he hired Ferdinand Zecca (a café-concert writer of comic and dramatic monologues) to handle the company's film production; within a year, with films such as *Histoire d'un crime* (1901), *Victimes de l'alcoolisme* (1902), and *L'Eruption du Mont Pélé* (1902),[15] its output of negative surpassed even that of Méliès. By 1902, the company was constructing a "glass house" studio in Vin-

3. Ferdinand Zecca and Charles Pathé

cennes, producing eight thousand meters of negative film stock per year, and, with the aid of Faria's posters (*Victimes de l'alcoolisme* was the first to draw praise),[16] launching a drive to make Pathé films the principal cinema attraction of the popular fairgrounds.[17]

By the time of Pathé's drive, films were being exhibited in a variety of locations, nearly all of them established sites of spectacle attractions.[18] In Paris, besides Méliès's Robert-Houdin Théâtre, there was another magic theater near the Grand Café, the Salle des Capucines (owned by the Isola brothers), which included films on its programs. Similarly, there were wax museums like the one directed by Léonard Béguiné on the Boulevard de Bonne Nouvelle and, especially, the Musée Grévin (founded by a prominent journalist, Arthur Meyer), which was openly promoted as "a newspaper in waxwork."[19] There, beginning in 1892, for three hours every afternoon and evening, Emile Reynaud had projected "Pantomimes lumineuses" such as *Pauvre Pierrot* and *Autour d'une cabine* (twenty- to fifty-meter bands of hand-painted images on gelatin sheets), to the music of Gaston Paulin, by means of a Théâtre-Optique.[20] Then, in 1899, Gaumont actualités were added to the variety of performances in the Grévin's theater. Another site in the capital was the Dufayel department store (on the northern edge of the city), which had a small theater that presented Lumière actualités as early as 1896 and then continued to exhibit publicity films as well as others by Pathé and Méliès, especially for children, until just before the war. Lumière itself ran two permanent cinemas in Paris between 1896 and 1897—one at the Grand Café (directed by Clément Maurice) and the other at the Théâtre Saint-Denis, the latter of which Mesguisch would later manage as the Select Cinéma Saint-Denis. Small cinemas also were located in the Café de la Paix and on the Boulevard de Bonne Nouvelle (where the respected photographer Eu-

15

4. Cinématographe Grenier (c. 1900)

gène Pirou exhibited films produced by his inventor-assistant, Léar) and in the passage de l'Opéra (operated by Gabriel Kaiser) right next to Méliès's open-air publicity cinema.

The primary locations for exhibition, however, were the café-concerts or music halls and fêtes foraines. In Paris again, the Eldorado, the Olympia, and the Casino de Paris, for instance, all began to include short films on their programs in 1896 or 1897. And the Folies-Bergère added films as an entr'acte in 1898. Soon, films were beginning to appear regularly on café-concert programs in most of the large cities and towns throughout France. That many of the top Paris café-concerts were owned by the Isola brothers and that they seem to have usually bought Méliès and Pathé films perhaps contributed to the latter's initial success in this major sector of the urban market. As the most popular spectacle among France's largely rural population, the fairgrounds were even more important than the café-concerts because, much like the weekly supplement to *Le Petit Journal*, in their annual or semiannual circuit of towns, they disseminated the news, fashions, and "scientific wonders" of the larger cities throughout the provinces. Nine fairs were presenting film programs as early as 1896; the number doubled the next year, and it had more than doubled again by 1899. By 1902, nearly every fair had one or two cinemas—one of the largest was Dulaar—mixing together a variety of short films with live acts and magic lantern slides in more or less continuous programs. The inventor-entrepreneur, Georges Mendel, initially enjoyed some success in producing films for the fairs;

but his real interest, like Gaumont's, lay elsewhere, in the area of apparatuses and accessories. Instead, it was Pathé, probably because he knew the interrelated network of petit-bourgeois families that owned and managed the French fairs so well, who would most take advantage of the fêtes foraines as the broadest, most integrated market for exhibiting films.

Two much publicized events during this period deserve attention for their reputed effect on the development of the early French cinema industry. One was the catastrophic fire, in May 1897, at the annual Bazar de la Charité in Paris (organized by the Catholic bourgeoisie), a fire that broke out in the fair's large temporary cinema (made of wood, cardboard, and papier-mâché) and killed 121 people—many survivors owed their lives to the courageous rescue efforts of nearby hotel employees. That the fire was caused by an exploding oxygen-ether projection lamp (of Joly's design) rather than a film projector powered by electricity probably saved the industry from irreparable damage. But that most of the victims were high society women may well have curtailed the cinema's appeal to a "respectable" audience—although the public debate provoked by the disaster virtually ignored the cinema to focus on issues of harmony or dissension within the French social hierarchy. Along with the fading fascination for the cinema as a technological novelty and the relatively high ticket prices for the cinemas and café-concerts of Paris,[21] the fire seemed momentarily to brake public interest in the new spectacle around 1897–1898.[22] And it may well have affected early scientific efforts to use cinema equipment—such as Dr. Eugène Louis Doyen's experiments in Paris, beginning in 1897, to record surgical operations for pedagogical purposes (with a Lumière camera modified by Clément Maurice).[23]

The 1900 Paris Exposition served to revive public interest, however, at least in terms of the cinema's technological possibilities. Besides the Lumières's giant-screen cinema (using 50mm film stock) and the Phono-Cinéma-Théâtre, there were seven panoramas projecting film images, the most popular being the Panorama du Tour du Monde. There was also the enigma of Raoul Grimoin-Sanson's Cinéorama, employing ten camera-projectors covering a 360-degree circular screen—which, according to legend, the authorities closed down after only four performances, but which recently discovered financial documents disclose posed so many technical difficulties that it never opened.[24] And there were more conventional "Visions d'art," which combined beautifully composed film images (by Lumière) or color photographs (by Gaumont) of various regions of France with recited or sung poetic texts. By privileging the educational and artistic as well as technological aspects of the cinema (and subsuming it under the category of photography), as Emmanuelle Toulet argues, the Exposition ultimately encouraged further experimenting with the cinema as an apparatus and spectacle, yet without calling attention to the areas of its real, consistent expansion in the café-concerts and fairgrounds.[25] It was there that Pathé and then Gaumont—both of whose companies were well positioned financially—saw the best chance of the cinema's immediate exploitation.

5. *Le Petit Journal* (16 May 1897): The fire at the Bazar de la Charité

Pathé Comes to Power, 1902-1907

Of the four major French companies originally involved in the cinema business, Lumière abandoned everything but the production of film stock during this period, while the other three all expanded their efforts in one way or another. The least successful of these was Méliès, whose family firm reached a kind of apogee around 1903–1904. That year, Méliès's Star-Film produced forty-five films, totaling 2,880 meters of negative film stock, and added distribution agents in Berlin and Barcelona (from the latter, Segundo de Chómon also covered Latin America) to those already in operation in England and the United States.[26] Along with his short trick films, Méliès now began to concentrate on longer féerie films whose elaborate decors involved several months of production— *Damnation du Docteur Faust* (1904), *Le Voyage à travers l'impossible* (1904), and *Le Palais des mille et une nuits* (1905), the last of which reached 460 meters in length.[27] Increasingly, however, such longer films as *Le Raid Paris-Monte-Carlo en deux heures* (1905) and *Les Quatre Cent Farces du diable* (1906) were geared to exclusive end-of-the-program screenings at the Folies-Bergère or Olympia music halls and even the Châtelet theater (a real sign of prestige for a "mere illusionist").[28] Although hugely successful—*Le Raid Paris-Monte-Carlo en deux heures* played for six months straight at the Folies-Bergère—these costly, hand-colored spectacle films returned less profit to Méliès than expected, for the fêtes foraines cinemas could hardly afford to pay the high prices such works demanded. As a result, Méliès's financial position became more and more precarious, even though his brother Gaston seems to have protected the company's interests well enough in the growing American market. Despite a decided reluctance to change his prior formulas for success, now Méliès also felt forced to adopt subjects made popular by others—for instance, melodramas such as *Détresse et charité* (1904) or *Les Incendiaires* (1906) and chase films such as *Jack le ramoneur* (1906). Finally, in February 1906, Star-Film ads began appearing in the trade journal of the fairs, *L'Industriel forain*, in what seemed a belated attempt to recover some part of the lucrative market that had been taken over by Pathé and Gaumont.

In contrast to its earlier strategy of privileging technological innovation, Gaumont, during this period, invested more and more of its capital in film production.[29] In 1903, much of that production was still given over to actualités; and Léon Gaumont was still seeking to exploit his sound-synchronization system through special *phonoscènes* screened at the Musée Grévin and the Théâtre du Gymnase, but without much success. Thereafter, Guy turned increasingly to mise-en-scène or story films, initially in imitation of those beginning to be produced in England by Bromhead's independent firm, Gaumont Ltd. Partly for economic reasons, Guy quickly established a "house style" that depended on fitting subjects and stories to real locations, whether in historical dramas such as *L'Assassinat du courrier de Lyon* (1904), comic sketches like *Le Bébé embarrassant* (1905), or serial gags such as *Le Matelas alcoolique*, with Roméo Bosetti (1906). By 1905, Gaumont had achieved a secure enough position to construct, next to the Buttes-Chaumont park, a "glass cathedral" studio ten times bigger than that of Méliès, with mercury vapor lamps (the first in France) to supplement the sunlight in winter, and an adjacent factory capable of printing up to ten thousand meters of positive film stock a day.[30] At the same time, Gaumont began to hire added personnel such as Etienne Arnaud and Louis Feuillade—whom Guy could then train as scriptwriters and filmmakers—along with set designer Henri Ménessier and his assistant, Benjamin Carré. Guy herself took on the task of producing longer films such as *La Esmeralda* (1905) and the 660-meter *La Vie du Christ* (1906), with sets and costumes designed by Victorin Jasset, a popular director of spectacles at the Hippodrome as well as various café-concerts. The company prospered to the point that, in December 1906, Gaumont could be reorganized as a joint-stock corporation (with two and a half million francs of capital stock) in alliance with the Banque suisse et française, whose directorate had important links to the French electrical industry.[31] And within that corporation, the cinema division now contributed almost 90 percent of Gaumont's overall profits.

The changes that Léon Gaumont set in motion in 1905–1906 (the point at which French industry in general entered a period of rapid growth), Charles Pathé had already initiated three or four years before, and on an even grander scale. In 1900, the cinema division of Pathé-Frères was little more than a workshop of artisans; by 1906–1907, it was the central component of a major industrial corporation, a veritable *usine aux images* or "image factory"—more than double the size of brother Emile's phonograph division—and dedicated to proving that the cinema was indeed, as Pathé's chief engineer, Franz Dussaud, seems to have first predicted, "the schoolhouse, newspaper, and theater of tomorrow."[32] Near the company's original offices in Vincennes, in 1902, with support now from banks such as Adam et cie, Pathé erected a "glass house" studio and then, two years later, added another, as well as constructing two more at nearby Joinville-le-pont and an even larger one at Montreuil.[33] At Joinville-le-pont, a maze of factories grew up for perforating, developing, printing, and splicing film stock; at Vincennes, a special laboratory created stencil-colored positive prints, a process that Pathé first introduced in 1903 and that soon became a company trademark.[34] By 1905, Pathé was turning out two hundred projectors, cameras, and other apparatuses per month at yet another factory in Belleville, in Paris, and printing twelve thousand meters of positive film stock per day (based on twelve thousand meters of negative per year), most of it story films rather than actualités.[35] And by the end of 1906, as advertised in *Phono-Ciné-Gazette*, the manufacture of apparatuses had increased to 250 per month while the production of positive film stock had tripled to an astonishing forty thousand meters a day.[36] According to Pathé's 1907 catalog, the cinema division alone had more than 1,200 employees, many of them women, whose repetitive "detail" work in splicing and coloring prints was probably quite similar to what they would have done in a textile factory.[37] That almost none of Pathé's employees was allied with a trade union was typical of the cinema industry in general (and would be until well

6. Pathé's Vincennes studio

after the war), so that the industry could be assured of cheap labor and also avoid the threat of the work stoppages and strikes then breaking out all over France.[38]

As the most visible of Pathé's employees, Zecca now served primarily as supervisor for an increasing number of filmmakers, many of them newly hired away from the other spectacle attractions in Paris. Although the evidence is still scanty, each one seems to have specialized in a particular film subject or genre, all of which together closely matched the range of acts making up the fairground and music hall programs. Lucien Nonguet (a former crowd-scene manager at several theaters, including the Ambigu and Châtelet), for instance, specialized in actualités and historical reconstructions such as *L'Epopée napoléonienne* (1903) and *La Révolution en Russie* (1905); Gaston Velle in féeries and trick films like *Rêve à la lune* and *La Poule aux oeufs d'or* (both 1905); Zecca himself in "realist dramas" like *L'Honneur d'un père* and *Au pays noir* (both 1905); Hatot (the former Lumière filmmaker) in chase films such as *Dix Femmes pour un mari* (1905); and Albert Capellani (a former actor with André Antoine and Firmin Gémier) in "sentimental dramas" like *La Loi du pardon* (1906). Moreover, many scenarios, especially those for Zecca and Capellani, now were the responsibility of either G. Rollini (Zecca's brother-in-law) or André Heuzé (a former publicity agent); and troupes of actors were being recruited from the music halls, circuses, and

7. Pathé's film splicing lab

theaters such as the Ambigu (where Zecca's parents still served as concierges). Something very much like what Janet Staiger has called the "director-unit" system of production—in which each of several filmmakers regularly worked with a small unit (including cameraman and cast) to produce a quasi-independent series of films—thus seems to have been instituted at Pathé, in contrast to the "collaborative" system that Charles Musser has described as more characteristic of the American cinema industry.[39] And at least by the summer of 1905, according to ads in *L'Industriel forain* and the *New York Clipper* (as well as its own monthly catalogs), Pathé's "director-unit" system was capable of turning out a half dozen film titles per week, making the French company probably the first to achieve a standardized mode of production of such volume.

Pathé's success came chiefly from exploiting the cheap costs of early film production, establishing the first worldwide network of film distribution, taking advantage of the proliferating American nickelodeons, and monopolizing the French fêtes foraines. In 1905, throughout the French industry, the printing cost of both negative and positive film stock was standardized at fifty centimes (or half a franc) per meter, while the basic price charged to clients for a meter of positive film was double or triple that—and any added color, of course, cost even more. Cast and crew salaries, construction materials for decors, and studio overhead, however, constituted the largest percentage of production costs; and it was there that differences emerged, for instance, between Pathé and Méliès. While Méliès was paying between thirty and fifty francs per meter to produce his spectacular féerie films, Pathé was restricting Zecca to an average production budget of fourteen to fifteen francs per meter. Differences in production costs also began to give an advantage to story films over actualités. According to Sadoul, for instance, comic films such as *Les Effets du melon* (1906)[40] cost a mere four francs per meter, a figure below that of the usual cost of an actualité. And the cost of simply duping others' films, of course, was still less. This cost-effectiveness, along with the desire to increase and regularize production as well as extend the "shelf life" of a film's distribution, undoubtedly fueled the overall shift from actualités to story films during the period.[41] In order to break even on any one film title, then, Pathé normally had to sell only a dozen or more positive prints of a story film, and actual sales averaged thirty times that number. As a result, the corporation's profits grew at a remarkable rate, with stockholder dividends quadrupling between 1904–1905 and 1906–1907. And Pathé's success repeatedly was trumpeted in the pages of *Phono-Ciné-Gazette* (1905–1908), the first French trade journal devoted to promoting the new industry, whose editor, Edmond Benoît-Lévy, just happened to be a Paris lawyer and educator associated with the company.[42]

These phenomenal sales were largely the result of the network of distribution agencies that Pathé rapidly put in place between 1904 and 1906, perhaps in imitation of the French automobile industry, whose export earnings throughout the world had leaped from two million francs in 1899 to 51 million francs in 1903.[43] The analogy was a familiar one—as in Benoît-Lévy's boast, in 1905, that, "in ten years, the industry of the phonograph and cinema will be more important than that of the automobile."[44] The first Pathé agencies spread out through the "First World" of developed nations and client states such as Russia, the latter of which absorbed nearly a quarter of France's export capital: Moscow (February 1904), New York, represented by J. A. Berst (August 1904), Brussels (October 1904), Berlin (March 1905), Vienna (July 1905), Chicago (August 1905), Saint Petersburg (December 1905), Amsterdam (January 1906), Barcelona (February 1906), Milan (May 1906), London (July 1906), and Odessa (July 1906).[45] Within another year, Pathé offices were monopolizing Central Europe as well as opening up the colonized areas of India, Southeast Asia, Central and South America, and Africa. In the United States, when Pathé wrote to Edison of its intention to open an office in New York and sought an agreement against duplicating one another's films, the American company interpreted this move as a threat.[46] As Pathé quickly prospered (aided by George Kleine Optical of Chicago, who dropped Edison dupes in favor of buying Pathé imports),[47] Edison included the French company (along with Méliès) within its string of patent suits, which, although the specific one against Pathé never came to trial, clearly was intended to curtail the French company's expansion.[48] Pathé retaliated by marketing its films in the United States several weeks prior to their release in Europe[49] and then by underselling its chief competitor—charging twelve cents for a foot of positive film stock versus Edison's fifteen cents per foot—effectively erasing the distinction the American company had been trying to establish between class A and class B films.[50] These actions, *Moving Picture World* later suggested, were responsible for the fact that, by October 1906, Pathé's film sales averaged around seventy-five copies each of a half-dozen or more film titles per week, constituting anywhere from one-third to one-half of the growing American nickelodeon market.[51] Throughout the following year, magazine articles devoted to the "nickel craze" consistently noted how prominent and popular were the French films; Edward Wagenknecht even recalled that "all the films shown" at his neighborhood nickelodeon in Chicago "were French Pathé."[52] Consequently, it was no idle boast for the French company to proclaim that it had "boomed the film business" in the United States and that, for both the quality and quantity of its films, Pathé-Frères was "tops in the world."[53]

Within France itself, Pathé's principal market was the fêtes foraines or fairs, which the company deliberately targeted as the basis for its expansion around 1902. In the larger French cities, films were becoming an increasingly significant part of established spectacle programs, most notably in the café-concerts or music halls—as evidenced by the exclusive screenings of Méliès's féerie films and reports in mass dailies such as *Le Petit Parisien*.[54] Permanent cinemas apparently were still quite rare. The only new ones were the remodeled Cinématographe-Théâtre du Boulevard Bonne Nouvelle (a former wax museum), which opened in Paris in 1904, and the Populaire Cinéma, opened in Marseille the same year and operated by the Richebé family. In the provinces and city faubourgs or outskirts, however, fairground cinemas were everywhere, displaying their wares as a marvelous spectacle of electricity produced by their own generators (electrical power had come to very few French towns of less than ten thousand inhabitants) to a large, cross-class family clientele.[55] The principal fairground cinemas worked within regional circuits, traveling by train and encamping in designated public spaces for three to four weeks each—for instance, Pierre Unik to the west and north of Paris, Alexandre Camby to the east, the Dulaar brothers around Lyon, and Charles and Schélmo Katorza around Nantes. By 1905, ten separate cinemas were operating on the fairgrounds in Lille and Havre, and in Bordeaux at least four were advertising their programs in the major regional newspaper, *La Gironde*.[56] Their business was so successful by then that some fairground cinemas were beginning to settle permanently in town or city squares, becoming French versions of the nickelodeons then springing up in the United States—which Pathé, along with Vitagraph, was particularly quick to exploit.[57]

Although constituting a rather tightly interrelated community, with its own trade journal, *L'Industriel forain*, the fairground cinemas operated as independent petit-bourgeois family businesses. Generally, they chose and arranged their own two-hour programs—sometimes headlining Méliès's longer films—and presented their reels of film as a major attraction, interspersing them with lantern slides and live acts, in relatively plush temporary theaters that might seat up to five hundred people. Variety was essential to these programs—as it was in other popular spectacles such as the circus, wax museum, and music hall as well as newspapers and illustrated magazines or even the profuse displays of the French department stores. And specific conditions—frequent reel changes and the sometimes irritating flicker-effect of early film projection, caused by irregular perforations in the film stock and unsteady hand cranking—simply confirmed the established model of constant program breaks. By the summer of 1905, however, most fairground cinemas were using Pathé projectors and films, whose dozen genre subjects and sheer numbers allowed their owners to acquire a vast stock from which to draw their programs and even change them once a week.[58] At least one competitor, Mendel, abandoned film production altogether at this time in order to concentrate on cinema equipment, including synchronized sound apparatuses. Within another year or so, Pathé films (now often serviced by Pathé projectionists) comprised at least 75 percent of the fairground cinema programs in France and sometimes dominated them to the exclusion of all others.[59] Yet it was precisely at this point that, following the logic of capitalist expansion, Charles Pathé chose to desert them—despite the fact that they had been so responsible for the cinema's success as a spectacle attraction—in a major campaign to consolidate and extend the corporation's economic advantage as well as to upgrade its prestige. And, as one of the first signs of that move, in the summer of 1906 Pathé-Frères won an exclusive contract to project its actualités at the prestigious French Colonial Expositions in both Paris and Marseille.[60]

Strategies of Dominance, 1907-1911

If, during the four years prior to 1907, a single French corporation rose to dominate the cinema industry in France and elsewhere, during the next four years a host of smaller "image factories" as well as hundreds of new permanent cinemas emerged to exploit the markets opened up by Pathé-Frères. So many of these were established in 1907 that the French press repeatedly expressed astonishment at the speed with which the cinema was supplanting the café-concerts and music halls and the extent to which it was threatening to displace the theater.[61] As one song from the popular revue, "Tu l'as l'allure!" put it:

> So when will the Ciné drop and die?
> Who knows.
> So when will the "Café-conc" revive?
> Who knows.[62]

Whatever the positions assumed—and they ranged from exhilaration to resigned dismay—there was no doubt that, in France, 1907 was "the year of the cinema," or even "the dawn of a new age of Humanity."[63] Within a matter of months, enthused *Phono-Ciné-Gazette,* a film produced by Pathé-Frères would be seen by 300 million people around the world.[64] Or as one satirist put it,

VILLE D'AUBERVILLIERS
SALLE DES FÊTES, Avenue de la République (SQUARE)

Samedi 24, Dimanche 25 et Lundi 26 Juin à 8 h. 1|2, SOIRÉE

REPRÉSENTATIONS DU

CINEMATOGRAPHE "PATHÉ"

Grand Prix — PARIS 1900
Le plus beau Spectacle Cinématographique du monde

PROGRAMME DES 24 & 26 JUIN

RAMONEUR & PATISSIER	*Le premier Cigare du Collégien*
L'épopée Napoléonienne	**Le Singe " August "**
Dispute de Joueurs	**Drame dans les Airs**
Chasse au Sanglier	*Indiens et Cow-Boys*
LE NÈGRE GOURMAND	*Coup d'œil par étage*
Nuit Epouvantable	**EN COULEURS**
GUERRE RUSSO - JAPONAISE	**LA FÉE AUX FLEURS**
Au Bivouac — Attaque d'un Village	*La Ruche merveilleuse*
MARIE - ANTOINETTE	**LE RÊVE A LA LUNE**
Les Devaliseurs nocturnes	*(Dernière création)*

PROGRAMME DU 25 JUIN

Le Mitron	**La Purge**
Barcelone au Crépuscule	**Baignade impossible**
COURSE DE TAUREAUX	**Fée Printemps**
Fumeur trop petit, Paravent Mystérieux	**LA VALISE DE BARNUM**
Guerre Russo-Japonaise	**LA GRÈVE**
Combats sur le Yalou. — Combat naval devant Port-Arthur	L'Ane Lutteur Statuettes vivantes
La Statue et l'Ivrogne	**Les Cambrioleurs modernes**
Roman d'Amour	La Fée aux fleurs, La Ruche Merveilleuse
L'AMOUREUX ENSORCELÉ	*Le Rêve à la Lune*
Les Dénicheurs d'Oiseaux	

ALFONSE XIII A BARCELONE — (SON ARRIVÉE A PARIS)

PRIX DES PLACES :
PREMIÈRES, 1 FR. — SECONDES, 0.75 — TROISIÈMES, 0.50
Les Enfants ne paient que moitié prix à toutes les places
Ouverture des portes, 8 heures — Le Spectacle dure environ 2 heures.
Le Cinématographe Pathé *vient pour la première fois à Aubervilliers.*

Imprimerie J. Couturier, 3 et 45, rue de Paris, Vincennes

Pathé rules the roost everywhere,
from the most dismal back street
to the finest, widest boulevards.[65]

So limitless seemed the future of the French cinema industry that it ignited what can only be described as an explosion of entrepreneurial activity.

Although this activity coincided with a general trend toward rapid industrial growth in France, it exceeded that in most other segments of the country's economy, even if remaining relatively small in scale. And the direction of the cinema's growth, interestingly, was shaped by certain legal decisions concerning its status as a public spectacle as well as a commodity or form of property. In defining the cinema as a public spectacle, French law followed the nineteenth-century tradition of distinguishing between two categories of spectacle. While the so-called legitimate theater was under the direct control of the French state, the *spectacle de curiosité* or "amusement attraction" was under the control of municipal officials, whether mayors or provincial prefects.[66] At least as early as 1901, the cinema had been classed among the spectacles de curiosité (along with the fairs, then its principal venue of exhibition)—evidence for which comes from the Paris prefect's decision to suppress the final tableau of a criminal's execution in Pathé's *Histoire d'un crime* (1901).[67] In June 1906, a new Finance Law passed by the National Assembly cut funding for the national censors' staff and effectively removed the theater from any censorship restrictions whatsoever. This created a sharp disparity between the legal status of the cinema and that of the theater as public spectacles, precisely at the moment when the French cinema industry was undergoing a rapid expansion. And that disparity deepened, in January 1909, when the Interior Minister circulated a directive reminding local mayors and prefects that they had the power to ban the screening of films—especially those, whether actualité or fiction, which represented criminal executions.[68] His rationale was simple: "There must be an absolute ban on all spectacles of this kind—spectacles liable to provoke demonstrations which disturb the public order and the public space."[69] As a consequence, the cinema's restricted categorization as a public spectacle gave rise to what many in the industry perceived as a "crisis of film subjects"—films seemed to be becoming increasingly repetitive and cinema programs more monotonous, supposedly because they were so tied to the fairground format.[70]

In defining film as a form of property, however, French law followed a course similar to the one taken during the previous half century when, to use Bernard Edelman's phrase, it was "surprised" by the technical innovation of photography. Up until 1905, the law considered film to be merely the work of a machine, incapable of intelligence or interpretation.[71] In February 1905, however, a Paris court took the opposite position on a case involving the famous Sorbonne surgeon, Dr. Doyen, and the cameraman-inventor, A.-F. Parnaland, the latter of whom was selling as his own the few teaching-aid films he had made for Doyen of his surgical operations several years before.[72] Here, the court

27

ruled that, because he had "first arranged his subject . . . and planned the setting," Doyen was the principal author of these films, which were indeed worthy of legal protection. As short fiction films replaced actualités as the major component of cinema programs, which now began to compete with those of the urban music halls and melodrama theaters, French law had to confront the conflicting claims resulting from that competition. Now, rather than extend the precedent set in the Doyen case, the courts initially sought to protect literary authors against unauthorized film versions of *their* work as intellectual property. A linked series of cases, in Paris, between 1906 and 1908, established that, if a film closely resembled an original literary work (which was complicated by early film's inability to record dialogue), it constituted a form of that work's publication and performance—and so involved an author's permission and right to royalty fees.[73] Had Urban Trading, for instance, not used *Les Deux Gosses* for the title of a 1906 film and had it also varied the conception of that film's story, it would have escaped Pierre Decourcelle's suit against the company for violating his rights to one of his more popular plays.[74] These court decisions had the effect of extending legal protection to fictional films, but primarily to authorized adaptations. A film's status as intellectual property depended, consequently, on the prior legal status of the literary work from which it derived. Moreover, while granting a kind of author's rights to film, these decisions also assumed, as in publishing, the primary right of the company whose capital produced the film.

Although diametrically opposed, these two legal definitions, in their insistence on the cinema's relation to the theater, turned out to be complementary in directing the French cinema's development. Whereas one, in terms of production, granted films protection according to their literary source, most of which turned out to be plays—for adaptations of novels often derived from already existing theatrical adaptations—the other, in terms of exhibition, separated the cinema from the theater, subjecting it to much greater censorship restrictions. This had the effect, I would argue, of provoking a series of efforts within the industry that, while asserting the cinema's autonomy as a mass cultural practice, would grant it a legal status commensurate with that of the theater, its "high culture" rival. In 1907, Benoît-Lévy laid out the position underlying these industry efforts quite clearly. "Film does not constitute an ordinary sort of merchandise," he asserted, "but a literary and artistic property."[75] "It is a literary and artistic property in a double sense," he added, "for a film consists of an idea and its application simultaneously. Invention makes it a non-written literary property, and photography makes it incontestably an artistic property."[76] Or, as E. Maugras and M. Guégan put it, one year later, a film possesses the two elements required of any work of art: production, the creation of mental work or the imagination, and execution, the skill of professional craftsmanship or artistry.[77] The sum total of the efforts this discourse supported might best be described as a strategy of legitimation for the French cinema as a cultural practice. That strategy gained official recognition in early 1909, when the Berlin Commission—responsible for revising the 1886 Berne Convention on the international protection of scientific, literary, and artistic production—formally granted protection, not only to the author whose work was reproduced on film, but to the film property itself as *une production de l'esprit* (to use the language of the relevant 1793 French law).[78]

As the editor of *Phono-Ciné-Gazette*, which came close to serving as a publicity organ for Pathé-Frères at the time, Benoît-Lévy served as a crucial, yet now largely forgotten agent of this French strategy. A model civic leader of the turn-of-the-century Third Republic, he was a lawyer and journalist who had founded the Société populaire des beaux-arts (1894) and an active member of the Ligue d'enseignement (the organization most responsible for initiating the secular education system).[79] From 1905 to 1908, his work was devoted almost exclusively to promoting the cinema as the fulfillment of the long-cherished dream of a "people's theater" and to convincing Parisians that the twentieth century would indeed be "the century of the cinema."[80] In May 1906, for instance, the Société populaire des beaux-arts organized a special *fête cinématographique* at the Trocadéro Théâtre in Paris, whose three-hour program was comprised of seventeen recent Pathé films.[81] So successful was the 13 May program (four thousand people apparently attended) that a second program was scheduled two weeks later, with a dozen additional new Pathé films.[82] The following year, also in Paris, on 11 May, *Phono-Ciné-Gazette* organized another festival in the Salle Elysées-Montmartre at the Théâtre Trianon (two thousand people attended), this time with a program of recent Gaumont, Raleigh & Robert, Vitagraph, Méliès, and Pathé films.[83] Under Benoît-Lévy's editorship, *Phono-Ciné-Gazette* reported, of course, on all the court cases concerning the cinema; and he himself repeatedly argued the industry's position that film was a "literary and artistic property."[84] His own contribution to this cause was to avert a protracted war with French playwrights by negotiating with the Société des auteurs dramatiques—specifically with the aging dramatist and opera librettist, Michel Carré—to make a film version of the popular pantomime, *L'Enfant prodigue.*[85] Recorded at the Gaumont studio in May 1907, this early feature-length film (1,600 meters) was projected through the summer months at the Théâtre des Variétés in Paris and met with a somewhat mixed response (at the time, Carré knew very little about filmmaking).[86] By then, however, Benoît-Lévy and *Phono-Ciné-Gazette* had helped prepare the way for Pathé-Frères to move on several fronts at once in an effort to secure its dominant economic position through restructuring and extending its proliferating operations.

Simply put, in 1906–1907, Charles Pathé sought to establish a near monopoly within the French cinema industry by dividing his corporation into more or less separate sectors of film production, distribution, and exhibition, thus extending its already "horizontal" structure to the point where control could be exercised "vertically" over every stage from the production to the consumption of films.[87] The initial front on which Pathé moved was the exhibition sector, perhaps impelled by the example of "nickel madness" sweeping the United States. A further spur to this strategy, however, came in July 1906, when the National Assembly passed legislation mandating a weekly day off from work for all employees in France, which created conditions for a regular period of "weekend"

9. Cinéma Pathé poster (c. 1907)

entertainment. In order to expand its market base beyond the clientele of the fairs and to attract a large urban white-collar and bourgeois audience on a more consistent basis, in November 1906, Pathé-Frères, in association with a new Benoît-Lévy company, embarked on a long-range project of constructing a circuit of permanent cinemas throughout France.[88] The first in Paris, the three-hundred-seat Omnia-Pathé (its facade a melange of metro entrance and oriental palace), opened on 15 December 1906, right next to the Théâtre des Variétés and across from the Musée Grévin.[89] Within weeks, other Pathé cinemas began springing up across the capital and as far away as Lyon, Marseille, Bordeaux, and Toulouse. In Paris itself, entrepreneurs quickly got wind of Pathé's plans and began either constructing their own cinemas or converting café-concerts, music halls, theaters, and even churches—one of the earliest being Kaiser's Gab-Ka, on the Boulevard des Italiens.[90] By the summer of 1907 (which coincidentally saw the closing of the Paris morgue to the public),[91] there were at least fifty new or converted cinemas throughout the city, many of them in the shopping and entertainment districts. Pathé ads and posters extolled the Omnia-Pathé's appeal to everyone in the family as well as every social class.[92] One 1908 poster—in which a smiling gendarme seemed to be directing the cross-class "traffic" of a cinema queue—even suggested that going to the cinema not only was respectable and safe but had the blessing of the state authorities.[93]

With characteristic caution, Gaumont waited until the summer of 1908 to open its first Paris cinema, the Cinéma-Palace,[94] and then slowly put up others, reaching Bordeaux only in 1910. In conjunction with his plans for Film d'Art, Paul Lafitte founded the Compagnie des Cinéma-Halls (absorbing, in the process, the small French distributor, American Kinetograph) and leased the giant Hippodrome theater (a former circus arena, among other things), on the Place Clichy, which debuted as a cinema in late 1907.[95] Although the Hippodrome led all other Paris cinemas in box office receipts (the Omnia-Pathé was a close second) through 1908 and 1909, according to *Comoedia*, Lafitte's financial problems at Film d'Art forced him to close it down, after which the huge arena reverted briefly to a skating rink.[96] Permanent cinemas expanded in Paris to more than one hundred by 1909, of which twenty (including the Cirque d'hiver, which began featuring films in December 1907)[97] were owned by Pathé-Frères, whose national circuit, by then, had reached a total of two hundred cinemas. Cinema construction slowed somewhat in 1909 and 1910,[98] apparently due to a leveling off in attendance, but then it exploded again in 1911, culminating in Gaumont's purchase and renovation of the Hippodrome (under the management of Edgar Costil, head of Gaumont's cinema circuit), which opened to much fanfare as the Gaumont-Palace, the largest cinema in the world (with 3,400 seats), on 29 September 1911.[99]

Although hardly trouble-free, Pathé's transformation of the exhibition sector quickly established the first component of his corporation's security, at least within France. Despite their popularity around 1907–1908,[100] the fairground cinemas could mount only a feeble resistance to Pathé's strategy, even with the support of such trade journals as *Argus-Phono-Cinéma* and *Ciné-Journal*.[101] In the face of the urban cinema explosion, their share of the market quickly declined. Although *Ciné-Journal* announced their immanent demise as early as the winter of 1908–1909, fairground cinema advertisements did not disappear from Bordeaux newspapers, for instance, until 1910, and many small traveling exhibitors actually survived up to the beginning of the war.[102] Similarly, the new permanent cinemas began to displace the café-concerts or music halls as the most popular urban spectacle. In part, this came about through a change within the more established institution itself, as the leading Paris music halls, around 1903, began turning into "luxury-category entertainments." The Folies-Bergère, for instance, now demanded a minimum of three francs, the newly renovated Moulin Rouge charged four francs and up, and both the Scala and Olympia cost as much as seven or eight francs.[103] By contrast, ticket prices at the new cinemas ranged from just fifty centimes to one or two francs, and music hall entrepreneurs found that, by adding matinee film screenings to their regular programs or shifting entirely to cinema programs, they actually increased their profits.[104] The slowest areas to evidence this change apparently were working-class faubourgs such as Saint-Denis, according to the municipal archive and local newspaper, whose population preferred the local music hall to the cinema as

10. Gaumont-Palace (renovated, 1911)

late as 1910.[105] By 1911, however, annual cinema attendance in Paris reached more than three million, a figure nearly equal to that of the café-concerts and music halls combined;[106] and Benoît-Lévy had persuaded many exhibitors to join him in founding a professional organization, the Association française du cinématographe.

Cinema programs also were settling into a relatively stable format, but one more restricted than the morning-to-midnight screenings so characteristic of the American nickelodeons.[107] French programs tended to follow the format of the music hall and melodrama theater, with differences developing between the fixed and mobile cinemas as well as between the large and small urban cinemas. The fairground cinemas generally presented a two-hour program each evening, with an added matinee on Thursday and Sunday. Moreover, the Thursday matinee, instituted at least as early as 1905, was specifically designed for children who attended school only in the morning that day.[108] The smaller urban cinemas adopted a similar program schedule, with those in the working-class faubourgs often open only Thursday through Monday—their hours conforming with the newly instituted "weekend" of entertainment as well as the more traditional habit of "Saint Monday" as a working-class day of rest.[109] There, the selection of films sometimes appealed to quite different constituencies, depending on the place and time. The small cinema operated by the Dufayel department store, for instance, located near the city's northern outskirts, screened films every afternoon, primarily for women and children, while the nearby Saint-Denis cinema, as Berlanstein suggests, attracted "merchants and employers" on Friday nights and workers the rest of the time.[110] The larger or more prestigious urban cinemas, situated in the shopping and entertainment districts and catering to the various strata of the bourgeoisie, offered at least two complete programs per day—both the Omnia-Pathé and Cirque d'hiver, for instance, advertised starting times of 2:30 P.M. and 8:30 P.M.—in direct competition with the music halls and theaters, which, as early as the summer of 1906, were doing matinee film screenings.[111] Their programs also comprised at least two hours of highly diverse films (numbering anywhere from a half-dozen to a dozen), with the American Biograph cinema, which opened in April 1910, being perhaps the first to offer three-hour programs every afternoon and evening.[112] And, once they became available, certain Boulevard cinemas began featuring the attraction of two- or three-reel dramatic films. As Charles Pathé himself later confessed, the permanent cinemas were essential to the development of longer films as well as a regular white-collar and bourgeois audience. By 1911, Georges Dureau agreed, the new cinemas indeed had succeeded in shifting the locus of exhibition away from the provinces and small towns to the larger cities and won over the "elegant people" of urban France.[113]

The second, and perhaps even more important, front on which Pathé moved was the distribution sector. *Phono-Ciné-Gazette* first announced Charles Pathé's surprising decision in July 1907: henceforth, Pathé-Frères films, rather than being sold outright, would be rented in weekly programs for a fixed percentage of exhibitor receipts.[114] And they would be disseminated, especially in France, through a network of regional companies spun off from the parent corporation and closely allied with its exhibition circuit.[115] Essentially, this was an early form of block-booking. By early 1908, various partners and surrogates had formed six new companies to handle Pathé-Frères films on an exclusive basis:

Cinéma-Omnia: northern and northwestern France, Algeria, Switzerland.
Cinéma-Exploitation: Paris and eastern France.
Cinéma-Monopole: east central and southeastern France.
Cinéma-Théâtre: west central France.
Cinéma-National: southwestern France.
La Belge Cinéma: Belgium, Holland, Luxembourg.[116]

Of these, no less than four came under the supervision of Benoît-Lévy, most of their offices being located in Paris, right above the Omnia-Pathé cinema. Crucial to this distribution network was another company in which Benoît-Lévy had an interest, the Société de cinématographe automobile, which assured the transport required for a weekly change of cinema programs.[117]

Although Pathé's transition to a distribution system based on film rentals was not always smooth—sales continued outside the territory of the regional companies and sometimes even within as well—the gamble seems to have paid off, at least according to the corporation's figures of doubled profits and dividends for 1907–1908.[118] And the move was officially sanctioned by the International Congress of Film Producers, early in 1909, which accepted the film rental system as its new standard of operation. In one sense, Pathé's shift to film rentals was an attempt to curtail the fairground showmen who were using the company's name without authorization and to reduce the high number of old, badly worn film prints in circulation.[119] In another, it can be seen as an effort to challenge the legal definition of the cinema as a spectacle de curiosité and align it with the theater. Although the move clearly was meant to advance Pathé-Frères's prestige, ultimately, however, its objective was economic—to standardize exploitation of the market created by the new permanent cinemas. The network of regional distribution companies, which to some extent still followed the territorial boundaries of the fairground circuits, suggested that Charles Pathé already saw that the future of his "empire" depended on the control of film distribution and exhibition perhaps even more than on film production. To that end, Pathé-Frères increasingly took on the structure of a monopolistic holding company at the head of nearly a dozen more or less separate affiliates, making it perhaps the most extensively vertically integrated film company ever.

In the meantime, however, Pathé continued to augment other sectors of the company, most especially that of film production. In 1907, Pathé mechanized its unique stencil color process and increased its output of projectors, cameras, and other apparatuses to four hundred per month.[120] The following year, at Belleville, Continsouza introduced a new projector, whose sales quickly made it one of the most widely used models in the world, almost achieving the professional popularity of the Pathé studio camera.[121] Another small studio was erected in the south of France, near Nice, joining the five "glass house" studios already in full operation at Vincennes, Joinville, and Montreuil. By early 1909, the printing of positive film stock had again doubled, to eighty thousand meters per day, and the manufacture of apparatuses had reached five hundred per month.[122] Over the course of that year, the company could boast of having produced eight hundred new film titles, or 20 million meters of positive film stock, and of having built six thousand cameras, projectors, and other related material.[123] With close to four thousand employees now among its various affiliates, Pathé could easily fulfill its advertised promise of a full new program of films each week, or a total of anywhere from fifteen hundred to two thousand meters of negative film stock.[124]

To achieve this high level, of course, meant hiring more filmmakers, scriptwriters, and actors as well, all of whom were integrated into an increasingly independent "director-unit" system of production. In 1907, the popular novelist Daniel Riche, for instance, accepted Pathé's offer to join Rollini and Heuzé in writing scenarios on a regular basis.[125] That same year, Pathé's studio administrator, Charles Lépine, took over the production of féeries and trick films from Velle (who had left for Cinès in Italy), only to be replaced soon after (when Lépine himself followed Velle) by the Spanish cameraman and former Méliès agent, Segundo de Chomón. In 1908, Georges Monca (a director at the Théâtre de la République) also came on board and soon was producing one-reel dramas and comedies written for René Leprince. Later that year, André Andréani (a Pathé actor) began collaborating with Zecca himself on historical films. At the same time, Camille de Morlhon (an established playwright) directed several adaptations and then began specializing in contemporary dramas drawn from his own scenarios. The really consistent money-making films for Pathé during this period, however, were the series of comic films written specifically for the company's first three "star" actors. The *Boireau* series, featuring André Deed (a former music hall acrobat and clown), established the genre between 1906 and 1908, after which he left for Italy to perform in a similar series under the name of *Cretinetti* or *Gribouille*. Shortly thereafter, the *Max* series, starring Max Linder and directed by Louis Gasnier (a former assistant to Nonguet), more than took the place of the *Boireau* series. By 1910, a third series, *Rigadin,* starring Prince and directed by Monca, was launched to complement the increasingly popular films of Linder, whose publicity status as "the king of cinema" made him the earliest French film "star."[126] And in 1910, Bosetti left Gaumont to direct several comic series—especially, *Rosalie* and *Little Moritz*—for Pathé's new Comica affiliate at the Nice studio.[127] Finally, in 1908, Pathé provided laboratory space, in its educational film division, for Dr. Jean Comandon to begin research in microscopic cinematography, research that was then introduced to the Académie des Sciences, in November 1909.[128] And the company's production schedule was rounded out with the earliest weekly newsreel, *Pathé-Journal,*[129] whose half-hour episodes were edited by Armand Verhylle and Lucien Doublon.

With its new studio (the biggest in the world), its new corporate structure, and its films now being marketed in the United States by George Kleine Optical (now a major foreign film distributor),[130] Gaumont was well positioned to respond, in 1907, to Pathé's challenge. A further technological advance, for instance, came that year with the development of the first automatic process for printing film stock, which pushed sales of positive film stock to fifteen thousand meters per day.[131] Three years later, demonstrations of the latest model of Gaumont's "Chronophone" system were given in Paris, at the Congrès international de la photographie as well as the Académie des Sciences. More important to Gaumont's return on investments, the now serious business of filmmaking was placed in the hands of a man, as Feuillade took over as head of production from Guy (who had married Herbert Blaché, an English cameraman newly hired by the company).[132] Gaumont himself supervised the transition to a director-unit system of production, as is evident from his letters to Feuillade,[133] during his 1908 and 1909 visits to the United States. Bosetti, for instance, specialized in Gaumont's chase films and then directed two comic series of his own creation, *Romeo* (1908) and *Calino* (1909-1910). In early 1908, the caricaturist Emile Cohl was hired to help Arnaud produce chase films and soon was making a series of original animation films.[134] In 1909, Léonce Perret (an actor who had worked with Antoine and Réjane) was sent to Berlin by Gaumont to produce phonoscènes for Oskar Messter and then was recalled to Paris, the following year, to direct comic and dramatic films for which he himself served as scriptwriter and chief performer. Both Arnaud and Feuillade, finally, made films across a range of genres. For his part, Feuillade directed his own scenarios for chase films, biblical films, historical reconstructions, melodramas, and the comic *Bébé* series (1910–1912). By late 1910, Gaumont, too, was releasing its own weekly newsreel, *Gaumont-Actualités*, edited by Henri Lefragette, and also was beginning to specialize in polar expedition films.[135] With this system of production, which relied much less than did Pathé on relatively strict divisions of labor, Gaumont soon made good on his promise, in 1907, to provide exhibitors with a program of at least six new films each week. And the lighting effects of the company's films were taken as exemplary of the best work in black-and-white cinematography.[136] Moreover, because Gaumont films continued to be sold outright directly to exhibitors, they quickly increased their share of the still important fairground market. Only in 1909 did Gaumont institute a separate distribution company, Comptoir Ciné-Location,[137] and begin to rent its films according to the principles first established by Pathé. By then, the corporation had weathered a year of no profits at all, in 1908 (partly due to heavy investments),[138] and resumed the spectacular growth it experienced in 1906–1907.

Unlike Gaumont, Méliès was poorly positioned to respond to the Pathé-led drive to industrialize the French cinema. In fact, he proudly refused to consider himself a businessman and vainly tried to maintain his status as an independent artist.[139] In late 1907, however, perhaps seizing on the expanding American market as an opportunity to regain some of the ground lost to his competitors, Méliès constructed a second studio at Montreuil.[140] As a consequence, in 1908, his output suddenly jumped to a total of fifty-five films and nine thousand meters of negative film stock. Méliès continued to make films specially geared to the Paris music halls—spectacular one-reelers such as *Le Tunnel sous la manche* (1907) or *La Civilisation à travers les âges* (1908). But most of his shorter trick films and comics now were destined for the fêtes foraines cinemas (following Pathé's withdrawal) and, increasingly, the American nickelodeon market. There Gaston Méliès served his brother well, at first, despite considerable odds. The theft of three hundred film print negatives from Méliès's New York factory, in May 1907, for instance, held up distribution for several months.[141] Yet Gaston rebounded with special ads in the new trade magazine, *Moving Picture World*, and, in early 1908, wrangled membership in the Film Service Association, Edison's initial organization restricting film imports into the United States. When the Motion Picture Patents Company was formed later that year, however, the

Méliès membership license was granted to Gaston (who was now keeping any profits for himself), but only after a six-month delay.[142] So dependent had he now become on the American market that this delay, together with his brother's shenanigans, forced Georges to close down the Montreuil studio through most of 1909.[143] Thereafter, without his brother's knowledge, Gaston began producing films under his own name, first in Brooklyn and then in San Antonio. As for Georges himself, he went back to creating féerie spectacles, such as *Les Fantômes du Nil* at the Alhambra, and did not resume film production until 1911, and then only under a contractual agreement dictated by Pathé, whose company would distribute such films as *Les Hallucinations du Baron de Münchhausen* (1911) and *A la conquîete du pôle* (1912).[144] Within another two years, nearly bankrupt and with his second wife dead, the once popular filmmaker would "retire" from an industry that no longer had any place for him.

While Pathé and, to a lesser extent, Gaumont sought to control every stage of film production, distribution, and exhibition, other new firms concentrated on carving out a niche within just one sector of the industry. Within the production sector, soon to be vacated involuntarily by Méliès, the earliest of these to emerge was Eclipse, in August 1906, out of the Paris branch of England's then largest film company, Urban Trading.[145] In order to initiate production of the company's first films, Hatot and Jasset were hired away from Pathé and Gaumont, respectively, to work at a small rented studio in Courbevoie.[146] After two years, however, the company remained little more than a "financial affair," with capital stock of one and a half million francs,[147] most of it underwritten by Ernest May, who was on the directorates of several French banks and electrical companies. All that changed, in 1908, when Eclipse moved to absorb its former parent company, contracted to help produce and distribute the films of a smaller French firm, Radios, which recently had been founded by Georges Maurice and Jules Dumien (the Olympia café-concert manager), and began renovating the latter's "glass house" studio in Boulogne-sur-Seine.[148] Within another two years, aided by George Kleine's distribution of its product in the United States, the company slowly established itself as the fourth largest French producer of films (at least in quantity).[149] Among them were Joë Hamman's earliest westerns (directed by Gaston Roudès), the *Arthème* comic series (starring Ernest Servaes), and a weekly newsreel, *Eclipse-Journal* (put together by Mesguisch and Emile Pierre). Furthermore, Henri Desfontaines (a former actor for Antoine at the Odéon and then for Capellani at Pathé) assumed the direction of the company's "serious" films under the Radios label.

Soon after its founding, Eclipse was joined by other, even smaller Paris firms.[150] In January 1907, for instance, Théophile Pathé founded a production company under his own name (with two million francs of capital).[151] Directed by Promio, these films were intended to supplant those of his more famous brothers in the fairground cinemas—although, on the basis of one surviving print, they turned out to be of much lower quality.[152] About the same time, Joly (Pathé's former partner) launched Société Lux (with one million francs of capital), whose film stock developing factory was run by Léopold Löbel and whose principal director-scriptwriter was Gérard Bourgeois (a former "Porte St. Martin" actor), assisted by a young caricaturist and journalist, Jean Durand.[153] Within a year, from its studio in Gentilly, Lux was releasing several films per week and scoring hits, not only at Paris's largest cinemas, but throughout the world[154]—the most popular titles apparently were in the *Patouillard* or *Bill* comic series, starring Paul Bertho. Some measure of the company's success can be gathered from its foreign distribution offices, which stretched from North and South America across Europe to Russia.[155] In 1908, the Galand company was reorganized (with one million francs of capital) as Le Lion, which secured a tenuous niche within the industry for the next two years by producing just one or two films per week.[156] And, in 1909, Raleigh & Robert, an early Anglo-French distributor of British, Danish, and Italian films, went into film production even more briefly, in conjunction with Hatot's own new company, Société du film négatif (in a Montreuil studio destroyed by fire not long after its construction), for whom Jasset directed the *Docteur Phantom* series (1910).[157]

The most successful of these new production companies clearly was Eclair. When first founded in May 1907, by two Paris lawyers, Charles Jourjon and Marcel Vandal, the company's fortunes did not seem propitious, for their capital investment amounted to only 150,000 francs.[158] Initially, Eclair may have been "banking" on the productivity of its chief engineer, Parnaland, the inventor and entrepreneur who had been involved in an important court case with Dr. Doyen. That changed early in 1908, when Jourjon and Vandal amassed another five hundred thousand francs to invest in the company, acquired an exotic garden estate from the celebrated naturalist, Etienne de Lacépède, in Epinay-sur-Seine, and there erected a "glass house" studio (whose dimensions were about one quarter those of Gaumont's giant studio constructed just two years before).[159] At the same time, their chief engineer retired (or was pushed aside) and was replaced by Georges Maurice (whose company, Radios, had been acquired by Eclipse), and Jourjon and Vandal set about renovating Parnaland's former laboratories for developing and printing film stock.[160] Finally, they hired the team of Jasset and Hatot, both of whom had experience working for Gaumont and Eclipse, to initiate a more regular schedule of fiction film production.[161] Under the new team's direction, Eclair's strategy was to exploit the formula of producing a series of short films built around a single character and actor, a principle of standardization which Pathé already had experimented with in its comic *Boireau* series. The formula they seized on, the *Nick Carter* detective series, was based on the popular American dime novels just then being issued in France.[162] By year's end, with considerable support from *Ciné-Journal*,[163] the gamble paid off in a profitable series of films starring Pierre Bressol as Nick Carter.[164] Soon Jasset and Hatot were cranking out other *films en série* as well—such as the *Riffle Bill* westerns (1908–1909) and *Morgan le pirate* adventures (1909)—and adding more titles to the *Nick Carter* series in 1909.[165]

It was at this juncture, probably based on a perceived opportunity in the American cinema market, that Jourjon and Vandal decided on a second major infusion of capital. In November 1909, for instance, Eclair's studio and laboratory at Epinay-sur-Seine were enlarged and new equipment was installed—from automatic developing machines to color printing machines—apparatuses that the company also now set out to manufacture for the world market.[166] Following the model of other new French producers, the company initiated production of a series of literary adaptations, carrying the label of ACAD (Association des compositeurs et des auteurs dramatiques), under the initial supervision of Numès (a former Variétés actor).[167] Furthermore, after briefly working for Raleigh & Robert, Jasset and Hatot resumed their relationship with Eclair by contracting to produce a series of fiction films in North Africa, establishing what would become a unique site of location shooting for the company.[168] In the summer of 1910, Jasset returned to the company's studio outside Paris and, that fall, assumed the role of "artistic director"—which meant that, while overseeing film production, he would have his own filmmaking unit.[169] Eclair's production schedule now was geared to the regular release of three or four films per week. The ACAD films or "serious dramas," whose direction by Numès, Bussy, and Agnel was now supervised by Emile Chautard (a former Odéon and Variétés actor), generally served as the "feature attraction" and introduced into the cinema a host of new theater actors, from Germaine Dermoz and Maryse Dauvray to Charles Krauss and Henry Roussel.[170] And they were supplemented by contemporary melodramas or historical dramas such as Jasset's own *Hérodiade* (1910). The other staples of Eclair's weekly program included either a short travelogue or documentary (usually shot by R. Moreau)[171] and a comic series—either *Gontran* (1910–1914), starring the smoothly polished René Grehan, or *Willy* (1911–1914), starring a mop-headed English boy named Willy Sanders. By the end of 1910, Eclair had passed Eclipse to rank third among French film producers and was well positioned (having opened distribution offices and printing laboratories in Milan, London, and New York)[172] to extend its operations throughout Europe and overseas.

Of all these new production companies, undoubtedly Film d'Art had more than its share of problems, perhaps because of its unusual ambitions. Although not officially announced until May, Film d'Art was founded in February 1908 (with just a half-million francs of capital) by businessman Paul Lafitte, who had close ties to the Paris press and theater world.[173] With Pathé's financial assistance, Lafitte built and equipped a "glass house" studio in Neuilly, after convincing playwright Henri Lavedan, along with Charles Le Bargy of the prestigious Comédie Française, to produce a series of one-reel dramatic films. One of the first of these, *L'Assassinat du Duc de Guise*, had a sensational premiere at the Salle Charras, on 17 November 1908[174]—the result of a well-orchestrated publicity campaign in the press, especially in *L'Illustration*[175]—and was followed by others such as *Le Retour d'Ulysse* and *La Tosca* (both 1909). However, the costs of making these few films exceeded even those of Méliès's spectacular féerie films—*La Tosca,* for instance, had to be reshot completely after Sarah Bernhardt refused to release the version she starred in—and box office receipts fell below expectations.[176] By the summer of 1909, Film d'Art was more than two hundred thousand francs in debt (some of which was paid off by Pathé), and Paul Gavault (a popular playwright) replaced Lafitte as head of production. André Calmettes, Le Bargy's assistant, took over direction of the company's films, abandoning original scenarios for literary adaptations—for instance, *Rival de son fils* (1909), *Carmen* (1910), and *Madame Sans-Gêne* (1911)—and adopting a more orderly and less costly production schedule, often with less-well-known actors. In early 1910, after the company finally broke with Pathé, he was joined by Henri Pouctal (a former associate of Antoine and Gémier) whose films included *Werther* (1910) and a quite popular *Camille Desmoulins* (1911). Despite Gavault and Calmettes's efforts, by the end of 1911, Film d'Art's debts had mounted to more than four hundred thousand francs, and the company had to be sold. One of the reasons for Film d'Art's commercial failure—other than its exhorbitant investment costs early on—was the limited and sometimes erratic distribution of its films. And the responsibility for that probably lay with Pathé-Frères, the company's initial distributor, for Pathé deliberately seems to have put the interests of a new competitor above those of Film d'Art, and not only in France.[177]

That company was SCAGL (Société cinématographique des auteurs et gens de lettres), one of the cornerstones of Pathé's attempt to redefine the cinema and attract a white-collar and bourgeois audience.[178] Crucial support for this effort was needed from French writers, especially dramatists, one of whose organizations successfully had sued Pathé, around 1905, over copyright infringements in the production of phonographs. It was Benoît-Lévy who, in response to the threat of open warfare between the theater and the cinema, in 1907, negotiated a reconciliation through the Société française des auteurs dramatiques, to produce a film version of Michel Carré's *L'Enfant prodigue*. When that project proved less successful than anticipated, Pathé himself then turned to the Société des gens de lettres, where the popular novelist Decourcelle had some influence.[179] In June 1908, with financial backing from the Banque de Merzbach, Decourcelle founded SCAGL as another Pathé affiliate, under an agreement that gave the company the right to adapt works by SGL authors.[180] Pathé assigned Capellani—after such recent successes as *Le Légende de Polichinelle* (1907) and *La Vestale* (1908)—to head SCAGL's production, at a newly constructed Vincennes studio, and assumed exclusive rights to distribute its films.[181] Several Capellani films proved quite successful—*L'Arlèsienne* (1908), which actually preceded Film d'Art's first releases by more than a month, and *L'Homme aux gants blancs* (1908)[182]—all of which convinced Pathé and Decourcelle to set the company on a course of adapting recent popular French "classics" for the screen. Soon other filmmakers were being transferred to SCAGL, including Monca, with a series of dramas and comedies starring Prince and the music hall singer-actress Mistinguett, as well as Carré, who could draw on his extensive connections to both theater and opera. So successful was SCAGL that, in 1910, Pathé launched its own *Séries d'Art Pathé-Frères*, through which two former actors, Andréani and Georges Denola, "graduated" to directing such "historical" adaptations as *Cléopatre* (1910), alongside the established director Morlhon who contributed contemporary dramas such as *Le Bon Patron* (1910).

Through SCAGL and, to a lesser extent, Film d'Art, Pathé's ambition to turn the cinema into a more reputable as well as more profitable enterprise came one step closer to being realized. Other companies, for instance, supported the move with their own special line of "artistic" films—from Eclair's ACAD series, Gaumont's *Grands Films Artistiques*, and Eclipse's *Série d'Art* to the short-lived efforts of Maurice de Féraudy (from the Comédie Française) for Théâtro-Films and Heuzé for Le Film des auteurs.[183] And nearly all took to displaying, in their advertisements, the names of the actors and actresses they were luring away from prestigious theaters. All this led to a debate between Dureau and Georges Fagot in *Ciné-Journal* (which, by 1910, had become the industry's principal trade journal) over whose company's films were the best "films d'art." SCAGL's success also had the effect of lengthening films, slowly standardizing the concept of having at least one "feature attraction" among a company's weekly program of releases. Beginning in 1909, with Capellani's *L'Assommoir* (735 meters)[184] and the Zecca-Andréani *Napoléon* (750 meters), longer films were becoming commonplace by 1911—for instance, Capellani's *Le Courrier de Lyon* (750 meters), Bourgeois's *Victimes d'alcool* (795 meters), Jasset's *Zigomar* (935 meters), and even Feuillade's *La Tare* (900 meters).[185] Finally, SCAGL seems to have confirmed Charles Pathé's strategy of shifting the locus of his "empire" to film distribution. The strategy solidified even further in response to what Pathé and others perceived as a French crisis of overproduction in 1908 (reportedly, it had tripled),[186] the result he implied, in rather self-serving letters printed in *Ciné-Journal*, of the new companies entering the industry.[187] Yet it had been his decision, after all, to construct permanent cinemas and rent films, thus abandoning the fêtes foraines market, which, at least in part, encouraged those very producers to emerge. Gradually, he began diverting the risks of production to the corporation's stable of smaller, quasi-independent affiliates—whose number had grown, by 1911, to include a half-dozen foreign companies as well as the meager remains of Méliès's French company—all of whose product (which now totaled an average length of 2,500 meters per week)[188] was then channeled through Pathé-Frères and its worldwide distribution agencies, eventually reaching up to 500 million people.[189] The strategy secured a high, steady rate of dividends for Pathé stockholders, at least from 1908 to 1911, and helped to raise the corporation's capital stock to 15 million francs.

Following in the wake of Pathé's strategic shift, several other French companies began staking out territory within the distribution sector of the industry. Monofilm, for instance, was a small company that concentrated on distributing foreign films in the French market until, in February 1910, it acquired the distribution rights to most Film d'Art productions.[190] By 1911, after Monofilm's coup in gaining French distribution rights to Milano-Films's epic *L'Enfer* (2,000 meters),[191] owner Charles Delac was able to buy out the debt-ridden French company through a process by which Monofilm was absorbed into Film d'Art. In the summer of 1909, Louis Aubert entered the distribution market and slowly wrested, from Raleigh & Robert, French rights to the increasingly longer Italian and Danish films.[192] Within two years, his company had prospered to the point of being reorganized as the Société Etablissements L. Aubert, with a half-million francs of capital stock. Aubert now had exclusive distribution contracts with most of the major Italian film producers—Cinès, Italia, Pasquali, Ambrosia—as well as the Danish producer, Nordisk, and was poised to enter both the exhibition and production sectors of the industry.[193] In 1910, out of the breakup of Compagnie des Cinéma-Halls, and under the joint ownership of Astaix, Kastor, and Lallement, emerged another important distributor, AGC or Agence Générale Cinématographique, in what soon became a successful attempt to market a wide variety of French, Italian, and American films.[194] The only significant non-French distributor was Vitagraph, which, in contrast to the other American companies (which chose to settle in London),[195] had established Paris as its principal foreign office as early as 1906–1907.[196] Within a year, Vitagraph was releasing up to six films a week in France—*The Haunted Hotel* (1907) was the first to have some impact, in April 1907—and was constructing a laboratory for printing positive film stock in order to use the Paris office to market its films throughout Europe.[197] By 1910–1911, the company's weekly releases often surpassed one thousand meters in total length, and its *Scènes muettes de la vie réele* were beginning to attract the attention of French filmmakers.[198]

One last company staked out a very different territory within the French cinema industry during this period—the leading Catholic publisher, La Bonne Presse. In 1903, La Bonne Presse had launched *Le Fascinateur*, a monthly educational guide edited by G.-Michel Coissac, whose objective was to extend the project, begun several years before, of promoting "religious learning by means of images," which initially meant magic lantern slides.[199] Encouraged by Coissac, in late 1905, La Bonne Presse opened its own office in Paris for selling or renting film projectors (of its own design) and selected programs of films—as "teaching aids" in Catholic diocese schools and as "illuminated sermons" in the churches.[200] Business was brisk from the start—460 projectors and 67,500 meters of positive film stock were sold the first year—no doubt spurred by the December 1905 law separating church and state. By 1907–1908, at least according to its ads in *Le Fascinateur*, La Bonne Presse had a cooperative exchange that may well have rivaled those supplying the fairground cinemas.[201] In conjunction with this service, the press published the first manual for film projectionists, Coissac's own *La Théorie et la pratique des projections* (1906).[202] Not all French Catholics, of course, accepted La Bonne Presse's efforts; the Jansenist orders, for instance, assumed a more Manichean position that the cinema was a major corrupting influence on contemporary moral life. If *Le Fascinateur* chose to emphasize the cinema's potential for pedagogical purposes, perhaps it was to publicize how different (and even progressive) a Catholic education could be from that provided by the Third Republic's recently instituted secular school system. For Coissac and La Bonne Presse were instrumental in introducing films as an educational tool into Catholic schools well before Benoît-Lévy, the Société populaire des beaux arts, and the Ligue d'enseignement (which already had an extensive lantern slide service) could begin, in 1909, to organize their own efforts to incorporate the cinema into education.[203]

If Pathé's position seemed secure within France itself, such was not always the case elsewhere; and that eventually would spell trouble, for the corporation had become increasingly dependent on the foreign market for its sales and rentals.[204] As one means of making the film product it distributed more attractive on the international market, Pathé adopted the "imperialist" strategy of having affiliate companies produce culturally specific films within the major nationally defined circuits of its distribution network. Launched in France itself with the founding of Film d'Art and SCAGL, the strategy was tested in Russia, Italy, and Belgium, before being introduced into the United States, the real locus of the company's problems. As Jay Leyda has argued, Pathé's branch offices in a sense created a Russian market for the cinema through the practice of selling its projectors and its expanding stock of films, initially, to touring showmen and, after 1906, increasingly, to urban exhibitors with permanent cinemas.[205] By early 1908, the French company's profits from its Russian sales were nearly half of what it took in from the United States and considerably greater than its profits from any other foreign country.[206] When demands for "native films" began to appear in the Russian press, this distribution network as well as the French company's previous films on Russian subjects—for instance, *Le Nihiliste* (1906) and *L'Espionne* (1907)—seemed to give it a distinct advantage. After the earliest Film d'Art and SCAGL imports, along with several local productions, had established a Russian market for adaptations of literary classics or familiar folktales, in the spring of 1909, Pathé set up its first foreign production unit in Moscow, under the direction of Maurice-André Maître and Kai Hansen, with cameraman Joseph Mundviller.[207] Within two years, the success of Pathé russe films such as *Peter the Great* (1909), *Princess Tarakanova* (1910), and *Lekhaim* (1911)[208]—in both the national and international market (and there were as many cinemas in Russia as in France, by 1911)—suggested that the strategy, though costly, indeed had some merit. Pathé's affiliate in Belgium, Belge-Cinéma-Film, headed by Alfred Machin, seemed to confirm that strategy on a much smaller scale.[209]

In a country such as Italy, however, which developed its own indigenous industry, around 1905–1906, Pathé's position was more complicated.[210] Pathé's distribution agencies—in Milan and Rome—so successfully orchestrated exhibition of the company's films that they set off alarms of protest in the fledgling corporate press as well as threats of boycotts among local exhibitors. Yet despite this opposition, by 1909, Pathé was able to set up an efficient, profitable system of distribution throughout the peninsula, adapting the rental system already in place in France.[211] This advantage was partially offset, however, by the loss of key Paris production personnel to major Italian companies: Velle to Cinès (1906), Lépine to Carlo Rossi (1907), and Deed to Italia (1908). As if to compensate, in the spring of 1909, Pathé founded FAI (Film d'Arte Italiana) in Rome, following the model of Film d'Art and SCAGL in France.[212] With Gerolamo Lo Savio as head of production, and Re Ricardi directing completely Italian casts and crews, FAI specialized in adaptations of cross-cultural masterpieces—for instance, *Othello* (1909), *Salomé* (1910), and *Françoise de Rimini* (1910), with Francesca Bertini. The competition between Pathé and the Italian companies, at least at the production level, reached its peak in 1909–1910, particularly after

Pathé refused to join the effort to create a European cartel paralleling the American Motion Picture Patents Company. By 1911, the result of these battles was a standoff. Pathé's role as a producer was prestigious but miniscule; as a distributor, however, the French firm enjoyed a sizable portion of the Italian market.

The most serious difficulties for Pathé as well as other French companies, of course, came in the United States, whose more than 8,500 cinemas (most of them nickelodeons) by 1908 now provided much of their income and profits.[213] Over the course of the previous year, evidence suggests that Pathé continued to supply about one-third of the total American market, averaging more than twice the number of film titles and footage of its competitors, Vitagraph and Edison, and selling as many as two hundred copies of each released film.[214] Despite its prominent position, augmented by a new factory (in Bound Brook, New Jersey) for printing postive film stock, Pathé felt vulnerable enough to support Edison's efforts to set up an organization that might monopolize the American cinema industry. After fruitless negotiations between the two companies in the spring of 1907,[215] the threat of Edison's film patent suits (one of which, in October 1907, was decided in Edison's favor) persuaded Pathé to sign on as a member of the Film Service Association (FSA), which licensed a select number of producers to operate in the United States.[216] That this licensing agreement excluded other foreign producers (except Méliès), however, probably appealed to Charles Pathé because it could only have strengthened his own strategies of dominance in France.[217] And the company's popularity in the nickelodeons continued unabated, as was evident in Joseph McCoy's survey, for the Edison company, of the films projected in the New York area, in June 1908.[218] Yet when Biograph set up its own rival licensing group to serve those companies excluded from the FSA, Pathé showed signs of disaffection. During that summer, J. A. Berst floated several ideas for Pathé—such as opening a rental agency (including Vitagraph, along with the "independents") modeled on the system the company recently had put in place in France and Belgium.[219] These came to naught, however, because of the company's already overextended investment and its perception as "foreign," and Pathé fell back on similar exclusionary conditions in its agreement to join Edison's more powerful Motion Picture Patents Company (MPPC), in December 1908.[220] Although restricting each affiliated company to releasing no more than four thousand feet of positive film stock per week, the MPPC shut out all other foreign films—with the exception initially of Gaumont and Eclipse, whose films could be distributed through George Kleine.[221] And its success was such that, of the nearly four million meters of film stock imported into the United States, between August 1909 and June 1910, nearly 70 percent came from France (and most of that from Pathé).[222]

Pathé's loyalty was hardly unqualified, however, for it soon became clear that the Trust—that is, the MPPC and its distribution affiliate, the General Film Company—would be unable to restrict "independent" producers and distributors for long. Although the French company's share of MPPC released films in 1910 at least continued to equal that of the leading American producers, Biograph and Vitagraph, the increasingly active "independents" were eroding the

Trust's position.[223] By May 1910, for instance, the Sales Company was formed (with Jules Brulator, the former Lumière representative as president)[224] in order to serve as a central distribution agency for the major independents as well as French (Eclair, Film d'Art, and Lux), Danish, and Italian films.[225] Then, one month later, most of the foreign producers, including Eclair and Lux (which now had an office in New York), broke away to set up the Associated Independent Film Manufacturers.[226] Just as important were the repeated attacks in the American trade press on foreign films, and those of Pathé in particular, as morbid, gruesome, indecent, or simply in "bad taste," especially in comparison to the growing demand for "good, clean, wholesome, national, patriotic, educational" American films.[227] So widespread was this "condition of mind which one can only call Pathé-mentia," wrote a correspondent for *Bioscope*,[228] that, when the National Board of Censorship was established jointly by the People's Institute and the MPPC, in 1909, the French company's films were either rejected outright or else forced to be cut or retitled, in what were clearly disproportionate numbers.[229] In other words, "educating the public taste" often meant restricting foreign competition, especially from France. In response, Pathé turned to the strategy that its affiliates had already tested in Russia and Italy rather than the one used in England, where its branch office controlled perhaps 40 percent of the market, releasing a dozen French films per week by late 1909.[230] First of all, the company sought to publicize its release of "artistic films" (issuing special booklets for Film d'Art and SCAGL productions) as well as religious films and educational subjects.[231] Second, Pathé set out to produce its own American films—and promptly began specializing in westerns or "Indian and Cowboy pictures"[232]—eventually constructing a new studio in Jersey City, in the fall of 1910.[233] Then, in June, that same year, it cut back its releases of French and other foreign films to less than three thousand feet per week, the better to complement its American product with educational films, comedies, dramas, and eventually newsreels.[234] In other words, Pathé reorganized its American affiliate to more closely match the "home" market, a move that successfully kept the company competitive for another year or so in the dangerously fluid conditions of the American cinema industry.

Pathé's decisions also were influenced by a behind-the-scenes power struggle that pitted the French company against the American giant, Eastman Kodak.[235] By 1908, the American company was manufacturing close to 90 percent of the world's supply of negative film stock and was perceived in France as a distinct threat, even by *Ciné-Journal*.[236] Increasingly irritated by Eastman Kodak's refusal to help curtail the growth of the "independents" in the United States,[237] Charles Pathé determined, in 1909, to manufacture his own supply of film negative and quietly initiated a plan to purchase and renovate a small film-stock factory (Blair) in England. That factory's initial product proved unsatisfactory, however, and Pathé resolved to build his own factory in Vincennes, despite the reservations of his own board of directors. At the time, Eastman Kodak and Pathé were still arguing over the merits of forming a European cartel in imitation of the MPPC. Eastman Kodak, after all, helped convene the February 1909 International Congress of Film Producers in Paris (presided over, ironically, by Mé-liès), with the intention of founding just such a cartel, after an initial congress the year before had ended inconclusively.[238] Pathé, however, refused to abandon its own monopolistic ambitions to a European cartel, particularly one that might easily end up under Eastman Kodak's control. Although the congress established international standards for film stock perforation as well as film distribution through rentals and sanctioned the development of longer films, no cartel emerged. Instead, Charles Pathé finally convinced his partners to go ahead with this last component of his empire, and, after the French company refused to be a party to the MPPC contract with Eastman Kodak, the American company promptly made good on its threat to cut off deliveries of film negative.[239] With its factory not yet under construction, Pathé resorted to draconian measures in order to keep producing films. In what was probably (to use Vincent Pinel's words) the first act of "genocide" perpetrated by the cinema industry, many of the old and not-so-old Pathé positive prints were recalled and "recycled"—the film stock stripped and recoated with emulsion—and turned into "new" nega-tive film stock.[240] When this too proved less than satisfactory, however, as did the strategy of rereleasing or adding material to earlier films, Pathé apparently turned to the Lumière company, which suddenly increased its share of the mar-ket for film negative.[241] Only in 1911, apparently, did Pathé's film stock factory finally begin functioning at a capacity sufficient to come close to fulfilling his pledge of turning out nearly as much film stock as Eastman Kodak and the German firm, AGFA, at least in Europe.[242] The cost, however, was devastat-ing—for Pathé-Frères was forced to "devour its own children"—and the com-pany's dividends, for the first time ever, suffered a decline.[243]

Strategies of Survival, 1911-1914

The year 1911 seems to have been a turning point for the French cinema indus-try, largely because of decisions either taken by or else forced on Pathé-Frères. Worldwide, France's position as the leading producer and distributor of films began to slip. First, and most significantly, that slippage was evident in the Ameri-can market, where, by the end of 1911, according to a report in *Ciné-Journal*, the explosion of "independent" companies was so squeezing Pathé that its film titles accounted for less than 10 percent of the total metrage released annually in the United States.[244] By the last three months of 1913, the slippage was even noticeable in France itself: both in numbers of film titles (308 to 268) and total metrage (121,000 to 86,000), the Americans had surpassed the French on their home territory, at least in Paris.[245] Only in Central and Eastern Europe and in the less developed or colonized countries was Pathé able to maintain its former dominance.[246] As the cost of film production rose—due to increases in salaries, higher costs of film stock and developing, and the steadily growing length of films—Pathé and the other French companies sought ways to economize. At SCAGL, for instance, the cost of producing a meter of film negative rarely rose above fifteen francs (which had been Zecca's budgetary allowance ten years before), even for prestigious films such as Capellani's *Germinal* (1913).[247] Charles Pathé took the added step, in 1913, of gradually abandoning direct involvement in film production altogether and loosening the ties between the parent company and its affiliates—effectively reversing the strategy of extended vertical integration he had pioneered in 1906–1907—probably as a means of satisfying his cautious bank partners and stockholders. The move paid off in that the company's capital stock, by 1914, would rise to 30 million francs.[248] Instead, with his quest for legitimacy as strong as ever, Pathé saw himself more and more as equivalent to a book publisher: Pathé-Frères would concentrate on distributing and exhibiting the product of more than a dozen affiliates and subsidiaries (which together now included at least five thousand and perhaps as many as seven thousand employees) scattered not only around Paris but from Moscow to Jersey City, each of which had to secure much of its own financing.[249] The result was a decentralization of the French cinema industry into a kind of "cottage industry" structure, which was exactly the reverse of the consolidation and specialization then going on in the American cinema industry.

This decentralization was even visible on the technological side of the industry. Gaumont continued to make progress, not so much now in sound synchronization—although short "talking films" were often shown at the Gaumont-Palace in Paris—but in color film processes. In 1912, for instance, a Chronochrome-Gaumont projector (developed by engineers Decaux and Lemoine) was presented to the public for the first time, after which "Gaumont-Color" films were screened regularly at one of the company's smaller Paris cinemas and occasionally even at the Gaumont-Palace.[250] A more lasting advance, however, came from the precision tool work of the Debrie company in Paris, which had developed high quality machines for both perforating and printing film stock. In 1909, André Debrie had designed an extremely compact camera, using a lightweight all-metal chassis encased in wood, which the company marketed as the Debrie Parvo.[251] So impressed were cameramen with the Parvo, despite its relatively high cost, that it soon became the standard camera used for location shooting worldwide; and, in order to keep up with this demand, Debrie had to enlarge its physical plant and triple its number of personnel.[252] Pathé itself sought to reach into an area still dominated by various magic lantern devices—the French bourgeois home. The company had evidenced some interest in this market as early as 1908, but it was not until 1910 that Arthur Roussel was given the task of developing an apparatus that could use a narrow-gauge film stock.[253] In 1912, in France, Pathé finally introduced its new projector, the KOK, and a large selection of the company's extensive library of films (for sale or rental), on 28mm film stock.[254] A year later, the company began marketing the same machine in the United States.[255] The KOK system proved to be a commercial success—not only in the home, but in schools, churches, and clubs—and it easily bested Edison's competing Home Projecting Kinetoscope in the United States.[256] Finally, despite Pathé's success (or perhaps because of it), just before the war, Eclair came up with its own version of a relatively lightweight projector, the Kinéclair, to compete with both Pathé and La Bonne Presse's apparatuses in schools, churches, and town lecture halls.[257]

Pathé's advocacy of decentralization was most pronounced, of course, at the level of film production. It was during this period that the company's director-unit system became standard in the French production sector, yet significant differences remained between this system and the one Staiger and Musser have described as characteristic of the United States. The specialized division of labor which American companies developed in order to promote efficiency only went so far in France. Perhaps most significantly, despite Pathé's insistence on carefully worked-out plots and detailed decoupages, there were no scenario departments.[258] Instead, the filmmaker usually was still responsible for writing or adapting his own scripts, a condition that would later provide the basis for the polemical notion of the filmmaker as *auteur*.[259] Moreover, the French director-units tended to be organized as small companies rather than as divisions within a single large company and to be involved, at least in part, in their own financing and production planning. In other words, there were no moves to institute anything like a central producer who would exercise strict control over a company's director-units, especially those engaged in feature-film production—as Universal first did in 1912, followed by the New York Motion Picture Company (with Thomas Ince), in 1913. By contrast, to cite W. Stephen Bush's report, the French companies continued to rely on the camaraderie of their production teams (especially at Gaumont) or on a "merit system" of responsibility and compensation rather than on "scientific management"—apparently there were no "clock watchers" at Pathé-Frères.[260]

Evidence of these director-units abounds, particularly among the host of new companies now being launched by individual filmmakers and even stars. One of the earliest of these was young Abel Gance's Le Film français, which produced only four short films between late 1911 and early 1912, the last of which starred Gance's patron, the actor Edouard de Max.[261] In the summer of 1912, based on his work at Pathé—from *Victimes d'alcool* (1911) to *Le Roman d'une pauvre fille* (1912)—Bourgeois announced formation of Kron-Lambert,[262] a company that seems never to have released a single film, forcing Bourgeois to accept a directing position at Eclair. More successfully, Charles Burguet located his Société des Films Azur in Nice, where he turned out more than a dozen films, starring Regina Badet, within two years.[263] Andréani and Heuzé both moved out from under the Pathé-Frères umbrella, providing the nucleus, primarily, for Georges Lordier's Les Grands Films Populaires (which first used a new studio in Parc-Montsouris and then took over the Lux studio in 1913)[264] as well as more ephemeral firms such as Cosmograph, Minerva, and Eclectic Films. Perhaps prompted by Lordier's success, Joseph Menchen and Louis Aubert separately took steps to move into film production by erecting studios at Epinay-sur-Seine and Joinville (rue des Réservoirs), respectively; and Aubert deliberately concentrated on making feature-length films.[265] By the spring of 1914, filmmakers André Hugon and René Plaissetty had set up their own companies, the latter specifically to produce detective films.[266] Two of the most popular

French female stars, Suzanne Grandais and Yvette Andreyor (both at Gaumont), attempted to spin off separate series of films—the one through Charles Mary and publisher Jules Tallandier, the other through Géo Janin.[267] With the exception of Burguet, Andréani, and Heuzé—whose *Le Bossu* (1913), starring Henry Krauss, was a box office hit[268]—most of these independent companies were not all that successful; but the efforts of those launched in 1914, of course, were quickly cut off by the outbreak of war.

Medium- and small-sized companies, many of them restricted to a specific genre, also proliferated within the orbit of Pathé-Frères. SCAGL, for instance, continued to specialize in longer dramas and comedies—from Capellani's Victor Hugo adaptations such as *Notre-Dame de Paris* (1911) and *Les Misérables* (1912), both starring Krauss, to Monca's more recent melodramas such as *L'Epouvante* (1911) and *Le Petit Chose* (1912) and Leprince's *Scènes de la vie cruelle* series (1911–1914), many of which starred either Mistinguett or the Comédie Française actress Gabrielle Robinne. Then, just before the war came Denola's *Rocambole* series as well as contemporary subjects directed by Desfontaines from Paul Garbagni scripts.[269] All of these films were produced at the SCAGL studio in Vincennes which, according to cameraman Pierre Trimbach, was widely admired for its balance of natural and artificial lighting (only one side, along with the roof, was of glass).[270] Beginning in 1912, de Morlhon (one of the few filmmakers whose name actually appeared on the film title) had his own production company, Films Valetta, for directing "modern pictures" from his own scenarios—for instance, *La Broyeuse des coeurs* (1913) and *La Fleuriste de Toneso* (1913).[271] Similarly, Andréani (who took over one of Pathé's studios at Vincennes) specialized in period dramas such as *Le Siège de Calais* (1911) and biblical films such as *Caïn et Abel* (1911), before adventuring off on his own.[272] And Machin contributed both shorts and features, such as *L'Ame des moulins* (1912) and *Maudite soit la guerre!* (1914), from a new subsidiary, Hollandsche Film.[273] Pathé-Frères confined direct investment chiefly to its popular comic series: *Max* (now often scripted and directed by Max Linder himself, and listed as such on the film title), *Rigadin* (still directed by Monca), and *Boireau* (once Deed returned to Pathé in 1912).[274] And, with its own stable of writers and actors, Bosetti's Comica company in Nice kept turning out new comic series to complement those made in Paris—for instance, *Rosalie* (1911–1912), starring Sarah Duhamel, and *Bigorno* (1912–1914). As this spectrum suggests, Charles Pathé seems to have opted to continue making films of one reel in length—from a half-dozen comic series to *Pathé-Journal* (the newsreel was now so popular that it was released twice weekly)—as the most reliable base for his company's production.[275] Although the benefits of this strategy would be quite substantial, at least until 1913–1914, they would not prove lasting in the face of the increasing shift to feature-length films.

Gaumont generally followed the strategies that had impelled the company into a position second only to Pathé in France. In 1913, for instance, now that its capital stock had risen to four million francs, Gaumont also expanded its production facilities by constructing a new "Victorine" studio near Nice. This provided needed space for the company's increasing number of director-units, which, unlike at Pathé, worked under relatively close, but friendly supervision. Feuillade remained head of production, directing a range of films from period dramas such as *La Fille de Margrave* (1912), with Andreyor, or *L'Agonie de Byzance* (1913) and the celebrated *Scènes de la vie telle qu'elle est* series (1911–1913), particularly those with Renée Carl, to the even more famous *Fantômas* crime series (1913–1914), starring René Navarre. Perret turned to longer dramatic films—for instance, *Le Mystère des Roches de Kador* (1912), *L'Enfant de Paris* (1913), and *Le Roman d'un mousse* (1914). New directors came on board each year: Georges Lacroix in 1911, Henri Fescourt in 1912, Maurice Mariaud and René Le Somptier in 1913, and Gaston Ravel, Léon Poirier, and Emile Violet in 1914. Perhaps the most important of these was Durand, who left Lux in 1910, to continue the *Calino* series (with the comic Clément Migé). Soon Durand was adding two more comic series—*Zigoto* (1911–1912), with Lucien Bataille, and the zany *Onésime* series (1912–1914), starring Ernest Bourbon. Both Feuillade and Perret also worked on major comic series—respectively, *Bout-de-zan* (1912–1916), with another child actor, René Poyen, and *Léonce* (1912–1916), starring Perret himself, with either Grandais or his wife, Valentine Petit. In this regard, Gaumont, too, seems to have made these regularly released comic series, along with *Gaumont-Actualités* (which, in early 1912, joined Pathé's as the only weekly newsreel to be distributed in the United States),[276] a solid cornerstone of production. And, supplementing the newsreel, there were not only the popular polar expedition films but special "topicals" like those documenting the Durbar ceremonies in India—280 prints of which allegedly circulated in England alone.[277]

All three of the other major French companies experienced a similar expansion in production (apparently without needing to augment their facilities) as well as radical changes in personnel. At Film d'Art, Delac, who had assumed control of management in the company's reorganization, took a different tack from the one adopted by Pathé and Gaumont. Rather than attempt to fill a broad production schedule that ultimately favored the short comic series, Delac determined to stick with literary adaptations, but in films of close to feature length. His first step was to hire Louis Nalpas (who had distributed the company's films in the Balkans and the Middle East) as head of production.[278] Working under Nalpas's supervision, Pouctal (who replaced Calmettes as Film d'Art's principal filmmaker) succeeded in turning out a consistent series of profitable films from classic adaptations such as *Les Trois Mousequetaires* (1913) to modern melodramas such as *Le Maître de forges* (1913) and *L'Alibi* (1914). By 1914, Film d'Art was in a secure enough position for Nalpas to hire Lacroix away from Gaumont and add yet another filmmaker, Jean Manoussi, to its production team.[279] Eclipse, on the other hand, followed Pathé and Gaumont's strategy more closely. Hamman, for instance, wrote, directed (along with Gaston Roudès), and starred in the popular western series, *Arizona Bill* (1911–1913), which had evolved out of his earlier western films. Similarly, after leaving Eclair, Bressol directed (again along with Roudès) and starred in the *Nat Pinkerton* detective series. In 1912, with the financial support of Frank Brockliss and Adolphe Zukor, Eclipse set up a special Franco-Anglo-American affiliate, the Histrionic Film Company, to make *Queen Elizabeth*, starring the aging Bernhardt in a reprise of her stage role.[280] Based on that film's worldwide success, Desfontaines went on to produce further historical films at the Boulogne-sur-Seine studios, many now in collaboration with Louis Mercanton, a former Bernhardt associate—for instance, *Shylock* (1913) and *Anne Boleyn* (1914). And to Eclipse's comic series—*Arthème* (1911–1916) and *Polycarpe* (1912–1916), both of which were directed by Servaes—René Hervil (a former actor under Bourgeois at Lux) added two others, *Maud* (1913–1914) and *Fred* (1914–1916), in the latter of which he himself played the leading role.

Eclair probably prospered the most throughout this period. First of all, the company "acquired" several well-known comics to start up new series—*Pétronille* (1912–1914), with Duhamel from Comica, *Gavroche* (1912–1914), with Bertho from Lux, and *Casimir* (1913–1914), with Bataille from Gaumont. In 1912, following strategies initiated by Pathé and Gaumont, Eclair assigned two of its technicians, J. Javault and André Bayard, to produce a series of short scientific and educational films under the label of "Scientia" (a series that would total nearly eighty titles by 1914)[281] and then announced the assemblage of a weekly half-hour newsreel called *Eclair-Journal*.[282] The same year, again in imitation of its chief rivals, the company introduced a series of "social dramas" ranging from *Au pays des ténèbres* (1912) to *Gerval, le maître de forges* (1912). Late in 1912, Chautard turned over supervision of the ACAD film series to Maurice Tourneur (a former theater director at the Odéon and Renaissance),[283] who quickly became skillful at adapting everything from Grand Guignol plays such as André de Lorde's *Figures de cire* (1912) to modern melodramas or farces such as Georges Courteline's *Les Gaîtes de l'escadron* (1913) and even historical epics such as Dumas's *La Dame de Monsoreau* (1913). However, it was Jasset's crime films, beginning with the feature-length *Zigomar* (1911), based on Léon Sazie's popular serial novel and starring Alexandre Arquillière, that probably distinguished Eclair's product most clearly from that of its competitors. So successful was this film that, within another six months, Eclair had a second title ready for release, *Zigomar contre Nick Carter* (1912),[284] in what turned out to be a deluge of crime films, consistently using a trio of actors—Arquillière, André Liabel, and Josette Andriot—from *Le Cercueil de verre* (1912) and *Tom Butler* (1912) to *Balaoo* (1913), *Zigomar, peau d'anguille* (1913), and *Protéa* (1913). Despite the sudden death of Jasset, its leading producer-director, in the summer of 1913, the company seemed stable and secure: the Paris offices and laboratories alone had eight hundred employees (excluding the filmmaking teams), and net profits (on total assets of more than five million francs) were reaching close to one million francs a year.[285] Indeed, Eclair was the only French company other than Pathé and Gaumont which had the financial resources and the foreign distribution agencies (in Moscow, London, Berlin, and Milan, as well as New York) to make an attempt to produce its own films in the lucrative American market.

As a result of the battle between the "independents" and the Edison Trust, the major French companies soon realized that it was in their best interests to establish their own subsidiaries within the American cinema industry. Early in 1910, for instance, while continuing to distribute its French films through George Kleine, Gaumont had opened a printing plant in Flushing, New York, run by Herbert and Alice Guy Blaché, who, for the previous three years, had been marketing the company's films and equipment (especially its sound projection system) out of Cleveland.[286] Later that year, Guy Blaché set up her own company, Solax (and two years later, her own studio), in Fort Lee, New Jersey, in a move that seems to have kept Gaumont from developing the Flushing site into a production studio.[287] In any case, after Gaumont left Kleine, in late 1911, the American branch office (still run by Herbert Blaché) soon contracted to distribute the company's French films through the Film Supply Company and, later, the Exclusive Film Corporation.[288]

Pathé's American affiliate also had begun film production in the spring of 1910, first on various locations and then in a studio constructed in Jersey City (near Bound Brook and Fort Lee).[289] Within a year, using that studio as well as an outdoor studio in Edendale, near Los Angeles, the company reached a production capacity of two or three one-reelers per week, most of them westerns and Indian films directed by either Louis Gasnier or James Young Deer.[290] Together with the *Pathé-Weekly* newsreel (now standard on most American cinema programs), these westerns constituted the most popular portion of Pathé's weekly five-reel package of releases, and drew fairly consistent praise until the market became glutted with the genre by late 1911.[291] At that point, Pathé set up its own distribution office, CGPC, for imported French films, especially features such as *In the Grip of Alcohol* (1911),[292] and used General Film, whose policies tended to discourage feature film distribution, to release its American product, including *Pathé-Weekly* (a new version of which, just before the war, was being issued daily).[293] Within a year or so, perhaps in response to continued criticism of its "foreign dramas," CGPC was reorganized as the Eclectic Film Company, headed by K. W. Linn and Arthur Roussel, and, by late 1913, was releasing three French features per month.[294] Finally, it was Roussel who arranged, with the help of the Hearst newspaper empire, for Gasnier to produce the famous *Perils of Pauline* serial (1914), starring Pearl White, which may well have instituted a new practice of releasing film prints en masse.[295] Thereafter, Pathé's American subsidiary (Pathé-Exchange would replace Eclectic in January 1915) concentrated exclusively on serials and short comic films, which, as Kristin Thompson has argued, locked Pathé into what proved to be, in the long run, an increasingly marginalized segment of the American cinema industry.[296]

Eclair chose an opposite strategy, but at the wrong moment, unfortunately, in 1914. After winning consistent praise from *Moving Picture World* for its French titles,[297] the company's American affiliate opened a long-delayed studio in Fort Lee, New Jersey, in the fall of 1911.[298] Within weeks, Arnaud was hired away from Gaumont to replace Gaston Larry (who had died) and to set about more efficiently organizing the studio's production schedule of films, most of them melodramas and comedies that were much less risqué than the films Eclair produced in France.[299] Among the other French staff "imported" to work in Fort Lee were René Guissart and Georges Benoit (cameramen), Benjamin Carré (set designer), Emile Cohl (animation filmmaker), and Francis Doublier (head lab technician).[300] As the company prospered, an American version of Eclair's newsreel was added to its production schedule, and the studio was augmented with a new wing to accommodate three directors working simultaneously.[301] After the affiliate was registered as American Standard Films, in October 1912, Jourjon seems to have sent Chautard to Fort Lee in order to work out new contracts to assure the distribution of French films—the shorter ones primarily through Universal (formed out of the breakup of the Sales Company) and the longer ones through World Special.[302] In March 1914, however, disaster struck when the Fort Lee studio and laboratory were destroyed in a fire.[303] Losing the physical plant and equipment was bad enough, but the destruction of all the positive prints and many of the negatives was catastrophic. Despite this setback, Jourjon announced that the facilities at Fort Lee would be rebuilt—while Eclair shifted production to its location unit in Tucson, Arizona (run by Webster Cullison).[304] In May, he dispatched Tourneur to the United States to replace Arnaud as the chief producer-director of the new studio. The war intervened, however, and Eclair was forced to turn over its still uncompleted studio to Peerless Pictures, newly organized by Brulatour (probably a silent partner in Eclair's American affiliate)[305] in association with World Pictures, the company through which Tourneur would then produce his earliest American films, such as *The Wishing Ring* (1914).[306] So, by the end of 1914, the French companies—with the exception of Pathé, which would soon be little more than a minor player—effectively were closed out of the American cinema industry.

Within France itself, the film distribution sector, which Pathé had revolutionized in 1907, perhaps most resembled its counterpart in the United States, at least in terms of the general move toward concentration. Of the major distributors, both Pathé-Frères and Gaumont (Comptoir Ciné-Location) served as conduits, not only for their own shorts and features (and, in the case of Pathé, the product of farflung subsidiaries such as the Jersey City studio's "American Kinema" films or the Moscow studio's "Films Russes"), but also for films from smaller independent producers in Italy, England, the United States, and elsewhere. While Gaumont, for instance, distributed special documentaries such as that recording Robert Scott's expedition to the South Pole in 1912, Pathé filled out its programs with short comedies and dramas drawn from nearly two dozen sources, consistently printing and distributing up to eighty kilometers of film per day.[307] About the same time that American producers began to publicize "star" actors, in 1910, Pathé also introduced publicity photos confirming its "star system," beginning with an ad expressing best wishes to Linder (after an appendectomy) and later continued with full-page ads of everyone from Rigadin and Little Moritz to Berthe Bovy and Mistinguett.[308] But, by 1912, every new weekly Pathé program featured, even more than its "stars," at least one film of three reels or more, most of them from either SCAGL, Films Valetta, or *Scènes de la vie cruelle*.[309] The other two "majors" concentrated on amassing very different sources of film product. AGC established a solid foothold by gaining distribution rights to Film d'Art productions (after the company's buy-out by Monofilm), particularly titles such as *Camille Desmoulins* (1911) and *Madame Sans-Gêne* (1911).[310] A year later, after signing contracts with Eclipse and Eclair, AGC assumed the enviable position of being the exclusive distributor for the three principal French film producers after Pathé and Gaumont; and its agencies spread through France and into Belgium and Algeria.[311] Aubert, on the other hand, was dealing ever more successfully in Italian and Danish films.[312] In the spring of 1913, for instance, the company hit the jackpot with the release of Cinès's *Quo Vadis?*, followed in the fall by the same company's *Marc Antoine et Cléopatre*.[313] At the same time, Aubert began to contract with independent French producers such as Les Grands Films Populaires and soon enjoyed a similar success with *Le Bossu*.[314]

By the summer of 1913, the four major French distributors were so assured of their contractual arrangements as well as the cinema exhibition market that, much like book publishers or theatrical managers, they began to conceive of a "season" of film releases.[315] Aubert, Pathé, and AGC, followed quickly by Gaumont, placed ads in *Ciné-Journal* announcing the film titles they would be distributing for the 1913–1914 "season" (the fall through spring months).[316] And AGC drew repeated attention, from August through October, to the highlight of its "season," Film d'Art's *Les Trois Mousquetaires*. So great were the number of films available for distribution in France by this time that the "majors" could not begin to handle them all, and smaller firms—for instance, France-Cinéma, Exclusif Agency, and P. Hodel—began to emerge on the industry's margins. As American films in particular grew ever more popular—from Vitagraph's melodramas to D. W. Griffith's *The Battle of Elderbush Gulch* (1913) and Selig's Tom Mix westerns[317]—confirming *Moving Picture World*'s view that the cinema was "Americanizing" the world, first the Sales Company (Biograph, Kalem, Lubin, Selig, Essanay) and then Edison joined Vitagraph in extending their distribution outlets to Paris.[318] But the number of films produced by the American "independents" swelled to such proportions that other American agencies such as Trans-Oceanic (Universal) and especially Western Imports/Jacques Haik (Mutual) were able to begin encroaching on the French market.[319] By early 1914, even AGC and Aubert were expanding their slate of releases to include American films—see, for instance, Aubert's decision to release the feature films of Famous Players, which itself had been established with the profits generated from Zukor's wildly successful French-British import, *Queen Elizabeth*.[320]

The exhibition sector of the industry also underwent changes in the early 1910s, but those changes, while no doubt further legitimizing the industry, led to much less concentration than was characteristic of the distribution sector. From 1911 through 1913, there was another boom in cinema construction across France, with new cinemas opening in Paris, for example, at the rate of forty per year. The most distinctive of these were the luxury cinemas—such as the Gaumont-Palace and Electric-Palace (both opened by Gaumont in October, 1911)—whose size and architectural design were reminiscent of the 1900 Exposition's "palaces of electricity" and also closely emulated the principal Parisian theaters. Pathé probably erected the majority of these "palaces"—from the Tivoli and Pathé-Palace (in 1911) to the newly renovated Omnia-Pathé (in late 1912)[321] and the Artistic-Cinéma and the Lutetia-Wagram (in 1913)—in order to maintain the supremacy of its circuit. But Aubert, expanding into the exhibition sector on the strength of its distribution profits, contributed its share as well with no less than five Aubert-Palaces, all constructed in 1913. So lucrative was the market that even "independent" luxury cinemas began to appear—such as the Parisiana (which Léon Brézillon finally converted from a top-ranking music hall in 1911) and the Colisée Cinéma on the Champs-Elysées, which soon became the site of "high society" afternoon parties and consistently featured American films, such as Ince's *The Battle of Gettysburg* (1914).[322] By 1913, the receipts garnered by the cinemas, at least in Paris, had surpassed those of the music halls and café-concerts and were closing in fast on those of the subsidized theaters.[323] That year alone, the Gaumont-Palace and Pathé-Palace (both of which had large, renowned orchestras)[324] took in nearly two million and one million francs, respectively. Even those writers who deplored the phenomenon agreed that, for the sheer variety of films offered, the conveniently informal "rules" of attendance, and especially the low cost of a ticket, the cinema clearly had an advantage in its competition with other spectacles.[325] By 1914, even the prominent drama critic Adolphe Brisson admitted that the battle was lost, that the cinema indeed had achieved an economic if not artistic status equal to that of the theater.[326]

Programs now varied according to the nature and location of the cinema. At one end of the scale, several inexpensive Paris boulevard cinemas such as the Pathé-Journal specialized exclusively in newsreels averaging one half-hour in length.[327] At the other end, the Gaumont-Palace offered programs divided into three approximately hour-long segments (with fifteen-minute entr'actes) and comprised of more than a dozen films, including at least one feature. Most cinemas, however, generally scheduled two-hour programs of a half-dozen films, with perhaps one entr'acte; and it was the Electric-Palace, quickly followed by the Pathé-Palace, which first established the practice of continuous program screenings, from early afternoon to midnight.[328] Some of the Paris "palaces," perhaps in imitation of the theaters, were finding it possible to restrict their programs almost exclusively to one or two feature-length films.[329] The increasing number and length of feature films presented problems for exhibitors, perhaps best articulated in Dureau's columns in *Ciné-Journal*, between 1911 and 1913.[330] One solution, instituted at the level of production and distribution, was to divide such films into parts to be screened consecutively over two or more weeks—as was Capellani's *Les Misérables* (3,400 meters), from 30 November to 21 December 1912. Another was to screen the film all in one program, but divided by an entr'acte—as was Perret's *Le Roman d'un mousse* (approximately 2,400 meters) at the Gaumont-Palace, the week of 13 February 1914. Such feature films also led to the strategy of preview screenings, several weeks to a month before the general release date, which seems to have become common

II. Omnia-Pathé exterior (remodeled, 1912)

12. Omnia-Pathé interior (remodeled, 1912)

practice, at least for major films, in the fall of 1913—see, for instance, Perret's *L'Enfant de Paris* (2,325 meters) at the Gaumont-Palace and Pouctal's *Les Trois Mousquetaires* (approximately 4,000 meters) at the Majestic.[331] And they were sometimes showcased in exclusive screenings at just a single cinema—as was Feuillade's *L'Agonie de Byzance* (with a special score composed by Henri Février and Léon Moreau) at the Gaumont-Palace. Finally, the more popular features even prompted some cinemas to break the long-established pattern of weekly program changes, such as when both *L'Enfant de Paris* and Capellani's *Germinal* were held over the same week in October 1913.[332]

The 1913–1914 "season" of films suggested that the French cinema's legitimacy was no longer in question. The Société des auteurs et compositeurs seemed to confirm that legitimacy, in November 1913, by agreeing to consider cinemas on a par with "legitimate" theaters and as worthy of inclusion in its statutes.[333] This was not entirely the case, however, at least in terms of the law. The most drastic instance of this occurred in the summer of 1912, when many mayors in southeastern France (in Lyon, Marseilles, Avignon, and elsewhere) banned the exhibition of crime films such as Eclair's *Bandits en automobile*. The mayors' action was based on the 1909 directive sent out by the Interior Ministry which reminded them of their power over the cinema as a spectacle de curiosité. This provoked a debate over film censorship in the press—perhaps best evidenced in Dureau's editorials defending the cinema in *Ciné-Journal*.[334] It prompted producers such as Gaumont to redouble their "reformist" tendencies in films such as Perret's *Le Mystère des Roches de Kador* (1912) and Feuillade's *L'Erreur tragique* (1913) without sacrificing the popular crime series, of course—witness the phenomenal success of Feuillade's *Fantômas* (1913–1914).[335] In the court cases that ensued from these bannings—especially the one in Hyères involving Eclair's *Tom Butler* (1912)—the judges ruled consistently in favor of the state. And, in 1914, those rulings were upheld by a decision of the Conseil d'Etat in Paris.[336] Despite the efforts of Benoît-Lévy, Pathé, and others over the previous six years, the cinema remained a spectacle de curiosité according to French law, at least in terms of exhibition.

In almost every other way, however, the French cinema's legitimacy seemed assured. Even its harshest critics, such as Louis Haugmard and René Doumic, had to admit to the cinema's "educational" value, especially evident in its newsreels and documentaries.[337] In fact, by 1913–1914, documentaries, scientific films, and even historical and biblical films were being used not only in Catholic diocese schools but at almost every level of French secular education; and some, such as André Chalopin, even believed that films would soon become "the *principal apparatus* of the modern school teacher."[338] While writers on the political right accepted the cinema as a new form of propaganda that could shape the French national consciousness and even help control the country's colonies, those on the left extolled the cinema as a new form of universal language that could promote international unity and harmony. Discourse on the cinema now extended beyond the industry's trade journals, which numbered at least a half-dozen,[339] to the major daily newspapers as well as prominent intellectual reviews. Both *Le Figaro* and *Excelsior*, for instance, ran special inquiries on the cinema, in 1912 and 1913, respectively; and, by the fall of 1913, *Le Journal* was publishing each Friday a full page of information, interviews, and capsule film reviews. In 1913, the trade journals also formed their own professional organization, the Association professionnelle de la presse cinématographique (directed by Lordier), following the model of those already established the year before—the Chambre syndicale française de la cinématographie (for producers and distributors) and the Syndicat française des directeurs de cinématographes (for exhibitors)—both of which superseded earlier and less powerful organizations founded, respectively, by Gaumont and Benoît-Lévy. As a final, conclusive sign of the industry's legitimacy, the 1913–1914 "season" seemed to culminate, on 12 June 1914, in an official gala celebration at the Gaumont-Palace, sponsored by the city of Paris and attended by the president of the French Republic.[340] Benoît-Lévy's earlier vision of the cinema—that is, the *French* cinema—as the popular art form of the century seemed on the verge of realization.

At the time, despite no longer being top-ranked in the world, the French cinema industry seemed healthy and relatively secure. Led by Pathé's strategy of decentralization, the industry's locus of economic strength shifted from film production to distribution and exhibition. Just six years earlier, Pathé and other French producers had supplied a significant portion of all films exhibited in the United States; now the process was being reversed, yet the major French companies were well situated to exercise some control over—and share in the profits of—the American imports. The Great War, of course, would change all that. The industry would be forced to shut down completely, and when it resumed business at year's end, the already established shift to American film imports would only accelerate. Now that its distribution system had contracted, its production base was relocated in the United States (Pathé himself remained there from the fall of 1914 to the spring of 1915), and it was tacitly encouraging American imports, Pathé-Frères no longer could play the same leadership role as before. For the rest of the decade and through the 1920s, the French would fight a valiant battle to resist becoming what Henri Diamant-Berger accurately called "an American film colony."[341] Their success in doing so, against considerable odds, however, is another story.

The Cinema of Attractions,
1896–1904

*All the visible universe is nothing
but a shop of images and signs.*
CHARLES BAUDELAIRE

EARLY FRENCH FILMS were produced and exhibited within a categorical framework already established by the Third Republic's institutions of mass culture.
The most important of these were the café-concerts and music halls of the larger
urban centers and the fairground theaters that circulated throughout the country,
setting up temporary sites of exhibition in cities and towns. Others, however,
included screened spectacles (from small-scale magic lantern shows to giant dioramas), mass-produced images printed on paper (from versions of traditional
images Epinal to illustrated magazines), and even photographs (whether for public or private distribution). Many of these offered a *variety* of subjects to view
(and consume), as mass culture equivalents to the display of either consumer
goods in the metropolitan department stores (and their catalogs) or postcards at
the major tourist sites. The pleasure of such "distractions" or "diversions," Miriam Hansen writes, promised a "modern" form of "short-term but incessant
sensorial stimulation" instead of requiring the extended contemplation more
characteristic of the traditional arts.[1] As cinema programs became common in
the fairs and elsewhere, films also were presented in this variety format, in what
seemed to be a discontinuous series of attractions (underscored by constant reel
changes) whose selection and order already tended to be maximally inclusive, in
terms of not only the subjects offered but also the class, gender, and generation
of the spectators addressed. In 1901, for instance, in his Grand Biorama, Charles
Sckramson offered three different evening programs per week, mixing actualités, dances, trick films, féeries, and religious films from different sources,
including Lumière, Méliès, and R. W. Paul (London). Toward the end of the
period, in 1904, Van Langendonck arranged lengthy programs of both live and
recorded performances in Le Palais de l'Art Nouveau, the last of which included
historical and biblical films, melodramas, comedies and féeries, most of them
now supplied by Pathé-Frères.

From the beginning, as evidenced by the Lumière 1897 catalog of film
titles or *vues,*[2] French companies also adopted this exhibition model of subject variety—or product differentiation—to determine their production of films

in terms of particular *genres*. If some companies tended to specialize in certain genres—Lumière in actualités and travel films, Méliès in trick films and féeries[3]—the largest and most successful corporation, Pathé-Frères, instead quickly moved to encompass the widest spectrum of subjects possible. "For better or worse," an early commentator concluded, "the great merit of the Pathé company is chiefly to have broken new ground and tackled every single genre, whatever the cost."[4] Among the earliest surviving Pathé catalogs, those from 1902 to 1904 already define that spectrum in terms of nearly a dozen genres or *scènes: plein air* films, comic films, trick films, sports films, historical films and actualités, erotic films, dance films, dramatic and realist films, féeries, religious or biblical films, and synchronized-phonograph films.[5] Even so, the company's specialties within the spectrum emerge clearly—in early 1904, for instance, the Pathé catalog listed 81 comic films, 63 trick films, 41 religious or biblical films, 25 dramatic and realist films, and some dozen historical films whose average length belied their small number.[6] Given Pathé's dominant position in the industry by 1904–1905, its classification of film genres (issued in monthly catalog supplements) undoubtedly served to solidify the variety model of program composition in the fairground cinemas as well as in the earliest permanent cinemas.

If the genre and variety formats function as congruent frameworks to describe early French film production and exhibition, a third framework recently constituted by historians can serve to distinguish the early cinema and what Noël Burch has called its distinctive *otherness*[7] from the kind of cinema which became increasingly dominant after 1904, and not only in France. The "cinema of attractions," to use Tom Gunning and André Gaudreault's formulation,[8] is perhaps the best term for the mode of representation governing early film production and exhibition, and it has at least four principal components. First, early cinema was presentational, equating camera and spectator in what Jean-Louis Baudry and Christian Metz have called simply "the gaze that sees."[9] That is, rather than narrate or, more precisely, focus on narrative and characterization, it tended to show or display—as an "attraction"—either the technical possibilities of the new medium or the spectacle of human figures, natural landscapes, and constructed decors. Such a cinema, Hansen argues, was predicated "on distracting the viewer with a variety of competing spectacles . . . rather than absorbing him or her into a coherent narrative" or a "classical" diegesis of spatial-temporal continuity.[10] As a corollary, it often addressed the spectator directly, not only through frontal staging, but also through the recurring looks actors gave to the camera, perhaps in order to create a degree of audience collaboration with that display. Second, the tableau in early cinema generally was considered to be autonomous, for it assumed, in Burch's words, the "*unicity* of the frame"— "any given tableau remain[ed] unchanged in its framing throughout its passage on the screen and from one appearance to the next."[11] The objective, to quote Gaudreault, was "to present not a small *temporal* segment of action but rather the totality of an action unfolding in an *homogenous* space."[12] Consequently, to use Gunning's concise phrasing, early films might be seen as "enframed rather than emplotted."[13] Third, such a single, unified viewpoint assumed a camera distance that usually described that enframed space in LS, one of whose consequences was to make human figures primarily performers of physical action rather than "characters" with psychological motivations.[14] And fourth, early films were sold as "semi-finished products," in Thomas Elsaesser's apt phrase, which could be "finished" in exhibition in very different ways.[15] All kinds of practices—variable projection speed (due to hand cranking), music and sound effects accompanying the film images, *bonisseurs* or commentators providing explanations, exhibitors asserting the right to reedit and color the film prints they purchased[16]—actively promoted a wide range of textual variance rather than anything like a definitive film text. In fact, as Musser argues, that exhibitors rather than producers ultimately exercised "editorial control" over films crucially determined the mode of representation in the cinema of attractions.[17]

Guided by this set of conceptual frameworks, my analysis of early French cinema focuses on its patterns of development within particular film genres accepted by both producers and exhibitors. These include the trick film and féerie, the comic film, the actualité, the historical and biblical film, and the "dramatic and realist" film. Although, by singling out discrete film texts as more or less fixed objects of study, this discussion does violence to the way the cinema was experienced by spectators at the time, it recognizes the conditions of their performative practice as cultural forms and thus encourages inquiry into the intertextual web of relations between the cinema and other cultural and social practices in France. Such an approach also emphasizes the differences between French production companies, most notably between Méliès and Pathé, particularly as the latter moved to dominate the industry. What is even more important, this analysis of genre films can pinpoint specifically how, as a mode of representation, the early cinema of attractions, to some extent, actually overlapped with the later narrative cinema. As Gunning has argued recently, early films are probably best defined as a dialectical interplay of attraction and narrative elements, in which an aesthetics of spectacle or display was generally, but not always, dominant.[18]

Trick Films and *Féeries*

Perhaps the most successful genre for French exhibitors during this early period was what they themselves called "transformation views" or "transformation scenes." Generally, these included anything from the short trick film of apparently no more than a single shot (none lasted more than three minutes) to the longer féerie comprising multiple tableaux. Although none of these films lent themselves to all that much manipulation by exhibitors, they more than made up for this with an amazing display of spectacular feats on the screen, the result of a seemingly miraculous filmmaking process. By 1898, such "transformations" constituted the bulk of Méliès's production; and, with some justification, he claimed the genre as his own and one reason for the cinema's success, even if he would have preferred the term "fantastical scenes."[19] This, of course, did not keep other companies such as Pathé from producing trick films and féeries; but the genre did provide Méliès with some measure of authority within the industry (and some control over the exhibition of his films), at least until Pathé moved into mass production. And it was within the "transformation" genre that Méliès established his own distinctive form of a "cinema of attractions." A film's scenario never amounted to much, he would later insist, because it merely served as a "pretext" for *trucs* or tricks and striking tableaux.[20] In fact, he claimed that his first task in preparing a film production always was to come up with a series of magical tricks, a central "grand effect," and a final *clou* of spectacle. Only after constructing the decors and costuming his actors did he actually work out the details of the scenario—using the thread of the story to assemble what was really significant, the trick effects and tableaux of spectacle. As a representative figure of the period, Méliès saw himself, then, not as a storyteller, but rather, and especially in the féeries, as an innovative composer of cinematic *revues.*

The trick film genre includes the principal films in which Méliès performed as himself—that is, as a celebrated magician. Yet in none, not even in an early one entitled *Le Magicien* (1898), was he content to simply record any of the illusionist acts he was known for at the Robert-Houdin Théâtre. Instead he invented tricks that displayed the "magical" properties of the cinematic apparatus as well as his own body as spectacle—whether dismembered or transformed.[21] Perhaps the earliest of these properties or cinematic techniques, already visible in *Le Manoir du diable* (1896–1897), was stop motion, which created a series of abrupt appearances, disappearances, or substitutions. In *L'Auberge ensorcelé* (1897), for instance, a traveler systematically "loses" first his clothes and then all of the furniture in a hotel room. At the conclusion of *Illusions fantastiques* (1898), by contrast, a simple box turns into a dove, a boy, then twin boys, and finally huge British and American flags—indirectly providing evidence that the market for Méliès's films quickly extended beyond France. Another technique was reverse motion that, in *Salle à manger fantastique* (1898), allowed a flipped dinner table magically to right itself. A third technique was multiple exposure, which combined rewinding and reexposing the film stock with the use of black cloth covering certain background areas of the set, resulting in such bizarre marvels as the three singing Méliès heads on a table in *Un Homme de tête* (1898) or the young man's head sticking out of a vase in *Le Chevalier mystère* (1899). This also was coupled with a matte device masking off a specific area of the camera lens, which, in *Le Portait mystérieux* (1899), produced the delightful image of Méliès talking to a life-size portrait duplicate of himself. In film after film, Méliès obsessively repeated himself "like a fetishist," writes Linda Williams, "making the game of presence and absence the very source of . . . the spectator's pleasure, while privileging . . . his own perverse pleasure in the tricks" of that game.[22]

L'Homme-orchestre (1900) offers an especially striking instance of this game of doubled spectacle, with a "hidden" trick effect and a cleverly orchestrated mix of theatrical and cinematic devices. On a bare stage framed by painted-flat curtains are seven simple chairs lined up in a horizontal row against a black background. Méliès appears in white shirt and trousers, sits on the far left chair, and, moving from chair to chair, replicates himself into six musicians (each with a different instrument) and a centered orchestra conductor (with baton). The six musicians chat among themselves, perform under the conductor's guidance, and then "fold" back, in pairs, into the conductor (stage center). After a wave of the baton seems to make the chairs vanish and reappear and then condense into one, a huge decorative fan rises up in the background, and a puzzled Méliès sits on the remaining chair, only to promptly disappear through a "trap" in the floor. This series of actions depends, of course, on an unusual number of multiple exposures and superimpositions, in order to magically multiply the magician himself.[23] Yet it also depends, not on stop-motion filming (as might be assumed), but, as Jacques Malthête discovered, on cutting different strips of film or "takes" together.[24] Cuts or splices, for instance, are what actually cause the chairs to vanish and reappear; the cuts seem invisible simply because the exact duplication of framing, from take to take, maintains a strict continuity of space and action—making this perhaps the very first form of "invisible" editing.[25] These cinematic devices then give way, however, in the film's conclusion, to theatrical devices—the hydraulics of lifting and lowering props and even people. But the final clou of spectacle replicates the magician once more, this time stressing foreground-background contrasts through the cinematic device of the cut. After apparently disappearing through the trapdoor (cut), Méliès leaps out over the fan toward the camera and, just as he hits the floor (another cut), vanishes in stage smoke. Finally, as the smoke clears, the fan descends to reveal, now behind it again, the magician walking forward, already anticipating the audience's applause.

Later Méliès trick films continue to work variations on this double spectacle of the visible magician and the "invisible" apparatus, mixing theatrical and cinematic devices and sometimes turning the trick back on its perpetrator. *L'Homme à la tête de caoutchouc* (1902), for instance, features the trick of a doubled Méliès head that the magician-scientist places on a laboratory table, the "grand effect" of a bellows expanding it to gigantic proportions, and the concluding spectacle of a "clown" assistant who takes over the bellows and literally blows the head to smithereens. These effects are produced, not only by invisible cuts and multiple exposures using a matte device, but also by the consistent movement of Méliès's detached head toward the camera (in the illusion of a dolly shot), until it is displayed as spectacle in MCU. *L'Homme-mouche* (1902) organizes its tricks within the context of a vaguely oriental stage set in which a Russian dancer performs for a half-dozen women dressed in peasant costumes, finally doing handstands and somersaults up the back wall and across the ceiling. The "grand effect" here is achieved by combining a matte device for multiple exposure with a lightweight camera (probably a Lumière) moved to an unusual position perpendicular to and looking down on the painted studio floor. Although less innovative technically than the previous two films, *Le Bourreau turc* (1904) does work out a clever pun on the device of the straight cut. Against the painted flat of a generic Middle Eastern marketplace, four men are lined up in a stockade, and, with a single stroke of his huge sword (and an invisible cut), an old man lops off their heads and tosses them into a barrel. After the old man goes to sleep, one by one, the heads pop up out of the barrel and fly over to reattach themselves to their bodies, which come back to life. Quickly they seize the executioner and, with another sword stroke, neatly cut him in half and run off— so that the film ends with the spectacle of his immobile upper torso flailing its arms in the background while the legs stagger about helplessly in the foreground.

Perhaps the most charmingly inventive of these trick films is *Le Mélomane* (1903), which returns to the musical format of *L'Homme-orchestre*.[26] Here, against a dark country skyline, crossed by five telegraph wires, in marches Méliès as a band leader carrying a baton and a huge G clef, followed by six women and a drummer boy. While the players line up (frame right), Méliès throws the G clef up to hang on the wires (in the far left corner) and, after drawing a face on a large white board, goes to stand under the wires (frame left), taking off his head and tossing it up to be attached to the middle wire. This he repeats five more times, with the help of straight cuts and multiple exposures, so that eventually a half-dozen faces are strung out along the telegraph wires in the upper third of the frame. Then, using his own baton as well as others taken from the waiting women, he turns the faces into half notes and quarter notes in an imaginary two-bar staff of music. After this elaborate preparation comes the real tour de force of the film as the women, now lined up under the wires, display flip cards spelling out each note (solfeggio), and Méliès, standing off to the right, leads them all in a rendition of "God Save the King." Once each line of the song is completed, the face-notes change position on the staff (at Méliès's command), and the women flip their cards to indicate the note changes—suggesting that the cinema audience itself was being asked to join in the celebration, not only of a king (probably the newly crowned Edward VII) but of the magician who could so perfectly synchronize these truc effects.[27] In a final magical twist, after Méliès has led his performers off, each of his face-notes (in a straight cut) turns into a dove that wings away in a white blur. Compared to this deftly sustained, mechanical sleight of hand, *Le Roi du maquillage* (1904) looks almost pedestrian as Méliès himself, directly addressing the camera, undergoes five transformations in succession (through dissolves) which imitate simple, stereotypical chalk figures he has quickly sketched on a blackboard. Yet the film's one special cinematic trick of a consistent MS camera position, which accentuates the magician's skill at disguise, does end with a kind of confessional signature—Méliès's favorite disguise as the devil.

Indeed, the mask of Satan is the one Méliès wears with most delight in several of these early trick films. To some extent, in this choice of disguise, the magician shares the anticlerical attitude of many of his contemporaries in the Third Republic. But, perhaps more important, this diabolical figure—whose "frolics" proliferated in such nineteenth-century pantomimes as *Les Pilules du diable* (revived at the Châtelet in 1880, and again in 1905)[28]—came to epitomize Méliès's own desire to evade the strictures of the French social order and perhaps celebrate his successful escape from the family business into magic and fantasy.[29]

In that mask, he could mobilize a recurring, yet continually shifting bricolage of "otherness"—particularly in terms of religion, race, and gender—in order to invert the hierarchical values of modern French society and hold them up to ridicule in a riot of the carnivalesque. *Le Diable au couvent* (1899), for instance, produces Satan right out of the sacramental font in a convent chapel, whose cluttered decor nearly threatens to overwhelm the action. Transformed into a priest who speaks to an assembled group of nuns, he reveals himself and scatters them, repopulating the chapel with his minions, culminating in a tableau in which he rides a giant frog (an emblem of fertility) while smaller devils and women prance around him. Then, after a struggle with various priests and angels, Christ himself enters, carrying a spear, to triumph over Satan in a final *clou* that echoes the emblematic image of Saint George killing the dragon. A similar demonstration of playfully devilish power marks *Les Trésors de Satan* (1902) and especially *Le Chaudron infernal* (1903), where the castle interior set is quite spare, the better to foreground a strongly gendered "beauty of erasure"— where the hand-inked yellows and reds of the cauldron and its flames consume the softly superimposed apparitions of the women victimized by Satan.[30]

Le Cake-Walk infernal (1903) is perhaps the most interesting of these films, not so much for its cinematic trick effects, but for the gendered and ethnic "otherness" of its spectacle. The film's hellish cavern of a stage set, for instance, is thronged with women performing for a satyrlike Satan, doing everything from Rockette-like chorus-line kicks to "oriental" dances. The first centerpiece, however, features a couple in blackface doing the cakewalk as it supposedly should be done; and the second features Satan himself doing it on a cauldron lid, as first his lumpy goat legs and then his arms detach and leap rhythmically around his happily writhing and eventually exploding body. The final tableau brings the entire cast back into the frame with Satan now centered at the top, his command unchallenged and unchecked. This is one of the few moments in Méliès's films when his penchant for the carnivalesque is not reined in by the forces of a social order he seems to have continually sought to evade. Nevertheless, the film remains far from a serious threat, partly because it cannot keep from reproducing, in travesty form, some of the very differences that determine the conventions of that order's representation.

The patriarchal order of power and control which informs Méliès's trick films becomes even more explicit—and also more explicitly called into question—in those predicated on a specifically male vision of the fetishized female body. Perhaps the earliest of these, *Tentation de Saint Antoine* (1898), parodies the saint's story by confronting him, first with a host of loosely clad dancing women and then with one who, in an astonishing cut, replaces Christ and steps down from the huge crucifix before which he kneels in prayer. Later films abandon the shock of this blasphemous transformation for more secular and more conventional deceptions. In *Equilibre impossible* (1902), for instance, before the startled eyes of an old man sketching in a grotto garden, a vase dissolves into a veiled young woman who, with the aid of several others, steps down to dance briefly with him. Costumed now as a circus high-wire artiste, she moves toward

the black background and begins a marvelous aerial dance until, as her atten-
dents form a tableau around her, she drifts upward, blowing kisses, and dissolves away—and the old man is pushed offscreen. The spectacle of the fetishized female body is multiplied in *Le Rêve du maître de ballet* (1903). Here, a
sleeping ballet master imagines (through a dissolve) that several female dancers
in Tyrolean costumes appear in his bedroom. Then, as the room turns into a
cavern (through another dissolve), the women are replaced by a dainty, white-
clad shepherdess. Once this last figure goes to kiss the ballet master, however,
she turns into an ugly matron dressed in black, whom he thrashes mercilessly
until another cut abruptly ends the dream—and he falls out of bed pounding on
a pillow.[31]

In other Méliès films, the filmmaker himself appears as a medium to manipulate these fantasies of frustrated male desire. *Le Monstre* (1903), for instance,
takes place against a painted flat of the Sphinx and the pyramids, as an old man
introduces a young man to the marvelous abilities of a mummy—after being
taken out of its coffin, it dances and doubles in height. In the end, by means of
straight cuts, the old man turns the mummy into a beautiful young woman to
enchant his companion and then, wrapping her in a veil, lifts and throws her
body—and the mummy skeleton falls into the young man's arms. *Le Merveilleux
Eventeil vivant* (1904) recapitulates this fantasy in spades, with a fat magician now
producing the fetishistic vision of female bodies for another man. Out of a large
oblong box emerges an ornate golden fan that unfolds into seven panels resembling peacock feathers, each of which then turns into a woman, the central one
in a bright red gown. After several further transformations, the women, now
skimpily clad in white, perform a dance for the man and then are turned into
statues that dissolve back into the giant fan and, finally, into the original box.
Suddenly, the box's four sides fall away (it is empty), the man dances angrily on
it, the sides fold back up, entrapping him—only his head struggles out of a small
hole near the top—and the fat magician bows and exits.

If, in *Le Merveilleux Eventeil vivant*, the spectacle of barely disguised castration fear is "solved" through displacement onto another, *La Parapluie fantastique*
(1903) eliminates any such threat through an excess of transformation. Against
a painted flat of the outdoor Galathea Theatre, Méliès the magician turns his top
hat into a soccer ball and then into an open umbrella, out of which he produces
ten classically draped women in succession, positioning them one by one in a
symmetrical tableau. After the theater background is transformed into a Greek
temple (through a dissolve) and the magician admires his composition comes
the climactic clou: the ten women line up across the frame, toss off their togas
in a single motion, and prance off in fashionable 1900 outfits. Finally, in a rapid
series of reverse transformations, Méliès undoes all his work, with the added
detail of a huge flower tucked into his buttonhole. *La Sirène* (1904) reasserts male
control through self-transformation and suggests one of the appeals that magic
must have had in turn-of-the-century France—the illusion of transcending or
evading the barriers of class difference. The first half of this film presents a stage
magic act, involving substitutions produced by simple cuts. The second half,

however, turns into an unexpected fantasy of metamorphosis in which a fish tank used by the magician (who changes from peasant to bourgeois gentleman in his costuming) enlarges to almost fill the screen (thus becoming analogous to it), and within which a mermaid dissolves in, floating in space. The mermaid turns into a Greek-gowned figure and, as the fish tank frame dissolves away, the magician leads her to a large centered couch where she reclines (with three other women at her feet) as he goes to sit above her and turns into Neptune. Here again woman is presented as a body displayed for exhibition, and the specifically bourgeois patriarchal control of that fetishizing (and the apparatus that reproduces it) is sanctioned, not by a pantomime Satan, but by a highly respected heroic god of classical myth.[32]

In its representation of the voyeuristic pleasure of these early trick films, perhaps the most complex, the most reflexive, is *La Lanterne magique* (1903). Yet that reflexivity is playfully oblique, for the film forms a pastiche of nineteenth-century pantomime, ballet, music hall performance, and magic lantern show, the last of which offers a substitute device for the film camera-projector. At night, in the miniature set of a children's playroom, two pantomime clowns, Pulcinella and Pierrot, build a magic lantern and project a short series of circular-framed moving images on a black background wall. The images include a landscape, a MCU of a flirting young couple in eighteenth-century wigs, then a MCU of an older couple arguing, and finally MCUs of each of the clowns themselves. Whether one reads this series, with Linda Williams, as a minihistory of film art[33] or as the pretext for a story of romantic rivalry, the trick certainly draws attention to the reproductive or replicative power of the machine. Curious about their apparatus, the clowns dismantle the lantern, out of which emerge a half-dozen dancing shepherdesses (one of whom, Mlle Zizi Papillon, does an acrobatic number), Harlequin and Colombine (two other pantomime figures), and ten ballerinas in tutus, along with Mlle Papillon doing the cancan. In one sense, as Lucy Fischer argues, the apparatus seems to function here as a womb, in its appropriation of female procreative power,[34] but, in another, as Williams concludes, this "spewing forth of identical female bodies only calls attention" to their "status as totally mastered, infinitely reproducible *images*."[35] Indeed, the final moment of spectacle does fix the symbolic gender of the magic lantern or camera-projector clearly as masculine. The two clowns now begin to fight over the principal dancer, but toy soldiers march in, forcing them to climb into the lantern and pull up its sides behind them. When the soldiers manage to open the lantern again, inside is a large jack-in-the-box Pulcinella, around whose rising and falling motion (once the soldiers exit) the women join hands and dance. Revealed by the cinematic device of the simple cut, the undulating phallus ultimately hidden in the apparatus (which is itself disguised as a child's toy) receives the ecstatic worship of its own progeny—the encircling bodies of women.[36]

Not all of Méliès's films are so exclusively "masculinized" in the way they subjectify men and objectify women. The earliest of the longer féerie films, in particular, deviate from this pattern, at least to the extent that several either place a female figure in a position of power or take a woman's story as their subject.

13. *Rêve de Noël*, 1900 (production photo)

La Lune à un mètre (1898), for instance, presents a male astronomer's dream in which the moon assumes not unrelated guises—as a seductive woman lounging within a suspended crescent and a monstrous head filling the astronomer's study window and threatening to devour anything that comes near. Once the man is swallowed, however, the moon goddess Phoebe intervenes to reconstruct him out of the indigestible bits tossed out of the monster's mouth—and literally dispels his nightmare of dismemberment. *Cendrillon* (1899), of course, cannot escape the process of fetishizing—for instance, transforming Cinderella into a bejeweled and begowned princess and concluding in a spectacle of dancing women—and it has to marry her off to the prince.[37] But another fairy god-mother (Jehanne d'Alcy), not a male magician or Satan, rules over this fairyland and assumes the highest, centered position in the film's final tableau. More significantly, the centerpiece of *Cendrillon* is Cinderella's nightmare, in which a grandfather clock in her bedroom leaps on a table, disgorges a gnomelike clown (who had disrupted the ball at midnight) and five dancing women who themselves turn into clocks and are finally condensed into a menacing giant clock in the center of the room. What is interesting here is that a concrete image of the fairy godmother's warning about not violating a temporal deadline seems to displace any other threat, such as the class barrier Cinderella has sought to violate in the fantasy experience of the ball. Of these early féeries, *Rêve de Noël* (1900) is perhaps the most idiosyncratic as well as the most benign. Although its loosely connected "dream" images—ranging from a fantasy procession through

14. *Barbe-bleue*, 1901 (production photo)

a palatial cavern to a banquet where an old beggar is invited in from the cold to dine—are framed by a repeated LS tableau in which two bourgeois boys first go to sleep and then awaken, no other sign indicates that the dream specifically is theirs rather than that of the nurse who attends them. Moreover, appended to the final frame image is yet another tableau of dancing women and children, centered around a Christmas tree—which, in the original print, apparently ended in an apotheosis of "Saint Nicholas in all his glory."

The most threatening, oppressive vision recurs with a vengeance in *Barbe-bleue* (1901), whose story focuses less on Bluebeard (played by Méliès himself) than on his new bride and eighth wife.[38] The centerpiece of this film, too, is a nightmare provoked by Bluebeard warning his bride not to enter the chamber next to her bedroom, her temptation to do so, and the sudden appearance of a devil who eggs her on. Once inside, she discovers his secret—the hanging corpses of his previous seven wives—a forbidden vision of male prerogative, the horrifying result of actions stretching back into the past and which predict her own future. Startled, she drops the chamber key in a pool of blood, which causes it to enlarge—as a sign of her husband's murderous potency and, paradoxically, not of his but *her* guilt. Another fairy godmother (Bleuette Bernon) comes to the rescue, however, dispatching the devil (twice); and, before Bluebeard can make the bride his eighth victim, a shining knight shows up with his army to run a sword through him, pinning his body to a courtyard post. Eventually, at the fairy godmother's command, even the ghosts of the seven other victims appear, to attack their murderer, and then become corporeal and join the rescued bride in quickly finding suitable new husbands from among the saviors. And the nightmare seems to evaporate, to be forgotten, except for Bluebeard's body still lying in the foreground of the final tableau. In its staging and erasure of a psychosexual trauma, *Barbe-bleue* presents an intriguing analogue to the celebrated "theatrical" seances of hypnosis performed by the Paris psychologist, Charcot, in which a hysterical patient, usually a woman, was magically cured of her problems, sometimes with the preparatory aid of a photographic device that produced multiple, split-second images of the actual hysterical state.[39]

In that they constitute a special category of transformation films, Méliès's féeries assume a contextual frame for reading which differs slightly from that of the shorter trick films. For one, they were less ephemeral than the trick films, sometimes playing for months at a single site—as did *Le Voyage dans la lune* at the Olympia music hall in 1902.[40] For another, although some of their subjects had circulated widely throughout the nineteenth century in simple pictures sold by itinerant peddlers,[41] they were all tied more closely to recent stage spectacles. *La Lune à un mètre*, after all, was closely based on one of Méliès's own miniature fantasy shows first presented at the Théâtre-Robert Houdin. *Cendrillon* appeared shortly after Jules Massenet's opera of the same name in Paris, and both were drawn from a popular 1895 pantomime that constantly was being revived on British theater programs for the New Year's holidays and once had even played at the Robert-Houdin.[42] Similarly, *Rêve de Noël* may have been inspired by an 1897 pantomime produced at the Olympia.[43] And both *Barbe-bleue* and *Le Voyage dans la lune* were based on Jacques Offenbach operettas, with the latter film also drawing on Adolphe Dennery's melodrama adaptation of the original Jules Verne novel as well as a current H. G. Wells story.[44] For that reason, the visual rhythm of the féeries may have been partly determined by musical accompaniment, whether by condensed versions of original scores or by newly written compositions, as was apparently the case with *Le Voyage dans la lune,* at least at the Olympia.[45] And, unlike the trick films, they may have encouraged the use of a bonisseur, especially in the fairground cinemas, either to summarize the story beforehand or else to designate each of the film's unfolding tableaux.

Furthermore, the féeries were marked by a somewhat different mode of representation. Partly because they were constructed of multiple shot-scenes and recorded exclusively in LS, their elaborate decors acquired an even more privileged role—as tableaux and clous of spectacle—much in the manner of late nineteenth-century French stage productions, on which the popular dioramas had such an impact—the most relevant being Louis Daguerre's "fairy work" projections.[46] Méliès himself alluded to the significance of these decors, whose construction consumed more time and money than any other component of his production.[47] Some even presented an intriguing bricolage of past and present in their mise-en-scène. *Barbe-bleue,* for instance, eclectically combines Renaissance and Second Empire architectural details, Belle Epoque fashions in women's clothing, and, for publicity purposes, a giant bottle of Mercier champagne.[48] *Rêve de Noël* summarizes the gist of its dream through the toys the two boys receive, combining the Christian emblems of the sheep and lion with one much more congenial to Méliès, the jester. Yet the féeries also forced Méliès to consider various means of producing spatial coherence through an episodic sequence

15. *Le Voyage dans la lune,* 1902

of tableaux. In *La Lune à un mètre,* two slightly different decors of the astronomer's study were constructed in order to simulate how, within the larger, less
cluttered space of the nightmare, a telescope could literally bring the moon
closer to the astronomer.[49] In *Rêve de Noël,* by contrast, adjacent spaces are connected in the transition between shot-scenes: a church interior, where several
boys are pulling on a bell rope, is followed by the church tower interior, where
a large bell is ringing. In *Barbe-bleue,* such a connection is made twice: first, when
the bride goes from her bedroom into the chamber of horrors (moving from left
to right in both rooms), and second, when Bluebeard drags her down stairs
from the tower ramparts and out the castle door into the courtyard.[50] Finally,
beginning with *Cendrillon,* in order to link individual shot-scenes of tableaux,
Méliès introduced a consistent device drawn from scene-change practices in the
theater and magic lantern shows—the dissolve.[51] Because it risked ruining an already costly prior shot-scene of spectacle, the dissolve seems to have had an important secondary function for Méliès—to restrict exhibitors from making alter-
ations in the length and order of shots in the prints they purchased from him.[52]

As the longest and most expensive of the early féeries, *Le Voyage dans la lune*
constitutes not only a culmination of Méliès's work but also a significant advance.[53] It mixes theatrical and cinematic devices in both old and new ways, it
privileges clous of spectacle by means of extended narrative continuity, and,
surprisingly, it experiments with dividing up and reconstituting the autonomous
shot-scene. Nearly twenty decors provide the principal spectacle material for the

film's thirty shots and the raison d'être for its parodic story of a half-dozen scientists who rocket off to the moon, have a series of harrowing encounters with the lunar Selenites, and barely escape to rocket back to public acclaim. The sets range from rather flat spaces of public ceremony (resembling several paintings by Méliès's contemporary, Henri Rousseau) to the "deep space" of the actual rocket launch (out of a huge, telescoping "Big Bertha" cannon) and the rugged lunar surface (with its multiple flyaway flats).[54] The adventuring scientists (who begin as medieval magicians) are all men, of course, with women serving either to help launch the rocket (as a sailor-suited corps de ballet) or to decorate a brief dream of space; the Selenite enemy, half crustacean and half primate in their costumes and behavior (they are played by Folies-Bergère acrobats),[55] seem a neutered composite "other," both biological and colonial. The narrative divides somewhat unevenly into three parts, bookended by a kind of expository prologue and the usual celebratory epilogue. And each of the three evidences a slightly different negotiation between the demands of spectacle "attractions," spatial coherence, and temporal linearity.

The middle section of Le Voyage dans la lune, where the scientists actually explore the moon, may break no new ground in its display of trick effects and spectacular decors, yet that hardly detracts from its achievement. The rocket sinks below the lunar surface, for instance, while the earth seems to rise in the far background sky, a "dream" of celestial bodies hovers over the sleeping scientists, ending in a shower of snowflakes, and Selenites keep disappearing in puffs of smoke. The initial section of the rocket launch, however, develops further some of the editing techniques from Barbe-bleue and L'Homme à la tête de caoutchouc. Three separate decors, for instance, loosely link adjacent spaces, in which the characters repeatedly exit frame left and enter frame right—from the interior of the factory manufacturing the rocket to the exterior rooftop where it is to be launched.[56] The launch itself is represented in two separate shots in which the perspective on the site shifts almost ninety degrees—first looking at the cannon from one side (as the women slide in the rocket) and then looking along the barrel from a point near its base.[57] The "trip to the moon" is condensed into a single tableau, using a matte shot of the enlargening moon, along with cuts to "awaken" the moon's face to the approaching rocket and then to imbed it like a huge shell casing in one eye.[58] And, in this supposedly uninterrupted tableau, what at first seems to be a POV shot (the spectator shares the view of the voyaging scientists) turns into an omniscient view of the crash landing.[59] Finally, the rocket landing is repeated in the following shot, this time from a perspective on the lunar surface, as strict temporal sequentiality is sacrificed for the effect of a doubled spectacle. The third and shortest section, the scientists' return to earth, presents a final, unexpected marvel. Not only does the rocket pass smoothly—by means of repeated descending movements—through four separate spaces (from a cliff on the lunar surface, through space and then the sea surface, to the sea bottom), it does so with amazing speed.[60] Lasting just two and two-and-a-half seconds, respectively, and joined by a cut, the second and third shots of this sequence produce an effect of "rapid montage" that matches, if not surpasses,

16. *Le Voyage dans la lune,* 1902

the earlier comic surprise of the lunar landing.[61] That all these innovations and recapitulated spectacle effects were so successfully structured in the scenario Méliès patched together goes a long way to explaining the worldwide popularity the film so quickly achieved.

In *Le Royaume des fées* (1903), Méliès returned to the earlier fairy pantomime tradition predating the science fantasy format represented by *Le Voyage dans la lune*.[62] The film's scenario was freely adapted from *Biche au bois*, a French fairy pantomime frequently revived in the latter half of the nineteenth century.[63] It tells the classic tale of Prince Bel-Azor (Méliès) who, with the aid of Aurora (Bernon), must rescue his fiancée, Princess Azurine, whom an ogre has stolen away to his isolated island castle. This simple tale serves as a pretext for some of the most spectacular decors in all of Méliès's films. The princess's bedroom, for instance, is a discreetly erotic space of gaudy baroque columns and soft draperies surrounding a huge seashell bed, and she is abducted in a bright yellow and red car composed of disjointed animal parts.[64] The undersea cavern into which the prince has to descend is a "deep space" of multiple fly-away flats (perhaps modeled on the drawings of Gustave Doré)[65] and sea creatures providing transport (a sailfish, a lobster, and a dolphin-drawn chariot); for their final journey to the ogre's castle, he and his men eventually climb into a giant black whale. Yet the film also displays and even extends some of Méliès's earlier cinematic innovations. In the painted "deep space" of the armaments room, for instance, the ogre confronts the prince with a simultaneous vision (through a dissolve that matches their foreground position in the frame) in which the princess is being lifted up

17. *Le Royaume des fées,* 1903

into his distant castle tower in the background. In the lurid green and red storm scene, the prince's (miniature) ship sinks and drifts down to settle on the sea bottom in a shot sequence that replicates the rocket's descent in *Le Voyage dans la lune.* Finally, as Gaudreault has shown, the concluding rescue sequence is broken down into shots that offer a half-dozen different perspectives on a seacoast peninsula and the island castle.[66] The prince moves from the castle exterior (after setting it afire) to a flaming, debris-filled interior hall, where he carries the princess down a staircase and off. When the couple returns to the peninsula, where Aurora is waiting, the perspective has shifted almost 180 degrees, perhaps in order to remove the castle, which previously had been visible in the background. Then, after the prince, confronting the ogre one last time, stuffs him in a barrel and tosses it off the peninsula cliff, there is an insert shot (again shifting nearly 180 degrees) of the ogre floundering in a rocky pool, presumably at the cliff base. In the end, however, even this cinematic construction of a space-time continuum has to give way to a final theatrical tableau of spectacle—with flying flats, ballerinas, and superimposed angels surrounding Aurora and her blessed couple.

If, in their construction of multiple-shot scenes, *Le Voyage dans la lune* and *Le Royaume des fées* exemplify one line of development in Méliès's féeries, *Dam-*

18. *Le Royaume des fées*, 1903

nation de Docteur Faust and *Faust et Marguerite* constitute another, which relies much more extensively on the representational system of autonomous tableaux. Unlike previous féeries drawn from operettas and pantomimes, both of
these films derive from well-known operas, by Charles Gounod (according to the
French catalog) and Hector Berlioz (according to the American catalog), and thus
evidence some aspiration to "high art."[67] *Damnation de Docteur Faust* (1903) is
somewhat unusual for Méliès in that its slight story builds rather slowly and
single-mindedly toward an interrelated series of climactic moments of spectacle. Essentially, Mephistopheles (played by Méliès, of course) leads Faust down
through one empty cavern after another (their sharp black and white features
linked smoothly by dissolves) in order to force his victim to witness several
spectacular displays of his power. These include dancing ballerinas, cavorting
devils with pitchforks, suspended women momentarily replaced by a furry monster sprouting tenacles and stamping goat feet, and a "waterfall" that turns into
a wall of flames. The final descent, however, is conveyed through the truc effect
of having Mephistopheles and Faust suspended against a dark background, seeming to drift from the top of the frame to the bottom, past parallel painted-flat
rock walls. Then, in the concluding tableau, Mephistopheles quickly tosses Faust
down another hole and gives his attention to his lively consort of devils and

dancing women, rising above them in a splendid cape that unfolds like great black wings. In short, Faust's story here is little more than a pretext for Méliès, through Mephistopheles, to let spectators indulge in all sorts of visual pleasure, without fear of retribution.

Faust et Marguerite (1904), by contrast, condenses into a similar number of tableaux the much more complicated prior story of Faust's infatuation with Marguerite, their violent courtship, and her abandonment and death. Compared to Méliès's previous féeries, most of this film's tableaux seem rather static and conventional, probably because they attempt to emulate the painted-flat decors used in staging Gounod's opera. Moreover, their size sometimes overwhelms the actors, strongly suggesting that spectators may have required either inter-titles or a bonisseur (most of the tableaux are joined by cuts rather than dis-solves) in order to understand the film. Yet, despite its dependence on a series of autonomous tableaux, with whatever kind of musical and verbal support, this Méliès film clearly is concerned with foregrounding its story. The best evidence for this is that Mephistopheles's tricks, which are few and far between, all serve Faust's cause and advance his story. First, in Faust's study, he produces the allur-ing vision of Marguerite demurely working at her spinning wheel; in Faust's duel with a rival, he diverts the other with magic flames; then, in the village church, he dissolves out of a wall to interrupt Marguerite's retreat to a life of prayer. Only in the final moments does this pattern shift as the film juxtaposes a tableau of Mephistopheles and Faust ruling over a bacchic feast among Greek temple ruins and another tableau of Marguerite near death in a medieval dun-geon, where Mephistopheles finally seizes Faust and they disappear through a trap in the floor. Ultimately, rather than celebrate the devil's prowess, this film exalts Marguerite's suffering. As smoke obscures the dungeon, the walls fly out and the painted-flat background dissolves to sky. Angels slowly ascend, bear-ing Marguerite completely clothed in white, to be surrounded by saints with golden halos. This climactic spectacle puts Mephistopheles's tricks to shame and strongly allies *Faust et Marguerite* with the apotheosis finales of the French bibli-cal and historical films.

A similar dual-focus narrative provides the pretext for some unusual magic in the short féerie, *Au Clair de la lune* (1904). Here, in an uncharacteristic move, Méliès focuses on the traditional pantomime figure of Pierrot who, in his search for love, comes into conflict with an inhospitable landowner. The film begins much like the recording of a stage performance as, one night, Pierrot enters a garden next to the man's house (frame right) and sings a sad love song, accom-panying himself on the guitar. The man comes out of his house to complain; and, after he goes back in, Pierrot comes forward to address the camera, miming his frustrated love as well as his anger. Then, as he goes to sleep on a background bench, a simple lunar fantasy brings his search to a successful end: in the sky above, clouds move off to reveal the full moon steadily increasing in size until it dissolves into a new moon with Phoebe herself reclining within its sickle curve. With this fantasy transformation, the film suddenly shifts into another mode, producing a series of surprising truc effects. Pierrot awakens and, after Phoebe tosses him her floral bouquet, takes up his guitar to sing to her. The landowner returns and orders his servants to seize the singer, but Pierrot simply leaps up into the sky to sit beside his beloved. Stunned, the servants run back in the house; and, to his astonishment, the landowner turns (in a straight cut) into a decrepit old man. Now, in a highly unusual climactic clou, the figure of the moon-lovers dissolves into an iris-masked ECU of a single eye, whose glance seems to reprimand the old man cowering in the foreground. Quickly, the eye turns back into the full moon, which diminishes in size and vanishes in the dark night sky. Finally, in a comic reversal of the earlier rejection, *Au Clair de la lune* concentrates on its moral lesson: when the old man knocks on his own house door, the servants fail to recognize him and send him off with blows from their juggler's clubs. In one last truc, the moon reappears, full-faced, to laugh heartily over the now empty garden. Through a loosely linked series of subject positions—in which an initially divided subject and object combine to become a whole new subject, with near omniscience—Pierrot not only appeals directly to the spectator but gets to condemn his antagonist and (in one last mirrorlike appearance) join in the cinema audience's laughter.

Late in 1904, Méliès returned once more to science fantasy and to the construction of multiple-shot scenes, in *Le Voyage à travers l'impossible*.[68] Although loosely based on a popular Dennery-Verne stage production (1882),[69] with an added opening attack on women's suffrage, the film also reworks material from *Le Voyage dans la lune*—especially in the opening shot-scenes, in the change of destination for the journey (from the center of the earth to the sun), and in the illusion of approaching the sun itself. Much like its predecessor, the new film lampoons scientific exploration, giving its travelers comic-opera names (Méliès, for instance, plays a Professor Mabouloff) and calling their organization the Institute of Incoherent Geography.[70] The scenario is divided into four parts, each of which involves a different modern mode of transportation—train, automobile, train again, and dirigible-submarine—and the last three all end in spectacular crashes. The decors are no less numerous than in the previous longer féeries, but here the action often seems as important as the spectacle, which again calls attention to Méliès's increasingly flexible system of creating continuity. The initial train journey, for instance, is a three-shot pastiche, including a miniature model, a stage-flat car with one side cut away, and a three-dimensional stage railway station. Several editing techniques are recapitulated from earlier films— the double spectacle of the automobile crashing into and through a mountain cabin (in overlapping exterior and interior shots), the cuts that "animate" the sun's face as it disgorges red smoke and pieces of the train that has sped into its mouth, and the descent of the dirigible through four different shots to turn into a submarine undersea. At least two things, however, seem new to the Méliès system. One plays on the spatial contrast between foreground and background and probably derives from theatrical practice—within the decor of a small Breton village there is an explosion out at sea, and the nose cone of the dirigible-submarine soon after drops from above onto the foreground beach. The other involves a strict orchestration of repeated movement throughout the film, in which the first three journeys consistently pass from right to left across the frame, while the last reverses direction, in order to better suggest a return to the institute's banquet hall at the beginning. And it is here (in a point to be taken up later) that Méliès's practice intersects with and yet diverges from the chase film as it is soon to be developed by Pathé, Gaumont, and others.

Prior to that development, however, both Gaumont and Pathé were producing "transformation scenes," in imitation of Méliès. Because scarcely any of Gaumont's early films apparently survive, their relation to those of the master magician remains unclear. Francis Lacassin's filmography of Guy, however, suggests that the company specialized in one feature of the genre that Méliès often incorporated into his films—dance performances.[71] Nearly half of Gaumont's production, between 1900 and 1902, was given over to dance films—from serpentine, Spanish, Bohemian, Basque, and Japanese dances to short ballets such as *Vénus et Adonis* and *Danse des saisons*. That all were performed by women from the Olympia or the Opéra (at least one of whom also worked for Méliès) obviously raises questions about the context of their exhibition. One would like to know, for instance, if such films were read and received differently, depending on whether they were screened in the music halls or fairs and whether the audience was principally male or female. Pathé also included dance films among its early productions, and those few that survive suggest that, in exploiting the marvel of cinematic movement, they, too, displayed it as a gendered spectacle. *The Dancers* (1900), for instance, stages familiar performance routines in the open air, before a crude painted-flat interior, against which leans a small white plaque bearing the company's initial trademark, PF, in black letters. In one, a couple in eighteenth-century costumes engages in a brief pas de deux; in the other, a woman does a flamenco dance, accompanied by two men playing a guitar and tambourine. Later Pathé films strive for more authenticity. In an eye-level LS of a painted-flat drawing room, for instance, *Valse excentrique* (1903) offers the Eldorado dancers Boldoni and Solinski, dressed in contemporary formal attire, performing a series of acrobatic spins, tosses, and flips. Here, the company's new stencil color process accentuates the woman as an object of spectacle by marking her full skirt and petticoats with bright yellow. *Danse des apaches* (1904), by contrast, serves to display the power of an underworld tough guy through his rough, abusive handling of a female partner. This spectacle of machismo is staged not only for his fellows but for several slumming bourgeois gentlemen.

Pathé's more numerous trick films followed those of Méliès to the extent that they focused attention on the spectacle of cinematic truc effects. *Peinture animée* (1903) does this with perhaps more art than craft. An artist spins a crank-wheel at the edge of a large painting on a gallery wall and then watches as his landscape study of a windmill beside a stream dissolves into a motion picture (through double exposure), with the suggestion of a story—a man leading a donkey brings grain sacks to the mill, and two lovers meet at its door. Simply and concisely, this film finds a source for the cinema in art (and not photography), equating the painter's and filmmaker's skill in creating the illusion of life-

19. *La Soubrette ingénieuse*, 1903

likeness. As this literal *tableau vivant* suggests, most Pathé trick films, unlike those of Méliès, tended to concentrate on a single cinematic device. In *La Soubrette ingénieuse* (1903), for instance, an overhead camera looking down on a set flat painted on the floor, along with a simple cut, gives a maid the ability to climb a wall and hang pictures for an absent master. In *The Wonderful Hair Restorer* (1903), a barber discovers the source of a client's baldness in cut-in, iris-masked POV shots, one of which, in ECU, magnifies an irregular hair filament.[72] Then, through simple cuts, his magic lotion not only gives the man a shaggy head of long hair but also sprouts patches of hair on his own palms. The most consistent truc that these films exploited, however, was reverse motion, beginning as early as *An Intelligent Waiter* (1901), where a man creates a full table setting out of porcelain fragments. In *Pêche miraculeuse* (1902), fights between two and then three fishermen are resolved when the antagonists, in unison, leap out of the foreground canal (or Pathé studio tank) into which they have fallen. *Baignade impossible* (1902) then uses the same painted-flat landscape (which miniature trains repeatedly cross) in tricking a man who undresses down to his underwear in order to take a swim—each time he is set to dive, a sudden cut endows him with a different costume. Eventually, after seven failed attempts to undress, he jumps in fully clothed. Finally, in *Les Mésaventures d'un artiste* (1903), a Sunday painter daubing at an easel alongside a foreground stream (shot on location) suffers a different kind of dressing down. After a half-dozen men sneak up and push the unsuspecting painter into the water, reverse motion tosses him back

20. *Metamorphose du papillon,* 1904

into their clutches for repeated pummeling. Unike *Peinture animée,* this film bur-lesques the "high art" pretentions of painting through the truc effect and, for good measure, frames this within the cinema's "natural" ability to reproduce reality.

Other Pathé trick films combine theatrical and cinematic effects to extend the spectacle of stage magic acts. *Metamorphoses du roi de pique* (1903–1904), for instance, has a magician do a few card tricks, after which the king of spades enlarges in size and comes to life, indulges in a card game, gets angry at losing, and then vanishes in a cinematic sleight of hand, emerging as a regular playing card from his master's sleeve. *Paravent mystérieux* (1904) has a servant tie up a different magician inside a folding screen, placed in front of a "Jardin des plantes" painted flat, where he can undress down to his long johns, without loosening the ropes, and then be replaced by the now-tied-up servant. For his last trick, the magician takes a scimitar inside the screen, which reopens to reveal his dismembered trunk and limbs suspended above his head on the floor (scimi-tar still in mouth); when the body parts all fall at once, in a straight cut, he springs up whole again. *Metamorphose du papillon* (1904), by contrast, reworks the transformation of a popular dance performance, turning a stage caterpillar and its paper chrysalis into what at first looks like a stage butterfly but then is revealed as a woman, as she straightens up from a bent-backward position, with huge fluttering wings. Her figure then becomes a site of display for the spectacle

21. *Le Cakewalk chez les nains,* 1903

of Pathé's unique stencil color process—as she revolves and ripples, a dozen combinations of rose, green, blue, and yellow shimmer across her wings and body. Perhaps the most interesting of these early trick films is *Le Cakewalk chez les nains* (1903), which opens quite simply (in AS) with an American minstrel figure seated in a dark velvet chair. The performance begins when he goes behind the chair and, with a downward sweep of his light-colored top hat, along with the technique of double exposure, creates a miniature couple in peasant costumes dancing on the chair seat. The sweep of a handkerchief changes this couple into another one with the woman now dressed in a long full skirt and a huge flower hat. Finally, the minstrel places an oblong box on end on the chair, out of which crawls a miniscule version of himself to perform the cakewalk while his "master" watches in admiration. Much like Méliès's *Le Cakewalk infernal* and *La Lanterne magique,* this Pathé film attributes a masculine authority to the reproductive power of the camera.

In its production of féeries, Pathé also followed Méliès closely, yet certain deviations from the "norm" the latter had established began to crop up quite early. This is evident in one of the earliest surviving Pathé films, *Ali Baba et les quarante voleurs* (1901–1902), which Zecca may well have drawn from popular pantomime adaptations of *The Thousand and One Nights.*[73] First of all, *Ali Baba's* seven autonomous tableaux are linked by fades rather than dissolves, and the first two tableaux join the exterior and interior of the thieves' secret cave through a ninety-degree shift in camera position.[74] Second, the representational space of these tableaux seems consistently flatter than in Méliès films, perhaps because of the full-length painted-canvas backgrounds and the relatively restricted choreography of actor movement. Furthermore, Zecca relies on theatrical devices to produce most of the film's few transformations—flyaway flats, for instance, open and close over the cave mouth—yet he uses a simple cut to effect Ali Baba's rather graphic beheading of Cassim, who is caught stealing some of the thieves' hidden treasure.[75] In the next-to-last tableau, much like Méliès, he too displays a troupe of dancing women (from the Paris Opéra)—for the gaze of a wealthy merchant and his disguised guest, Ali Baba, as well as the spectator. Here the spectacle serves, if only briefly, a narrative function, for one of the dancers, knowing of Ali Baba's plan to rob his host, stabs and kills him under the pretense of collecting money for the entertainment. Narrative closure, however, quickly gives way to a finale of spectacle in which Ali Baba is invited to gaze upon a tableau of skimpily clad women, backed by spinning wheels and stars around a centered sun. This finale not only attaches an apotheosis ending closely associated with "occidental" religious and historical representations to the story of a legendary "oriental" thief, à la Méliès, but also strangely reverses the gender relations of his death—although killed by a woman, he is "rewarded" with a paradise of women, almost as a substitute for all the earthly treasure he has lost.

One of Pathé's earliest biblical films, *Samson et Delila* (1902), resembles *Ali Baba* quite closely, in both subject and mode of representation. Here, eight separate episodes (only the last four of which survive) stage the familiar story of Delilah's deception of Samson—she cuts his long hair, the source of his superhuman strength, while he sleeps—and his eventual revenge, toppling the stone columns of his Egyptian captors' palace. These autonomous tableaux also are linked by fades, and flyaway flats along with a theatrical lift create the only instances of transformation—collapsing the palace walls and letting Samson emerge from the wreckage in an apotheosis tableau. As evidence of Pathé's new insistence on the specially constructed nature of each separate studio decor for its films,[76] however, *Samson et Delila*'s tableaux are distinguished by greater detail and depth. In the "castration" scene, for instance, hieroglyphs cover nearly every painted-flat stone surface, two priests encourage Delilah from behind background curtains, and she herself deliberately circles the sleeping giant before disempowering him.[77] This film concludes, too, with a troupe of dancing women, but their spectacle diverts the attention of the Egyptian rulers and priests and pushes Samson to the background, giving him the opportunity to stage an even more spectacular finish. Now "shorn" of all earthly delights and despair, he can become a model of the "true" subject as spectacle for the spectator.

Slightly later Pathé féeries—*La Fée des roches noires, Les Sept Chateaux du diable*, and *La Fée printemps* (all 1902–1903), directed by Zecca, with decors attributed to Lorant-Heilbronn—seem to have come under Méliès's influence more directly, yet in crucial ways remain distinct. In *La Fée des roches noires,* a peasant refuses to help an old woman carrying a bundle of sticks and goes to sleep at the foot of a huge rock. She promptly turns into a fairy and confronts him with a series of threats: a sudden waterfall spurting from the rock, grotesquely masked gnomes cavorting under the laughing profile of a rock face, a rope noose hanging from a signpost, and a vision of ghosts and skeletons in a cemetery. Terrified and repentant, he finally begs her forgiveness, as she now sits triumphant in a swan-drawn chariot. Unlike *Ali Baba* and *Samson et Delila*, the sudden transformations here are created almost exclusively by simple cuts, and the peasant's vision occurs through a dissolve to a separate tableau in which his sleeping body is replaced by a tomb, out of which he rises, much puzzled, to face the ghoulish apparitions.

The explicit moralizing of this film—in contrast to both *Ali Baba* and Méliès's *Barbe-bleue,* for example—then takes on a strongly religious cast in *Les Sept Chateaux du diable,* which was drawn from a popular pantomime revived at the Châtlelet in 1897. Introduced by the CU spectacle of a florid face with rolling eyes and a huge mouth holding the title, *Les Sept Chateaux du diable* uses the story of the devil promising a young woodcutter all manner of riches in order to present an episodic series of tableau spectacles of the seven deadly sins—all of which are linked by dissolves and marked by identifying signs within the frame which change from French to English to German. Among these tableaux are a pastry shop in which a huge gluttonous face (as in the title shot) engulfs a whole roast pig, a mammoth baguette, and even two boys and a servant; a hall where the statues of Luxury and Idleness turn into beautiful women; and finally a cavern opening onto a foreground sea across which several boats speed by (one bears Napoleon) on their way to hell. Although, in the beginning, the woodcutter's wife is turned into a coatrack, from which he in turn gets a new suit of clothes, she inexplicably reappears in the end to rescue him from the devil. In the final tableau, a painting of Saint George and the dragon dissolves in, transforming the background painted flat of the devil's rocky castle; and flats fly away to reveal a spectacle of paradise with God himself reigning over a spinning wheel of time, angels, soldiers, and the reunited couple. Sanctioned by this "revelation," the woodcutter is returned to his social position, and he and his wife are blessed, not with riches, but with children flocking in from both sides of the frame—in a kind of visual polemic against the unusually low birthrate of late nineteenth- and early twentieth-century France.

A similar polemical appeal to fecundity is much more simply and effectively staged in *La Fée printemps.*[78] Here again a woodcutter and his wife are the principal characters, but now they come to the aid of an old woman traveling through the countryside one winter evening by offering her food and shelter. Their reward is immediate as the old woman dissolves into a fairy woman who, in turn, transforms winter to spring and presents the couple with a huge bouquet of flowers, out of which emerges not one child but twins. Much like *La Fée des roches noires,* this film includes only two LS tableaux, yet one depicts an exterior landscape with the couple's cottage (frame right) and the other represents the cottage interior. Moreover, unlike previous Pathé and Méliès films, the shifts from one to the other adjacent space are done by straight cuts that loosely

22. *Don Quichotte,* 1903

match the exits and entrances of the characters. Significant as these features are, the chief pleasure of *La Fée printemps* comes from its spectacle—and not so much from its miraculously produced children as from its marvelous changes in color. For the blue tint of the opening tableaux, both exterior and interior, gives way to black and white when the fairy woman appears, the better to highlight her pale green dress dotted with yellow flowers and the massive yellow bouquet (some of the flowers fly in from offscreen) she gathers for the couple. What this does, of course, is "naturalize" Pathé's own special processes of reproduction; and, in staging this "miracle" of morally conceived fertility, *La Fée printemps* slyly invokes the "high purpose" of the company's own transformative powers.

Several Pathé films produced during the following year show marked signs of deviating even further from the "norms" of Méliès's féeries. One of these is *Don Quichotte* (1903), a féerie adaptation of the Cervantes novel, originally comprised of fifteen shot-scenes, of which only seven seem to survive.[79] Nearly all of these emphasize the novel's farcical or burlesque episodes—as when Quixote and Sancho are turned into music hall clowns, in white- and black-face, respectively, for their horseback ride into the cosmos. Pathé's new stencil color process plays an important role in the film's spectacle—ending the horseback ride with a big red explosion, for instance, highlighting Sancho's brief royal reign in garish reds and yellows, and then tinting the final tableau of Quixote's death in somber greens and blues. What is especially unusual about this *Don Quichotte,* however,

84

is its strategy of repeatedly representing two different spaces within the same tableau. In the opening, Quixote's book-crammed study interior includes a matte shot of inspirational heroes from the past lined up across the background wall, just above the door through which he and Sancho depart on their adventures. The inn they then come to has an interior decor of both upper and lower levels, which are complemented by a third enclosed space—a puppet theater that is brought in to distract the two adventurers while Sancho is robbed of his wineskin. The shot-scene in which the two fall out of their boat and are rescued by mill workers is composed of a foreground lake, a big revolving mill wheel to the right, and a matte shot (not a studio decor) of the cutaway mill interior in the background. This composite shot is so organized that, when the mill workers run left to exit from the matte interior (passing through an apparent door in the wall), they appear just a couple of frames later, and in the order of their exit, on the exterior studio dock, from which they can reach the struggling heroes. Finally, *Don Quichotte* may well be the earliest surviving Pathé féerie that contains intertitles.[80] Rather than link shot-scenes with dissolves, here they are all introduced by a cut to a brief intertitle: from "He sets out to defend the oppressors" to "The hero's death." This strategy may have allowed exhibitors a bit more freedom in cutting the films they purchased, but it also probably reduced the need—already slight, given the familiarity of the novel and its various "realizations"—for a bonisseur to summarize or explain the spectacle.

Introducing LS tableaux with brief intertitles soon became a standard mode of representation and narration for Pathé's longer films, as is evident in *Le Chat botté* (1903).[81] In eight tableaux, this film presents episodes from the fairy tale of Puss-in-boots (perhaps based on one of several stage pantomimes),[82] concluding with his clever outwitting of a powerful ogre and the ensuing betrothal of his young peasant master to the Marquis de Carabas's daughter. Puss-in-boots is played throughout by the pantomime actor Bretteau dressed up in a soft, white cat suit, and the transformations through cuts and dissolves are restricted to the final shot-scenes—as when the ogre shows the cat a vision of the dancing skeletons of his victims. The shot-scenes in this film are unusually varied in their mode of representation. In a wooded glen, for instance, the cat watches a group of "greeting card" rabbits (probably children in bunny suits) doing a "patticake" dance; while in the enemy's castle, by contrast, the ogre plucks small children out of jars by their heels and drops them into a steaming cauldron—his nonchalance makes the violence as shocking as anything in Méliès's films. Other shot-scenes aim for a kind of studio verisimilitude: the Millet-like tableau of peasants against a painted-flat hay field, which the Marquis and Puss-in-boots pass through, and the opening tableau of the peasant's farmyard (including a real donkey and chickens), whose "deep space" is extended by an immense painted flat of woods and a stream with a distant windmill (again).[83] Two shot-scenes also shift the camera to an unusual HA LS position: the first in the cat's initial appearance to "console his master" (whose father has died) and the other in the final tableau of the Marquis's banquet room, which dissolves into a vision of "Fiançailles apothéose," anchored by the cat's foreground position, in which

23. *Le Chat botté,* 1903

angels on a staircase look down on yet another procession of children. If couples in these early Pathé féeries are consistently united or reunited through the intervention of a magical agent, they themselves also become a celebrated locus of generation.

As perhaps the most significant genres of this early period of filmmaking, the trick film and féerie exemplified several crucial components of the French "cinema of attractions." The shorter trick films presented a series of either marvelous or comic trucs, most of them produced by uniquely cinematic techniques—"invisible" cuts, stop motion, reverse motion, dissolves, multiple exposures, superimpositions, and magnification through close framing. The longer féeries, often in conjunction with such trick effects, displayed for contemplation elaborate, even "deep space" decors in spectacular tableaux, accentuated by either hand-inked or stencil process colors. Although both Méliès and Pathé privileged such "attractions" in their films, the two companies also diverged in significant ways, most obviously in Méliès's consistent use of the dissolve to link shot-scenes and in Pathé's shift to intertitles as a means of transition and nomination. Interestingly, it was Méliès that experimented in constructing scenes of two or more shots or tableaux—connecting adjacent spaces through matching exits and entrances, creating temporal sequentiality through several different spaces by means of the consistent direction of movement, and building separate decors of a single space to be viewed from a multiplicity of perspectives. And it was Pathé that tended to resist such scene construction, at least in the féeries (with the exception of *Ali Baba* and *La Fée printemps*), and, while mixing different modes of representation, remained bound to the more traditional conventions of theatrical or painterly tableaux. Moreover, Méliès characteristically mounted energetic, mildly subversive spectacles of "otherness," often in various forms of the carnivalesque, and produced protean displays of metamorphosis, in which procreative power was relocated in a male magician (both before and behind the camera), yet without greatly eroding the boundaries of gender difference. By contrast, Pathé generally sought to provide a more ideologically stable, moralizing discourse, one that sided with the "normal" as opposed to a "deviant other," as if already in search of legitimacy with a petit-bourgeois or bourgeois family audience. Such differences between the two companies would not hold across all genres, however, and certainly not in the transition years of 1904 to 1907.

Comic Films

From the scant evidence available in surviving catalogs and archive prints, French comic films were not all that numerous before Pathé's move to mass production around 1902. And, even after that date, the genre sometimes overlapped with the trick film, because the latter's cinematic trucs often had a decidedly comic effect—as in Méliès's *L'Homme à la tête de caoutchouc* (1902) or Pathé's *Baignade impossible* (1902). Donald Crafton has shown that Lumière's first comic film, *Arroseur et arrosé* (1895), actually reworked an old joke whose most immediate source was a Christophe comic strip published in *Le Petit Français Illustré* (3 August 1889), and he suggests that such strips provided "a virtually unlimited supply of gags and story material" for early French films.[84] Sadoul, on the other hand, has argued that early comic films were drawn primarily from and sometimes simply recorded short, familiar music hall routines in a single tableau—that is, they put on display a well-known comic's performance of one or more gags—and his thesis, complemented by Crafton's, still makes sense.[85] Certain early Méliès film titles, such as *Chicot, dentiste américaine* (1897) and *Guillaume Tell,* with "clowns" (1898), for instance, suggest an origin in variety numbers.[86] Guy's filmography includes titles such as *Saut humidifié de M. Plick* (1900), performed by Plick and Plock, as well as *Les Clowns* (1902) and several others starring a monkey named Jocko.[87] And it should not be forgotten that, from 1896 to 1901, Hatot produced several series of single-shot comic films for Lumière, using circus acrobats, famous clowns such as Footit and Chocolat, and the pantomime artist Bretteau.[88] But it was through Pathé principally that a teeming crowd of nineteenth-century comic stereotypes was imported into French films, along with the music hall's irreverent, knockabout humor.

The earliest of Pathé's comic films presented a simple gag or routine, recorded in LS or FS, and in the open air against the company's generic painted-flat interior. In *The Artist* (1900), for instance, a bourgeois fellow accidentally knocks over and ruins a painting he is appraising and then unquestioningly buys it from the angry painter. In *Une Dispute* (1900), one man repeatedly slaps and kicks another man (knocking their boaters onto the floor), until the latter seems to agree with his attacker, and they walk off, smiling, arm in arm. Yet this film begins with the boaters already on the floor, after which the two men dissolve in, so that the ensuing argument seems to explain something like a topical riddle or "comic strip" puzzle (the cause coming after the effect). When Zecca took control of Pathé's production, he initially mined the popular acts he knew so well from his own café-concert days—such as those of the Six Daïneuf Sisters, the Omers, the English comic Little Tich, and the clowns Anverino and Antonio.[89] And the performers quickly recognized that the cinema could serve them as a new form of publicity. One of these films, *Rêve et réalité* (1901), predicates its sexist gag on a single dissolve—from an elder man, in MS, pouring champagne for and then kissing a lovely young woman to his "awakening" to discover he is in bed with his horse-faced, toothless wife. Another, *Chez le dentiste* (1902), uses an "invisible cut" to produce out of a poor patient's mouth an uprooted tooth the size of his head. A third, *Une Bonne Histoire* (1903), offers evidence of the company's anticlerical politics (it is well to remember that the Pathé family was Protestant)—constructing the incongruous image of a Catholic bishop and priest, reading and chuckling at the republican newspaper, *Le Journal*.

Soon Zecca was exploiting the reputation of famous stage comics, by presenting them in uniquely "intimate" MSs. In *Première Cigare du collegien* (1903), for instance, Félix Galipaux performs one of his better known music hall routines—that of a young man "enjoying" his first cigar.[90] In *Ma Tante* (1903), Dranem dresses up in "auntie" drag and indulges in a little snuff while sewing, only to have a cat jump on the table and swish its tail in his face; in *Le Mitron* (1904), he appears disguised as a baker blithely plastering dough all over his head and dropping a plug of tobacco into the mixing tub.[91] *La Bonne Purge* (1904), again with Dranem, this time taking some awful medicine, adds the dubious "attraction" of a cut-in CU of his face and extended tongue reflected in a mirror (actually, a cut-out oval mask) to justify the distasteful remedy. Finally, *Rêve de Dranem* (1904) adds a racist touch to the bedroom gag in *Rêve et réalité*, repeatedly substituting, through cuts, a laughing black woman for the lovely brunette he imagines he is kissing. For reasons that remain unclear, neither of these comics, however, was to become a regular performer for Pathé.

Other Zecca comic films presented slightly more elaborate music hall numbers, even if sometimes still recorded in a single tableau. *Le Chien et la pipe* (1902), for instance, takes place in the interior of a train compartment, where a man and woman, traveling separately, argue over her repositioning of his luggage and his pipe smoking until he simply picks up her little dog and tosses it out the window. A dissolve to a reverse-angle exterior of the train (presumably

24. *Ma Tante*, 1903 (Dranem)

at journey's end) resolves the conflict when, surprising them both as they descend from the compartment, the dog is there sitting on the station platform, the man's pipe in its mouth, which the woman kindly returns to him. In the painted-flat LS of a Paris street corner, *Ramoneur et patissier* (1903) has a boy who is supposed to be delivering pastries stop to play dice with a policeman, until the latter loses and is replaced by a passing chimney sweep. The loser's consolation, however, is the chance to gobble up a pastry from the basket the first boy has left on a nearby bench. The two boys soon begin arguing over the dice game, and another policeman stops by to laugh at them. The first boy grabs a cream tart and throws it at the sweep, who ducks, and it splatters all over the laughing "intruder." According to this film's premise, conventional authority figures such as policemen are no more than children and easily can be made the butt of their jokes. Finally, *Erreur de porte* (1904) stages a very different kind of railway station gag involving a clownish country bumpkin traveler. In the initial LS tableau, a passing porter points the man, who is suffering intestinal distress, toward a "water closet," but he mistakenly enters a nearby door marked "telephone" instead. A FS of the interior, matchcutting his exit and entrance, shows the traveler now mistaking the wall phone and its pad for a toilet seat, before which he steps up on a stool and drops his pants. The gag then concludes in a cut back to the LS exterior, as a fashionably dressed gentleman enters the telephone booth—once the traveler has exited, with a big grin—only to stumble out with a handkerchief to his nose. This was just the kind of French humor, sensitive to tastes and smells, that prim and proper American reviewers, waving their own figurative handkerchiefs, would later find so excruciatingly unbearable.

Besides the comic trick films that displayed his own prowess as a magician, Méliès produced other less explicitly self-referential comic films. At least one of these, *Tom Tight et Dum Dum* (1903), through "invisible" cuts, turns a music hall number involving "eccentric clowns" into a fascinating spectacle of dismemberment and gender crossing. Dum Dum (a fat man played by Méliès) and Tom Tight (a drunken bourgeois gentleman) meet in a conventional painted-flat park setting, and the one promptly pounds the other into the ground with two swings of a giant mallet until only his head sticks out, which Dum Dum then pushes under with his foot. Two women enter and toss him first the drunk's head—which he bounces a bit and balances on a cane—and then the other body parts, all of which he wraps in a white sheet, out of which miraculously emerges a live woman. They dance briefly in one another's arms, until she disintegrates into pieces; and, when he stands on a chair, the two women assistants (in a doubly peculiar substitution) turn into French and American flags for him to wave vigorously. Tom Tight reappears and, as soon as Dum Dum lifts and shakes him, disintegrates as well; then he mixes the pieces with those of the woman in a pile and runs off. In the final clou, out of the pieces rises a figure split down the middle into a half-man, half-woman, who drunkenly staggers off after him. Here, unlike Pathé's comic films, not only is the human body for Méliès under constant threat of breakdown and disintegration, but it also is so malleable as to be capable of instantaneously switching gender, its identity finally defined as equally male and female.

If *Tom Tight et Dum Dum* takes Méliès's obsession with the metamorphosis of bodies to one kind of logical conclusion, erasing gender difference, other films point in a different direction. *Chirurgie fin-de-siècle* (1902), for instance, offers a delightful parody of the earliest films publicizing Dr. Doyen's surgical skills. To quiet his patient, this doctor (played by Méliès) systematically lops off each of his arms and legs and then, reaching into a huge incision in the man's stomach, pulls out an amazing array of objects—from live rabbits and giant utensils to a working tire pump. Exasperated by his inability to "unblock" his patient, the doctor finally ends the operation by chopping off the man's head. In contrast to the centered action of *Chirurgie fin-de-siècle, Un Maleur n'arrive pas jamais seule* (1903) uses a water hose to kick off a series of ricocheting gags—in a homage to Lumière's *Arroseur et arrosé,* which Méliès himself had copied in 1896.[92] In the film's LS painted-flat of a Paris street corner, a workman is standing on a ladder to clean a street lamp and a soldier is slumped asleep beside his barracks door. A man sneaks in to replace the latter's rifle with a water hose that a fireman has dragged in (and left behind at his exit), and then, with a look to the camera, he runs off to turn on the water. The sudden stream of water sends the workman sprawling, and the lamp falls and hits a passing policeman. The workman grabs the hose and sprays a couple who stick their heads out a second-floor window and then douses the laughing soldier. One after another, the soldier, workman, and policeman climb the wall to go in and out of windows and finally all tumble out together onto a kiosk (conveniently carried in, and bearing a Méliès poster advertisement!), which collapses and adds a woman (from inside) to the writhing bodies filling the screen. It would be another several years, however, before this gradually accumulating frenzy of physical mayhem would become a staple of Pathé and Gaumont comic films.[93]

Diverging Paths:
From *Actualités* to Historical and Realist Films

The other particularly successful film genre for French exhibitors during this early period, whether in the music halls or the fairground cinemas, was the actualité. From the beginning, Lumière produced these films in such profitable numbers that Méliès, Gaumont, and Pathé all took to making them as soon as each, in turn, began producing films. The Lumière actualités covered a range of subjects from "current events" to French ceremonies such as the seemingly endless military parades or President Félix Faure's visit to naval bases (late in 1896), and from travelogue footage of foreign countries (including the colonies) to shots of French daily life in either the city streets or around the Lumière's own bourgeois home, such as *Repas de bébé* (1895).[94] The genre's success was due in part to the prior popularity of such topical subjects in photographs and postcards as well as in the new illustrated magazines such as *Le Petit Journal Illustré* and *L'Illustration*. For actualités participated in the industrial production of images associated with travel and tourism, as Gunning argues, in which "appropriating the world" through a technological extension of seeing had become a thoroughly "modern" source of pleasure.[95] But the genre also depended on the low cost of the films' production and, especially, on the ease with which exhibitors could select and edit their own sequences of such films. In 1897, for instance, an exhibitor could buy from Lumière any combination of at least a dozen different vues of a bullfight in Spain, and three years later he could pick and choose from seventeen different shots of the 1900 Paris Exposition.[96] And, because actualités could be recorded and printed the same day, on the very site of a fairground cinema, they served as a novel form of publicity for the more enterprising exhibitors.

The Lumière catalogs distinguished this broad category of actualités from other kinds of films, including what the company labeled *vues historiques* or "historical scenes." These latter films, although never making up more than a miniscule fraction of Lumière's production, covered a wide range of subjects—from *Execution de Jeanne d'Arc* and *Assassinat du Duc de Guise* to *Mort de Robespierre* and *Entrevue de Napoléon et du Pape*, all directed by Hatot, in 1897.[97] *Mort de Marat* (1897), for instance, condenses into a single, sunlit LS tableau Charlotte

Corday's assassination of the Revolutionary leader (trapped in a boot-shaped bathtub) and her immediate arrest—during which several among the crowd flocking into the high-ceilinged room seem to protest her seizure. Pathé's first catalogs, however, conflated actualités and "historical scenes" into a single category for the purposes of distribution. This conflation assumed, at least until sometime shortly before the appearance of Pathé's newsreel, in 1908, that the difference between recording a current public event as it was happening and reconstructing a past (or even present) historical event in a studio was much less significant than Lumière would have it. What did apparently matter, however, was that a representation of the "historical" differed from a representation of the "purely fictive" or imaginary—which meant that referential differences mattered more than differences in modes of representation.[98] Although the indexical link between image and referent was sufficiently established for spectators, the cinema's overwhelming illusion of "reality" as spectacle must have had an effect that exceeded the discriminatory norms of *vraisemblance* then currently operating in the related medium of photography.[99] In other words, the "historical scene" was bound to the actualité within an unbroken continuum uniting historical past and present, each of which could be dissected and displayed as "attractions" of autonomous tableaux. If, in this early period, Pathé enjoyed a good deal of success in exploiting the shared "family resemblance" between historical reconstructions and actualités, his company was hardly alone, for Méliès had already set a precedent, if only marginally, in his own film practice.

In 1899, Méliès made a "historical film" that was nothing less than an anomaly in his early filmmaking career. Although reconstructed actualités such as *Combat naval en Grèce* (1897) or *Visite sous-marine du "Maine"* (1898) were hardly foreign to him, *L'Affaire Dreyfus* (1899) was unique for several reasons.[100] First of all, unlike Méliès's other films, it took a controversial historical event as its subject, the arrest and conviction of the Jewish army officer, Alfred Dreyfus, on what turned out to be false charges of treason—whose retrial at Rennes, in August and September 1899, coming after a long, acrimonious debate in the French press, seems to have provoked the film's production.[101] That Méliès would go out of his way to make such a film—and his first long film, totaling 240 meters—attests to the intensity of his political views as a Dreyfus supporter.[102] Second, the film's eleven autonomous tableaux (recorded in chronological order) were sold both separately and in series, so that exhibitors could assemble as many tableaux as they wished—and Méliès's catalog provided captions to help bonisseurs identify and describe each of the affair's represented episodes.[103] This sales strategy indicates how similar the film's tableaux were to actualités of the period, not only in France—where the film apparently was quickly suppressed—but also in England and the United States.[104] All of these tableaux were studio reconstructions, however, and their immediate sources were illustrations in the popular Paris weekly magazines—the final tableau of Dreyfus leaving the Rennes lycée for prison, for instance, was drawn from a photograph published in *L'Illustration* (15 September 1899).[105] The film's mode of representation, consequently, was somewhat subdued in contrast to that of

Méliès's other films, particularly in its "realistic" decors and costumes and relatively restrained acting style.[106] And, in at least two shot-scenes, the actors' movements deviated from Méliès's norm.[107] In the assassination attempt on Fernand Labori (one of Dreyfus's lawyers, played by Méliès), the lawyer and several friends enter the frame from the right foreground, quite close to the camera. In the courtroom fight among the journalists covering the trial (which pit the Dreyfusards led by Mme Séverine of *La Fronde* against the anti-Dreyfusards led by Arthur Meyer of *Le Gaulois*), the movement is much more dramatic—the journalists lunge toward the camera, exiting the frame left and right, some almost in MCU.[108] Rather than approximate the movement of passersby in actualités (as in the first shot-scene), this sudden rush toward the camera seems designed to produce a shock effect, as spectacle, one which Méliès would, thereafter, in both his trick films and féeries, always contain within the frame.[109]

After several other "staged" actualités—his "documentary" footage of the 1900 Paris Exposition and *Eruption volcanique à la Martinique* (1902), for instance—Méliès contributed one last film to the genre, *The Coronation of Edward VII* (1902), which was quite different from *L'Affaire Dreyfus* and much closer to the tableau vivant style that would soon characterize the historical film.[110] This film was commissioned and financed by the Warwick Trading Company—whose director, Urban, managed Méliès's sales in England—for the purpose of exhibiting a sensational actualité that would "record" the first coronation of a British monarch in sixty years. Because Urban stipulated that the film should be ready on the evening of the coronation and the ceremony should be reproduced in a single tableau, Méliès visited Westminster Abbey, with his coproducer, in order to reconstruct an exact replica of the site's decors and costumes in his Montreuil studio. After a month or more of preparation, Méliès and Urban (who insisted on using his own camera)[111] completed the film on time, by 26 June, but then shelved it for over a month because the real public ceremony had to be rescheduled for 9 August. The film was an instant success, however, headlining the Alhambra music hall program in London, making the circuit of Empire Palace music halls around England, and then touring the world. That success depended on the alleged significance of the event, of course, but also on the meticulous detail with which it was reproduced for spectators in a single "long-take" LS tableau. The decors re-created the "deep space" of the abbey's north transept, as viewed from the nave, while composing several enclosed areas within the frame for the participants, with the new king privileged either in the foreground or on a dais to the right. The ceremony itself was condensed into a stately, paced ritual sequence: a procession of gifts, the taking of the oath, the presentation of the sword of justice, and the adornment of the new king with sceptre, orb, and crown. And what seemed to assure the film's solemnity was that the ritual unfolded without interruption, without drawing undue attention to either the performers (the king, for instance, was played by a washroom attendant)[112] or the cinematic apparatus itself.

The tableau style of *The Coronation of Edward VII* was taken up in one of Pathé's earliest surviving historical films, *Epopée napoléonienne* (1903), whose success securely established the single, unified viewpoint of the autonomous shot-scene as a characteristic feature of the genre.[113] *Epopée napoléonienne* was divided into two unequal parts: the first subtitled *Napoléon Bonaparte* (in 5 tableaux, 160 meters in length) and the second, *L'Empire, Grandeur et Décadence* (in 10 tableaux, 270 meters).[114] Whereas one focused on Napoleon's early years as a boy, a young army officer, and a property owner, the other highlighted his years as emperor, concluding with his failure, death, and apotheosis. As a chronological sequence of episodes from Napoleon's life which would have been familiar to almost any-one (at least in France), this film constituted less a history or even a chronicle than a series of spectacle attractions, much like either wax museum tableaux or historical paintings. And each tableau or shot-scene was introduced, as was the case in *Don Quichotte* and *Le Chat botté*, by a brief intertitle, in order to set off the episodes as autonomous moments of animated spectacle. Although the film's shot-scenes are consistently composed in LS, with a camera positioned at eye level, they alternate between studio and location backgrounds—perhaps analogous to the paintings and photographs printed side by side in illustrated magazines—providing further evidence of Pathé's conflation of actualité and historical reconstruction. One battle, at Arcole bridge, occurs on a real wooden bridge, for instance; another, at Waterloo, has soldiers rushing back and forth against the painted flat of a small hill. Generally, however, the most spectacular of the shot-scenes take place in the studio, with either diorama-sized backdrops (for the Malmaison garden party and the coronation ceremony) or multiplaned, "deep space" decors (for the crossing of Mount St-Bernard and the burning of Moscow).

Epopée napoléonienne seems to have provided the impetus for a series of Pathé historical films in 1903–1904: see, for instance, *Guillaume Tell* (5 tableaux, 145 meters), *Marie Antoinette* (9 tableaux, 175 meters), and *Christophe Colomb* (8 tableaux, 265 meters).[115] And some measure of its success can be gathered from the fact that it was still being exhibited in the summer of 1905[116] and that, according to the company catalog, prints were still available for purchase in 1907. What is most intriguing, however, is that during its four years of exhibition, the film seems to have existed in more than one version. Initially, its two parts were sold as a single package, making it one of the earliest two-reel films produced anywhere in the world. Yet Pathé obviously also sold the two parts as separate single reels (they had different catalog numbers), each of which could be exhibited on its own. And, by 1907, the company was virtually ignoring part two and instead was advertising *Napoléon Bonaparte* as a separate film—a marketing strategy that privileged Napoleon's rise to power and affluence. In addition, Pathé seems to have sold at least some, if not all, of the tableaux individually—*Sentinelle endormie*, for instance, was listed separately in the 1907 catalog, and the coronation scene may have been available as *Le Sacre de Napoléon* in the 1913 catalog of KOK 28mm prints.[117] Finally, exhibitors were free, of course, to reduce the film's length and slightly rearrange the order of shot-scenes—as is evident in the surviving Library of Congress print from Australia.[118] Here again, for Pathé, the early historical film shared an affinity with the actualité, in that a film such as *Epopée napoléonienne* constituted not a "finished product" or commodity, but a relatively malleable, multiple text.

This textual flexibility was shared with another important Pathé film of the same period, *La Vie et la Passion de Jésus-Christ* (1903), which superseded prior versions of the same subject—Lumière's *La Vie et la Passion de Jésus-Christ*, in thirteen tableaux (Hatot, 1897), Gaumont's *La Vie de Christ*, in eleven tableaux (Guy, 1899), and Pathé's own *La Vie et Passion du Christ*, in sixteen tableaux (1900). Unlike American films on this subject, which tended either to record or to reconstruct the famous Oberammergau passion play, Pathé seems to have avoided any reference to prior theatrical productions and composed its own "original" scenario.[119] Moreover, according to the company's early catalogs, Pathé's film was distributed in at least three *séries* or versions.[120] The longest version comprised thirty-two tableaux (all introduced by intertitles) and ran to nearly six hundred meters in length. The first four tableaux cover the period from the annunciation to the flight into Egypt, two more present episodes from Jesus' childhood, and the next seven depict various miracles from the water being turned into wine in Cana to the resurrection of Lazarus. The remaining nineteen tableaux then represent Jesus' final days from his triumphant entry into Jerusalem and the Last Supper to his ascension and apotheosis. A shorter série of twenty tableaux focused exclusively on this latter section of the film, after beginning with the adoration of the magi. And a third série of twelve tableaux reduced this second version even further. A certain diversity of representation thus marked *La Vie et La Passion*, as well as *Epopée napoléonienne*, but here it was due to differences in production and exhibition more than differences in shooting on location or in the studio (the latter of which clearly dominated). The thirty-two tableaux were not recorded all at once or in chronological order but at three different periods, and the actors in the final period of shooting were different from those in the first period and even wore different costumes. Moreover, as is evident from surviving prints, exhibitors did not necessarily purchase all the tableaux Pathé offered, and some may well have added their own color rather than pay the extra cost of the company's stencil color process.[121] What held the film together as a more or less coherent text, of course, was the familiarity of the story as a centuries-old tradition of iconic episodes. And, in contrast to the company's usual anticlericalism, the iconography of the studio decors and character groupings consistently seemed to imitate the Saint-Sulpice style of painted statuary so characteristic of the French Catholic Church in the Second Empire and Third Republic and which was also being promulgated in color prints by La Bonne Presse.[122]

La Vie et la Passion may have provided one model for both the structure and style of Pathé's early historical films, but there were others within French cultural practice probably even more significant in determining the characteristics of the genre. One of these was located in the tradition of historical painting, the most highly valued French genre throughout the nineteenth century, a tradition especially relevant to *Epopée napoléonienne* because of the famous Versailles Historical Museum (first opened in the 1830s), which included nineteen rooms com-memorating the glory of Napoleon, principally in huge battle pictures.[123] A sec-ond model was the closely related practice in the theater of what Martin Meisel has aptly called "realizations," by which spectacular tableaux literally re-created well-known paintings and produced some of the most fascinating "effects" on the nineteenth-century French stage.[124] This practice had a long tradition, beginning at least as early as the Napoleon plays that filled the Paris theaters after the July 1830 Revolution and which offered climactic tableaux re-creating Horace Vernet's famous paintings.[125] Pathé's *Epopée napoléonienne* itself "realizes" or "makes more real" at least four such paintings: Vernet's "Farewell at Fon-tainebleau" and "The Apotheosis" as well as David's "Crossing Mount Saint-Bernard" and von Steuben's "The Death of Napoleon." Although the Pathé catalog descriptions do not insist on these "realizations," the Pathé KOK list-ing for the undated, single shot-scene film, *Le Sacre de Napoléon,* does advertise it as "a faithful reconstruction of the celebrated painting by David." The practice of pictorial "realization" in the theater, therefore, seems to have offered the early cinema an important means of achieving a "persistence of effect" in a "historical series," without relying on the principles of narrative causality.[126]

A third model, more recent in origin, was located in the Third Republic's secular system of education, which had been established just twenty years be-fore. Specifically, this involved the interplay between visual illustrations and verbal captions, probably based on popular engravings, in the new French pri-mary school textbooks on history.[127] Pierre Guibbert has argued that such text-books—and their strategies of memorization for a newly secularized genera-tion—provided a model for the first Film d'Art and SCAGL historical films, but that interplay clearly was already operative five years earlier in the tableau style of *Epopée napoléonienne.*[128] Consequently, the early history film may well have served those theories of education for a general public which relied heavily on instruction through images, whether advocated by Benoît-Lévy (a strong secu-lar proselytizer) or Coissac (a rival Catholic proponent). In any case, the school textbook model underscored the ideological function of a film like *Epopée na-poléonienne* (especially given Pathé's decision to market only part one in 1907) as a ritual spectacle of collective identity for the state nationalism that became so characteristic of the French Third Republic during this prewar period, and whose patriotic appeal increasingly would be taken over by the political right.

Although classified as a distinct genre in Pathé's catalogs, the "dramatic and realist film" also shared an affinity with the actualité and the historical film dur-ing this period. Yet the genre gradually began to diverge from the latter in sev-eral ways—"experimenting" with a more continuous narrative line, a more il-lusionist diegesis, and even a rudimentary character psychology. The earliest of these films, now lost, seems to have been *Mariage de raison* (1900), which, ac-cording to the first Pathé catalog, comprised five separate tableaux.[129] Another, *Un Drame au fond de la mer* (1901), however, survives in a nearly complete print, beginning with perhaps the earliest film title card, printed in French, German, and English. As this title scrolls upward, first revealing a painted seascape and

25. *Un Drame au fond de la mer,* 1901

then giving the illusion of a descent into the depths, there is a cut (rather than a dissolve) to a LS painted flat of the rocky seafloor, where several dead bodies lay next to the wreck of a sunken ship. What ensues is a terse, cruel tale of simple greed as a deep-sea diver (with deliberately slowed gestures) descends a background rope ladder to find a treasure chest of coins and then is attacked by another diver from behind. In a reworking of the underwater sensation scene from a then current British play, *The White Heather* (1897),[130] the second diver quickly cuts the airhose of the first, who is left to stagger around and collapse, while the murderer grabs the booty and begins to ascend. Unencumbered by moralizing, this short film introduces into the French cinema a *grand guignol* form of melodrama, whose *fait divers* stories of crime and violence or spectacular moments of what, in England, was called the sensation drama[131] would often characterize the genre throughout the prewar period.

The most noteworthy of these early films was *Histoire d'un crime* (1901), which, based on Pathé's own publicity, has sometimes been called Zecca's first really successful film.[132] Again, the subject is a contemporary fait divers involving a violent crime—this time among the "lower classes"—and the surviving print's attached title is given in French, German, and English. Unlike *Un Drame au fond de la mer* or even Méliès's *L'Affaire Dreyfus,* whose episodic tableaux came from topical magazine illustrations, however, *Histoire d'un crime* reconstructs the continuous narrative of a waxworks exhibit first installed in the Musée Grévin in 1899.[133] The film tells the story of an anonymous carpenter, representing his

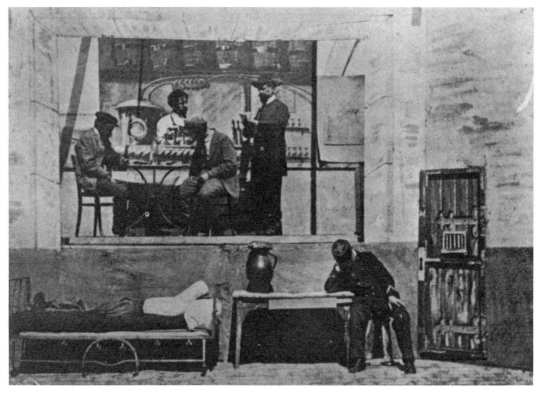

26. *Histoire d'un crime*, 1901

crime of theft and murder, followed by his arrest, conviction, and execution (all within seven LS painted-flat tableaux, linked by dissolves).[134] It also clearly takes its ambivalent attitude of moralizing mixed with fascination from the waxworks exhibit as well as the Paris morgue—confronting the criminal with the murdered man's corpse, for instance, and concluding with the truc spectacle of a beheading by guillotine. Perhaps the most interesting feature of the film, however, occurs in the prison shot-scene, when a series of three "dream" images appears in the upper background area of the frame as the convict sleeps, watched over by a dozing guard at a foreground table. Based on the borrowed theatrical device of the "vision scene" (requiring an enclosed stage built into the set),[135] each of the three images is marked off by a quickly dropped curtain or shutter, yet the pretext for their spectacle effect is a relatively complex narrative strategy. For these dream scenes retell the man's past story sequentially, from the point when he was happily interrupted in his work by his wife and child to the moment when he lost all his money in a café card game. Although this inserted "flashback" story obviously serves as a warning against gambling (which is then trumped by the sensational execution scene), Zecca's attempt, in *Histoire d'un crime,* to narrate two stories simultaneously and to represent the interior life of a character (and a working-class character, at that) makes the film no less anomalous and forward-looking than *L'Affaire Dreyfus* in early French cinema.

Other Pathé "dramatic and realist films" soon followed on the heels of *Histoire d'un crime*. *Victimes de l'alcoolisme* (1902), for instance, reproduces the familiar nineteenth-century "fable" of a worker whose uncontrollable drinking pushes his family into poverty and him into madness. The scenario probably was adapted from Zola's *L'Assommoir,* as Sadoul claims, but it could just as easily have been drawn from any one of several series of popular lithograph prints or their theatrical versions on the music hall or melodrama stage.[136] Each of the film's five LS tableaux constitutes an autonomous shot-scene, illustrating a different stage in the worker's fall from "happiness and prosperity" to "misery" and "madness." At least two things distinguish *Victimes de l'alcoolisme,* however, from *Histoire d'un crime.* First of all, several of the studio decors are much more detailed in their composition. The painted flat of the street corner where the Au Père Colomb bar is located, for instance, depicts a series of sharply defined shops stretching off along a narrow street into the distance. The initial family dining room has not only a window looking out over the city rooftops but a door opening onto a kitchen. Moreover, it includes a good number of "real" props— a sewing machine at which the wife does "put-out" work, a table that she and her mother set with dishes and utensils, and a large gas lamp suspended overhead. Second, each tableau is separated from the others by a straight cut and an intertitle, whose text is printed out in black letters on white strips, like labels roughly pasted on a dark surface.[137] Here, then, is the earliest extant evidence of Pathé's intertitle "innovation," which, within another year—in *Don Quichotte, Le Chat botté, Epopée napoléonienne,* and *La Vie et la Passion de Jésus Christ*— would take the form of a Pathé trademark: terse phrases in large red block letters on a black background.[138] As in those films, a strongly didactic principle governs the interrelation between verbal caption and visual illustration.

Although none of the "dramatic and realist" films Pathé produced during the subsequent two years seems to have survived, the company's catalogs provide some sense of the genre's trajectory. *La Vie d'un joueur* (1903), for instance, presented another warning against gambling (in eight tableaux), apparently this time drawn from a waxworks exhibit at Madame Tussaud's in London.[139] The extremely successful *Roman d'amour* (1904) told the story of a young working-class woman who is seduced by a wealthy client of the dress shop where she works.[140] After a brief life of pleasure, she is abandoned and soon starves; the final LS tableaux focus on her parents' despair, her "terrible atonement," and their reconciliation at her hospital deathbed. Given such descriptions, together with a few surviving publicity stills and posters, these Pathé films seem to have adopted the fait divers subjects and tableau style of autonomous shot-scenes in *Histoire d'un crime,* but without the narrative complexity of an inserted "flash-back" story. The studio decors, however, as in *Victimes de l'alcoolisme,* seemed quite detailed in construction and included "authentic" props, as if the principle of verisimilitude, perhaps emanating from the naturalist theater of Antoine, were beginning to infiltrate the genre's tableaux. Yet the overwhelming moral tone of these early films—preaching the virtues of close family bonds and disciplined work—surely kept them from being "proletarian" works that could serve class

27. *Victimes de l'alcoolisme*, 1902 (poster)

28. *Victimes de l'alcoolisme*, 1902

ends, as Sadoul once argued.[141] Rather, as the special supplement advertising *Victimes de l'alcoolisme* strongly suggests, they much more likely served to ensure working-class and artisan (as well as petit-bourgeois and white collar) assent to the domestic and public harmony of a bourgeois social order. By 1904–1905, however, certain Pathé films in the genre would not be so reassuring, and the "dramatic and realist film" would play a significant role in the shift from a cinema of *attractions* to a *narrative* cinema.

4

The Transition to a Narrative Cinema,
1904-1907

The cinema will be the schoolhouse,
newspaper, and theatre of tomorrow.
PATHÉ-FRÈRES

BETWEEN 1904 AND 1907, the French cinema industry and its products' dominant mode of representation underwent a radical, reciprocal transformation.
Pathé-Frères, followed eventually by Gaumont, moved into mass production
and, in an attempt to standardize and exert greater control over that production
as well as its consumption, turned increasingly, and successfully, from actualités
to story films. At the same time, the company expanded the markets for its
commodities by means of a worldwide network of distribution agencies, with
the result that sales of positive film prints tripled, the increase coming particularly in the American market of nickelodeons. The pressure of mass production,
along with the desire to exercise control over the profitable circulation of products, would finally, in 1906–1907, compel Pathé to begin restructuring film
distribution and exhibition within France itself—through such measures as the
construction of a circuit of permanent cinemas and the shift from selling to renting films. But, before that step of legitimation would be taken, the company's
filmmakers already would be working within a much transformed system of
representation and narration.

For the mass production and marketing that Pathé pioneered between 1904
and 1907 coincided with the waning of the cinema of attractions and the emergence of an increasingly narrativized cinema. Early cinema historians differ over
how to conceptualize this transformation. Some such as Burch, Thompson, and
Barry Salt have tended to assume a binary model of film practice and to posit a
break or rupture between a "primitive" and "classical" cinema. For all their
differences, Salt and Thompson have been concerned with tracing the development—and celebrating the achievement—of the textual system of narrative continuity which ultimately came to dominate the American cinema during the
middle to late 1910s; while Burch has continued to privilege the so-called primitive cinema as a basis for resistance, through a variety of filmic avant-gardes, to
the monolithic "institutional mode of representation" of a bourgeois cinema.
Other historians have tended, instead, to assume a tripartite model and to posit
a transitional period distinct from, while sharing characteristics with, both the

cinema of attractions and the later classical narrative cinema. On the one hand, Gunning, Gaudreault, and Ben Brewster have been concerned with defining this transitional cinema textually in terms of an uneven, fluctuating shift in the dialectical interplay between presentation and representation, spectacle and narrative, showing and telling. On the other, Musser and Elsaesser have focused on how its constitution as a mode of representation was determined by a historically specific interplay of economic, social, and cultural forces. Ultimately, they argue, the cinema turned to narrative as an economic solution to a number of contending exigencies involved in the representation of space and time as well as in the positioning of spectators within a new spatial-temporal continuum.

If one assumes such a tripartite model, this period of transition, as Gunning suggests, can best be described as a gradual process of narrativization in which film's initial predisposition toward showing was channeled or deflected toward mimesis and storytelling.[1] This involved, first, a change in the concept of spatial coherence as the autonomous tableau gave way to a synthetic space no longer bound to a pro-filmic event or scene but constructed out of interrelated, discrete shots. Perhaps the clearest systematic example of this occurred in the early chase film where the repeated movement of characters into and out of the frame, through a series of shots, redefined screen space as "a metonymic part of a larger [diegetic] whole."[2] Correlating with this was a change in the conception of temporality—the crucial problem, writes Musser, for filmmakers in early cinema[3]—with greater attention now being given to issues of succession, simultaneity, and internally generated causality. Both of these changes produced a new, interrelated form of contiguity and sequentiality in which the significance of a shot became increasingly dependent on those that preceded and followed it and, ultimately, on even larger patterns of organization. Here, the articulation of linearity, especially in the serial structure of the chase film, seems to have preceded and probably conditioned the emergence of narrative causality as a crucial organizing principle. As narrativization extended to every level of film discourse, certain spectacle attractions that once had served an aesthetics of display—for instance, pans, cut-ins, POV shots—now came under its sway as well. In other words, such attractions became "remotivated" as filmic signs,[4] to be subordinated to and incorporated within a causal narrative chain whose governing principle of unified action would depend on the conventional devices of repetition, delay, surprise, suspense, and, above all, resolution or closure. Eventually, Gunning concludes, narrativization came to "regulate the balance between mimetic and narrative functions in the filmic sign" or, in Stephen Heath's words, "between the photographic image as a reproduction of reality and the narrative as the sense, the intelligibility, of that reality."[5]

One of the consequences of these changes—and perhaps their chief motivation, as Musser and Elsaesser would argue—was to wrest control over the process of "making meaning" in the cinema away from the exhibitor. This transformation of film discourse would construct a different kind of "film narrator" or position from which to narrate a story. No longer would a film's intelligibility as a story need to rely on either prior knowledge or familiarity or else an exhibitor's narrativizing commentary—a move already underway through the increasing use of intertitles (which Pathé had pioneered in 1902). Instead, that could come from what Gunning calls "a sort of interiorized film lecturer," through the way a film told its story, selecting and organizing "narratively important elements from a mass of contingent details" and creating a hierarchy of knowledge or point of view concerning that material.[6] As a corollary, this transformation also positioned viewers differently—actively engaging spectators in "stitching" together a synthetic spatial-temporal whole, ultimately according to a narrative logic. In fact, as Elsaesser puts it, this turn to narrative assumed a significant change in spectatorship in that the earlier collective audience that had experienced a physical, performative space now turned into isolated spectators, each of which was bound up with the imaginary representations or diegesis of a constructed screen space.[7] This new relationship between spectator and screen clearly diminished the power of the exhibitor, for it tended to situate both narrator and spectator at the apex of a hierarchy of knowledge, especially the "narrative knowledge," to use Elsaesser's reformulation of Brewster, accumulated by the temporality of the filmic process itself.[8]

My own work on this period of transition focuses on the particular terms of transformation—both textual and intertextual—within the French cinema or, more precisely, within a range of Pathé films released between 1904 and 1907. Based on surviving Pathé film prints, supplemented by the few Gaumont titles still extant, several simultaneous yet relatively distinct "models" of transformation seem to have developed during this period to negotiate beween the competing interests of spectacle attractions and those of spatial contiguity, temporal linearity, and narrative continuity. Let me call them the bricolage model, the redundancy model, the alternation model, and (for want of a better term) the compound model, the latter of which involved a range of contiguous changes in framing, or a more or less systematic form of editing. Although two or perhaps even three of these, as the previous chapter has demonstrated, occasionally could be found in Méliès's early féeries, they either disappeared from his work after 1904 or else continued to circulate in such a way that, even in his later films, narrative served primarily as a pretext for spectacle attractions.[9] In Pathé's films, however, that relationship was reversed. The redundancy and alternation models, at least initially, each came to characterize a particular film genre from among the dozen the company advertised—the one, the comic chase film, and the other, the erotic film. And all but the bricolage model eventually coalesced into a loosely integrated system of representation and narration in perhaps the most significant of Pathé's genres, the dramatic and realist film, especially the domestic melodrama and its grand guignol variant. By 1906, it is clear, Pathé was making specific categories of story films within a mode of representation that allowed the company a greater degree of product standardization and differentiation than ever before. Perhaps more important, its filmmakers were deploying most of the components so basic to the system of narrative continuity which historians consistently have attributed to Vitagraph and Biograph (or

Griffith) several years later. And certain films articulating that system began to assume either a clearly defined moral or even ironic "voice" of narration.[10]

To some extent, I would argue, the transition to a narrative cinema in France can be mapped according to the generic distinctions marking Pathé-Frères's film production. However, within the genre of dramatic and realist films, the referential body of Third Republic social relations on which that system worked consistently hinged on such concepts as the criminally or morally deviant and the family, and often (but not always) on their structural opposition. In fact, those relations tended to coalesce around particular sets of binary oppositions—lawful or normal versus deviant, public versus private, male versus female—all of which culminated in that of bourgeois versus "other" and thereby provided crucial axes of subject construction for the existing French social order. If narrative transgression within the genre could sometimes interrogate or even subvert those relations, its principal function was to reproduce and legitimize that order—almost in parallel with Pathé's own desire for legitimation—through circulation as much as containment. As an ideological form of emerging influence, then, the early narrative cinema in France can be seen as mapped onto a specific historical site of Third Republic social relations of difference.[11] This is especially interesting in that a narrative cinema began to emerge, in France, well before any serious attempt was being made to recruit a specifically bourgeois audience—for instance, through constructing permanent cinemas and promoting "film d'art" productions.[12] In fact, within the public sphere of fairs and music halls, an increasingly large segment of the French cinema's relatively mixed mass audience seems already to have been comprised of urban women and children.

The *Bricolage* Model

The least successful, or long-lasting, of these models, the bricolage model, seems to have developed as a *combinatoire* of prior genres.[13] In one sense, this model could be seen as an offshoot of the féerie, in which relatively "real" spaces replaced that genre's typically fantastical decors. In another sense, however, it worked a variation on the historical reconstruction film by joining actualité footage to contemporary fictional scenes. And it often drew on the travel film genre that, as Musser has demonstrated, was so popular among American producers such as Edison around 1903–1904—see, for instance, *Rube and Mandy at Coney Island* (1903) and *European Rest Cure* (1904).[14] In this hybrid format, Pathé essentially cobbled together different genre elements and conventions, as if in an attempt to condense the variety of "acts" on a music hall or cinema program into a single marketable form.[15] In other words, any such film constituted a microcosm of what Hansen has called "the larger field of intertextual *bricolage*" marking the early cinema program and tended "to preserve the stylistic heterogeneity of the genres" within that field.[16] Although narrative could still sometimes serve as a pretext to assemble a series of spectacle effects (from divergent sources), inversely, those effects could also serve, in turn, as crucial links or causal shifts in the film's linear continuity. Perhaps in no other films was the negotiation between attractions and narrative so visibly in flux.

One of the earliest instances of this hybrid format occurs in *Un Drame dans les airs* (1904), which begins with two actualité shots of a balloon launch for pleasure-seeking tourists. The following sequence then alternates between shots of a gondola basket in which two men take turns looking through a telescope (against a studio background of a moving diorama sky) and actualité shots (framed by a circular iris) of French warships at sea. The slight story of a sight-seeing balloon trip thus serves to display a series of patriotic images—whose sense of military preparedness probably had some topical relevance, given the then current French conflict with Germany over Morocco and perhaps even the Russo-Japanese war. The last irised actualité shot of sea waves pounding against a rocky shoreline, however, sets up a causal chain of action that puts the very act of viewing at risk, and the film ends in a fictional sequence produced entirely in the studio. In one tableau, a miniature model of the balloon runs into a storm (of moving painted flats), is hit by lightning (scratched on the film stock), and explodes in flames (tinted bright red); in the next, the gondola falls into the Pathé studio pool (backed by a painted canvas of hills and sky), and the two sightseers drift into the frame to be rescued by a man in a rowboat. Here, the balloon disaster serves a double function in the film's textual negotiation—acting as the climax to a series of spectacle attractions and, at the same time, generating a final brief moment of narrative crisis and suspense. And, in having its sightseers encounter and survive a "natural" catastrophe, the film lets the spectator experience what Gunning has called both the "shock" of a new technological means of travel and the dissipation of its dangers.[17]

L'Incendiaire (1905) offers a somewhat different combinatoire of genres and a slightly stronger sense of closure. This film opens with a LS of a gypsy camp, which, while introducing what might seem a documentary tour of the unfamiliar, also evokes the late nineteenth-century French obsession with vagrancy as a threat to the social order.[18] In the deep space of what seems an actual location, a couple (the woman is carrying a baby) moves from their makeshift hut (frame left) toward the background—because the surviving copy lacks intertitles, exactly where they are going remains unclear. The second shot then sets up a narrative premise as the man falls asleep against a haystack, and the pipe he is smoking sets the straw on fire. What follows, however, is the spectacle attraction of a half-dozen actualité shots, displaying a burning haystack and various efforts to control the blaze—which include water hoses from a single fire engine as well as a bucket brigade. Suddenly, inexplicably (again, perhaps because an intertitle is missing), the film shifts into a chase, and a mob of peasants pursues the "accidental" arsonist through ten consecutive location shots, with a good deal of variation in both the direction of movement across the frame and the locus of characters' entrances and exits. The pursued "arsonist" manages to out-maneuver a train and cross several walls and a bridge, only to be captured as he emerges from wading a shallow pond in a rather flat, dreary landscape. And there, in a stunning narrative resolution, he is promptly strung up to a lone tree by his pursuers. A woman nearby appears as soon as the mob leaves, however, uses the scythe she is carrying to cut the man down and drags him to the foreground, where he seems to revive. The film's concluding shot then returns to the gypsy camp as the man is carried in (followed by the woman and baby) and is placed on a foreground cart in front of their hut, where he shakes his fist angrily, presumably levying a curse on his tormentors. Although the circularity of this return to the beginning serves as a further sign of narrative resolution, the film text as it survives remains somewhat indeterminate. This suggests just how important intertitles or a lecturer's comments could be, at the time, in determining the ideological slant of a film. *L'Incendiaire* seems to take an ambiguous position on the so-called vagrancy problem: which of the two—the alien gypsy "arsonist" or the French peasant mob—is to be exonerated, ultimately, and which is to be judged guilty? And Pathé's catalog description is equally ambiguous—while it sides, at the end, with the gypsy against an "ingrate, egoistic society," it also admits, at the beginning, that he may be looking for something to steal as well as searching futilely for work.[19]

Perhaps the most complicated of these bricolage films was *Un Tour du monde d'un policier* (1906). Unlike the previous two films, this one begins with a clear-cut narrative premise, articulated through alternating studio and location shots: a Paris banker embezzles from his own bank safe and flees in disguise (dressed like Sherlock Holmes, no less), a detective is sent off in pursuit of him, and the thief escapes (in another disguise), partly because he seems to know more than the detective does about train schedules. Introduced by the intertitle "Suez Canal," the following sequence further delays the narrative resolution (with the comic reversal of the detective's arrest) and shifts to a kind of travelogue as studio shots of the sightseeing banker-embezzler, looking through binoculars, alternate, in a POV-shot structure, with actualité shots of boats, palaces, camels and desert sands, supposedly along the canal. This colonialist spectacle of the "exotic"—in which Egypt serves as "the entry point to the East," from the perspective of the European master[20]—moves on to India, China, and Japan (again in a mixture of actualité and studio footage, some of which is tinted), within which the detective suddenly reappears to reintroduce the narrative of pursuit (without the least regard for what causes his reappearance). And, in the midst of this colonial "tour," an "Opium Smokers" scene imports the device of multiple exposure from the trick film and féerie in order to contrast the two men's dreams of desire—the one of women pouring wine, the other of cops seizing the thief, neither of which ever seems to be realized. The travelogue and the subordinated pursuit continue through the studio reconstruction of an "American Election" campaign, only to cut abruptly to a western drama (shot on location) in which the banker-embezzler unexpectedly rescues the detective from certain death at the hands of hostile Indians. This implicitly racist resolution of the film's episodic and repeatedly delayed narrative effectively concludes their joint world tour, and the two men return, no longer antagonists, but now partners to a studio bank office (presumably in Paris). There, the attraction of a CU insert of a letter (one of the earliest in surviving Pathé prints) serves to resolve any lingering questions about the money the banker had initially stolen. In the film's final shot, however, spectacle supersedes narrative once more, in a stencil color "curtain call" tableau that is remarkably similar to the apotheosis finales that typically concluded Pathé's féeries as well as its biblical and historical films. This finale concisely allegorizes the ideological underpinnings of the film, for the two male Europeans shepherd groups of extras dressed in a variety of "native" costumes into a ceremonial procession in front of a huge globe—with the ambiguous figure of the banker-embezzler uncannily exposing the imperialist appropriation of the world by France as well as Pathé itself.[21]

One of the last of the bricolage films, *La Jeteuse de sorts* (1907), returns to the "alien" threat of *L'Incendiaire*, but evidences an even more contradictory view of that threat. Pathé's description of the film for *Phono-Ciné-Gazette* vilifies the title's gypsy woman "who casts spells"—for seducing a young peasant away from his wife and farm—and seems to justify the violent action of the neighbors who take revenge on the villainess. The surviving film prints, however, are equally, if not more, interested in creating empathy for the gypsy woman and implicitly criticizing the peasants' racial prejudice. The film opens, for instance, with a nondiegetic MS introducing the title character who stands in front of a painted-flat wall with a bunch of flowers in her hand.[22] A double narrative premise is then worked out in a sequence of loosely matched LSs. The peasant leaves his young blonde wife and house by a canal and, in walking to the village, accepts a flower from the dark gypsy woman; and when she is taunted and chased down a lane and over a small bridge by a group of peasants, he rushes to rescue her from their bullying. Prefaced by an intertitle, "The witch has her victim," the next sequence shifts to narrate the seduction as the gypsy woman leads the dazed peasant to her dilapidated cottage (surprising her mother), from which even his wife is unable to free him. In what seems to be a final sequence, the peasants, spurred by the wife, set fire to the steps of the cottage (the husband stumbles out), pursue the gypsy woman when she tries to flee in a rowboat on the canal, and, seizing her, toss her into the water, presumably to drown. Although an intertitle, "Chastised and pardoned," inserted at the beginning of the chase, suggests an eventual reconciliation between husband and wife, the film's last three shots instead focus on how the gypsy woman is rescued by her mother. And her rescue is accentuated by the cut-in from a HA LS—on the canal bank, the mother enters from the left foreground, as the woman drifts in from the right background—to a FS, showing her being pulled out of the water just as she is about to go under. Moreover, once she is carried back to the cottage interior, the peasant couple comes to pay their respects—an action that further complicates the meaning of the intertitle. As a parable of either tolerance (affirming the peasants' pardon) or purification ("cleansing" the peasant community of a "virus"), *La Jeteuse de sorts* seems constructed for sharply different audiences. Yet it also could assume a distinctly urban audience that would view either of the antagonists here from a "superior" social position.[23]

Despite such striking concoctions as *Un Tour du monde d'un policier* and *La Jeteuse de sorts*, the bricolage model of negotiating between an aesthetics of display and an aesthetics of narrative never presented a viable, exclusive option for Pathé during this period.[24] Rather than condense increasingly heterogeneous forms of representation into a single format, the dominant trend in the French cinema, in both production and exhibition, was toward sustaining that heterogeneity through generic distinctions and even toward creating a hierarchy of genres and film titles within a cinema program. And, as greater control began to be exercised over exhibition, the ambiguity of subject positioning could be more subtly articulated. These examples of the bricolage model, however, can serve to introduce the principles of redundancy and alternation which would consistently organize Pathé's comic chase films and erotic films, respectively, as well as certain features such as cut-in close shots and letter inserts that would characterize the company's melodrama films. Moreover, in their insistence on defining Frenchness in terms of an alien other, these films introduce at least one ideological axis of difference governing Third Republic social relations as crucial to the French cinema's system of representation and narration. Such a model suggests, then, that a certain ideological as well as textual ambiguity would persist in the company's production, particularly within the relatively loose boundaries of the dramatic and realist film.

The Comic Chase Film and Company

A second, much more successful model of transformation emerged in the comic chase film. This model worked simply on what Musser has called the principle of redundancy or "repetition with slight variation."[25] Rather than accumulate a variety of genre elements around a unifying action or theme, it constructed a synthetic space through a series of loosely linked shots in which one character was pursued by another (or else a whole bunch of others), each of which repeatedly moved into and out of one frame after another in a continuous line of action. This constant rehearsal of synthetic spatial continuity, Gunning notes, partially accounts for audiences everywhere being fascinated with the genre.[26] Chase films, as Jasset was one of the first to point out,[27] seem to have originated in the British and American cinemas—see, for example, the Mottershaws's *A Daring Daylight Burglary* (1903), William Haggar's *Desperate Poaching Affray* (1903), Lubin's *Meet Me at the Fountain* (1904), and especially Biograph's *Personal* (1904)[28]—but Pathé and then Gaumont quickly picked up on their enormous popularity. This model superseded both companies' earlier strategy of having a comic musical hall routine performed within an autonomous shot-scene—a strategy that continued, of course, in a few films such as Pathé's *Joyeuses lavendières* (1905) or, better yet, *Opération chirugicale* (1905), whose burlesque of a patient's belly as a cornucopia of bizarre objects and creatures the 1905 Doyen court case again made freshly topical. This new strategy, however, allowed the simplest of stories to be extended clearly and efficiently into quite marketable

29. *Dix Femmes pour un mari*, 1905 (production photo)

film lengths, without the need for either inserted intertitles or an exhibitor's commentary. And it was economical—whole films could be shot rather easily and cheaply on location. By 1905, the leading French company was exploiting the strategy in its own comic chase films, and, within another year at least, a variation on the strategy was predicating both Pathé and Gaumont's other numerous short comic films.[29]

The earliest surviving copy of a Pathé comic chase film seems to be *Dix Femmes pour un mari* (1905),[30] which obviously derives from either Biograph's *Personal* (1904) or Edison's plagiarized version, *How a French Nobleman Got a Wife Through the New York Herald Personal Columns* (1904). Much like its predecessors, this film begins with a simple narrative premise: a man advertises in a newspaper for a wife and sets up a rendezvous site for any prospective candidates. When he arrives, however, he finds ten women waiting, which then prompts his flight and their pursuit through the rest of the film. Similar premises mark a series of Pathé films over the next year or two.[31] In the provincial setting of *Vot' permis? Viens l'chercher!* (1905), for instance, a man is caught snaring a rabbit on a country estate, apparently without a permit. That premise gets repeated in *The Strong Arm of the Law* (1905), where a vagabond boldly lifts a rabbit out of a hutch as a little gendarme looks on, and in *Les Petits Vagabonds* (1905), where two boys steal a couple of rabbits, chickens, and eggs from a peasant, and then is varied in *Poor Pig* (1907), where two boys release a large pig tied to a farmyard trough. Likewise, in the city setting of *Le Voleur de bicyclettes* (1906), a young man is seen riding off on someone else's bicycle in front of a theater; and in *La Course de sergents de ville* (1907) a dog is spotted snatching a leg of lamb from the open window of a butcher shop. In another variation, in *Chien de garde* (1906), a provincial bourgeois woman seeking a watchdog is so swamped with offers that she has to flee her own house and grounds, whereas, in *Chien récalcitrant* (1907), a provincial couple has to retrieve their watchdog after robbers have frightened it into seeking refuge in the local pound. Then, in *La Course de parasol* (1907), a petit-bourgeois fellow goes out for a walk on a hot day, only to lose his umbrella in a gust of wind; and, in *La Course à la perruque* (1906), some boys attach a bunch of balloons to the hat of an old woman sitting on a park bench, and the balloons sail off bearing not only the hat but her wig as well. Finally, in a twist on the genre's beginnings, *La Course des belles-mères* (1907) opens with a newspaper ad announcing a "mother-in-law race," the winner of which will acquire a "handsome son-in-law."

These comic chases followed an easily replicated pattern in which obstacle after obstacle confronted both pursued and pursuers. In *Le Course des belles-mères*, the women race up and down hills, clamber over walls and farm wagons, weave around trains and cars, and pile into and out of different doorways in a building. In *The Strong Arm of the Law*, the vagabond thief escapes from an increasing number of pursuers by "borrowing" one vehicle after another—a rowboat, bicycle, and automobile—the last of which drags a half-dozen gendarmes linked together in a chain down a long hill. In *Poor Pig*, the unloosed pig drags some dozen pursuers over walls, into a well, and through a stream (all conveyed by the old trick of reverse motion); and, in *Chien récalcitrant*, the watchdog drags its master back to its new "home" at the pound (once using the new trick of a backward-dollying camera to record the man's reluctant slide down a country road).[32] In *La Course de sergents de ville*, the dog "thief" leads a herd of policemen on a merry chase through the Paris streets, in and out of cellars and bedrooms, and up and down the facade of a five-story building (the truc effect, this time, of an overhead camera tracking across a set flat painted on the floor). In *La Course à la perruque*, with the furious woman and a crowd in hot pursuit, the hat and wig fly over woods and fields, cross the Seine, enter an apartment window, and finally escape up a fireplace chimney. And, in *La Course de parasol*, the fugitive umbrella leads its owner and a half-dozen others up and down the scaffolding at a construction site, in and around an amusement park Ferris wheel, into and out of a river, and finally up into the air—with all of the pursuers linked together like the long tail on a kite. Even one of the earliest surviving Gaumont films, *Un Coup de vent* (1906), works a variation on this chase by having a man come out of a Paris railway station, lose his hat in a gust of wind, and then futilely pursue it in and around a river barge, a multitiered fountain, a sidewalk café, and a coal loading site.[33]

In order to keep these stories clear and simple, the comic chase film made most of its characters into easily recognizable stereotypes—for instance, the strolling bourgeois or petit-bourgeois, the artisan at work, the maid with baby carriage, the strutting city policeman or provincial gendarme, the "country bumpkin" just arrived in the city—supplemented by an array of animals. Through what happened to such stereotypical figures, of course, the genre also caricatured the so-called leveling process considered to be a hallmark of Third Republic France; and it was particularly insistent on putting down figures of authority and respect, whether public (policemen) or domestic (women). Moreover, because circus acrobats and clowns usually played the pursuers, often cross-dressed as women, their exaggerated pratfalls constantly interrupted the flow of movement and often kept them from ever catching their prey. Such obstacles and pratfalls, Gunning writes, provided "mini-spectacle pauses in the unfolding of [the chase] narrative."[34] Consequently, although the comic chase film certainly established a rudimentary form of linear continuity, involving the spectator in simply defined and quickly resolved narrative expectations, its popularity probably depended just as much, if not more, on the spectacle attraction of these repeated gags or delays. These could be accentuated by truc camera movements, as in *Poor Pig, Chien récalcitrant,* and *La Course de sergents de ville* or, as Doug Riblet suggests, by added sound effects.[35] Furthermore, with very few exceptions, Burch argues, the comic chase tended to "exhaust" the space of each shot (which could not end until the last participant had left the frame) and to encourage variety, from shot to shot, in "suturing" the direction of movement across the frame and in characters' entrances and exits.[36] And the chase often closed off rather arbitrarily. In *Un Coup de vent,* for instance, there is no compelling reason why the man should finally capture his hat in the coal pile—except for the racist joke of having him walk off in blackface. This arbitrariness was one crucial feature that carried over from the cinema of attractions and gave exhibitors a good deal of latitude in screening such films, perhaps almost as much as they had with actualités, for they could easily cut shots as well as rearrange them—the better to fit their programs—and still maintain the linear action of the chase.

Based on the comic chase film's success, Pathé soon began to use redundancy as a structuring principle for many of its other comic films. Here, the initial shot, with or without an introductory intertitle, set up the premise for a gag that could be repeated in one situation after another, in what Gunning has called "linked vignettes."[37] And the gags or "vignettes" tended to be organized serially rather than in a causal, sequential chain. This pattern can be seen developing through several films between the spring of 1905 and that of 1906. Both *L'Automobile et le cul-de-jatte* (1905) and *La Perruque* (1905), for instance, resemble comic strips in which one or more shots set up a gag and then a final shot brings it off. The first film has four well-dressed men leave a park café table to get into a waiting car and then refuse to drop a coin in the hand of a legless cripple who stops by in his pushcart. Yet, when the car breaks down, having traveled from background to foreground in a deep space LS, they collar him (after he has traversed the same space) into playing a draft horse to pull the car offscreen. The second film begins with a young boy spotting his bald uncle putting on a wig in order to go off to a rendezvous. A second shot of a hallway shows the boy lining the inside of his uncle's top hat with some kind of glue so that, in the final shot, when the man meets his lady love next to a park bench and sweeps off his hat in a decorous bow, the wig comes off, too—and the woman falls over in a faint.

Slightly later films simply add on situations in which the gag can be repeated, with some variation. *Le Voyage irréalisable* (1905) has a petit-bourgeois fellow try to leave his house on a bicycle, which suddenly, in a truc cut, shrinks to a miniature toy. This trick recurs each time he tries a different means of transportation—trolley, horse carriage, train, and taxi—and, incredulous, he shows off each toy vehicle to the camera. *Cache toi dans la malle* (1905) locks a would-be lover, wearing a fine white suit, in a lady's trunk to escape her husband, and then sends it off on a perilous journey. As two workmen struggle to transport it, the trunk rolls down a staircase, drops off a carriage, falls into a pond, and finally tumbles end over end down the stairs leading to a railroad crossing—and disgorges a man in rags. *J'ai perdu mon l'orgnon* (1906) has a petit-bourgeois bachelor lose his eyeglasses while eating breakfast and then rush out into the street for an appointment—to bump into a post, a man reading a newspaper, a bicyclist, and a horse and carriage—until he finally gets a ride from a woman with a vegetable cart. *L'Histoire d'un pantalon* (1906), by contrast, is of a different class of fait divers (given the labor unrest that year) and is unusually brutal. Here, a workman hides his pay in a pair of trousers, to keep the money out of his wife's hands; but she unknowingly sells the trousers to a peddler, which sends him off in desperate pursuit. So obsessed is he that not only does he beat his wife but everyone he comes across, no matter how innocent, including the peddler and the man who has bought them from him (after tearing a hole in his own pants).

Over the course of the following year, such films became a staple of French film production, sometimes repeating gags and situations from earlier films. In *Un Jour de paye* (1906), for instance, a man spends his paycheck getting drunk in a bistro and then sets out to navigate the streets of Paris, with disastrous results. In *Automobile à vendre* (1906), a bourgeois couple invite some friends out for a ride in the country in their new automobile, where it promptly dies, and they end up pushing it into a village and hitching it to a horse. In *The Short-Sighted Cyclist* (1907), one of the earliest surviving Eclipse films, a messenger trying to deliver a letter loses his eyeglasses and keeps running into workmen, horse carts, shop displays, and café tables before toppling off of a bridge into a river. In Pathé's *Grève des bonnes* (1906), a drunken group of maids goes on strike (carrying signs in both French and English), but the mayhem they create in Paris seems to ridicule the targets of their anger—a bourgeois family, Bourse businessmen, policemen, and soldiers—as much as it does them. In *Vengéance de nègre* (1906), a well-dressed black man turns the tables on a Parisian newspaper vendor, a woman who has repeatedly snubbed him and refused his money, by paying a boy to blacken her face as she sleeps so that she suffers even worse indignities. Despite its rough attempt to promote racial equality, this film is caught in a vicious circle—not only does it recirculate the stigma of blackness, but it demonizes a woman in the process. *Les Mésaventures d'une mission nègre à Paris*

(1907), by contrast, reverts to the usual prejudicial stereotypes. Here, a half-dozen caricatured Africans (whites in blackface) violate all sorts of Parisian standards of behavior and then are chased past the city's monuments and pursued into and finally seized in the park housing a zoo. Perhaps the most finely honed, and least offensive, example of this pattern of simple replication occurs in *Le Bailleur* (1907). This film opens with a LS of a bedroom interior in which a Monsieur Patissot, preparing to go out for the day, begins to yawn broadly, which his maid, helping him with his overcoat and top hat, promptly echoes. Patissot then passes by some soldiers lined up in front of a barracks, stops in a crowd standing around a street corner kiosk, sits briefly at a sidewalk café table, and joins several relatives (presumably) in a drawing room—and in each situation, his yawn "ricochets" from one character to another around the frame.

A good number of these films, interestingly enough, involve children or "bad boys" perpetrating "serial gags" at the expense of adults.[38] Pathé's *Les Farces de Toto gâte-sauce* (1905), for instance, has a pastry shop assistant out making a delivery meet a friend so that together they can play tricks on various people on the street—such as tripping a bourgeois gentleman and pouring flour in his hat or opening the valve on a water wagon to soak a sleeping workman. In the same company's *En Vacances* (1906), a factory owner sends his two children out of Paris to his brother's farm, where they quickly create havoc—nailing a peasant's clogs to the floor, putting firecrackers in drainpipes, knocking the spouts off cellar wine barrels, and shooing all the animals out of the barn. By contrast, in *Ecole buissonnière* (1906), a boy supposedly doing schoolwork in a typical bourgeois dining room instead sets off with several friends to play hooky and "tour" Paris, where they indulge in such pranks as guzzling a man's beer while he is reading *Le Journal*, at a café table, and then trading him a cigarette for his cigar. In *Les Debuts d'un chauffeur* (1906), one of the first films to exploit the dangers of modern city traffic, two boys start a car left parked outside the Demaria photography factory, and it sets off to "tour" Paris, repeatedly running into people, including the mayor, but politely stopping for a passing cripple.[39] In Gaumont's *The Glue Pot* (1907), a boy steals a bucket of sticky liquid, which a poacher has been using to trap birds in an orchard, and spreads it on some house steps, a park bench, and a bicycle seat to "trap" various people in awkward positions. Finally, Pathé's *Toto fait de la peinture* (1907) has two boys steal a sleeping painter's bucket and brush and indulge in a "crime spree" of blackening a statue and then a park bench (on which two women sit unsuspectingly), pouring paint into a soldier's cap while he's busy courting, and drawing a face on another sleeping man's bald head. In that all of these films seem designed to appeal to an audience of children as well as adults, they provide significant, if indirect, evidence of a growing "youth market" for the cinema in France during this period. And Pathé's two *Toto* films, along with *La Perruque* (where the same boy performs), specifically suggest the beginnings of a move to organize a comic film series around a single character or actor.

Much as did the obstacles and pratfalls in the comic chase films, the repeated gags in these comic films served as "minispectacle" attractions of ridicule, which

30. *Toto fait de la peinture,* 1907

consistently were represented in LS through rather broad gestures of behavior. And the primacy of the gags often did nothing to encourage any greater consistency in "suturing" the direction of characters' movements, from shot to shot, especially in their entrances and exits. Whether the films deployed comic chases or serial gags, or both, however, increasingly they were coming to more definite narrative and rhetorical conclusions. There are signs of this already in *Vot' permis? Viens l'chercher!*—where the "poacher" simply stops at a village outdoor café and nonchalantly reveals his permit to the puffing, pursuing gendarme— and particularly in *Les Petits Vagabonds,* where, after the younger of the two boys has been caught by gendarmes on horseback, the older sneaks up from behind to release him (in a surprisingly early reverse-angle shot). *En Vacances* deploys repeated letter inserts (again, some of the earliest such intertitles to survive) in order to accentuate the opening and closing of its narrative: in the first shot, the father writes a letter to his brother, and in the next-to-last shot, the brother writes back to him. Yet the letters, which contain one of the few film references to the many strikes then going on in Paris, belittle their significance by having the brother request some "revolutionary strikers" in exchange for the children. Other films begin to use the notion of a comic reversal in which the gag is turned back on its perpetrator. In *The Glue Pot,* for instance, the cyclist races up from a "deep space" background and knocks the boy over onto the glue pot, leaving

31. *Les Petits Vagabonds*, 1905   **32.** *Les Petits Vagabonds*, 1905

both of them crawling about with rear-end attachments. And, in *La Course de sergents de ville*, the dog, after successfully reaching its doghouse, bursts out to now chase all the policemen back to their headquarters at the Hôtel de Ville, in a LS gag that will be extended and refined much later in Buster Keaton's *Cops*. *Le Bailleur* comes to perhaps the least arbitrary resolution of all. Happily ensconced in his relatives' drawing room, Patissot is stunned by the truc of two wall portraits yawning back at him, in succession, which leads him, in the next shot, to a hardware store where he buys a snaffle in order to clamp his mouth shut.

Finally, many of these films close with what Salt and Burch have called an "emblematic shot," in a possible variation on the féerie or historical film's apotheosis tableau.[40] Whereas *Toto gâte-sauce* ends with a MS of the two boys laughing at having escaped any kind of retribution, *Toto fait de la peinture* concludes with the boys' victims coming forward into MS (after they have awakened the painter) and laughing at their shared comic plight. Similarly, *Poor Pig* has the pursuers carry their captured prey forward so that the pig's face becomes the center of a concluding group portrait. At the end of *J'ai perdu mon l'orgnon*, which also returns to its beginning, the harried man sits down at his table again and, sipping his coffee, in MCU, nearly inhales his lost eyeglasses, which he then wipes and dons with pleasure. Likewise, *Le Bailleur* closes with a MS of its "hero," now happily muzzled; but suddenly his smile extends into a yawn that snaps his chin strap. *Les Mésaventures d'une mission négre à Paris* ends with a similar MS of one African (in a white robe and crown) hooting like a monkey behind bars. Because the chase preceding this final shot had finished near a zoo, only a missing intertitle or an exhibitor's commentary could determine whether the bars represent a jail cell or, more condescendingly, a monkey cage. In contrast, then, to its somewhat arbitrary function in earlier American and British films—such as Edison's *The Great Train Robbery* (1903) or *Rube and Mandy at Coney Island* (1903) and Hepworth's *Rescued by Rover* (1905)—in these Pathé films the final "emblematic shot" actually continues the simple narrative beyond

33. *En Vacances*, 1906 (title frame)   34. *En Vacances*, 1906

the apparent resolution of the preceding shot while also condensing that narrative into a kind of synecdochical figure.

The Pleasure and Pain of Just Looking:
Erotic Films and Others

A third model of transformation, somewhat more unique to Pathé, was based on the principle of alternation. This developed most clearly out of Pathé's early erotic films,[41] some of which—for instance, *Peintre et modèle* (1902), *Borgia s'amuse* (1902), and *Le Bain des dames de la cour* (1904)—"realized" well-known paintings of one or more nude or partially nude women and perhaps unintentionally exposed the voyeurism inherent to "classical" art. Others, however, included the act of gazing itself and were constructed along the lines of what has become known as the cinematic device of the POV-shot sequence.[42] Minimally, of course, the POV-shot sequence is composed of at least two discrete shots: one shot of a person looking and another, separate shot of what the person is looking at. In the cinema of attractions paradigm, Gunning argues, the continuing alternation of such sequences was governed by *ocularization* rather than *focalization*—the desire to put something on display for a spectator rather than construct a character within a narrative—so that their "power [was] projective rather than absorptive, relishing hidden dramas and spectacles."[43] Accordingly, Elena Dagrada suggests, the "matte shot" or "keyhole shot" in such films may represent "the visual experience of a spectator in the midst of a perceptual revolution . . . exceed[ing] the ordinary limits of vision."[44] Yet what was seen or exposed in these shots often served as a particular kind of "pleasure point" of attraction, presumably but not exclusively, for a male clientele.[45] For such films may have circulated as fetishized tableaux vivants within what Emily Apter has called the "technical arsenal of pleasure" of the *cabinet* or peep show that had long been popular in French houses of prostitution.[46] In any case, the early erotic film turned the act of spectating itself into spectacle and made the voyeuristic nature of the cinema all that much more explicit.[47]

One of the earliest of these films to survive, Pathé's *Ce que l'on voit de mon sixième* (1901), can be taken as an exemplum of the genre. Its six shots alternate three shots of a man on a balcony looking through a telescope with three black-iris-masked images of what he sees. The first and third viewed images display, respectively, a couple kissing (at a studio garret window) and a woman undressing (in an ornate studio window frame); and they are connected by a second, panning shot over the rooftops, which both serves as an actualité attraction and creates a minimal diegetic space.[48] In the final shot, the man turns to the camera and mimes his pleasure, in a kind of mirror image of the male spectator. Many of Pathé's early erotic films, however, placed a mischievous character (usually male) in the public space of either a hotel or an apartment building corridor, looking through door keyholes into different private spaces—see, for instance, *Peeping Tom* (1901) and *L'Amour à tous les étages* (1903).[49] One of the last of these, *Par le trou de la serrure* (1905), actually seems to have been a remake of *Peeping Tom*. Here, three waist-level FSs of a man peering through three doors on the same floor alternate with three MSs (each framed in a keyhole mask) of what he sees in the separate rooms. Whereas the first keyhole shot gives him a privileged view of a young woman at her dressing table and the third lets him spy on a boy embracing a hefty, older woman, the second offers a "deconstructive" striptease as a woman, getting ready for bed, removes her breasts (small sacks), nose, teeth, and wig. This series (actually comprised of earlier single-shot Pathé films)[50] then ends with a comic, moralizing twist as another man unexpectedly comes out of the fourth door, punches the voyeur, knocks him down the foreground stairs, and then throws a self-satisfied glance at the camera. As both Burch and Gunning point out, such an overt act of repression at the end of these erotic films—a kind of uncanny joke on the "subjecting" power of surveillance[51]—may well have provoked as much pleasure and laughter as did the views and antics of the voyeur,[52] especially, I might add, for female spectators.

Les Cartes lumineuses (1905) repeats the voyeuristic spectacle so characteristic of this kind of film, but as a male fantasy of sexual initiation within a much more intimate household setting. A young man enters the foreground of a bourgeois salon, after a woman, presumably a maid, has left through a rear door. Almost immediately he goes to a small box sitting on a foreground table, takes out and lights a cigar, picks up a packet of cards, and sits to look at them closely. A POV CU of the first card in his hands signals the spectacle to come, and the card surface dissolves to a FS of a woman who "comes alive" and begins a striptease.[53] The film continues through three more cards—the same woman appears in different poses and stages of undress—which alternate with the same shot of the salon, where the young man conveys his pleasure with looks to the camera. In the last shot, the maid returns to sit on the young man's knee and asks to see the cards. Then, just as he is about to show her one, the film cuts to the Pathé trademark of a crowing rooster.[54] At least two points are of interest here. The spectacle attraction of the POV shot is accentuated by dissolves and especially CUs as well as, of course, by the "forbidden" nature of the fetishized female body. Moreover, the return of the maid and her gestures of familiarity promise a continuation of the young man's erotic fantasy—the "excess" of spectacle seems about to stimulate a story of sexual activity, one that, given the film's probable site of exhibition, may even exceed the bounds of the frame.

POV-shot sequences, of course, were not restricted to Pathé's erotic films—as is evident in *Un Drame dans les airs* and *Un Tour du monde d'un policier*. And, as such sequences began to be incorporated into other film genres, a perceptible shift occurred in the POV shot's function. Advertised as a dramatic and realist film, *Un Coup d'oeil par étage* (1904) exemplifies this shift from spectacle attraction to narrative revelation quite clearly. The first ten shots of this film describe a situation analogous to that of *Par le trou de la serrure*. A concierge ascends the hallway stairs of a four-story apartment building, making a pretense of dusting and delivering mail, but actually peering through the keyhole of a door on each floor. What he sees are three unrelated comic private scenes, again from earlier Pathé films—a man angrily beating on a telephone at his desk, three children engaged in a pillow fight in their bedroom, and a woman whose cat is swishing its tail in her face (Dranem's *Ma Tante*). After each view, the concierge then comes forward (as if on a public stage) and laughingly mimics what he has just seen. This series is unusually redundant—in the way the man traverses the frame, in the alternation of hallway and room interior shots, and in the miming reenactment of the comedy. As the concierge reaches the fourth floor and peers in the garret room keyhole, however, the film changes radically. What he sees now is a young man desperately fighting a fire that has broken out in his room. The remaining six shots then turn into a continuous narrative sequence of escape as the young man bursts out of the room and collapses, the concierge rushes back down the stairway, where he is joined by the people he has spied on, floor by floor, and they all finally reach the ground floor where several firemen are already working a pumping machine. *Un Coup d'oeil par étage*, not unlike *Un Drame dans les airs*, literally grafts one kind of cinema onto another to produce a single film. An initial series of comic views suddenly turns into a prototype of what would soon become the popular chase film. And the turning point comes precisely in the last POV shot, in which the spectacle of a fire unexpectedly takes on a narrative function that generates the action in the rest of the film.[55]

Sequences dominated by spectacle and narrative respectively, are also grafted together, but in reversed order, in the historical reconstruction film, *La Révolution en Russie* (1905).[56] The first part of this film links three separate tableaux into a loosely continuous narrative. Actualité footage of a battleship, perhaps even the battleship Potemkin, precedes and establishes a historical context for two fictional shot-scenes. In the first, on the deck of a ship, a sailor is shot after complaining about bad food, and a mutiny breaks out. In the second, on a harbor dock (presumably in Odessa), the sailor's body is displayed and galvanizes a crowd of townspeople into sympathy with the sailors. The remaining five shots of the film shift into a different mode of representation that unites the two spaces of ship and city (although now we are on another ship) and reverses the action of the film's opening. Three of these shots represent a ship deck in the foreground and a painted cityscape in the background: a ship cannon fires and sets the city ablaze, and an officer with a telescope exults in what he sees. These shots alternate, however, with two separate POV shots that are inserted each time the officer looks through his telescope. The first depicts a family running out of a smoking building, and the second shows a group of people struggling up a grassy slope to escape a Cossack attack. These two POV shots seem to serve a double function. On the one hand, they are located at the end of a causal narrative chain, representing the effect of the cannon firing. Moreover, the telescope links them into a loose narrative sequence: the townspeople flee the city and are hunted down by the Cossacks. On the other hand, the two shots are presented as moments of spectacle equivalent to the background explosions and fires depicted in the alternating shots in the series. And the officer calls attention to their status as attractions with his exuberant gestures. Perhaps most interesting, the officer's privileged role as spectator (even more than narrative agent or character) seems to direct the cinema audience's sympathies away from the townspeople—which the film initially seems to promote—and align them instead with the military forces of czarist Russia (which, of course, would conform closely with France's heavy capital investment in that country). That is, unless the commentary of an exhibitor would have redirected that alignment by condemning or ridiculing the officer.[57]

Finally, the POV-shot sequence's shift in function became apparent in Pathé's comic films as well. A film such as *Le Dejeuner du savant* (1905), for instance, remained within the cinema of attractions paradigm by simply turning the "pleasure point" of attraction into its opposite. This film alternates three MSs of a biology professor preparing to eat lunch at his desk with ECUs (each with a circular iris mask) of what he sees when he places a bit of cheese and some water under his microscope. First, maggots writhing on the cheese and, then, tadpolelike creatures swimming about in the water cause him to react in disgust; but the learned professor, unlike the spectator, seems incapable of making connections and resumes his reading, munching unwittingly on a piece of bread. Within less than a year, however, in another comic film, *Richesse d'un jour* (1906), the POV-shot sequence had begun to lose its status as an attraction and taken on a more exclusively narrative function. This film narrates the story of a clochard who finds a wallet full of money, spends it all during a day (on clothing, gambling, women, and drink), and, confronted by the wallet's owner in a police station, presumably ends up in jail—a kind of comic Third Republic fable of social mobility in which one's status is measured by a certain style of consumption. A single POV shot appears about midway through the film's nineteen shots as the newly attired clochard goes to bet on the horses at a racetrack.[58] There, an actualité LS of bunched horses racing around a fence turn at first merely seems to describe the location more specifically. But the next shot of the clochard standing in a crowd at the racetrack rail and looking through binoculars implies—through the direction of the clochard's look and the matching direction of the horses' movement across the frame—that the first image has been seen through the clochard's binoculars and that the horses are rounding the turn to the final stretch of their run. The two shots together generate narrative inter-est—will the horse the clochard has bet on win? Yet, just as important, they also produce a striking sense of verisimilitude that positions the clochard "naturally" within a milieu otherwise foreign to him. Unlike previous Pathé films, which displayed the POV shot principally as spectacle, *Richesse d'un jour* tends to stress its diegetic and narrative function. As Judith Mayne argues—and the argument certainly holds for these Pathé films—"the articulation of space, particularly in terms of alternation, and the implicit assumption of point of view for the spec-tator, [would be] key features in the evolution of cinema as a narrative form."[59]

The Dramatic and Realist Films

The final model of transformation which I want to consider includes several distinctive features generally not found in either Pathé's comic or erotic films. This, the compound model, depended on contiguous changes in framing or camera position—whether through camera movement or through cutting to a different perspective of either the same space or else an adjacent space. In the cinema of attractions, such frame changes had served as trucs or spectacle ef-fects—as in Lumière's tracking shots of the 1900 Paris Exposition or the cut-in HA CU of a man's bald head in Pathé's *The Wonderful Hair Restorer* (1902). Now, the function of these frame changes began to shift, somewhat along the lines of the previously discussed POV shot. That is, they became narrativized or remo-tivated within a continuous flow of action, not only to construct a synthetic, diegetic space for that action, but also to elicit, suspend, and fulfill narrative expectations. In those films where a story now served as the dominant principle of organization, any sense of disruption resulting from a frame change was "naturalized" in terms of a narrative logic. Taken together, camera movement, cut-ins, reverse-angle cutting, and other forms of alternation gradually became integrated into a relatively flexible system of continuity editing. And the prin-cipal locus of this model's development was Pathé's dramatic and realist films, especially during the period of the company's expansion beginning around 1904.

As already discussed, several 1904 Pathé films in the genre provide evidence for this kind of transformation in film discourse. Both *Un Coup d'oeil par étage* and *Un Drame dans l'air*, for instance, include POV shots whose function oscil-lates between offering an attraction and telling a story. At least two other films released in August 1904, however, deploy different changes in framing and par-tially for narrative ends. In line with *Histoire d'un crime* and *Victimes de l'alcoo-lisme*—and a long tradition of factory strike plays in both England and France, including Louise Michel's *The Strike* (1890)[60]—*La Grève* takes up the topical issue of labor unrest in France. Its faits divers story warns against the horrible effects of a strike—a striking worker is killed by the police, a factory owner is beaten in retaliation, and a trade union leader is arrested—in order to envision, in the final tableau, a future "union of Capital and Labor."[61] Although relying

35. *La Grève*, 1904 (poster)

on just five autonomous LS tableaux, the film repeatedly creates an unusually "deep space" playing area—in the office interior whose background doors open onto a foyer, and in the factory exterior where a foreground iron fence and gate initially distance the striking workers (and their families) from the owner as he speaks from a centered background doorway. Moreover, in the latter tableau, the camera pans back and forth in order to follow the crowd as they surge around the policemen arresting the union leader, perhaps in an attempt to reproduce the verisimilitude of an *actualité*. *Les Dénicheurs d'oiseaux* tells a much simpler story of three boys stealing a bird nest full of eggs in some woods and then being chased briefly by a gamekeeper. This film begins with a LS of the boys coming to a large tree that the oldest of them scales, but the theft then is represented in a cut-in LA MS of him climbing into the treetop and descending with the nest. Although this cut-in serves to display the boy's prowess in a dangerous position, it also completes a minimal narrative action and establishes the basis for the subsequent chase. Although the chase itself lasts only one shot, a pan away from the wooded path up which the boys are running serves economically to introduce an adjacent stream, through which they splash to safety, leaving their pursuer on the background bank.[62]

This remotivation of frame changes in the dramatic and realist film occurs with some regularity in surviving Pathé film prints from the next year or so.

Yet certain titles participate in the process less fully than do others. In order to tell its story of a servant's remorse for killing his miserly peasant master, *Le Remords* (1905), for instance, sticks to a short series of alternating interior and exterior tableaux, along with truc cuts and superimpositions that turn a coveted farm into a cemetery. *Vendetta* (1905) tells the more complicated, if no less familiar, story of a Corsican bandit who, after killing a hated rival, flees the gendarmes, takes refuge with his family, holds off his pursuers with rifles reloaded by his wife, and finally, rather than be captured, shoots himself. Slight pans reframe the gendarmes early on as they exit the bandit's house and then pursue him across a stream. The chase (along a picturesque seacoast) generally follows a pattern of temporal continuity, but the film shifts to temporal repetition in its moments of confrontation—the gendarmes' action of first rushing out of the house and later breaking into the same place is repeated in full, in both exterior and interior tableaux. Yet, for the final confrontation, both exterior and interior are represented from a slightly different camera position than before—the interior tableau, for instance, now excludes the fireplace up which the bandit earlier escaped and instead emphasizes the wide window and door through which the gendarmes threaten to enter.

Comparing other pairs of Pathé films, especially those involving the figure of the *apache*, rather than peasant murderers or bandits, can bring the uneven development of such frame changes into even sharper focus. If the genre initially drew on newspaper reports of class conflict, as in *La Grève*, now, as France entered a period of increasing strike activity in 1905–1906, such conflicts disappeared, to be replaced by the threat of apache street gang crimes, which, to a large extent, also displaced the earlier "problem" of vagrancy. Although most of those crimes were actually confined to the new working-class suburbs of Paris and other cities, the apache soon became a figure of fascination and revulsion—first in the daily newspapers and then in the cinema—as a "universalized" sign of random terror and violence.[63] Here, real social tension and conflict could be resolved through a process of condensation and displacement onto the most publicized deviant "other" supposedly threatening the French bourgeois social order.

One such pair of films, *Indiens et cow-boys* (1904) and *Brigandage moderne* (1905), aptly contrasts one kind of apache with another. *Indians and Cowboys* probably draws part of its story from *The Great Train Robbery* (1903), for it locates its threat quite literally in the exotic American West, where a so-called "Indian Marauder" attacks a stagecoach, kidnapping a woman and child, who then have to be rescued by a posse of cowboys and scouts in a climactic gun battle. Although shot entirely on location (exactly where is not clear),[64] this film generally adheres to the parameters of the cinema of attractions, illustrating its brief expository intertitles with LS tableaux full of "authentic" costumes and props. However, in a remarkably consistent strategy, nearly every one of these tableaux is marked by some kind of panning camera movement, and all but one has a clear narrative function. In the second tableau, for instance, a pan reframes the passengers getting into the stagecoach before it exits the frame and then follows an Indian who suddenly emerges from hiding on the background roof of a low building and runs off in pursuit. Similar pans help to narrate, first, the robbery of the stage by a band of outlaws (after which stage and outlaws exit in opposite directions) and, then, the attack by the Indians. Perhaps the most interesting occurs in the final tableau as the posse creeps out of a background woods toward a foreground Indian teepee—now, another pan reveals the object of their quest, the woman and child sitting in the middle of the Indian camp. The use of camera movement to introduce offscreen space for narrative purposes certainly makes *Indiens et cow-boys*, like *Les Dénicheurs d'oiseaux*, a unique film for 1904, yet it is no less unusual for its explicit racism. Although the stage is attacked twice, only the Indians are pursued and punished—not only for killing several whites but for abducting the woman and child and thus threatening family figures crucial to the social order of the "colonizers"—while the white outlaws simply ride off with their loot. Furthermore, because an Indian is whipped by the cowboys in the opening tableau, providing some justification for the later attack as revenge, only the initial intertitle labeling the Indian a "Marauder" secures, if somewhat tenuously, the boundary separating victim from victimizer in the film.

Brigandage moderne (1905) offers perhaps an even more appropriate early example of this model because, in its much more sustained chase, the pursued apache is a "modern highwayman" and the pursuers, the police.[65] The narrative premise is set up in the opening shot, in the deep space of a country road, as a man on a motorbike stops an automobile in the foreground, robs its three wealthy passengers, and then speeds off before a policeman on a bicycle can arrive from the far background. In contrast to the chases in Pathé's comic films, this one takes a much more consistent course, following the pattern of the initial scene. Although the police pursue the apache on bikes and in cars through no more than four subsequent shots, the chase is accentuated (in all but one of them) by the spectacle effect of having the characters traverse extremely deep spaces. And both the thief and the police repeatedly move from the background to the foreground of these spaces, in loosely matched entrances and exits. It is just this kind of regularity in the criminal pursuit film—a "disciplined" mode of representation which works here to the advantage of the police (in the end, they get their man)—which would eventually establish the general principle of matching action or movement across adjacent or proximate spaces within a strict linear time frame.[66] Perhaps even more important in *Brigandage moderne*, however, is the cut-in occurring in the middle of the chase. In a MS, which matches action across the cut (unlike the similar cut-in in *Les Dénicheurs d'oiseux*), one policeman, having shinnied up a roadside pole, talks into a phone he has patched into a telephone line.[67] At first, this might seem just a way to display, through magnification, the latest gadgetry for catching apaches (à la James Bond), but the phone call turns out to have a narrative purpose. It alerts other policemen along the regularized route of the chase, several of whom, in the last shot, after the apache has poled a rowboat across a stream in the background, "magically" step in from offscreen, in the foreground, to finally apprehend him.[68]

36a. *Au pays noir*, 1905   **36b.** *Au pays noir*, 1905

Another pair of films exemplifies a different shift from working-class to criminal: *Au pays noir* (1905)[69] and *Au bagne* (1905–1906), the latter a rather grim reworking of *Histoire d'un crime*. As one of Pathé's more popular films during the summer of 1905[70] (and yet one of the last to depict male working-class conditions for several years), *Au pays noir* still remains closely tied to the cinema of attractions. Eight brief intertitles introduce an equal number of autonomous shot-scenes, all of which rely on Lorant-Heilbronn's decors constructed at Pathé's new Montreuil studio.[71] Some of these tableaux are quite detailed in representing a working-class milieu—for example, the open entrance gate to the mine includes a distant painted flat of the town, railway tracks on the ground, and a catwalk above, within whose space a complicated choreography unfolds involving mine workers, the owner and his managers, a horse-drawn rail cart, and a woman and boy scavenging for loose pieces of coal. The principal "attraction" of the film, however—and a Pathé trademark by then[72]—is the 180-degree pan across a painted panorama which follows a group of miners (including a father and son) from their houses through the town square to the mine entrance, and the ninety-degree pan across the deep-space working tunnels leading off from a central shaft underground, at the end of which father and son come forward to sit and eat lunch with their fellows. Unlike *Indiens et cow-boys*, in both of these shots, the function of the pan is more descriptive than narrative, offering a kind of simulated documentary tour of a coal mine site. Only in the sixth tableau does the story seem to come to the fore, in an accidental "pit gas" explosion; but even this provides the occasion for the truc of scratches on the filmstrip, to simulate the explosion, and the spectacle of water pouring out of the rock ceiling and walls of the studio tunnel. Moreover, in the two copies of *Au pays noir* that survive, the following rescue scene seems to have given different exhibitors the license—as if in imitation of the bricolage model of construction—to insert actualité footage of real rescue teams preparing to descend into the mine.[73] Both copies, however, conclude in a LS of the miners' bodies laid out around the coal pit entrance, against the painted flat of a high slag slope; and, when the surviving father emerges, he pushes away the owner and doctor in order to stand over his dead son as the rest of his family clusters around him.[74]

37. *Au pays noir,* 1905

38. *Au pays noir,* 1905

Although the film clearly valorizes patriarchal family bonds, this "tragic" tableau—the very antithesis of the féerie or historical film's apotheosis ending—strongly suggests that working-class men (and women) endure suffering simply in "the order of things."[75]

Released six months later, following the success of *Les Apaches de Paris* (1905), which seems not to survive, *Au bagne* initially emulates *Au pays noir* quite closely in its mode of representation.[76] In the film's first half, brief intertitles introduce autonomous shot-scenes that "document," in studio decors, episodes in the life of a convict from the moment he enters a penal colony prison, focusing on his shackling and branding, hard labor, and punishment by whipping.[77] One of these tableaux even includes the spectacle attraction of a ninety-degree pan across the painted panorama of a naval port facility which follows some prisoners who have been conscripted to load a docked ship. The subsequent escape of a specific convict from prison, however, is represented quite differently.[78] First of all, as the convict goes to his cell window and jumps out (he has used a file to break both the bars and his shackles), there is a 180-degree shift to a LA LS of the prison exterior just as he emerges from the window. Not only does this reverse-angle shift matchcut his movement from one space to another adjacent space,[79] but the second shot continues to follow his movement by tilting down as he drops to the ground and simultaneously reveals another guard in the foreground whom he must subdue before running off. Then a reverse tilt of the camera reveals yet another guard coming out of the same window to yell off after him and order a cannon to be fired as an alarm. In sharp contrast to the descriptive function of the earlier pan, this camera movement serves to link three consecutive stages in a narrative line of action.[80] The convict's escape carries over through two further shots (now filmed on location), only one of which matches his frame exits and entrances; and, finally, an intertitle announces his arrest, which is handled by having the boat he has stolen be captured by the police in two pursuing launches. The narrative excitement generated in this four-shot sequence is even further contained, not only by the studio tableau of his execution by a firing squad (staged for the other prisoners as well as the spectator) but also in a final shot (again on location) of his weighted body being dumped unceremoniously from a breakwater into the sea.[81] This moralizing excess of representation in *Au bagne* could have served either of two radically opposed public debates in France, in 1906. On the one hand, it reported in graphic detail the consequences of the archaic French policy of transporting criminals to penal colonies in the South Pacific, a policy that was becoming an increasing political embarrassment.[82] On the other, by reinscribing penal torture and execution as public spectacle—and thus suggesting it was an effective means of "social defense" against criminal deviance—the film also could have helped to provoke the 1906–1908 debate over reinstating capital punishment in France.[83]

That this remotivation of frame changes did not always follow a chronological progression is also evident in another pair of Pathé films, *L'Honneur d'un père* (1905) and *L'Effet de l'orage* (1906), both of which involve petit-bourgeois or bourgeois families with property. *L'Effet de l'orage*, for instance, adheres to the cinema of attractions by representing and resolving the antagonism between neighboring fathers in just three emblematic shot-scenes, all of which are recorded in studio decors. The first shot presents two side-by-side country houses, with a high wall between them, dividing the frame into two equal halves. One father is working on a ladder against the wall, when the other comes out to quarrel with him. Each is taken back into his house—the one by a son, the other by a daughter—and the young man uses the ladder to declare his love for the young woman, a moment that is disrupted when the fathers return, sequester their children, and resume the quarrel. The second shot "releases" the young couple into a blue-tinted natural landscape, and a descriptive pan follows them as they stroll arm-in-arm across a wooded glen, against a painted panorama of distant hills and moon-filled sky. Once they exit, however, the truc of several inserted orange-red frames signals the first of a series of changes: the painted flat of a now cloudy sky transforms the background, scratches on the filmstrip simulate rain falling, and orange zigzags of lightning flash across the frame. The couple returns to shelter by a foreground tree; suddenly, lightning strikes the tree (which bursts into flames), and a large limb breaks off and falls on the young man, who collapses and has to be carried off. The last shot depicts the amber-tinted interior of one house, where, under the care of his father and the young woman, the young man revives. According to narrative expectation, the other father rushes in, and the older men angrily square off before the centered couple. The young woman speaks to her father and, as the couple moves into the background, the two fathers come to the foreground and finally shake hands. Young love and a natural disaster combine in typical melodramatic fashion to reconcile the differences between the two privileged figures (strangely, neither family has a mother) of a strongly patriarchal social order.

Produced more than a half-year earlier, *Honneur d'un père* (1905), also focuses ultimately on a propertied father (again, the mother is absent), but in far less happy circumstances. And it continues the strategy of *Les Dénicheurs d'oiseaux*, *Indiens et cow-boys*, and *Brigandage moderne* in that all of its eight shots are filmed on location. The first two shots establish the narrative premise: a young woman receives a letter and leaves her father's country house apparently to meet a man by an old stone bridge, a man who inexplicably strangles her in anger (without an insert CU of the letter, the motive remains unclear). The next four shots, which constitute at least half of the film, trace the discovery and return of the daughter's body; and here, in contrast to *L'Effet de l'orage*, is where specific frame changes serve to advance the narrative. The first comes in the LS of a boy apparently checking his traps along a stream, where a pan, which at first seems merely descriptive, leads to a narrative question: what has he discovered at the water's edge? Two shots later, when the boy returns with several men, a slightly closer LS reveals that it is a woman's body, which they place on a stretcher; and a reverse pan describes their journey, which will be completed in the next shot, where the father recognizes his daughter and also reads the initial letter. Here the pan and then the slightly closer LS are essential in con-

128

39. *Honneur d'un père, 1905*

structing a chain of simultaneously revealed and withheld information—an advance over the repeated pattern of simple revelation in *Les Dénicheurs d'oiseaux* or *Indiens et cow-boys*—which is crucial to this patriarchal narrative. In the final two shots, the killer is recognized and pursued by the police, only to be shot and killed, as he runs up a wooded path from the background, by the father who has concealed himself by a foreground tree. The father's successful vengeance, to restore his "honor," is clearly sanctioned by the male authorities, who come up to check the body and take his hand.

These last two films in particular suggest that a slightly different kind of story was beginning to define Pathé's dramatic and realist films—that of the domestic melodrama. "Scenes of domestic life," Rémy de Gourmont called them, and the sheer number of such films within the genre prior to his 1907 essay seemed to confirm their dominance.[84] Many of these films, like the Sunday supplements of *Le Petit Journal* and *Le Petit Parisien*,[85] told stories of contemporary family traumas, of the threatened loss to the family of a father or child—and less often, at least initially, the mother—usually through twists of fate or coincidence involving either an accident or else an apache crime. And the traumatic loss of a child was particularly relevant in France, given the country's increasingly accepted one-child-family ideal (especially among white-collar workers)[86] and its uniquely low birthrate at the turn of the century. As in both *L'Honneur d'un père* and *L'Effet de l'orage*, the accident or criminal act that threatened the family usually occurred in a "public space," but the resolution, especially if it restored family harmony, tended to return to the sanctified "private space" of the home.[87] The families in these domestic melodramas ranged from working-class and white collar to bourgeois, a spectrum that still seems to have assumed a mass audience "in which different classes and social groups [could] meet and find an identity."[88] However, those families were almost always explicitly patriarchal, privileging the father's position in the hierarchy of character relations. And that position was, as in *L'Honneur d'un père*, sometimes sanctioned in the end by the police—in an aptly ideological gesture that reaffirmed its significance to the French social order.

As Peter Brooks has suggested,[89] the cinema was the twentieth-century popular art form that most relayed and supplanted nineteenth-century melodrama, and Pathé's early domestic melodramas certainly constitute a specfic instance of such a transposition in that they rework many of the conventions of French stage melodrama. From its inception, in the aftermath of the French Revolution, Brooks argues, "melodrama [took] as its concern and raison d'être the location, expression, and imposition of basic ethical and psychic truths," becoming the principal cultural form through which the essentially moral universe of a "desacralized" French society was demonstrated and made operative—specifically, within the family and its domestic sphere.[90] Accordingly, its characters assumed "primary psychic roles, father, mother, child"; and its narrative threatened to block or eclipse the virtue "inherent" to those roles, before its eventual restitution.[91] If Pathé's domestic melodramas drew on this long tradition of French stage melodrama for both their narrative economy and symbolic configuration—even to the point of giving the characters generic names—they also shared in that tradition's mode of representation. For melodrama strove, in Brooks's words, "to make the 'real' and the 'ordinary' and 'private life' interesting through heightened utterance and gesture" as well as to "make its representations clear and legible for everyone."[92] And, in the specific domain of the theater, it transformed the stage into an "arena for represented, visual meaning [accompanied by music] . . . most especially at the end of scenes and acts," where meaning was resolved in tableau, "in a visual summary of the emotional situation."[93] Although a tableau style of representation obviously was widely disseminated throughout early French cinema, the combination of rhetorical intensification and representational clarity in nineteenth-century melodrama, I would argue, more specifically informed Pathé's domestic melodrama, especially through discursive features such as changes in framing.[94] Camera movement, cut-ins, reverse-angle cutting, as well as other forms of alternation all began to turn into the symptoms, to appropriate Brooks's terms, of that melodramatic pressure being exerted "upon the surface of things" in order to extract a so-called moral truth.[95]

Just how crucial these patterns of alternation and changes in framing were to the development of a narrativized cinema is evident in a wide range of domestic melodramas released by Pathé in 1906. Some of these continued to focus on the criminally deviant and their perceived threat to the patriarchal family.

Le Braconnier (1906) and *La Revanche de l'enfant* (1906), for instance, both tell a story that would be familiar to those who had joined the recent migration from country to city in France. In the first film, a poacher is threatening a country estate and the old gamekeeper (and his daughter) who manages it along with a young assistant. After learning that a man is setting traps illegally on the estate, the old gamekeeper goes to check and is shot by the poacher; the young man then proves himself by apprehending the poacher and reaching a doctor in time for the wounded man to be treated successfully. In the second film, the game-keeper surprises two poachers and, in the chase that follows, falls off a plank stretching over a ravine to his death. Seeking revenge, his son pursues the poach-ers, with the help of gendarmes, until the pursued men, too, are dead. One of the interesting features of both these films is their use of "bridge" shots, perhaps modeled on the POV-shot sequence, which connect a character in one space to another, adjacent space, not through sight, but through sound cues (probably provided by the exhibitor). The second shot of *Le Braconnier*, for example, pre-sents the young man (after he has left the gamekeeper's house) coming up a ravine path and stopping to listen; in the next shot he discovers a trap set by the poacher (who has exited the frame just before he enters).[96] Such a shot is not repeated when the gamekeeper leaves the house to find the poacher; but one does occur immediately after the shooting, in order to place several men nearby so that, when the young man finds the gamekeeper and calls out, they can ap-pear and help carry the wounded man off. A similar sequence occurs near the opening of *La Revanche de l'enfant*. Here it is the gamekeeper who, coming for-ward along a path, stops to listen, after which a slight pan follows him as he exits. In the next shot (some of whose action seems to overlap with that of the previous one), the gamekeeper runs in (his entrance matching his exit), to dis-cover the poachers just having shot some rabbits—and the chase begins.

From then on, however, the two films deviate in their outcome and, to some extent, in their manner of getting there. The remaining four shots of *Le Bracon-nier*, for instance, organize space according to the young man's heroic actions, in a tightly condensed rather than expanded sequence. In the deep-space LS of a path running through an open field, for instance, he surprises the poacher, quickly subdues him, and loads the now bound man onto a passing cart. And in the equally deep space of the following shot, the cart stops by a gate and the young man runs into the background courtyard to accost a doctor, whose car-riage then comes forward and follows the cart off. Two lines of action are neatly combined in the last shots—the poacher is taken to the local police station, the doctor follows along to treat the gamekeeper—and, in the final tableau, the young man can recount his "adventure" to the gamekeeper and receive his daughter's hand in marriage, in the newly secured space of the home. *La Re-vanche de l'enfant* organizes its space similarly, according to the vengeful action of the gamekeeper's son, but it integrates several other characters into his pursuit as well—and not without some awkwardness. The boy first attacks the poachers outside a country inn, and, although they elude him, his attempt alerts several gendarmes who, in the following deep-space LS of another open field, successfully shoot one. As if imitating the pattern of circularity already marking some Pathé comic films (but under the sign of "poetic justice"), the other poacher is now chased back to the same ravine edge, where the boy strikes him with a knife, causing him to fall to his death as well. The ending FS tableau, rather than continue to follow the movement of the boy, however, in grand guignol fashion focuses on the mother (earlier, she, too, had gone off in apparent pursuit of the poachers) as she comes up to cradle her dead husband's head.[97]

Even more ambivalent in their treatment of crime were other Pathé films such as those involving pursuit dogs (which were especially popular),[98] for the dogs served both sides of the law with equal enthusiasm. In *Les Chiens contrebandiers* (1906), for instance, a team of greyhounds works as carriers for a small band of gypsy smugglers in the Pyrenees, near the Spanish border. The film's initial two sequences set up a contraband run using alternations between adjacent interior and exterior spaces—the first in a gypsy cabin, the second in a mountain cave—each of which is consistently marked by ninety-degree shifts in camera position. The second sequence also includes a man spying on the smugglers and dogs at the mouth of the cave so that parallel lines of action can develop: in the following exterior shot of the local police station, the spy informs the gendarmes (the men inside the door are represented in silhouettes against a background window), then the film cuts back to pick up the dog's run. Halfway through the first leg of the run, the two lines of action come together as the gendarmes jump out of some woods and give chase; they diverge, after a half-dozen shots, when the dogs lay down in some foreground bushes, and the gendarmes pass by in the background. At this point, in an early instance of temporal simultaneity through crosscutting, a second parallel line of action develops as a gypsy woman (first seen in the cabin) goes to the mountain cave (in another alternating sequence) to warn the smugglers of the police chase.[99] The last leg of the run thus pits the gendarmes against five smugglers in a shoot-out—first in some trees by an open field, and then on a treeless border ridge (marked by a small sign)—in which all but one of the smugglers are killed, while the dogs escape unscathed. In the final sequence, again alternating adjacent exterior and interior spaces, the dogs, followed by one young man, come to another cabin across the border; and the survivor tells his story to the remaining smugglers, including the woman who earlier spread the warning. In order to narrate its story, *Les Chiens contrebandiers* consistently deploys two different patterns of alternation, one of them involving crosscutting, and with considerable clarity and economy.[100] Yet it concludes with a puzzling emblematic MS of a smiling old gypsy with two greyhounds—an image that seems quite at odds with the losses the smugglers have suffered.

Le Détective (1906), by contrast, is much more certain in its handling of a threat to an urban bourgeois family. Here, a young girl (an only child) is seized by apaches in order to extract a ransom from her father and mother—and the girl's action, interestingly enough, proves as crucial as the hired detective's to the film's happy ending. The kidnapping is narrated in three loosely linked shots—of the family drawing room, a country lane where the girl and a family maid are walking, and the kidnappers' cabin in a wood—and in the fourth, the ransom note is delivered to the house and displayed in an early CU insert.[101] The note kicks off the search for the girl by a detective, whose disguise unfortunately fails to keep him from being captured by the kidnappers as well. Most of the rest of the film is devoted to two set pieces of action, each of which is organized according to the principle of alternation, but this time, as in *Au bagne*, the alternation is between exterior and interior views of, first, the kidnappers' cabin and, then, a barn with a loft.[102] Six shots comprise the first sequence, in which the girl escapes from the apaches and then returns to rescue the detective (who has been tied to a barrel marked "explosives"); and, given the position of the cabin door used for entrances and exits, the camera seems consistently to shift 180 degrees from inside to outside and back. Moreover, the recurring exterior view of the cabin is marked by a HA LS, which serves to "hide" the girl's tiny figure within the space of the frame (from both the kidnappers and the spectator). The second sequence at the barn, where the girl and detective now elude the pursuing apaches, is less precise in its shift of camera position, but it pivots on the detective's ruse of a rope leading out a background window in the loft interior (while the two escapees hide in the foreground). This leads the apaches off in one direction in the final shot, while the girl and detective can escape in the other. Although, in its alternation of exterior and interior views, *Le Détective* represents a relatively sophisticated instance of a continuous flow of action across a constructed diegetic space, at least for 1906, it also concludes with an attraction—an isolated MS of the girl at home, framed by her two smiling parents. Much like the emblematic shots concluding Pathé's comic films, in that it condenses the narrative into a synecdochical figure, this "family portrait" concisely summarizes the ideological project that these French domestic melodramas seemed determined to serve.[103]

In a slight deviation from these films, *Un Drame en express* (1906) locates its threat in one of the chief icons of modernity, the express train, and directs its violence against a young bourgeois woman traveling alone.[104] Here, the apache figure comes dressed like a gentleman, which makes it easier for him (in the first LS) to spot his prey entering a rail station and (in the second) to follow her onto a departing train. In a long-take AS of the first-class compartment the woman has reserved, he quickly renders her unconscious (with chloroform), steals her money and rings, and, when she suddenly awakens, seizes her by the throat and throws her off the train. After this act of grand guignol brutality, the film suspends this line of action to follow another through three more elliptical shots. First, the woman is discovered lying on the train tracks by several peasants, who revive her and learn of the robbery; then, one peasant runs off to the closest train station and its telegraph office. There, in an unusual MS of the office interior (there is no prior "establishing shot" of that space), he has the telegraph operator tap out a message on his machine. The film's two lines of action now converge in the last two tableaux. Apparently informed by the telegraphed message, detectives arrest the disguised gentleman when the train stops at another station farther along the line, and later the woman is brought into this station's interior

40. *La Loi du pardon*, 1906

to positively identify him. If, somewhat as in *Brigandage moderne*, the modern technology of the train in *Un Drame en express* creates a space in which the individual—especially a lone woman—becomes isolated and vulnerable, prone to unexpected eruptions of violence, that of the telegraph serves to contain and suppress that violence, and in the process links all classes together in a restored, properly authorized social order.

In contrast to Pathé's previous films, *La Loi du pardon* (1906), which Jasset singled out as one of the first popular successes in the genre, focuses on moral deviance as a threat to the family from within.[105] This threat comes from the wife or mother, who is guilty of infidelity, and its resolution turns on the daughter's health and desire (again she is an only child) as well as the husband's judgment. The film's opening shot succinctly narrates the family's disintegration: in a rather modern drawing room,[106] the husband discovers the wife writing a note in response to a love letter she has just received (there is no CU insert of explanation) and, despite the pleas of both mother and daughter, angrily orders her to leave. And it closes in a triangulated tableau summarizing the emotional situation: the husband in despair (frame left), the daughter weeping (frame right), and an empty background space where the wife has exited. The next shot recapitulates this private moment of the couple's separation in a public courtroom, where several judges reaffirm the father's right to the daughter, but not before the girl expresses her own desire to be with her mother. The third shot then recapitulates the initial emotional situation, in a slight change of framing: father and daughter are sitting alone on a park bench, but in a relatively empty LS that contrasts with the rather full, condensed spaces of the previous tableaux. The last five shots of the film are organized around an alternation (with mismatched exits and entrances) between a LS of the bedroom interior where the girl now lies ill and a LS of the exterior street entrance to the family townhouse. The father leaves the girl sleeping in the company of a nun (he is going to buy her some gifts, it turns out), and, as he exits the exterior shot, the mother gets out of a background carriage and comes to the townhouse door and enters. What happens now constitutes an intriguing ideological twist on the function of disguise—for the mother persuades the nun to exchange clothes behind a background door. Her objective presumably is to sit with her daughter undetected, yet when the girl awakens, they immediately embrace. More important, the nun's habit has the effect of masking or even erasing the mother's guilt. And this disguise proves significant when the husband returns to recognize and again reject her (although she kneels to plead with him), that is, until the daughter gets out of bed to join his reluctant hand with her mother's in a centered, but very uneasy reconciliation. In the private space of the child's room, the earlier public verdict is overturned as the bond between mother and daughter forces the father to accept the mother's value to the bourgeois family.

Pauvre Mère (1906), which was released just two months later, also focuses on the bond between mother and daughter, but in a different class milieu. In just eleven shots, it narrates the story of a working-class mother (the father now is conspicuously absent) who loses her only daughter in an accident, takes to drink, falls ill, and soon dies in a convent hospital. Here, a POV-shot sequence is crucial in representing the accident that opens the film.[107] The first shot describes the simple room in which the mother and daughter live: the woman does put-out work at a sewing machine while the girl plays with a doll and runs to the room's single window. The cut to a HA LS of a military band marching through the street then reveals what the girl is seeing, and the camera position, along with the direction of the girl's look, quickly establish that the room is located several stories above the street. The next shot returns to the room as the woman anxiously pulls the girl away from the window and resumes her sewing, but the girl goes back to the window, leans too far out, and, to the mother's horror, tumbles out. In contrast to Pathé's previous films, then, *Pauvre Mère* uses the spectacle of a POV-shot sequence (observed by a female rather than a male) as the pretext or narrative premise for an unrelenting series of moments of frustrated desire. To that end, in its final six shots, the film repeatedly deploys the dissolve and superimposition in a pattern markedly different from that of the POV-shot sequence. The mother's obsessive desire for her lost daughter is represented through three separate superimpositions of the child, the most interesting of which appears, in conjunction with a cut-in, as the mother is sitting dejectedly on a park bench—in a FS, the girl dissolves in to replace another girl whom the mother has noticed playing nearby and taken onto her lap. Then, in the last shot, the girl materializes over her mother, who lies in a hospital bed, and they reach out toward one another just before the mother falls back and dies, as if to signal a promised reunion. Rather than exploit the sense of magical illusion often previously associated with superimpositions, as in *Le Remords*, *Pauvre Mère* uses them instead as a rhetorical figure to heighten the subjective, emotional intensity of the mother's condition.

While exemplifying the domestic melodrama's significance to the development of a narrativized cinema, these last two Pathé films also raise questions about the composition of French cinema audiences and how exhibition practices affected the reception of particular films. In privileging the relationship between mother and daughter and the emotional appeal of their shared desire, for instance, both *La Loi du pardon* and *Pauvre Mère* seem to address a specifically female spectator.[108] This suggests that, by 1906, women—as well as children— were beginning to constitute an increasingly important segment of those who regularly attended cinema programs in France.[109] Attracting and holding their interest with such women-centered melodramas, particularly those appealing to white-collar families, may well have been one of Pathé's earliest strategies for "legitimizing" the French cinema industry, strategies that would eventually include the construction of permanent cinemas and the promotion of "film d'art" productions. Yet, as a textual system, both films address the spectator somewhat ambiguously at the end. Is the concluding tableau of *Pauvre Mère*, for instance, to be read, within a conservative Catholic tradition, as a legitimate religious "reward" for the mother's suffering or, rather, as an implicit appeal for social measures to redress the near-poverty conditions of the single working-class woman? In *La Loi du pardon*, is the wife or mother to be read as a kind of sanctified Mary Magdalene, a figure of innocence represented from her daughter's point of view,[110] or a woman who has literally taken a vow of chastity? And what about the husband-father's attitude, for only he and not the judge can fulfill the real "law of pardon"—has the family actually been restored? The answer might have depended on where and in what context one saw the film. How would either have been read, for instance, if screened, as some films were beginning to be, in a Catholic diocese? Despite all of Pathé's advances in storytelling efficiency and clarity, by 1906, the cinema exhibitor could still play a significant role in determining the spectator's experience and reading of a film—through adding or cutting intertitles, prefatory commentary, accompanying music, and even positioning on his program.

Dissemination and Difference

During the period of 1905–1906, as the previous pages demonstrate, a loose system of representation and narration—dependent on camera movements, cut-ins, reverse-angle cutting, and various forms of redundancy and alternation— began to coalesce in Pathé's dramatic and realist films and especially its domestic melodramas. Within another year, and well before the company decided to adopt a new rental strategy of film distribution, that system was being disseminated through Pathé's other genres as well as Gaumont's expanding film production. At least two representational features clearly distinguished the two French companies, however [111]—Pathé's "trademark" of a now standardized waist-level camera position [112] and its logo of a rooster "branding" one or more interior decors of almost every film (see, for instance, the frame still from *En Vacances*) as a further safeguard against duping by competitors. [113] Although the dissemination of this representational system can be traced in a few historical films, it was particularly evident in those comic films that did more than simply construct a series of repeated gags in one shot-scene after another. Moreover, in both comic films and domestic melodramas, the system seemed to encourage tighter constructions of spatial-temporal continuity (through repetition and alternation), slightly more complicated narrative structures (without abandoning the "logic" of co-incidence and the generic nature of the characters), as well as more resonating registers of rhetorical intensification. Yet the Third Republic social relations of difference on which this system was mapped continued, particularly in Pathé's films, to be defined in terms of the patriarchal family, as a crucial French site of social legitimation.

A number of Pathé comic films began to use frame changes inventively to construct, elaborate, and accentuate their gags. Both *La Chaussette* (1905) and *Lévres collées* (1906), for instance, take advantage of the cut-in close shot to place the spectator in a privileged position of knowledge. [114] *La Chaussette* emphasizes its construction of an appropriately deep space from the beginning, as a bourgeois gentleman, after dancing with several other couples in a background room, comes gingerly forward through an arch doorway to rest in an adjacent drawing room. When he slips unnoticed behind a foreground screen, a cut-in AS sets up the film's gag—he removes a troublesome sock and stuffs it in his pants' pocket. A return to the "establishing" shot shows him dancing energetically with another woman, whom he then leads back into the foreground room to rest again on a couch. Now a cut-in MS springs the gag as he absentmindedly pulls out the sock to wipe his forehead and fan his face—at which the woman sniffs in disgust, spots the offending "hankie," and faints away. *Lévres collées* constructs a slightly different deep space in a post office interior, where several customers (among them, Linder), one after another, conduct business at a series of background teller windows. Out of this group, a bourgeois woman and her maid come to a foreground table, where the latter's tongue gets used, almost like a mechanical device, to wet some dozen stamps. A suitor comes up to admire the maid, and, when her mistress goes back to purchase more stamps, the two fall into a kiss—from which they cannot get unstuck. A cut-in MCU isolates and magnifies their predicament for the spectator, as they struggle back and forth against a black background. An elliptical return to the "establishing" shot shows various people failing to free the couple until a boy succeeds in cutting them apart with a pair of scissors—and, in a comic feat of reproduction, a duplicate of the man's mustache now adorns the maid's upper lip. This sends them both into gales of laughter in a concluding emblematic MCU.

Several Pathé films with longer, repetitive narrative structures rely on similar changes in framing to wrap up their gags. *Pitou amoureux* (1906),[115] for instance, plays a series of jokes on a lovesick soldier, culminating in a neatly matched reverse-angle cut in which he gets tossed from outside a police station, into a jail cell, and straight into a large bin, from which he emerges completely covered with coal dust. The racist nature of the gag is then underlined in a concluding MCU of his tear-stained, blackened face. *Le Nettoyeur de devantures* (1907) begins quite differently with a window cleaner setting out slightly drunk from his neighborhood café, so that his ladder and bucket turn into deadly weapons as he traipses through the Paris streets. This film also climaxes in a reverse-angle cut, however, as he leans his ladder against a restaurant exterior, crashes through the front window, and gets thrashed by the angry bourgeois diners. And it, too, closes in an emblematic MCU—with the window cleaner pulling a fork and then a hunk of bread out of his disheveled head. *Mariage enfantine* (1906) uses the gimmick of child actors to send up another conventional love story, this one involving a young peasant couple and a rival soldier.[116] The first part of this film narrates a leisurely "chase" through various woodland locations, only to end in the ruins of a castle with the girl's father rejecting the boy, who then inexplicably gains the magical aid of the soldier in his love quest. The second part then quickly reverses the narrative—the father suddenly agrees to the boy and girl's marriage (on the advice of an officer supplied by the soldier)—and accentuates this fantasy resolution by now shifting to studio decors, even for the palace garden finale. In the wedding banquet scene, however, the soldier's role as rival returns briefly in a cut-in MS of him, under the table, stealing the bride's garter, which he happily brandishes in the subsequent LS, just as she stands on a chair to deliver a speech. But harmony is restored in the convention of a final emblematic MCU—of the child bride and groom holding hands, pecking at one another's lips, and chattering away merrily.

Other Pathé comic films use frame changes either to set up or to elaborate a gag through an unusual play on spatial-temporal continuity. *L'Accordéon* (1906), for instance, focuses as much attention on its premise as on what follows. The first half of the film is restricted to a single FS of a painted-flat cottage exterior, with a centered door; and it works out a cleverly timed series of gags based on a simple situation—a young man is serenading a young woman whose father is opposed to any suitors. After dismounting from his bicycle and briefly playing a huge accordian, the young man lays the instrument on its side and, using a bicycle pump, fills it with air, lifting himself up to the level of the young woman's balcony window—with the spectacle of his elevation accentuated by the truc effect of a tilting camera movement. Once the couple embrace and he climbs in her window, a reverse tilt reveals a second man coming up to let the air out of the accordian and ride off on the suitor's bicycle. Just as the suitor begins to climb back down (completely unaware of his losses), the father comes out of the cottage door and, spying the man's feet at the top of the frame, gives him a whack with his broom. Then, another man enters to help the father pump up the accordian again, and they knock the suitor into what now becomes a "closed box"—where he receives another good whack. The film's remaining two LS tableaux present the comic spectacle of this giant upright accordian slowly shuffling past a family picnicking in the park and then along a city street. In the latter shot, two men sit on it in order to tie their shoelaces and are thrown off by its convulsive shrug; in retaliation, they squash the accordian down to normal size and lift it up, pushing and pulling, until a paper-thin image of the young man falls out. When they give the image a shake, the young man materializes (in a straight cut) and kicks both of them offscreen, then wipes his brow and strides off in the opposite direction. Falling in love in the movies, *L'Accordéon* suggests, can be hilariously dangerous, entrapping one in the spectacle of a male "castration" nightmare.

Le Concierge bat son tapis (1906) and *Médor au téléphone* (1907), by contrast, use relatively complicated editing strategies to set up or work out their gags. The fait-divers story in the first film takes place in the working-class outskirts of Paris, where an apartment building concierge is simply trying to clean an old carpet. After his wife refuses to let him do the job in their backyard plot (where she is raising chickens, turkeys, and rabbits), he takes the carpet into an empty room inside and begins beating away at it, producing huge clouds of dust. Here, the film shifts to the street-front exterior of the building where two men come round a corner, stop before the door, and look up. A POV shot reveals what they see—what seems to be smoke pouring out of an apartment window. This misperception, which depends for its comic effect on the spectator knowing more than any of the characters, spurs the two men to action—ringing the doorbell (it goes unanswered) and calling in others, among them several policemen who run off to get a fireman. Instead of dwelling on what could have been a lengthy "chase," the film returns quickly to the apartment building exterior and then to the room full of dust for its payoff. First in the room and then outside, the poor, startled concierge undergoes his own excessive beating—not only at the hands of the fireman and policemen but those of his own wife and neighbors as well. In *Médor au téléphone*, a man goes to have a drink at a sidewalk café, realizes he has left his dog at home, and calls the dog on the telephone to tell it where to find him. In this extremely short film, the gag comes neither at the beginning nor at the end, but in the middle—with an unabashedly "modern" dog, perched on a high stool, talking into a wall telephone. This is accentuated, first of all, through magnification, in the spectacle of a MS, probably augmented by sound effects. But that spectacle is doubled through its alternation with a parallel MS of the man talking into the café telephone. Then, to suggest the length and ease of their conversation, this alternation is repeated through six shots, in an early instance of parallel editing that constructs a clear sense of temporal simultaneity and spatial distance. And that distance is confirmed by the subsequent, and more conventional, shots of the dog running through several streets, in loosely matched exits and entrances, to reach the café and sit comfortably in a chair beside its master.

Similar editing patterns repeatedly linking adjacent spaces also begin to transform Pathé's "serial gag" films.[117] *Tommy in Society* (1907), for instance, opens with a conventional "bad boys" routine as two boys move successively through three rooms in their parents' apartment—stuffing a cat into the piano, shooting dinner plates tossed in the air, and tricking the maid into dumping a pot off the stove. The following three shots then repeat these spaces in order, as an older sister and the parents discover their handiwork. The film's final sequence takes the boys out into the hallway and into another upstairs apartment to set up their last gag. Now, an alternation of closer shots, on each side of the apartment door, connects a neighbor woman who crosses the hallway to visit and the boys who pour water into their end of a speaking tube. Their action in one space has its effect in the other as the woman, speaking into her end of the tube, gets sprayed full in the face. *Diabolo* (1907) creates a variation on this structure, but turns the butler of the family into the "destructive child." Here, the mother sets up the premise by bringing home a Diabolo, a popular Japanese spinning top, ostensibly for her two daughters. Infatuated with the toy, the butler orders mother and daughters out of the dining room, pushes the table and chairs after them, and soon demolishes the rest of the furniture with his erratic, exuberant play. His wrecking performance carries over into the study and bedroom and then out into the hallway, where the mother finally hits him over the head and throws him to the floor. What is especially interesting in *Diabolo*, however, is the way the intercutting of adjacent spaces shifts from temporal simultaneity to sequentiality, neatly timing the right-to-left trajectory of the mother and daughters in pursuit of the out-of-control butler. In the first shot, only after he exits do they enter and cross the dining room, horrified. Then, after he leaves the wrecked study, the film cuts back to the dining room where they push open the door that, in a matchcut, lets them cross through the study. Finally, in the bedroom, their entrance coincides with his exit so that, in the hallway, the mother is close on the butler's heels as, wild-eyed, he descends the stairs. Deployed in embryonic form here in *Diabolo* is the parallel editing structure that will become crucial to later films ending in the last-minute rescue.

The regularity with which this new representational system could operate in Pathé's comic films by 1907 is especially evident in *A Hooligan Idea* and *Ruse de mari*. The first film has two apaches rob a bourgeois gentleman (played by Linder), not once but twice. The initial tableaux show them bartering with a Jewish pawnshop proprietor for a used army officer's uniform (the Dreyfus affair gives this transaction an ironic twist) and then the larger of the two donning the uniform in disguise (adding a bit of clipped hair for a mustache). The scam itself is worked out in a simple alternation between the LS exterior of an apartment building—where the "officer" paces, while the other apache sneaks in through a window—and the FS interior of a dining room, matchcutting the latter's entrance. After snatching some money from a cabinet, the apache faces down the whole household, one after another, by nonchalantly puffing on a cigarette—the butler hides in the cabinet (after brandishing a knife), the gentleman backs out of the room, quavering (although armed with a gun). The maid runs outside to get the "officer," who quickly seizes the unprotesting apache and takes him off; but the two stop once they have rounded a nearby street corner, and the "officer" returns to the scene of the crime. The sequence of exterior and interior shots is repeated as the "officer" is invited to share lunch with the gentleman, but now a cut-in MS accentuates the ironic offer and acceptance of reward money. In the cut back to FS, the gentleman is called out of the room for a moment, and the "officer" stuffs his uniform with food, along with several pieces of china from the cabinet. And when he returns to the street corner to share his booty, another cut-in MS of the two partners underscores their success at "double dipping." With a deft, deceptive economy, this film hollows out one of the crucial public figures of authority which usually serves, at least in the domestic melodramas, to shore up the bourgeois basis of the French social order.

Ruse de mari extends this kind of structural repetition in a very different story of a timid clerk or artisan who evades his angry wife's order that he not stay out too late playing cards with his friends (again, Linder is one of them) at his local café. The initial LS of the couple arguing in their dining room establishes the premise when the wife points to the background wall clock, which is followed by a cut-in CU of the clock face at 8:00. In two subsequent exterior shots, where the husband regains his composure, he leaves their apartment building and, in a matchcut exit and entrance, arrives at the café. This sequential structure is then repeated as the wife awakens in their garret bedroom to discover, in another cut-in CU of a clock, that it is 12:55, after which she follows her husband's route to the same café, where she stops to look in the window. At this point, the film shifts to alternating interior and exterior LSs of the café in order to facilitate a smoothly choreographed series of moves. The bartender spots her and warns the husband who, glancing at another background wall clock, exits offscreen and, just as his wife enters, reappears outside at what turns out be a second background door. After the bartender and cardplayers deny seeing the husband and the wife leaves the café, the film returns to its initial sequential structure of three repeated shots, but in reverse order. First the husband arrives home, then his wife follows and is shocked to find him asleep in bed. This time, when she awakens him to complain, he can point to the clock (now there is no need for a cut-in), reprimand *her* for staying out late, and begin to beat her—in a deceptive reversal whose apparent justification the film assumes the spectator undoubtedly will share. A concluding MCU of the couple in bed—she cries into a handkerchief, while he alternately smiles and threatens—caps this condensed version of "the taming of a shrew" and restores patriarchal power in the private sphere where it counts, in the bedroom.

Based on surviving prints, Gaumont's comic films also began to pick up on Pathé's system of representation. In one of Guy's last French films, *Le Matelas alcoolique* (1906), Bosetti plays a drunken sailor who inadvertently gets sewn up in the used mattress a woman is airing and mending in an open field.[118] This absurd premise is set up by a brief sequence of alternating shots in which the woman goes off to a nearby café and the sailor wanders up from the far background and falls asleep on the mattress.[119] Much of the film then focuses on the difficulties she has in carrying the mattress through town and into the bedroom of the old couple who have bought it (all the characters seem to be artisan or working class). During this journey, the mattress grows increasingly restive—

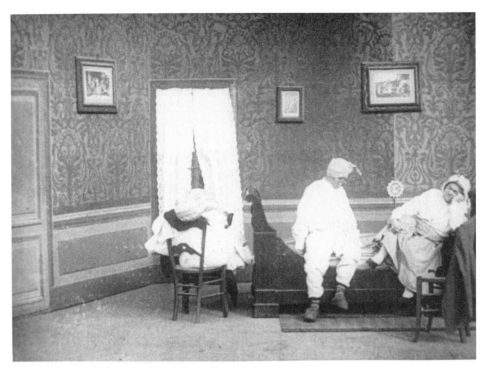

41. *Le Matelas alcoolique*, 1906

after being rolled down a hill, slipped off a bridge onto a road, dragged up some steps, dropped into a construction site hole, and banged into some men carrying heavy dresser cabinets. Most of these gags are worked out in loosely linked eye-level LS tableaux,[120] but one is carried through the synthetic space of several interrelated LSs: the woman drapes the mattress over a bridge railing, and it begins to fall; she rushes down some stone steps; and the mattress falls onto a street and is run over by a passing car.[121] This gag depends on the temporal simultaneity of the second and third shots and on the consequent delay, through their order, in knowing what happens to the mattress. And it is capped by a cut-in FS of the woman pulling the mattress out from under one wheel of the stopped car. The final gag occurs in a long-take LS of the old couple's bedroom as the mattress twice tosses them off the bed. And it is topped by a matchcut, as they throw the mattress out the background window, to the street outside where it drops on a woman pushing a wheelbarrow in front of the door to their building. She rips it open, and the sailor wanders away now dazed as well as drunk; a gendarme comes up and arrests her, and the couple drag their ruined possession back inside.

Several other films produced by Gaumont's new team of filmmakers— Bosetti, Arnaud, Feuillade—deploy this representational system with even more assurance. *Un Homme aimanté* (1907), for instance, reworks the premise of the

42. *L'Homme animanté*, 1907 (production photo)

absurdly transformed object, from *Le Matelas alcoolique*, in order to ridicule the efforts of an old bourgeois gentleman to regain some respect by drawing on a "heroic" past.[122] This film opens with several LSs of the old gentleman being harassed by two men as he is out walking—a comically matched exit and entrance has him escape from them only to run smack into them again coming from the opposite direction. Back in his drawing room, he looks at a suit of armor "guarding" a background door and mimes getting an idea. Reverse-angle cutting (on location) takes him from the exterior to the interior of a pawnshop, where from among an amazing clutter of objects he purchases a coat of chain mail. Two boys then take the chain mail to a small factory to be worked on before delivering it to the old gentleman. Because the location factory interior is rather dark (only "natural" light is falling from the right), what is being done to the chain mail is withheld until the next shot when the boys run past a cart full of metal cans that spring toward them—they have turned the chain mail into a giant magnet. This, of course, sets up a series of gags involving the old man after he dresses in the chain mail and stalks about his house and along several streets. The drawing room suit of armor, for instance, leaps out and knocks him over, everything from shop signs and manhole covers to pots and pans attach themselves to him, and even a lamppost bends over to stick momentarily to his back. Finally, literally encrusted with objects—the good bourgeois burdened with possessions, or rather stolen goods—he is taken to a police station and, after doffing the chain mail, is sent home. Circulating like a comic form of surplus capital through the film, the chain mail and its magical power eventually end up in the hands of the police. And the last image is of the police chief playing with the magnetized metal, as it causes a truncheon to magically dance up and down.

In *The Bomb* (1907), by contrast, Arnaud structures a single, repeated gag within a sequence of sustained alternation, beginning with the unlikely premise of a woman who comes out of her house to find a bomb on her doorstep. The space of this opening LS—with the doorstep (frame left) and a lane angling off into the background—recurs in alternation with various other locations, as one group of characters after another is summoned to defuse the bomb, approaches up the lane, and flees in fright without doing a thing. Each of the other locations introduces a local stereotypical figure of authority—gendarmes on a street corner, soldiers at a barracks gate, the mayor and his wife in their dining room (she is lashed into the armor and helmet of Brunehilde for their combat!). Eventually, the townspeople offer the task to their most expendable member—a prisoner already condemned to death—but even he panics and races back to hammer at his prison cell to be let in again. This repetition of the cell space allows a final twist on the alternating series for, as the opening space returns once more, a dog now approaches on its own to sniff at the bomb. Instead of letting the dog simply snuff out the threat by urinating on the bomb, the film produces a sanitized substitute, in keeping with its strategy of alternation—in the next shot of another house front, the animal runs in to grab a watering can in its mouth and exit. Success finally comes, then, in a cut-in FS of the dog tilting the can so that water pours out over the bomb, followed by a matchcut LS as the townspeople come up to thank their canine savior. And the film concludes in a conventional emblematic shot: dog and bomb are sitting on a table, with the "hero" decorated with a soldier's cap and a watering-can medal.[123]

Finally, *The Inlaid Floor Polisher* (1907) works a variation on the spatial-temporal gag structure of Pathé's *Tommy in Society* and *Diabolo*. This film begins with a couple ousted from their study in order that a workman can polish the floor—what he does, however, is toss the furniture into a corner and begin scrubbing the rug. In the second shot, another couple is eating at their dining room table when the overhead lamp begins to sway—this and their looks serve to place their room in an apartment building just below the workman in the study. As plaster starts to drop from the ceiling, they rush to a window and call for a cop, who enters just as the lamp crashes down on the table. The film now returns to the study and rug polished so smooth that workman, wife, and husband all slip and slide around as if on ice, finally falling so hard they go right through the floor—quickly followed by the cop and other couple who now come bursting through the study door. A cut back to the dining room, in a slightly closer shot, overlaps this action as the workman disappears through a hole in this floor (where the table used to be), with the others falling after him. The final shot places a third room below the other two, into which the half-dozen characters tumble and then stagger out, leaving a man cowering behind a pillow in the corner of what used to be his bedroom. In redirecting the movement across adjacent spaces from the lateral to the vertical, *The Inlaid Floor Pol-*

isher intensifies the mayhem created by its initial causal agent to nightmarish proportions.

If this system of representation was producing new structures of continuity in many of Pathé's and Gaumont's comic films, it also was sometimes altering the shape of Pathé's historical films. Again, a pair of film titles can help to map this deviance from the genre's traditional tableau style. *L'Assassinat du Grand-Duc Serge* (1905) and *Le Nihiliste* (1906) both tell the story of anarchist rebellions located, not in France—where anarchist attacks had been notorious just a dozen years earlier, and syndicalist strikes just then were breaking out in record numbers—but, more safely, in distant Russia. The earlier film, directed by Nonguet,[124] is comprised of only two LS tableaux—the first in a cellar where a dozen men are planning the assassination attempt, and the second on a street (with a painted-flat building across the background) where one of the anarchists tosses a bomb under the duke's halted carriage. Simple truc effects convey the explosion and segue into the same tableau now cluttered with wreckage (several carriage fragments are still falling from above, while ragged holes scar the background building), and policemen rush in to arrest the stunned bomber. *Le Nihilist* is more complicated, partly in that its anarchist rebellion turns into a family plot of vengeance. Briefly, a young woman named Nadia is arrested for anarchist activity, sent to Siberia, and dies en route; then her brother avenges her death by bombing the Saint Petersburg palace. Consistent with the genre's prior conventions, all but the last of this film's eight tableaux are introduced by brief intertitles. And most of these—for example, the opening arrest in a clandestine printing press room and the departure from a prison on Saint Petersburg's main square—are recorded in long-take LSs, in which the characters' movements, as in *L'Assassinat du Grand-Duc Serge*, are choreographed within the deep space of relatively detailed studio decors.

After Nadia's death (in the fourth shot), however, the brother's transformation into a "nihilist" is articulated in a synecdochical MS of him testing some explosive materials and constructing a bomb. His act of revenge is then narrated in a 150-degree reverse-angle cut from a LS of the palace courtyard exterior—where his mother hands him the bomb, once he has climbed up to a second-story window—to a ballroom interior (differentiated even more by an eye-level LS) where the czar is hosting a diplomatic reception. Only at the end of this tableau, after all the officials have paraded in from a background door, does the brother finally break in through the window (frame right) and explode his bomb. Through the smoke a final tableau dissolves in to reveal a heap of rubble against a painted flat of the distant Saint Petersburg square, including the prison from which Nadia originally left the city and over which a heavy snow steadily falls. Unlike Pathé's earlier Russian films, then, *Le Nihiliste* concludes in an unambiguous tone of moral judgment. This empty, emblematic tableau poignantly echoes the earlier LS tableau of Nadia's death near a cabin in a spruce forest clearing, which, after the other prisoners and guards have gone on, holds for a long moment on the snow falling over her abandoned body.

Un Drame à Venise (1907), one of the earliest films attributed to Capellani,[125]

43. *Le Nihiliste*, 1906

44. *Le Nihiliste*, 1906

relies even more on such features as close shots and matchcutting from one adjacent space to another. Its subject, too, is a family plot of alleged infidelity and grand guignol violence, but set in the "exotic" milieu of Renaissance Venice. An old beggar discovers the initial signs of a noblewoman's clandestine affair and exposes her would-be lover to the husband, who then kills him and attacks his own wife. This film, of course, makes much of its painted-flat decors, combined with the company's studio pool, to represent the public spaces of Venice—for instance, a gondola landing on one of the main canals and a tiny bridge over a canal just outside the family house—where the wife and "lover" rendezvous and are spied on and pursued. But the relationship between public and private spaces (almost all within the house) proves even more interesting, and right from the beginning. For the film opens with an alternation between exterior and interior spaces, based initially, as in *Le Braconnier* and *La Revanche de l'enfant*, on a sound cue. First, in a LS of the canal outside the family house, the "lover" poles a gondola forward from under the background bridge and, once centered in the frame, begins playing the mandolin. Next, an unusual AS introduces the woman at a tiny reading table in a small tapestried room, as she stands (in response to the mandolin) and exits right; and, in a ninety-degree shift of camera position, an eye-level LS of the bedroom matchcuts her entrance from a background door as she goes past a canopied bed to a window (frame right) and blows a kiss. In the recurring exterior shot, the "lover" returns her gesture toward the window, where she is now visible (upper frame left). After an ellipsis, presumably for a missing intertitle, another AS shows her writing a letter at her table—the overall effect of which is not only to set up the rendezvous but to define that small room as her own closeted space and the locus of her illicit desire. After receiving the letter in a public square, however, the "lover" stupidly tears it up—and an old beggar whom he has rudely rejected earlier quickly retrieves the pieces— setting up a counteraction to the narrative trajectory of the expected affair.

This counteraction begins, ironically, in a space just as marginal as the woman's. Now, the beggar sits at a small table in his garret room and, in a cut-in HA MS, pieces the letter back together, to discover its meaning for his own desire—revenge.[126] The husband, followed by the beggar, then pursues the "lover" to his own house and, from the background bridge, sees his wife let down a rope ladder from the window so that his rival can climb up from the gondola and into the bedroom. The anticipated climax comes as the husband breaks in on the couple: the two men draw knives, the wife flees into her reading room, and the husband finally stabs the intruder repeatedly at the window and pushes him out. A last shot of the house exterior then matchcuts the body falling from the window into the canal, while the beggar now gleefully watches from the bridge, and the shot holds until the canal surface becomes smooth and calm once again. And what happens to the woman? The husband breaks down the door to her room and discovers his wife, in a matchcut final FS, standing wrapped in a white robe, a dagger in her upraised hand. When he moves to touch her, however, she opens the robe to reveal that she is costumed in ornate Amazonian breastplates, with a heart pierced by an arrow positioned over her

45. *L'Espionne*, 1907

navel—and at this stunningly bizarre sight, the husband falls to his knees and weeps. Here, the woman's body becomes the textual site of wildly contradictory signs, as emblems of eros or passion war with those of chastity or fidelity. After her own writing has been destroyed and then reconstituted to be used against her, she herself, in the end, becomes a flagrantly torn figure whose spectacular textual excess seems more open to multiple reading than even that of the wife in *La Loi du pardon*.

L'Espionne (1907) tells another brutal story of thwarted passion and vengeance, somewhere in southern Russia. Here, a young woman named Vera spies on her own father, a Cossack chieftain, for a nearby Tartar encampment and, after a battle between the two forces, is caught and put to death. The film begins with a LS studio interior of the chieftain's tent where Vera overhears her father's plans and steals a map detailing the Cossacks' movements the following day. A simple form of reverse-angle matchcutting takes her up a gorge and onto a ridge where a Tartar lookout quickly seizes her. The Tartar camp to which he then takes Vera is at the bottom of another gorge, so that the latter camp is distinguished by location shooting rather than studio decors. Despite its use of locations, the film is quite concerned with spatial composition and lighting—most especially in the single battle shot-scene where a natural arching rock gateway throws the Tartars into silhouette, waiting in ambush in the foreground, as the Cossack chieftain's horsemen ride up from the background on the sunlit trail. In three subsequent shots, Vera is captured with the map, condemned in the chief-

46. *La Fille du Corse*, 1907   **47.** *La Fille du Corse*, 1907

tain's tent (despite her mother's attempt to intercede), and taken to an open field to be stabbed to death by a half-dozen men. As if this brutal act of "justice" were not enough, they then send a horse dragging her body off to the Tartar camp. This sets up the chase that concludes the film, for Vera and the young Tartar leader apparently have been lovers—it was he who took her to a hiding place (and kissed her goodbye) just before the battle, a place that failed to conceal her from the Cossacks. The chase sequence, consequently, is driven by the Tartar leader's love for her and not any desire to fight the Cossacks again, and the spectacle of her body being dragged repeatedly across more than a half-dozen shots is probably as shocking to the spectator as to him.[127] In that the final LS tableau focuses on his grief over her body in an open field, *L'Espionne* turns a story of intrigue into a cruelly tragic romance, not only implicitly condemning the Cossacks' cruelty, as well as the ethnic hatred determining it, but exaggerating the dangers of romantic love by "trapping" it in an "alien" culture.

La Fille du Corse (1907) uses a suitably "exotic" locale to stage yet another version of jealous passion, but in a clearly delineated two-part narrative structure. Here, a man discovers that his wife has a lover and shoots them both, then flees from the authorities into the hills. Bringing food and drink to her father, the young daughter eludes the pursuing gendarmes as well; but they surprise the two, and, rather than be taken, the father commits suicide. Much like *L'Espionne*, this film exploits the "attraction" of its location shooting—as in the LS of a sharply cornered hillside path in the village, where the man shoots the surreptitious lovers, and in the echoing LS of a similar path out in the country, where he finally turns the gun on himself. Some unusual framing choices also make economical use of one particular location: a sandy road running along a hillside bank covered in vegetation and broken only by wooden steps that lead up to the family's small house. The opening diagonal LS of this space introduces the Corsican family (and, once the father leaves, a letter from the lover), but, after the shooting, a closer shot focuses on the steps up which the wounded wife is carried, followed dutifully by the daughter. A third, even more distant LS of the same space then introduces the second half of the film, revealing a previously unseen door in the left foreground, out of which emerge the gendarmes to pursue the daughter. Perhaps the most interesting choice of framing accentuates the meeting between father and daughter—a HA FS/ELS of the two on a rocky hillside high above a sailing ship on a distant bay. And a cut-in MS of them eating bread dipped in a tin of soup underscores the privileged nature of their relationship, which, in the end, will pit them both against the authorities. Despite its apparent contradictions (how is it that the daughter can serve both her mother and father?), the film goes to great lengths to protect the patriarchal nature of its Corsican family.

All three of these "exotic," luridly violent films can be said to fall within an important variant of the French melodrama tradition, that of grand guignol.[128] This variant had its origins in the fait divers of bizarre crime stories whose grisly details and grotesquely marked bodies newspaper dailies such as *Le Petit Journal* or *Le Petit Parisien* and special "showcases" such as the Paris morgue, respectively, put on display for the amusement of readers and spectators during the latter part of the nineteenth century. Such faits divers also provided the basis for the *rosse* or "nasty" plays performed at Antoine's Théâtre Libre and other theaters in the 1880s and 1890s.[129] These were short plays of no more than one or two acts that, in re-creating "naturalistic" slices of life in Paris or in the provinces, almost always climaxed in violent crimes committed out of greed, passion, or despair, carrying the threat to the family or the bourgeois social order to the most horrifying conclusions. When the Théâtre du Grand Guignol opened in Paris, in 1897, rosse plays quickly became a staple of its popular programs, and many of these short works of agonizing suspense and horror were written by de Lorde, who claimed that grand guignol was as essential to modern life as gladiator contests and guillotine beheadings had been in earlier times.[130]

Now, some of Pathé's earliest successful films—*Histoire d'un crime, Un Drame au fond de la mer*—already had exploited the sensational stories of the *faits divers*. By 1906-1907, however, Pathé was beginning to draw directly on the rosse plays of Grand Guignol. Here, the best example is *Terrible Angoisse* (1906), which condenses one of de Lorde's more popular plays, *Au Téléphone* (first performed in 1902), into a screen version of less than five minutes.[131] According to Pathé's 1907 catalog, the story focuses on a Paris lawyer who is called to court, leaving his wife and son alone at their country house. When apaches break in, the terrified woman calls her husband on the telephone, but he can only listen helplessly as she and her child are strangled. Here, the new technological device of the telephone, as Gunning argues, serves to intensify the modern experience of the separated and threatened family rather than to circumscribe that experience and resecure their safety—for all the husband can do in the concluding tableau is throw himself abjectly on the corpses of his wife and son.[132]

Pour un collier! (1907) follows the same grand guignol trajectory in its story of passion, greed, and envy which ends badly, sending another distraught bourgeois gentleman into the depths of despair. Here, a woman is so infatuated with a string of pearls which her husband cannot afford that, one night at a party, he is driven to stealing a similar necklace from their hostess's bedroom. Unfortunately, she surprises him there, and, in desperation, he strangles her. The film does not end here, however; nor does it end with the husband's arrest, exoneration, or reconciliation with his wife. Instead, it returns to the setting of the opening scene, the couple's drawing room, where a jeweler (played by Linder) had first elicited the woman's desire for the pearls. After the killing, the husband passes through several "bridge" shots, which have the effect of accentuating his disheveled, distraught state and delaying the denouement, and he reappears in the drawing room to offer the stolen necklace to his wife. Suddenly (in a straight cut) she is replaced by the dead woman, and he backs away startled to the background window and falls out. Much as in *Pauvre Mère*, the truc effect here serves to objectify the husband's subjective sense of guilt and motivate his fall,[133] which continues through a matchcut reverse-angle shot of his body hitting the sidewalk below. The final tableaux then deftly summarize the cruelly ironic "moral" of this story in distinctly gendered looks. While the badly injured husband, who has been laid out on a centered couch, reaches out toward his wife in anguished desire and supplication, she simply turns away from him and, placing the pearls around her neck, stands admiring herself in a mirror (frame right). Boldly defying convention, *Pour un collier!* then caps this "misrecognition" of bourgeois morality and family harmony with an emblematic MS of the woman, proudly bejeweled, blithely smiling at the camera.

The greater percentage of Pathé's domestic melodramas, however, continued to fulfill the genre's convention of a "happy ending," with single children now playing a crucial role in both resolving narrative conflict and containing transgression. Although most adopted the new system of representation, a few still adhered more closely to the cinema of attractions. *Mauvaise Mère* (1907), for instance, deploys nearly a dozen LSs to narrate a working-class story of family union and disunion—involving a man with a school-age son and a woman with a younger daughter.[134] The film eschews any kind of cutting within scenes in favor of quite detailed decors, particularly for the garret rooms each pair of characters first inhabits. And it relies on concise gestures to represent their relationships: the marriage agreement is signaled by the woman plucking the petals of a flower and then accepting the gift of a ring, and she quickly begins cuffing the boy (once his father has left for work). After school one day, an old gendarme finds the boy crying before a cemetery gravestone (apparently his mother's), and, at the local police station, father and son are reconciled after beating marks are discovered on the boy's body—which leads the man to shove the woman and her daughter out of their new rooms in the final tableau. In its concern with exposing child abuse, however, *Mauvaise Mère* confines the problem to the working class and stakes out an extreme patriarchal position by unrelentingly villifying a woman and her relation to her daughter so as to valorize a father and son, with the public support of the police.

Some of the same elements figure in *Distress* (1907), but in a more complicated narrative and correspondingly complex system of representation. This film focuses on the relationship between an unemployed working-class father and his young daughter, beginning with his theft of a baguette and his quick arrest and conviction. In a telling detail at the police station, the father and daughter are roughly separated while a woman happily exits with her recovered baguette. In a brief sequence of crosscutting, the girl is introduced to a convent orphanage school classroom, and the father escapes from his prison cell and returns to steal the girl willingly away from the convent school playground. Reunited with his daughter, the man now becomes a "good father" (a "repentant" rather than an "incorrigible" ex-convict, as in the earlier *Au bagne*)[135] and, in two autonomous shots, gets a construction job and brings some food home to the girl in a simple garret room. This restored family is threatened, however, in a sequence of intercut adjacent spaces as a gendarme comes to the construction site in search of the escaped convict. He surprises the father working on the roof, which causes him to slip, and a matchcut describes his fatal fall to the ground below, where the gendarme tries to comfort the girl after her father is carried off on a stretcher. *Distress* then concludes in two more autonomous shot-scenes. First, the gendarme takes the girl home to his wife and two children, where she is immediately welcomed in a bourgeois-style dining room, and they all sit down to supper in a tableau that echoes the scene of the more spartan meal she and her father shared earlier. The last, much more static tableau, however, is of a cemetery, with snow falling, as the girl, in the company of the gendarme, places flowers and prays at her father's simple grave marker. By the end, this film has criticized an unfeeling public system of justice, while praising the private action of a "civil servant" family in taking in an orphan, and honored a "good" working-class father, while also eliminating him in order to move his daughter into a slightly higher social class.

A quite different catastrophe separates a child from her parents in *La Petite Aveugle* (1907), but then another inadvertently serves to reunite the family once again. This film begins with a series of autonomous LSs that establish the family's bourgeois status and the inability of a team of doctors to restore the young girl's eyesight. In several similar tableaux, but now on location, the girl's mother is struck and knocked unconscious by a passing automobile, and a gypsy woman who happens by seizes the girl and "recruits" her for begging. The last part of the film, however, combines intercutting and cut-in close shots to create not, as in *Médor au téléphone*, a comic attraction but a heightening of suspense. First of all, in a LS interior of the gypsy woman's shack, the girl escapes her captor (who drunkenly falls asleep at a table) by tying strips of cloth together and going out a background window. But, in a 180-degree reverse-angle cut to a LS of the shack's exterior, the girl drops, due to her blindness, from the window straight down into a well. An unusual FS of the well interior shows her struggling in knee-deep water and calling out. On this sound cue, now a new alternation begins as people run up to the shack exterior and a gendarme descends into the well on a rope to pluck the girl out of the water.[136] An even longer LS of the shack exterior then caps this sequence in order to show the gendarme and girl being brought out of the well and going offscreen, after which the gypsy woman appears at her door to yell in protest, only to be seized and taken off in the opposite direction. Much like *Le Détective, La Petite Aveugle* returns, in its final tableau, to the bourgeois drawing room of its opening, where the girl's father is sitting anxiously beside her mother who is recuperating on a couch. The disheveled gendarme brings their daughter through the background door and then tactfully exits as the family gratefully comes together in a foreground "portrait." If the medical profession cannot cure every threatening physical ailment, this film suggests, at least the police are there to protect nice bourgeois children from far worse social "defects."

Lutte pour la vie (1907), by contrast, tells a rags-to-riches story in which romance and marriage serve as a final reward for hard work—and, through its tramp hero, the film traces one reason for the then current French migration from the provinces to Paris. This vagrant, much like Hugo's Jean Valjean, wants to work but is refused in one of the initial shots that describe his wandering through the countryside. Moreover, when he comes upon a better suit of clothes at the side of a road, his desire to improve himself, in more than appearance, is accentuated in a cut-in AS of his transformation. In Paris, he follows a woman in a carriage from the Gare du Nord (making a brief "tour" of the city) and then offers to carry her bags into her apartment. Next, he sells some newspapers on the street, but gives all the coins he earns to a destitute woman with two children. Finally, his generosity and determination pay off when he finds a dropped wallet and, in a cut-in MS, takes out a business card, further magnified in an ECU insert, for A. Heuzé (an in-joke reference to Pathé's chief scriptwriter). The card lets him return the wallet and its money and get a white-collar desk job as a reward, in a scene that also introduces the daughter of the grateful factory owner. Her presence then becomes important in the film's climactic sequence when a fire breaks out in the nearby family house. For, in an elliptical series of shots, the new employee spots the young woman at an upper-floor window, rushes into the smoke-filled house, finds her collapsed in a bedroom, and carries her downstairs and outside to her anxious father. After two autonomous LSs, which quickly narrate the father blessing the couple, followed by their wedding, the film concludes with the former tramp driving his new bride into the country, to the very spot where he initially changed his clothes and began his journey to respectability. In *Lutte pour la vie*, social mobility is realized through the fable of an individual of good character who can take advantage of coincidence, complemented by the verisimilitude of consistent location shooting—and Pathé implicitly acknowledges its own ideological stake in such a fable of success.

A final pair of films neatly summarize the social relations of class, gender, and generation in Pathé's domestic melodramas and, in their elaboration of a two-part narrative structure, demonstrate just how accomplished these films had become by the summer of 1907. The first, *Le Bon Grand-père*, poses the question of whether a young man's bourgeois parents can accept his marriage to a woman who does seamstress work for the family. The first five shots of the film (all but one of them LSs) focus on the young woman: in the family dining room (where she resists the son's advances one evening), for instance, and, in "bridge" shots, as she journeys the next morning from her tiny one-room apartment to the family townhouse.[137] The exception is a FS of her dressing and sipping coffee in her own room that morning, which succinctly contrasts the cramped limitations of her world with the spaciousness of the bourgeois family milieu. The next sequence then focuses on the young man, who happens to be a painter, as he continues to court the young woman (an intertitle describes him as her "first love"), ending eventually in her room where she extracts a promise from him. "Seven months later," in the room in which he is painting, she tells him she is pregnant; and, after his mother angrily orders her out of the house, the son follows.

Two subsequent autonomous shot-scenes, introduced by intertitles, close off the first half of the film and open up the second, concisely narrating a change in the young couple's situation. First, they are forced to send the baby off to a wet nurse in the country (the woman is ill, the man spends all of his time painting); three years later, having prospered, they go to the rough dwelling of a peasant couple, who sadly returns their daughter to them. By chance, one day, the son's father meets the young woman and her daughter in a city park, and his kind greeting sets up a resolution to the family rift by shifting it somewhat comically onto the grandparents. In a FS, the old couple argues over a dice board game they are playing (still costumed in bed clothes), and then each surreptitiously, in a separate MS, writes a letter to Amalie, the granddaughter—and each letter, in a CU insert, asks her to keep it a secret from the other. A further FS shows them continuing the argument, while getting dressed in good bourgeois black, and exiting separately. As its title suggests, the film then follows the grandfather (not the grandmother), again through "bridge" shots, as he goes to a toyshop and comes out laden with two dolls, a drum, a little chair, and a hobby horse. Multiple reconciliations are now played out in a single tableau of the young couple's new drawing room: the grandfather arrives first to play with Amalie and is then hidden by her mother, the grandmother arrives to play with the child and embrace the woman she once rejected, then Amalie (somewhat like the girl in *Le Loi du pardon*) brings the grandparents together to sit on a central couch, and, finally, their son arrives to express his surprise and pleasure. In a sense, the daughter "legitimates" the older generation, and hence herself as well; once the embodiment of a *mésalliance*, she now marks its erasure.[138] And to conclude its continually shifting *focalization* of character, *Le Bon Grand-père* ends, much like *Le Détective*, on an emblematic MS family portrait, with the young girl at the center.

Les Deux Soeurs tells a very different story of mésalliance between social classes. This film focuses on two sisters and their sick mother who all live together in a garret room (described in the opening LS), where the young women (whose light-colored costumes contrast with the mother's black dress) also do "put-out" work as seamstresses. Delivering a bundle of clothes to a shop one day, the elder sister, Lucy, meets a man who drives her home in his touring car, in a sequence of matched exits and entrances across three LSs. Back in the garret room, Lucy argues with her mother and angrily leaves to join the man who is still waiting for her outside. In matched exterior and interior LSs, he takes her to his modern white stucco house and into a large drawing room. There she writes a letter that, in a CU insert, expresses her frustration over the "privations" and "disappointments" of her life and asks her mother to "forget and forgive" her. An intertitle, "A fatal letter," introduces a closer FS of the garret room, which serves to heighten the now bedridden mother's reaction to the letter—she collapses in shock—and the younger sister's grief at her death.

This tableau effectively closes the first "act" of *Les Deux Soeurs*, and another intertitle, "A year later," marks the beginning of the second half. The younger sister is now selling flowers on the street, and she meets Lucy, dressed in the latest fashion, coming out of a jewelry shop. Lucy invites her sister into a waiting carriage, takes her "home," and, in an exterior LS, introduces her to the man whose wife she has now become[139]—his reaction is to rub his hands together in anticipation and follow them into the house. What follows, intriguingly, is a FS of the younger sister at a dressing table being transformed by new clothes, makeup, and hairstyle.[140] Although Lucy seems to be responsible for this change, it also serves to fulfill the man's desire, as revealed in the following LS, where the two women now join him in the drawing room. After Lucy is called away by a maid, he quickly propositions the frightened sister and is only stopped from attacking her by Lucy's return. She believes her sister's explanation rather than his and, in a moment that is recapitulated outside the house, leaves him to go off with her sister. In a final tableau, preceded by an intertitle translated as "The return to duty," the two sisters resume their work as seamstresses in the same garret room where the film began. Now that any explicit male presence has been erased, however, the newly reaffirmed bond between sisters is determined by their shared relationship to the dead mother. Both are dressed in black—as if replicating the mother's figure—and her chair sits conspicuously empty in the room's background.[141] In the end, a double absence or erasure seems to "lock" them into the "woman's part" of suffering victim. However, although social mobility through illicit means seems roundly condemned as dangerous in *Les Deux Soeurs*, it is less certain whether the sisters' final position should be read as a punishment for disobedience, as a working-class "fate" to be endured, or, perhaps less likely, as a sign of social injustice.

Between 1905 and 1907, I have argued, Pathé's domestic melodramas and their grand guignol variants played a critical role in the emergence of a narrativized cinema in France. Initially, several relatively distinct models of transformation—involving redundancy, alternation, and other changes in framing—worked to subordinate spectacle attractions within a linear and then a narrative logic, across a range of generic categories. These then coalesced—in conjunction with inserted intertitles and letters and accompanying sound effects—to form a new system of representation within Pathé's dramatic and realist films as well as its comic films. And, as the features of this system came to be disseminated, increasingly they were organized according to a principle of sequential repetition, sometimes within the format of a two-part narrative structure. The overall effect of this system of fragmentation and succession was to guarantee, as Burch would say, the *legibility* of a film story, especially an unfamiliar one, no matter where or how a Pathé film was exhibited.[142] In other words, this turn to narrative in the French cinema became a crucial strategy of standardization for the company to ensure a measure of editorial control over its product. And that control increasingly shaped the discourse of its films so that they now addressed the spectator in either a conventionally moral voice or even, as in *Pour un collier!*, a distinctly "ironic" voice. Furthermore, within Pathé's dramatic and realist films, this new system of representation was mapped onto a specific historical site of French social relations, coalescing around crucial axes of difference according to class and gender, particularly in terms of criminal or moral deviance from bourgeois social norms. And the patriarchal family served as the principal site that was threatened and ultimately legitimated by that deviance. Finally, in that a number of Pathé's domestic melodramas, beginning in the summer of 1906, seem specifically to address a female spectator, they point to an apparent shift in the composition of the French cinema audience, as well as a possible strategy of legitimation within the industry. Here, as Heidi Schlupmann suggests, in her study of the German cinema audience,[143] the significance of the early female spectator demands further consideration—especially given that, unlike the Pathé films that reach conclusions explicitly valorizing patriarchal family relations, women-centered melodramas such as *La Loi du pardon*, *Pauvre Mère*, and *Les Deux Soeurs* consistently seem to end in less firmly coded, ambiguously legible tableaux.

The Cinema of Attractions (continued)

During this complex process of transformation in France, the cinema of attractions refused to simply and abruptly vanish, like an interchangeable prop or body in a Méliès film. In fact, both Méliès and Pathé perpetuated its characteristic mode of representation throughout this period, partly because the exhibition format of the music halls and fairgrounds still provided a viable venue for such a cinema. Perhaps as might be expected, both companies did so precisely in those early film genres most closely identified with spectacle attractions—the trick film and féerie as well as the biblical film and, to a lesser extent, the historical film. And, in the case of Pathé, particularly, some of these films achieved a remarkable degree of artistry.

Méliès, for instance, continued to celebrate both his power as a magician and the cinematic *truc* of the simple cut in such single-tableau trick films as *La Chaise à porteurs enchantée* (1905). Here, in what is essentially a smoothly timed stage act, Méliès produces a couple in eighteenth-century costumes out of an empty sedan chair, transforms each one of the pair into the other, replaces them with himself as well as servants, and finally folds all of them back into himself and then makes even the chair disappear. In *Les Cartes vivantes* (1905), which survives in a beautifully hand-colored print, Méliès re-creates another stage act, but plays knowingly on the size and status of his props. After leaning forward and holding out a playing card so that it is "readable" to the camera, he produces (through cuts and dissolves) huge versions of several cards on a stand, from which, successively, a "real" queen of hearts and king of spades step forward and then return to their places. Then, in a clever reversal—which will be re-worked at the end of René Clair's *Entr'Acte* (1924)—a "real" king bursts through the huge paper card, unrobes to reveal himself as the magician, and rushes back at the card, only to vanish (on a cut) and finally poke his head back out through the card and laugh. In *Bulles de savon* (1906), the stage act has Méliès creating, from blown soap bubbles, several women's faces that float suspended against a black background and then dissolve into full-length women (posed on a pedes-tal), whose butterfly wings, in a further truc cut, he grabs and appropriates for himself. At the end, he indulges in another characteristic and narcissistic rever-sal—after a large soap bubble dissolves in around his seated, bowed figure and lifts slowly off the pedestal, he himself runs in from offscreen to admire this image of his own engendering.

Other Méliès trick films set in a single decor stage more obviously night-marish visions. *L'Alchimiste Parafaragamus* or *La Cornue infernale* (1906), for in-stance, turns the magic of transformation against a sleeping medieval alchemist. In a barrage of superimpositions, simple cuts, and multiple exposures, a host of creatures—from a serpent and spider to a white ghost and the spiky figure of Satan—converge on the alchemist's study in a frenzy that culminates in the spec-tacle of a giant flask exploding and killing the alchemist, over whose body Satan poses in triumph. In *L'Ile de Calypso: Ulysse et Polyphème* (1905), this magical power is framed within the féerie decor of the legendary Greek tale, but the violence is no less grotesque. Surrounded by female musicians, Calypso lures the hero toward a cave, only to dissolve away and be replaced by a huge clutch-ing hand and then by the Cyclops's face, into whose central eye Ulysses plunges his spear—and blood oozes out to cover the monster's nose and beard. The hero flees the returning Calypso, who along with her attendants creates an oddly conventional "curtain call" tableau against the black void where a deeply mi-sogynist nightmare had just been played. Although Méliès obviously had lost none of his playful, fetishistic exuberance in these short films, his bag of cine-matic tricks remained largely unchanged.

In the féeries, Méliès seems to have reached a similar plateau of develop-ment. Here, he even abandoned some of the cinematic components of the con-tinuity system he had exploited in *Le Royaume des fées* (1903) and *Le Voyage à travers l'impossible* (1904) and instead adhered more closely to a theatrical form of spectacle. Evidence of this can be seen in the hugely successful *Le Raid Paris-Monte Carlo en deux heures* (1905), which drew its episodic story from the increas-ingly popular French pastime of touring by automobile, or in *Rip Van Winkle* (1905), a colorful forest fanstasy based on Robert Planquette's 1884 comic-opera version of the Washington Irving tale.[144] But the shift is even more clear in *La Palais des mille et une nuits* (1905), inspired as much by an 1880 pantomime of *Aladdin* as by Pixerécourt's early nineteenth-century adaptation of the tale.[145] The latter film consistently privileges the spectacle of elaborate "oriental" decors and trick effects done within rather than across tableaux. Particularly striking are the deep-space decors of a jungle garden transformed by layers of flyaway flats and accentuated by left and right foreground entrances as well as a cavern palace interior populated, in turn, by dancing skeletons, a fire-breathing serpent, strange frog-men, and finally a bevy of classically draped women and ballerinas in tutus. Because of their frequent internal dissolves, the film's shot-scenes seem to be longer than ever; and the prince's quest for the treasure that will assure his marriage to the princess repeatedly turns into a kind of world tour, eclectically combining (in good bricolage fashion) imaginary realms such as an ice palace with the "real" sites of supposedly exotic, uncolonized cultures—from India, Indochina, and Indonesia. And, in a clever twist that exposes the mask of the "other" and its dangers, the Palace of the Arabian Nights, where the treasure is hidden, turns out to look much like the Musée Grévin in Paris.[146]

Based on an Arthurian legend, *La Fée carabosse* (1906) presents a similar quest through the rocky wilderness and ruined castles of a medieval landscape. Here, a troubadour tricks a witch (offering a bag of sand instead of coins) into granting him the magical power to rescue a trapped princess; and then a fairy spirit, in the form of an old man, inexplicably protects them both from the witch's revenge. The premise for this narrative is established in a single LS tableau of a castle interior, which takes up nearly one-third of the entire film's length. Color rather than deep space provides the chief attraction in this initial encounter between the troubadour and the witch, especially in the costumes of the latter's clown assistants—bold striped sweaters of green, red, and black, with bald heads topped by tufts of red hair—and the huge golden picture frame they bring in, within which the desired princess materializes in a red, blue-green, and white gown. The quest then takes the troubadour in a consistent lateral movement, across a series of spaces, culminating not so much in his release of the chained princess (which seems perfunctory) but in his confrontation with a host of creatures—a giant frog, owl, and griffin—outside the second castle's walls. The rest of the film simply sends the troubadour and princess in the opposite direction, with the witch taking a short parallel flight through a single skyscape, until the climax comes quickly in what looks like the same tableau that concluded *Le Royaume des fées*. Perhaps the only unique feature of *La Fée carabosse* is the way the film opens and closes with its title arching in glowing red and yellow letters across the top of the frame. Initially, the witch appears, in AS, looking anxiously up at the words; at the end, the couple, also in AS, kisses under what now reads as a garlanded blessing.

Perhaps the most telling evidence of this change, or lack of change, in Méliès's work comes in *Les Quatre Cent Farces du diable* (1906), which derived in part from the Châtelet's revival, *Les Quatre Cent Coups du diable*, opening on 23 December 1905.[147] Once the show closed after a successful run, the following summer, Méliès produced a one-reel (or 300-meter) film of his own around the episode of "the phantom carriage" which he had been asked to film and screen as an integral part of the Châtelet stage féerie.[148] His film presents an English engineer, William Crackford, who acquires a quantity of exploding magic pills

48. *Les Quatre Cent Farces du diable*, 1906 (production photo)

by signing a pact with the alchemist Alcofrisbas (alias Satan/Méliès) and then embarks enthusiastically on a series of travels with his assistant. This narrative, of course, serves as a pretext for displaying all manner of spectacle and for "sending up" once more a male representative of the "rational" and "modern" through the forces of Satan, who is seconded here by a Jewish messenger, the "seven deadly sins" (all female), and assorted animals. The film's initial tableau of Crackford's laboratory is cluttered with model vehicles—a train engine, automobile, dirigible, balloon—so many of them major props from previous Méliès films, in fact, that it looks like a personal museum. Indeed, this sense of representing and reworking the past is picked up in the subsequent dozen or so tableaux, especially in the use of large-scale models, multiple exposures, and intercut adjacent spaces to represent the phantom carriage's journey through the heavens, drawn by an apocalyptic, skeletal horse. Surprisingly, however, Méliès uses theatrical rather than cinematic trucs here in order to achieve most of the genre's requisite transformations, which almost has the effect of turning much of the film into the record of a stage performance. And, in the tableau of an Italian inn's kitchen, the paired entrances and exits of frolicking chimpanzees, black cats, and cooks become so repetitious that the frenetic mayhem they produce frankly grows tiresome. The one provocative moment that recaptures some of Méliès's former diabolical exuberance in this otherwise disappointing, although well-crafted film comes in the final clou of spectacle, when a huge painted-flat cat face rises up in hell to disgorge Satan's minions through its mouth (in the form of women in either black cat skins or bat wings) and Crackford is literally skewered and roasted over a well-fanned fire.

What accounts for this decisive shift or "stagnation" in Méliès's féeries? One reason may have been economic. Until recently, it has been assumed that *La Palais des mille et une nuits* was the first film produced in the new studio erected at Montreuil, and that the costs of its construction may have forced Méliès to concentrate his efforts more narrowly in the production of his later "big films"—specifically on their mise-en-scène.[149] Yet Malthête has now determined that the second Méliès studio was not constructed until late 1907.[150] Moreover, earlier féeries, such as *Damnation de Docteur Faust* and *Faust et Marguerite*—which derived from operas by Berlioz and Gounod—already evidenced such a commitment to "theatrical" spectacle.[151] *Faust et Marguerite*, for instance, eschewed transformations until the finale and instead privileged spectacular decors as well as choreographed actor movement, whose rhythmic effects probably depended, as Malthête has suggested, on the musical accompaniment of familiar operatic excerpts.[152] More significant perhaps, then, was the special status Méliès's féeries were achieving as "feature attractions" in the best music halls and theaters of Paris—which led to exclusive exhibition contracts with the Olympia, the Folies-Bergère, and the Châtelet. That may well have encouraged him to emulate the stricter standards and practices of a high art tradition—which, in France, meant the theater[153]—a tradition that also strongly marked the genres of historical and biblical films. Whatever the case, together with his continued reliance on a more or less artisan mode of production, Méliès's increasingly fixed mode of representation and narration tended to set off his films as different from those of his rivals, Pathé and Gaumont.

Yet even when Méliès tried to respond, by imitation, to Pathé's newly acquired dominance in the fairground cinemas and elsewhere, the results were mixed. Beginning in late 1905, many of Méliès's trick films suddenly adopted the contemporary settings of Pathé's popular melodramas as well as comic chase films (with their recurring hapless gendarmes), and some eschewed cinematic trucs altogether. Unfortunately, this sometimes had the effect of reducing the spectacle attraction of the tricks without any compensatory heightening of interest in either the decors or the narrative. *L'Hôtel des voyageurs de commerce* (1906), for instance, divides its simple hotel decors into a short corridor (frame left) and a room (frame right), within which a drunken traveler is tricked by the other hotel guests. One problem here is that occasionally all the action is confined to just half of the frame, leaving the other empty and devoid of interest. Another, more important, is that the tricks are few and either visibly contrived rather than hidden (a dummy in the bed, a ghost appearing out of a cabinet) or even pointless (a huge key unlocks the drunk's room).[154] The only surprise comes at the end, when the drunk seems to explode as he is being tossed in the air. Although no more full of tricks, *Le Tripot clandestin* (1905–1906) works somewhat better simply because there are surprises in the decors and a concluding twist in the slight narrative. Here, at the warning of a police raid, an elaborate gambling room that has attracted a dozen or more people changes, in seconds, into a fully equipped woman's clothing store—through a series of stunning transformations built into the set as well as rapid costume changes. Once the gendarmes leave, the clothing store reverts to a gambling den again; but then they return, now accompanied by the mayor, and too quickly for any transformation other than the gamblers' flight and a dowsing of the lights. After the mayor relights the lamp over the roulette table, however, he soon convinces everyone to join him as the civic authorities take the gamblers' places and reproduce the tableau of illicit pleasure which opened the film.

In some films with a contemporary setting, however, Méliès continued to exploit specifically cinematic trucs, but here the effects were not always well managed. In *Le Maestro Do-Mi-Sol-Do* (1906), for instance, a clown-faced musician tries to practice in a music room where the instruments keep moving about and changing in size or identity (and some of those moves are not all that well timed).[155] It is his own initial kicks and shoves that set off the series of gags, and the reciprocal violence done to him culminates in an unlikely flaming piano and exploding drum. The most successful of these later trick films, *Les Affiches en goguettes* (1906), again works at the expense of several gendarmes. Here the frame is filled with a large billboard, advertising such things as corsets, face powder, meat extract, and genuine cocoa to the sidewalk passersby in the foreground. At the billboard's center is a graffiti, "Mort aux flics," over which Méliès himself papers a poster for the Parisiana show, *L'Amour à crédit*. Through simple cuts and multiple mattes, the figures in the various posters come to life—the Parisiana couple step forward, breathe deeply, and try some of the advertised products—but return to poster form when a pair of gendarmes saunter by. Once again animated, they pelt an old gentleman reading a newspaper, quickly followed by the gendarmes—with plates and bottles, feathers and flour, and confetti snow. Now the center poster vanishes, exposing the graffiti to the gendarmes; and the whole billboard suddenly falls forward, flattening them, to reveal all the poster people jeering from behind a park fence. When the gendarmes try to scramble over the fence, the billboard springs back up, pinning them in place with their heads poking out of holes, and the poster people merrily dance through in the foreground. Extremely witty in its play on both cinematic and theatrical trucs and on the foreground/background unmaskings so characteristic of French stage farce, *Les Affiches en goguettes* pushes the cinema of attractions to the point of reflexivity. Its climatic attraction directly invites the spectator to join the poster people in thumbing their noses at the hapless authorities—through the revealing mirror image that erases any difference between what lies before and behind the screen.

Less successfully, Méliès also sought to imitate Pathé's dramatic and realist films more directly in such films as *Jack le ramoneur* (1906) and *Les Incendiaires* (1906).[156] In a sense, *Jack le ramoneur* could be said to follow the bricolage model of combining several different genres into a single format, perhaps explicitly for an audience of children.[157] A chimney sweep dreams of becoming a prince in a fairy kingdom and, the next day, discovers a hidden box of "treasure" with which he tries to run off. At least half of this film is devoted to depicting Jack's dream, making him a kind of mirror image of the spectator as the central subject within and the chief spectator for Méliès's sumptuous tableaux of spectacle. A dissolve replaces the boy's barren garret room with a painted-flat castle beyond a lake over which swans draw a fairy godmother reclining on a couch. Another dissolve replaces that with a cavern interior studded with jewels and stars, into which the fairy godmother and the boy ride on a huge snail; there she transforms him into a prince with a throne, from which he can view a procession of heralds and soldiers who do a formal dance ending with a ballerina's pirouettes. The dream comes to an end, however, with a dissolve back to the garret room, where a man kicks Jack awake and sends him off to work. In the following LS tableau of an exterior brick wall (also linked by a dissolve), Jack crawls up the inside of an exposed chimney flue and discovers the box of "treasure" in a niche near the top. Suddenly the film shifts into a chase as Jack confronts the house's owner in a drawing room and, after a brief struggle, flees with the box, pursued by servants and gendarmes. Using location settings (a rare strategy for Méliès), the chase itself is interesting because it eschews the usual comic gags (let alone trick effects) and also consistently directs the characters' movements from foreground to background in at least four separate shots—the first two of which are even linked by a dissolve rather than a cut. Although the film apparently ends in Jack's capture, he is pardoned and rewarded—in a kind of moral admonition as to how good little boys should act when their dreams come close to being realized.

Within Pathé's production output during this period, the cinema of attractions model continued to dominate certain film genres as well. Interestingly, this was perhaps more true of the company's biblical films and trick films than its popular féeries. Indeed, throughout 1905–1906, Pathé's biblical films seem to have taken precedence over its historical films, perhaps in response to the Catholic Church's increasing interest in the cinema for educational purposes. In their deployment of autonomous LS tableaux (recorded from an eye-level camera), however, both *Le Regne de Louis XIV* (1905) and *Les Martyrs chrétiens* (1905) equally exemplify Pathé's now standardized system of representation within the latter two genres. Only two tableaux survive from *Le Regne de Louis XIV*, but each displays an array of meticulously detailed costumes on human figures artfully arranged within a deep-space landscape. And a slow pan extends one painterly composition into a panorama of the Versailles gardens. By contrast, *Les Martyrs chrétiens* uses studio decors rather than locations to compose its three, even more autonomous tableaux. In the first, "Les Martyrs," against a painted-flat background of the Roman Coliseum arena (including a cardboard horse and chariot),[158] a band of soldiers marches in with several Christian prisoners—their movement described in a slight pan—and, once the emperor (seated in the background) has given the signal, hoists one onto a foreground cross. After a straight cut replaces the man with a mannequin, lions are set loose in the arena, and one beast quickly begins tearing at the garroted body. A similar painted flat provides the setting for "Daniel dans la fosse aux lions," with Daniel chained to a centered post against a darkened background area, out of which emerge several lions, followed by the superimposition of a protective angel. Daniel's chains miraculously fall away so that he can walk among the lions, even patting and kissing one as if it were a dog. The third and last tableau, "Le Festin de Balthazar," describes a palace interior with arched, darkened background areas, before which the king and his courtesans are lolling drunkenly across the floor. Suddenly, a superimposed hand (in CU) begins writing, "Mane, Thecel, Phares," against the darkened left background; and Persian soldiers quickly rush in to stab the terrified king and carry off the women, as chunks of the palace walls begin to collapse.

The same style of representation marks *La Vie de Moïse* (1905). Brief inter-titles—"Moses Saved from the River" or "The Burning Bush"—introduce each of this film's six autonomous shot-scenes, which reproduce familar "Bible lesson" episodes from Moses' story. The tableaux rely exclusively on painted-flat decors, recorded in LS in the studio, and the supernatural moments are generally created by simple cinematic trucs: either cuts or dissolves. The one exception to this pattern occurs in "The Parting of the Red Sea." This episode is comprised of three tableaux, and the transitions between them are marked by very brief sections of heavily scratched film stock (as crude signs of a supernatural effect), separating the Hebrews' successful sea crossing (between huge painted-flat waves) from the Egyptians' drowning (apparently in the real water of Pathé's studio pool). That difference is further marked in the third tableau by a change in camera position to HA LS, perhaps in order to better represent the struggle of the Egyptian soldiers and horsemen. The very next tableau—in which Moses produces drinking water out of the desert rocks—then is set off by the return to a waist-level camera position. Framing and editing, consequently, serve equally with the mise-en-scène to differentiate two crucial moments of the film's spec-tacle. And the gender difference determining that spectacle finally is made ex-plicit in the last tableau—the women dancing in ritual adoration around the golden calf are dispersed by Moses and his stone tablets, after which he himself turns into a radiant white figure, in front of whom a single male worshiper remaining next to the broken idol kneels in supplication.

If *La Vie de Moïse* seems calculated to appeal to a broad spectrum of Chris-tians (and perhaps those of the Jewish faith as well), it is possible to read the final tableau—with its focus on a single worshiper in a rather "spartan" setting—as anticlerical, and pitched more directly to Protestants than to Catholics. There is no such equivocation in *L'Inquisition* (1905), in which the anticlericalism that sometimes marked Pathé's films is unmistakable. Here, the torture chambers of the Inquisition are put on display as a spectacle of terror, in a half-dozen studio tableaux, one of which deploys the company's trademark pan—like those in *Au pays noir* and *Au bagne*—to follow the head inquisitor and his priestly pro-cession through three adjacent cells. The various "interrogation" devices they inspect on their rounds produce the kind of luridly fascinating horror usually associated with grand guignol—for instance, a revolving wooden wheel finally rakes the body of one man across a "boxed set" of spears.[159] And the film con-cludes in the sensation of an auto-de-fé, where two "martyrs" are burned in a public square before a massed group of priests and their followers.

The provocative anticlericalism of *L'Inquisition* may have proved too offensive to market successfully—for the title was dropped in Pathé's 1907 catalog. In any case, the company's next religious film, *Le Miracle de Noël* (1905), specially produced for that year's Christmas season, was much milder in tone and almost secular in subject. Here, a half-dozen LSs stage the spectacle of an updated fairy tale whose charm is reminiscent of *La Fée printemps*. The film begins on a winter night with snow falling over a small church (frame left), in front of which a boy is begging, not too successfully, from the parishioners who have been attending midnight Mass. In the second tableau of the nave interior, the boy kneels in the foreground before collapsing, after which the stained glass figure of a saint comes alive, steps down from its background window, and carries him off. Once outside, the saint magically revives the boy (giving him a new suit of clothes as well) and places him on a donkey. In exchange, the boy is asked to help the saint distribute Christmas presents to children, and the last half of the film aptly repeats the first half's alternating exterior and interior spaces. Now, however, the two figures (along with the donkey) cross the rooftops of the city, stopping so that the boy can crawl down a chimney, which leads, in the next tableau, to a bedroom where two girls are sleeping. There, the boy himself magically produces a tree laden with gifts and decorations, delighting the two girls when they awaken. In the final tableau of the same rooftop, the saint simply helps the boy crawl out of the chimney; and they slowly go off, presumably to continue their work—perhaps even, the film implies, in the houses of the very children who may be watching in the audience. By offering a moral for children not only about receiving but giving as well, *Le Miracle de Noël* served Pathé nicely in defending the legitimacy of its films as "wholesome" family entertainment.

One year later, undoubtedly prompted by the popularity of its 1903 film as well as by Gaumont's new *La Vie du Christ* (1906), Pathé produced a second version of *La Vie et la Passion de N. S. J. C.* (1907). Although this version continues to adhere to the genre's tableau style, it also incorporates some elements of Pathé's new system of representation and narration. Brief intertitles again introduce each of the film's forty-three autonomous tableaux, which, in contrast to the earlier version, give added attention to the "Naissance de Jésus" and the "Enfance de Jésus." Nearly all of these tableaux have been recorded in LS in the studio, with painted-flat decors that sometimes describe a strikingly deep space for the choreography of actor movement—as in "The Adoration of the Magi," where Joseph exits a large barn interior through an open door (center background) and stands on a distant rock, in order to call the shepherds and magi in to cluster around Mary and baby Jesus. The decors also often seem darker than before—perhaps to better set off those costumes and props selectively marked by stencil color. Specific representational strategies are deployed at particular moments, however, as if to distinguish one series of episodes more clearly from another. Artificial light, for instance, seems to clear a foreground desert space for the procession of magi against a darkened sky. Cut-in MSs isolate, first, Jesus against a flat, neutral background (after Pilate's intertitle, "Ecce Homo") and, later, Saint Veronica displaying the magically imprinted icon of his face. Finally, although some truc dissolves and superimpositions occur earlier, the best are

49. *La Vie du Christ,* 1906

50. *La Vie du Christ,* 1906

51. *La Vie du Christ,* 1906

52. *La Vie du Christ,* 1906

saved for the end. Once Jesus dies on the cross, for instance, the stencil color is replaced by a light blue tinting, which carries over into the tomb, where artificial light through a background arch now singles out the soldiers sleeping in the foreground until Jesus slowly rises out of a centered crypt. Only after he vanishes does the stencil color return in the stunning golden figure of an angel, whose halo seems to have been constructed out of a brightly polished film reel. And, for the ascension, Jesus turns into a white-robed figure surrounded by golden rays, all framed by a doughnut-shaped cloud, which progressively grows smaller as he lifts into the heavens.

Gaumont's *La Vie du Christ*, directed by Guy and Jasset, also generally adheres to the tableau conventions but, otherwise, differs greatly from either of the Pathé films. Brief intertitles, for instance, introduce each of its twenty-five tableaux, segregating them into autonomous shot-scenes, which consistently end in fades to black.[160] At least half of these tableaux rely on painted-flat studio decors, most of them supposedly in emulation of James Tissot's famous Bible illustrations.[161] Yet this film, too, uses specific cinematic techniques quite selectively. In "Jesus before Caiaphas," for instance, a short pan describes Jesus' movement toward and then away from the Palestine ruler who turns him over to Pilate. Something close to a reverse-angle shift then marks the transition from the first-floor interior where Pilate washes his hands before the mob (framed in a background window) to the exterior where Jesus is flogged while Pilate watches from a background balcony. The miracle of Saint Veronica, likewise, is emphasized in a cut-in MS display. The principal distinction of Gaumont's *La Vie du Christ*, however, is its unique combination of realist and melodramatic elements, or what might be called "masculine" and "feminine" discourses. On the one hand, there is a deliberate effort to achieve some measure of verisimilitude—through both shooting on location and using authentic props. This is especially true of the scenes in the manger or in the Garden of Gethsemane or during the journey to the crucifixion, one shot from which describes the long procession (curving up a rocky hillside) by means of a ninety-degree pan. On the other hand, the film repeatedly insists on privileging women in relation to Jesus. Only three miracles are represented, for instance, and all of them involve women: the Samaritan, the daughter of Jaïre, and Mary Magdalene. The scene in which Peter denies Jesus also focuses on the women around the disciple as much as on him. And it is a half-dozen women, not Simon, who come to Jesus' aid when he collapses beneath the weight of the cross. Not only is this emphasis on women suggestive of Guy's involvement in the film's production, but, much like Pathé's domestic melodramas of the same period, it raises questions about what audience was expected for its exhibition.

Despite these differences, however, the Gaumont and Pathé versions, along with the latter's earlier biblical and historical films, shared one significant characteristic: they were sold in a variety of lengths, including versions of multiple reels. Pathé's *La Vie et la Passion*, for instance, was released in four parts (totaling 950 meters), the last of which, "Passion et Mort de N. S. J. C.," was then subdivided into five separate short reels (comprising 410 meters of the complete film).[162] In whatever length or form it was exhibited, this new "passion play" was extremely popular in the United States.[163] Gaumont's *La Vie du Christ* seems to have been available either in individual shot-scenes (anywhere from fifteen to forty-three meters in length) or else as a full-length 600-meter film.[164] Much like their predecessors, then, neither film constituted a "finished product" or commodity; instead, they encouraged exhibitors to purchase and exhibit whatever combination of tableaux would best suit their programs.[165] In the context of the transition to narrative films in France, the biblical film thus continued to promulgate a form of cinema based on the principle of a spectacle series rather than one of spatial contiguity and temporal sequentiality organized according to a narrative logic.

Shortly after the production of its new *Passion* film, Pathé also began to reinvest its resources in the historical film genre. One of the more prestigious films in Pathé's 1907 production schedule was *Amour d'esclave*, which drew on the nineteenth-century "Neo-Grec" or "Olympian" classical revival in painting and its penchant for sentimental Greek or Roman subjects depicted, as Caroline Dunant writes, "in brilliantly colored, potent, and accessible images."[166] For the subject of *Amour d'esclave* is the tragic consequences of Polymos's obsessive love for Chloë, a beautiful slave dancer, in ancient Athens. More than half of the film is played out in the painted-flat decors of just three autonomous tableaux, all but one of which are recorded by a camera positioned at eye level. The high point of this series makes much of the company's tinting and toning process in combination with stencil color: in a blue-toned dream scene (opened and closed by dissolves), Chloë dances with twenty other women on the floor of a sunlit rocky cavern, climaxing when their long white veils are transformed into a "wheel" of rainbow colors. Yet even this film evidences some signs of Pathé's new system of representation and narration. The final sequence, for instance, is composed of four shots that alternate between an exterior prison gate and an interior cell, into which Polymos follows Chloë (his wife Chrysis has ordered her arrest)—and both die there from drinking poison. One striking feature of *Amour d'esclave*, however, is the exaggerated gestures of its principal actors, not only in comparison to the relatively restrained acting style of Pathé's dramatic and realist films but even to that of the biblical films.[167] Asking the actors to emulate a "high art" form of melodramatic pantomime, perhaps associated with the "toga play,"[168] was symptomatic of yet one more strategy in Pathé's drive for legitimation in 1907. And the film's production closely coincided with Benoît-Lévy's arrangement to have Michel Carré record on film his own pantomime drama, *L'Enfant prodigue*, for screenings at the Variétés and the Châtelet theaters that summer.

Pathé's trick films during this period also remained largely within the cinema of attractions model. Those produced by Velle, between 1904 and 1905, exploited the full spectrum of truc effects, but often continued to concentrate on a single cinematic device per film. *L'Amoureux ensorcelé* (1905), for instance, relies on stop motion and straight cuts to turn its simple story of a dandified petit-bourgeois suitor into a spectacle of increasing mayhem. Thoroughly bewitched, when the woman he is wooing suddenly is replaced by the devil (nattily attired in matching Renaissance jacket and pantaloons, with two long feather "horns"), the suitor blindly attacks him, systematically destroying every single object in her drawing room, and finally has to be hauled away by the police. *D'Où vient-il?* (1905) then literally inverts this process by using reverse motion to let a man in long johns leap out of a lake onto a dock (on location) and gradually dress up as a strolling petit bourgeois (complete with top hat, umbrella, pipe, and dog) and walk jauntily off. *Créations renversantes* and *La Poule phénomène* (both 1905), by contrast, depend on the attraction of a MS or AS, together with "invisible" cuts, to extend a stage magic act—the latter of which reworks the chicken-or-egg argument as a recipe puzzle. In rapid succession, a white-wigged clown produces a full-grown hen out of a large egg and chicks out of her own eggs, stuffs the hen into parchment paper and burns it in a bowl, turns the chicks back into eggs cracked over the bowl, stirs the contents and flips out the hen once more. *La Fée aux fleurs* (1905) uses a similar LA MS to display the unmediated, voyeuristic view of a woman dressed like Madame de Pompadour, opening a window to water some plants (all against a black background). Through dissolves, brightly colored flowers and vine leaves appear and disappear; she blows a kiss and fades out to be replaced by a rose bouquet that finally turns into a giant red bloom at whose center she reappears—the former politically suspect emblem of decadent artifice transformed into a goddess of fecund, if fanciful, metamorphosis. And, in *Cascades de feu* (1905), such marvelous transformations turn abstract as, first, a spiraling and, then, a cascading fireworks display shifts through a rainbow of brightly tinted colors.

Several other Velle trick films not only are more elaborate in design but their "magic" serves as a kind of publicity. Essentially, *La Ruche merveilleuse* (1905), for instance, is a dance film in which a painted-flat beehive becomes home to a troupe of female dancers playing a queen bee and her helpers. Although the queen bee is threatened by a giant spider, in a brief fable of fidelity and cooperation, the principal function of the film's decors, costumes, and truc effects, much as in *Metamorphose du papillon*, is to publicize the unique Pathé stencil color process. Restricted to a single painted-flat tableau of an eighteenth-century chateau garden, with an unusually deep perspective, *L'Album merveilleuse* (1905) is even more overt. It begins with an artist displaying a special album of illustrations to a less-than-interested aristocrat—his initial trick is to get the album to stand on end and increase in size. Once the album is opened to reveal a human figure drawn to scale, his next trick is to tear off the page, crumple it, and toss it on the ground, from which a real person leaps up in the very same costume. This proceeds to the point where six different men and women are lined up before the aristocrat, who is now excited presumably by the prospect of peopling his empty garden (and life). The interesting thing here is that the first book page bears the anachronistic title, "Album Pathé-Frères," which transforms the film's magic into a blatant form of self-advertising—except, as the Pathé catalog indicates, that the artist turns out to be a charlatan.

Looking much like a condensed féerie, *La Peine du talon* (1905), by contrast, comes off as an explicitly didactic fable. Here, in a LS studio forest of multiple, stencil colored flats, a vaudeville "professor" (dressed in a yellow plaid coat, black top hat, and white shoes) is happily collecting butterfly specimens. Each time he catches one and examines it in his magnifying glass, a cut-in POV CU displays the brightly colored insect fluttering within a white ring against a black background. Suddenly he is seized by a pair of giant grasshoppers and surrounded by a host of female dancers in bee, butterfly, and dragonfly wings. The latter take him off to a cavern where, in another LS tableau, he is accused, convicted, and punished by being impaled on a toadstool with a golden pin—and, in order to emphasize the "poetic justice" of this revenge, a matching overhead FS exhibits him wriggling against a gray background. After being released, the professor vows never again to harm any of nature's creatures, providing a proper model of sentimental morality for all the children in the presumed audience. Yet the film itself ends in a tableau of posed women, with a kaleidoscope of shifting color rippling across their bodies and wings, oblivious to its own fixed display of fetishized female figures.

The genre reached probably its highest level of achievement, however, after Velle left Pathé to work in Italy and the Spanish cameraman, Chomón, took over direction of the company's trick films. Several of these films deftly extend the stage magic acts that had been a staple of Méliès productions (which Chomón once distributed), but with an intriguingly gendered twist. *Le Sorcier arabe* (1906), for instance, stars a big, heavily bearded magician (in an "oriental" costume of turban, yellow cloak, and red trousers) who, against a painted-flat oasis, uses a scimitar to create a row of flames, out of which dissolve four women who dance around him. After repeating this trick, in which the women reappear with huge colored flowers over their heads and then dissolve back into flames, the magician produces a couch on which one of the women is reclining and gazes down at her. Suddenly, in a straight cut, the two figures are reversed; the magician admonishes the woman, who hides her eyes, and, after he tosses her in the air, a cascade of flowers falls around him. This gendered "drama" of gazes—which empowers his gaze at the expense of hers—then concludes in an emblematic tableau as the magician reclines on the couch again, surrounded by his women, and smoking a hookah pipe. *Les Roses magiques* (1907) involves a similar performance, but in modern dress. Here, against a painted flat of stone columns, leaves, and flowers, a slim, trimly bearded magician transforms bouquets of roses into three dancing women and back again with ease, before producing a half-shell radiating streamers on which one of the women reclines. Then, once the women have disappeared, the magician gets up from the shell to uncover, in a straight-cut reversal, a veiled figure that has replaced him—it is one of the women—and, in a sweeping gesture, spills her two companions out of the veil as well. Finally, he reduces the women into single roses, folds them into one, tucks it in his buttonhole, and, with a satisfied look, sits back on the shell.

If such films, much like Méliès's earlier trick films, seemed to depict women as little more than malleable images controlled by the transformative power of men, others directed by Chomón did more than momentarily reverse those gender positions. Within the single tableau of a dark stage-jungle clearing, *Le Charmeur* (1907), for instance, orchestrates both theatrical and cinematic trucs in order to turn the tables on an "oriental" magician. Here, the magician lures a huge yellow caterpillar out of the jungle with his flute-playing and stuffs it, once subdued, into a large white chrysalis suddenly standing center stage, out of which a woman with black and yellow butterfly wings emerges (through a dissolve) to leap and soar about, easily eluding his grasp. She, rather than the magician, then produces five more butterfly women out of the chrysalis, who all perform a dance that ends with them suspended and fluttering in midair. In the finale, the magician himself is turned into a caterpillar (which hops off, perhaps to begin a new cycle of transformation); and the butterfly women, joined by garland strands, continue to dance and soar on their own. An even more spectacular reversal occurs in *La Scarabée d'or* (1907). Again, within a single-tableau studio decor (a stone staircase of European design), an even older "Arab" magician captures a golden beetle and tosses it into a cauldron, where out of the bursting yellow flames emerges a female figure decked out in a gold beetle headdress and multiple dragonfly wings, suspended in the air. The flaming cauldron quickly turns into an elaborate fountain, behind which the figure descends, and jets of water arc out in pulsing red, blue, yellow, and green. Suddenly, an eruption of smoke transforms the fountain of water into a fireworks display of whirling colors almost filling the frame. The dragonfly woman, along with two cohorts, reappears to challenge the old man and now tosses him into an iron bowl, which has replaced the fountain and fireworks; in a final display of power, she hovers over it in triumph.

The most elaborate of Chomón's early trick films (co-directed with Velle) was *Les Invisibles* (1906), which, while incorporating certain features of Pathé's new system of representation, also experimented with original spectacle effects. The story initially involves an alchemist and his assistant who discover a magic potion that causes anyone who drinks it to disappear. The potion is quickly stolen by a pair of thieves, however, and that sets up a series of comic trucs, concluding in a courtroom where the alchemist regains control. In the opening scene, *Les Invisibles* uses a cut-in MCU of the alchemist, as he experiments with a liquid concoction, to magnify the gag of having the top of his bald head blown off—the assistant then stuffs things back in and sews him up in the following LS. After the discovery of the magic potion, the thieves (dressed in commedia dell'arte outfits) break into the alchemist's now empty study, in a sequence of 180-degree reverse-angle cutting, and watch in amazement as the various parts of a human skeleton dance out of a background closet. There they find a flask of the potion and, once having divined its secret, go off to steal some new clothes and get a free meal. The last part of *Les Invisibles* then introduces several new truc effects for its final tableaux of spectacle. Against the painted flat of a town square, the two thieves magically flip off the lights in the foreground and turn into silhouettes to lead their pursuers off on a "Chinese shadow puppet" chase, as the painted flat becomes a moving diorama background.[169] The alchemist and his assistant are mistakenly arrested (the thieves get off scot-free), but they quickly take over the studio set courtroom of the final tableau. The magic potion makes one of the three judges disappear, and the alchemist and his assistant replace them on the bench, where their white features stand out now against a darkened set (in contrast to the thieves' earlier silhouette figures). In a comic variation on the apotheosis finale, the remaining judges and lawyers are transformed into large dancing vegetables (apparently stencil colored in the original) and then vanish, leaving the two men all by themselves, brightly lit and laughing, in a frame that is otherwise completely black.

As these titles demonstrate, Pathé's trick films seemed to have challenged—in quality as well as quantity—and triumphed over Méliès on his own terrain. This was no less true of the company's féeries. Although these films, too, generally adhered to the spectacle conventions of the cinema of attractions, they relied much more on cinematic trucs (contra Méliès) and also began to incorporate certain innovations developed in the dramatic and realist films. In the summer of 1905, probably the most successful of Pathé's films was *La Rêve à la lune*, in which a fantastical "trip to the moon" becomes the last clou in a bricolage series of drunken hallucinations.[170] This féerie begins as a drunk (Zecca himself) staggers up the stairs of an apartment building to his room, dropping an empty wine bottle as he reaches his door.[171] And a cut-in MCU comically magnifies his difficulties in inserting a key into the door's keyhole. Once inside the room (which is unusually spare), he reaches for another bottle on a centered table, and both vanish—in their place stands a woman with a huge bottle for a body. What ensues is a little spectacle summing up the highs and lows of drinking. Two other bottle women magically appear from behind the first, and they all dance around the drunk until one turns into a barrel on which is painted a glaring, angry face. This conscious hallucination is followed by an unconscious one as the drunk falls asleep in bed and, through a dissolve, awakens on a park bench in the LS of an empty city square. There he yells at the moon, tosses a brick that chips it into a quarter moon, climbs up a nearby lamppost, and clambers onto a window ledge. A truc FS then shows him climbing up the side of a building, tossing down potted window plants and unhinging shutters, until he reaches the roof. Now a wind begins blowing across the LS of painted-flat rooftops and sends the drunk, who grabs onto a drainpipe, flying off on an "impossible voyage" and the last stage of his nightmare.[172] Still clutching the detached drainpipe, he speeds across a moving diorama sky-and-landscape background, is nearly obliterated by bursts of lightning and rain, and finally disappears behind a flat of heavy clouds. The clouds then part to frame the moon as it enlarges into a giant face. The drunk climbs out of the lower clouds and into the moon's open mouth, the moon smacks its lips with pleasure, and the drunk reemerges to lean tipsily out of its mouth and fall out. In a single truc FS, suspended upside down against a background sky of stars, comets, and planets, he now drifts slowly from top to bottom across the frame. A straight cut rather than a dissolve rudely reintroduces the final tableau of his room as the drunk falls out of bed, picks up an empty bottle, and tosses it at a grandfather clock—and, in an echo of the gag in the city square, its moon-shaped face shatters. In effect, *La Rêve à la lune* remotivates the fantasy of the féerie (à la Méliès) within the "real world" aberrations of an individual, but leaves it up to the spectator, or exhibitor, to decide, in the end, whether drinking is something to be enjoyed or condemned.

Undoubtedly the most popular of Pathé's féeries, however, was *La Poule aux oeufs d'or* (1905), which was still taking up seven pages of promotional material in the 1907 Pathé catalog.[173] La Fontaine's fable of a peasant who gains and loses a fortune by acquiring a white hen that lays eggs full of gold coins serves here as the pretext for a four-part, stencil color film, in which each part, introduced by a brief intertitle, presents its own climax of spectacle.[174] The opening tableau, for instance, is marked by a Pathé trademark: a long pan across the "deep space" painted-flat decors of a medieval city follows two pickpockets from the city gate to the small stage where a magician is performing for a crowd.

53. *La Poule aux oeufs d'or*, 1905 (poster)

Replacing them there, a peasant wins the hen in a lottery, and a reverse pan follows him back to and out the same gate. Later, in the peasant's henhouse, the chickens are transformed into women skimpily clad in either green or yellow feathers and red cockscomb caps who, against a backdrop of two red rooster heads arching toward the sun, perform a ballet that concludes in a mound of large golden eggs.[175] This second section intercuts adjacent spaces—the relatively "realistic" farmyard and henhouse—on matched exits and entrances,[176] just as the next intercuts the peasant's new palatial interior and, beneath its floor, the cellar where he hides his treasure. The major spectacle of this third section, however, turns out to be, not the huge rolling eyes and grasping arms that seem to threaten the miserly peasant in the cellar, but—once the pickpockets have discovered his secret—a revelatory ECU insert of an egg held in one thief's (painted-in) hands. There, inside the egg, a devil's head dissolves in, literally spitting out coins in a thin golden stream[177]—an image that may dissuade the thieves from stealing the hen but not the hidden bags of money. In the film's final section, after the peasant has killed the hen in despair and broken the last egg open in a yellow explosion,[178] an evil fairy reduces him to rags and then sends him, through another dissolve, into the Grand Palais–like decors of the concluding ballet.

This "Ballet de la poule aux oeufs d'or" condenses several strands of significance in the film. For one, it reworks components of the earlier ballet—with an even greater number of the same female dancers now performing before an immense golden egg, and framed by a row of rooster heads on tall gold-tinsel bodies. Here, however, the peasant is quickly excluded as further punishment for his miserliness, and the ballet is staged directly for the spectator's pleasure. Intriguingly, in the last part of the ballet, after the arching glass and ironwork background has gone dark, the golden egg turns into a woman costumed in a veil of coins before a huge yellow sun and two women (one wearing a rooster's cockscomb) perform a pas de deux ending in a foreground embrace, while the remaining women stand in rows (left and right) and hold large eggs aloft, each of which pours out a stream of gold coins. The devil, along with the miserly peasant, is strangely erased from this fantasy of plenty and replaced by eroticized women whose production of eggs and coins constitutes a fetishizing of the "natural" as an "unnatural" spectacle for consumption. This spectacle, of course, presents a perfect emblem for the Pathé company itself at the time, in that its own films (bearing the Pathé rooster trademark) seemed to be producing profits as abundantly as the eggs here produced coins. And, as a spectacle encouraging consumption (rather than miserliness), this dazzling golden show also draws a mask over the actual circulation of money within the film. Not only do the thieves successfully make off with all of the peasant's wealth, they are already present at the opening magic show, picking the pocket of someone in the audience, just as the magician is making a child disappear by means of a cinematic truc. And there, in miniature, and considerably displaced, is a privileged trace of the cinema industry's own story of profit-taking.

Several other Pathé féeries of approximately the same date offer striking

54. *La Poule aux oeufs d'or*, 1905

differences in tone and mode of representation. *L'Antre de la sorcière* (1906) tells the story of a clownish peasant who leaves his fiancée after an argument and is drawn into a tavern that looks more like the devil's lair. Most of the usual cinematic and theatrical trucs occur in this one LS tableau, befuddling the peasant, until his fiancée reappears as the last of a series of "dream" women—and now a godsend. An ending emblematic MS encapsulates the film as the couple stand sullenly back to back, then turn together, and kiss. Although surviving in an incomplete print, *L'Obsession d'or* (1906) seems to tell a similar story of desire and despair. In the LS of a garret room, which he can no longer afford to rent, a struggling artist imagines, through dissolves, that one of his paintings turns into a chest full of moneybags and that he is invited into a fairyland of dancing women. While this dream narrative is condensed into a cut-in MS, in which, seated at a table, he revels in a shower of golden coins, a parallel narrative turns on a contrasting AS of his female model exchanging her earrings with a pawnbroker for some real coins. In the final LS tableau, she returns to the garret room, not only with enough money to pay the rent, but in time to save the artist from hanging himself—her role as savior closely linked to her sacrificial exchange value. *Voyage autour d'une étoile* (1906) combines elements from previous Pathé as well as Méliès films to send an astronomer off to a not-so-distant star, a trip that ends in an unexpectedly wry catastrophe. A relatively lengthy LS tableau lets the astronomer decide exactly which planet or star to visit—his choices are presented in POV shots, ostensibly through a telescope—and how to get there; his mode of travel turns out to be a giant soap bubble. Yet nearly as much attention is given to the running gags that the astronomer and his assistant engage in as a vaudeville team. The women of the star he visits inhabit a space very similar to the one concluding *La Poule aux oeufs d'or*, but a Saturn figure quickly boots him out of its "door"—and he drifts back to earth under his trusty open umbrella. In the final FS tableau, however, he falls onto and is speared by a rooftop weathervane capped by the Pathé rooster, so that his wriggling, spitted body looks ready for roasting.

The most intriguing of these féeries, *Le Fils du diable à Paris* (1906), rivals *Les Invisibles* in energy and inventiveness.[179] The premise for this film's witty script is that young Satan has grown so bored with hell that his exasperated parents send him off to Paris, with Molière's good Doctor Sganerelle as a guide, in hopes that a little vacation will revive him. This leads to an irreverent fantasy, studded with cinematic truc effects. Young Satan and Sganerelle journey to "the capital of the world" by automobile, for instance, one segment of which includes a LS of a deep tunnel through which they come forward, lit only by wildly swinging flares. Once they arrive in Paris, a crowd quickly gathers around this charmingly surreal vehicle with its travelers dressed in medieval costumes and its strange driver sporting an owl's head, topped by goggles. Then, when young Satan gets drunk in a restaurant and cannot pay, a brief alternating sequence—soon to be extended in *Médor au téléphone*—lets Sganerelle use his giant syringe like a telephone to call up hell, where, in MS, Satan answers at his office desk and resignedly mails off extra money. Satan's messenger immediately shows up at the restaurant, of course, and the good doctor, in a cut-in MS/FS, now conjures up for his protégé a series of women in what looks like a glass display case. Bored with all of them, from an exotic dancer to a coy bourgeois shopper, he suddenly perks up at the image of a simple peasant woman (even devils are not immune to cultural stereotypes) and falls in love. Staging a car wreck, Sganerelle conspires for the two lovers to meet; but when young Satan tries to marry the woman, a church crucifix causes him to flee for his life, straight back to his parents. Relieved to be in hell again, our hero is doubly delighted when the peasant woman shows up among a procession of the "damned" (disgraced and in despair, she had committed suicide), and this audacious plot twist lets the couple "live happily ever after."

In 1906–1907, along with its production of *La Vie et la Passion de N. S. J. C.*, Pathé began to either remake its earlier féeries—such as *La Fée des roches noires* and *La Fée printemps* (both 1907)—or else rerelease them (see, for instance, its 1907 stencil color version of *Ali Baba*). In conjunction with this strategy of remakes, Pathé returned to *The Thousand and One Nights* stories for a féerie version of *Aladdin* (1907), photographed by Chomón apparently under the direction of Capellani. *Aladdin* fulfills the conventions of the genre in measuring out its clous of spectacle, sometimes in the form of unexpected cinematic trucs. In the opening tableau, for instance, Aladdin's desire is represented in an unusual dream image: while he sleeps in the foreground, a globular-edged frame fades in (as if attached, like a plaque) over the background wall, within which his double lifts a bedside curtain in order to pledge his love to the reclining princess. Subsequently, his lateral path through an underground temple garden decor (to discover the magic lamp that will make him a "prince") is traced by pans, while simple cuts produce the miraculous transformations that threaten to trap him there. Rubbing the magic lamp calls up not one but a menagerie of genies whose shape seems to depend on the occasion—a gnome with yellow wings and a red grass skirt to release Aladdin from the underground temple; a scaly green, blond-haired giant (an offscreen platform in the foreground produces the illusion of his size) to transform him and his mother along with their humble house; a half-dozen black slaves to serve the "prince" and princess after their wedding; and a fairy godmother to foil the evil magician's theft of the princess at the end. In the apotheosis finale, this latter figure then reappears from within a huge replica of the lamp to preside over the other genies and dancing women who perform for the reunited couple. Only six intertitles demarcate the film's sixteen tableaux, so that certain scenes are composed of multiple shots that trace Aladdin's movement through adjacent spaces—the rocky desert canyon and underground temple garden, the exterior and interior of his house—linked by cuts and often, but not always, by matched exits and entrances. What is perhaps most interesting here, however, is that the camera angles change slightly (shifting twenty or thirty degrees) for the interior and exterior tableaux of Aladdin's house, precisely when he is transformed into a "prince," and they revert to the original position when the magician intervenes to undo him. Differences in framing thus seem to accentuate crucial differences in the mise-en-scène, according to the demands of narrative as well as those of spectacle.

One last Pathé féerie, Capellani's *Cendrillon* (1907), extended even further the interest in narrative continuity which was becoming evident in *Le Fils du diable* and *Aladdin*. This adaptation of the Cinderella story, of course, contains its requisite moments of spectacle—as in the fairy godmother's transformation of the poor girl into a princess (a half-dozen girls in cupid wings quickly weave a network of thread into a costume around her) and of the pumpkin into a carriage (through a "rapid montage" of several shots). The most accomplished of these comes in the final tableau, after Cinderella is brought to the palace interior, only to be rejected by the prince—as the fairy godmother dissolves in, the prince spins Cinderella in a pirouette, and precisely midway through she is again transformed into a princess, before whom he kneels in recognition. Perhaps the most intriguing, however, reworks the device of the internally framed image, from *Aladdin*, once Cinderella has had to return to her stepmother's home in rags from the ball. As she sits weeping in the kitchen, the background wall explodes out to reveal, in the small-scale dimensions of a distant set, the beginning of the prince's search for the woman whose foot will fit the glass slipper, after which the wall returns to normal, through reverse motion. Here, perhaps even more clearly than in *Aladdin*, spectacle serves a double function, one in which its effect as an attraction comes close to being subordinated to, and redirected to accommodate, the demands of a parallel strand of narrative. And

55. *Cendrillon*, 1907 (poster)

the film does this—much as do its counterparts in the domestic melodrama—by seeming to address a female spectator.

Within the féerie genre, the cinema of attractions, in fact, seemed close to dissolving away in *Cendrillon*, in that the film's textual system was so full of features "imported" from Pathé's dramatic and realist films. First of all, although *Cendrillon* opens in the deep-space studio decors of the stepmother's kitchen and salon, several scenes are shot on location, most notably the ball that takes place on the grounds of an actual chateau and during which a pan follows Cinderella and the prince as they move in a semicircular arc among the other dancers.[180] Moreover, not only is character movement smoothly traced through adjacent spaces—for instance, the studio kitchen and salon—by means of matched exits and entrances, but it also flows through linked location exteriors and studio interiors.[181] The most striking of these represents Cinderella's escape across four shots: up a garden path and then a country road, to a door in the house exterior, and finally into the kitchen. Although the first two shots in this sequence are necessary to the narrative (the prince's men pursue Cinderella in one and then turn back in the other), the third shot of the house exterior is not, except in that it stresses a continuous action through more and more contiguous spaces. Finally, this film sometimes substitutes narrative details for spectacle attractions— as in the fairy godmother's creation of a dance teacher who instructs Cinderella for the ball. Toward the end of the film, this narrative detailing verges on a kind of emblematic significance. In distinctive back-to-back HA LSs (in different wooded clearings), the prince's representative comes from background to foreground in search of the lost slipper's owner—approaching first a reclining diva figure surrounded by her female servants or admirers and then a lone peasant girl feeding a flock of geese and chickens. Although the one assumes a pose of extreme diffidence (she has no need of the prince's love or his class status), the other weeps in desolation. Taken together, these new strategies of representation in *Cendrillon* encapsulate some of the more important strands of development, particularly for Pathé, in the transition to a narrativized cinema in France.

5

The Pre-Feature, Single-Reel Story Film,
1907-1911

I love the cinema because I find in it an intense description of contemporary history.
The film unreeling upon the screen often teaches us better than does the printed page.
ANATOLE FRANCE

As I remember it, all the films shown at . . . my own first neighborhood theater
[the Family Electric, in Chicago] . . . were French Pathé, and if I loved the posters
I loved the titles and subtitles even more. They were always tinted red, with enormous lettering,
and there were two of the famous Pathé roosters at the bottom of each title,
one at the right and the other at the left.
EDWARD WAGENKNECHT

BETWEEN 1907 AND 1911, the French cinema industry underwent a further transformation that had complicated repercussions for the narrative cinema model that had recently emerged, especially in Pathé's melodramas as well as its short comic films. Impelled by Pathé's successful strategy of expansion, the industry divided into relatively distinct sectors of production, distribution, and exhibition. Permanent cinemas, most of them in the larger urban centers, became the chief site of exhibition, with Pathé and Gaumont each controlling its own circuit of cinemas. New production companies such as Eclair, Eclipse, and Lux formed in order to supply those cinemas outside Pathé's and Gaumont's orbit as well as the fairground cinemas Pathé had largely abandoned and, perhaps most significantly, the huge number of nickelodeons that had grown up in the United States. Others such as Film d'Art and SCAGL were established as part of Pathé's attempt to attract a more regular white-collar and bourgeois audience and further legitimize the cinema industry. And, in the process, Méliès found himself squeezed out of production completely. As a consequence of the shift away from direct sales to a system of film rentals, distribution soon became the linchpin of Pathé's empire, and the company contracted to market not only the product of its foreign subsidiaries, such as Film d'Arte Italiana in Italy, but also that of Film d'Art and SCAGL. Moreover, companies like Aubert and AGC arose to distribute the increasingly numerous films produced in Italy and Denmark, and Vitagraph opened its own distribution center in Paris. While tentatively securing its position as the world's largest film producer and distributor, Pathé's moves also had the effect of provoking more competition than it per-

179

haps had bargained for, especially encouraging an increasing quantity of film production.

Pathé's expansion strategy also led to a much greater degree of standardization, regularizing each sector of the industry in quite specific ways. French cinemas could screen a completely new program each week now that a half-dozen companies were producing and distributing weekly packages of different films on a regular basis. The single reel of 200 to 300 meters gradually became the standard story film format,[1] particularly for the more "serious" genres (approximating a one-act play), while the half-reel of approximately 100 to 150 meters became standard for the increasingly popular comic films. And once the rental system had begun to wrest control from the exhibitor, the producer-distributor could ensure that each screening of a film was more or less uniform from cinema to cinema. Perhaps the most innovative form of standardization to appear was the continuing series, a marketing strategy that came to dominate those genres whose production, in film after film, could be organized around a single central character now identified by name—and by an actor or nascent star. Beginning as early as 1907, Pathé, for instance, was releasing a comic series named after the recurring character of *Boireau*, which led to the later, even more regular series of *Max* and *Rigadin*. In 1908, Eclair began drawing on the popular fiction of the dime novel, to initiate a wildly successful detective series, *Nick Carter*, as well as other adventure series, including the western, *Riffle Bill*. And Gaumont soon followed with its own comic series, *Calino* and *Bébé*. Yet other genres continued to maintain their popularity without necessarily resorting to the marketing strategy of the series, most notably the contemporary story films of Pathé, Gaumont, and, now, Lux.

This standardization suggests at least two lines of inquiry for an historical study of the pre-feature, single-reel film in France. One involves questions about the system of representation first developed in Pathé's dramatic and realist films and rapidly disseminated throughout other genres as well. First of all, did this system remain relatively stable and in wide circulation during this period, or did it undergo further changes, and, if so, what was the specific nature of those changes? Similarly, whether the changes appeared in the form of either new strategies or re-emerging elements of the cinema of attractions, did they result in anything like a radical reconstitution of the narrative cinema model? For instance, did most films continue to insist on an indirect form of address, constructing a consistent spatial-temporal orientation for the spectator through a variety of viewing angles and distances, more or less regulated by the new rules of continuity editing? Second, what attitude or "voice" did this system tend to adopt toward the stories it narrated and how did it position spectators? Specifically, did the French model continue to be marked—as already has been shown—by the kind of moral, psychologizing voice Gunning has argued was an essential element of Griffith's Biograph films of the period,[2] or was it marked more and more by the ironic voice of grand guignol films like *Pour un collier!*? And, what role, vis-à-vis the images, did intertitles[3]—whether expository or dialogue—and musical accompaniment[4] play in constructing a narrational position and controlling the flow of narrative information? All in all, to what degree did this model, appropriating the language of a *Moving Picture World* reviewer, allow a specific film to "show the plot so clearly that no trouble [was] experienced in understanding the theme of the story," no matter where it was shown?[5] Finally, in what ways did the French system of representation continue to be mapped onto the referential body of Third Republic social relations and the axes of difference which constructed the "normal" and the "deviant?" Did that mapping undergo any crucial shifts or realignments, and how was it shaped—for the purposes of distribution—by the increasingly prominent "foreign" body of American social relations and by the growing demands of film censorship in the United States?

A second line of inquiry concerns the development of models of narrative construction in the pre-feature or single-reel film.[6] Besides the episodic structure associated with the early féeries and historical or biblical films as well as the simple structure of repetition associated with the chase film, at least two general models of narrative construction seem to have vied for dominance during this period.[7] One was what could be called the model of the one-act play which, to some extent, already was established in Pathé's dramatic and realist films. According to this model, a single, central incident formed the basis for a steadily rising line of action that culminated in a strongly affecting climax. An important variant of this model was the two-part narrative structure in which the second half of the film initiated another steadily rising line of action that then reversed the first half's conclusion. A different model, however, was provided by the well-made play, particularly as it had been refined by French playwrights like Victorin Sardou. Here, a tightly unified, five-part structure—intrigue, rising action, climax, falling action, catastrophe—produced a more or less symmetrical, pyramidlike model of construction. And, following the principles made famous by Fernand Brunetière, dramatic conflict in this model was located in the clash of wills of highly individualized characters. Given the admittedly schematic delineation of these models, what particular forms of narrative structure came to define the single-reel story film in France? How did these differ, from genre to genre, in their negotiation between models? And were the endings of French films all that different, as Jasset suggested, as early as 1911 (perhaps accepting the judgment of American reviewers), from the "bright, happy denouements" so characteristic of American films?[8] These questions are especially pertinent for the French literary adaptations as well as the historical films they spawned, which suddenly began to command public attention in late 1908 and early 1909.

For perhaps the most important "innovation" during this period was the large-scale introduction of literary adaptations as a strategy to legitimize the cinema industry.[9] The production and exhibition of such "films d'art" was determined, in part, by the development of two different legal definitions of the French cinema. Between 1906 and 1908, a series of court decisions agreed with the cinema industry's claim that it was involved in the creation of "literary and artistic properties," for which a company could collect the equivalent of "royalty fees"—and which, not so coincidentally, provided a legal basis for Pathé's shift to renting films. By classifying plot as distinct from character psychology and style,[10] these decisions also differentiated between the primary right of the company whose capital produced the film and that of the author (of the scenario or original source work). In terms of exhibition, however, other court cases implicitly classed the cinema, not as a theatrical enterprise, but among the spectacles de curiosités, which came under the censorship control of municipal officials. When, in 1906, the theater was removed from any censorship restrictions, the resulting disparity between the legal status of the cinema and that of the theater provoked a move within the industry—heavily promoted by Benoît-Lévy—to demonstrate that such a disparity was unwarranted. The move to change or nullify this legal definition was crucial for the French cinema's development. It allowed Pathé, first of all, to cast its strategy of expansion as an attempt to legitimize the cinema industry, in that its circuit of permanent cinemas was constructed to induce, not only the white-collar and civil servant strata of the bourgeoisie with middle-class pretensions but the bourgeoisie itself "to want to go to the cinema" on a more regular basis. And, beginning in 1908, it encouraged Pathé to subsidize, both directly and indirectly, new production companies such as Film d'Art and SCAGL, both of which had close ties to the most prestigious Paris theaters. The films these companies produced then served as a means of acquiring a greater degree of cultural capital or social prestige, which in turn would produce an increase in Pathé's overall capital accumulation.[11]

The sudden surge of literary adaptations—like "a wave of artistic inspiration," to use Dureau's phrase[12]—particularly in the production of SCAGL, along with the original scenarios that Film d'Art initially commissioned from playwrights, served to revive the historical film and make it one of the more influential genres of the French cinema. And by concentrating on stories drawn from either classics or nineteenth-century drama and fiction and even opera— often set in past periods, from Greco-Roman times up through the French Revolution—literary adaptations came close to being synonymous with historical films. This had a profound effect on the French system of representation for, through the historical film (and its corollary, the biblical and "oriental" film), I would argue, certain features of the cinema of attractions reemerged to challenge and be reabsorbed into the newly narrativized cinema. Specifically, there was a return of the autonomous shot-scene or tableau with the spectacle attraction of studio decors and costumes, sometimes heightened by lighting effects, providing a context for the choreography of increasingly detailed, even stylized actor movement. Acting assumed a privileged importance as reputable actors from the Comédie Française and other Paris theaters were contracted to perform for the camera, which, in turn, contributed to the development of a star system. And the specific gendering of performance in these films—in contrast to that, for instance, in the comic series—raised questions not only of representation but of spectatorship. Mise-en-scène and its interpretation or consumption, in other words, took on as much significance as framing and editing, especially, as Brewster has argued, in the form of an optical space of "deep space" compositions—within which characters seemed intent on thoroughly exploring, to adapt Burch's language, "the circumscribed, geometrical nature of the perspective box."[13] It was as if the "theatrical" spectacle of Méliès's earlier opera adaptations and féeries had returned in a more accomplished "high art" form.

The cultural capital of the historical film genre also drew on a particular spectrum of subjects and authors. On the one hand, SCAGL tended, somewhat more than the others, to specialize in subjects drawn from French history, from the time of ancient Gaul to the French Revolution and its aftermath. On the other hand, Film d'Art and Pathé's Film d'Arte Italiana often went outside French history and culture, whether in the former's "operatic" films or in the latter's line of Shakespeare adaptations. Yet every major French film company contributed stories from the Greco-Roman and biblical period. Generally, then, the genre's "re-collection of past (and present) images, movements, and practices rearranged for the cultural present"[14] could be said to coincide with the conservative Nationalist Revival, and corollary Catholic Revival and Classical Renaissance movements, just then beginning to dominate French cultural and political life.[15] In its quest for legitimation, the French cinema industry seemed to accommodate itself to the love of "great subjects" and the taste for academicism which, according to Henri Dujardin-Beaumetz, minister of fine arts (1905–1910), privileged France as *the* country of classicism.[16] "The classical spirit belongs to all countries," Georges Leygues, a minister of education, had once said, "but it belongs above all to us."[17] Yet that accommodation was hardly unqualified, for specific historical films either resisted this trend or else articulated contradictory positions. Consequently, during the first two or three years of its "restoration," the genre constituted a crucial site of contestation, not only between the interests of spectacle attraction and narrative continuity, but also among the antagonistic social representations vying for ideological dominance in Third Republic France.

Contemporary Melodramas:
Light and Dark Variants

Prior to 1907, Pathé's dramatic and realist films may have led the way in transforming or narrativizing the French cinema, yet they passed virtually unnoticed—except as simple "sentimental scenes"—in Jasset's 1911 survey of the major worldwide developments in the art of cinematography.[18] Likewise absent from this account were those pre-feature contemporary melodramas produced by Pathé during the subsequent three-year period, as Jasset instead celebrated the "happy ending" dramatic "masterpieces" that Vitagraph had begun to release in France.[19] Jasset may not have had much of an excuse for this lacuna—other than that he was writing as the principal filmmaker of a rival production company, Eclair, and in France's most important trade journal, *Ciné-Journal*, which had excluded the leading French company from its pages throughout its first two years of publication. Yet the task of reconsidering the contemporary story films produced by Pathé and others between 1907 and 1911 is not simply one of putting back what Jasset left out. The survival rate of film prints within the genre is perhaps even less than that for the preceding period—several dozen prints from Pathé, a half-dozen from Gaumont, and even fewer from Eclair and Lux. And relatively little seems to have survived of the more prestigious, "headliner" films—from Monca's early SCAGL series starring Mistinguett or Prince (1909–1910) to de Morlhon's first films from his own scenarios for SAPF (1910), with one or two exceptions. What remains collected in archives, consequently, constitutes not so much a cross section of the genre as a more or less random sample of its pre-feature standard fare, and perhaps especially in terms of those films that would have been available in the foreign (American) market.

Given such a sample of surviving contemporary story films, any conclusions about the genre's contribution to sustaining and modifying the new French system of representation can only be tentative. Yet certain questions still have to be addressed. Did the genre generally continue to operate, for instance, according to its recently established "rules" of spatial-temporal continuity, or did it make further "advances," especially in editing practices, and thereby constitute an analytically cohesive mode of representation? How did it negotiate between the one-act play model of narrative construction, especially the two-part structure developed most clearly in *La Fille du Corse, Le Bon Grand-père*, and *Les Deux Soeurs*, and that of the well-made play, whose influence was increasing because of the turn to literary adaptations? And did it take up the same domestic melodrama or grand guignol subjects as before, involving patriarchal family traumas and love triangles, or else somewhat different ones, and to whom did they seem addressed? Finally, how did the French contemporary films of the period compare with those produced concurrently in the United States, not only by Vitagraph, now a major French distributor, but also by Biograph, where Griffith was directing his first films?

To begin with, some films either continued to work within the older tableau system of representation or else repeated, without much variation, what had become standard practice. Not unexpectedly, this was true of Méliès's few films in the genre. *L'Avare* (1908), for example, relies on a limited number of long-take LSs to tell its story of a miserly old man who loses his hoard of gold and, when it is found, refuses to offer a reward. *Not Guilty* (1908) does likewise, in just three studio decors, with a story of robbery, murder, and deception in a peasant village.[20] In the first LS tableau, which condenses village life into a series of social rituals—men indulging in a potato-sack race, soldiers passing through, peasants going to work in the fields—three men conspire to rob a wealthy peasant couple (whose house occupies part of the background) and are overheard by a neighbor woman getting water from a well. In the following interior LS, the conspirators brutally attack the couple and blind the young woman; when the couple's grown son returns to find their bodies, he is arrested. In the last two LSs, once a simple cup of well water somehow restores the young woman's sight, she accuses the conspirators in the local courtroom; then the mother miraculously recovers to support the accusation and present the heroic woman to her exonerated son. Although there is some effort to achieve a degree of verisimilitude in the decors and costumes, that is contradicted by an acting style that is as exaggerated as *Not Guilty*'s miraculous plot turns. Moreover, so much is going on in the first two tableaux that actions overlap inconsistently from one to the other (in a late example of temporal repetition), and they are orchestrated in such a way that even cutting each tableau into multiple shots, in order to create a sequence of alternation, would render the story incoherent.

Although much more competent, of course, certain Pathé films do little more than work variations on the company's previous releases in the genre. *Le Bagne de gosses* (1907), for instance, stitches together the story of an orphan boy's wandering from village to village with that of a convict's incarceration and escape, as in the earlier *Au bagne*. After enduring one hardship after another, in several series of location LSs, the boy finally comes under the benevolent protection of an old man, whose guidance and instruction restore his inherent goodness. As a melodramatic warning against lawbreaking, no matter how dire one's situation, *Le Bagne de gosses* recycles the comforting, patriarchally inflected myth of "natural" redemption. *The Little Chimney Sweep* (1908) reworks the story of a lost child—this one is kidnapped from his bourgeois home by a man infatuated with but spurned by the child's mother. Indentured as a chimney sweep, he and an older boy who befriends him later chance to stop by the family house at whose gate a gypsy is playing a violin. When the boy asks to play, his rendition of "Jocelyn" carries over, as a sound bridge, into the subsequent shot of the house interior, where the mother recognizes the music he first performed in the opening tableau. Not only is the son restored to his family, but the older orphan boy is taken in, too, as if in compensation. In order to reach a similar resolution, *The Waif* (1908) borrows the narrativized device of the dream from the féerie. This film traces another orphan boy wandering through the mountain villages of southeastern France in a half-dozen LSs, until he settles down to sleep in the doorway to a shop. There, an angel dissolves in and out over him (marking the shift to dream), after which a wealthy woman drives up in a car and takes the boy off to her villa, where she feeds him and puts him to bed. And a cut-in MCU singles out the high point of this maternal fantasy: the boy savoring the delicacy of a poached egg in a cup. After the angel reappears to close off the dream, the shop owner kicks the boy awake; but a young couple happen by (the woman is carrying a baby), reprimand him, and invite the boy to join them. As one miracle fades away, it is matched by another, less fanciful one—the boy may not ascend the socioeconomic ladder, but he does become part of a family, even if a poor one.

By contrast, Gaumont's *The Old Woodcutter* (1909) uses a character's dream to narrate, in flashback, the elliptical story of a peasant family's suffering. Anchored by several ballad intertitles, the frame story focuses on an old man who, in a short series of LSs matching his exits and entrances, struggles through a forest with a heavy load of wood until he collapses. Thereafter, while the woodcutter lies near death in a triangular area at the bottom left foreground of the frame, a sequence of five LS tableaux fades in and out "behind" him.[21] The first two tableaux represent the simple life of the old man and his wife, along with their son and daughter-in-law and small granddaughter (one bed, the cooking fireplace, and some drying laundry are all crammed into one interior room). In the third tableau, the son is called to military service, presumably for the Franco-Prussian War; in the fourth, the family is informed of his death, and the daughter-in-law collapses in grief. In the last tableau, only the grandparents and granddaughter are left, and the latter's hunger prompts the old man to go off with his ax, providing the motive for his action in the beginning of the film. This memory of the past seems to revive the old man; when a spectral death figure approaches from a background wooded clearing, he stands to confront it (the figure dissolves away), grabs the load of wood, and runs off with renewed vigor. Although the surviving film print breaks off at this point, it suggests rather strongly that this child's needs, too, will be answered, at least for the moment, by the efforts of a conscientious family.

A good number of Pathé films, however, take up the concerns of the family melodrama more explicitly, and in the increasingly standardized format of a two-part narrative structure. They also tend to tell stories in which a father is mistakenly accused of a crime but eventually is exonerated through either his own actions or those of an only child. *Le Roman d'un malheureux* (1908), for instance, uses a double coincidence to compound its story of family disruption.[22] Not only is a young girl (an only child) struck and injured by a passing automobile on her way to school, but her father (there is no mother) is fired from his white-collar clerical job and then mistakenly arrested for robbing the office safe, which results in the girl being sent to an orphanage. Once released from prison, the father finds that his criminal record keeps him from holding a job even as an unskilled laborer, and he is forced to join a gang of apaches. When one of the gang attacks a lone woman in a modern bourgeois house they plan to rob, he turns on the apaches and assists several policemen in their arrest. In recompense, the woman promptly hires him as her gardener and then introduces him to his daughter whom, in a final coincidence, she has adopted. All of these twists of fate and reversals of fortune occur in just nineteen shots, almost exclusively recorded in LS, and they are measured out in relatively discrete sequences that divide each half of the film into more or less equal parts. Moreover, the midpoint is marked by separate yet parallel summary tableaux—first, the father in the prison shop repairing a stool and, then, in a privileged AS, the girl sadly writing a letter in an orphanage bed before going to sleep—whose effect is to accentuate the emotional destitution of the two characters. In the end, father and daughter are reunited and a quasi family is restored, with an unusual shift upward in socioeconomic position, at least for the daughter, through the benevolence of a bourgeois "mother" figure. What is not unusual, however, is that just as the father's sense of virtue is tested and triumphs, despite all odds, it is sanctioned by the state in the form of the police.

The False Coin (1908), by contrast, focuses on a destitute working-class or artisan family living in a garret room, probably in some provincial town. With his mother ill in bed and his father presumably out of work, a young boy (another only child) goes to a nearby corner café to buy what looks like a bowl of gruel. There he is accused of paying with a fake coin, and the local gendarmes arrest his father as a counterfeiter. The boy returns to the café to discover the café owner and his wife minting fake coins in the cellar; and, after he has guided the gendarmes back to the café to seize the real counterfeiters, the father is released and reunited with his son.[23] In constructing its narrative sequences, this film relies extensively on intercutting adjacent exteriors and interiors of the family apartment dwelling, the café, and the local police station. What is most interesting, however, is that the sequence in which the boy discovers the counterfeiters receives greater attention than the "climactic" one where they are captured by the gendarmes. This sequence alternates between a LS of the corner café exterior, as the boy peers through a street-level window (frame left), and a LS of the cellar interior, where the owner and his wife are at a foreground table and the boy's face is visible at an upper background window. Rather than construct a POV-shot sequence, this 180-degree shift in camera position withholds narrative information by presenting both viewer and viewed, at a distance, within the same tableau. Only then does a cut-in MS of the café owner, breaking open a mold to reveal a dozen newly minted coins, substitute the eyes of the spectator for those of the boy in order to expose the counterfeiting operation. Despite this rather idiosyncratic construction of suspense, *The False Coin*, much like *Le Roman d'un malheureux*, has the police sanction the restoration of the patriarchal family in the end, this time literally within the office of the local police chief.

The Little Cripple (1908) makes a homeless orphan boy the hero of another story of false accusation over an apache crime. Remarkable for the gray desolation of both its studio interiors and its location shooting, this film systematically structures its narrative in terms of recurring spaces and actions, with a minimum of intertitles.[24] An initial AS introduces the orphan boy sitting against a wall and strapping on his wooden legs (with his crutches nearby), its matter-of-fact tone sustained in the following LS of a workers' *pension* as he and a younger boy sit on the curb outside. A simple 180-degree alternation of exterior and interior spaces matchcuts the movements of two apaches into the pension's first floor bar (a drunk is asleep at one table) and then out (at closing time), after which the woman who runs the pension gives some food to the crippled boy and takes the other inside. What follows economically intercuts three different sets of characters moving through these spaces, plus the woman's garret bedroom, as the apaches return to crawl through a shuttered window, sneak past the drunk and the boy sleeping at separate tables, and rob and strangle the woman. The boy awakens and rushes upstairs only to be seized and carried off by the apaches, who exit by a side stairway (revealed in an exterior shift in camera position); then the drunk staggers upstairs and collapses next to the woman's body. These spaces are repeated the next morning as two policemen discover the dead woman and arrest the drunk, all of which the crippled boy learns when he arrives outside the pension. This sets up a short sequence of pursuit as the crippled boy follows the apaches to an unused dock and sees them row out into a bay and toss the boy overboard. Once again, the film plays out sequential actions in parallel as, first, the crippled boy removes his wooden legs and swims out to rescue the other boy and, then, the policemen swim out to capture the apaches (who, in order for the repetition to work, have abandoned their boat). Finally, in the local police station the two boys exonerate the drunk, who, in return, promises to take responsibility for them, as well as himself. Although this ending produces an authorized patriarchal "family," the film's real interest comes prior to that, when it holds on the younger boy helping his rescuer with his wooden legs and crutches, and then holds again on the crippled boy sitting alone on a low wall overlooking the bay—the actualité "portrait" of the opening now doubly charged with emotion.

Perhaps even more of these melodrama films focus on relations among adults, sometimes setting their stories of loss through death or abduction in more distant, "exotic" locales. Pathé's *La Vengeance du forgeron* (1907), for instance, exhibits as much interest in its location shooting as in its early nineteenth-century story of a provincial blacksmith whose wife is seduced by a local aristocrat. When the latter brazenly returns to pace the shop courtyard (whose deep-space composition extends through a background open gate), the blacksmith draws him inside and takes his violent revenge with a heavy mallet. Gaumont's *In the Hands of the Enemy* (1907), by contrast, tells a more conciliatory, if no less melodramatic, story set during the 1871 Franco-Prussian War. After an opening LS of a typical bourgeois drawing room, where a French officer receives a ring from his fiancée as he is going off to war, this film moves swiftly to the battlefield, where in the deep space of a wooded clearing the French officer and his men retreat in the face of a larger number of German soldiers. Soon, the French are holed up in a LS bedroom interior and dying one by one; when the Germans finally break in, the severely wounded officer is the only Frenchman still alive. After an intertitle, "In the Enemy's Hands," a cut-in FS of the French officer shows him giving the ring to his German counterpart and dictating a short note before dying. Another intertitle, "The Irony of Fate," introduces a LS of another battlefield strewn with wreckage and bodies, among which the (now wounded) German officer is discovered by a nurse and carried off on a stretcher. The stretcher bearing the German officer, of course, is brought to the French woman's house, setting up the final tableau—a long-take LS of the bedroom, which echoes the earlier bedroom space where the French officer died. Here, perhaps in the young woman's own bed, the German awakens, speaks of her fiancé's death, and returns the ring. In horror, she seizes his nearby sword and then lets it fall. As he asks for the laudanum a doctor has left behind, she finally pours some for him to drink just before he, too, apparently dies. Here, the historical conflict between Germany and France, just then beginning to re-emerge, is resolved through a paralleled set of private spaces, in the characteristic fashion of melodrama—by means of the moral "truth" of individual forgiveness.

The most interesting of these "exotic" melodramas is Pathé's *The Pirates* (1907), in which a band of pirates kidnap a young woman on the coast of Brittany and take her off to their ship, where she is rescued by her fiancé after a

56a. *The Pirates,* 1907

56b. *The Pirates,* 1907

56c. *The Pirates,* 1907

fierce battle.[25] Although little about this story seems out of the ordinary, what is unusual is how strikingly and efficiently it is told. The opening tableaux—especially the long-take LS of the house interior, where the pirates seize the young woman at her spinning wheel and attack her parents—look almost deliberately conventional. The rest of the film, however, uses distinctive strategies—narrativized camera movement and two different kinds of intercutting—to set off each stage of its narrative. At the bottom of a flight of wooden steps on the beach, for instance, the young woman breaks away from her abductors, in LS, and a short pan follows her movement until she is again subdued (frame right) and placed, in FS, in a foreground rowboat. Then a ninety-degree reverse pan follows the rowboat, still in FS, as it is pushed off into the open sea, throwing the struggling villains and heroine into silhouette. After a brief journey, a series of shots establishes the three spaces that will provide the basis for the remaining action: the exterior starboard side of the pirates' ship, the main deck, and the rough cabin interior where the woman is chained. Instead of separately narrating

57. *The Pirates,* 1907

58. *The Pirates,* 1907

59. *The Pirates,* 1907

her rescuers' pursuit, the film instead focuses on the battle in 180-degree reverse-angle LSs as the pirates fire their cannons, the rescuers clamber up the side of the ship, and individual duels break out on the deck. While this is going on, the cabin boy rushes into the FS of the adjacent cabin interior (his exit and entrance matchcut) and frees the woman from her chains. Among the bodies strewn around the deck, the woman then falls into her fiancé's arms (he has led the rescuers and killed the pirate leader) so that *The Pirates* can conclude, as the boy flanks the couple, with the requisite "family portrait."

Finally, to return to Paris, the sheer diversity of Pathé's melodramas can be summarized in a trio of films. Unlike almost any other film from this period, *Le Contremaître incendiaire* (1908) exploits the outmoded bricolage model of construction; in addition, it takes on the subject of explicit class conflict within a large French factory.[26] An unmarried foreman by the name of Loisel envies the factory owner's life of ease and robs the payroll safe, covering his tracks by setting fire to the factory. Although he tries to blame a worker he has recently

60. *Le Contremaître incendiaire,* 1908

argued with and dismissed, Loisel is quickly found out and arrested. The beginning and ending sections of this film are composed of rather conventional FSs
and LSs, most of them preceded by simple intertitles. By contrast, the lengthy
middle section (like a "modern" version of the still popular pyrodrama)[27] is
largely comprised of actualité footage (there are over a dozen shots, with only a
single intertitle) in which a fire brigade supposedly fights the blaze Loisel has
started. What is interesting here is how the film negotiates between different
modes of representation according to fictional conventions. Loisel's theft and
arson, which begin this section, for instance, are narrated in a sequence of
six shots—uninterrupted by intertitles and loosely matching his exits and entrances—the most crucial of which has him actually setting the fire in an unusual
HA LS. Furthermore, at one point in the actualité footage, both the foreman and
the factory owner look on as a fireman enters a nearby building to rescue a
threatened child. The shift away from the firefighting to the discovery of the
theft then is handled more simply—through a huge background window in
Loisel's office, the painted flat of the factory shows it now in ruins.

    The ideological position *Le Contremaître incendiaire* takes on the class conflict
premising its narrative is no less intriguing. That conflict is first articulated
through juxtaposed tableaux—the factory owner and his family eating a sumptuous breakfast in their dining room, Loisel with a meager tray in his office—a

61. *Le Contremaître incendiaire*, 1908

"contrast edit" that Griffith would later deploy for extended symbolic effect in *A Corner in Wheat* (1909). In the Pathé film, however, the initial intertitle, "Good Master, Bad Assistant," strictly determines the moral significance of this opposition. The intertitle is especially fortuitous because the Pathé factory itself (two exterior shots of a loading dock have film cans sitting along a background wall) implicitly serves as the principal target of the foreman's anger.[28] In the end, of course, factory owner and worker (the suspect Loisel earlier dismissed is given his job back) share a bond of cooperation, each assuming his proper place in the socioeconomic order. And the film's villain becomes merely an ungrateful "middleman" who, as a lone figure without a family, deflects any critique of the social order by taking on all sorts of "bad" traits, including that of unjustly exploiting those beneath him. In its resolution of class conflict, *Le Contremaître incendiaire* probably was not all that unique, for it seems to have been a staple of the genre, beginning with *La Grève*, to celebrate the "good worker" who accepted the capitalist's factory ownership while demonizing the "bad worker" who resisted (usually violently). This is evident, for instance, in Eclair's recently rediscovered *Journée de grève* (1909), in which a mob of strikers attacks the home of a factory owner only to be halted and shamed by a family domestic who, although initially encouraging the workers' strike, now protects the owner's injured daughter and the "health" of the bourgeois family. Moreover, it is supported by trade press descriptions of other lost films such as Lux's *The Horrors of a Strike* (1909), Gaumont's *How to Settle a Labor Dispute* (1910), and Pathé's *The Iron Workers' Strike* (1910).

A different kind of conflict is worked out in the company's remake of *L'Affaire Dreyfus* (1908).[29] Here, somewhat surprisingly, the famous historical crisis of ten years before gets rewritten almost exclusively as a military affair. From the beginning, Colonel Henry and Major Esterhazy are shown to be guilty of the treason for which Captain Dreyfus is charged and condemned, so that the "plot" turns on the melodramatic issue of "misrecognition" and recognition. This film, too, is composed largely of autonomous LS tableaux, with a few exceptions. The characters move repeatedly through three linked spaces: a building exterior and two adjacent interior rooms representing the office of army intelligence; by contrast, Henry's bribery of Esterhazy occurs in the foreground of a deep-space ballroom (with dancing couples in the background). At one point, there is even the spectacle of an early triptych tableau, but it merely serves to link the intelligence and judicial sections of the army, by telephone. The most intriguing thing about this *L'Affaire Dreyfus*, however, is that its climactic moments come in two public ceremonies: first, Dreyfus's humiliation, as a military man, at being stripped of his rank and then his recovery of honor as he is reinstated in a concluding tableau. Shorn of the intense public debate over the "affair," especially the anti-Semitism underlying one side of that debate (as well as most of the military and political judgments), Pathé's film turns Dreyfus's story into a propagandistic argument for restoring faith in the French army.

A Narrow Escape or *The Physician of the Castle* (1908), by contrast, exploits the grand guignol formula of the family threatened by apaches in an unusually sustained structure of suspense.[30] Essentially a remake of *Terrible Angoisse*, Pathé's earlier adaptation of de Lorde's *Au Téléphone*, this film introduces a fake telegram to call a doctor away from his suburban home, and his wife and young son, supposedly to check on the sick baby of another bourgeois couple in a distant chateau. In his absence, an apache gang breaks into the house, the wife barricades the door and telephones her husband, and the doctor, in the company of several policemen, rushes back to the house. In contrast to both de Lorde's play and the earlier film, however, this adaptation rewrites the climax to conform with the conventions of melodrama—and the doctor apprehends the apaches just in time. One unusual feature of *A Narrow Escape* is its exclusive focus on the domestic milieu of the bourgeoisie and in its stark depiction of that milieu under criminal attack. And what is threatened is not only the private space of the home and its valuables but what that haven is most meant to protect—the mother and child at the center of the family. Besides this site of contestation, the conflict between bourgeois and apache also involves a struggle for control of some of the chief technological devices of modern life—while the apaches use the telegraph to deceive the doctor, the wife uses the telephone to inform him, and a white sports car both bears the doctor away and brings him back home. Moreover, that conflict involves the attempt to exercise control over sickness—for the physical illness the doctor is called away to treat serves to mask

62. *A Narrow Escape*, 1908   63. *A Narrow Escape*, 1908

the "social disease" threatening his own home, whose eradication he turns out to be well suited, as a professional, to perform.[31]

What most distinguishes *A Narrow Escape* from other films in the genre, however, is its sustained use of alternation or parallel editing. The delivery of the telegram and the doctor's consequent departure, for instance, carefully establish two pairs of adjacent spaces in and around the bourgeois house—exterior LSs of the gate and front entrance, interior FS/LSs of the dining room and study. The alternation then begins in the narration of two diverging, yet parallel lines of action, as a LS describing the doctor's car traveling up a hillside road is followed by a cut-back to the gate area where two apaches have been watching and waiting in the left foreground. In the following two shots, they attack the family maid before the front entrance (which the mother observes through a window), and mother and son barricade the background door leading into the dining room. At this crucial point, the film suspends this line of action in order to depict the doctor's arrival at the chateau, first, in an exterior LS and, then, in an interior FS/LS, where he goes to examine the baby and discovers that the couple did not send the telegram. This line of action is suspended, in turn, as the film cuts back to show the apaches breaking into the empty dining room and, next, the mother and son in the study, where she finds the telegram and frantically dials the telephone. Now, with a subsequent cut-back to the chateau interior, where a servant answering the phone hands it to the doctor, this pattern of alternation, and its building suspense, culminates in two parallel cut-in MCUs—first, the wife and, then, the doctor, in matching profile, talk excitedly on their respective phones. After this privileged moment of rhetorical intensification, the film traces the doctor's journey through four more shots, yet without once cutting back to the house.[32] And, in the next-to-last shot, soon after the apaches finally break into the study, the doctor and policemen rush in to seize them, in a highly condensed tableau conclusion. What this sequential order suggests is that alternation, in *A Narrow Escape*, serves not only to create suspense but, perhaps more important, to bind wife and husband together at the climactic

194

moment of their greatest vulnerability, in shots that seem to erase the distance between them. In another few months, Griffith would develop this strategy of parallel editing further as the basis for a subgenre of last-minute-rescue Biograph films, including such titles as *The Fatal Hour* (1908), *The Cord of Life* (1909), and especially *The Lonely Villa* (1909), the latter of which bears a very close resemblance to *A Narrow Escape*.

All of these films suggest that, during these two years, the contemporary melodrama generally adhered to and extended the system of representation staked out several years before. Particular Pathé films like *A Narrow Escape, Le Contremaître incendiaire, Le Roman d'un malheureux*, and *The Pirates* further exploited the strategies, respectively, of parallel editing, contrast edits, and narrativized camera movement. Other films such as Gaumont's *In the Hands of the Enemy* and Pathé's *The Little Cripple* deployed the strategy of repetition and variation to produce emotionally resonating, recurring images—which, along with the contrast edit, created a rudimentary form of what Gunning, referring to Griffith's later films, calls a "moral voice" in film discourse.[33] And, whatever the combination of strategies, nearly all adopted the format of the two-part narrative structure. With the significant exception of *A Narrow Escape*, the genre's subjects also remained bound up with a certain referential body of social relations. Major characters still tended to come from the lower classes, perhaps more frequently white-collar than either artisan or working class, and they continued to be relatively generic and sometimes even anonymous rather than individualized. Moreover, the narratives still relied extensively on melodramatic coincidence as well as moral or criminal deviance, with apaches most responsible for threatening the accepted bourgeois social order. What seems singularly different, at least in these surviving prints, is that men and boys were the principal agents or heroes of the stories. Unlike earlier Pathé films, here women consistently were secondary characters, whether as wives or mothers tied to the home, victims of violence, or, in a rare instance, benevolent "fairy godmothers." This relative lack of interest in women—let alone the relations between mother and daughter or between sisters—suggests that the genre no longer may have been specifically addressing women as spectators. If such an address once had been part of Pathé's strategy of legitimation, perhaps its moment was brief; for Pathé was about to adopt what would become a principal axiom of that strategy, privileging literary adaptations and their appeal to a white-collar and bourgeois clientele, whatever its gender. In a corollary move, Eclair was adopting the strategy of privileging the heroic exploits of a popular male detective.[34]

Eclair's *Nick Carter* films were different from most other French melodramas in that they were drawn from a popular series of "pamphlet novels" or "cheap stories" that were American in origin and all about the same fictional detective hero.[35] The "Nick Carter Library" of weekly stories, called "dime novels," had been in mass circulation for some twenty years in the United States before they first appeared in France, in March 1907, when Eichler (a Dresden publisher that recently had opened a branch office in Paris) began to issue them in translation, in biweekly booklets sporting boldly designed covers.[36] These "individualized" booklets, Lacassin has argued, introduced an inexpensive alternative to the lengthy *feuilleton* format that had long dominated French publishing (in which chapters were printed weekly in a mass-circulation newspaper over many months).[37] And it was the almost instant popularity of this French Nick Carter series on which Eclair chose to capitalize when the company set up a regular schedule of film production in the summer of 1908. The first six titles that Jasset directed for the series closely followed the format that Eichler had introduced. They were released at biweekly intervals between 8 September and 15 November, and each one narrated a complete story involving the detective hero in a single reel of 150 to 250 meters.

The first film, *Le Guet-Apens* or *The Doctor's Rescue*, offers a good example of the flexible strategies of representation on which Jasset depended for the series.[38] For one thing, in order to recount the story of a doctor's kidnapping and rescue, it adopts Pathé's newly standardized two-part narrative structure. In the first half, a band of apache beggars fix on a prosperous doctor (as he leaves church with his wife, no less) and lure him away to a garret room and then a warehouse, where he is forced to write a ransom note and is bound and gagged. In the second half, the wife hires Nick Carter who, by disguising himself as a beggar (twice), succeeds in tracking down and arresting the kidnappers and releasing the doctor. Jasset's film works smoothly back and forth between location exteriors and studio interiors, assuming the Pathé camera position of waist-level FS/LSs and LSs. Certain details of representation, however, contribute some suspense to part one: the doctor and his wife come up a street, followed by a beggar woman, and exit quite close to the camera, in MS; after the doctor accepts her note in the study, the beggar woman signals her offscreen partners by partly closing a background window curtain; and, inserted between shots of the garret room and the warehouse, is a FS of the doctor's wife pacing anxiously at home. Part two builds on this latter strategy of alternation by intercutting interior and exterior shots of the warehouse, as Carter briefly peers through a window, seizes the beggar woman when she comes out, and then, in order to get in, disguises himself in her clothes. The privileged moment in the film, however, is the MS of Carter, shortly after he is first introduced, demonstrating his expertise (synonymous with that of the cinema actor) in taking on the disreputable persona of the beggar. Legitimately attired for "slumming," the detective beats the apaches at their own game of deception and restores this typical bourgeois couple—and the social order they represent—for a characteristic final emblematic shot.

As *Le Guet-apens* suggests, the *Nick Carter* series was not all that different from Pathé's earlier domestic melodramas and their fascination with criminal deviance as a threat to the family—with two notable exceptions. Rather than being drawn from almost every class level of French society, the series' victims were consistently bourgeois, and they usually were adults without children. And, of course, they were always saved from financial ruin or death by an impeccably professional detective. In other words, it was a thoroughly modern professional milieu that the Eclair series reproduced, one that may well have

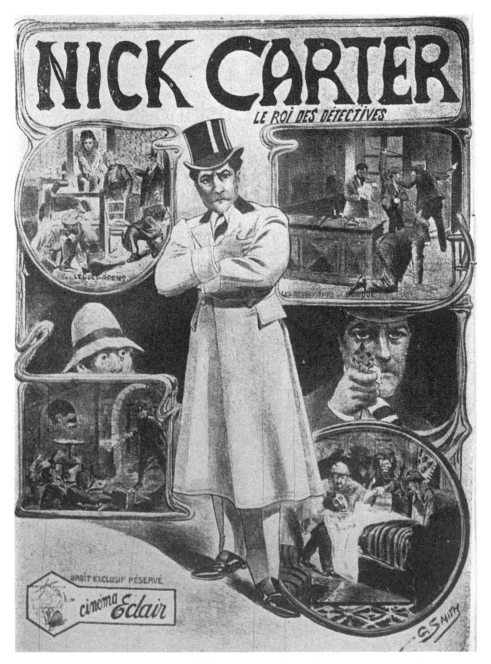

64. *Nick Carter,* 1908 (poster)

been geared to the bourgeois clientele (especially white-collar and civil servant) which the industry was attempting to attract to the new cinemas. As for Nick Carter himself, the French hero shared with his American original a penchant for disguises; but otherwise the two were radically different, especially in terms of the relative emphasis on their race and class. The dime novel detective, as

Michael Denning describes him, was "a young, muscular, white Anglo-Saxon man," and clearly a racist model for turn-of-the-century American national identity.[39] Eclair's film detective, by contrast, was thoroughly "Frenchified," most overtly in Bressol's compact, yet surprisingly agile figure and dark Mediterranean features. As scrupulously honest and class-minded as Sherlock Holmes (for all his detective work, no money ever changed hands), the Frenchman put his protean intelligence—the many disguises serving as a concise sign of his uncanny ability to master any social group's identity—at the service of his bourgeois clients, in order to allay their fears and terrors.

The initial six *Nick Carter* films were so successful that Eclair quickly put another four titles into production for the following year.[40] Each of these new films seems to have stuck with the series' bourgeois milieu and narrative economy—what the company's own planted article in *Ciné-Journal* described as "brisk, straightforward narration, [with] logically linked, rapidly sketched scenes unencumbered by psychological explanation"[41]—as well as its two-part narrative structure. All this is still evident in one of the last films in the series, *Le Club des suicides* (1909),[42] which reworks a well-known grand guignol play first staged just the year before.[43] Here, a journalist investigating a band of criminals, who are using an exclusive club as a front, is tricked, in a card game, into almost committing suicide and has to be rescued by Nick Carter and his assistants. Part one creates its suspense, first as the journalist chooses a playing card, by inserting a CU of the ace of spades (followed by an intertitle explaining its diabolical significance), and then by cutting away from him as he paces nervously in the darkened room where he is supposed to shoot himself. Part two, of course, narrates Carter's successful raid on the club, after he has been hired by the journalist's anxious wife. This time, accentuated by LS pans along a street, Carter and his men twice jump out of a car and seize a club member in order to use his coat and wallet to assume an appropriate false identity. And the by-now-expected MS of Carter adopting his full disguise—in this case, he and his men put on false mustaches—comes just before they penetrate the club and rescue the journalist at the last minute.

The unusual success of the *Nick Carter* series prompted Pathé and other companies to turn out new variations on the old story of apprehending apache villains. In Pathé's *La Petite Policière* (1909), one of de Morlhon's earliest extant films, for instance, a white-collar bank official is blamed for a robbery perpetrated by an apache gang, and his young daughter pursues the real culprits in order to exonerate him. Much as in *A Narrow Escape*, this film briefly sets up parallel lines of action in alternating shots—the gang breaks into a building while the bank official's family is gathered for breakfast—and brings both together in the father's office. Moreover, it adds an exterior shot of the bank building entrance, not only to trace the daughter's journey from home to office (carrying a forgotten bank ledger), but also to let her bump into one of the exiting apaches, which establishes the premise for her successful pursuit in the second half of the film. In *Dog Detective* (1909), the butler of a bourgeois family is in cahoots with a gang of apaches and helps in his master's abduction for ransom.[44]

The abducted man's wife, however, goes straight to the police, who send out a specially trained dog to track the man down to an abandoned warehouse, loosen the ropes with which he is tied, and smuggle in a gun for him to surprise and overwhelm his captors. Initially, this film, too, deploys parallel lines of action, which quickly culminate in the kidnapping. Thereafter, however, in a somewhat implausibly extended narrative, the police simply wait near the warehouse while the dog and the abducted man himself do all the work.[45]

At the same time Eclair was introducing the *Nick Carter* series, SCAGL was beginning to release its films as the "feature attraction" of Pathé's weekly programs. Very few of the contemporary subjects produced by this new company apparently survive from this period, but those that do suggest that the mode of representation marking SCAGL films was not all that consistent. One of these, Capellani's *L'Homme aux gants blancs* (1908)—whose title alludes to a de Lorde play staged at the Grand Guignol just one year before[46]—offers an interesting basis for assessment because it exists in the form of a two-page original scenario, written by Capellani himself, as well as an incomplete print.[47] According to the scenario, the film tells a wickedly ironic tale of double deception among the nouveau riche in Paris. A prosperous-looking, but nearly penniless, bourgeois gentleman (Jacques Grétillat) charms a wealthy young woman (Mlle Brésil) he has met at a fine restaurant, accompanies her home, and later happily emerges—with a very expensive pearl necklace in his pocket. In examining his catch, this "apache in polished boots" drops the white gloves he has bought for the occasion, and another, less elegant fellow (Desfontaines) who has been watching this charade picks them up to put on and enter the same house. As the second thief searches for money and valuables, however, the woman surprises him; and he strangles her, inadvertently dropping the gloves by her body. This evidence soon leads the police to the would-be gentleman, from whom they recover the necklace; as he is being led away to the police station, among the crowd looking on stands the real murderer.

Although Capellani's film follows the scenario outline closely, there are several unexpected choices in its representational strategy. Not only does it pick up on some of the scenario's details—most notably, the gentleman's white gloves—but engages in some inventing of its own. Perhaps the most unusual of these is the triptych tableau that introduces the crucial purchase of the white gloves. Separated by a "central panel"—a HA ELS of a Paris boulevard crowded with traffic—on the left (in AS), the gentleman speaks into a telephone while, on the right (also in AS), a saleswoman listens and takes down his order. This economically establishes his apparent mastery over the city and its resources (as well as women), but, when the gloves are delivered in the very next scene, that mastery has its flaws. A button comes loose on one of the gloves he tries on, and a cut-in CU of his gloved hand gives special significance to the saleswoman's quick fingers, sewing it back on. Later, at the woman's apartment, after she has gone to change clothes, what might seem a puzzling insert "interrupts" the gentleman's efforts to make certain he will remain unobserved in the drawing room. As he peers at an opening in the background drapes through which she has

65. *L'Homme aux gants blancs*, 1909

66. *L'Homme aux gants blancs*, 1909
(Jacques Grétillat)

67. *L'Homme aux gants blancs*, 1909

passed, there is a cut, not to her dressing (as in a POV shot), but to an exterior LS of the maid closing the shutters on one of the balconies—apparently a cross-cut to explain (both women are occupied) how he can steal the necklace that has been placed on a foreground table. As its narrative draws to a climax, the film relies increasingly on more conventional means, choreographing the actors' movements and gestures in long-take tableaux—such as the gentleman's hotel room, when the police interrupt his departure and the saleswoman is brought in to confirm that the gloves they have found are his. Yet, in the concluding FS/LS outside the woman's apartment, camera movement extends the film's coolly nasty scenario by springing one final surprise that opens up an ironic gap between the knowing spectator and the unsuspecting "hero." When the gentleman is brought out, the murderer exits the frame, as if running away; but a ninety-degree pan simply reveals him waiting by the paddy wagon, "graciously" holding open its rear door. And when the police inspector accidentally drops his cane, the murderer picks it up for him with a hypocritically obsequious gesture. This final ironic flourish serves *L'Homme aux gants blancs* well in its savage and probably quite topical exposé of Parisian high life, for not only do two men prey on one woman (who is doubly victimized) but the real apache, simply by imitating his "better" bourgeois counterpart, literally gets away with murder.

Another early SCAGL film, *L'Assomoir* (1909), provides a study in contrast. First of all, this film is drawn from Zola's celebrated novel of sexual jealousy and alcoholism among the French working class and closely follows either William Busnach's 1879 condensed stage adaptation, which ran for nearly a year in Paris, or Charles Reade's adaptation, *Drink*, which had a similar success in London.[48] Both of these stage productions reshaped the novel into the symmetrical, pyramidlike structure of the well-made play, and that structure is evident in the released film version of two separate parts of one full reel each—making it one of the earliest multiple-reel contemporary "features" produced in France. The first reel, which seems to be the only one extant, initiates the intrigue as Virginie (Catherine Fontenay) seduces Lantier (Grétillat) away from Gervaise (Eugénie Nau) and climaxes in her attempt to destroy the family Gervaise builds with Coupeau (Arquillière), by causing an "accident" at the construction site where he works as a roofer. The second reel then focuses on Coupeau's partial recovery and subsequent lack of employment, which drives him to drink, his apparent cure, which is reversed by Gervaise's own decline, and his "inevitable" death in a fit of delirium tremens.[49] Finally, on the evidence of the surviving nitrate print, *L'Assomoir* may have been shown exclusively in black and white, perhaps adopting a photographic convention in order to simulate the "realism" of Zola's story.[50]

Given the structure of the well-made play, perhaps it should not be surprising that the film relies so extensively on long-take FS/LS tableaux, often introduced by lengthy intertitles, and characterized by studio decors—from the one-room flat that Lantier, Virginie, and Coupeau initially share or the laundry room where Gervaise and Virginie fight over Lantier to the public park (with its painted-flat backdrop) where Coupeau proposes to Gervaise. Perhaps the most elaborate of these is the dance scene that mixes working class and bourgeoisie in another public park (this time shot on location) and has both Virginie and Lantier separately now try to draw Gervaise and Coupeau away from one another. The only major deviance from this mode of representation comes during the climactic scene of the accident. The construction site is divided into several contiguous spaces: three different levels of scaffolding, plus two adjacent spaces at its base. Through these spaces, Coupeau descends several ladders to meet Gervaise and their young daughter Nana for lunch; then Virginie sneaks in and up one ladder to loosen some scaffolding boards. The accident itself is conveyed through ellipses that seem to quicken the pace of the characters' movements—eliding part of Virginie's descent as well as Coupeau's ascent, and then letting the other workmen find his body after the anticipated but unseen fall. Whether later sections of *L'Assomoir* exploit such editing patterns is unclear but probably not likely, for this scene marks the climax or apex of the narrative structure—everything else constitutes a falling action to the final catastrophe that, according to reviewers, gave undivided attention to Arquillière's mad performance.

Although generalizations about SCAGL's contemporary films have to remain tentative,[51] it is instructive to compare these two films with other concurrent, less "prestigious" Pathé titles. Several of these make especially effective use of "exotic" location shooting—discrediting the notion that Pathé tended to confine its productions to the studio—for stories no less grim than those set in Paris. *Nuit de Noël* (1908), for instance, tells the familiar story of a woman's infidelity and her husband's revenge, but makes the main characters a simple fisherman, his wife, and a miller, in the "wilds" of Brittany.[52] As beautifully composed as is the opening rose-tinted HA LS of the Breton harbor where the fisherman puts out to sea in a small sailing ship, it takes on particular significance when the wife comes into the foreground, turns and waves, and then exits crying, quite close to the camera. This focus on her desolate state carries over into the next shots (now tinted amber) as she pauses at a cross marker on a barren hill, walks along an empty slope (with a windmill, bare tree, and lighthouse on the distant horizon), and approaches their two-story stone house. Another sequence of LSs (again the tinting shifts from rose to amber), takes her to the windmill, pulling a wheelbarrow through a landscape of scattered, huge upright stones, as if to mark the earth itself as a land of the dead—and perhaps evoke the threat of her husband's possible death at sea.[53]

As these images suggest, *Nuit de Noël* evidences some interest in exploring this woman's state of mind, especially in giving a motivation for the adultery she later commits. Although she resists the miller's advances, that night a stark black-and-white AS of the house interior shows her giving way to her own desire as she looks at herself in a dresser mirror and attaches a ribbon to her cap. Moreover, their illicit rendezvous is then situated within her community's legitimate rituals (again accentuated by color) as she joins a group of villagers in silhouette entering the amber-lit doorway of the local church and then takes part in a circular dance in the red light of a bonfire. After the two lovers steal back to the house in the miller's horse cart, a crosscut to the harbor, where the fisher-

68. *Nuit de Noël*, 1908 (poster)

man's ship is docking, sets up the narrative climax. Here, the film shifts again to focus exclusively on the action (and stunt work) as the fisherman drives up to the house and, noticing the cart, breaks in the door; a split second later the miller drops out of a small second-floor window into his cart and races off, quickly pursued by the fisherman. And, as the Pathé poster anticipates, the film ends in a bit of sensational violence, on another barren hilltop, where the fisherman beats the miller unconscious and, just as the print breaks off, is about to push the cart (and body) onto the surf-pounded rocks below. That this shocking story occurs on Christmas Eve—and recalls an earlier, even more horrifying rosse play, *A Christmas Story*[54]—does make the film almost deliberately blasphemous. And while this anticlerical attitude was typical of grand guignol—and of French culture during the Third Republic in general—it seemed distinctly "foreign" in the United States, where one reviewer was disturbed enough at the film's morbidity to call for its censorship.[55] But what was perhaps just as unsettling or "offensive" was the ambiguity of the film's attitude toward the woman in this story. For, if at least one intertitle condemns her as a coquette, many of the images lend her desire, even her subjectivity, some legitimacy—at least until her character is nearly erased in the sheer savagery and violence of the husband's revenge.

Le Moulin maudit (1909), which provoked the wrath of the National Censorship Board in the United States,[56] tells a remarkably similar story of provincial peasant life in which a newly married miller catches a rival named Wilhelm with his wife Joanna and, in a fit of rage, beats him to death. Although the exact time period of this story is unclear, it was shot by Machin, as was *Nuit de Noël*, entirely on location—this time near the Flemish town of Gand, in order to exploit the picturesqueness of an old, isolated windmill.[57] The film that the American censors allowed to be screened must have looked like a simple documentary of Flemish peasant life—from the opening tableau of a village dance, where Joanna accepts the miller's offer of marriage, to the series of tableaux (each introduced by a cryptic intertitle) depicting their life together over a six-month period. What American viewers would not have seen is the last half of the film, after Wilhelm comes to visit his rival's wife. When the miller returns and finds someone else's shoes at the base of the windmill ladder and Wilhelm descending the ladder, the film (uninterrupted by intertitles) explodes into one of the more memorable climaxes of grand guignol violence. Not only does the miller kill Wilhelm, but he drags the body back toward the ladder, lashes it to one of the windmill blades, and ties his terrified wife to a nearby post so that she has to face the consequences of her crime in the spectacle of her lover's circling corpse. Yet, as the miller tries to leave the murder scene, the windmill remains looming ironically in the background of the frame, like a spectral sign that he, too, cannot escape his crime. The economy of this resonant repetition in *Le Moulin maudit* then coalesces in one last ingenious tableau. In an unusual HA LS, the miller leaps into a pond; when the water once again grows still, there on its surface indelibly fixed is a reflection of the continually turning blades of the windmill. All three characters and their story of passion and vengeance are literally condensed into a single iconic image whose initial emanation of picturesque nostalgia has been replaced by a charge of unspeakable horror.

Pathé was not the only company, however, to release such grimly sensational films—at least on the evidence of two surviving Gaumont titles. Feuillade's *La Légende des phares* (1909), for instance, recounts an ironic folktale about an old Breton woman (played by Carl) and her fisherman son.[58] The opening LS of a rocky beach at night, with several corpses stranded by the ebbing tide, succinctly shows how the old woman makes her living—moving from one dead seaman to another, collecting coins from their pockets. Returning to the one-room house she shares with her son, she greedily hides the coins in a small casket and refuses to let him have any—and he angrily puts out to sea in a small boat. Later, in a LA LS of a rocky cliff overlooking the sea, where a warning lantern has been hung from a cross, the old woman deliberately knocks the signal off the crossbar and waits for her prey. Another corpse washes up on the beach, but the seaman she has "killed" turns out to be her own son. So stricken with remorse is the woman that she herself now takes up a fixed position on the cliff, holding a lantern high; and, in the final tableau, her figure dissolves into that of a memorial statue, with its own moral warning. In *Gardien de la Camargue* (1910), set on the southern coast, another young man suffers at the hands of a woman—only this time he is a refuge ranger, and she is a young actress from Paris named Arlette, visiting her aunt for the summer.[59] As if taking Arlette's perspective, this film initially seems most interested in "touring" the region's picturesque locations—from an old stone archway, through which she arrives in a carriage to meet her aunt and don a native costume, to a hillside olive orchard, where she first meets the ranger and then rides with him on horseback in a procession of peasants through several fields. The connotation of these images shifts, however, when a letter calls Arlette back to the capital—registered in the LS of her lone figure walking away from the camera toward the stone archway—but the rest of the film focuses on the ranger's despair over her leaving. In one sequence, he races through the countryside to plead with her before she departs in the carriage; in the next, he follows the train which bears her away, but halts in a tableau that includes a distant, deserted windmill. In the end, he turns his horse toward the sea and rides out into the surf; the final shot displays his body, like that of the son in the earlier film, washing up on the beach.

That Pathé released so many films in the tradition of grand guignol during this period, despite the howls of protest they raised in the United States, remains something of a puzzle. After all, Berst as well as Pathé himself must have been keenly aware of the newly voiced American insistence on "good, clean, wholesome" films and on the kind of melodrama that, as Owen Davis, one of its best practitioners, described it, "only ends when you have exhausted every calamity, but it ends happily; it *must* end happily."[60] When he visited the United States, in May 1908, indeed Charles Pathé seemed to be responding to this criticism for he insisted that he personally would select the films his company released in the American market.[61] It may be, however, that Pathé was still banking on the continued popularity of the kinds of films that had helped to establish its early dominance in the American market—that is, on the continuing "exportability" of sensational stories, whether set in "exotic" places, the provinces, or the capital, which had such a mass appeal in France. And that popularity may have seemed consistent with the long practice, in the American and British theater, of staging plays either translated or adapted from French sources.[62] Furthermore, in France itself, this was a period of *grand peur*, of heightened anxiety, about all kinds of threats to the French social order—from the wave of working-class strikes to feminist demands for women's equality—and that anxiety circulated, through displacement in the French daily press and its fixation on the lurid details of one apache crime or *crime passionnelle* after another.[63] One of the more notorious of these, in 1907, involved Albert Soleillade, a Paris laborer and family man who confessed to raping, killing, and mutilating a neighbor's eleven-year-old daughter.[64] A year later, another "starred" Marguerite Steinheil, an attractive bourgeois figure who was accused (and acquitted) of murdering not only her husband but her own mother.[65] And that same anxiety circulated, in condensed form (and sometimes transported to more "exotic" milieu) in the rosse plays and films exhibited in Paris theaters and cinemas. Indeed, by 1910, even English-language Parisian guidebooks listed the Théâtre du Grand Guignol as one of the city's best known tourist attractions.[66]

Yet, gradually, more and more Pathé and Gaumont titles did run counter to this fascination for grand guignol irony by imposing a more conventional moral voice as well as a relatively "happy ending," both of which were more conducive to American tastes.[67] Pathé's *Le Roman de l'écuyère* (1910), also directed by de Morlhon, for instance, returns to a contemporary urban setting for its story of marital infidelity and miraculous reunion. Here, a circus clown named Toddie (Jacquinet) learns that his wife, a bareback rider, is having an affair with a bourgeois gentleman and throws her out, keeping their only daughter (Renée Pré)—and this breakup soon leads to an accident that cripples him. A year later, the girl searches out her mother who, while still living with the gentleman, has a fit of remorse and returns to her husband—and the family is restored, much as in *La Loi du pardon*, with the daughter joining her parents' hands. This film initially alternates the family dressing room and the circus arena, the latter of which is viewed through an entrance curtain from backstage, thereby staging the development of the affair in the foreground of a doubled, deep-space playing area.[68] In preparation for Toddie's discovery, a third space is inserted between these two, as he comes to a door, listens, and then (on a matchcut) breaks in on the illicit couple. In the film's second half, a similar adjacent space is inserted as the girl comes to the gentleman's townhouse entrance, only now it is the wife who, after her drawing room "epiphany" of remorse, is reunited with her daughter outside. An even stronger structural rhyme links this recognition of guilt with Toddie's earlier accident at the circus.[69] Near the end of part one, as he stands on a platform ready to perform on the trapeze, a background memory image of his wife and her lover dissolves in, so upsetting him that he falls. Near the end of part two, the wife is seated in the foreground, turned away from a half-dozen party guests, when Toddie suddenly dissolves in to replace the man chatting beside her. This apparition so shocks her that she immediately takes off the jewelry the gentle-man has given her and leaves the room. Although unexpected psychologically, this latter climactic moment receives added melodramatic force from the way that it economically reworks particular elements from the dramatic climax con-cluding the first part of the film.

One of the principal means by which French melodramas during this period were assured of a moral voice, however, seems unique—through the incorpo-ration of mass-produced images, especially photographs. In contrast to the am-bivalence with which innovative technologies such as the railroad and the tele-phone were represented in the cinema—recall, for instance, *Un Drame en express* or *A Narrow Escape*—the experience of modernity associated with photography, at least initially, was consistently benevolent. Pathé's *Vues d'espagne en cartes pos-tales* (1907) provides a good introduction to this pattern of representation in that its travelogue vues are framed within the fictional "plot" of a French bourgeois family touring Spain. After their carriage drives up to a hotel, the mother visits a nearby market and examines a rack of postcard photographs. In three separate sequences, a postcard she holds in her hand, in CU, "magically" turns into a moving image. The first presents several comic Spanish "types," the second displays a lovely series of views of the Alhambra palace, and the third "climaxes" in a smooth tracking shot of the Barcelona Gardens. The family then leaves the hotel in their carriage, and the film ends—their tour apparently complete. With a good deal of craft and wit, *Vues d'espagne* suggests just how important post-card photos had become to the tourist industry in Europe—as both a "proof" of one's travel and a stimulus to others.[70] But it also shows how photographs can even become a substitute for travel. Moreover, as an advance on photogra-phy, the cinema is able to simulate travel itself, turning the spectator into a tourist—making any part of the world visible and available for appropriation. And, unlike the mother within the film, who at least travels to Spain, the film spectator never really has to leave home.

Similar CU photographs cropped up, shortly thereafter, in a surprising number of French films.[71] Here, they circulated within the narrative and sym-bolic economy of melodrama as a specific form of moral "truth"—their implicit authenticity producing in the words of Henri Matisse, "the most precious docu-ments in existence."[72] As a consequence, they also tended to stabilize identity, to fix the individual as a social subject, especially in the face of what Walter Benjamin, quoting Charles Baudelaire, called the "shocks and collisions" one experienced in "plunging into a crowd" or being caught up in the "traffic of a big city"—"like a *kaleidoscope* equipped with consciousness."[73] "Every photo-graph," Roland Barthes once wrote, "is a certificate of presence."[74] It names and compels belief in the "that-has-been," for it constitutes a "laminated object" to which "the referent adheres." Moreover, in that it stops or "embalms time," to use André Bazin's famous phrase, the "intense immobility" of the photograph can recirculate like a haunting or "return of the dead."[75]

Such a return figures prominently in one of the earliest French films to de-ploy the insert CU of a photograph, Gaumont's *Le Déraciné ou artiste* (1909).[76] This film tells the story of a young fisherman from Toulon who discovers that he has a talent for singing and steals his aged mother's rent money in order to embark on a career.[77] The old woman is forced to become a beggar and, sometime later, comes across her successful son. Shot entirely on location on the southern coast of France, this film opens with a simple spatial opposition, in exterior LSs, between the mother's shack and the outside stage at the Casino des Fleurs where the fisherman first is encouraged to perform. And that opposition is extended in further LSs that juxtapose the simple rowboats and fishing nets in front of the shack with the pleasure boats anchored in the harbor (before which the young man is invited to join a small touring company) and the train that carries him off to a modicum of fortune and fame. If these images of modern urban life serve as a lure to the young man—for his story follows the path of the French provincial attracted to the city—in the second part of the film, they constitute an ironically spectacular backdrop to the old woman's wanderings, which trace a very different path of exclusion and abandonment. Their opposite trajectories are then reconciled in two climactic moments of recognition mediated by specific public and private images. First, the old woman sees a poster advertising her son's performance at the Palais de Fêtes (probably in Nice) and begins to follow him. When she approaches him in a park one day, he shoves her away so hard that she falls, and in her hand he discovers an old photograph—a MCU of himself taken long ago in Toulon. This self-recognition economically conveys his acceptance of guilt, and he finally acts out the proper role of a son to a mother—and is exonerated.[78] Celebrating the "sacred" sphere of the private and familial, *Le Déraciné ou artiste* offers a moral exemplum of the third commandment, "Honor thy father and thy mother," through two interrelated media of mass-produced images.[79]

With the aid of a similar photograph, Pathé's *Le Grand-père* (1910) reworks the story of the company's similarly titled film from three years before. A young couple, Elizabeth and Hubert (as in the earlier film, he is an artist), wed against the wishes of Erdmann, her father; then, several years later, the old man is reconciled to the marriage through the intercession of their young daughter. Here, the photograph initially functions as a memorial fragment or, to adopt Susan Sontag's language, as a kind of "surrogate possession."[80] An early scene, for instance, has Elizabeth alone at a desk reading a letter from Erdmann (who remains adamant in his rejection) and includes an unusual cut-in HA MCU over her shoulder as she gazes at a photograph of her father and lifts it to her lips. This is followed by the requisite melodramatic coincidence in which, out walking with the family maid, the girl runs into Erdmann outside his townhouse and scrapes her knee (requiring him to bind the wound with a handkerchief). Back in her own apartment, she happens to notice the photograph left on the desk, and another cut-in HA MCU has her repeat her mother's look and gesture in a doubled rhetorical figure that turns the mother's loss and longing into the daughter's discovery and desire. Returning to Erdmann's townhouse, the girl's revelation of his letter and photograph stuns the old man, but her mission fails to dissuade him. That can only transpire after the girl fakes an illness and demands that he come to comfort her—and this, too, requires a corresponding "trick" of representation, articulated by means of the telephone. As she climbs a chair in the hallway to reach the wall phone, suddenly a triptych tableau connects FSs of the girl and her grandfather across a central panel, the HA ELS of a thronged Paris street—with the side panel "portraits" now replacing the earlier enframed photograph. Once Erdmann "comes back to life" in the apartment, the reconciliation can swiftly unfold, condensing all three generations into the concluding tableau of a restored family portrait, with the grandfather and grand-daughter at its compositional center.

So far I have been dealing with films in which photographs function as a source of recognition and revealed truth, not only restoring broken family relations but renewing the value of the patriarchal subject threatened by the exigencies of modern urban life. There are several melodramas, however, which include the photographic process itself—specifically, the lapse in time between the taking and printing (and viewing) of a photograph—as a mechanism of delay or suspense leading up to the film's resolution. One such film is Lux's *Les Lavendières* (1910), which uses the situation of picture taking for its narrative premise. Set in a provincial village, its story involves a young bourgeois tourist and his friend who are taking photos of the local washerwomen. After accosting one of them named Mary and being rejected, the tourist goes along with another washerwoman, Kate, who spreads a rumor that Mary was flirting with him. This enrages Mary's fiancé, a young peasant named John, who angrily breaks off their engagement and refuses to be reconciled with her until the ruse is exposed at a village festival. To narrate such a relatively complicated story, this short film relies heavily on a tableau mode of representation in which single shots illustrate intertitles such as "Furious at being repulsed by Mary, the young squire listens to Kate's maliciousness." Most of these are shot on location, and they follow a distinctive pattern in their deep-space choreography of the actors.[81] Even more interesting, however, is the way the film establishes its crucial enigma, for, inserted between the moments when the tourist chucks Mary under the chin and when she slaps him is a MS of his friend holding the camera up to shoot. Precisely what the resulting photograph records, of course, is delayed until, during the festival at an outdoor café, the two supposed rivals square off to fight. Then the friend steps in to show John his snapshot—a CU of Mary just about to hit the other man in the face. The final tableau presents one further delay in its resolution by having John explain himself to Mary's mother, before a short pan leads him to kneel beside the chair in which Mary is sleeping, so she can awaken and embrace him.

Pathé's *L'Intrigante* (1911) incorporates several steps in the photographic process, in an extremely condensed two-part narrative. The schemer of this film's titles is the governess of a provincial bourgeois household, whose plan is to marry (for money) the widowed father of her ward, a ten-year-old girl, who clearly dislikes her mother's "replacement." A note the governess writes to her lover (who is pretending to be her "cousin") discloses this plot to the spectator in the opening drawing room tableau; when the daughter inadvertently reads the so-called cousin's reply and learns of the deception, the governess locks the girl in a backyard shed in order to meet her lover alone. The shed turns out to be the father's amateur photography lab, however, where the girl stands on a stool to look out a slot in the background door, and the following rectangular-masked POV shot of the governess and lover kissing in the yard reads like a displaced "primal scene." The girl gets down to find a camera, but the governess returns to check on her, and the scene ends with the couple kissing again, apparently unobserved, and separating. Later, the father, who clearly is attracted to the governess, joins his daughter in the lab. Instead of telling him what she knows, the girl gets him to develop a roll of film, and a cut-in HA MS shows him taking a negative filmstrip out of a tray (the whole image tinted rose from an offscreen light source). As he steps forward to hold up the filmstrip, a cut-in ECU of the negative now reproduces the earlier POV image of the couple's kiss. The father's knowledge finally coincides with both the girl's and the spectator's, and in the concluding drawing room tableau the governess is dismissed. As documentary evidence, here the photograph is instrumental not only in maintaining a hierarchy of classes but in keeping sexuality at bay by associating it with potentially criminal behavior. Yet, as a kind of dream scene projection by the girl, it also creates a haunting disturbance in the final portrait of father and daughter as a proper bourgeois family. Nevertheless, like the previous films, *L'Intrigante* trades on the seeming veracity and consequent virtue of the photograph as a privileged source of knowledge and truth—and, by implication, those qualities extend to their own moving images. In effect, all four films seek to define the cinema as a thoroughly moral discourse.

By 1910–1911, French melodramas of both the light and dark variety were distributed across the full spectrum of available representational modes. On one end of the spectrum were those, following the practice of films such as *L'Assomoir*, that reverted in large part to an older, narrativized tableau system. Although there were exceptions, most of these were marketed as "headliners" or "prestige" films of one sort or another, which brought them in line with a significant body of concurrent historical films. In the middle of the spectrum were the majority of films, combining sequences of long-take, deep-space tableaux with others organized according to various changes in framing—from camera movement or cut-in close shots to parallel or contrast editing or even quick cutting—especially in two-part narrative structures that relied on the systematic repetition of selected spaces. At the other end were those few, following the example of *L'Homme aux gants blancs*, *Le Grand-père*, or *L'Intrigante* that deployed "new" representational strategies within their narrative and symbolic economy. Although it would be tempting to read this spectrum in terms of a nostalgia for the past versus an enthusiasm for the modern, the dichotomy does not hold when one considers specific film subjects. What is apparent, however, is that characters increasingly were being located within an urban bourgeois milieu, even if a good number of films continued to exploit the "exotic" culture of the provinces or of the "lower classes." Moreover, with the growing popularity of actresses such as Mistinguett, women once again began to assume prominent roles, even though they often still served as either the source of moral deviance or the means of restoring the patriarchal family. Perhaps most intriguing was the development, out of the grand guignol films, of an ironic voice of narration—from *L'Homme aux gants blancs* to *Le Moulin maudit*—in contrast to the moral voice so characteristic of the domestic melodrama. Indeed, the disjunction such an ironic voice creates between the spectator and a film's central character may constitute a major difference between the French cinema and its American counterpart during this period.

To disparage those films that continued to adhere closely to the older tableau system of representation would be unfair since they generally did so with a good deal of efficacy and craft. Pathé's *Le Bon Patron* (1910), for instance, another early film directed by de Morlhon, is a perfect example of how well that system could serve a "prestigious" film—even one that told a story of class conflict very much in line with *Le Contremaître incendiaire*.[82] The explicit basis of that conflict is unclear, however, because the only extant print begins with a working-class man (Gaston Moreau) already angry at a foreman in the lumber company where he is or was employed.[83] When he attacks the foreman one day, he himself is stabbed (with his own knife) and hospitalized; hearing of his condition, the lumber company owner (Mévisto) decides to help and personally gives some money to his family in compensation. This film is restricted to a minimum of decors—the family dining room, a hospital room, the owner's office, and an alley in the lumberyard (the only actual location)—all but the last of which are recorded consistently in waist-level FS/LS. The principal space, in fact, is a recurrent, symbolic space—the family dining room. It is there that the workman's anger is first expressed: before his horrified wife and daughter, he smashes one of their few porcelain dishes. It is there, too, that the owner comes to offer the money to the wife and daughter. And it is there that the workman returns to find a special vase of flowers on the table and perhaps even be reconciled with the foreman (although the extant print breaks off before this can be certain). Consequently, *Le Bon Patron* ends up celebrating not only the benevolent businessman as a solution to class conflict but also the older capitalist system that defined the small business as an extended family (with a doubly patriarchal boss) and which still largely characterized France before the war.

For its subject, Pathé's *La Mariée du château maudit* (1910) turns to a jeopardized love story, located in a different social space, and, more important, takes advantage of a much wider range of representational strategies. This story begins rather frivolously with a small bourgeois wedding party deciding to play a game of hide-and-seek on the grounds of a provincial, partly ruined chateau. The bride falls into a buried chamber, in which she discovers a deadly secret, and it takes a peasant girl's cat to help the groom and their friends locate and rescue her. Initially, the intercutting of contiguous spaces serves to organize this film, as in the sequence of shots where the bride splits off from a woman friend, disappears into a hidden cleft, and gets up off the floor of a dungeon, and the groom nonchalantly passes by the same spot. Thereafter, parallel editing takes over as the bride explores a series of rooms, the last of which (lit by a small window upper left) has a still figure seated at a foreground table, while the others in the wedding party discover she is missing and begin to search. This is complicated, however, when the bride realizes the figure is a skeleton and, after a momentary fainting spell, begins to read the book propped up before it on the table. Now a cut-in AS of her before the open book includes a device familiar from previous féerie films: a matted-in "live action" scene on the left and right pages. And this story-within-a-story tells of another married woman who, after her lover has been killed, was bound in that very chair and forced, as was the woman in *Le Moulin maudit*, to face her own guilt and its consequences. However, this grim "fairy tale" proves to be safely enframed in the past, its "embalmed figure" serving as a gender-specific warning against infidelity. The cat, first introduced in what seemed a throwaway shot early on and then shown, in CU, coming through the window (just before the reading), suddenly appears on the table so that, when the bride reawakens from another faint, she can tie a scarf around its neck and send it back out the window. In the reassuring coincidence of a happy ending, where the good bourgeois are supported by even better peasants, the film resumes the intercutting of contiguous spaces, and the groom swings into action, rappelling into the chamber, and reemerges reunited with his bride.

Using equally flexible editing strategies, Lux's *Un Drame sur une locomotive* (1910) tells a radically different story of love and jealousy in the urban milieu of railway workers, probably drawing its ending from Zola's *La Bête humaine*.[84] An engineer named Jack is in love with the daughter of a local café owner, but she herself is in love with his co-engineer, Tom. One day, after their scheduled departure, the two men begin fighting in the engine cab and fall out alongside the tracks, leaving their passenger train to rush on, derail, and crash—dramatizing one of the chief "modern" fears and traumas of the previous century.[85] Although comprised chiefly of FS/LSs, this film, unlike the earlier Zola adaptation, *L'Assomoir*, relies on sequences of interrelated shots rather than long-take tableaux, and is punctuated by just a few, brief intertitles. The fait divers nature of its story is accentuated by location shooting, as well as restrained action and a "natural" choreography of actor movement, including that of minor characters—for instance, the exterior shot of the café continues after the major characters have exited so that two men who have been drinking and chatting in the foreground also have time to get up and leave. What is most unique about *Une Drame sur une locomotive*, however, is the way it represents the fight and train crash. After the two men have quarreled beside their locomotive—over a flower the woman has given Tom—smoothly matched LSs show the train moving off on a diagonal into the background. A sudden cut-in AS of their struggle in the cab ends with both beginning to fall out, followed by a quick five-frame FS of them falling forward from the train, and then a LS of both lying together on the gravel roadbed. This unexpected prototype of quick cutting is then matched by another short sequence where, in LS, the "runaway train" rounds a curve and exits in the left foreground (in fast motion)[86] and, in LALS (accentuated by a pan), races along a slope toward the right background, climaxing in a sudden explosion of white smoke. The increasing suspense generated by this sequence is then broken by an intertitle, "After the accident," and two FSs of the wrecked engine and one passenger car (suggesting that all aboard the train have survived). Only after this "pause" do people begin running toward the crash site and does news of the disaster reach the woman in the café, who rushes off to find the two rivals dead, locked in one another's arms. In the end, *Une Drame sur une locomotive* privileges a personal tragedy at the same time that it opens up, in the sensational fashion of grand guignol, the possibility of a greater social catastrophe.

The sophistication with which these contemporary melodramas could exploit framing and editing strategies is no more apparent than in two final titles. Gaumont's *Le Vertige* (1910), one of Perret's earliest surviving films, skillfully blends irony and pathos in its tragic love story set in a seductively lush countryside (shot on location in Lorraine or Alsace, and tinted exclusively in green and amber).[87] Here, an innkeeper's daughter named Greta falls in love with Pierre (Perret), a Paris painter on holiday, who flirts with her but not all that seriously. Greta's growing interest in Pierre is articulated in a number of ways—within a deep-space FS/LS of the terrace fronting the inn (where Greta arranges flowers on a foreground table and glances at Pierre who sits smoking in a background window), through a closer eyeline matchcut between them, and finally through a smooth matchcut on her movement following Pierre to the inn's gate (to give him some brushes left behind), where a short pan separates them from the inn and her parents. This "love affair" culminates in two exceptionally composed tableaux—a FS/LS of the two strolling through a field of long grass (extended by a pan) to sit on a stone bench before a distant mill and pond, and an evening LS of the ivy-covered house by the gate, where Greta leans out a second-floor window to speak with Pierre below and lets fall a long white veil for him to kiss. That the spectator knows something that Greta does not renders these images all the more poignant—as well as doubly ironic, given the painter's profession—for the film's very first scene isolates Pierre at the inn window, in LA FS, declaring his boredom in the CU insert of a letter sending for his wife.

Le Vertige, in effect, is a perfect example of how, within a film's temporal construction, an ironic voice of narration can create a gap or discrepancy between what a principal character is allowed to know and what a spectator is led to understand. In the second half of the film, Greta's stunned reaction to the wife's arrival accumulates through a succinct repetition of prior spaces—in the FS/LS of the terrace, she sees the woman throw open Pierre's window; in the grassy field where he is painting (now distanced in LS), she is shocked by his delight at the news; and in the deep space of the terrace again, she watches him greet his wife warmly and close the window shutters. Thereafter, she follows the pleasure-seeking couple as they go boating on a nearby stream, through no less than three LSs, accentuated by short pans, which obsessively repeat her subjective position now as an excluded spectator at the foreground margin of a silhouetted screen of trees. The final LS focuses on Greta alone beside another stream, taking off the veil that once seemed to bind her to Pierre and wading out into the water, again conveyed through a pan, to drown herself. Through a masterly use of recurrent imagery, *Le Vertige* increases the distance between this victimized female figure and the painter who blithely remains unaware of her pain, while, simultaneously, it slowly closes the gap initially opened up between her and the knowing spectator—only to break that link, too, in one last frisson.

Every bit as remarkable is SCAGL's "terrifying cinedrama," *L'Epouvante* (1911), whose handling of suspense makes it the equal of any American film at the time.[88] This is one of the earliest surviving films starring Mistinguett, and Decourcelle's original script serves as an exemplary vehicle for her and her co-star, Emile Milo, by restricting its action to a very short period of time and to just a few adjacent spaces. In a self-referential gesture, Mistinguett plays herself as a well-known, but unnamed theater actress, who returns to her apartment one evening to find a jewel thief (Milo) in her bedroom. She calls the police, but the thief eludes them and ends up hanging precariously from a gutter; after they leave, she has to decide, now that the tables have turned, whether or not to rescue him. *L'Epouvante* begins succinctly with two brief intertitles (there are only four in all) introducing two separate LSs of the principal characters: Mistinguett, in a white fur, leaving a theater to get into a waiting car, and Milo casing a bedroom, hearing a sound through the door (frame right), and hiding under the bed. Only in the next two shots does the relationship between these two characters become clear as the actress (still in fur) and her maid enter the FS/LS of a drawing room, exit left, and come into the bedroom in a closer AS, which initially centers on the bed and then (through a short pan) reframes Mistinguett taking off her jewelry at a foreground table. A brief sequence of alternation takes the maid back into the drawing room, while Mistinguett climbs in bed, and ends with the maid turning out a gas lamp in the kitchen. Unlike *Le Vertige*, this film closes the gap between the spectator's knowledge and that of its central character with a shock. A FS of Mistinguett in bed, tossing aside a book and reaching for a cigarette, suddenly shifts, when she looks down at a dropped match, as the camera dollies away from her to LS. Although this unusual camera movement literalizes the distance between spectator and character, and accentuates the latter's vulnerability, the next shot closes that distance with almost Hitchcockian intensity. An overhead CU MS past her head frames the thief's hand emerging from underneath the bed and snatching the match. The LS that returns then focuses on the actors as Mistinguett struggles to control her fear and eventually uses the pretext of refilling a water glass to exit, after which Milo quickly gets up to find the door locked (and his presence known), grabs the jewelry, and exits through the background balcony doors.

For much of the film's second half, attention shifts to Milo, who finds himself in an equally, if not more, vulnerable position. The reason is that the exterior shots (all done on location) confine him to a narrow balcony running alongside the apartment—several MS/ELSs, with a park and cityscape in the distance, reveal that he is caught on a five-story building—and to the steeply sloping roof. The police pursue him in an extended sequence, uninterrupted by intertitles, which alternates between the bedroom and the balcony and then the balcony and the roof, as the actors' movements and the relatively quick cutting combine to keep the two proximate yet constantly separate. And while the police consistently are framed in FS and LS, Milo is privileged in closer shots—linking the spectator with his predicament and his deft performance. This sequence ends, after the police go back inside, with the thief dropping onto the balcony and climbing over the edge (conveyed in a downward tilt) to hang from the gutter; when one cop steps back onto the balcony, the LA shot reveals (but only to the spectator) no more than the thief's hands at the bottom of the frame. Just as the police leave Mistinguett sitting at the dressing table, the suspense cranks up a notch as a MS shows Milo now hanging by one hand and crying out in desperation—and, prompted by the sound cue, she goes to the balcony door. Although too afraid to step outside, Mistinguett extends a drape over the balcony railing so that Milo, at the last moment, can clutch it and haul himself up to safety. This unusually sustained alternation finally comes to rest in a long-take FS/LS of the bedroom as the two shakily come to an agreement—she allows him to go free and he returns her jewelry—one performer rewarding the other, under the mediating gaze of the spectator, with the gesture then being reciprocated. Although perhaps lacking the fever pitch of Griffith's last-minute rescue films, *L'Epouvante* certainly belies the widely held notion that the French cinema was incapable of producing exciting action films. Indeed, in its unique framing and editing strategies, it is every bit the equal of Phillip Smalley's later "classic" one-reeler for Universal, *Suspense* (1913).

Comics Come in Series

By 1907–1908, the short comic film was an established, increasingly profitable staple of French film production. Pathé, for instance, was usually releasing two or three comic films per week, and Gaumont sometimes came close to matching its rival's output. Although none of these films were ever advertised as "headliners" on either French or American cinema programs, their consistently popular appeal could be counted on to attract and sustain a more and more regular clientele.[89] Lacassin has described these years as the "formative period" of early French film comedy, and, to some extent, the label fits.[90] Some of Pathé's and Gaumont's comic films continued to exploit the earlier structuring principle of redundancy, whether in chases or in serially linked gags or vignettes. Even more films, however, consistently deployed changes in framing to elaborate their patterns of gag construction. And a few films varied their representational strategies in such a way as to produce relatively complicated comic structures. This strongly suggests, as Toulet argues, that the so-called classical period of French film comedy had already begun.[91] What demonstrates the case most clearly, of course, is the development of the comic series around a single male actor, which introduced a quite different, yet often complementary, structuring principle to the genre. Here, a comic type—and during this period, they were all male[92]—possessing relatively constant character traits confronted one challenging, awkward, or bizarre situation after another, in film after film. As previously mentioned, Pathé initiated the comic series strategy with Deed in the *Boireau* series (1906–1909), and Gaumont soon followed with Bosetti in *Roméo* (1907–1908), Clément Migé in *Calino* (1909–1913), and René Dary in *Bébé* (1910–1912). By 1910–1911, every major French company had at least one regular comic series: Lux with Bertho in *Patouillard*, Eclipse with Servaes in *Arthème*, Eclair with Gréhan in *Gontran* and Tommy Footit in *Tommy*, and Pathé with Charles Prince in *Rigadin* as well as Maurice Schwartz in *Little Moritz*. Moreover, Linder's series for Pathé was recognized around the world as the best of the lot.[93]

Before tracking the mainstream of French comic film production during this period, it is worth considering, if only briefly, those few films that constituted a "throwback" to the earlier strategy of the single-shot recording of an essentially stage performance. Most of these are Star Film releases from 1908, when Méliès was turning out double the usual number of films from his two Montreuil studios, in a desperate attempt to reverse his increasingly marginal status in the American market. *His First Job*, for instance, reworks a situation borrowed from one of the early *Boireau* series, but here, in the LS tableau of a grocery store set, the pacing and execution of the gags are almost as inept as the apprentice himself.[94] *The Mischances of a Photographer* is not much better, unfortunately, even though it employs two set decors (one is merely the wall of Montreuil studio B) to tell its simple story of a man who decides to become a photographer and so garbs his neighbors in assorted theatrical costumes. The film's single gag is delayed until the very end when, after a boy has shoved a water hose into the back of the camera, the photographer dowses his subjects—in a rather unfunny reprise of Lumière's first gag film, *Arroseur et arrosé*. Despite being confined to a single set, *French Cops Learning English* succeeds in being mildly amusing, perhaps because the strict geometrical arrangement of Miss Blackford's classroom provides a suitable backdrop for the schematic exercises she forces her five marionettelike gendarmes to run through. Their education advances rapidly once they all finally pair off with English girls in conversation lessons, and the film concludes in a celebratory dance that—as the school principal joins in the co-educational festivities, holding up a sign bearing the code words, "Entente Cordiale"—serves to reconfigure the 1904 French-British political alliance.

Still, the Méliès comic films seem oddly tame and even embarrassingly amateurish in comparison to a single-shot film such as Gaumont's *Le Bon Invalide et les enfants* (1908). In a characteristic eye-level LS studio decor of a park, an old man slowly paces about and sits exhausted on a background bench, and several boys come in to play with a ball in the foreground. Quickly tiring of their game, they go over to speak to the old man, who suddenly (in a straight cut) offers them his head, and they return to the foreground to toss it around. Gradually, they acquire both legs and an arm from the still sitting figure, and finally stand the body parts up like pins and bowl them over with the head. Once this ghoulish game is over, they simply return all the parts to their owner and exit—and the old man leaps up from the bench rejuvenated and strides off like a young man again. What initially might seem, in *Le Bon Invalide et les enfants*, a cruel expropriation of the aged by the young turns into a little fable of reciprocal exchange in which a "helping hand" and head are doubly regenerative. Likewise, in Gaumont's *Les Trois Mannequins* (1909), a love story and crime story neatly converge within the LS exterior of a pawnshop. Because the pawnshop proprietor cannot stand his daughter's suitor, the young man disguises himself as a clothes dummy in order to be near her. A thief comes by, swipes something from a display table, and takes on a second dummy's disguise so as to avoid the proprietor—who notices the missing item but not the watch the thief lifts from his pocket. Finally, a cop is called in and takes the place of a third dummy in order to nab the thief. A cut-in MS of the lined-up men shows them tiring of the game, which sets up the final gag in the returning LS: the suitor yawns, stretches, and loses his balance so that all three dummies topple over in a heap. The suitor grabs the thief; the cop finds the stolen goods; and the proprietor is pleased—and blesses his daughter's choice of a husband. Small gestures come across all that more comic and heroic, this film shows, within a doubly static tableau.

The comic chase film, one of the earliest innovative narrative forms, continued to enjoy a vogue, at least for another year or so. Pathé's *The Bathers' Race* (1907), for instance, uses the premise of having a man swipe a bicycle out of a bathhouse on the beach at Deauville, which leads to a rather loosely connected chase through a park, past some ruins, and into and out of a hotel. And it concludes with a FS of the thief, after having sicced two gendarmes on his pursuers, retrieving the stolen bicycle and riding off quite pleased with himself. The same company's *Adventures of a Madman* (1907) lets an asylum escapee do all sorts of crazy things—guzzle a mechanic's can of gasoline, chomp on a washerwoman's cake of soap—while being pursued halfheartedly by a token contingent of victims. His mad antics take on a satirical edge, however, when he dons a military uniform and duels with a cane-twirling dandy (Linder); then, after he is captured and dunked in a river, an emblematic MS poses him like Napoleon, but with a huge crab on his head. Gaumont, by contrast, seems to have produced variations on the comic chase strategy that were quite single-minded in their development of an initial premise. The well-known *La Course aux potirons* (1908), for instance, begins with a street vendor's cart collapsing and his half-dozen huge pumpkins rolling off down the road like ballooning automobile tires.[95] In the end, of course, the errant pumpkins all return to the cart and resume their natural form—as commodities for purchase and consumption—but for a while they lead the vendor and an assortment of townspeople on a merry chase. What is particularly striking in this film's relatively uncomplicated series of location LSs, however, is the range of the pumpkins' travels through French society. Not only do they mow down people in the street, they leap through a window to crash through a typical bourgeois dining room (the sole studio set decor) and then disappear down a manhole into the town's sewers. Anticipating the course they will inevitably take as food, the pumpkins also serve as comic leveling agents, erasing the spatial as well as social hierarchy of *above* and *below*.

A greater number of French comic films used the structuring principle of redundancy to follow up an initial premise with an accumulating series of re-peated gags, but in a context other than the chase. Star Film's *Why That Actor Was Late* (1908), for instance, loosely strings together a half-dozen LS tableaux depicting how an irritable fat actor is delayed in getting from his café table to the theater for a performance. Although most of these tableaux have no more than a single lame gag, the second one of a studio street set crams in several—the actor collides with a horse cart and deliveryman, he hails a sleepy driver who cannot start his car, and, once it does, a gendarme rushes in to halt them and issue a parking ticket—but their pacing and execution are as awkward as those in Méliès's other comic films that year. The only surviving Théophile Pathé film, *Governess Wanted* (1907), likewise, has a roughly finished look. Its simple premise is an ad for a governess, which brings a half-dozen women to "Sigh's Cottage," in "Blossom Delight Lane," where a fight breaks out in the corridor next to the interview room, spilling everyone down some stairs and into the street and off to a police station. Although this film does, if awkwardly, edit together adjacent spaces, it prefers either to hold on one space—such as the front garden of the cottage through which one character after another passes—or to pan back and forth from one space to another, for instance, when the women, one by one, go in to be interviewed. Unfortunately, this has the effect of slowing the pace of the gags interminably.

Pathé's "serial gag" films, by contrast, seem unusually fluid and consistently well paced. In *La Planche* (1907), for instance, a carpenter's assistant is sent off to deliver a long wooden plank, with the predictable results that, inadvertently, he knocks over a passerby, flattens a café table, smashes a crockery display and then a shop window, and finally runs into a cyclist and woman pushing a baby carriage. In *The Mattress* (1908), a clown-faced fellow does similar damage with a big mattress he has purchased until he decides to hire a carriage, which promptly breaks in two rounding a corner so that he has to play cart horse to get it to his apartment building. Once there, he uses his purchase like a tram-poline to bounce upward several floors to his apartment window, but in trying to draw it up with a rope, both he and the mattress fall on and flatten a pair of policemen. In *Hurry Up Please* (1908), a cameraman is taking moving pictures in various locations around Paris, and, as soon as he begins cranking his camera, the film shifts into extreme fast motion.[96] This truc effect gag is repeated in a snappy rhythm across a dozen deep-space LSs, with the camera always posi-tioned in the left or right foreground—speeding up strollers along the sidewalks and in the park, a couple in heated argument, several groups of lounging work-men, and traffic in the street—which not only simulate what the cameraman is recording but offer a concise analogy for the cinema's power to manipulate the real world. Yet that power turns out to be reversible, for the film concludes with an ironic twist—a boy sneaks up to the camera and, with a turn of the crank, makes the cameraman himself rapidly dance off into the depths of the frame.

Some of the earliest Pathé films in which Linder played a major role fall into the similar category of the extended situation. In *Les Débuts d'un patineur* (1907), for instance, he is a young dandy anxious to try out the new sport of ice skating but who approaches a wintery Paris park, incongruously, as if dressed for the theater.[97] There, he eagerly checks his overcoat (but keeps the top hat that will later distinguish his character), prances about, and, still smiling, sits down to have skates attached to his nimble feet. A series of three, loosely related shots quickly dispels his optimism. Reaching the ice, he takes a couple of shaky steps, falls in a heap, and has to be picked up and propped on a pyramidlike flurry of legs. After a short lesson, he promptly drops his top hat and, reaching down, sits on it in another desperate flurried dance. Finally, he pushes away a small boy who has run into him and then is pelted with snowballs, which send him hurtling into a woman being pushed about on a sled—and with that, a cop hustles him off the ice. Demoralized and unmasked, the disheveled dandy drops onto a bench to have his skates removed, as everyone close by ridicules him with laughter. And the film ends with him in an emblematic MS, "unmanned" and crying like a baby. In *Les Débuts d'un aéronaute* (1907), also obviously shot on location, Linder joins another man in the sport of riding a balloon over Paris. Once aloft, however, they fail to haul in an anchor attached to a trailing rope, which sets up a series of amazing gags. Ripping through the city streets, in a consistent pattern of movement from background to foreground, the anchor lifts an officer off his horse and drops him in the river, and then does likewise with a parked bicycle, a woman out shopping, a vegetable cart, a café table, and a doghouse complete with dog. Finally, the gondola itself begins smashing into chimneys and rooftops, eventually tearing away the side of a building to expose two rooms. When the balloon at last crashes in an open field, a horde of people rush in to trash the gondola and exit—leaving Linder alone to rise up entangled in the wreckage, his stunned dismay accentuated by a cut-in emblematic MS.

Again, Gaumont was especially adept at turning this kind of comic film into social commentary. *Buying a Cow* (1908), for instance, begins with the intriguingly absurd premise that a petit-bourgeois couple wants to buy a cow for their city apartment. Two location LSs are all it takes to get them from city to country, where they greedily test the cow's milk before purchase, but ten more are needed for their return. The cow has to be pushed and pulled up a village road; a driver will not allow it to be hitched to a bus, but it refuses to go on the metro; then, while its new owners stop at a café for a drink, it wanders off with two boys. Eventually, when the threesome do arrive back at the apartment building, the concierge refuses to let the cow in. The solution to this dilemma is just as absurd as the initial premise: while the couple argue, a passerby takes the cow off and leaves a toy pig in its place, which is perfectly acceptable to the concierge. In lampooning city folk who think they can acquire the "real thing," *Buying a Cow* suggests that all they can ever get for their troubles is the displaced nostalgia of a (probably mass-produced) replica. The premise for *Une Dame vraiment bien* (1908) is much more plausible and the satire more acute.[98] This film looses a leveling agent on French society quite different from that in *La Course aux potirons* by sending a fashionably dressed woman (Carl) out of a clothing shop to walk unescorted through the Paris streets. In a series of location LSs, the woman attracts the gaze of one man after another, each of whom promptly has an accident. A husband walks into a lamppost, a cyclist falls into a café table, a gardener sprays a man sitting on a park bench, a workman carrying a plank knocks out another man following him, and a line of soldiers stumbles and collapses in a heap. Finally, two cops give chase and seize the woman, putting a cloak over her shoulders, and escort her to the door of her apartment building. In one sense, *Une Dame vraiment bien* obviously mocks male desire with its continuous display of a female figure followed by recurring "castrating" gags. Yet, in another sense, the film simply endorses the cultural myth of the single, unattached woman's disruptive power and, consequently, her "taming" in a very condensed fashion—first, by suppressing her image as defined by clothing and, then, by enclosing her in an offscreen private space—in order to preserve the normal functioning of a male-dominated society.[99]

Several other concurrent Pathé films introduce changes in framing in order to better articulate their accumulating series of gags. One of the more novel of these was *Le Langage des pieds* (1909), which, at least according to the surviving scenario, narrated its simple story almost exclusively in MSs of a couple's legs and feet. *The Man Who Walked on Water* (1908), by contrast, opens with an enigma: a man is standing, in FS, in what seems to be an ankle-deep pond, with a pole in one hand and a net in the other, fishing. This enigma is situated within a larger space in the next shot, in which a boy coming along a path tosses pebbles into the pond and is chased off by the fisherman. Now the film begins to alternate between this initial space and a nearby village, where the boy persuades a rural postman and peasant farmer to follow him to the pond—and they see the fisherman land a boot. While the amused onlookers return to gather more villagers, another FS anticipates their pleasure by showing the fisherman reeling in a cooking pan. Finally, the mayor, a gendarme, and several local soldiers join the throng to gawk at the fisherman in the final tableau. One gag now caps another in close succession as the fisherman actually hooks and nets a large fish, but then (accentuated by a slight pan) climbs out of the pond on stilts and happily walks off, while the astonished villagers seize the boy who allegedly set up the spectacle and begin paddling him. Not only does *The Man Who Walked on Water* efficiently orchestrate its few gags by means of alternating spaces and crucially timed changes in framing,[100] it also creates, for those in the cinema audience, a surrogate body of onscreen observers, which allows the spectator to displace any resentment at this deliberate misperception onto a scapegoat and enjoy the film's trick with the assurance of the fisherman himself.

At least one other early Linder film also uses changes in framing and alternation to structure its gags. *His First Cigar* (1908) reworks Galipaux's *La Première Cigare du collegien* (1903) as well as Linder's own *Première Sortie* (1905) into a longer and more complicated, two-part format.[101] The first half of this film seems to duplicate *Première Sortie*, following Linder from one place to another and back, in a symmetrical sequence of six shots. It begins with a LS of a bourgeois dining room where an adolescent Linder stuffs some of his father's cigars in his pockets and, when his mother appears, pretends to be trying to catch a fly, before he exits decked out in his schoolboy's cap. Loosely matched exits and entrances take him out of his apartment building to a terrace restaurant where he sits to order a drink and, finally, light a cigar. In a cut-in MCU, Linder now re-creates Galipaux's gag of a boy trying to prove himself a man: puffing on the cigar and smiling and then looking at it strangely; puffing again, frowning, and looking a bit ill; puffing a third time, belching, and, with his eyes suddenly bulging, holding a handkerchief to his mouth. After Linder staggers back to his building, the film substitutes a LS of Pathé's ubiquitous stairway corridor for the expected dining room, and his efforts to negotiate this new space are articulated in a five-shot sequence of alternation. As he finally reaches a background door in the first stairway shot, another cut-in MCU focuses on his attempt to shove a cigar into the keyhole and eventually his successful insertion of a key. Reverse-angle cutting then takes him into an unfamiliar bedroom where a man jumps up to hide behind a bedside chair and then, recognizing the belching intruder, decks him with a pillow and kicks him back out into the corridor. The next-to-last shot quickly returns to the family dining room where Linder staggers about toppling rubber plants and pulling the cloth off a table, until his mother appears, sits him down, and gets out a bottle of medicine. Then comes the conventional emblematic shot, but this one echoes the restaurant gag with the cigar—in MCU, the mother forces Linder to gulp down a full glass of the medicine. The Oedipal comedy of *His First Cigar* thus ridicules "masculine" pleasure by turning the boy's oral fixation into an extended and then doubled displeasure, circumscribed in the end by the "home rule" of a humiliating maternal embrace.

All of these structuring strategies came together in two superb comic films. Pathé's *Le Cheval emballé* (1908) tells a simple, well-known story in two equal parts.[102] While serving a customer in an apartment building, a laundry deliveryman leaves his cart unattended next to a feedstore, and his horse consumes an open sack of oats sitting on the sidewalk outside. Suddenly endowed with spirit and energy, the horse races off through the Paris streets and repeatedly crashes into objects and people, attracting more and more pursuers. The first part of *Le Cheval emballé* begins with a sustained sequence of alternation. However, here, as in *A Narrow Escape*, the alternation is between two simultaneous lines of action, both recorded in LSs. While the horse consumes the oats (marked by the diminishing size of the sack), the man ascends the usual Pathé staircase, delivers a load of laundry to a bourgeois couple (who give him a glass of wine), and is then delayed by the concierge (who offers some snuff) as he descends. Moreover, the last two moments of alternation come precisely when the deliveryman himself is consuming the wine and snuff. The horse's feeding, of course, triggers the second half of the film, as if the swelling a spectator is asked to imagine going on in its belly explodes in a whirlwind chase. By means of slightly speeded-up filming and straight cuts, horse and cart swiftly plow through a series of obstacles—a nurse and baby carriage, a kiosk, some market stalls, two different workmen's scaffoldings—and reverse motion once even sends the cart into the glass windows of a pottery shop. Then, at the end of the chase, in a sequence of three shots that smoothly match its exits and entrances, the horse neatly eludes its pursuers and slips into its stable stall. The last two shots wrap up *Le Cheval emballé* with three gags, each of which tops the one before. At the stable gate, a man grabs a hose and dowses the pursuers, who flee the frame as the deliveryman turns to laugh at them, and then, unexpectedly, he gets dowsed as well. The only one to escape unscathed is the horse, which, in a final emblematic MS, is shown chomping contentedly at a box of hay and turning to look at the camera. Not only does the horse get away with considerable mayhem in this film, but, to cap its success, it has a last shared horselaugh with the audience.

A similarly concise strategy of sustained alternation structures Feuillade's *Le Thé chez le concierge* (1907) for Gaumont. Again, the premise is quite ordinary: a concierge and his wife are hosting an evening party, to which some of their neighbors are invited. The first two shots establish the crucial alternating spaces—a LS of the couple's single, dark-wallpapered room, as a half-dozen people gather to begin celebrating, and a LS of the street and apartment building entrance (frame right), as the concierge steps out, looks around, and goes back in, apparently content that all the building's tenants are gone for the night. But he is quickly proved wrong as one bourgeois tenant after another comes in to ring a newly installed apartment doorbell. Each time this new contraption is used, the film cuts to the interior room to explain (probably with the help of musical accompaniment) why neither the couple nor their guests hear the bell—a gendarme leads the group in singing, they applaud one another, and a woman begins dancing while the others stamp their feet to keep time. When two other gendarmes finally show up to question the angry crowd now gathered in the street, they are jeered, which gets everyone herded off to the police station. If the first half of this comedy of manners concludes in a doubled victimizing of the "innocent" bourgeois, in the second half, the victims are allowed their revenge as the concierge's guests take their leave, and the police prefect leads his men and the tenants back to the apartment building. Now a shorter sequence of alternation shows the concierge and his wife preparing for bed in complete ignorance of the irate crowd approaching (and being let in by the gendarmes), who, after bursting into their room, attack the couple and push them out onto the street. The final tableau neatly reverses the initial situation—now the concierge and his wife are locked out of the building, in their nightclothes—and then repeats the ironic gag ending the film's first half—a gendarme comes along to haul them off to jail for disturbing the peace. In *Le Thé chez le concierge*, a new technology gone awry turns a mild form of the carnivalesque into a "serious" social disorder, but in a reversible series in which proper order is re-righted—and made all the more amusing by the schematic symmetry with which it is articulated—and abetted by the police.

If Gaumont's subsequent comic films often fall back on the chase format, they do so, however, without any flagging of inventiveness. *Un Monsieur qui a mangé du taureau* (1909), for instance, has the host of a petit-bourgeois dinner party suddenly strap a mounted set of horns on his head and announce (in an intertitle inserted at the moment of utterance), "Do you realize you have eaten the meat of a bull!" With that, he goes into a mad rampage—smashing objects in the dining room and kitchen, pinning people into corners or on the floor, and bursting out onto the street to attack women and children, gendarmes, and even public statues in a series of deep-space LSs. A brief moment of alternation introduces a post office exterior and interior—where a telegram (signed by Lepine, the Paris police chief) urgently calls for a matador—but in the subsequent series of LSs, the crazed "bull" just whips into fast motion, repeatedly bouncing a gendarme between a tree and a lamppost.[103] In another, hilarious alternation that incorporates actualité footage, a whole contingent of matadors marches down the Champs Elysées (apparently in response to the telegram), while the mad "bull" battles a man dressed in a horse suit, who, when he is bested, simply sits down on his haunches.[104] Finally, before a semicircle of background onlookers, one matador finally steps in to bow to the camera and break the man's mad spell by simply swirling his cape and threatening him with a sword thrust. And the crowd, perhaps mirroring the cinema audience, cheers this "hero" who not only ends the mayhem but also reasserts the boundaries separating the human from the animal as well as the "real" from the fictional. American reviewers, however, saw such films—and they were more often Pathé's than Gaumont's—as one more example of the boundary separating American good sense from French "bad taste."[105]

Somewhat more narrowly and, for the Americans, more "responsibily" focused, Gaumont's *La Guêpe* (1910) begins with a man sitting at a sidewalk café table and, in a cut-in MCU, discovering a wasp on his glass of beer. In his efforts to kill the wasp, he enlists the help of his neighbors; soon their flailing pursuit overturns all the café tables and chairs (along with an interior billiard table) and sends them off through the streets, in a series of LSs, until they lose their way and have to straggle back to the café completely disheveled. Echoing the cut-in MCU that initiated this chase, another cut-in HA CU sets up the film's resolution—now several wasps are swimming in his beer. This time the man tries another tactic and swallows the entire contents of his glass, smiles, and suddenly goes into a contorted cakewalk dance. In a concluding HA FS, as people crowd around, his stomach bulges and—in a doubly inverted parody of giving birth—out of his mouth pops a fully formed wasps' nest. *Rembrandt de la rue Lepic* (1911), by contrast, uses the body of a woman to work out its gags, but through the premise of imprinting rather than ingestion. Here, an artist sells a "genuine" Rembrandt to a man in a crowded restaurant, a woman accidentally sits on it, the painted image transfers to her white dress, and the man rudely tries to reclaim his purchase. The woman will have none of this, of course, and a fight breaks out, clearing the restaurant and spilling out into the street. The ensuing chase, once enlivened by fast motion, destroys one social space after another—including a petit-bourgeois dining room, a garret bedroom, and a bourgeois drawing room (hosting a private concert)—and ends with the women rolled up in the canvas awning of a grocery shop, a literalized image of commodified representation. Despite getting his money back at the artist's studio, the obsessed buyer still cuts the "painting" out of the exhausted woman's backside as his rightful possession.[106]

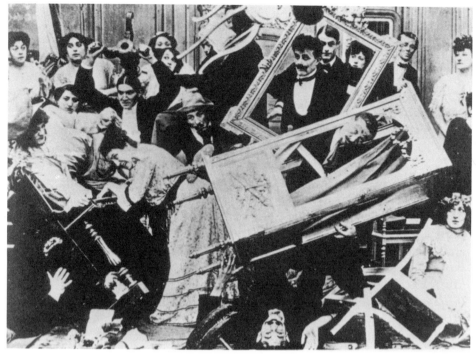

69. *Rembrandt de la rue Lepic*, 1911 (production photo)

Most of Pathé's other comic films are more complicated by comparison, at least in their representational strategies. One of these may be the sole surviving example of what might be called "woman on top" comedies, among which *La Rêve d'une feministe* (1909) was perhaps the most explicit—a wife daydreams about assuming men's roles and awakens to find her husband angrily demanding his dinner.[107] *The Cabman's Wife* (1908) is rather less certain of its ideological project. Here, when her husband staggers in drunk and penniless one morning, a woman becomes a horse carriage driver for a day. After he and a friend then go off in pursuit of her, their combined adventures come to an end when she collides with another woman driver and everyone is hauled off to the police station.[108] The film's initial parallel trajectories of action, much as in the earlier *Ruse de mari*, are set up in two evenly balanced sequences. In three matched LSs, the woman argues with her husband in their garret room, goes off in the carriage parked in front of their tenement building, and picks up her first customers— among them a fat woman with a baby. In the following three LSs, the friend pulls up in his carriage and, after both husband and friend fortify themselves with a bottle of wine, they jump in the second carriage and give chase. In the next sequence, each LS recapitulates a series of gags that almost bring the two lines of action together—the first carriage runs into something, the fat woman and baby tumble out, a cop issues a ticket, and the second carriage enters the shot just after the first has exited. This recurring pattern climaxes in a LS of the collision, and the two women drivers get into a fight, after which the police take them off separately in their carriages. The resolution comes in a sequence constructed exactly like that which sent the men off in pursuit. The three carriages drive up in succession outside the police station, the husband reasserts his authority over his wife in the public space of the police office (although he cannot escape responsibility for the tickets), and, outside on the street, he beats her until she begs him, on her knees, to stop. Instead of then reaffirming the husband's power in the private space of the couple's garret room, however, *The Cabman's Wife* concludes with a twist on the convention of the final emblematic shot. In MS, against a wallpaper background, they sit side by side, both dressed in driver's uniforms and smoking clay pipes—only he chokes on his, while she confidently puffs away on hers.[109]

At least one of Pathé's films subjecting adults to misrule by a child is no less unusual in its representational choices. In *Oncle Burton* (1909), a bourgeois couple called away on business leaves their young son in the care of an uncle, and the boy amuses himself by playing tricks on the older man.[110] The first tableau, for instance, sets up one of these: after receiving the letter begging him to visit, the uncle packs a favorite Venus de Milo statuette, which, with a bucket of paint, the boy later will turn into a black Venus. Before the young predator meets his prey, however, the film works out a similar extended gag at the house gate. After his parents have gone off, the boy passes through the gate (in a reverse-angle cut) with the help of a man painting the fence, and immediately repays him by smearing white paint all over his face. When the uncle arrives, in the next shot, the boy now has both hands ready and covers the old man with paint splotches as they embrace. Other gags follow in rapid succession, one of which involves cutting from an exterior FS of the boy leaning out of a window with a fishing pole to an interior FS of the uncle at another window (below), suddenly garroted by the snagged, dropped blinds. It is this intercutting of adjacent spaces, accentuated by camera movement, that sets up the most elaborate of the film's gags.[111] First of all, a "master" LS of two adjacent rooms shows the boy asleep (left background) as the uncle passes from one room to the other (his lateral movement traced by a pan) and gets in his own bed (frame right), and then a reverse pan reveals the boy getting up to do further mischief. In the insert LS of a stairway, the boy snakes a hose up a ladder through an opening onto the roof—and in the ensuing LS of the uncle's bedroom, water begins pouring out of the background fireplace. But this is only the beginning, for the camera tilts up to reveal the boy drilling a hole in the floor of the room above, and a reverse tilt describes the results—falling plaster awakens the uncle, who gets up and splashes around, then stands on the bed to look up at the hole, and now is drenched, not in water, but in black paint.[112] All this mayhem is finally capped by another pan, at the end of which the uncle finds the boy fast asleep in his bed. When his parents return, of course, their child is innocence personified, but the uncle suffers one last indignity—in the hallway, he grabs his hat to flee and is showered in flour. Although *Oncle Burton* creates a good deal of havoc, its destruction of the bourgeois home is slightly displaced, for its unrelenting attack is directed at a stereotype somewhat marginal to the family.

Pathé's *Un Match enragé* (1909) is perhaps the most sophisticated of all these short comic films, particularly in the way it reworks the loose structural design of *The Would-Be Juggler* (1908).[113] The earlier film has Linder playing a drunken Parisian dandy who, inspired by a stage juggler, doggedly attempts to perform his own balancing act, in one everyday situation after another. This premise is established in a long-take, slightly angled LS of a theater interior—the juggler balances a ladder and then a stack of chairs on his chin, and the dandy lurches onto the stage (from his box frame right) and, with an excited lunge at a chair, collapses everything into a heap. After he has been booted out of the theater, a sequence of loosely related LSs sends the dandy through the Paris streets, where he seizes a passing man's top hat to balance on his cane and then his nose, and does likewise with a carriage lantern—and, in return, takes a punch and a kick. The following sequence puts him in a post office telephone booth, in front of which a line of people impatiently gathers—in a pair of cut-in MSs, the dandy now tries to balance the receiver and then a cigarette on his chin. After two more unsuccessful juggling tricks in the street, he sits down at a café street table, fumbling an attempt to balance his beer and selzer, setting up the film's most elaborate gag through an alternation between the café exterior and interior. A waiter gets up on a ladder to wash a window that has been sprayed with selzer, and the dandy, imitating the earlier stage juggler, lifts the ladder-with-waiter and sends them crashing—in a perfect matchcut—onto the café tables inside. The final sequence then alternates between a stairway and a bedroom interior as the dandy runs over a woman in a doorway and, once inside, piles several vases, a tea set, and a bowl on a tiny table. Just as he at last succeeds in balancing these objects, the woman and her neighbors burst into the room and send him sprawling—after which, to reverse the pattern, he gets to beat them with some handy pillows.

The story of *Un Match enragé* is deceptively simple: on a bet, two men begin playing chess in a bourgeois drawing room and persist, almost literally, come hell and high water. Their game is narrated in three separate, concise stages, however, each of which is marked, much like *The Would-Be Juggler*, by somewhat different strategies of representation. In the initial long-take FS/LS of a dark-wallpapered drawing room, the two men—the taller one is all in black; the shorter, in a white jacket—sign a contract in the foreground and take over a central table, where several couples have been watching two other men play chess. After everyone else has left through a background door framing another room, the first of what will be a series of cut-in MSs shows the two chess players absorbed in their game. Servants bring in a small table of food to set behind the chess players, and after they exit, in comes a Saint Bernard. Another cut-in MS follows, showing the two men completely oblivious to the dog slurping up all the food behind them. One servant returns to take the dog off, and another cut-in MS shows the players still staring at the chessboard; then the servant returns with a lit candle and goes off yawning. Sometime later, several servants are surprised to find the chess game still going on and blow out the candle, prompting the chess players to find another room. The second stage of the game is then played out in a sequence of sustained alternation. Now, a thief breaks into the house only to find the chess players so absorbed that he can steal their wallets, watches, and even a cigar that he lights, tossing the match, which starts a fire. The alternation continues, anchored by the oblivious chess players, as the thief escapes from the house, a servant discovers the room filled with smoke and puts in a call at a corner firebox, and firemen rush in to escort the two men (protecting their chessboard) from the collapsing building. In a cleverly absurd epilogue, the final stage of the game occurs in a wooded area beside a lake, as the two men, in yet another FS/LS, set their board on a foreground tree stump. Suddenly, reacting to a move, the player in the white jacket jumps up excitedly and falls backward into the lake, and the other grabs the chessboard and steps into the lake after him. The climactic gag comes in a cut-in HA MS, as they finish their game up to their shoulders in the water, the chessboard floating between them. Then, in the final tableau, after the taller man wins, the two simply walk out of the lake, the one pays the other the bet money, and they stride off in opposite directions. The turn-of-the-century bourgeois gentleman, this film suggests, enjoys his sport with the same obsession that, according to legend, Nero did his fiddling.

This close analysis of surviving film prints demonstrates that, between 1907 and 1909, the French comic film, along with the contemporary melodrama, played a significant role in consolidating and extending the system of representation and narration developed just a year or two earlier. Increasingly, the genre's gags came to depend not only on the skill of one or more actors performing in a certain mise-en-scène or with specific props, but on the spatial contiguity and temporal linearity of a sequential ordering of shots. Particularly important were sustained sequences of alternation, between either adjacent or distant spaces, which could multiply the gags and funnel parallel lines of action into a comical climax. Strategically placed cut-in close shots could cap an accumulating series of gags—with a privileged moment of revelation, deception, or parody—or else construct a sequential framework for the gags. And films such as Pathé's *Le Cheval emballé*, *Oncle Burton*, and *Un Match enragé* could orchestrate their comedy in structures of multiple parts, each of which exploited a distinctly different representational strategy. Moreover, these films repeatedly mocked, without ever subverting or erasing, the hierarchies of class, gender, and generation crucial to the French social order. As the genre rapidly shifted to the comic series around 1909–1910, however, the center of attention from shot to shot throughout any one film focused on the performance of the star comic actor and often on a feature peculiar to the series—a conspiratorial direct address to the audience. The question is, whatever popularity the comic series may have gained by means of the continually returning performer as well as the specificity of its parody or social critique, did the newly established representational strategies continue to be as crucial as before, both to the articulation of individual films and to the genre as a whole?

The earliest French comic series, introduced rather irregularly at first, was Pathé's *Boireau* (1906–1909), in which Deed "starred" as an impulsive, slow-witted adolescent or young man who consistently gets into trouble by trying, unsuccessfully, to follow the behavior expected of a working-class or white-collar youth in French society. According to Sadoul, Deed had been a singer and acrobat on the café-concert circuit, performing at the Folies-Bergère and the Châtelet, and had occasionally even appeared as an extra in Méliès's films.[114] His Boireau character comes out of that stage tradition, both as a grotesquely bewildered clown and a skillful practitioner of physical gags. David Robinson has aptly described his habitual gait as "rather like a chicken, his bottom thrust out in a constant—and rarely disappointed—anticipation of a kick or a spanking."[115] Yet his small figure, blank face, and seemingly unconscious acrobatic moves also anticipate the later, more graceful and inventive Keaton.

L'Apprentissages de Boireau (1907), perhaps the earliest of these films to survive, seems typical of the series as a whole in that Deed plays a hapless adolescent whose father tries to apprentice him to a grocer, a hairdresser, a pastry cook, and finally a bistro owner—and each apprenticeship, of course, ends in a mini-disaster.[116] Much of the film's appeal comes from Deed's performance, from the way his character mishandles people as well as objects and immediately attempts to gratify his simple desires. In the hairdresser's shop, for instance, he lathers the whole side of a man's head, sharpens his razor with a huge file, and then cuts off the man's unlathered mustache. In the patisserie, after being given an apron and hat, he promptly grabs a cream tart, sits down at a table to devour it with relish, and (angry at being interrupted) tosses another one in a female customer's face. But his performance is framed significantly within the repeated structure of an alternating three-shot sequence. Each scene of apprenticeship (introduced by a brief intertitle) begins with an exterior location LS of Boireau and his father entering the door of the shop, plays out the comic business in a FS/LS of a painted-flat interior, and concludes with a matching LS of Boireau stumbling out the same exterior door. The last two scenes then vary this pattern by extending the comic business into a second interior shot. In the patisserie, after the cream tart toss, Boireau is put in the kitchen to knead dough in a large vat: there he picks his nose before plunging his hands into the dough and soon, covered with flour, is lying down to sleep on the vat's soft, sticky "bed." In the bistro, he is sent to the cellar where he unplugs barrel after barrel and laps up wine to his heart's content.

L'Apprenti architecte (1908), by contrast, focuses exclusively on Boireau's apprenticeship to a single trade.[117] Both parents this time use their influence to get him this job, and he is much more deferential in the architect's office (continually bowing to his new boss) and even timid—the man's rough handshake sends him leaping into his mother's arms. Much like the earlier film, *L'Apprenti architecte* initially highlights Deed's "clumsy" performance, extending his gags from one adjacent interior to another, all within the architect's studio. Asked to gather up the blueprints for a restoration project, Boireau gets punched about by several draughtsmen and ends up knocking over most of the room's tables and cabinets. The rest of the film, however, takes the architect and his new assistant to the restoration job site where the gags equally depend now on matchcutting movement across a series of LSs. A pratfall sets the pattern of gags to follow as Boireau stumbles into a hole in front of the site's scaffolding. The second gag has a workman at the top of the scaffolding accidentally drop a bag of cement which hits Boireau in the next shot (he has climbed up to the first level) and knocks him for a loop into a barrel on the ground. The third has him lifted up by pulley to the level just beneath the workman, where he promptly walks off a plank and flops into another barrel, full of water. The last has him crawl up to the scaffolding's top level, only to trip and fall into a metal chute and roll down into a bin of debris sitting on a cart. To extend this gag, a man pushes the cart off down the street, and at a nearby dump site Boireau drops out of the bin along with the rest of the trash—of less worth, despite his acrobatics, than the old building being renovated. By repeatedly stitching together adjacent spaces into short, unified scenes, the *Boireau* series—at least on the basis of these two films—seems to have established an economical narrative model that could continually prepare for, extend, and conclude its comic business and run at least as long as, if not longer than, Pathé's other comic films.

Somewhat belatedly, and only after Deed had left Pathé to work for Itala Films, Gaumont responded to the popular success of the *Boireau* series with a comic series of its own. In September 1908, Léon Gaumont wrote from New York to his production head, Feuillade, in Paris, commenting on how well Pathé's comic films were being received there. "We, too, must have some good, well-trained artists," he argued, for "what often—and perhaps always—saves a less-than-satisfactory film scenario are the nuanced details of a performance."[118] Since Bosetti's *Roméo* series (1907–1908) apparently had not done the trick for the company, in 1909, Feuillade arranged for Bosetti to initiate a second series called *Calino*, this time using Migé, another acrobatic veteran of the circus and music hall.[119] In the initial films in this series, Migé plays Calino as a cheerful, conscientious buffoon whose single-minded enthusiasm or careful attention to warnings—and masterful pratfalls—inadvertently lead to an escalating series of gags and, eventually, an orgy of destruction. And because quite often Calino is a newly recruited civil servant of one sort or another—for instance, *Calino bureaucrate* (1909), *Calino agent* (1910)—the story situations in the series seem to be mapped according to an increasing degree of specialization or fragmented division of labor, especially within the strata of "little people" in French society.[120] Indeed, one might say that Calino's destructive antics, in contrast to Nick Carter's professional restorative powers, result in a carnivalesque vision of French state bureaucracy wildly run amuck.

Calino pompier (1911), for instance, turns a French fire brigade into a bunch of Keystone Cops, with Calino as their gung ho "point" man. The slight story is a familiar one from early actualités and story films: the brigade responds to a call and goes off to fight a fire. Only here, the fire wagons are pulled by slow-moving donkeys (that repeatedly drag across the frame from background to foreground), and the firemen themselves are no less lethargic in their efforts to get to their destination. Although he is the last one out of the fire station (to his dismay and chagrin), Calino quickly races to the head of the straggling brigade and incites them to action—with the help of fast motion. Once they all reach the smoking house, this truc gag is repeated in one LS after another (across loosely adjacent spaces) as the firemen, at Calino's urging, speedily put up a ladder, pass buckets from one to another, and pump water out of a barrel. Eventually, this hyperactivity leads them to toss all the furniture out of the house and break down its walls, until the owner, horrified at the excessive damage, pleads with Calino to halt the mayhem—and everyone collapses in exhaustion. Then, in a parody of the final emblematic close shot, Calino is presented with an over-sized medal, despite having destroyed the house he was supposed to protect and preserve.

A similar kind of destruction concludes *Calino a peur du feu* (1910), but this film relies much more on intercutting adjacent spaces and on changes in framing. The opening tableau of a park in Paris presents Calino, uncharacteristically, as an eccentric dandy—in frock coat and vest, white trousers and black boots, topped by a raffish boater. In exchange for a coin, he receives a fortune card from a beggar woman, warning him, in a CU insert, that, unless he is careful, he is going to perish by fire. His frightened response is to immediately stamp out his cigarette in the gutter and, in a subsequent MS, strap a huge fire extinguisher on his back and, pleased with himself, smile at the camera. This premise sets up the expected series of gags as Calino strolls about the city, in LSs—spraying two workers sharing a cigarette on a park bench, a lamplighter going about his business, and a passing driver in an automobile belching smoke. Now comes the most complicated of the gags as Calino, having spotted several smoking chimneys (according to an intertitle), appears on a townhouse rooftop and begins to work on each threatening chimney in turn. An extended sequence follows, alternating between the rooftop, the townhouse dining room (where water pours out of a fireplace to soak a bourgeois couple), the adjacent kitchen (where water erupts out of the stove and splashes the maid), and finally the street below (where two smoking policemen are hit by a cascade of water). After Calino is seized, one last gag is played out in the ubiquitous police station—as the police chief lights a cigarette, Calino goes into a quaking fit and then sprays him, too, with his seemingly inexhaustible extinguisher. In this film, Calino's parodic attempt at self-expression flips into no less parodic efforts at self-preservation, and no space or level of the French social order seems safe from his manic behavior.

Not every film in the series, however, let Calino terrorize French society with his obsessions. Sometimes he himself ended up as the butt of a joke, as in *Calino achète un chien de garde* (1910), where, as a bourgeois married man, he one day discovers his own home wrecked by robbers. As a consequence, cut into the LS of the couple's plundered drawing room is a MCU of Calino explaining to his wife, in broadly mimed gestures, his plan to purchase a ferocious watchdog. In the subsequent shot, the whole household—husband, wife, butler, maid, and gardener—all prepare for this event by constructing a huge doghouse, with such accoutrements as barrels for the dog's soup and water as well as a "dangereux" warning sign. At the kennel, Calino chooses the largest, nastiest beast available—it takes two men to wrestle it into a crate on a cart—but fails to tip one of the dog handlers, and the man later mimes his revenge in talking with his fellows at a nearby café. Three interrelated LSs delay revealing what he has done as Calino and his cargo pass through the city streets to his house gate and the area of the doghouse. The revelation finally comes in an unusual POV-shot sequence, which neatly equates the spectator's discovery of the trick with that of the fearfully trembling characters. First, there is a MS of Calino and his "family" dressed in odd bits of armor, clasping guns, and looking off anxiously to the left foreground. Then comes a HA FS of the open crate, in which, at the end of a huge chain, a tiny dog barks off toward the right foreground. Coming as it does at the film's climax, these early eyeline-matched shots serve not only to fulfill comic narrative expectations but to provoke the surprise of a truc attraction.

Soon after the *Calino* films proved viable, Feuillade introduced a second comic series, *Bébé*, starring the five-year-old child actor, Dary. One of the first of the series' sixty-five films, *Bébé apache* (1910), suggests that, although Bébé's pranks may have exceeded those of Pathé's earlier films using child actors, they were firmly framed within a moral, socially correct discourse. This film begins with the mother (Carl) knitting and Bébé and his sister Fonfon reading a comic, in a quiet family tableau that is interrupted by two policemen, one of whom has been beaten up by apaches. Through his reading, of course, Bébé is familiar with the latest fashion in criminal disguises, so he and Fonfon quickly make themselves up as apaches—and the lack of an intertitle leaves their intentions ambiguous. This carries over into the long-take FS/LS of a rough cabaret where the two establish their credentials by performing an apache dance and Bébé wins their respect by drawing a knife to protect Fonfon. Then, in a cut-in AS of their table, Bébé persuades the cabaret gang of a robbery plan, for which Fonfon coughs up a huge set of keys. After she is sent off, another cut-in MS isolates Bébé spitting into his palms and wiping his face, just the right gesture of bravado in anticipation of the crime. But all this "criminal activity" turns out to be a ruse for he leads the gang into his own parents' drawing room where cops spring out of the background cabinets to seize them, while Bébé stalks proudly back and forth in the foreground. Much like his mentor Nick Carter, Bébé shows that even a good bourgeois boy can best apaches at their game, entrapping them within the very social space they supposedly threaten.

If Bébé often played "adult" figures early on in the series, a good number of the later films instead used everyday childhood experiences and fears as the basis for comic situations. *Bébé a la peste* (1911), for instance, has the precocious kid faking an illness to stay home from school, while *Le Noël de Bébé* (1911) has him adopt the guise of a ragged orphan in order to gain the attention and love of his mother. In *Bébé marchand des quatres saisons* (1911), he actually plays an orphan who takes over the street vendor's cart of a little girl who has been hit by a car. Later at the hospital, in a cut-in MS, the two kids take the time to tally up the day's accounts, and the girl shares the profits with him. In the end, Bébé shrewdly uses her accident to secure both of them a new home, where they soon are working as assistants to their adopted father, a doctor. Throughout the series, Bébé's desires and actions remain decidedly gendered: he is continually protecting his sister (adopted or not), seeking an exclusive relationship with his mother, and competing with all sorts of men and other boys. That competition is even evident in *Bébé fait visiter Marseille* (1911), which begins in Paris, at the end of summer vacation, with Bébé all decked out in a sailor suit, ready to visit his cousin Alex and tour the Mediterranean port city. No sooner has he arrived (now dressed more casually and with a cigarette dangling from his mouth), however, than the two start to argue over the relative merits of Marseille and Paris, an argument accentuated repeatedly by cut-in close shots. Bébé can only win with a gag, of course—sneaking a crab into the bed of his sleeping cousin—a gag that the spectator shares, in a privileged shot of Bébé listening outside the door for Alex's rude awakening. Yet this resolution also depends on the chauvinism of a punning intertitle that introduces Berlin as a third term, establishing both French cities as superior—for "fools" are even bigger in Germany.

Lux also bought into the comic series craze with *Patouillard* or *Bill*, as Bertho's character was known in both England and the United States. Bertho had been a comic opera singer and music hall comedian before signing briefly with Pathé, apparently to substitute for Deed in a brief continuation of the *Boireau* series and then appear in several films as Calino, prior to Gaumont's appropriation of the character.[121] In 1910, Lux hired Bertho to create a weekly comic series, which quickly became a favorite of cinema audiences worldwide.[122] Generally, Bill was an ambitious, but not all that talented young fellow who, much of the time, either sought out challenging tasks—mapped, as in *Calino*, according to a specialization of labor—or chased after women. *Bill as a Boxer* (1910), for instance, offers the challenge of twenty thousand francs to the man who can knock out a black boxer named Tapeford (a figure probably based on Jack Johnson), and Bill, a small, compact man dressed in a loud plaid jacket and matching trousers and sporting a boy's cap, eagerly leaves his amused mother to seek out the boxer's manager. Once in the office, he easily floors the manager, but a punching bag springs back to knock him across a desk; Tapeford himself (in blackface) simply takes four of Bill's punches, laughs heartily, and sends him sprawling with a soft jab. Bill signs up for a match anyway and, in training, encounters a Chinese vendor in a park, who quickly bests him, and then upends a lamppost, which promptly gets him arrested. In the end, he returns home undaunted to draw an outline of Tapeford on the dining room wall and hurts his hand punching at the figure—only to have the whole wall suddenly collapse and his angry mother emerge out of the rubble to pummel him. A comic "Horatio Alger" story of repeated failure, *Bill as a Boxer* does not organize its gags in a steadily intensifying series, as might be expected, but rather hits a peak early on (in Tapeford's office), falls off, and then rises to another peak at the end—without once deviating from its consistent FS/LSs and LSs. Despite a certain rhetorical flatness, however, the film does offer the provocative pleasure of reversing the usual relations of racial dominance (the "colored" and "colonized" consistently top the white European) and of turning Bill into little more than a naughty boy.

In *Patouillard amoureux* (1910), Bertho is no more successful as a suitor, until an unexpected denouement. This time, however, his antics are situated within a pattern of alternating adjacent spaces and spatial opposition within the frame. The film's initial shots establish the hallway and drawing room where Bill, ill at ease in top hat and tails, goes to meet the woman he loves just before a party begins—accidentally leaving a floral bouquet in the cane rack and doing a prat-fall, with tea cup, right in front of both her and her father. Meanwhile, another suitor—older and more elegant—appears in the hallway, takes the floral bouquet, and, sweeping into the drawing room, presents it to the woman over Bill's fallen body. After the woman goes off with her guests, Bill remains behind and, finding her dropped hankie, gets so excited that he sits on his own hat. In the next scene, another floral bouquet circulates in condensed fashion: discovering the woman and other suitor already in the drawing room, Bill hides this bouquet under a table (frame right), but, when he approaches the woman (frame left), the other man appropriates the flowers again and offers them to her. This provides a climactic duel, which Bill quickly wins by pinning to his foil a sudden love note from the woman (her own attitude has been withheld up to now) and waving it in his rival's face. Bill's success here as well as the film's construction of gags, however, seem unusual in the series. A later film, *That Horse Did Run* (c. 1911), for instance, simply reworks Pathé's *Le Cheval emballé*, but reduces the initial alternation of spaces and gives most of its attention to the destructive chase. And *Bill Pays His Debts* (1911), at least in the fragment that survives, seems to focus on Bertho's music hall turn in his "trademark" suit of loud plaid.

Of the other French comic series launched by Eclair and Eclipse during this period, almost nothing remains of the films released before 1912. One of the half-dozen films Tommy Footit made for Eclair in early 1911, however, has come down to us—*Tommy étrenne son cor de chasse*. Little is known of Footit other than that he was the son of Georges Footit, one of a pair of famous late nineteenth-century music hall clowns, Footit and Chocolat,[123] and this film certainly does not make much of his performance. In a sense, *Tommy étrenne son cor de chasse* is a throwback to the comic films of four or five years before, especially in that its premise—Tommy and a friend buy an old French horn from a caricature of a Jewish pawnbroker—sets up a series of repeated gags, in "linked vignettes," which conclude with a chase. Yet, unlike the earlier films, here the gags are structured according to different representational strategies. In a FS/LS of a generic room, for instance, Tommy first blows into the horn (in exhibition, probably accompanied by a sound-effects machine) and blasts his friend out a window—where he saves himself, in a cut to an iris-masked FS, by clinging to a nearby chimney. Then, in a LA LS that frames him within what seems to be an empty apartment building courtyard, Tommy's horn emits another blast, and all the windows fly open, as people retaliate by pelting him with vegetables, pillows, and cushions. Next, Tommy blows a group of strollers around a street corner, and the following LS of a park shows them, in superimposition, drifting over the treetops and tumbling down, one by one, as their umbrellas collapse. Finally, an alternating sequence pits Tommy and his friend playing wildly in one room against a bourgeois group gathered sedately around a piano in the room above; the latter room's floor suddenly buckles upward and splits, and piano and people come crashing down. It is this catastrophe that provokes the short chase, concluding in one last gag—running up into the foreground, Tommy turns on his pursuers as well as an advancing trolley and blasts them into the far background.

Although the most successful of the French comic series that followed *Boireau* were produced by Pathé, the company continued to distribute other short comic films, and it is worth glancing at several of these surviving titles. *Family Football* (1910), for instance, reactivates the structure of repeating gags through a loosely linked series of spaces. Here, the subject is sports and its transformation of French social life. Specifically, a doctor recommends exercise for an anemic bourgeois family entrapped in their dreary, stuffed interiors, and the father's sudden infatuation with soccer leads them all on a rampage—clearing their apartment of clutter and driving them out into the countryside, where they end up dunked in a canal. *La Poudre de valse* (1911) begins with another anemic bourgeois family whose prescription for health is a strong dose of special medicine. Their initial reaction is singled out in a cut-in MS—the stuff smells terrible—but it seems to work as they all begin dancing, faster and faster, around the dining room. The daughter and son then test the powder in adjacent spaces (with the help of stop motion)—the one on the shrubs and trees in the garden, the other on the furniture in the drawing room. All this finally leads to a wild carriage ride through the streets and parks after their horse is fed some of the same "dancing powder." *Une Belle-mère collante* (1910), by contrast, restricts its resolution of a "family problem" to the petit-bourgeois apartment where a husband and mother-in-law are locked in deadly combat. The husband has a plan involving a crocodile that he has ordered from Egypt and picks up at a shipping office; freed from its crate, the animal cordially seals their agreement with a handshake. Back at the apartment, he sends the crocodile into the mother-in-law's bedroom, where it slips under her bedcovers, in a cut-in close shot, and reduces her to flailing feet. Unseen up to now, the wife appears, asking for her mother, and the husband has a change of heart. In an outrageous displacement of guilt, he accuses the crocodile, draws a revolver and shoots the poor beast, then slices the body open and pulls the mother-in-law out intact—for the tongue-in-cheek requisite family portrait.

Perhaps the most intriguing of these Pathé titles is *Tom Pouce suite une femme* (1910). If its story seems familiar—a man pursues a woman he sees in the street and is rejected—the characters may not. Tommy, a modern bourgeois stroller (marked by a cigar), is played by a midget; the object of his attention, a shawl-draped spinster named Mary, is a lanky, long-faced fellow in drag. This mismatched pair cross one another's path in a succinct sequence of three FS/LSs, followed by three more that trace Mary's lateral movement into an apartment building (where the concierge tries to caress her in passing), an apartment hallway, and finally (in a ninety-degree shift in camera position) a kitchen. Tommy takes the same route (passing right under one of the other apartment residents) and sneaks into the kitchen to begin the flirtation. It is Mary, however, who is the star attraction in this music hall routine, her behavior fluctuating between the coy and the toying, her moves both sinuous and mechanical (the whole body seems hinged at right angles, yet loosely coiled), as she draws Tommy in and keeps him at bay, or shoves him down on the floor with one long, leverlike leg. And no less than three separate cut-in MSs accentuate her performance, repeatedly teasing him with the possibility of a kiss. In the end, she simply tires of the game and tosses poor Tommy right out the background window; in a subsequent shot, he drops onto a sidewalk and runs off relieved. A cut-in MCU then closes off this "woman on top" parody as Mary sits laughing at her kitchen table, her easy triumph circumscribed by the obvious gender of the actor playing her.

The general consensus among cinema historians is that the "least inspiring and today the least appealing" of Pathé's best known comic series during this period is *Rigadin* (or *Whiffles* as it was known in England and the United States), starring Prince.[124] For nearly ten years, Prince had been a Boulevard theater star, principally playing comic roles at the Variétés, so he was a big catch for the French cinema when, in late 1908, he agreed to work with Monca, Mistinguett, and others on many of SCAGL's contemporary story films.[125] By the summer of 1910, the comedian had acquired such a following that Pathé announced a special new weekly series for him,[126] and SCAGL soon turned over production of the *Rigadin* series to Prince himself. Unlike the previous comic characters, Rigadin was drawn from the tradition of vaudeville and light stage comedy—a white-collar Don Juan, who often clung to respectability and convention, while entangled in a love affair, and then was tyrannized either by his conquest or by an abusive mother-in-law. In other words, the *Rigadin* series, much like its stage equivalents, often parodied the serious bourgeois drama of the period and its principal subject of *amour*.[127] The earliest extant film in the series, *Les Timidités de Rigadin* (1910), offers a concise model of this format. Here, Mistinguett persuades the family servants to throw a party while her parents are out one evening, a party that sets them all to dancing "in style" in the drawing room. Into these festivities stumbles her shy suitor Rigadin, only to be seated on a tiny stool so that she can tower over him with her formidable crested headpiece. As Rigadin slowly warms to the party atmosphere, the dancing gives way to a "staging" of *Lohengrin*, and Mistinguett turns him into an outrageous parody of Wagner's warrior-hero with armor and weapons made out of all manner of pans, bowls, trays, rolling pins, and other utensils from the kitchen. In the end, Rigadin's animated "debut," which, of course, stuns Mistinguett's returning parents, looks like that of a discarded, bric-a-brac prototype for the Tin Man in *The Wizard of Oz*. Although Prince certainly did affect the look of a simpleton— "with turned-up nose, wide, grinning mouth and vacant eyes"[128]—he could also, as in *Les Timidités de Rigadin*, skillfully modulate the range of his comic performance, from deadpan restraint to exuberant excess. In fact, in an apt comparison that runs counter to received opinion, Gunning has said that Prince reminds him of the later Jean Renoir.

Another *Rigadin* film from 1910, *Le Negre blanc*, also sends up the serious bourgeois drama, but in an even more unconventional way. The opening longtake, FS/LS of a bourgeois drawing room establishes the premise: Prince plays a black man attending a social gathering for the marriageable daughter of the house, with whom he seems to fall in love, even though he cannot abide her singing. Soon after, on the street he meets a Monsieur Linseed Oil, whose calling card identifies him as an expert on "coloring of all kinds." In the next sequence, Prince comes to Linseed Oil's office for treatment: one glass of the man's concoction (in a cut-in CU) turns just half of his face white, so he orders one more (in another cut-in CU) and happily dances out the door transformed into a white man. The unexpected resolution to his desire comes in a final long-take tableau of the same drawing room, as Prince returns to startle everyone with his changed appearance. Learning that the young woman has already become engaged, he pours a concoction in her champagne glass (in one more cut-in CU) which, in a toast to the engagement, she drinks—and instantly turns black. Shocked, the fiancé now rejects her and storms out, whereupon the father, in disgust, offers her to the "white nigger"—and, to top his revenge, Prince haughtily rejects her as well and saunters off. There is an intriguing ambivalence to *Le Negre blanc*. In one sense, it is unusually explicit in satirically condemning racial discrimination, and the satire may even allude to the paradox of being attracted to and resenting the bourgeoisie that so characterized the petit-bourgeoisie and white-collar workers or civil servants, the classes with which Prince as a performer was usually identified. Yet, in another sense, the film simply confirms the dominant racial economy through gender difference.[129] Although the young woman is not the only one who condescends to Prince (who, after all, gets to "transcend" his color), she is the only one singled out irrevocably for tainting—the object of desire turned into its abject opposite, by both suitor and father.

The first French comic star to be heralded as "le roi du cinématographe"—and not just in Pathé's advertising[130]—was, of course, Max Linder. Unlike his competitors, Linder's reputation has survived virtually intact, along with a good number of his films, excerpts of which are readily available (even on videocassette) in the films recently compiled by his daughter, Maud Linder.[131] As already suggested, however, that reputation was slow to develop, for Linder first began appearing in Pathé films as early as 1905. He had had a short, relatively undistinguished stage career, playing minor roles in Bordeaux and then in Paris, when he signed on as a film actor,[132] and, over the course of the next four years with Pathé, he alternated between performing as the lead and simply walking on as an extra. Even when he played leading roles, however, as in the comedies apparently directed by Gasnier, his character fluctuated—from a schoolboy in *La Première Sortie* to the young dandy in *Les Débuts d'un patineur*. Yet one crucial character trait remained relatively constant: Linder often acted like what Eugen Weber has called the leisured French bourgeois rentier[133] or, at least, a lower-class bourgeois figure with pretentions to that status, and occasionally—as in *The Would-Be Juggler*—showed signs of the subtly affected elegance that would later become his trademark. Given the 1907–1908 films he appeared in as a presumptuous young dandy interested in sports and amusements, one can speculate that the Pathé company may have considered constructing a series around Linder that would complement the *Boireau* films. For some reason, however, these films did not establish Linder as a major comic, and Pathé seems to have turned to Gréhan, whose elegant, swaggering Parisian dandy, Gontran, might supplement Deed's work for the company. According to Jean Mitry, Gréhan's character apparently proved too dependent on music hall verbal comedy, at least initially, and Pathé turned back to Linder again, once Deed had gone off to Italy to star in the *Cretinelli* series, Gréhan had been hired at Eclair, and Gasnier had returned to Paris after helping establish the Pathé affiliate, Film d'Arte Italiana.[134]

In late summer, 1909, under Gasnier's direction, Linder began appearing in a regular series of Pathé comedies, with his name soon included in each film's advertisement.[135] Although initially he still assumed a different character from film to film, certain patterns began to emerge in the choice of situations as well as in the structuring and articulation of gags. *Le Conquête* (1909), for instance, highlights Linder's performance as a young dandy smitten with a lady passing on the street. In a comic reversal, he drops his handkerchief to get her attention and then follows her around as she shops (and tries to ignore him), burdening himself with flowers, plaster bust, dog, and long roll of cloth. These serial gags, all recorded in FS/LS, conclude with a twist when Linder reaches the woman's apartment only to find a huge husband installed there—who tips him for delivering her purchases. Produced to coincide with Pathé's release of several prestigious Shakespeare adaptations, *Roméo se fait Bandit* (1909), by contrast, evidences a penchant for parody.[136] According to this Tyrolean version of *Romeo and Juliet*, when Montacu refuses to let Romeo marry his daughter Juliet, the young man, played by Linder, tricks the father into believing that a bandit named after Hugo's Hernani has kidnapped her and then masterminds her rescue himself. That it was shot entirely on location, probably in the French Alps, and released in stencil color makes this film unique in the series. Generally, Linder's performance is subordinated to the film's many scenic mountain landscapes; moreover, certain strategies accentuate key moments of the story rather than the comedy. A cut-in MS, for example, privileges the young lovers sitting and kissing on the Montacu garden wall, and an unusual POV-shot sequence—in which two linked LSs are framed by a binocular-shaped iris mask—shows the "bandits" watching the father go off alone into the mountains, where they can seize and blindfold him, and leave a threatening note about Juliet's "kidnapping." Linder does, however, contribute something of his own to the parodic tone of *Roméo se fait Bandit*. In the beginning, he fails at least three different times to reach Juliet on top of the wall before finally succeeding, and, near the end, he appears smartly dressed in white trousers and boater, an incongruous image of the modern hero as tourist, poised in studied readiness for his rescue attempt.

La Petite rosse (1909) is more typical of these films, in part because of its studio bourgeois setting and characters. Here, Linder plays a timid young Frenchman courting Madeleine (Arlette d'Umès), an assertive, athletic "new woman," who challenges him to a test before she will consent to be his wife. And her test mocks his well-known skill as a performer—he has to successfully juggle three balls in the air at once. The opening deep-space FS/LS of a bourgeois drawing room establishes the unconventional relationship between these two: although elegantly dressed in a cape and top hat, Linder is meekly simpering in his approach, while Madeleine, set off in green against her rose-fabric furniture, angrily pounds a table (at which he trips backward over a couch) and roughly pushes him into a chair.[137] This contrast extends into the next sequence where, in her father's study, she perches on a desk to write her letter of challenge and, back in the drawing room, the letter delivered, Linder bursts out crying (using a lace handkerchief to pat his eyes) and then strikes a pose of determined acceptance. A nifty sequence of substitution follows—alternating between Madeleine at a balcony window and Linder coming out of the street door just below—to sum up her charming manipulation of his inadequacy. As she looks down from the balcony, Linder practices doing a trick with his cane and tosses it overhead. On a matchcut, she grabs it and steps inside; Linder looks around puzzled, suddenly lunges to catch an umbrella she has let fall (unseen), which he lays gently on the sidewalk, and rubs his eyes in disbelief. This deft use of ellipsis is also crucial to Linder's preparation for the test. Trying to juggle four apples at a green grocer's, he bumps into a man and is shoved into a whole rack of fruits and vegetables; "eight days later" (reads an intertitle), he is still doggedly trying, the disastrous effect of which is a room cluttered with broken furniture.[138] After these inventive gags, the film's conclusion comes almost as a letdown. A letter summons Madeleine and her father to Linder's room (now restored), and he demonstrates his skill by going behind a dressing screen, from whose sides two different arms poke out to juggle the three requisite balls (a neat trick in itself). Although the surviving prints break off at this point, the film goes on, according to *Film Index*,[139] to expose Linder's ruse—but there is no mention of whether the reversed gender difference marking this comic hero and heroine is sustained to the end.

Tout est bien qui finit bien (1910) also is typical of these early films, in character, setting, and story. Again, Linder is courting a young woman, but the obstacles to his success this time are the parents—his father and her mother. Instead of depending on physical gags, this film also exploits the couple's situation, accentuated by a distinctive strategy of framing and editing. Once Linder has decided to pursue the young woman, he discovers they are neighbors, in a deep-space LS of an empty Paris street. First, he retrieves her dropped purse in the foreground, and, then, they walk off in parallel trajectories—she to a background door on the left, and he (continually doffing his top hat in deference) to a door on the right. This sets up another parallel as Linder rushes in to plead with his father, as the latter sits at his dining room table, while the young woman greets her mother and nonchalantly sits to eat in a matching dining room (both have dark wallpaper and are presented in FS). The woman's resis-

70. *Tout est bien qui finit bien,* 1910

tance quickly fades, however, when Linder impresses her with his prowess—by paying a bum to attack her on the street, so he can come to her rescue. Back in their separate apartments, in a repeated alternation of spaces, Linder opens his dining room window (frame left) and calls out, while she opens her window (frame right) and responds. Then, in a repeated LS of the empty street, they lean out and gesture from matching windows in the upper corners of the frame, their mutual love metaphorically bridging the void between them. That "bridge" is broken when Linder's father quickly hustles him out of the dining room, and her mother does likewise, so that, in alternating FSs, the parents can angrily look out the windows and comically echo one another's threatening gestures. Unfortunately, the surviving print of *Tout est bien qui finit bien* also breaks off soon after the parents confront one another in the street, only to be interrupted as the young woman crawls out of a background window, joins Linder, and runs off. But, here again, *Film Index* offers a resolution: the film ends where it began, with the parents now on the verge of forming a parallel couple.[140]

In *Timidité vaincu* (1910), Linder plays another mild-mannered young man, this time a henpecked husband who suffers at the hands of not only his wife but her parents as well. The first three FSs succinctly describe his situation. In a bourgeois dining room, the mother-in-law makes Linder perform the tasks of a maid and pulls his hair when he drops a tray; in the drawing room, the father-in-law looks up from his newspaper and yells at him when he asks permission to go out; and, at the bottom of the hallway stairs, the concierge, without even noticing him, literally sweeps Linder out the door. Sitting on a park bench, Linder reads a newspaper story about an American doctor who can cure anyone of cowardice "by simple injections of pepper and water" and decides to try the treatment—but not before a streetcar passes him by, publicly confirming his status as a nonentity. Once Linder has entered the doctor's office, the physician, finding almost no pulse in his patient, orders an extra large dosage in a giant syringe—and a cut-in MCU graphically describes the injection. The prescription works instantly, however, giving Linder snappy new gestures and a perky step, and he refuses to pay more when the doctor demands a higher fee. The rest of the film restages each of the earlier situations, in reverse order, repeatedly testing Linder's transformation, in a model of the perfectly symmetrical comic structure. First, he dances about in front of a streetcar, forcing it to back off in the opposite direction. Next, he confronts the concierge, slapping her back into her room, and kicks the father-in-law out of the drawing room. Finally, in the dining room, he orders his wife out with a cane and, when the astonished mother-in-law enters, orders her to kneel at his feet. At the heart of this French male fantasy, then, lies a repressive mother-in-law, a stereotypical nemesis that can only be subdued by a strong dose of American virility. That the gendered imbalance of *Timidité vaincu*, in contrast to that of *La Petite rosse*, is righted by inverting the nationalistic hierarchy normally privileging the French (no matter how tongue-in-cheek) suggests that Pathé was already seeking ways to gear the Linder series to an American audience.[141]

By the spring of 1910, Linder's fame had reached such proportions that, using the comic's own name, Pathé retitled the series in which he starred as simply *Max*. His character now stabilized into that of an impeccably dressed young bourgeois—in frock coat, tie, and vest, with either striped or black trousers, spats, a top hat and cane. Consistently inhabiting well-appointed apartments, fully equipped with servants, as Sadoul points out, Max rarely ever worked; instead, he either courted young women (not always unmarried), frequented restaurants and nightclubs, or indulged in various sports.[142] In other words, he now epitomized the leisured French bourgeois rentier or young man living on an allowance and pursuing a life of "decadence." And the scenarios Linder himself now wrote, along with Fagot,[143] often were organized around a particular weakness or obsession of that character.

Max se trompe d'étage (1910), for instance, has Max play a drunken dandy whose sole objective is to get from the street entrance of his apartment building up several flights of stairs to his parents' apartment. In the opening FS, Linder defines his character with a short stage-drunk act: after dropping his frock coat in front of the street door, he picks up the doormat by mistake and tries to wrap it around his shoulders. Once inside, in linked pairs of LSs, Max begins ascending the Pathé staircase, adding bits of business as he goes—crawling at one point, turning his dropped top hat into a flattened porkpie at another. His ascent is divided into four sequences, as his drunken condition takes him into a wrong room on each of four floors, and each sequence is marked by a different strategy of representation. The first sequence is constructed around an alternation between stairway corridor and dining room, where Max frightens a couple and then gets kicked out the door by the woman while the man hides under the table. In the second, Max intrudes on three people fighting over the dining room table, takes a quick punch, and immediately returns to the corridor. The third involves another dining room, where a woman is serving dessert to six small children, and includes a cut-in MS of several of them greedily devouring cream tarts. When Max arrives, of course, he gets hit in the face, and another cut-in MCU, outside in the corridor, shows him stunned and splattered with cream.[144] In the last sequence, Max stumbles into a bedroom where a thief suddenly pulls out a gun and fires at him. This produces a climactic reversal of his "progress"—and one more variation in representational strategies—as Max tumbles back down all four flights of stairs, in slightly speeded-up motion, accentuated by relatively fast cutting. An ellipsis thankfully lets Max reach his own apartment at last, and, in a final emblematic MCU, his parents pamper their "baby" by wiping his face and offering him a steaming bowl of coffee. Eschewing the oedipal comedy of the earlier *His First Cigar, Max se trompe d'étage* does, however, satirize the alleged independence and insouciance of the young leisured rentier.

Although no less tightly organized, *Qui est l'assassin?* (1910) is much more strongly plotted. Again a drunken dandy living at home with his bourgeois parents, Max becomes both victim and villain in a parodic detective story. In the opening FS of his bedroom, Linder gets to perform another stage-drunk act: dancing with his frock coat, doing tricks with his top hat, taking a revolver out of a drawer and shooting wildly about, and finally collapsing over a dressing screen. The next several shots and intertitles present a model of succinct narration. "Somebody has been killed!" introduces Max's parents, who find their drawing room in ruins and then, in matched exits and entrances, discover their son apparently dead on the floor of his room. "Who is the murderer?" introduces a physician and gendarme, who also move between drawing room and bedroom and, after examining the "body" (now in bed) and revolver, have no explanation for the parents. The next sequence alternates between these two rooms, as Sherlock Holmes, preceded by a brief letter, arrives with a promise to solve the case and Max, all alone now, awakens to find himself covered by a floral wreath, realizes what has happened, and decides to continue the pretense. Consequently, Max gets to watch Holmes go about his investigation—wrapping a hair around his finger, measuring a section of floor—and then, after he leaves, imitate the famous detective before resuming his own daily routine. A short sequence of pursuit ensues as Holmes follows Max out a window, down a street (measuring a footprint on the way), and to a sidewalk café. There he confronts Max with the physical evidence of his "crime" and orders his arrest, which sets up the denouement as Holmes calls the parents from the police station. Once they have arrived, a final intertitle—"This is the murderer!"—boldly

71. *Max hypnotise*, 1910 (Max Linder)

announces his solution of the puzzle, to the astonishment of everyone but Max himself. In addition to its economical structure, then, *Qui est l'assassin?* owes a good deal of its success to its clever dual-focus narration, by which successive pursuits of information by the "authorities"—parents, physician, gendarme, and Holmes himself—are undercut by Max's more complete knowledge (shared with the audience) as a comic villain-victim.[145]

Max hypnotise (1910), by contrast, reverses this dual-focus narration to make Max the unconscious victim of his own servants' machinations. The narrative premise here is announced in a letter inserted into the opening shot: an older couple has agreed reluctantly to sign a contract—probably a marriage agreement—with their leisure-loving son-in-law-to-be, Max. When Max (still in bed) receives the letter, he leaps up to perform a little dance of ecstatic pleasure, but his manservant and maid are appalled and decide to render their master unfit for marriage. In preparation, they hypnotize Max, with incredible ease, in several "practice sessions." First, Max is turned into a mechanical mannequin to dust his own bedroom, while the manservant smokes a cigar and reads *Le Journal*—after which, unhexed, Max pronounces his job well done.[146] Then, at the dining room table, in mid-chew, Max is hypnotized into changing places again—and he is surprised, when unhexed, to find only one more bite of food on his plate. Finally, at the contract-signing ceremony in the drawing room, the manservant pops up from behind the piano to hypnotize Max just as he is about to put pen to paper. Suddenly, he turns into a dog, jumping all over the furniture and scattering his relatives and witnesses, after which the maid leads him docilely back to the bedroom. There the manservant dons his top hat and proposes to the maid, who accepts, and they unhex Max one last time before happily exiting. Max yawns and, still hungry, mistakenly tries to eat a candle the maid has given him; then exhaustion replaces his disgust, and he promptly falls asleep. Although *Max hypnotise* is confined to just four LS studio decors, this strategy works perfectly for such a simple story, both in structuring the accumulating series of hypnotic gags and calling attention to Linder's superb performance as three or four separate characters of descending "social worth." Not only does the film reverse the hierarchies of master and servant and of human and animal, it has the servants steal from Max the "happy ending" to his own story.

If the two previous films explore the comic potential of improbable situations, *Max prend son bain* (1910) pushes through to the patently, sublimely absurd. The film begins ordinarily enough with a physician giving Max a remedy for hiccups, but the remedy is peculiar—he is to immerse himself in water—and Max's response is even more so: he purchases a new porcelain bathtub. The hiccups nearly forgotten, his problem now is to get the tub home. After a carriage waiting outside the store goes off without him, Max reaches down to pick up the tub and falls in, then lifts it upside down over his head and staggers off. This leads to the marvelous image of the upended bathtub slowly crossing an apartment building courtyard like the white carapace of a giant, headless tortoise or snail. And, once Max has the tub in his apartment, there is another problem. Because the only water faucet is in the hallway, he has to move back and forth between the two spaces, trying, after he breaks a good-sized pitcher, to fill his tub with no more than a flask and glass. This quickly proves impractical, so Max pushes the tub into the hallway, where, once full of water, it becomes impossible to move—and he decides to take his bath there anyway. Once he is finally in the tub, a new sequence of alternation begins as several women come up the stairs: a slightly HA MCU shows Max ducking his head underwater, and, after they pass by the tub (strangely, without seeing him), another HA MCU shows his head popping out of the water.[147] Eventually, the concierge and several gendarmes appear, disbelieve his explanations, and carry the tub off with him in it. This leads to a second marvelous image of the tub borne aloft like a coffin by the gendarmes through the street, with a naked Max greeting two passing ladies of his acquaintance with insouciant courtesy.[148] From the police station, Max runs off inside the upended tub once again, but this time the earlier sight gag is topped by having, first, a yipping dog follow him and, then, in a trick shot, the tub crawl up the side of a building. In the end, Max seems to escape through a garret window on the roof, while the tub crashes down like a huge bowling ball to scatter the pursuing gendarmes. In a wonderfully structured, escalating series of gags, *Max prend son bain* obsessively binds man and bathtub together as one to produce a marvelously surreal image and satirize the most basic notions of social propriety.

Early in 1910, Linder had appeared as one of several spectators in a film entitled *At the Cinematograph Theatre*. Later that same year, the now famous star re-created his own early experience as a film actor in *Les Débuts de Max Linder au cinématographe* (1910). This film is somewhat unique in the *Max* series, partly because it provides a rare behind-the-scenes glimpse of Pathé-Frères's production personnel. Bearing a letter of recommendation from Decourcelle, for instance, Linder enters Charles Pathé's office where the company owner is so busy talking into several telephones that he barely has time to accept the actor on a trial basis. Soon after, Monca gives Linder a brief screen test—in a room dominated by a poster for *La Poule aux oeufs d'or*, Pathé's most popular film the year the actor first joined the company—and later Nonguet directs him in several scenes from a film allegedly entitled *The Son-in-Law and the Mother-in-Law*. In its representational strategies, *Les Debuts de Max Linder* is a throwback, in some ways, to the earlier period it seeks to re-create. Initially relying on autonomous FS/LSs of studio set offices, it concludes in a chase with Linder and an antagonist, locked together, rolling through one street after another, until they get soaked by a street cleaner. Yet it also includes an unusual number of letters and regulations, and, just prior to the chase, there is a sequence of alternation in which wife and mother throw a mattress and table out the dining room window to land on Linder in the street below—where a nearby cameraman blithely cranks a waist-level Pathé camera. Furthermore, Linder reverts to the timid character of his 1909–1910 films—evidencing extreme concern for a chair he inadvertently knocks over in Pathé's office, then carefully choosing not to sit in a similar chair in the next office, and hesitantly performing the "screen test" dance and somersault. Given the ordeal he endures in *The Son-in-Law and the Mother-in-Law*, however, his hesitancy is understandable; in the final emblematic FS, he stands disheveled and dripping wet between the unruffled cameraman and director. Even at this early date, the myth of the star is being constructed as the crucial creative figure in film production.

On the evidence of these surviving film prints, between 1909 and 1911, the French comic series largely fulfilled its potential as an innovative cultural form. First of all, the various series continued to consolidate the system of representation and narration which had come to characterize the genre. There were rare instances in which that system was extended—as in the eyeline-matched shots concluding *Calino achète un chien de garde* or the ironic dual-focus narration structuring Linder's *Qui est l'assassin?* For the most part, however, established strategies such as cut-in close shots and sequences of alternation served the comic series in at least two ways. On the one hand, they offered the comic star a better showcase for his performance, not only allowing for more nuanced gestures but orchestrating the rhythm of that performance across a series of interrelated spaces. On the other, they provided the material for structuring comic gags in

72. *Les Débuts de Max Linder au cinématographe,* 1910

more complicated ways—as is apparent in *Calino a peur du feu* and especially in Linder films from *La Petite rosse* to *Max prend son bain.* Whatever their degree of formal complexity or sophistication, however, the films in the French comic series generally were mapped according to a particular referential body of Third Republic social relations involving the petit-bourgeoisie and bourgeoisie. Whereas the *Calino* and *Patouillard* series tended to focus on the public sphere of labor or work (organized, in turn, according to an increasing specialization), the *Rigadin* and *Max* series focused more exclusively on the private sphere of leisure, whether the character was either pursuing or fleeing a woman or, in Linder's case, seeking the "decadent" pleasures supposedly due the bourgeois rentier. And the *Bébé* series oscillated back and forth between the two. In the *Calino* films, this sometimes led to an oblique attack on the growing power of the French state bureaucracy. In the *Max* films, a particular sphere of leisure circumscribed the films' frequent inversions of crucial social hierarchies (class, gender, and generation), often limiting them to the "deviant" behavior of the rentier dandy. Moreover, the threats such inversions could pose also usually were contained within a comedy of manners whose norms, in an increasingly consumer-oriented society, would be acceptable beyond the borders of what might be called French.

Film d'Art and Films d'Art:
The Historical Film and the Literary Adaptation

In 1911, Jasset argued that, just three years before, the first productions of Film d'Art had marked a significant break in the development of French filmmaking.

> People in the film industry understood that all the rules they had observed until then were passé. Well-known artists acted by standing still instead of running around; they achieved an increasing intensity of effect. It was amazing. One has to admit that the first film produced by Film d'Art was marvelously executed. Even if one criticized the technical flaws, which could be excused on the grounds that the actors had gone to great lengths to overcome difficulties they had never faced before, *L'Assassinat du Duc de Guise* was still a masterpiece. . . . Except for some technical rules, nothing remained of what the old school had so slowly built up. Doing things the old way was at an end.[149]

It is easy enough now to find fault with this claim—not the least of which is its failure to acknowledge the radically transformed mode of representation instituted by Pathé between 1904 and 1907. Yet, however polemically overstated they may now seem, his words do raise significant questions. Jasset himself, for instance, wondered about Film d'Art's alleged influence on subsequent film production and, for answers, pointed to the films of SCAGL and those of Vitagraph (which were widely distributed in France). But his text also can serve as a "positive lever" to pry open other, more general questions. In what ways did the revived genre of the historical film, whose status Film d'Art clearly helped to elevate, along with the new practice of deriving films from "classic" literary works, which both Film d'Art and SCAGL did so much to promulgate, make use of this new French mode of representation? That is, how did such historical films and literary adaptations sustain or deflect the developing course of this system of representational strategies—or perhaps even reconstitute that system? As adaptations, what particular negotiations did they make between the prior models of narrative construction provided by, on the one hand, the short story and, on the other, the well-made play? And how did they negotiate between the opposing moral and ironic "voices" of narration? Finally, in its representational mapping of subjects, how was the genre positioned ideologically, especially vis-à-vis the Nationalist Revival movement then emerging in France?

Any consideration of these questions has to begin with Film d'Art's *L'Assassinat du Duc de Guise*—whose premiere, on 19 November 1908, *Phono-Ciné-Gazette* called the most important cinema event since Lumière's first public screening in December 1895.[150] In order to understand that claim, however, it is important to recall that, on the eve of that premiere, Pathé's biblical and historical films still generally adhered to the older system of representation.[151] This is evident, for instance, in *Le Fils prodigue* (1907), which uses brief intertitles to introduce seven separate episodes from the well-known parable, all but two of which are staged in autonomous LS tableaux. The exceptions are a matchcut on the prodigal son's movement from the interior to the exterior of the inn where

73. *Le Fils prodigue*, 1907

he has squandered his money and an inserted FS of him praying on a desert slope before returning home. The usual painted flats define the interior of both the son's home and the inn, but, strangely, they occupy part of the location exteriors as well: the home is nothing more than a painted-flat facade set out in an open field, and the inn is likewise, but set among palm trees. This presents an interesting contradiction for the circular pattern of this story, for the similarity in facades nearly negates the difference that the film tries to make between the decadence of the inn—through its Egyptian motif decorations and dancing women—and the frugal (read Christian) conditions of the home. And that difference is further obliterated in the celebratory feast set in the unexpectedly elaborate decors of the final tableau. The prodigal son's home, in the end, turns out to encompass the best of all possible worlds.

A similar mode of representation marks Capellani's *La Vestale* (1908), which reworks the Greek story of forbidden love from *Amour d'esclave*, and its sentimental spectacle drawn from "Neo-Grec" paintings. Here, a young Roman couple, Cinna and Acté, are separated when he is sent off to war against the Gauls; and, when she receives news that he has been killed, she becomes a vestal virgin—each a virtuous subject to the king, according to his or her gender. After Cinna returns from the war a hero (the news was false), Acté breaks her vow in order to meet him, allowing the sacred flame in a temple vessel to go out, for which she is condemned to die. This story of female "infidelity" to a kind of "state religion" is narrated in ten intertitles, each of which then is illustrated by a LS tableau, in which the actors work out the details of the action with broad, mimetic gestures within painted-flat studio decors. The only exception to this comes in the final scenes, when the film twice cuts from exterior to interior shots—first, of the temple and, then, of the grotto where Acté is to be entombed—matchcutting the characters' background exits and entrances. Yet this merely sets up a concluding foreground miracle, accentuated by Pathé's stencil color. Through contact with the woman's veil, the temple vessel suddenly reignites, its flame ironically now consecrating her vow of love—and the king pardons her and reunites the couple.[152]

Capellani's *Samson* (1908) borrows even more elements from Pathé's new system of representation. Its story begins with Samson's birth and an example of his feats of physical strength; but it focuses on his seduction by Delilah, his capture, blinding, and imprisonment in Gaza, and, eventually, his revenge. Although this film, too, is shot entirely in LS tableaux of painted-flat studio decors,[153] it includes a good number of relatively realistic props—for instance, the heavy granary wheel that the blinded Samson is forced, like a beast of burden, to push in an unending circle around its axis. Perhaps its principal distinction is that it relies on several different changes in framing. The second shot-scene, celebrating Samson's birth, for instance (presumably separated from the first by a missing intertitle), frames the same walled-in garden interior from a camera position slightly to the right of and closer in than that of the opening tableau. Next, Samson's seduction is set up and carried out in an alternating sequence of adjacent exterior and interior spaces, with mismatched exits and entrances on the same side of the frame. Then, in its final sequence, the film introduces a slight degree of suspense by briefly crosscutting a shot of Samson's labor at the granary wheel with one of his captors' triumphant preparations in the Gaza palace. Whereas this pattern of changes in framing seems to mark off the beginning, middle, and ending of *Samson*, another pattern of repetition—resembling that in *Le Nihiliste*—reinforces its destructive resolution. In the third tableau, Samson had ripped the huge door guarding the city's gate from its hinges and carried it off on his back. In the deep space of the next-to-last tableau, he repeats this feat by standing between the background columns framing the entrance to the palace interior and pushing them off their base so that stone arches and roof beams come crashing down on the assembled throng of celebrants. Despite this patterning, the film concludes with a dissolve to a conventional apotheosis tableau, as Samson ascends into an arcing assembly of angels.

In the context of these films, *L'Assassinat du Duc de Guise* both reproduces the conventions of the historical genre and yet is strikingly different.[154] The film's subject—which already had been taken up in an early Lumière "historical scene" as well as in a lost 1902 Pathé film—is Henri III's plotting and murder of the Duc de Guise (on 23 December 1588), a leader of the Catholic Sainte Ligue who had begun to threaten the French king's power.[155] Here, formal and historical closure coincide in the violent death of the central male character and establish a precedent for ending most films in the genre. Following the principles of classical unity, Lavedan's original scenario confines the action to the morning of that day, within studio set decors representing six separate rooms in the Chateau du Blois. Although dependent on the conventional practice of using painted flats for walls, these studio spaces are specially decorated to achieve a sense of historical verisimilitude—with actual period furnishings, some of which extend offscreen to the left or right, richly designed costumes, intricate tile floors, and a huge stone fireplace into which the body is tossed at the end. The acting of Le Bargy (Henri III), Albert Lambert (Duc de Guise), Robinne (Marquise de Noirmoutier) and others, as both Jasset and Brisson claimed, is indeed economical and restrained, especially in comparison to that of earlier films in the genre.[156] There are scarcely any broad gestures or quick movements (until the murderous attack by a half-dozen armed men); no one looks at the camera, with the exception of de Guise, just moments before the assault, as he stands boldly but anxiously in the foreground of the frame—as if, momentarily, to further engage the spectator's empathy. In order to heighten this difference, the poster advertising the film was one of the first to draw the spectator's attention specifically to the actors, along with their theatrical association, by printing their names in bold letters.

Throughout the film's unusually few shots—there are only nine, most of them long takes—the camera is positioned consistently at waist level (following the practice of Pathé films), and just as consistently frames the actors in LS or FS/LS, illuminated with full, diffused lighting. Despite several rather flat tableaux—as in the scene where Henri III and his men prepare for the murder and later cluster around the body in his bedchamber—there are instances of a relatively deep-space mise-en-scène. The frame space sometimes extends into a second room visible through an open doorway in the background (again not uncharacteristic of earlier Pathé films),[157] as in the shot of the king's antechamber which reveals the background cabinet room. More important, in a form of theatrical blocking that verges on the balletic, figures are set off from one another through a choreography of diagonal foreground-background juxtapositions—as in the shot where Henri III, in hiding (frame left), pulls aside his bed curtain to watch de Guise exit through a background door, or where the latter, now through another background door, enters the cabinet room of conspirators, several of whom seem to "close off" both foreground "exits." Furthermore, in that last shot, de Guise's movement carries him forward into FS, perhaps (in conjunction with his glance at the camera) to heighten the "heroic" nature of his character just before the attack.[158] Finally, when Henri III is first introduced, as a figure dressed in black and set off against a light background, his decentered position in the frame even suggests how he controls other men's actions, much like a "bottled spider," from the edges of a space that has been turned into a deceptive trap.

In its mise-en-scène and framing, the *Duc de Guise* is quite characteristic of early Film d'Art productions. Somewhat unique to the film, however, are its pattern of cutting on de Guise's movement and its use of intertitles. The first of these serves to accentuate the film's dramatic structure. In three contiguous shots occurring at the narrative climax, de Guise passes through the king's bedchamber and adjacent antechamber to the cabinet room, where he is finally attacked. What is especially interesting here are the changes in camera position which

74. *L'Assassinat du Duc de Guise*, 1908 (poster)

75. *L'Assassinat du Duc de Guise,* 1908
(Charles Le Bargy, left)

76. *L'Assassinat du Duc de Guise,* 1908

77. *L'Assassinat du Duc de Guise,* 1908

smoothly matchcut his exits and entrances, so that he seems to circulate repeatedly from left to right, first into the depths of the frame and then back out to a vulnerable foreground position. And since those exits and entrances are always through doorways in background walls, they reinforce the sense of enclosed spaces through which he moves to his death. After the attack, de Guise tries to flee, and the matchcutting on his movement is now repeated in reverse, quickening in order to intensify his flight, so that he ends up dying back in the king's bedchamber. Neatly complementing the traplike description of space just prior to the murder, this pattern of cutting seems to play de Guise out and then draw him back as if he were snared on the hook of an invisible thread. A different kind of pattern seems at work in the film's ten intertitles. Most of these, in the tradition of the genre, occur between shot-scene changes and briefly summarize the visual action that ensues. Two, however, interrupt the first shot of the marquise and de Guise, concisely setting up opposite responses to Henri III's threat: a letter comes to her warning de Guise of a plot, on which he scrawls, with a flourish of bravado, "He would not dare!" The other three intertitles then interrupt the shot in which de Guise falls dead in Henri III's bedchamber, and the

78. *L'Assassinat du Duc de Guise*, 1908 (Gabrielle Robinne, Albert Lambert)

79. *L'Assassinat du Duc de Guise*, 1908

first two serve to privilege de Guise at the king's expense. The first notes that the king has to assure himself that de Guise is really dead, which Le Bargy then acts out with great caution. The second, "He is even larger in death than in life," offers a rare instance of dialogue cut in at the moment of utterance, in which Henri III's reported words serve to counterpoint the visual action in a kind of conclusive "history lesson."[159] But the third—a letter taken from the body which implicates de Guise in the Spanish war against France—seems to contradict this "lesson" and lends support to Henri's plotting, unless, of course, one assumes it has been planted.

If only momentarily, these intertitles produce a wavering in the film's attitude toward the assassination, a kind of ambiguity in its narrative "voice." Yet the effect of these strategies, in the end, is to represent the Duc de Guise as a framed, "innocent" Catholic martyr (although it was he who instigated the Bartholomew Eve's massacre of French Protestants in 1572) in contrast to a devious, cowardly, "appeasing" king. That contrast is drawn out further in the final stark tableau of the guards' underground chamber—the antithesis of an apotheosis tableau—as the conspirators nonchalantly wash their hands and Henri III unceremoniously tries to further reduce de Guise's "greatness" by burning his body. Moreover, the king enters the chamber with his face partially hidden by a black mask and only reveals himself once the marquise, in despair, has rushed in—so that the film ends with the two figures confronting one another across the foreground of the frame. Intriguingly, this final tableau seems to have been cut from both the British and American release prints.[160] In its complicity with what André Billy called "the cult of great men [or] the taste for exemplary figures"[161]—celebrating a "patriotic" Catholic against a "traitor" from within (even if a king)—such a representation is not without ideological ramifications at the moment when a conservative Nationalist Revival movement was on the verge of achieving ascendancy in French society.

The surviving Film d'Art productions that followed the *Duc de Guise* generally turned away from original scenarios, for their stories of violent death or imprisonment, to adaptations of dramas and operas.[162] Throughout the next year or so, they also seem to have developed in two divergent directions, the latter of which, despite *Ciné-Journal*'s praise for the company,[163] may well be responsible for the long-standing dismissal of its films as "too theatrical" and hence a dead end in cinema history. This divergence comes sharply into focus if one compares two pairs of films, *La Tosca* and *Rival de son fils* versus *Le Retour d'Ulysse* and *Héliogabale*.

La Tosca (1909)—which *Moving Picture World*'s reviewer proclaimed "a masterpiece, flawless from end to end"[164]—is drawn from a popular Sardou play and, possibly, also from a condensed version of Puccini's recent opera.[165] The story pits Mario Cavardossi (René Alexandre), who loves the celebrated singer, Florio Tosca (Cecile Sorel), against Baron Scarpia (Le Bargy), the malicious police chief of Rome. After coming to the aid of Angelotti, an old republican activist, Mario is arrested and sentenced to death. Scarpia writes a letter to halt the execution, on condition that Tosca become his mistress; instead, she stabs and kills him. Most of the film is composed of long-take LSs, with full, diffused lighting, recorded by a fixed camera consistently positioned at waist level (now also a Film d'Art trademark). Although the studio set decors may be slightly more spare and the final scene of execution even resorts to a painted cityscape backdrop, the acting is no less economical and restrained—"What acting!" a New York spectator is said to have exclaimed—and character movement is carefully choreographed within a relatively deep-space mise-en-scène. At times, that movement carries an actor forward into FS, in either the left or right foreground.[166] Tosca and Scarpia's "dance of death," for instance, is performed within the triangular playing area of his office (anchored by a table in one foreground corner, a chair in the other, and a background doorway and desk) and ends with a bizarre foreground ritual—first performed on stage by Bernhardt[167]—as she places a large crucifix on his chest and lighted candles on either side of his head. *La Tosca* deviates somewhat from the *Duc de Guise*, however, in eschewing dialogue intertitles as well as in adopting a slightly different strategy of editing and framing. Not only does it intercut interior and exterior shots (through a 180-degree shift in camera position), when Mario rescues Angelotti from prison, but it includes a rather unusual MS of the latter as he climbs out his cell window—perhaps one further sign of the displaced republicanism with which the film's story seems to empathize. And that attitude seems confirmed, in the end, when Scarpia's letter, despite Tosca's revenge, proves to be a ruse and actually seals Mario's death.[168]

Adapted from Schiller's famous historical drama, *Rival de son fils* (1910) also may have relied on a truncated version of Verdi's operatic score. Set in sixteenth-century Spain, this film makes rivals of King Philippe II (Paul Mounet) and his son Don Carlos (Roger Monteaux) for the hand of the French princess Elizabeth (Mlle Pacitti). The Grand Inquisitor (Gabriel Signoret) enflames the king's jealousy and, after the royal wedding of Philippe and Elizabeth (cementing the bonds of Spain and France), tricks Don Carlos with a false letter into entering her bedchamber and there has him killed. Letters are crucial to this story (there are four in all), not only in order to clarify advances or turning points in the narrative, but, as in *La Tosca*, to produce the deception that concludes the film in a tragic death. Perhaps even more interesting is the way that a large portrait of Elizabeth serves as an object of exchange in one central scene. Here, both the king and his son (one after the other, and mediated by the Inquisitor), convey their rival infatuation with the princess within the quadrangular playing area of a shot (with both left and right background exits): while Don Carlos's opening right foreground position is played off against Philippe's ending left foreground position, the portrait of Elizabeth consistently occupies the gravitational center of the frame. This studied choreography of movement within one FS/LS after another produces an unusual final tableau: in the foreground, the king stands with his back to the camera and orders the Inquisitor away, but then Elizabeth also moves away from him to the background, to weep with her back to the camera, and the king turns around to lift his arms in a gesture of helpless remorse. Such a framing and acting strategy—which was not all that un-common on the French stage at the time and which historians have associated with later Vitagraph and Biograph films[169]—not only intensifies the characters' private emotional states (giving the film's discourse a moral, psychologizing "voice") but also suggests that an irreconcilable gap has opened up between queen and king. That this domestic tragedy—again equating family and state—is the responsibility of a villainous Inquisitor gives the film an anticlerical edge, yet one softened by the displacement of time and space.

If *La Tosca* and *Rival de son fils* tend to integrate carefully orchestrated char-acter movement, within a relatively few enclosed spaces, and a variety of changes in framing, *Le Retour d'Ulysse* (1909), eschews the latter altogether. Adapted by Jules Lemaitre from the final chapter of *The Odyssey*, this film re-counts the story of how Penelope (Mme Bartet) keeps a horde of would-be suitors at bay in Ithaca, until Ulysses (Mounet) finally returns from the Trojan War and easily dispatches them. Two palace interiors recur most frequently among the LS tableaux of painted-flat decors—an open court area and the queen's bedroom (both probably based on "Neo-Grec" historical paintings)—with others representing a wooded glade on Calypso's island (where Ulysses has been stranded), the ruined city of Ithaca, and a rather plain entrance to the pal-ace. Expository and narrative intertitles introduce most of these,[170] but occasion-ally the film either cuts on Penelope or Ulysses's movement from one space to another or alternates between tableaux—for instance, between the suitors' ca-rousing and the queen's solitary work on a tapestry of her husband in full battle armor. *Le Retour d'Ulysse* is structured so as to highlight the intelligence and craft by which both Penelope and Ulysses outwit the suitors in related contests. For three years, she undoes at night the weaving she has done during the day (she has promised to choose a suitor once the tapestry is finished); then, on his return, he takes on the disguise of a beggar and surprises the suitors by being the only one capable of stringing the king's bow. Yet Penelope's domestic resis-tance ultimately is premised on the masculine ideal of Ulysses's power—while she sleeps (in one of the early scenes), he dissolves out of the tapestry as a dream figure exhorting her to go on awaiting his return. That power is explicitly mas-culinized in the final tableaux when he demonstrates his strength, not only by stringing the bow, but by shooting and killing Antinoüs (Lambert), whom an intertitle describes as weakened and made effeminate by a decadent life of leisure.

Héliogabale (1910) complements *Le Retour d'Ulysse* in several ways.[171] For most of its length, this film mounts its story of the cruel third-century Roman emperor in just three LS tableaux of painted-flat decors, placing it even more firmly within the tradition of nineteenth-century historical paintings, opera stagings, and earlier Pathé films.[172] The first two represent the exterior and in-terior of a Roman temple, while the third sets up the contrasting interior of the emperor's palace. There, amidst a throng of extras engaged in a ritual proces-sion, Héliogabale (Jacques Guilhème) becomes infatuated with one of the vestal virgins, Julia Aquilina-Severa (Olga Domidoff), and drags her off to his banquet hall, where he tries to fondle her before another throng, of "exotic" dancing women.[173] Into this spectacle of depravity breaks a horde of "citizens" led by an old man who earlier had tried to protect Julia, and they succeed in driving Héliogabale from the palace—in a loosely linked series of three new spaces. The latter's headlong flight through an underground passage involves a drop through a trapdoor and onto the bank of a diverted river channel (where he is finally seized), an action that rather than being matchcut is repeated across the cut. In a final tableau, with Julia and the old man present, Héliogabale is killed at the base of a bridge and his body thrown into the Tiber. At least two salient points can be made about the story this film tells. First, Héliogabale's historical violation of Rome's traditional religion is transformed into a sexual violation, displaced onto the body of a vestal virgin. Moreover, this is worked out in a family melodrama plot, with a "father" figure successfully protecting a "daughter" from a "bad son." Second, Héliogabale can be read as a kind of "oriental" despot threatening Rome and its heritage from within—much as the decadent suitors threatened Ithaca in *Le Retour d'Ulysse*. Indeed, the conflict between West and East, between the Greco-Roman and the Orient, mapped out in these two films—a conflict that was crucial to any nationalist notion of French civilization at the time—is one that will be staged repeatedly in the genre.[174]

The trajectory of that staging is evident in two sets of Gaumont and Pathé films, each of which can be differentiated according to the division marked out within Film d'Art. What is especially interesting about these films is that, in mapping the conflict between West and East, they often invoke cultural notions of gender difference—celebrating "masculine" values at the expense of the "feminine."[175] Moreover, they fall into specific subcategories—biblical films versus "oriental" tales—one of which adopts the moral, psychologizing "voice" of *Rival de son fils*, while the other, much like *Héliogabale*, eschews any sense of interiority altogether. The first set of biblical films—Gaumont's *Judith et Holophernes* (1909) and Pathé's *Moïse sauvé des eaux* (1911) and *Caïn et Abel* (1911)—is unusually inventive in its strategies of framing, lighting, and editing, and ultimately creates a rudimentary degree of subjectivity in its central characters.

In *Judith et Holophernes*, Feuillade divides the Old Testament story into two equal, rather static parts. Judith (Carl) prepares to leave the city of Bethulia, as a ransom for its safety, and she arrives in Holophernes's camp in the midst of a night of drunken revelry, which provides her with the opportunity to kill him. The first half of the film focuses on Judith's singularity—most notably when she is being dressed for her journey, in a LS that is literally framed by a simulated wooden border, as if to "realize" or bring a well-known painting to life. The second half deploys a similar framing device for contrast, using curtains and a low foreground railing, in order to compose the tableau of Holophernes's feast, but now an arc light (from the right) accentuates the king (left foreground) against a crowd of revelers.[176] The final moment of spectacle provides an ingenious analogy to the actual killing. As Holophernes draws her away from the background festivities and into a separate foreground room (and then exits alone, frame right), Judith sharply closes the curtained doorway behind her, redefining the space as hers. A matchcut on that movement shifts to a longer shot of the same space with Holophernes now stretched out asleep on a bed (right foreground), and Judith pushes the top part of his body offscreen in order to behead him. Rather than be represented directly "on stage," Holophernes's beheading is articulated across several interrelated rhetorical figures—the drawn curtains, the matchcut, and the right frame line. Closing off a space, redefining its boundaries, is refigured in the cutting of a body, and the dismembering serves to embody Judith's subjectivity with power. Much as it does in Pathé and Gaumont's contemporary melodramas as well as Griffith's films of this period, the filmic discourse in *Judith et Holophernes* "conspires" to judge and justify its heroine's action—and leaves the spectator little choice but to do likewise.

Similarly focused on a woman, *Moise sauvé des eaux* deploys a slightly different strategy of representation. This film, from a script by Carré, tells the story of how Amron (Jacquinet) and Jokebed (Madeleine Roch)[177] save their only child from the pharaoh's order to execute all the exiled Hebrews' newborn babies in Egypt, and how Jokebed is allowed to continue nursing him after the pharaoh's daughter finds and adopts the infant. Initially, the story relies heavily on lengthy intertitles, at least one of which is a direct quotation from Hebrews, chapter 11. Likewise, the film privileges the stylized movements and gestures of the principal actors in long-take, stencil color tableaux. Yet its two major sequences are organized strictly in terms of alternating adjacent spaces. The first shifts back and forth between an open area in front of the city gate and Amron and Jokebed's living quarters (both studio decors), matching exits and entrances as the pharaoh's soldiers search one space (while the parents hide the infant) and then the other, eventually coming away empty-handed. The second sequence begins with an AS/LS of a riverbank lined with bullrushes (now shot on location), where Jokebed and her daughter come forward, and (coincident with a slight pan) the girl goes to the water's edge and puts the infant in a basket (frame left). At this precise moment, the camera shifts ninety degrees and cuts in to an AS of her setting the basket on the water among the rushes, her figure glowing softly in the backlight and reflected fill light. After a return to the initial AS/LS (matchcutting the girl's movement), in which mother and daughter reluctantly exit (frame right), the pharaoh's daughter and her servants replace them in the tableau (following an intertitle); and, in exactly the same sequential changes in framing, she discovers the child and asks Jokebed, who has returned as a supplicant, to wetnurse the infant as her own adopted and protected son. Although the pharaoh ratifies this personal arrangement in the public court of the final tableau, this river sequence is crucial, not only for Moses' survival and the Hebrews' future destiny, but also for the way it depends on the conventions of gender difference—using the pacific bonds between women, as mothers and daughters, to resolve the hateful antagonism between men.

Caïn et Abel continues this pyschologizing tendency, within the tightly unified format of the well-made play. The first half of this film leads up to the killing, while the second half focuses on Cain's despair. Shot entirely on location, the film initially seems quite conventional in its waist-level, stencil color tableaux that quickly establish Cain's envy of his brother. In a separate shot before the killing, however, Cain moves off alone among some boulders to think and comes forward into MS, as if his decision were being made, in a silent soliloquy, in conjunction with the audience. Once he does the deed, in the next shot, and covers Abel's body with stones, Pathé's patented special effects briefly take over—lightning flashes and red smoke give way to a painted flat of golden rays before which an angel dissolves in to cause the stones magically to roll away. Although a similar "vision" of the dead Abel and the sword-bearing angel confronts Cain later at one point, most of the rest of the film describes his lonely wandering. A variety of framing strategies now accentuate his suffering—a pan traces his stumbling path along a rocky hillside, and a HA shot shows him scrambling forward into FS in a narrow rock cleft. This concludes in another FS of Cain collapsing in fear and exhaustion, and kneeling to pray, but the surviving print breaks off before it is certain whether he is answered or not. Although the principles of restrained acting seem less binding here than in most historical films, *Caïn et Abel* is somewhat unusual for its attempt to depict its central character's psychological state through a kind of sustained objectification—fixing that character consistently within a single, resonant "wilderness" environment.

Unlike these biblical films, Pathé and Gaumont's "oriental" films not only remain firmly locked into the old tableau system of narration, refusing their central characters any kind of subjectivy, but also consistently devalue and even demonize the "East" as "feminine." A good example of such films is Pathé's *Cléopatre* (1910), which played a small role in what can only be called a world-wide "Cleopatra craze" beginning that year—her figure was appropriated to hawk everything from cigarettes to beauty soap and light bulbs.[178] Based on a 1890 Sardou play adapted from Shakespeare for Bernhardt, this film focuses on the ending of its original source—where Antony, another Roman emperor seduced by the "Orient," dies along with his seducer, Cleopatra, the queen of Egypt (played by Roch). Following convention, the film's twelve LS tableaux combine painted flats—a seascape, for instance, beyond Cleopatra's palace terrace—with rather spectacular props such as the scaled-down sailing ship that seems to carry her from the first shot to Antony's camp in the second.[179] And, because this was the company's initial "séries d'art" production, all these decors (including the costumes) are showcased in stencil color. The acting within these spaces, however, is nowhere as economical as that so characteristic of Film d'Art productions and instead resorts to the tradition of broadly stylized gestures, divorced from the verbal declamation supporting them on stage. In fact, after reporting the lost battle at sea, the poisoned messenger (Stacia Napierkowska) goes into a writhing "dance of death" that momentarily upstages Cleopatra herself. But that death also epitomizes the exotic cruelty and "otherness" of Egypt which the film seeks to put on display.

That "otherness" re-genders another familiar story of death and destruction in Gaumont's *Le Festin de Balthazar* (1910). Here, Balthazar (Perret, in a nicely nuanced bit of acting) is warned not once but three times before Cyrus's army quickly overruns his palace and kills him. The first occurs in the opening long-

80. *Cléopatre*, 1910 (Stacia Napierkowska, Madeleine Roch)

take LS tableau of a simple palace interior (with the painted-flat of a distant cityscape framed in a wide background doorway), where a messenger confronts a quite indolent Balthazar, who hesitates and then recovers his insouciance. The second comes from a soldier, after a sinuous female dancer (apparently Napierkowska again) has performed for the king in another interior, whose foreground, like all the others, is edged round in darkness.[180] The film then delays the third warning with an added LS tableau (using a set decor from *Judith et Holophernes*), accentuated by an offscreen arc light again, where the servants gather up more wine jars from a large storage room. Finally, as Balthazar carouses with several women, in yet another interior, a magnified hand writes, "Mane, Thecel, Phares," against a black background wall—a spectacle that is then doubled when an angel (replacing the words) steps down to confront the king, whose pleas of mercy are ignored. A crosscut to a dark LS palace exterior, lit only by an arc lamp offscreen, then shows a horde of soldiers rushing from left to right, who, in the next tableau, burst in to stab Balthazar. The next-to-last tableau returns, with a difference, to the beginning: against a smoking background cityscape, a soldier slowly paces among the bodies scattered across a palace balcony and, then leaning on a column with a nonchalance to match Balthazar's, watches parts of the city burn and collapse. If much of the film seems designed to condemn the passive, "feminine" Balthazar in contrast to the active, "masculine" Cyrus, this soldier's lassitude suggests that the latter's victory may be brief, given the seductive power of the "feminized" Orient.[181]

Just as intriguing in its display of gender difference is Pathé's *Sémiramis* (1910).[182] Drawn from a script by Carré and directed by de Morlhon, this film recounts the legend of the famous Babylonian queen (Roch, again) in a series of autonomous, stencil color LS tableaux, nearly all of which are introduced by intertitles. The first part of this relatively static film has King Nimus bring Sémiramis to Babylon as his new queen, after which she quickly conspires to kill him, making herself the sole ruler. Much attention is lavished on the painted-flat decors, of which one of the palace exterior is reminiscent of *Héliogabale*, and on the actors' choreographed movements in a deep-space mise-en-scène—perhaps most strikingly in the large, empty room over whose background wall soldiers bearing swords crawl to enter a curtained-off area (frame right), and from which the king emerges all bloodied to collapse before the "shocked" queen (left foreground). In a variation on the structure of the well-made play, the second part shifts to unadulterated spectacle, highlighting Sémiramis's successful efforts to gain her people's trust, which culminate in a splendid tableau (drawn from Puvis de Chavannes) of her renowned hanging gardens. And those gardens are full of women laden with flowers, in a "feminized" utopian fantasy of peaceful social harmony. In typical apotheosis fashion, *Sémiramis* then concludes (at least in the only extant print) with the queen's own death as she collapses on a huge griffin-shaped altar, from which a superimposition of her regal figure lifts off into the heavens. A final missing tableau, however, seems to have staged a further spectacle of gender-reversal revenge, as in *Le Festin de Balthazar*, with a horde of Arabian soldiers sacking the city and reducing the famous gardens to ruins.[183]

In sharp contrast to these bibical films and "oriental" spectacles, certain historical films, especially those of Film d'Art, extend the narrational stance already marking the final moments of the *Duc de Guise* and *La Tosca* into a kind of ironic "voice"—in parallel with that developed even more strongly in several grand guignol films. *L'Arrestation de la Duchesse de Berry* (1910), for instance, recounts the Legitimist plot, in 1832, to overthrow Louis-Philippe and restore the Bourbon throne. The first half of the film, in which the Duchesse de Berry (Nelly Cormon) unsuccessfully leads an insurrection in Southern France, is missing from the only extant print; the second part focuses on her escape to the Vendée region, where she is betrayed by an informer named Dantz (Levesques), in the pay of the Orleanist police. Like its predecessors, this film generally relies on choreographing its actors' restrained gestures and movement within the deep-space mise-en-scène of long-take LSs. The climax, however, is articulated through an alternation of spaces, between the formal drawing room of the Guigny sisters, who have taken the duchess in, and the secret chamber behind the fireplace where she hides (in AS) from Dantz and the police—who inadvertently smoke her out of hiding simply by calling for a fire to be lit. The film also uses a drawing-room studio decor that is constructed in an unusual way; instead of having a flat back wall, ending in open corners, this set angles its principal wall into a ninety-degree-angle corner in the right-center background. While preserving a sense of deep space, this design produces an added degree of

81. *L'Arrestation de la Duchesse de Berry*, 1910

"realism" and accentuates the characters' dynamic movements. The final tableau incorporates a similar design for the local prefect's office and emphasizes its relatively empty space with a strong arc light (from the right), all of which throw into stark relief Dantz's acceptance of the reward money the prefect disdainfully holds out to him on the tip of a dueling foil. Not only does *L'Arrestation de la Duchesse de Berry* turn what is now commonly considered a farcical coup attempt into a heroic drama, but it even has the Orleanist authorities, in an ironical postscript, contemptuously condemn their own informer as a coward.

Such an ironic "voice" is even more sharply pronounced in *Werther* (1910), Pouctal's earliest surviving work for Film d'Art. Drawn from Massenet's opera (based on Goethe's famous novel) by Charles Decroix, this film narrates the story of Werther (André Brulé), a young German student, and his passionate love for his childhood friend, Charlotte (Laurence Dulac), whose marriage to another man, Albert (Philippe Garnier), eventually prompts him to suicide. Although it, too, shares features with its predecessors and was specifically advertised for "the higher class of audience" in the United States,[184] *Werther* also includes unusual strategies of representation. The first of these involves a deliberate pattern of camera movement in one of the last shots of the film, representing the interior of Charlotte's home. A pan follows Charlotte laterally from the central room to an adjacent one on the left and center-frames the wall between them, as she closes the door that keeps Werther from joining her (both of them moving forward into FS here). A reverse pan then reframes the central room as

82. *Werther*, 1910

Werther returns to a background door and exits past her husband as the latter enters. Another pan now follows Albert as he comes forward and passes through the crucial door in the wall, with the camera now center-framing the second room as he embraces his wife. These pans seem to function symbolically as much as narratively, in order to mark just who can and cannot be with or possess Charlotte. A second strategy involves an unexpected change in framing for the film's final shot. Immediately after Werther's suicide—represented in LS with his back turned to the camera (the pistol he fires at his head produces a small cloud of smoke drawn or etched on the film)—there is a cut to a shot of Charlotte, her husband and children clustered around a decorated Christmas tree in the middle of the same central room. This time, however, instead of repeating the usual LS, the camera frames the family in FS, as if literally to magnify the joy they share. Yet, juxtaposing these two shots, unmediated by an intertitle, compromises that sense of joy through an ironic disjuncture between the spectators who know and the characters who remain ignorant of Werther's death.[185]

Within this spectrum of divergence within the genre, it was the films drawn from biblical stories, classical mythology, or "oriental" tales that most tended to recuperate features of the cinema of attractions. Although Film d'Art released several such titles in its first year of production—*Le Baiser de Judas* (1909), for instance, survives only in scenario form[186]—most of them came from Pathé and Gaumont. Arguably, it was Pathé's biblical films that stuck more closely to what Jasset called "the old way" of doing things—at least if *Joseph vendu par ses frères* (1909) can be taken as representative.[187] Like the earlier *Le Fils prodigue*,[188] this film tells a circular story of loss and redemption—Joseph is betrayed by his brothers in Palestine, then resists the seductive lure of Potiphar and prospers in Egypt. It, too, is staged in just eight FS/LS tableaux, most of which illustrate a half-dozen expository intertitles. Moreover, for the crucial moment of Joseph's forgiveness of his brothers, the film falls back on the "dream vision" of his father Jacob weeping over his lost son's many-colored coat. Reversing the familial hierarchy of the earlier film, here Joseph, in playing the "good son," eventually assumes the role of the father in relation to his own brothers.

The Arcadian subjects that briefly became a staple of Gaumont's production about this time also held fast to the "old way"—on the evidence of *Idylle corinthienne* (1909).[189] In yet another celebration of the "classical" over the "oriental," this story separates a young Greek shepherd and shepherdess when the latter's parents sell her into slavery but then reunites them by means of a benevolent prince. The film's half-dozen set decors are recorded consistently in LS, and the opening long-take tableau can be taken as exemplary in its choreography of actor movement within the space of a simple peasant courtyard. First, the lovers define the space as their own—after wreathing a "classical" marble bust and pouring some wine, he plays his pipe in the background while she dances before him. Then, a rich Egyptian merchant enters to successfully bargain with her parents; once he goes off with the shepherdess, the shepherd is left to exit the empty space alone. Much of the film thereafter traces the shepherdess through the "exotic" milieu of a slave market and palace in Alexandria. In a slight deviation from convention, however, a FS of the palace terrace exterior reintroduces the disguised shepherd (in search of his love) as he confronts the rich merchant and asks what has become of her. In preparation for its narrative climax, the film now intercuts two separate spaces—an interior where the young woman is being costumed for a celebration and the terrace exterior where the shepherd is waiting—before bringing the two together in a LS of the central palace hall. Their moment of recognition, intriguingly, is keyed by musical accompaniment—the shepherd's pipe, which he is asked to play in the left foreground. His music draws the shepherdess forward to dance and then move to the right, from which positions across the foreground of the frame the two lovers recognize one another and finally come forward to embrace. In its last tableau, *Idylle corinthienne* returns to the opening courtyard (the parents now conspicuously absent), where the lovers can again play and dance in a "fantasy" space of their own making.

Even Eclair, with its penchant for the adventure film series, took to the French fashion for biblical films. Jasset himself produced at least two of these, *La Résurrection de Lazare* and *Hériodiade* (both 1910), the latter of which was drawn from a Massenet opera.[190] Apparently the only Eclair film to survive, however, is *La Parabol de l'enfant prodigue* (1911). This film draws directly on Luke chapter 15 for its seven intertitles, which essentially serve to narrate the familiar fable of the prodigal son. Consequently, its eleven tableaux are selected and composed explicitly to illustrate this verbal text. Despite this restricted mode of representation and narration, the Eclair film is distinctive in several ways. First of all, it is shot entirely on location; and, because its tableaux some-times "realize" specific paintings (such as those of Tissot), they consistently achieve a harmonious balance of graphic and representational elements—as in the alley of a biblical village, where ascending and descending stone steps are framed by multiple doorways and arches.[191] Second, each tableau is defined by a deep-space mise-en-scène, accentuated often by having the characters circu-late within the frame from LS to AS. What is especially striking is that, from tableau to tableau, the son repeatedly exits in the right foreground, in pursuit of his prodigal ways. This pattern of movement is broken, not when he himself realizes his condition, but in the next-to-last tableau, when he returns to his father, who accepts and embraces him—and they go off together toward the right background. The final tableau then recapitulates the opening, again fol-lowing the domestic melodrama, by anchoring the son in the right foreground, his body turned around toward and his gaze fixed securely on his father and younger brother centered in the background.

This recuperation of the older tableau style carried over as well into the French adaptations of Shakespeare's plays. As Robert Hamilton Ball was one of the first to point out, Shakespeare films proliferated during this period, not only in France but in England, Italy, Denmark, and the United States.[192] Film com-pany after film company appropriated Shakespeare's name and play texts, much as they did classic opera titles, in order to acquire a kind of cultural capital, and to increase their profits in the process of enhancing their social prestige.[193] Be-cause Shakespeare's plays were in the public domain and accessible to a wide audience, Roberta Pearson and William Uricchio argue, they could serve, in the United States, to both demonstrate the cinema industry's commitment to moral education and also more regularly attract a middle-class audience.[194] Vitagraph, for instance, used a series of one-reel adaptations—*Macbeth* (April 1908), *Romeo and Juliet* (June 1908), *Richard III* (September 1908), *Antony and Cleopatra* (No-vember 1908), *Julius Caesar* (December 1908), *The Merchant of Venice* (December 1908), and *King Lear* (March 1909)—to establish what the company called its "quality film" production.[195] And Bush did much to promote such Shakespeare adaptations in *Moving Picture World*.[196] The effect these films had in France re-mains uncertain, but it must not have been all that extensive because—other than Méliès's *Hamlet* and *La Mort du Jules César* (both 1907)—the earliest French Shakespeare adaptations did not appear until late 1909.[197] Then, however, several French companies (Gaumont and Eclair were the exceptions) rushed into pro-duction, with Pathé prompting Film d'Arte Italiana in particular to initiate a series of the English playwright's "Italian" works. And what may well have impelled this appropriation was the persistent complaint from American re-viewers that audiences too often found the historical stories in French films incomprehensible.[198]

One of the first of these Shakespeare adaptations was Film d'Art's *Macbeth*, directed by Calmettes and released in late 1909.[199] This *Macbeth* claims a "high art" status from the beginning by calling attention to its Comédie Française actors—Mounet (Macbeth) and Jeanne Delvair (Lady Macbeth). Each is introduced separately, in costume and in MS, preceded by an intertitle, in one of the earliest instances of preliminary "credits"—a strategy of introduction which eventually would become widespread in such "theatrical" films. Otherwise, the film generally follows the Film d'Art model of long-take LSs, deep-space studio set decors, relatively restrained acting, and strongly choreographed character movement. What is most intriguing, however, is which moments in the play the adaptation chooses to represent and highlight. Not unexpectedly, perhaps, the film includes most of the supernatural scenes: the trucs of invisible editing and dissolving superimpositions work satisfactorily enough in studio sets for the witches (twice) and Banquo's ghost, but disguising Macduff's army in skimpy little trees in an actual wooded clearing considerably deflates the concluding miracle. Yet *Macbeth* gives so much attention to the early sequence of Duncan's murder (eight shots altogether, and interrupted by only one intertitle) that its structure resembles that of the well-made play rather than Shakespeare's—after this climax, the falling action and catastrophe are wrapped up summarily in just four tableaux. The murder sequence is unique in that it involves an alternation between adjacent rooms in Macbeth's castle interior and smoothly matchcuts the movement of servants and masters from one to the other. Moreover, immediately after the alarm is sounded, a crosscut exterior LS describes Malcolm and Donalbain's escape from the castle. The most striking detail, however, comes in Lady Macbeth's choreographed moves after the murder: first, she wrests the bloody daggers from Macbeth in the foreground, and places them in the hands of Duncan's sleeping servants (on opposite sides of the frame); next, she exits left background (into Duncan's room) and returns with blood all over her own hands to further smear the servants. This excess of blood then resonates in the slightly closer LS tableau of her later "sleepwalking" scene within the same room, which immediately precedes and upstages Macbeth's own speedy death in the final tableau.

Although produced by Pathé outside France, the first of Film d'Arte Italiana's Shakespeare adaptations, *Othello* (1909), deserves some attention for the way it both conforms to and differs from those made in France. This *Othello* strips the drama down to a condensed playlet, concentrated on the opposition of Desdemona's father, Brabantio, to her marriage to the Moor, Iago's manipulation of the "intrigue" involving Cassio to enflame Othello's jealousy, and the final confrontation in which Othello shames Desdemona in public and kills first her and then himself. Comprised of eighteen shots, most of which are recorded in LS, the film also includes fifteen intertitles, twelve of which simply summarize the narrative action visualized in the subsequent shot. The others are letters—two from the Doge of Venice with orders for Othello, plus Cassio's letter to Desdemona, which arouses the Moor's jealousy. Whether set up in the studio or on location, the film's decors rely extensively on rather flimsy painted flats, sometimes with no more than a chair or two for props, and are illuminated with full, diffused lighting. Several shot-scenes depend on choreographed actor movement within a relatively deep-space mise-en-scène, as in the shot of the doge's palace interior—but here the movement of Othello, Desdemona, and

Brabantio back and forth through a crowd of people, from background to foreground, seems flattened by the waist-level camera position. Finally, the acting of the principals, divorced from Shakespeare's language, is no less exaggerated than that in earlier Pathé historical films. Iago (Cesare Dondini) is portrayed as a comic corpulent figure whose seeming lack of motivation makes his actions seem devilish pranks that simply get out of hand, while Othello (Ferrucio Garavaglia) goes from being a stock warrior hero who can show compassion for his enemies to a wild-eyed wretch who, in a racist caricature of the role, even writhes on the floor of Desdemona's sitting room, much to Iago's amusement.

What is especially interesting about *Othello*, however, is that, much as in *Macbeth*, the first half is much more inventive than the rest of the film. For one thing, the initial shot-scenes display Venice itself as an attraction, substituting "The Queen of the Adriatic" and its architectural jewels for Desdemona (Vittoria Lepanto) as a site of spectatorly pleasure.[200] After the first LS tableau introducing Othello and Desdemona in front of a townhouse facade, the next three shots describe Iago and Rodrigo in a gondola passing through Venice's canals to the house of Brabantio. Each shot seems to dolly forward across the water, in a jumpcut series (uninterrupted by intertitles) that would be familiar from actualité films or travelogues. And Iago and Rodrigo sit conversing in MS, occasionally glancing at the camera and once, as the gondola passes under the Bridge of Sighs, even briefly turning into silhouettes. The effect of this series is unsettling: not only does it suggest Iago's ability to maneuver in this "exotic" space, it links the spectator to him as a surrogate viewer. Eventually, of course, this guided tour of the city is subordinated to the logic of the film's narrative—as Iago comes to meet Othello and Desdemona, his action proves to have been simultaneous with that of the opening tableau. The subsequent shots then extend this sense of simultaneity through further crosscutting—Iago pulls Othello away from Desdemona in front of the townhouse, Brabantio and his men disembark from a gondola on a canal dockside—and all of the major male characters confront one another in a formal garden. After this long exposition, the film settles down to reenact its famous story in conventional LS tableaux, with the characters' actions governed closely by intertitles. The one remaining point of interest comes in the final tableau, where Desdemona is strangled beside a heavily carved Victorian bed (frame right), so that Othello can die, at some length, "center stage." And the murder-suicide is played out under the portrait of a woman in white (with two children at her side) enshrined over the background doorway—a maternal icon through which Iago's initial sightseeing voyeurism is turned into a moral vision of the domestic sphere (and the proper role for a married woman) which encompasses Desdemona herself within its condemnation.

Later Film d'Arte Italiana adaptations such as *The Merchant of Venice* (1911) also doubled their pleasure by appropriating Venice as a spectacle attraction, while others such as *King Lear* (1910–1911) attempted to enact their stories in the relatively "tamed" exteriors of natural locations. And because both films adhered closely to the older tableau system of representation, audiences would have had to rely heavily on either the frequent intertitles or else their familiarity with "famous bits" of text in order to comprehend them at all. The earliest Shakespeare adaptation from Eclipse to survive, *The Taming of the Shrew* (1911), generally followed this model as well.[201] Much like its predecessors, this film is almost completely comprised of FS/LS studio decors recorded by a waist-level camera. Long-takes first introduce Katherine (Madeleine Barjac), who rages throughout the space of the frame—beating a servant girl, shouting at and shoving her father, ripping off her sister Bianca's necklace, and bashing Lucentio (her sister's suitor) with his lute—and then present her confrontation with Petruchio (Romuald Joubé), as they circle warily, smash vases together, and threaten one another with slaps and punches. Thereafter, this adaptation continually depends on the displays of Petruchio's outrageous behavior—for instance, he saunters into his wedding, held in a great hall with checkerboard floors, in a ragged harlequin outfit topped by a huge feather. But it also shifts away from such public spectacle to link two specific moments of intimacy through a change-in-framing technique taken over from Pathé's domestic melodramas. The first comes, in Petruchio's house, after he has kept Katherine from eating supper and ordered her to sleep in a chair: in a cut-in AS, he opens a window behind her sleeping figure (a soft light from the upper right floods over her) and then kneels beside her to kiss her temple. The second is inserted at the end, as the husbands wager on whose wife is most obedient. Now, an AS of the women in a separate room (the newly married Bianca is seated in a center chair, while Kate is seated at her feet) privileges Katherine's rising and turning to face the camera before she goes off, in the final tableau, to kneel to Petruchio. Although still operating securely within a patriarchal system of dominance, the closer camera position seems to suggest a motivation for Katherine's decision by recalling the earlier private gestures of Petruchio's love.

While the other French companies were either filming adaptations of famous operas and Shakespeare plays or flooding the market with biblical and "oriental" films, SCAGL was concentrating on subjects (many of them adaptations as well) dealing specifically with French history. Films focusing on significant figures or events in a nation's history, of course, were not restricted to France—see, for instance, Ambrosia's *The Last Days of Pompeii* (1908), Itala's *Ugolin* (1909), Vitagraph's *Washington* (1909), and Biograph's *1776* (1909). But SCAGL's production of historical films easily outnumbered its competitors elsewhere and presented a broad panorama of French history, from its Gallic beginnings in *Vercingétorix* (1909), through *La Tour de Nesle* (1909) and a new longer *Napoléon* (1909)—whose release coincided closely with Vitagraph's own version of the same title[202]—to the more modern *L'Arlésienne* (1908) and *La Grande Bréteche* (1909). Much of SCAGL's early output, including all of the previous titles, has been lost, but enough prints survive to give credence to Fagot's polemical celebration of the company as the best French producer of early "films d'art."[203] Whether or not one agrees with Fagot, however, SCAGL's historical films are of particular interest not only for their representational strategies but for the ideological positions they negotiate.

Capellani's *Jeanne d'Arc* (1909) is of unusual topical interest because its release seems to have followed closely on the beatification of Jeanne d'Arc, 18 April 1909.[204] The scenario, by Capellani and Carré, covers several key moments in Jeanne's short life, from her angelic visions as a shepherdess (in 1428) to her burning at the stake in Rouen (in 1431), within the pyramidal design of the well-made play. To some degree, the film adheres to the older tableau style in that its range of tableaux often illustrate specifically dated intertitles. Yet, within that system, the shots recorded on location mesh smoothly with those recorded in the studio, perhaps largely because the latter's decors are designed to achieve a sense of verisimilitude. Both are often defined by a deep-space mise-en-scène—as in the great hall at Chinon where Jeanne easily picks out a disguised Charles VII or in the arch-framed dry moat bed through which Jeanne's army rides to attack the English at Patay. And, most strikingly, the foreground of this latter tableau is left empty, except for the poignant detail of a lone cart with a soldier's corpse just off to the side.[205] The real emphasis of the film is on Jeanne's military prowess, and that is conveyed most clearly at the midpoint climax, in the battle of "Les Tourelles" at Orléans (7 May 1429). Here, an alternating sequence of LSs depicting the base and top of the fortress's walls presents Jeanne's soldiers attempting to scale the wall with ladders, Jeanne's wounding, and her quick recovery to lead another charge up the ladders and display the French flag in triumph.

Thereafter, *Jeanne d'Arc* moves succinctly to its conclusion through a series of what seem to be deliberate visual echoes and contrasts, deploying rhetorical strategies of closure to complement those of its narrative. In contrast to the successful battle at Orléans, Jeanne's capture at Compiegne, for instance, is represented in a single, somewhat flattened tableau.[206] The subsequent procession into Rouen reverses the direction of her earlier triumphant procession out of Chinon. Her dungeon cell recalls her family's simple farmhouse interior (from the film's second shot), and the superimposed guardian angel that now appears to her resembles the knighted figure superimposed against a grove of trees (in the very first shot) and occupies the same background position in the frame. Finally, the last tableau where Jeanne is burned at the stake is set off from the rest of the film in its highly condensed representation of characters in space (significantly, the French bishop rather than an English officer is prominently displayed on a canopied platform),[207] yet the presence of authentic foreground props and the absence of supernatural effects continue to stress the film's sense of verisimilitude. Negotiating skillfully between location and studio shooting, between old and new modes of representation, *Jeanne d'Arc* also carefully negotiates between the Catholic, Royalist view of Jeanne's beatification and the republican view of her as a popular military leader, and ultimately seems to come down on the side of the latter's concept of patriotism.[208]

Capellani's *La Mort du Duc d'Enghien* (1909) invokes representational strategies similar to those of *Jeanne d'Arc* in order to tell a story of injustice from the early period of Napoleon's rule.[209] In 1804, the Duc d'Enghien (Georges Grand) is living with Charlotte de Rohan (Dermoz) in exile in Germany, near Baden,

83. *La Mort du Duc d'Enghien*, 1909 (Georges Grand, right)

when he is kidnapped and secretly brought to the Chateau de Vincennes, wrongly charged with plotting to overthrow Napoleon, and executed at midnight. This film, too, relies on intertitles (some of them quite lengthy) to narrate its story, illustrating them with LS tableaux. Much like *Jeanne d'Arc*, it also deftly integrates studio decors and locations according to the principle of verisimilitude—the duke's German chalet, for instance, is decorated with guns, bugles, and stuffed animal heads on the walls, he is introduced returning from the hunt with a brace of rabbits, and his favorite dog roams freely around the chalet interior. Yet *La Mort du Duc d'Enghien* also deviates considerably from the tableau style. The sequence in which Napoleon's soldiers capture the duke briefly alternates interior and exterior shots. A sequence of four location shots then articulates the journey of the carriage bearing the duke to Vincennes, mapping a consistent pattern of lateral movement from left to right, the last shot matchcutting its exit and entrance from one side of the chateau gate to the other. Furthermore, the final sequence creates a degree of pathos and suspense—as *Bioscope* implied in its praise of the film's scenario—by crosscutting the duke's lengthy walk from prison cell to court martial to execution with shots of Charlotte and his dog anxiously waiting in his cell.[210] The moral, even political position that this filmic discourse takes then culminates in the last tableau, as the duke stands in the right foreground, facing a background line of armed soldiers, poised on the lip of his own open grave. As an essentially apolitical figure mistakenly caught up in a political intrigue, the Duc d'Enghien could have served either republican or antirepublican interests, depending on whether the spectator read the Napoleonic state historically or simply as representative of the current French state.

A similar story of injustice propelled by jealousy is told in SCAGL's *Fouquet, l'homme au masque de fer* (1910), which confounds the imprisonment of financier Nicolas Fouquet (in 1661) with that of the mysterious "Man in the Iron Mask" (in 1679), both of whom had been arrested at the order of young Louis XIV.[211] Much like *La Mort du Duc d'Enghien, Fouquet* is strongly marked by matched exits and entrances as well as by sequences of alternation. The first sequence, for instance, intercuts three contiguous spaces in and around Fouquet's Chateau de Vaux, where the king's lover, Mlle de la Vallière, draws the minister away from his own festivities (for the king) in an indiscreet rendezvous. Saint-Mars, a rival jealous of Fouquet's power, spots the couple and informs the king, who recognizes a handkerchief he once had given Vallière now in Fouquet's hand—and orders his arrest. The next sequence then crosscuts Vallière's secret visit to Fouquet in prison and a spy informing Saint-Mars, which leads to an angry confrontation with the couple. And in the final sequence, the camera shifts ninety degrees from exterior to interior, as Saint-Mars places Fouquet in an isolated cell and (devising a clever means of carrying out the king's order that the disgraced man neither be able to see nor be seen) condemns him to wear a special iron mask. Perhaps even more interesting, however, is the way *Fouquet* handles the political or ideological implications of its story. In one sense, it partially deflects attention from the political by introducing a love triangle to motivate the action—and this is emphasized by the MS preliminary "credits" of Alexandre as Fouquet and Yvonne Mirval as Vallière. Yet, in another sense, following the *Duc de Guise*, it empathizes with an "innocent" victim of the French court's political machinations, perhaps even suggesting a parallel between Fouquet and the "little people" against the power of the French state. That empathy is further charged in the final tableau of the cell, after Saint-Mars has exited, as Fouquet stands alone and sightless, with the iron mask locked firmly onto his head.

SCAGL, of course, was not the only French company producing films whose subjects were drawn from French history. Among its popular adventure series, Eclair slipped in several historical films. One of the few surviving examples is Jasset's *Fleur empoisonnée* (1909), whose story of chivalry betrayed and revenged is set in seventeenth-century France. The first part of this film climaxes in a duel (one aristocrat has defended a dancer from another's attack in an inn), which ends with the chivalrous defender treacherously stabbed in the back. The second takes up the revenge of the dead man's wife, in which she lures the murderer to her chateau where he inhales the poison of a white flower she "graciously" bestows on him. Two things are of particular interest during the scenes leading up to the duel. The musicians who entertain at the inn (and who later find the dead man's body and return it to the chateau) are first shown traveling through a snowy wood to their destination. This touch of "realism" (focusing on a "servant" class, in an actual location)[212] then establishes the setting for the duel, whose effect probably depends on its echo of a famous Jean-Léon Gérôme painting that sometimes was "realized" in stage productions of Dion Boucicault's *Corsican Brothers*.[213] The rest of the film is played out in the studio interiors of the chateau, but here, too, there are several points of interest. The wife disguises her maid as a male page in order to invite the murderer to a rendezvous, and a cut-in MS accentuates the cross-dressing—just as it does sometimes in the *Nick Carter* series. Furthermore, her poisoning of the flower is singled out in an unusual insert CU.[214] That the romance the murderer is expecting is doubly deceptive makes the wife's revenge a striking counterpoint to the initial attack on the dancer. And the final tableau—in which masked figures with drawn swords and hooded hangmen with nooses are revealed behind the tapestries and doorways—turns the death scene into a quasi-subjective nightmare worthy of grand guignol.

Gaumont also included several historical films on its schedule of releases during this perod, several of which survive to give radically different examples of the company's product. Arnaud's *Le Dernier Requiem de Mozart* (1909), for instance, seems to follow Film d'Art in its dependence on famous operas and non-French historical figures, yet the film is also distinctive in its own right.[215] First of all, its nine tableaux are restricted to a single studio set space—"realizing" a Mounchaski painting of Mozart's last room—which is filmed consistently in LS by a camera positioned at eye level. Each of these tableaux is preceded by an intertitle: the date (5 December 1791), a mysterious messenger, a threat of death, a doctor's warning, Mozart listening to his last score, and the titles of three of his more celebrated compositions. Moreover, near the end, this tableau style is accentuated by the spectacle of matted insert vignettes in the upper left background of the frame, corresponding to the preceding intertitles—a childhood composition, "Don Juan," "The Magic Flute"—and representing what Mozart is thinking as he stands in the right foreground.[216] The single set thus literally becomes a kind of memory machine, probably supported by familiar musical excerpts, putting Mozart's life, in terms of his musical creativity, on dramatic display.[217] Furthermore, although the last tableau does not include an insert vignette, the intertitle that precedes it, "Requiem," seems to ask the spectator to furnish just such an image from memory—and specifically recall, perhaps keyed by the recurrence of music, an earlier insert vignette of a funeral bier being blessed by a priest.

By contrast, Feuillade's *Le Huguenot* (1909), which shares several points of affinity with Giacomo Meyerbeer's opera, focuses on an especially disturbing event in French history and relies on representational strategies that ally it much more closely with SCAGL's historical films.[218] This film opens with a Huguenot Protestant, Raoul de Nangis, being wounded in a duel and left for dead by the Catholic Maréchal de Tavannes, whose daughter then orders a nearby café owner to look after his recovery. What follows then alternates loosely between several parallel plot lines: Nangis goes to Admiral de Coligny to be awarded a commission, he tracks down his benefactor to express his gratitude, and King

Charles IX, in league with Tavannes, endorses the policy of stigmatizing the Huguenots by having men paint an *X* on the window shutters of their houses. This concludes in the massacre of Huguenots on Bartholomew's Eve, 24 August 1572, and a final duel between Nangis and Tavannes, who has killed Coligny, in the latter's house. Most of *Le Huguenot*'s twenty-four shots are filmed in LS, yet the opening duel (fought in a park near a village café) occurs in FS, and several subsequent shots have one or more characters come into FS in either the left or right foreground of the frame. Here, too, are several instances of a relatively deep-space mise-en-scène, but with a difference—most notably in the repeated shot of the café exterior, which uses the two roads angling away from its corner (center frame) for background entrances and exits. A number of studio interiors also reveal a second space in the background of the frame—such as the window of Nangis's room which opens onto a street where soldiers can be seen in LS attacking the Huguenots.

Much like Capellani's films for SCAGL, *Le Huguenot* exhibits a system of narration that relies on repeated editing patterns and changes in framing. One sign of this is the loose form of crosscutting, clearly marked by intertitles, between the simultaneous lines of action that converge in the massacre and duel. Another, however, is quite unique. Those shots in the film not connected or bridged by an intertitle are usually marked either by matchcutting on the exit or entrance of a major character or by cut-in CUs of a significant object or detail. That there are three of these CUs is somewhat unusual (given the prior examples in *L'Homme aux gants blancs, Fleur empoisonnée,* and *Le Déraciné au artiste*), and all come early in the film. In the first two, at the site of the duel, Tavannes's daughter discovers a small book printed in 1553 by the Geneva Institute of Jean Calvin, which contains a letter from Coligny to Nangis about his commission. And in the third, Nangis discovers the emblem of the Tavannes family on the money purse that the daughter had given to the nearby café owner to pay for his recovery. The corresponding CUs (and the privileged information they bear) thus bind these two characters together, and, at their meeting, the daughter accepts the purse in exchange for an arm band (and apparent love token) which protects Nangis until the duel at the end. The coherence of *Le Huguenot* is determined, then, not only by the development of parallel plot lines and by the symmetry of a climactic duel that reenacts the opening, but also by the sustained circulation, in CU, of crucial objects or emblems. Furthermore, despite Gaumont's penchant for "Catholic" biblical films, the construction of a story around the shameful spectacle of the Huguenot massacre situates this film in stark opposition to the story of a Catholic aristocrat's martyrdom in the *Duc de Guise*, as does its melodramatic attempt to reconcile Protestant and Catholic through romantic love and, more persuasively, in the climactic duel, through the miraculous revelation of a crucifix within the Huguenot's house.

As a contested site of representation, the French historical film perhaps best can be summarized by considering four different titles produced by Gaumont, Pathé, and SCAGL, in 1910. The two of these from Gaumont are rather episodic

84. *Christophe Colomb*, 1910

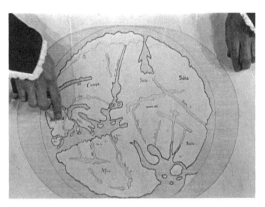

85. *Christophe Colomb*, 1910

86. *Christophe Colomb*, 1910

87. *Christophe Colomb*, 1910

films chronicling the lives of "famous men." Feuillade's *Christophe Colomb*, for instance, covers fifteen years in the life of the fifteenth-century Italian explorer—from his initial expedition plans set forth in Genoa, in 1485, to his imprisonment by the King of Spain, in 1500. This film uses eighteen intertitles—providing place names, character names, dates, or summaries of the action to come—in conjunction with two dozen tableaux, most of them recorded in LS. Generally, the characters' movements are choreographed within a deep-space mise-en-scène (whether natural location or studio set), and at one point, a short pan even reframes Columbus alone on a beach (after several friends have left him), looking out to sea. The most distinctive sections of the film, however, come in the opening and especially in the closing prison scene tableau. The first scene, in which Columbus explains his plan to the Genoa officials, is filmed in FS, but includes a cut-in to an unusual HA CU of a map (approximating a POV shot), with his hands coming in from the top of the frame to point and gesture. The final scene of Columbus in prison in LS, by contrast, includes a clearly demarcated POV-shot sequence (through a ninety-degree shift in camera position), after a guard calls him to look out of his cell window (frame right). A

HA LS, enframed by the silhouetted mask of foreground window bars, shows us what Columbus presumably sees—the rival explorer, Amerigo Vespucci, riding in triumph through the town square. The final LS then offers a variation on this ironic contrast edit by filling the left half of the darkened prison cell with an insert vignette of a monument to Columbus (framed by "heavenly" cumulus), while the old explorer himself stands barely visible on the right, at first reaching out toward this imaginary image and then turning in despair to the window, which seems the only source of light.[219] Here a series of "attractions"—selective arc lighting, an insert vignette, a POV shot—all serve to condense the narrative conclusion, not unlike that of a Griffith film, into a highly symbolic tableau. In contrast to the "real" image of Amerigo's triumph, which seems "enclosed" in the past, this dream image opens onto a future that will confirm Columbus's public recognition and fame, suturing the spectator into identification with the explorer himself as a once victimized, but now exonerated hero.

Perret's *La Vie de Molière* covers an even longer period in the life of the seventeenth-century French dramatist (played by Perret himself)—from his first surreptitious efforts at writing, as a young law student, to his death on stage some thirty years later. At least four particular episodes are given special attention in this film, and each is distinctive in its mode of representation. The fifteen years Molière spent with a provincial troupe of traveling players, for instance, is condensed into just three location tableaux, yet all focus, not on their performances, but on the work involved in traveling—and one LA FS/LS accentuates their weariness in trying to maneuver through a woods. The playwright's acceptance of Louis XIV's patronage, by contrast, is represented in a spectacle series of LSs that offer a "tour" of the Versailles gardens, in the company of the king and his courtiers. The scene that dramatizes Molière's infatuation with his actress-wife, however, includes melodramatic cut-in MCUs—first of the playwright at his desk and then of the wife who, though an inspiration to his work, cruelly rejects him. The final scene stages a performance of *Le Malade imaginaire*, but it is shot from backstage, with Molière himself in the title role seated before the curtain (right background), which rises to reveal the court's box seats. Another cut-in MCU then singles out the moment when he suffers the stroke from which, after being returned to his study, he soon dies. Given the way the film has "documented" Molière's life, it is disconcerting (and very possibly ironic) to have the final tableau present his figure as a memorial statue in the Versailles gardens, surrounded not only by aristocrats but by angels waving olive branches and strumming harps.

At least a half-dozen films, in 1910, took up the subject of the French Revolution or its aftermath in Napoleon's reign—including not only Gaumont's *André Chenier* but Pathé's *A Secret Incident in the Life of Marie Antoinette, In the Realm of Terror*, and *An Episode of 1812*. The earliest of Pathé's that survive is *Cagliostro*, with its somewhat ambivalent story (scripted and directed by de Morlhon) of the charlatan who charmed the French court in the last years of the *ancien régime*. Rather than link Cagliostro to the famous "Diamond Necklace Affair," this film focuses on his prowess as a magician who can hypnotize a gypsy dancer, Lorenza, and, presenting her at court, predict the death of Marie Antoinette as well as others—which promptly sends him to prison. This highly condensed, probably invented story offers a satisfying blend of both old and new systems of representation. Several scenes call on Henry Krauss, as Cagliostro, and Napierkowska, as Lorenza, to perform a complicated choreography of moves within long-take LSs—for instance, the café interior where Cagliostro fights a duel over Lorenza, and the palace interior where he exhibits his magic for the queen.[220] Others deploy various truc effects—as in the opening scene of an alchemist's study, where Lorenza appears as a tantalizing figure superimposed against a background wall, and again, at court, where Cagliostro turns a lighted candle into a bouquet of flowers and produces the dancer from beneath a veil floating in the air. The most intriguing feature of the film, however, involves the spectacle of repeated CUs as insert POV shots. The first introduces Lorenza's face as a blurred and then sharply focused image, when the alchemist holds up a magic mirror that he has dipped in a special liquid and at which Cagliostro stares in wonder. When he himself hypnotizes Lorenza and has her gaze into the same liquid in a flask, the film opens up a paradoxical space of spectatorly desire by deliberately withholding the image that seems to frighten her. Only later, at the film's climax, when Cagliostro holds the same flask up for Marie Antoinette, is that desire fulfilled in a revealing CU—the Revolution is made emblematic in the superimposed image of the guillotine on a scaffold encircled by a crowd of people. Here, the heavily gendered lure of the imaginary turns deadly, as the initial erotic figure of the dancer serves to expose a horrifying vision of historical destiny. And, in the darkness of his prison cell (softly lit by filtered arc lights), after confronting a dream image of Lorenza meeting a new lover, Cagliostro commits suicide with a poison ring—in a condensed resolution of the film's *liebestod* theme.

SCAGL's *L'Evadé des Tuileries* tells a different invented story, this one of escape and reconciliation in the midst of the Revolution, in a kind of dress rehearsal for *Madame Sans-Gêne* (1911).[221] The escapee is an aristocrat, Count de Champcenetz (Grand), who, after surviving the historic attack on the Tuileries palace, conceals himself three separate times before being able to flee Paris with the English woman he loves, Grace Elliott (Robinne). This film repeats and varies its representational strategies within an essentially two-part narrative structure. A letter from Elliott to the count, for instance, serves as a "bridge" between the public space of the national convention (where it is read) and the private space where the count has come in answer to Elliott's letter. Following this economical introduction, the attack itself is condensed into a single, long-take FS/LS tableau of a palace interior, with a series of people—the count, several children, then the revolutionaries—bursting through a background door to warn or confront the king and queen and other aristocrats in the foreground. Wounded during the fighting and looting, the count revives at the end of this tableau and escapes into a fireplace, after which another FS/LS of a hidden pas-

88. *Cagliostro*, 1910 (Henry Krauss, Stacia Napierkowska)

sage shows him and several pursuers, now in striking silhouette, approach a foreground grille and exit in opposite directions. The next sequence, by contrast, repeatedly alternates adjacent spaces as the count escapes out a window and hides himself among some corpses in the street below, followed by the revolutionaries who fail to spot him. A woman among them remains behind to protect him, however, and, in another long-take FS/LS interior, she conceals the count in a background laundry basket until her husband (still wearing his Phrygian cap) discovers the ruse and unexpectedly welcomes him as a friend. The last sequence returns to alternating adjacent spaces as the count, pursued again, reaches Elliott's bedroom, but now cut-in closer shots first reveal his hiding place under the mattress and then nearly turn this story of repeated evasion into sexual farce, when Elliott gets into bed on top of him. In *L'Evadé des Tuileries*, historical conflict gets resolved within the space of domestic melodrama, and an aristocratic hero undergoes a radical transformation, or even witty resurrection—reborn out of his lady love's bed as a disguised coachman to drive them both into the "happy ending" of exile.

By early 1911, well before Jasset's paean of praise to Film d'Art in *Ciné-Journal*, the historical film had indeed had a significant impact on the French cinema. First of all, in terms of the industry's promotional strategy of legitimation, the genre served as a showcase for introducing well-known actors—with women nearly equal in number and stature to men—from the Paris theaters to cinema audiences and for drawing bourgeois spectators of both genders more regularly to the cinemas. In turn, as Jasset and others claimed, those who worked for Film d'Art and SCAGL generally imposed a model of restrained, economical acting in opposition to the style of broad pantomime formerly associated with the genre. In privileging "star" actors, along with period set decors and costumes, sometimes accentuated by stencil color or lighting effects, the genre did encourage a return to the older mode of representation characterized by the autonomous tableau. Certain films especially reverted to this system—most notably, Pathé's "oriental" films, which tended to privilege spectacular display over narrative development and to deny subjectivity to its "exotic" characters. Yet even more films—whether made by Pathé, Gaumont, SCAGL, Film d'Art, or Eclair—worked just as much, if not more, within the newer system of representation, negotiating a balanced orchestration of mise-en-scène, framing, editing patterns, and even sound accompaniment. In their logical plotting of action (sometimes involving double plots), careful pacing of dramatic moments, and resolutions based on sustained suspense or strong character identification, films such as *La Tosca, Fleur empoisonnée, Jeanne d'Arc, Le Huguenot, La Mort du Duc d'Enghien, Cagliostro*, and *L'Evadé des Tuileries* produced especially effective models of narrative construction, sometimes within the highly structured format of the well-made play. And some such as *Judith et Holophernes, L'Arrestation de la Duchess de Berry*, and *Werther* even inflected their narratives with either the strongly moral voice of the contemporary melodrama or the bitterly ironic voice of grand guignol.

Finally, the genre encompassed a broad spectrum of ideological positions in relation to the Nationalist Revival beginning to dominate French political and cultural life. While some films—*L'Assassinat du Duc de Guise, Duchesse de Berry, Fouquet, L'Evadé des Tuileries*—seemed, like Pathé's earlier *L'Affaire Dreyfus*, at least to offer support for the antirepublican attitudes of the Nationalist Revival, just as many—*La Tosca, Jeanne d'Arc, Le Huguenot, Rival de son fils*—continued to circulate what could be called republican attitudes of patriotism and anticlericalism. Others such as *Duc d'Enghien, Cagliostro*, and *La Vie de Molière* took up a more ambiguous position. Yet films as diverse as *Le Fils prodigue, Le Retour d'Ulysse, Idylle Corinthienne, La Festin de Balthazar, Héliogabale*, and *Cléopatre* all enacted stories in which the power of the East and its "feminized" seductive vices were no match for the classical virtues of the more "masculinized" West. Finally, although *Sémiramis* may have offered the countervision of a "feminized" social utopia, it bracketed that vision within a very gender-specific story of violent retribution. If the French cinema industry was generally successful in using the historical film to capture a bourgeois audience, or at least those aspiring to be bourgeois, it seems to have done so by hedging its bets, circulating the genre's cultural capital through distinctly different refigurings of the ideological premises of the Third Republic.

Trick Films and *Féeries*

By this time, trick films clearly had been relegated to a secondary status on French as well as American cinema programs. Moreover, the genre constituted no more than a small percentage of both Pathé's and Gaumont's production, was virtually absent from the other companies' output, and no longer was the major form it had once been even for Méliès. Similarly, féeries were being issued less frequently as either historical or contemporary "dramas" came to headline Pathé's and Gaumont's weekly packages of film releases. In fact, Jasset described this as the period when "the *féerie* softly, quietly flickered out."[222] Yet the genre's depreciation in value did not keep Pathé, in particular, as Fagot put it,[223] from upholding the féerie tradition into the teens—with such Velle films as *La Rose d'or* (1910) and *Amour de page* (1911) to Méliès's own *Les Hallucinations du Baron de Münchhausen* (1911) and *A la conquête du pôle* (1912). Nor did it discourage Chomón from turning out a rich concoction of trick films, whose skill and charm consistently drew favorable notices in the British and American press. And both the féeries and trick films focused disproportionately on women, in contrast to the contemporary melodramas, suggesting that the genre may have been sustained in cinemas or on cinema programs that specifically catered to women and children. Nor did this apparent devaluation forestall innovations in the genre. At least three proved to be significant—Chomón's use of sustained stop motion to make inanimate objects "come alive" in various situations of daily life, his work with mattes to bring miniature human figures into the same frame with normal-sized figures, and Cohl's frame-by-frame recording of hundreds of sheets of line drawings to create perhaps the earliest animation films at Gaumont.

To provide a context for these innovations, it is worth noting that a number of Pathé films simply extended the earlier trick film format, especially for comic effects. In *A Cabman's Delusion* (1908), for instance, straight cuts keep changing what a horse carriage driver sees, after he picks up a sportily dressed passenger. At one point, as they argue, the passenger disappears and the driver takes his place, only to find a double of himself in the driver's seat; the double then turns into a coat that gets tossed back into the carriage, becoming a woman in black and, finally, the original passenger. After the horse goes through similar changes, the carriage arrives at its destination, only to have the passenger vanish again, without paying the driver. *Tormented by His Mother-in-law* (1908) involves Linder and his wife's mother in a similar series of transformations, after the two have argued at the dining room table and she has dropped a potted plant from a window onto his head. Wherever he goes—to a sidewalk café, a kiosk, a park bench, or a carriage—people magically turn into the daunting mother-in-law. So enraged is he, by the end, that he is plunging a sword into a large portrait of her in the bedroom and ripping pillows inside out, engulfing himself in a thick cloud of feathers. *Traveling on the Cheap* (1907) confines its truc to an initial shot, where a man stuffs two women into a small suitcase. Unlike the previous films, however, this one is not restricted to LSs—once he settles in a compartment on

89. *Tormented by His Mother-in-law,* 1908 (production photo: Max Linder)

the train and opens his lunch, the women's heads pop out of the suitcase over-head—and a cut-in MCU shows him feeding each in turn. Finally, in *L'Aspira-teur* (1908), two men come upon a special mechanical cart designed to vacuum up litter and garbage and use it instead to inhale passersby as well as dogs. The film comes to a kind of climax in a sequence of alternating exterior and interior LSs, when they empty an apartment of its furniture and even pull in a maid from the next room. But this is not all, for, when they pause to relax at a sidewalk café, two other men turn the machine, and the trick, back on them.

The first innovation to occur in such trick films—animating objects by means of sustained stop motion—has a controversial chronology. In early 1906, Pathé released Chomón's *Le Théâtre du Petit Bob,* which apparently used stop-motion cinematography (rather than invisible wires or hands) to animate an extended puppet-theater scene staged by a young boy named Bob (clearly from a bourgeois family) for a group of his friends. The film's status was com-plicated, however, because it seemed to exist in two quite different versions, the second one dating from 1909. When he discovered this discrepancy, Carlo Montanaro argued that the surviving Spanish copy was the earlier version: there, the puppet-theater performance comprises just four separate tableaux, each of which involves no more than two puppets—in a sword fight, a box-ing match, a struggle over a smoking pipe, and "a complicated feat of acrobat-ics."[224] Recently, Crafton and Elias Savada established that the longer English copy indeed was the one released in 1906.[225] In this version, popular characters in the form of the latest windup toys serve to rationalize the animation effects.

And they "star" in the story of a miniature automobile that races through a city and out into the countryside to catapault into a building from which the toy driver is taken off by gendarmes to be chastised by a judge. Although this version would seem to end with a blatantly moral lesson, its final few tableaux (the last is an emblematic shot of the boy bowing and smiling) instead let the children as well as the cinema audience applaud Bob's ingenuity (and Chomón's) in staging the automobile's reckless run. As Crafton suggests, *Le Théâtre du Petit Bob* strengthen's Chomón's position among the vanguard of animation pioneers—which include Edwin S. Porter, *The Whole Dam Family and the Dam Dog* (1905), and J. Stuart Blackton, *Humorous Phases of Funny Faces* (1906). Yet, for reasons that remain unclear, the stop-motion technique used in Chomón's film evidently had little immediate effect on French trick films.

That changed with Vitagraph's release of *The Haunted Hotel* in Paris, in April 1907.[226] This film introduced a new variation into the "haunted hotel" stage act that had long been a staple in both European and American theaters and music halls.[227] What was new here was the truc shot of a tabletop on which plates, cups, and utensils arranged themselves, a pitcher poured wine into a glass, and a knife sliced up a loaf of bread. *The Haunted Hotel* was an immediate success in France, partly, as Crafton has argued, because of Vitagraph's aggressive advertising campaign—which included a screening at *Phono-Ciné-Gazette*'s May 1907 film festival—and partly, as Jasset pointed out, because the long-take close shot of the table emphasized the spectacle of the truc.[228] And, according to Frederick Talbot, Vitagraph's Paris office sold 150 prints of the film throughout Europe.[229] The Paris press speculated a good deal about how the tricks in *The Haunted Hotel* were achieved, with Gustave Babin of *L'Illustration*, for instance, tenaciously trying to extract the secret from Thiberville, one of Gaumont's principal cameramen.[230] But to no avail, except that his "failure" may have served to deflect publicity about the cinema and its marvels away from the American company and, with debatable success, to Gaumont.

Despite *The Haunted Hotel*'s success, it seems to have taken the French several months to exploit the attraction of stop-motion cinematography. The first to do so, not unexpectedly, came in a Pathé series of Chomón trick films, several of which focused on animating objects in a room, but usually in LS.[231] *La Maison ensorcelé* (c. 1907–1908)[232] may well have been the earliest of these for, inserted within its story of three men on a dare trying to stay the night in a haunted house, is a tabletop sequence quite similar to that in the Vitagraph film. *Le Démenagement* (1908) is more characteristic in that it moves a couple from one townhouse to another by means of a special electrical device that animates their furniture. After various objects have packed themselves into boxes, everything from the bedroom, kitchen, dining room, and salon files out of the door in order and down several streets, enters the new townhouse, and moves into its proper place. And the spectacle disguises another story, as it does in several other films—the socioeconomic history of an industrial technology displacing a group of artisans or service workers. *Electric Hotel* (1908) works a variation on the "haunted hotel" act by equipping a new establishment with an electrical system

that whisks a couple's luggage in and out of an elevator, sends it into their assigned room, and even hangs up their clothes. A drunk wanders into the hotel
lobby, however, and disrupts the system, which tosses the guests, followed by
their luggage, out the window. Oddly, Gaumont's three-shot version of this
skit, *Hôtel du silence* (1908),[233] uses no animation at all. In this film's rather spare
hotel, a single male traveler's needs are catered to instead by a wide range of
conventional trucs, both theatrical (his bags move unaided ahead of him from
lobby to room, a food-laden table rises up out of the floor, a coffee tray springs
out of one wall) and cinematic (a mobile dressing screen magically puts him in
pajamas at night and suits him up again in the morning).

This animation of objects provided the chief spectacle attraction in other
kinds of Pathé trick films as well. Some of these, as in *The Haunted Hotel*, were
little more than single-shot stage acts with cut-in close shots of stop-motion
effects. *Rêve des marmitons* (1908), for instance, opens with a chef and his kitchen
workers much more interested in drinking than in doing their tasks, and an elf
hiding in a laundry basket puts them all to sleep. After the elf cuts off the hand
of one character after another, each detached hand, in a half-dozen MSs and
MCUs, then goes about slicing up vegetables, washing and drying dishes, polishing utensils, or computing costs on a blackboard. In the final shot of the
series, a man's bald head becomes the surface on which several comic faces are
sketched, ending with a scrawled "Pathé-Frères Paris." The characters awaken
to find all their tasks miraculously accomplished, except for those of the bald-
headed man, who is tossed into a flour barrel and pelted with vegetables. A
nightmare of dismemberment turns into a fantasy of playful labor, yet the
kitchen workers themselves as a body strangely turn on one of their own members and ridicule him for unconsciously "deviating" from the game. *The Idler*
(1908) multiplies a similar fantasy of work through several spaces, unfortunately
with flagging inventiveness. Tossed out of bed and pummeled by his wife, a
man is ordered to clean up the bedroom, but instead falls asleep and imagines
the task done. As he sits on a chair, in a LS tableau, the objects strewn about the
room dutifully return to their normal positions—a boot, for instance, smooths
out a pillow before the latter jumps back on the bed. A cut-in CU then shows a
pair of boots slipping on the man's feet and lacing themselves up, while another
LS shows his coat arranging itself around his sleeping body. Finally, in a cut-in
MCU, a comb straightens his hair, a tie loops around his neck, and a hat perches
on his head—which then all dissolves back to him sleeping in LS, the room
unchanged. A shorter fantasy sequence follows in his workshop, and his exasperated wife sends him off to do the marketing. He doesn't get far, of course,
before falling asleep again, so now the basket and pan he is carrying can seem to
speed off to the grocery shop and return full of food. Two men come along to
trip over the still empty basket, however, and smash it to bits, which leaves the
wife, out searching for her lost husband, to end the film with a cliché—beating
him over the head with the pan.

Chiffonniers caricaturistes (1908) plays out a different game of labor in the cluttered interior of a shack, as a couple of ragpickers brandish paintbrushes, paper

fragments, and clay to create a collection of "artworks" for hawking. Their "mode of production"—which may have derived from Vitagraph's *Humorous Phases of Funny Faces* (1906) and *Lightning Sketches* (1907)[234]—involves reverse motion, collage animation, and "claymation" (one of the earliest instances of the technique), in a repeated series of CUs. The ease with which they turn out this art, while perhaps intended to satirize recent developments in modern art, also serves as a fit analogue for mass culture—for instance, the cinema itself—in an "age of mechanical reproduction." All of these works are "portraits"—most of them military officers, political figures, and music hall comics (at least one of these can be identified as Deed)—and both their selection and the ragpickers' attitudes toward them are located securely in the ideological drift of the period. The caricature of a Jewish usurer (which receives their condemnation) interrupts the series on French soldiers, and the German emperor (who startles them) is set off against the French president, the Russian czar, Teddy Roosevelt, and a British statesman. Although partially deflected by the antics of the clay-figure comics concluding the film, these faces clearly speak to and for an audience of "little people" already receptive to the French Nationalist Revival movement.

Even Pathé films pitting the police against formidable criminals, and hence more dependent on narrative development, began to exploit the stop-motion technique. *Rêves d'agent* (1908), for instance, begins with a MS of two gendarmes falling asleep at a table.[235] A fade (one of the earliest uses of the device to mark off fantasy from reality) leads into what seems to be a collective nightmare, divided into four separate sequences, each of which displays the prowess of a particularly elusive thief through a different truc effect. The first sequence, which alternates between the exterior and interior of a jewelry store, has a cut-in CU of banknotes slipping out of a desk drawer, folding themselves neatly, and jumping into the thief's waiting hand. The second has him turn into a paper-thin white cutout that can slip under an office door; inside, a cut-in MS shows him magically commanding the gold coins inside a safe to migrate through its steel plates and drop into his hat. The third then resorts to dissolves and reverse motion so that he can escape the pursuing gendarmes. And in the fourth, staged on the ubiquitous Pathé staircase, he erupts out of the camera lens in the form of a white silhouette that turns into a superimposition and goads the gendarmes into attacking one another—from which, through another fade, they awaken exhausted at their table.[236] *Jim le glisseur* or *Slippery Jim* (1910) uses similar trucs to tell the story of another thief (a Houdini-like escape artist), but without the dream frame. After magically twisting out of his leg irons in prison, Jim emerges completely dry out of a tied-up sack tossed into the prison moat and then, like James Bond, casually lights a cigarette. In a chase through the countryside, he eludes a flock of prison guards by constructing a bicycle out of a single inner tube, then turning into a black cutout to ride along the top of a moving train, and finally, after being captured, snaking out of a ragpicker's basket (into which he has been stuffed) as the long white thread of an unraveling costume. Back in prison, in the final shot, Jim performs an acrobatic whirl away from his captors and, before they can recover, locks them all in his cell and simply walks off. In contrast to *Chiffonniers caricaturistes*, both *Rêves d'agent* and *Jim le glisseur* follow the established pattern of using truc effects to belittle the police as representatives of state authority.

A second innovation—the spectacle of miniature human figures, done by means of mattes or double exposures—has a somewhat more certain chronology. Although the representation of differently scaled figures goes back at least as far as Méliès's *Voyages de Gulliver* (1902) and Pathé's *Le Cakewalk chez les nains*, sustained use of the process again can be associated with Chomón's early trick films for Pathé. *Bobby et sa famille* (1906), for instance, makes the antics of two miniature clowns the centerpiece of an extended stage magic act. In a painted-flat forest clearing, a bright yellow clown disencumbers himself of his traveling gear (including a bird cage) and constructs a large white paper moon against the darkened background sky. After adding eyes, nose, and mouth, he snaps a whip and the moon face turns into a magnified CU version of his own. Now two smaller white clowns somersault out of his suitcase (frame right), vault and vanish into the background, only to reappear, suddenly miniaturized, popping in and out of the moon's eyes and mouth. When the moon disappears, these miniscule figures perform acrobatic feats in the sky at their master's command, until he grabs them, one by one, and stuffs them back in his suitcase. *The Black Witch* (1908), much like *Le Charmeur* and *La Scarabée d'or*, shifts the gender (and race) of the magician creating such spectacle displays, but within the serene interior of an Arabian palace. There, a black woman stages a hallucinatory "light show" for a couple by tossing mysterious ingredients into a flaming cauldron. Accentuated by a cut-in AS (and probably Pathé's stencil color process), her performance produces one miniature figure after another (all but one of them women) arising from the cauldron and dissolving away—within a high-contrast, "solarized" image whose only illumination comes from the fire. After a cut back to LS, the palace interior dissolves into a cavern where a similar performance of ascending figures is followed by another set of women who spiral upward within a fountain of falling water. In the finale, two more superimposed fountains or waterfalls frame the first, within each of which women spiral down and come forward to stand with their creator. Back in the palace, the couple purchases the cauldron, like naive spectators under the spell of a fairground showman, in a many-layered mystification of the cinema's (and Pathé's) power.

The question of who exercises control over such magical power is perhaps no more strikingly resolved than in Chomón's *Red Spectre* (1907), all of whose cleverly structured spectacle effects take place within a single tableau, a painted-flat cavern over which Satan supposedly rules. Appearing out of a coffin as a kind of skeletal devil, this Satan initially indulges in some Méliès-like tricks—making painted-flat rocks fly away to deepen the cavern space, conjuring up a half-dozen dancing women who turn into flames, and producing two more women out of cauldrons in order to wrap them in black sheets, suspend them in midair, and burn each one to nothing. These preliminaries then lead to a series of increasingly unusual cinematic trucs. Three bottles on a stand are brought foward into CU (as the camera rack focuses), each of which holds a superimposed miniature woman, over which Satan pours dark wine.[237] A box bearing the Pathé rooster trademark is brought into a close shot, each of whose three panels revolves, one by one, to reveal the MS of a composite woman "inside." A framed image of three female dancers is suspended in midair, all of whom are transformed, through up-and-down wipes, into a woman's face in MCU and then an elderly couple in MS. Finally, through reverse motion, a set of black blocks are constructed into a "screen" on which appear an old woman and her dog in FS. Each of these spectacle effects, however, is magically dispatched by a young woman in hunting togs and wings (played by Julienne Mathieu) who, as Satan's antagonist, keeps popping in and eluding his attempts to catch her. In the ending clou of spectacle, she triumphantly assumes his powers—opening up and closing down the cavern's "deep space," creating smoke and fireworks everywhere, raising up an array of women goddesses, perhaps for support—and eventually transforms Satan into a mere skeleton on the floor, wraps herself in his cloak, and vanishes in a burst of red fire. Although this gender war of revenge seems to conclude with the misogynist trickster or magician outwitted by a deceptive stand-in for his women victims, Mathieu also, it should be noted, simply assumes the guise of the "red spectre" she has overthrown.

Given Pathé's diverse marketing strategies during this transitional period of 1907–1908, it is probably no wonder that at least two Chomón trick films grant almost complete authority to female rather than male magicians.[238] And both make extensive use of the framing device of miniaturized human figures. In *Les Chrysanthèmes* (1907), a pair of women in bright yellow dresses enact a series of deftly executed, if conventional, transformations involving vaguely "oriental" dancers, yellow parasols, and white flowers. For their climactic spectacle, however, they bring a circular frame of flowers forward into MS, within which diminutive female dancers perform as if suspended in the air, to be replaced, finally, like an ironic afterthought or echo of previous trick films, by one tiny man. Returning the flower frame to the background, where it dissolves away, the two women step forward again and fill the frame with their spinning parasols, which then dissolve into an emblematic MS of the two smiling and bowing to the camera. More elaborately, *The Wonderful Mirror* (1908) opens in LS, with a large triptych mirror set in an art nouveau, painted-flat frame on a dark stage.[239] A woman magician (Mathieu again) dissolves in and steps forward, suddenly reflected in the center panel, then opens the left and right panels to introduce a girl and boy. Within a cut-in FS of the framed center panel, Mathieu commands a succession of figures to dissolve in and out, as if practicing her scales. As the LS returns, the girl steps out of the left panel and opens the other to let out three dancing replicas of herself with bar staffs crowning their heads. In turn, the boy steps forward to change into an Asian warrior figure and let out four dancing replicas of himself. Then, Mathieu takes over, producing a half-dozen dancers whose gender shifts back and forth, and the girl and boy join her in several further transformations. Finally, assisted by the girl, she causes diminutive figures to dance within the center panel, ending in a tableau of women, after which

90. *Les Chrysanthèmes*, 1907

the two pose together before the mirror as yellow flowers erupt along its rim and the boy materializes in to sit at their feet.[240]

Two other Chomón trick films, however, serve to restore a kind of patriarchal order to these new conjuring tricks. *Cuisine magnétique* (1908) uses all kinds of cooking implements to create an energetic musical revue conducted by an acrobatic male chef, within the confines of a darkened kitchen stage set. In the initial sequence, the chef transforms hand towels into assistant chefs that, in turn, become upright spoons, knives, and forks that, together with a set of dancing pans with faces, do a brief chorus line number. In the next, he lets a huge knife and fork chop his body into bits and toss them into a pot, only to have the body parts return and spring back together. Finally, dancers bearing giant spoons and forks, one by one, leap out of a background cauldron to perform in groups and exit, leaving behind one small boy with a fork who is hustled off by a man with a threatening knife. For an encore, the chef calls everyone back "onstage" within an arching frame of corks, stoppers, and other magnified utensils. If *Cuisine magnétique* locates its magic on the countertop of a fantastical kitchen, *Toula's Dream* (1908) is situated within a more "realistic" domestic space. Here, a black female cook preparing dinner for a white woman falls asleep at a foreground table, and a devilish white male chef leaps out of a cloud of smoke to provoke a series of dream episodes. In the first, a cut-in MS of the table shows several grotesque clown faces appearing over the pan into which the cook is tossing chopped vegetables—one of which has a Pathé trademark affixed to its pointed forehead. In the second, another cut-in FS lets her watch two miniature chefs mount ladders to saw a pumpkin face in half. When the white woman returns to the kitchen, the two women look in the oven; and cut-in MCUs show them watching three tiny couples dancing in peasant costumes, after which the chef, now a miniature pied piper, leads a group of children in a dance of prop vegetables. At the conclusion of each of these visions of sponta-neous cooking, the women happily bring a tart or pie out of the oven and back to the table. Suddenly, however, all the objects in the room begin to jump about and collapse in a heap—and the cook awakens to find her mistress angry at all the work that remains undone. Whatever the site of fantasy, these films suggest, in good French tradition the magical power of cooking belongs to men.

If some debate still simmers over the development of these first two inno-vations, scarcely any remains concerning the third, the beginnings of the ani-mation cartoon. Just as Méliès could be said to have revived and transformed both the magic act and the féerie tradition in early French cinema, so, too, could Cohl, a respected Paris graphic artist and caricaturist who had contracted to write scenarios for Gaumont in early 1908, be said to have "reinvented" the comic strip on film. When Cohl received Gaumont's permission to experiment with animation, in the summer of 1908, instead of relying on the "lightning sketches" or animated objects of earlier films, he turned to the more refined technique of India-ink line drawings on white rice paper. For his first film, ac-cording to Crafton, Cohl made more than seven hundred individual line draw-ings, recorded each twice (frame by frame), and had the laboratory print the footage in negative in order to produce a white-on-black chalk-line effect.[241] The finished product, *Fantasmagorie*, was released in Paris, in August 1908, and en-joyed an immediate success. *Fantasmagorie* is clearly a trick film in that it uses a slight narrative—a stick-figure clown and bourgeois gentleman suffer one ca-lamity after another—as a pretext to display a series of spectacle effects. Here the spectacle takes the form of frequent and amazingly illogical metamorpho-ses—for instance, the gentleman's top hat and umbrella turn into a cinema inte-rior, and the clown emerges out of the ballooning head of a woman sitting in front of the gentleman and engulfs him; later, an elephant whose tusks are cradling the clown changes into a house, whereupon the clown plunges out of a window and loses his head—which Cohl's hand quickly reattaches with a paste brush. Underlying this non-sequitur imagery, as Crafton has shown, was the iconoclastic, antirational aesthetic of the Incoherents, a Paris circle of anarchist artists to which Cohl had belonged some fifteen to twenty years before.[242] That *Fantasmagorie*'s hallucinatory images had such an impact, however, was probably due to their seeming spontaneity and to the unusual fluidity of the transforma-tions—perhaps not unlike the gracefully multiplying white lines of Marey's "chronophotographs."

91. *Fantasmagorie*, 1908

Several other short animation films quickly followed, including the lost *Le Cauchemar du fantoche* (1908), from which even the hand of the animator was now absent.[243] The only one of these to survive, *Un Drame chez les fantoches* (1908), organizes its uninterrupted flow of moving lines and forms around a more familiar, yet not entirely coherent, melodramatic story. A man attacks a woman twice, and each time a policeman rescues her; the man escapes from prison only to be doubled and turned into a long stole for the woman, who then literally gives her heart to the policeman. The first episode eschews any transformations apparently in order to establish the three central characters, but the second is full of them—a walk-in closet turns into a grinding wheel on which the man sharpens a knife, blocks form a column topped by a potted fern, out of which comes a snake to keep him from stabbing the woman, and after the policeman arrives, a cage materializes around the man to lift him up and away. The third episode has fewer changes, and instead constructs the illusion of a 180-degree reverse-angle shift from inside to outside the prison cell for the man's escape. In the final episode, the transformations return—for instance, a shower head sprays the woman and causes the stole to shrink into two little piles on the floor—and conclude in an encore bow in which the characters metamorphosize into the Gaumont trademark, an encircled capital G. Perhaps the first of Cohl's films to be distributed in the United States, *Un Drame chez les fantoches* was described in *Moving Picture World* as "a unique and exceptionally attractive Gaumont film" that won "rounds of applause wherever it [was shown]."[244]

Yet despite such accolades, for reasons of economy,[245] Cohl's subsequent animation work for Gaumont lost its autonomy and was consistently framed by some kind of live-action narrative. *Clair de lune espagnol* (1909), for instance, begins in the studio decor of a Spanish cabaret where a matador named Pedro argues with his fiancée, a dancer, and leaves, only to return, in the end, and reconcile with her. Most of the film unfolds in the realm of fantasy, however, much like *Rêve à la lune*, when Pedro is then abducted by a flying machine and taken off to the moon. This central section is intriguing in several ways. First of all, as Crafton has argued, the moon constitutes a perfect decor to further narrativize Pedro's emotional state of *amour fou* because of its double association not only with "eros and insanity" but also with "female inconstancy."[246] For the moon figure (as if, in exemplary form, taking on attributes of the other) to mediate the lover's return to his fiancée, as female acrobats (initially appearing (male) lover attacks the "inconstant" (female) moon with a rifle and hatchet. The pantomime figure of Pierrot intervenes to show Pedro that he has unbalanced the universe by injuring the moon, and he himself is turned into a half-moon figure (as if, in exemplary form, taking on attributes of the other) to mediate the lover's return to his fiancée, as female acrobats (initially appearing as stars) launch him earthward toward the cabaret. Finally, much of this central section is articulated through an early example of the synchronized combination of live action and matte animation.[247] Midway through the flight of the real hatchet that Pedro throws, for instance, an animated hatchet smoothly replaces it and buries itself in the moon's nose. *Clair de lune espagnole* thus seems to renovate the bricolage format of mixing generic conventions by means of a new conjunction of production techniques.

For some of these frame stories, Cohl returned to his own earlier work as an illustrator. *Les Joyeux Microbes* (1909), for instance, seems to derive from an 1896 cartoon, "A Diagnosis; or, Looking for a Bacillus," which Cohl had done for a British humor magazine, as much as it does from Pathé's *Le Dejeuner du savant* or *Opération chirigucale*.[248] The frame story is set in an old doctor's office, which a young man enters in order to be diagnosed for an illness. The doctor takes samples from his patient's skin, examines them under a microscope, and then has the young man look for himself. A series of five animated shots (now printed in positive black-on-white), each introduced by an identifying intertitle and masked by a circular iris, reveals that he is "full of microbes"—plague, sleeping sickness, rabies, cholera, and tetanus. After these revelations, the young man, understandably, rushes off in a panic. Here, the animation sequence follows the pattern Cohl had established in *Clair de lune espagnol* in that it combines a variety of techniques including line drawings, cut-outs, and even real objects. And now, according to Crafton, he could do the requisite frame-by-frame recording with an electrically driven camera.[249] However, what is just as interesting is that all the intertitles comprise a short dialogue between patient and doctor (as they would in a comic strip), and that the first two or three are inserted at the moment one character or the other is speaking them. The rest of the intertitles introducing the animation shots then equate each microbe (parenthetically) with a "social illness"—politicians, bureaucrats, mothers-in-law, taxi drivers, and drunks—each of which is represented as a figure of ridicule. A loose alliance of antirepublican, antifemale, antimodern attitudes underpin these satirical sketches, attitudes that, not unlike those in *Chiffonniers caricaturistes*, constitute part and parcel of the Nationalist Revival movement.[250] When Cohl returned to this kind of frame story in a later film he made for Pathé, *Le Retapeur de cervelles* (1911), however, the "illnesses" represented were confined to those of the stereotypical "henpecked" husband.[251] And even those were submerged in the exhuberant metamorphoses of an exceptionally fluid animation.

Cohl left Gaumont for Pathé, in the fall of 1910, partly because the pressure of cranking out biweekly trick films forced him to rely too often on shortcuts. Yet the films he produced rather successfully masked his frustration. Some such as *Le Garde-Meuble automatique* (1910) simply recycled the truc effects of earlier films, like *Le Déménagement*. Others such as *Le Binetoscope* (1910) made the animation of faces and bodies seem to originate in the whims of an animated clown. Perhaps the most interesting of these later Gaumont films depended on the frame story of an eccentric painter, *Le Peintre néo-impressioniste* (1910). The opening studio shot concisely sketches a satirical situation—a woman dressed in a toga and holding a broom is modeling for the painter whose canvas has nothing on it but a comic stick figure. A dialogue intertitle—"Cleopatra, someone's at the door . . . back to work!"—caps the caricature, and a prospective buyer enters to look at the painter's work and set up the spectacle of an animation sequence. Here, as Crafton has shown, the film's paintings are indebted to Cohl's past experience as an Incoherent—for instance, the first canvas is completely blank, reproducing an illustration from *Le Charivari* (30 October 1884).[252] Eight differently tinted "animation" paintings seem to be mapped on blank canvases, and each one is introduced by a descriptive intertitle, and a witty play on words and colors. The first one, for instance, using cutout figures and line drawings, depicts "A cardinal eating lobster in tomato sauce beside the Red Sea." Another represents "Negroes making shoe polish in a tunnel at night" with a brief segment of black leader. And the last uses both tinting and toning to present a red devil shooting pool with green balls and drinking through his cue stick. Such visual and verbal playfulness not only re-created Cohl's Incoherent past, of course, but also looked ahead to the next decade's discovery of the marvelously incongruous by the French Dadaists and Surrealists. In the last shot of *Le Peintre néo-impressioniste* (with Cohl undoubtedly laughing up his sleeve), the buyer happily purchases every one of the paintings he has looked at, as well as the model's broomstick.

Meanwhile, at Pathé, where Chomón, even earlier, experienced some of the same frustrations as Cohl did at Gaumont, trick films declined in number if not in interest, however peculiar. *Une Excursion incohérente* (1910), for instance, deploys a barrage of cinematic trucs against a bourgeois couple and their two ser-

92. *Une Excursion incohérente*, 1910

vants who dare to embark on a simple country outing.[253] Their first bad experience comes when they stop for a picnic in the gothic studio set of a wooded clearing: cut-in CUs reveal that grasshoppers fill the sausages, mice are hiding in the
hard-boiled eggs, and maggots teem in the cheese. As if that were not enough,
it begins to rain, and the travelers take shelter in an empty cottage nearby. In the
kitchen, the servants soon are beset by exploding pots, one of which (in CU) turns
into a grotesque head, and then by ghostly female dancers who turn into spec-
ters. In the bedroom, the couple take to single beds separated by the barrier of a
white sheet, which sets up a bizarre dream sequence aptly organized in terms of
an obsessive repetition. A FS of the sleeping man (in profile) serves to anchor the
increasingly sexual nightmare that now unfolds in silhouette on the background
sheet. Once the woman has settled in bed, a cut-in FS of her begins to metamorphose by means of cutout figures. A bridge is erected to span the bed
(topped by Pathé's rooster trademark), while a miniature train pops out of her
mouth, races across her body, crosses back over the bridge, and returns to its
origins. Next, in a cut-in MCU, a dove escapes from a bird cage to plant a kiss
on her forehead and dive into her mouth. Then a house rises from her head,
trees sprout from her feet, and a tiny couple exchange kisses by means of detached, mobile heads. Finally, two demons rise up to pour libations on the
woman, and, in the returning FS of the sleeping man, they turn into devils who
seem about to rape her. Fleeing to the cottage courtyard (as if to escape his own
guilt), the man comes face to face with various creatures erupting out of a well;

he and his wife and the servants race about and plunge in and out of the cottage windows, until he himself, of course, tumbles into the well. Rescued and pumped free of well water, he is about to revive when the surviving print breaks off, but not before this disturbingly outrageous film has circulated, in the deceptive guise of mere child's play, a bad dream of consumption and (male) sexual repression which might have delighted the Surrealists.

If Pathé's short trick films sputtered out in bizarre "omnibus" structures like *Une Excursion incohérente*, more conventional féerie films continued to be produced in significant numbers. As before, their subjects were drawn from fairy tales and fantastic adventure stories, and several were even remakes—such as *La Belle au bois dormant* and *Le Chat botté* (both 1908). Some of these films gave credence to those reviewers, especially in the United States,[254] who considered the genre *démodé* or perhaps worthy of interest only to children. *Geneviève Brabant* (1907), for instance, recounts the medieval legend of a banished, but faithful, and eventually exonerated wife in LS painted-flat tableaux, generally preceded by intertitles.[255] However, at several crucial points, matchcutting on movement links adjacent exterior and interior spaces—as when her husband discovers the cavern where she and her daughter are hiding. Similarly, *The Clockmaker's Secret* (1907) works a variation on the Faust story, in which its title character signs a pact with the devil so as to win a competition (dated 1648) for a new town hall clock. The clockmaker's daughter, however, not only exposes his secret but saves her father when the devil comes to collect him. This film even more consistently adheres to the convention of LS painted-flat tableaux, introduced by intertitles. The devil controls the spectacle effects of the first half—presenting visions of heaven (female dancers with huge numbers fixed to their dresses) and hell against the back wall of the clockmaker's shop and putting the finished clock in place at night in the midst of his cohorts dancing about with flares. Then, for the sake of moral and aesthetic balance, an angelic knight comes to the aid of the daughter in her climactic struggle with the devil and transforms the last tableau into an apotheosis finale. A giant clock face turns into the moon and then the sun (with a woman at the center of its swirling rays), and the daughter and her knight are joined by an array of female dancers (including those bearing numbers). Interestingly, the clockmaker himself is banished, along with the devil, from this "happy ending," its romantic coupling blessed by a sign of the maternal.

Other Pathé féeries were either more inventive or more accomplished, but also reasserted maleness as the explicit subject of their fantasies. *Le Petit Poucet* (1909), for instance, somewhat like the earlier *Aladdin*, uses the distorted space of a LA AS/LS to exaggerate the size of, first, a threatening giant and, then, his boots (in a cut-in closer shot), which the boy hero steals in order to save his many brothers and sisters. *Le Pêcheur des perles* (1907), for which Chomón probably did the cinematography, uses a rags-to-riches story to mount a feast of spectacle attractions, accentuated by tinting and stencil color.[256] The first occurs in the opening shot (tinted rose) as a simple fisherman falls asleep (in the foreground) on some rocks overlooking the sea: in the background a huge rainbow framing several women around a waterfall dissolves in, and the fisherman awakens, enchanted, and dives into the water. A transition truc shot shows him swimming down through schools of passing fish and upward floating medusas, and then a pan describes his marvelous passage across the sea floor—a sun mysteriously rises in the far background, and he is greeted by an undulating octopus, which is replaced by a waving starfish. In a large painted-flat cavern, a fairy queen and her female attendants (some of whom emerge out of seashells) stage a dance for the fisherman and then place him inside a giant oyster. In a cut-in HA FS of the oyster, the outer shell dissolves away to reveal him sleeping curled up inside, and a further dissolve rings him round with a string of unusually large pearls. After the fairy queen has lifted him out of the oyster and sent him back toward the surface (with his prize), the fisherman emerges from the sea (now tinted deep green), to stand as a dark silhouette on the foreground rocks. The film's final shot then creates a kind of apotheosis in the fisherman's own simple cabin interior—with the aid of a fairy godmother, he and his wife receive rich courtly clothes, the cabin turns into a palace grotto with seashell fountains in the foreground, and strings of pearls glow along the vaulting arches of the dark background walls. Virtually lacking any narrative tension or conflict, *Le Pêcheur des perles* stages its hero's easy rise to wealth in a fantasy land of maternal plenitude whose source is coded stereotypically as nature itself.

Chomón's *Voyage au planete Jupiter* (1909) returns once more to an exclusively male realm—with a king and his astronomer—and to the fantastical trip into space popularized by *Un Voyage dans la lune*. Unlike prior féeries, however, this film relies extensively on constructing sequences out of multiple shots, organized particularly around the POV shot, and it even "invents" several new truc effects. The opening sequence in the astronomer's study introduces the first POV shot: in LS, the king looks through a telescope, and there is a cut to a FS of the moon making faces. Disgruntled, the king asks the astronomer to let him examine a large book on a centered stand in the study, and a cut-in AS reveals, inside the open book (in a technique resembling that used in Cohl's *Clair de lune espagnol*), a matte shot of the sky with the planets scrolling neatly downward in an orderly procession. This prompts the two men to go to a balcony (presumably for a better look), and the journey takes them through three different shots of matched exits and entrances: a LS representing a diagonal line of church columns, a MS of a doorway framed in silhouette and opening out onto the balcony, and a 180-degree reverse-angle LS of them standing on the balcony itself. The actual sequence of viewing then alternates between an AS of the two men using a telescope to look off to the right (the camera has shifted ninety degrees) and a series of LSs: flames erupt out of a rocky landscape over which snow then falls, a woman lounges languidly within the crescent of the moon, Saturn makes bold gestures from inside his planet's rings, and Jupiter stands guard with fire flashing out of both his planet and shield. This final image seems to most excite the king, and the two men go back the way they came, in another three-shot sequence (the two shots of the balcony repeated in reverse order).

After this carefully constructed, almost tongue-in-cheek preparation, the actual "voyage to Jupiter" begins in a LS of the king's bedroom and unfolds as a dream. A dissolve removes the interior walls and places the bed with the sleeping king against a painted cloudscape, with a rope ladder conveniently hanging down from above for him to climb when he awakens. A LS shows him ascending, in very condensed fashion (just as the book indicated), past the moon and Saturn and finally approaching Jupiter—the truc effect probably created by stage machinery rather than by a moving overhead camera. In the next shot, he is suspended horizontally (center frame) with arms flailing toward the background as flyaway cloud flats successively rush past him toward the camera—rather effectively producing a sense of vertiginous movement. However, his visit to the planet, in sharp contrast to earlier films, is surprisingly brief. He dispatches several creatures in the usual manner, in bursts of yellow smoke, but is quickly overpowered. And, in the LS of Jupiter's court, the god uses his thunderbolts to make the king race around helplessly in fast motion. Jupiter's men then drop the exhausted king off a rock ledge, and another shot with flyaway cloud flats rushing away from the camera creates the effect of having him sail in the opposite direction. Now, as he climbs down the ladder in terror, Saturn grabs a giant pair of scissors and cuts the rope after he passes. The final shot has painted-flat clouds fly away to reveal the king falling out of bed, calling the astronomer in to complain, and then sitting disconsolate with his jester. There is no apotheosis finale to *Voyage au planete Jupiter* for there is nothing to celebrate in this story of "royal" failure—an absence perhaps fitting for what seemed to be the genre's own approaching end.[257]

Fairy tales continued to be made primarily for children during this period, principally by Velle who had resumed work at Pathé—see, for instance, *Barbe-bleue* (1910), *La Petite Blanche-Neige* (1910), and *La Petite Bergère* (1910), the latter of which returned to the practice of having child actors play adult characters.[258] Yet another kind of féerie for adults enjoyed a short-lived revival—that of the more traditional pantomime featuring the characters of Pierrot, Columbine, and Polichinelle or Harlequin. Pathé's *La Légende de Polichinelle* (1907) offers an early, rather inventive example and may well have been intended for children. As in other recent Pathé féeries such as *Aladdin* and *Cendrillon*, this story of a youth pursuing and rescuing the girl he loves (who has been "abducted" by older aristocrats) does more than display a series of spectacle effects. The opening LS tableau represents a museum of mechanical toys and mannequins, from among which Columbine is dusted off by a servant, cranked into motion, and carried out in a box. Polichinelle (played by Linder)[259] calls after her and weeps until a fairy reveals—in a background miniature scene reminiscent of *Cendrillon*—a ballroom where she has been set on a pedestal surrounded by aristocrats; then he rushes off after her, riding a toy horse. His journey takes him through a series of fairyland spaces—a country inn (and a scene of vanishing objects), a bridge collapsing into a rocky gorge (from which he escapes, with the help of a dragon-lady, on rising mushrooms), and a hill topped by a gnarled tree (on whose limbs he suspends a couple of the aristocrats' servants).

When Polichinelle, joined by a group of elves, reaches the aristocrats' castle, the film abandons these autonomous shot-scenes and instead constructs his rescue of Columbine through a sequence of adjacent exterior and interior spaces, once matching exits and entrances and twice matching the characters' position (within the frame) in 180-degree reverse-angle cuts. Then, in an alternating sequence, Polichinelle sets the room below the one in which Columbine is performing on fire (as if reenacting the French Revolution in miniature), and, after the building collapses, he rushes in to collect the pieces of her body in a bundle. The return journey takes him across the bridge (reconstructed in reverse motion) through the added space of a formal garden (where the wave of a wand magically restores Columbine) and back to the museum for the traditional apotheosis finale. All the figures in the museum "come to life," and a fairy godmother appears to bless the reunited couple. In a final transformation, she stages a series of dances by quartets of women, concluding with a serpentine dancer bursting out from behind the backdrop of an immense shell bordered by a rainbow arch of flowers. *La Légende de Polichinelle* condenses any number of social conflicts or resentments—servants versus masters, children versus parents, young men versus older, more powerful men—into Polichinelle's rescue-revenge and resolves them in the imaginary space of a museum cum playroom.

Later féerie films seem to address adults rather than children in the way they either complicate their stories or draw attention to the pantomime performance. Lux's *Le Retour de Colombine* (1909), for instance, tells what seems to be the simple tale of Harlequin's loss of Columbine to a rival and their belated reunion years later, as he lies dying. That story is complicated, however, by the verisimilitude of the film's sets—from Harlequin's shabby garret room to an outside café entrance—and particularly by its ambiguous narrative structure, which involves "dream visions" similar to those in Gaumont's *The Old Woodcutter*. The film opens in a LS of the garret room, where Harlequin, aged and alone and penniless, falls asleep on a foreground couch. A dissolve repositions the couch in front of a fashionable townhouse, as Harlequin's younger double (in superimposition) rises up to play a guitar, and Columbine (after tossing some flowers out of a window) comes out on the arm of another clown. A second dissolve positions the couch in a wooded clearing, as Harlequin watches his double come up to Columbine, sitting alone on a stone bench, and exit with her. After a quick dissolve back to the garret room, a cut now repositions the couch in a "respectable" room, and Harlequin watches in dismay as Columbine accepts some flowers from his double without a trace of emotion, after which the double discovers and reads a letter and orders her out. The sequence closes with a cut back to the older Harlequin, now hungry, deciding to leave the garret room. In one sense (supported by *Bioscope*'s description of the film's story), this sequence reads as a chronological flashback of Harlequin's prior relationship with Columbine, with the cuts indicating where explanatory intertitles once marked time shifts. In another sense, however, the detail of Columbine tossing out the flowers suggests that, chronologically, the initial flashback shot may actually follow the last shot in the series. This ambiguity returns in the film's conclusion, after Harlequin has given a coin, acquired by begging, to a poor old woman. She follows him back to his garret room and, with a wave of her cane, the "respectable" room dissolves in, and she herself turns into the young Columbine to beg forgiveness. Given the earlier embedded flashback, is this reconciliation imaginary or real and who exactly experiences this climactic moment of recognition—Columbine, as *Bioscope* suggests (apparently following the missing intertitle), or rather, as the visual tableau itself suggests, the dying Harlequin?

Le Retour de Colombine suggests that the féerie genre was still serving to sustain a long-standing pantomime tradition, but now under the direction of a strategy of legitimation in which the French cinema was increasingly seeking to imitate the theater.[260] This is especially evident in Pathé's *Le Cauchemar de Pierrot* (1911), which tells a rather violent version of the same story, from Pierrot's point of view. This Velle film opens with a long-take FS/LS of a simple, all-purpose room where Columbine seems to be living with Pierrot (played by the mime Séverin), but is attracted to Harlequin, who first appears at a background window and then invites himself in.[261] She and Harlequin ask Pierrot for something to drink, which forces him reluctantly to descend through a cellar trapdoor, and the two perform a short sensuous dance in the foreground before Pierrot reappears and spots them in one another's arms. After chasing Harlequin out the window, Pierrot strangles Columbine and slowly staggers off in remorse—at which point she sits up, goes to the window, and smiles at her clever deceit. The rest of the film traces Pierrot through a series of eighteenth-century city spaces—a street café, a formal garden, a public square—as he obsessively imagines confronting the two lovers. Each time, a straight cut replaces a nearby couple with Columbine and Harlequin, which sends Pierrot into a rage—in the garden, he destroys a statue—accumulating, in effect, further humiliation and guilt. And, although at least one sequence involves the intercutting of adjacent exterior and interior spaces, the emphasis throughout is on Séverin's performance as Pierrot, thus reproducing and privileging, as on stage, his mimed gestures of love and despair, his gestural summaries of or preludes to the narrative action. Appropriately, *Le Cauchemar de Pierrot* ends in another long-take FS/LS of a public square, where Pierrot's guilt finally reaches the point of producing, through a dissolve, his own trial and execution by hanging—from which he only escapes by rolling off the bench on which he has been sleeping. This tableau then concludes in a cleverly choreographed reconciliation between Pierrot and Columbine in the foreground as he kneels to kiss her right hand, oblivious to Harlequin who has sneaked in behind her to kiss the other, proffered hand. This triangular composition simply reproduces the beginning, through the distancing device of ironic mockery—in order to serve, not Pierrot's, but Columbine's desire.

A different strategy of legitimation serves as a subtext in one last féerie film, Pathé's *Le Miracle des fleurs* (1912), directed by Leprince. Its slight story, also set in vaguely eighteenth-century decors, has Pierrot fall in love with a Columbine who has left her peasant village to sell flowers in the city market. They share his simple artist's studio until one day, when he is out trying to sell a painting, a gentleman lures her away with the gift of a pearl necklace. Pierrot sinks into such despair that he is about to commit suicide, but Columbine, rejecting the gentleman's advances, returns to her "true love," just in time for their reconciliation. Although this film includes several location shots and a single instance of alternation at the end, for suspense, it typically foregrounds the smoothly choreographed pantomime of its actors in long-take AS/LS tableaux. The film's chief interest lies in the ambiguous gender of this Pierrot, for it adopts the French stage tradition in which women perform both the male and female roles. Here, Pierrot and Columbine are played, respectively, by Napierkowska and Mlle Bordoni, both of whose expertise as dancers turn the film into something like a ballet. That Napierkowska seems to have been part of a lesbian community within the Paris theater world, however, makes the film available for a double reading, one of which runs counter to the harlequin story's usual spectacle of male desire.[262] In this alternative reading, Napierkowska's androgynous figure becomes the means to put female desire on display, giving expression to the physical and emotional love between two women, openly, legitimately. Yet however sensuous is the lovers' intimacy, it remains chaste throughout, at most polymorphous, the actors' bodies ultimately governed by the gestural economy of pantomime, and further confined by a conventionally gendered symbolic economy of objects—the pearl necklace (artifice) versus the ever-renewed flowers (nature). If, in *Le Miracle des fleurs*, the féerie tradition opens up the possibility of celebrating a "deviant" love, it sets severe limits on its representation.

And what of the trick films and féeries from Méliès during this period? Do they deserve more than an ironic, appended note? On the basis of surviving trick film prints, the answer is probably a heavily qualified yes. *François 1er et Triboulet* (1908), for instance, is little more than a single-set stage act in which magical transformations have been sacrificed almost completely to a series of lame jokes perpetrated by a jester on his king. One flickering point of interest, however, comes at the end when the jester produces an "oriental" dancer and sets her on the king's lap, then himself replaces her (in a straight cut) and laughs at his master. Similarly, *The Genii of Fire* (1908) uses just two set decors to mock a bourgeois couple's desire to experience the exotic or unusual, which tempts them into a grotto despite an old man's warning at the entrance. Once inside, they are assaulted by torch-bearing genie and a chalice of fire which leave them blind—at the end of this second tableau, the couple comes forward into AS, in order to emphasize their plight—that is, until they stumble outside and the old man heals them with a special potion. Although the truc effects orchestrated by the grotto's black-clad master magician are unexceptional by Méliès's standards, what is peculiar is that, in luring the couple into the darkness of a fun house nightmare, *The Genii of Fire* seems to be attacking characters who closely resemble the cinema's own spectators. The trucs in *Satan en prison* (1907), by contrast, seem effortless and build to a revelatory climax. A gendarme pushes a bearded man into a barren cell that he meticulously furnishes, through simple cuts, with a fireplace, wall paintings, matching table and chairs, place settings, bread and wine, and finally a woman to dine with him. Discovered by the astonished gendarme (who calls in reinforcements), he quickly "erases" his handiwork and eludes the pursuing gendarmes through a series of metamorphoses in and around the fireplace, finally stepping forth as Satan in a white cloak and vanishing into the wall. Despite its carefully crafted trucs, however, *Satan en prison* ultimately comes off as an ascetic, even "Protestant" version of Méliès's earlier diabolical extravaganzas—especially in contrast to Pathé's *Red Spectre* of the same period—perhaps because by then his trick films were being produced explicitly for the American market.

Although Méliès's féerie films also suffer technically in comparison to Pathé's, they are scarcely devoid of interest. In *Le Tunnel sous la manche* (1907), for instance, the topical subject of constructing a tunnel under the English channel is turned into a fantasy shared by both King Edward VII and President Fallières. Despite its relatively slow pace, the film does deploy crosscutting in order to represent the tunnel's construction and, perhaps more important, "uses a divided set to show the two leaders retiring simultaneously" and, after a train collision destroys the tunnel, awakening from their dream at the end.[263] Ultimately, of course, the dream-turned-to-nightmare burlesques both republican politicians and scientific advances in technology. *La Bonne Bergère et la méchante princesse* (1908) tells a version of the Cinderella story in which a young shepherdess wins the love of a handsome prince at the expense of a fat, ugly, bad-tempered princess. Much like Pathé's earlier *Cendrillon*, Méliès juxtaposes these antagonists not only in terms of action and gesture (the princess hits and kicks anyone who comes near her) but also in terms of space—the one's rough, plain cottage interior versus the other's huge palatial drawing room. Although the tableau of the shepherdess's transformation is full of truc effects, the real clou of spectacle comes in the scene of retribution that falls on the demonized, unlady-like princess. A fairy godmother turns her palace to ruins, looses grotesque male heads and dragons to threaten her, and eventually orders black-cat figures to trap the villainess in an iron-fence cage and push her down a well. Finally, *La Civilisation à travers les âges* (1908) takes on a subject quite different from any in the master magician's previous films.[264] In just eleven long-take tableaux, Méliès sketches human history as a series of injustices, beginning with Cain's killing of Abel, which is miraculously transformed in the end by a "triumphant" Peace Congress meeting at La Haye, in 1907. The film's interest lies, not only in its expression of the current international hopes for peace (which failed to avert the Great War) and its establishment of one model for Griffith's *Intolerance* (1916), but also for its selection of a 1906 labor strike and street battle to represent "modern times." In *La Civilisation à travers les âges*, then, Méliès made the unusual move of confronting the reality of French social conflict directly, something his films had not done since *L'Affaire Dreyfus*, even if he could only resolve it through another, more historically specific fantasy.

6

The Rise of the Feature Film, 1911-1914

As for me, I wanted to see the film as close up as possible. I had learned in the equalitarian discomfort of the neighborhood houses that this new art was mine, just as it was everyone else's. We had the same mental age: I was seven and knew how to read; it was twelve and did not know how to talk. People said that it was in its early stages, that it had progress to make; I thought that we would grow up together. I have not forgotten our common childhood: whenever I am offered a hard candy, whenever a woman varnishes her nails near me, whenever I inhale a certain smell of disinfectant in the toilet of a provincial hotel, whenever I see the violet bulb on the ceiling of a night train, my eyes, nostrils, and tongue recapture the lights and odors of those bygone halls; four years ago, in rough weather off the coast of Fingal's Cave, I heard a piano in the wind.

JEAN-PAUL SARTRE

THE THREE YEARS just prior to the outbreak of the Great War saw another crucial change in the French cinema industry which impinged on the representational system then governing the narrative cinema. In the face of increasing competition, especially from the United States, Pathé-Frères redefined and even abandoned parts of the strategy of concentration which, for a half-dozen years, had sustained its preeminent position worldwide. Although the Pathé "empire" continued to expand, if at a slower rate than before, the distribution sector clearly now played the dominant role in its operations. This encouraged a similar concentration of film distribution within France, with Gaumont, AGC, and Aubert joining Pathé to exercise control over the weekly release of product, at least until the supply of American films began to overwhelm even them by early 1914. Although far less concentrated, the exhibition sector of the industry steadily grew in importance, as more and more permanent cinemas were constructed and ticket sales challenged or surpassed those of the music halls and theaters. Increasingly, cinemas also were divided into "classes," depending on their location, the composition of their programs, and their clientele—enforcing a greater degree of distinct markets and possible reading positions. Finally, as Pathé further decentralized its own film production, a "cottage industry" of medium- and small-sized companies arose in France, with many tending to specialize in a specific genre of film—for instance, SCAGL in historical reconstructions, Eclair in criminal adventures, and Valetta in modern bourgeois melodramas—with perhaps only Gaumont proving an exception to the trend. This specialization was also determined, however, by a significant difference that emerged between the now standard format of the single-reel film and its increasingly popular rival, the feature-length film.

Indeed, the feature-length film was, arguably, the principal innovation during this period. Multiple-reel films had appeared irregularly in France at least since *Epopée napoléonienne* and *La Vie et la Passion de Jésus-Christ*, and they were becoming more frequent by 1909. In 1911, the cinema industries of France, Italy, and Denmark almost simultaneously launched a concerted effort to produce multiple-reel films on a more regular basis. This effort was driven, at least in France, not only by the continuing desire for legitimacy vis-à-vis the theater, but by the growing output of single-reel films made in the United States, which verged on monopolizing the market there, and the consequent demand for a new, distinctive European or, rather, national product or "special attraction." While producers such as Cinès in Italy concentrated on lavish historical reconstructions and those in Denmark specialized in sometimes risqué, contemporary films, the French ranged across the spectrum of so-called serious dramas. At SCAGL, for instance, Capellani turned out bigger and bigger historical films, some of them adaptations of Victor Hugo, like *Notre Dame de Paris* (1911) and *Les Misérables* (1912). For Pathé itself, Bourgeois initially gave his attention to "social dramas" such as *Les Victimes d'alcool* (1911). And at Eclair, Jasset used the multiple-reel format for a new series of crime films, beginning with *Zigomar* (1911). This production and marketing strategy proved so successful that, by the fall of 1912, Pathé was releasing at least one film of anywhere from two to five or more reels in length per week. Furthermore, French films such as Pathé's *Notre Dame de Paris*, Gaumont's *La Fille du Margrave* (1912), and Eclipse's *Queen Elizabeth* (1912), along with other imports such as the Italian version of *Dante's Inferno* (1911), were achieving such popularity and critical acclaim in the United States that, by 1913, the American cinema industry itself was forced to embark in earnest on the production of longer films. On the eve of the war, in Paris, spectators could count on viewing a different four- to six-reel film each week at the more prestigious cinemas. The feature-length film was close to becoming standard fare.

As the multiple-reel film was transformed into an increasingly standardized feature-length format, French filmmakers were forced to rethink the models of narrative construction which regulated the single-reel film.[1] Their range of options were several. It was unlikely, for instance, that the short story model, in which one central incident formed the basis for a steadily rising line of action that culminated in a strongly affecting climax, could be expanded across several reels, especially if exhibition practice still included breaks between reels. They could, however, extend the two-part narrative structure, in which the central line of action developed in the first half of a film was challenged and reversed by another in the second half. Given the frequently drawn analogy between the cinema and theater, they could also exploit the symmetrical five-part structure of the well-made play, already an established model for the historical film. And, for film adaptations of novels such as *Zigomar* and *Fantômas* (1913–1914), which had not already been adapted to the stage, they might emulate the original serial format of their publication. Indeed, a crucial question here is whether the narrative structure of the early French feature generally followed a serial format determined by reel breaks or whether any film constructed an unbroken line of action across several reels—the best example being, as Brewster has demonstrated so well, Universal's *Traffic in Souls* (1913).[2] One of the problems in tracing the development of the French feature-length film is that, in contrast to the United States, where scriptwriting manuals first began to appear during this period,[3] in France such manuals seem to have been nonexistent. This suggests that the scriptwriting process and its consequence, the detailed continuity script,[4] were nowhere as standardized in France as they were in the United States. It means, at least for now, that the French models of narrative construction have to be teased out of surviving film prints as well as descriptions and reviews in the period's press.

The emergence of the feature-length film also raises questions about the system of representation which had come to more or less characterize the French cinema. If the principal strategies of that system remained relatively stable, what further, specific changes did the system undergo? Were those changes dispersed across the mise-en-scène, framing, and editing of film discourse or concentrated within a single area? How did they involve the composition and deployment of intertitles and musical accompaniment? Perhaps most important, did developments in the French system parallel those in the United States, particularly in terms of analytical editing—eyeline matches, shot–reverse shots, crosscutting—all of which would become central to the so-called classical Hollywood cinema?[5] Or rather, as Brewster and others have suggested,[6] did the French system increasingly differ from the American, especially in its emphasis on long-take, deep-space tableaux, to the point of constituting an alternative model of representation and narration? As before, did any further differences emerge in the strategies employed by one company versus another or in one genre versus another, especially now that female stars were beginning to come to the fore in both the historical film and the modern bourgeois drama? And were such strategies of representation, along with choices in subject matter, beginning to distinguish particular filmmakers from one another? Finally, now that the trade press was acknowledging the importance of the director's role—although his name rarely ever appeared in either the publicity or credits of a film (de Morlhon being an early exception)[7]—was it possible to tell the difference, for instance, between films directed by Feuillade and Perret at Gaumont or between those made by de Morlhon and Leprince for Pathé?

Despite the innovation of the feature-length film, most French companies remained convinced of the viability of the single-reel format. After all, it satisfied what a *Bioscope* writer described as the era's "increasing desire for condensation," whether in snappy newspaper paragraphs, short stories, or variety acts.[8] This was especially true of the comic series, which served Pathé, Gaumont, Eclair, and Eclipse as a reliably profitable staple of production, for the comic series could easily exploit the growing appeal of stars, guaranteeing that favorite actors (most of them still men) returned to the cinemas week after week in a restricted format that would highlight their performances. In addition to its popular *Max* and *Rigadin* films, for instance, Pathé got Deed to come back from Italy to star in another round of *Boireau* films (1912–1914) and supplemented all three with a variety of series—perhaps most notably *Little Moritz* (1911–1912), with Schwartz, and *Rosalie* (1911–1912), with Duhamel—from Comica in Nice. As the *Calino* series began to run out of steam, Gaumont introduced a zany new series, *Onésime* (1912–1914), starring Bourbon, developed a highly sophisticated one, *Léonce* (1912–1914), starring Perret himself, and replaced *Bébé* with another kid series, *Bout-de-Zan* (1912–1914). Eclair continued its *Gontran* series with Gréhan, created its own kid series around Sanders as *Willy* (1911–1914), and picked up Bertho from Lux (just as the company began to fold) for a new series called *Gavroche* (1912–1914), while Eclipse weighed in with Servaes as *Arthème* (1911–1914). Other kinds of continuing series organized around a central character also used the single-reel format, most notably the detective series exemplified by Pathé's *Nick Winter* and Eclipse's *Nat Pinkerton* (played by the former Nick Carter, Bressol). Perhaps the most intriguing of these series, however, was Feuillade's *La Vie telle qu'elle est* (1911–1913) for Gaumont, which eschewed a recurring central character and put its trust in an ensemble of its best actors. Gaumont's stated intention here was to create "slices of life" in specific social milieus or situations, as simply and starkly as possible, representing "people and things as they are and not as they should be."[9]

The *La Vie telle qu'elle est* series, along with various detective series and corollary crime films, introduce several important issues concerning representation and reception in the French cinema during this period. According to the company's advertising, the Gaumont films sought to interject an aesthetic of realism or naturalism into the cinema, as if to erase the melodramatic origins of the "dramatic and realist film" genre. In one sense, this alleged intervention simply served a legitimizing function, calling further attention to the cinema as a respectable art form. In another sense, however, in both written discourse and actual film practice, Gaumont again put in play the close interconnection that existed between melodrama, realism, and grand guignol sensationalism in late nineteenth-century French drama and fiction. Yet, here and in certain Pathé and Eclair "social dramas," perhaps impelled by realist concerns, the threat of destitution and its social causes often now came to the fore, unmasked by the supposed threat of criminal deviance which earlier so dominated the genre.[10] And, in Feuillade's films, that threat consistently was framed in terms of gender relations, frequently seeming to take the woman's part. The exploration of criminal deviance and its corrective counterpoint of police regulation and discipline shifted instead to the detective series and crime films. And, according to many conservative critics as well as moral reformists across the political spectrum, the French cinema's exploration of crime so exceeded the limits of bourgeois slumming as to threaten the social order. Given that children—among them the impressionable Jean-Paul Sartre—may have constituted 25 percent of cinema audiences, to these critics and reformers, films such as Eclair's *Tom Butler* (1912) and

Gaumont's *Main de fer* (1912) contradicted the ideological effort to make French youth into good subjects and citizens of the state.[11] This view, in effect, assumed that, as a textual space of representation and cultural space of interaction, the cinema was dangerous in that it fostered reading positions of deviance and even resistance. In fact, both the popular crime films and the *La Vie telle qu'elle est* series, perhaps more than any other film genres of the period, became crucial ideological sites of struggle over the class, gender, and generational relations defining Third Republic France.

The Historical Film Comes of Age

By 1911, the historical film constituted one of the French cinema's more distinctive genres. Such films—whether produced by SCAGL or Pathé itself—were often prominently featured among the company's weekly releases in France, and they were given special attention, as imports, in the company's advertising as well as trade press reviews, especially in England but also in the United States. Other French companies also continued to give a privileged status to the genre: Film d'Art, for instance, devoted much of its resources to historical films, while Gaumont, Eclair, and Eclipse all made them an important component of their production. One reason for the genre's significance during this period, of course, was that it served as the chief vehicle for the development of the feature-length film and, as a consequence, of the cinema as a formidable rival to the legitimate theater. Scarcely any French historical film produced after 1911 ran less than two reels; at the other extreme, some were reaching lengths of up to twelve reels—as in Capellani's *Les Misérables* (1912) and Pouctal's lost *Les Trois Mousquetaires* (1913). The multiple-reel format of the historical film raises crucial questions about the French system of representation and its models of narrative construction, and those questions, in turn, take on added weight in the context of the genre's ideological relation to the Nationalist Revival movement then dominating French political and cultural life. Addressing these questions is again complicated, however, by a relative dearth of surviving film prints, especially after 1912. Although at least three of Capellani's major films for SCAGL are still extant, along with a couple other Pathé titles and several English "classics" from Eclipse, very few survive from Film d'Art, Gaumont, or Eclair. This has the effect of inadvertently skewing any analysis of the French historical film, but that skewing does have the advantage of focusing attention on the early stages of the transition to multiple-reel films, beginning with Capellani's contribution at SCAGL.

The earliest of Capellani's multiple-reel films to survive seems to be *Le Courrier de Lyon* (1911), whose apparent lack of influence remains puzzling. Although publicized for a spring release in France and England, there is little evidence of its actual screening in either country—did cinemas balk at having one long film dominate their programs instead of screening its three reels consecutively over several weeks, as they had done with previous lengthy films like

L'Assomoir?[12] Furthermore, its release was delayed in the United States for over a year, until the summer of 1912, long after other feature-length European films had broken into the American market. The uncertain impact of Capellani's film is unfortunate because the complicated story it tells, adapted by playwright Emile Moreau from a popular nineteenth-century stage melodrama,[13] involves eight major characters and is surprisingly well constructed. Set during the transitional years of 1795–1796, that story is premised on a duplicitous double plot in which a band of criminals threaten a respectable bourgeois figure as well as the French state. First, a merchant named Lesurques (Ravet) rides out of Paris on the road to Lyons in order to hide some money intended for his failing father (Albert Dieudonné) in the old man's roadside inn at Lieusaint; simultaneously, a former friend of Lesurques named Courriol (Georges Tréville) sends Dubosc, an escaped criminal, and several accomplices to the same inn in order to rob the Lyon mail coach of a huge sum being shipped by the Revolutionary government to Napoleon's army in Italy. Because Dubosc (also played by Ravet) closely resembles Lesurques, the latter is misrecognized at the inn, arrested, and convicted of the crime. When Didier (Paul Capellani), the fiancé of Lesurques's daughter (Andrée Pascal), discovers evidence proving his innocence, Dubosc secretly has it destroyed. Finally, just before Lesurques's execution, the confession of an accomplice, Chopard (Mévisto), sets the police on the trail of the real villains and promises to exonerate the victim of their clever deception. However, in one of the more infamous French miscarriages of justice, Lesurques goes to the guillotine even though demonstrably innocent, much like the earlier Duc d'Enghien.

Le Courrier de Lyon seems to confirm Brewster's hypothesis that European feature-length films initially used reel breaks to separate their narratives into large segments,[14] for its narrative does divide into three more or less distinct parts, each of which corresponds to a break between reels. What is interesting, however, is the way the film's narrative structure doubles the intrigue, rising action, and climax of the familiar well-made play. In an initial sequence of exposition (laid out in eight intertitles and eleven shots), Courriol and Dubosc set up the robbery scheme at a Paris restaurant nicknamed the Tin Dish (on 28 May 1895). Lesurques and his daughter and future son-in-law also happen to be dining there, and Courriol notices the two men's resemblance and plans to turn it to their advantage. The subsequent sequence (five intertitles, eleven shots) traces Lesurques's journey from Chopard's small stable (he hires a horse from Chopard's wife, played by Nau) to Lieusaint, where he stealthily leaves the money for his father, and then his return to the capital. This is followed, in turn, by the climactic sequence (three intertitles, six shots) in which the mail coach is attacked and Dubosc wounds Lesurques's father, who believes his attacker to be his own son. Reworking this sequential pattern of action, part two begins with the investigation of the crime, which quickly leads to Lesurques's arrest, accused by his own father as well as Courriol and Dubosc. This provokes Didier's own investigation in a sequence that parallels Lesurques's earlier journey: he goes to Chopard's wife and gets a ledger proving that his future father-in-law returned the horse four hours before the robbery was committed. This, in turn, produces

Dubosc's counteraction in an overlapping sequence that parallels his earlier action as well: now he follows Didier home and sneaks in, at night, to ink out any reference to Lesurques in the ledger. A brief court scene then confirms Lesurques's guilt, as the stunned couple discover the ledger has been tampered with. Here, the conclusion to part two seems to coincide with the last reel break, for the slightly shorter part three focuses on the suspense leading up to Lesurques's scheduled execution (on 30 October 1796).[15] This section, too, relies on crucial information from Chopard, this time a confession that apparently clears the condemned man and shifts the blame to Courriol and Dubosc. Concerned about shoring up its authority, the Paris court stands by its decision, however, and this final "act" works out a heavily ironic version of the well-made play's falling action and catastrophe.

Le Courrier de Lyon also distributes various strategies of representation in such a way as to distinguish its three segments one from another, much in the manner of earlier Pathé films. To be sure, certain strategies are deployed throughout. A strong sense of verisimilitude, for instance, governs the studio decors and props as well as the choice of locations (the actual historical sites, according to Pathé's publicity)[16] to create a consistently spare, unostentatious Revolutionary world. Interiors and even some exteriors are usually framed in AS/LSs or FS/LSs, and the characters circulate within and between these framed spaces in matched exits and entrances as well as in contrasting left-right and foreground-background positions. Part one, however, is especially marked by pans—not only to reframe the characters as they approach the Tin Dish, for instance, but also, once the inn is "established," to reveal Lesurques coming down the Lyon road toward it from the distant background. Moreover, the two sequences at the inn both include 120-degree reverse-angle matchcuts from exterior to interior as, first, Lesurques climbs in a window and, later, Dubosc crashes in the door and hides in order to surprise the coach driver. In a sense, this strategy of representation conspires in the substitution of bodies essential to the film's duplicitous narrative.

Part two then adopts the strategy of the cut-in CU to reveal crucial clues in the crime plot. What seems to be the first clue actually comes up in part one, when an intertitle mentions that Lesurques has broken a spur from his boot, a detail that is reiterated visually when he returns the horse to Chopard's wife and when the spur is given back to him just prior to his arrest—but at no point is either boot or spur shown in close shot. Instead, the first cut-in CU unexpectedly occurs in the investigating judge's office when, without advance warning in an intertitle, a servant brings a whip he has found near the inn—imprinted with Chopard's name and address—but this the judge (unlike the spectator) reads as a ruse or "purloined letter," the name of one owner masking another. In the following sequence, in another cut-in CU, the discovery of Lesurques's name in Chopard's ledger sets up the expectation that the "letter" of the whip will be reread. However, in the very next sequence, Dubosc eliminates that possibility in a gesture that extends the spectacular effect of the scene's single-source sidelighting. In a third cut-in CU, he obliterates Lesurques's name with ink, in a kind of double synecdoche—again blackening his reputation and consigning him to darkness, and death. Finally, perhaps more conventionally, part three deploys the strategy of alternation or crosscutting—between the condemned man in his cell, Chopard confessing, and Courrisol and Dubosc waiting in a room overlooking the courtyard in which the guillotine stands—to intensify the suspense over whether or not the villains will be caught and Lesurques will die. If names or "letters" circulate in a melodramatic game of substitution and erasure throughout the middle of this film, the last "act" returns to the physical action of the beginning, in a quasi-royalist resolution (the "injustices" of the Revolution or Directorate would be "righted" by Napoleon) to what ultimately can be read as a displaced threat to the benevolent bourgeois body of the French state.

Le Courrier de Lyon may have been an anomaly in the spring of 1911, its release strategy out of synch with the diversified single-reel and split-reel format of French cinema programs. That was not the case six months later, when Pathé released Capellani's *Notre Dame de Paris*. For SCAGL, Capellani had already directed several single-reel adaptations of Hugo historical dramas, including *Marie Stuart* (1908) and *Le Roi s'amuse* (1909). *Notre Dame de Paris*, however, proved the most successful of these, in England and the United States as well as in France.[17] That success stemmed, in part, from worldwide familiarity with Hugo's melodramatic story of abusive church power in fifteenth-century Paris, but also from the way the film exploited Napierkowska's dancing prowess, playing the part of Esméralda, "queen of the Paris gypsies and vagabonds," and Henry Krauss's acting and extensive makeup, as the deformed hero, Quasimodo. Unlike *Le Courrier de Lyon*, this film's scenario (written by Carré) focused on only three major characters and—in what *Moving Picture World* called a model of construction—condensed the novel's action into three parts, each of which seems to have corresponded to a reel break.[18] In the first reel, Archdeacon Frollo (Claude Garry) plots Esméralda's abduction in front of Notre Dame cathedral, using the hunchback bell-ringer, Quasimodo; but the Captain of the Royal Archers, Phébus (Alexandre), intervenes, and Quasimodo is punished by being pilloried in a public square. In the second, at the "Apple of Eve" inn, Frollo is again foiled in a more direct attempt to abduct Esméralda, yet succeeds in killing Phébus and pinning the blame on her. In the third and final reel, Esméralda is being returned to Notre Dame to do penance when Quasimodo rescues her; however, Frollo discovers her hiding place by accident, and she is taken to the same public square for execution, as Quasimodo, enraged, throws his master from the cathedral tower. In a series of structural parallels that give the film a degree of unity and coherence that surpasses even *Le Courrier de Lyon*, part two reworks the narrative materials of part one, but more concentratedly and in a different space, while part three reprises both the cathedral and public square set pieces from part one, with Quasimodo now defending Esméralda against Frollo rather than blindly serving his master's desire.

Notre Dame de Paris begins with separate introductions to each of its three principal characters. In fact, Napierkowska is singled out as the star in an initial iris-masked MS, which then dissolves to an iris-masked LS of the cathedral

93. *Notre Dame de Paris*, 1911 (Henry Krauss, left)

facade, as if to equate her, as a representative of the common people, with
the church itself. Preceded by intertitles, long-take LSs then present Esméralda
dancing for the street people who have "elected" her queen and Frollo condescendingly ordering Quasimodo about in his study, from which the latter exits
to ring the bells in the cathedral tower, glowingly transformed by single-source
lighting from a background window. In the following sequence, these figures
are quickly brought together by sight and sound: coming from the steps of
Notre Dame, where Esméralda is now dancing, her jangling tambourine interrupts Frollo at his desk, draws him to a background window, and stirs his desire,
in an approximation of a POV shot. In a series of mismatched exits and entrances, he moves along the cathedral ramparts to seek out and startle Quasimodo, who himself is gazing out the window of the bell tower. Then, in repeated movements toward the foreground, across several shots, the two men
finally pose against Notre Dame's facade to confront Esméralda, who hesitantly
collects her pet goat and exits, pursued. After this relatively complicated sequence of eight shots, the abduction is narrated in two long-take tableaux (each
preceded by an intertitle), as Phébus and his archers pass Esméralda at a street
corner and then return to rescue her and seize Quasimodo in a nearby alley. The
climax of this initial line of action, articulated almost exclusively in studio decors
(accentuated by stencil color), comes in the spectacular tableau of the public

94. *Notre Dame de Paris*, 1911 (Claude Garry, Stacia Napierkowska)

square, where the heads of spectators in the lower foreground, together with a half-dozen background painted flats (including a hazy image of Notre Dame), create an illusion of unusually deep space for Quasimodo's whipping on an off-center platform.[19] And the scene is capped by a cut-in FS, as Esméralda, having passed through the crowd, offers him a drink of water, in a public display of compassion and near intimacy. Contrasting sharply with Frollo's coolly distant observation of his accomplice, her action sets one conception of Christianity against another, along the schematic axis of gender difference.

The incompleteness of the surviving print's other two reels compromises any close analysis of how their strategies of representation comply with or differ from those of the first reel. What remains of reel two, however, suggests that the "Apple of Eve" sequence is constructed in terms of alternation—initially of exterior and interior reverse-angle shots, as Phébus and Esméralda, followed by Frollo, arrive at the inn. This continues as the couple climb some stairs to one of the inn's rooms while Frollo enters the inn and then, drawing a crucifix dagger, magically ascends a background wall. In the third reel, a series of long-take tableaux (again preceded by intertitles) describe Esméralda's torture and journey in a horse cart back to Notre Dame, her figure now set apart from the others in a stunning white robe. From the moment Quasimodo rushes to her rescue,

307

however, the film shifts to intercutting adjacent spaces and matching exits and entrances, all the while relying less and less on intertitles. Appropriately, for instance, Quasimodo tosses a rope out the bell-tower window, where he has been sequestered, and, in a reverse-angle shot, rappels down the cathedral wall to carry an unconscious Esméralda off to his room. Then Frollo—his agony at her escape revealed in an unusual sidelit MS of him standing at his study window—suddenly spots her on the cathedral ramparts, pursues her to her hiding place, and drags her toward the bed. And when Quasimodo rushes in to save her once more, she has to restrain him from killing Frollo outright. But Quasimodo is no match for the soldiers Frollo soon hires, and Esméralda is carried off to be hung in the same public square, while Frollo watches gloating from the bell-tower window. It is there, in the only other space defined as his own, that Quasimodo attacks his master in revenge. If *Notre Dame de Paris* eschews any possibility of popular resistance (from Esméralda's street people)[20] in order to celebrate its hero and heroine as an "outlaw couple," it does so without sacrificing the anticlericalism central to the "republican" ideology of Hugo's source novel—and still occasionally a strong suit of the prewar historical film.

Pathé's *Le Siege de Calais*—along with *Notre Dame de Paris*, one of the most publicized French historical films in the fall of 1911[21]—deploys strategies similar to both of Capellani's big productions, but according to a slightly different model of narrative construction. Based on an original scenario by Eugène Creissel and Andréani (who also directed), this two-reel film narrates "an incident in the Hundred Year's War" between England and France, when the army of Edward III successfully besieged the French town of Calais in 1347. Much of the shooting was done on location around an unspecified castle, elaborate studio decors were built for Calais's town center, and the harbor set from *Cléopatre* seems to have been resurrected for the English queen's arrival after the siege has succeeded. Perhaps in imitation of the Italian *Dante's Inferno*, the production also used several hundred extras, many of them on horseback in medieval battle gear,[22] making *Le Siege de Calais* one of the first French historical films to exploit the spectacle of mass crowd movement. The scenario insists on strictly following the lines of the well-made play, with the climax coming at midpoint: the battle over the besieged town is decided toward the end of reel one, and the rest of the film is devoted to negotiations over the terms of surrender. What is intriguing, however, is that not only are the falling action and catastrophe developed at much greater length than are the initial three parts, in contrast to *Le Courrier de Lyon*, but the falling action actually seems to begin prior to the break between reels: reel one ends with the townspeople of Calais, already defeated, waiting for Edward III to set his conditions of surrender, in an early example of narrative continuity divorced from and overriding the organizing principle of the reel break.[23]

This film, too, introduces its star actors separately—Henri Etiévant as Edward III, Léontine Massart as Queen Phillipa, and Georges Dorival as Governor of Calais—each framed in MCU against a painted backdrop of royal emblems, like a Holbein portrait. The narrative then begins *in medias res* with an

95. *Le Siege de Calais*, 1911 (production photo)

assault on Calais, articulated in a four-shot sequence of alternation similar to that in the earlier *Jeanne d'Arc*: French soldiers hurl stones and water from the top of the town's walls at the English army massed below, attempting to scale the walls with ladders. Although the assault is repelled, the townspeople are close to starvation and, in a three-shot sequence, send a messenger off to the French king for assistance. This sequence depicting the messenger's descent over the walls creates suspense by starting with an isolated FS as he shinnies down a rope, followed by a FS/LS of the English soldiers marching off along the base of a diagonal wall as he suddenly descends in the foreground, just around a corner, and rushes off undetected. From the French king's camp, with its white tents lining a grassy hilltop, in a lovely deep-space LS tableau, the French army of horsemen and foot soldiers marches off in a matchcut pair of framed movements that carry over into the battle at Villeneuve-la-Hardie. Although an intertitle announces that the French army is repulsed, the battle itself is choreographed in a stunning sequence that matchcuts the mass movements of hundreds of soldiers across four LSs.[24] First, the armies rush at one another from the left and right, until the center line of battle wavers and is obscured; then a horde of soldiers pours straight down two different slopes in succession (toward the camera), the second framed in such a way that they flow toward the right before looping and hurtling off (frame left). Finally they rush in from the right to overrun the French king's encampment. Out of the initial standoff of forces comes a doubly charged movement within the frame—from background to foreground

96. *Le Siege de Calais*, 1911

and top to bottom—whose trajectory curves like a bent bow, its skillfully orchestrated flow of energy a dynamic figure of the English army's power.

The second part of *Le Siege de Calais* then shifts to a much more static mode of representation, relying on a limited number of deep-space LS tableaux. After a two-shot sequence on the town walls, one of which echoes the previous battles in a pan on some marching soldiers, the film is restricted to just three spaces in Calais—the city gate, the public square, the council chamber—and only one of the English king and queen in the harbor. Once Edward III sends off his demands, the townspeople's deliberations move from the public square to the private chamber; only there are the specific details of the surrender terms revealed in an intertitle: to avoid total destruction, Calais must hand over six prominent citizens, each linked to the others by a rope round his neck, with one bearing the keys to the town. In the film's last three tableaux, these six men then move forward repeatedly from public square to city gate to harbor, the slow rhythm of their journey toward expected death in striking contrast to the earlier battle at Villeneuve-la-Hardie. And it is accentuated by the graphic matching of the final deep-space tableaux, as the men first emerge from the background gate to pass between flanked soldiers and exit (frame right) and then pass again through flanked soldiers in the harbor to confront the English king in the left foreground.

Here, in the concluding tableau, as the suspense builds to the catastrophe of the Calais men's execution by beheading, comes an unexpected reversal. Suddenly Queen Phillipa steps forward to appeal for mercy to the king, who not only relents but exits—so that the final image has the Calais men kneeling at the queen's feet in gratitude. This seeming shift in power suggests that the contrasting modes of representation in *Le Siege de Calais* are ultimately organized according to the conventions of gender difference—the "masculine" action of the first part set against the "feminine" stasis of the second, its last tableaux even reminiscent of the earlier *Sémararis*. The queen's act of mediation resolves the long hostility between French and English in a displaced ideological emblem of the 1904 Entente Cordiale, stressing the peaceful consequences of the alliance between the two nations rather than its further incitement to war.

If these three French historical films from 1911 are marked by considerable flexibility in their strategies of representation, just as many titles, at least among those that survive, seem restrictive, even regressive. A good example is the final reel of Pathé's three-part *La Rivale de Richelieu* (1911), which was released in the same month as *Notre Dame de Paris*. This film, scripted and directed by Bourgeois, uses the political figures of Cardinal Richelieu (Auguste Volny) and young Louis XV as the antagonists in a domestic melodrama plot, in which Richelieu has to defend his ward, Julie de Mortimer, and her newlywed husband, Chevalier de Mauprat, against the king's favorite, Baradas. These plot deceptions require frequent intertitles, including several notes, and are played out exclusively within interiors, recorded in AS/LS or FS/LS. And those interiors often consist of little more than dark, heavy drapes and a scattering of props, perhaps the better to focus on the actors' performances. Only two moments in this reel stand out: an intercutting of adjacent spaces as Richelieu toys with the young couple, and the choreography of all the major characters in the final deep-space tableau of the throne room, in a chess game of moves which reunites king and cardinal. Similar strategies mark the surviving fragment of de Morlhon's three-part *Une Intrigue à la cour d'Henry VIII* (1912), which dramatizes Jane Seymour's successful plotting against Anne Boleyn to become Queen of England. This film also relies on large tapestries, painted flats, and a minimum of props, for its interior decors. It uses fewer intertitles, however, and, in the scene where Henry (Volny again) discovers an apparent rendezvous between Anne Boleyn (Roch) and a lover, two different reverse-angle cuts between rooms prepare him for and then snare him in Seymour's trap. In the end, the former queen goes to her execution in a tableau similar to that ending *Notre Dame de Paris*, but in much plainer surroundings and in the company of fewer spectators.

These two Pathé films provide some evidence for Burch's argument that French historical films remained committed to the tableau system of representation because of low production budgets.[25] When Pathé instituted such budget restrictions and how widely they were enforced are not yet clear—*Le Siege de Calais*, released just prior to de Morlhon's film, for instance, certainly was not filmed under such constraints. But the commitment to an older mode of representation did not depend solely on cost-cutting measures, as is evident from at least two Film d'Art productions still extant. Although it is difficult to say whether they are representative of Film d'Art's output, both films closely follow the pattern already established the previous year by *Le Retour d'Ulysse, Héliogable*, and others.[26] Released concurrently with *Notre Dame de Paris* in France, *Madame Sans-Gêne* (1911) generated even more publicity than did its competitor.[27] Not only was Calmettes's three-reel film version drawn from Sardou's celebrated 1893 three-act play of the same title, but Film d'Art convinced Réjane, probably the best light comic actress of her generation, to reprise her starring role from the original stage production and then arranged to release the film immediately after a special revival of the play closed at the Théâtre Réjane. After introductory ASs of the star actors—Réjane, Edmond Duquesne as Napoleon, Dorival as Lefebvre, Jacques Volnys as Comte de Neipperg, and Rablet as Fouché—the story focuses on three episodes in the meteoric career of Madame Sans-Gêne. She begins as an opportunistic laundress in the early days of the Revolution, saving de Neipperg from being killed by a mob in the Tuileries and, at the same time, gaining a husband in Lefebvre (who later becomes a field marshal to Napoleon). Once attached to the emperor's court, she scandalizes Napoleon's sisters but gets on famously with the "great man" himself. Finally, she outwits the emperor, when he discovers an alleged affair between de Neipperg and the empress, by manipulating a series of letters, with the help of Fouché, to demonstrate that the "affair" is no more than an innocent friendship. Although neatly divided according to reel breaks, the film's episodes offer a model of narrative construction somewhat different from other historical films, by having a comic interlude separate the intrigue of reel one from another, more serious intrigue in reel three.

Much like the original play, the film version of *Madame Sans-Gêne* gives particular attention to the spectacle of its studio decors and costumes as well as Réjane's high-spirited performance—which, despite the loss of Sardou's dialogue, confessed Dureau, suffered not in the least.[28] In the initial sequence, for instance, she pauses outside Napoleon's garret apartment door to throw a conspiratorial glance at the camera before stuffing a laundry bill in her bodice, rearranging her basket, unbuttoning her blouse a little, and slowly opening the door—yet she still fails to arouse his interest. Then, during reel two, she offends Napoleon's pretentious sisters with her "vulgar" behavior—coming to the palace dressed sloppily, chatting with the servants, and shaking hands with the guards. With one major exception, the film consistently follows the tableau mode of representation, using long-take LSs to illustrate expository and narrative intertitles. That exception occurs in reel one, when Madame Sans-Gêne protects de Neipperg and wins Lefebvre's respect and love. The sequence begins with a deep-space FS/LS of a street, through which Napoleon passes in a procession from foreground to background, in front of her laundry shop (frame right). Then, in a ninety-degree shift in camera position, another FS/LS displays the shop interior, with the procession visible through a door and window in the background, as Lefebvre stops by briefly to get her consent to be his fiancée. The sequence alternates between these two spaces until de Neipperg appears,

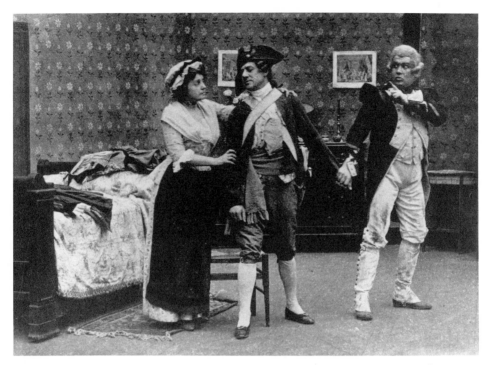

97. *Madame Sans-Gêne*, 1911 (production photo: Gabrielle Réjane, Jacques Volnys, Georges Dorival)

and Madame Sans-Gêne hides him in a room to the left of her shop interior—which, when Lefebvre returns, in a further alternation of spaces, turns out to be her bedroom. And, instead of a rival, he finds a wounded man and agrees to aid in his escape. The third reel then reworks this intrigue, after Napoleon and Madame Sans-Gêne (in a night scene, with the added detail of a fireplace glowing in the left foreground) surprise de Neipperg apparently about to enter the empress's bedroom. Here, instead of intercutting adjacent spaces, however, the film simply alternates between the emperor's study and the empress's bedroom, as Madame Sans-Gêne and Fouché orchestrate the timing of four inserted letters, which restore the illusion of everyone occupying his or her proper social position. And, in the final tableau, as Réjane prepares to exit, she smiles coyly and turns away, slyly flouncing the train of her gown. If *Madame Sans-Gêne* offers a comic fantasy of upward social mobility, as a result of the Revolution, its central figure also glances knowingly, yet gently, at the caricatured "opportunists" making the most, for themselves, of the Third Republic.

Buoyed by *Madame Sans-Gêne*'s success, Film d'Art finally persuaded Bernhardt, after the supposed disaster of her unreleased *La Tosca*, to appear in a film version of *La Dame aux camélias* (1912).[29] This celebrated Alexander Dumas fils melodrama had been frequently revived ever since its 1852 stage production, most significantly by Bernhardt herself in the 1880s and 1890s.[30] Now nearing the end of her theatrical career, she reprised the role of Camille de Gautier once more, along with Lou Tellegen as Armand Duval, in a condensed, two-reel version of the five-act play, directed again by Calmettes. The first reel traces the progress of Camille and Armand's passionate affair, which has the effect of transforming her, and concludes by introducing Duval's father, who sets out to separate the lovers. Convinced of the father's appeals to morality as a "sacred law" of secular French society, at the beginning of the second reel, Camille abandons Armand to return to her old ways, as the mistress of the Comte de Varville, which provokes a violent outburst by the spurned lover at a prominent social gathering and a subsequent duel. Realizing that Camille has sacrificed her health to honor her pledge, the older Duval finally allows Armand to return to the stricken woman and seek her pardon, and their reconciliation comes just before she dies in his arms. In the film version, therefore, the play's third act begins near the end of reel one and carries over into reel two, the reel break further disguised by similar studio decors for Duval's and Camille's drawing rooms, both of which look out on background gardens. And as a further consequence, the second reel is packed with three climactic confrontations.

In its mode of representation, *La Dame aux camélias* is perhaps the most regressive of all surviving Film d'Art productions. Essentially, the film comprises just eleven FS/LS tableaux, all but two of which—brief shots of the entrance to Camille's townhouse and the dueling site—are shot in studio decors, probably designed in imitation of the well-known (at least to Parisians) stage sets. Moreover, nearly all are introduced by narrative intertitles, and more than half include further inserted intertitles and letters. Not once is there an instance of intercutting or cutting-in to a close shot. The highly static quality of these long-take tableaux may well have been determined by an impulse to preserve a famous theatrical performance on film—for Bernhardt acted before the camera, she admitted at the time,[31] exactly as she would have in the theater, even to the point of speaking all her lines (which went unrecorded). Yet the strategy was also the result of her deteriorating physical condition (one leg eventually would be amputated in 1915), which severely restricted her movement. Still, a certain stasis is quite appropriate to this story of frustrated passion and desire for personal happiness. The confining spaces of the various bourgeois drawing rooms and salons serve as splendid cages for the characters, giving a material existence to the rigid moral authority ultimately governing their action. The effect of these enclosed hothouse spaces is to make even more poignant the emotional gestures of defiance and resistance—from Camille, all alone, clinging to a background curtain after Armand's departure in the first scene to his public display of anger, flinging his gambling money in her face just before the final scene. And those gestures culminate in the famous "dance of death" at the end, where, as they finally embrace, her face hidden by his head, the handkerchief flutters and drops from her hand resting on his shoulder, her arm slowly falls limp, and, as she herself begins to fall back, he catches her, smoothly pivoting in a 180-degree turn, and lays her gently on the bedroom floor.[32] The hesitancy that once marked the play—between endorsing or critiquing the moral authority of a pa-

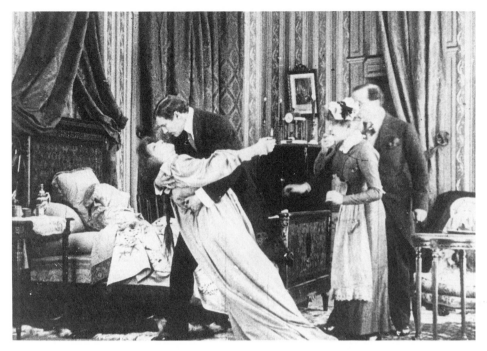

98. *La Dame aux camélias*, 1912 (Sarah Bernhardt, Lou Tellegen)

triarchal bourgeois social order—is dispelled, by the time of the film, in an all-too-familiar spectacle of sentimental pathos.

Shortly after the successful release of *La Dame aux camélias*,[33] Bernhardt appeared on stage in Emile Moreau's *La Reine Elisabeth*, which ran for only twelve performances in Paris, making it the worst failure of her long career. To recoup her financial losses, Bernhardt agreed to reenact the role on screen for Histrionic Films, in a special Franco-Anglo-American production that was filmed in London and premiered at the Lyceum Theater in Chicago on 12 July 1912.[34] Thereafter, *Queen Elizabeth* toured the United States and elsewhere, with great success[35]—accumulating much of the capital that would later finance Zukor's Famous Players—until Eclipse finally released it in France on 31 January 1913.[36] The film focuses exclusively on the legendary relationship between Elizabeth and Essex (Tellegen), who incites her jealousy by having an affair with the Countess of Nottingham (Mlle Romain), whose husband, the Earl of Nottingham (Maxudian) then frames Essex with a counterfeit letter. Essentially a melodrama of intersecting, duplicitous love triangles, the scenario is constructed according to the conventions of the well-made play. The first reel establishes Essex as the Queen's favorite in a scene that includes a brief staging of Shakespeare's *The Merry Wives of Windsor* (Falstaff escapes detection for an amorous dalliance by hiding in a laundry basket), but it concludes with a fortune-teller prophesying her unhappiness and his doom. The second reel works out the intrigue between

Essex and the Countess and Earl of Nottingham, climaxing in a public court scene where the queen confronts Essex with the incriminating evidence (from which, unlike Falstaff, he cannot escape). The third then stages a series of spectacular moments as the predicted catastrophe falls on Essex, the countess, and eventually the queen herself.

For the most part, *Queen Elizabeth* adheres to the older tableau mode of representation. First of all, the producers insisted on using the dozen or more set decors of the Paris theatrical production, along with its "dresses, armor, and furniture." And the costumes contributed greatly to the emphasis on spectacle—the last one worn by Bernhardt, for instance, is a long ermine robe "with sleeves so widely bell-shaped that when her arms are horizontally extended, the bottom of the bell reaches the knees."[37] Second, the narrative is fully articulated in no less than twenty-six intertitles, most of them quite lengthy, so that the action within the FS/LS tableaux largely illustrates a set of prior verbal texts. Moreover, some of the intertitles make a claim for historical accuracy, particularly those exhibiting Elizabeth's "authentic" signature on two documents, privileged in CU: Essex's Irish commission and his "death warrant" (both preserved in the British Museum). The film does, however, deviate slightly from this discursive mode and, more important, makes an intriguing shift in the gendered nature of its spectacle. The one significant change occurs in the scene where Nottingham discovers his wife and Essex alone together—in an alternation of interior spaces that show him looking through a curtained doorway, from one side and then the other. His point-of-view image of the illicit couple is then transformed into words, in an unusual AS where the counterfeit letter gets written, and, in the very next scene, the queen establishes the apparent "truth" of the correspondence.

This climaxes in two scenes of spectacle in the final reel, in which Essex becomes an object of display, but of a different sort, for the queen. In the first, she stands with her back to the camera in the foreground, watching through a full-length window as Essex, in the background, passes from left to right toward the tower; as the executioner comes on behind him, she orders the curtains drawn—so that the whole scene appears as a theatrical construction staged by the queen herself. In the second, now dressed all in white, she enters a tower chamber to view Essex's body prominently laid out in the foreground. The last scene then tops this exhibition of the male body (for an "unseeing" woman's eyes) with a final clou of spectacle in which the queen almost literally takes Essex's place in staging her own death. Before an enormous pile of cushions centered just in front of the throne, Bernhardt stands unsteadily, surrounded by servants, sips from an offered cup of wine, shakes her head at her image reflected in a mirror, stretches her arms out, suddenly clutches at her breast, staggers, recovers momentarily, and then pitches face forward into the cushions. "Sic transit gloria mundi," concludes the final intertitle, as if to confirm the "justice" of this self-construction in which the dead woman becomes the proper object of spectacle.[38]

In its subsequent historical films, Eclipse continued to exploit the cultural

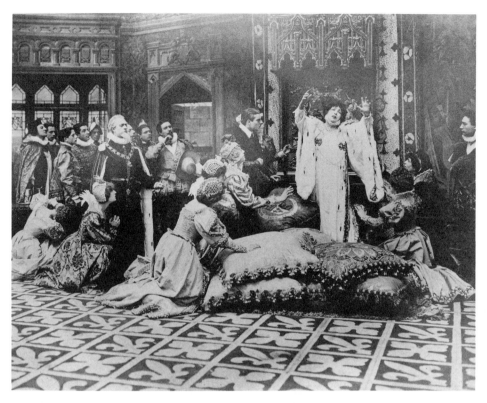

99. *Queen Elizabeth*, 1912 (production photo: Sarah Bernhardt)

capital afforded by its ties to England. Yet this led Desfontaines and Mercanton to extremes of "theatricality" in mounting *Shylock* (1913), the last of the company's Shakespeare films.[39] This three-reel adaptation streamlines *The Merchant of Venice* to focus on the contract binding Antonio (Joubé) to Shylock (Harry Bauer) and the romance of Bassanio (Jean Hervé) and Portia (Pépa Bonafé).[40] Except for a brief tour of Venice by gondola, in the opening reel, the film's dramatic conflicts are confined to studio decors, recorded consistently in FS/LS, and there are only eight of these. The first reel has three, moving from one of Antonio's rooms to the street in front of Shylock's house and then inside, where he borrows three thousand ducats so that Bassanio can court Portia. The second reel includes three different interiors in Portia's house—for her meeting with Bassanio, the casket scene (where he chooses the right one), and their wedding. The last reel then is restricted to the climactic court scene—where Shylock wins his pound of flesh from Antonio, but Portia (disguised as a lawyer) gets him to admit that he cannot take it without spilling blood—and the final scene at Portia's house. What this means is that the film is constructed of exceptionally long takes—the casket and trial scenes each run ten minutes or longer—which follow one another en bloc. However, they are all interrupted frequently by intertitles, many of them lines of dialogue (the casket scene, for instance, has fourteen), which only accentuate each scene's highly static quality. Consequently, in the tradition of French "classical" theater, *Shylock* relies heavily on the verbal text of its source play as well as the performances of its actors. And, partly because of the crowded staging and uniformly dark costumes,[41] Bauer alone stands out, but in an unwaveringly anti-Semitic portrayal of the Jew as an object of ridicule and even contempt. Antonio, in particular, taunts him throughout—for instance, placing his foot condescendingly on the money-lender's chest of ducats. And the final scene endorses this anti-Semitism by making Shylock literally grovel before Portia, begging for the principal on his loan, and, then, by ending with a saccharine intertitle—"the famous lovers of Shakespeare live 'happily ever after' "—which blithely erases the origins of their own blood money.

The weight of respect for its own cultural capital continued to fall, perhaps in conjunction with reduced production budgets, on Pathé's attempts to turn classics of the French theater into "marvels of cinematographic art." This is especially evident in de Morlhon's 1912 adaptation of a masterpiece of French tragedy, Racine's *Britannicus*, whose subject might be said to epitomize the notion, so dear to the Nationalist Revival movement, that France was the country best suited to wear the mantle of Greco-Roman classicism. Dispossessed of the Roman throne by his mother, Agrippine (Jeanne Grumbach), in favor of Nero (Hervé), Britannicus (Joubé) seeks to marry Junie (Mlle Sylvie), a descendant of the family of Augustus. Attracted to the young woman himself and fearing a conspiracy, Nero, with the aid of Britannicus's treacherous tutor, Narcisse (Signoret), threatens the couple, but relents, when Agrippine intervenes, and then finally poisons them both at the wedding feast. Shot exclusively in painted-flat studio decors, this film, too, is comprised chiefly of AS/LS or FS/LS tableaux.[42] Although the acting style tends toward the declamatory, the seasoned dramatist and theater director consistently uses the deep space of the interiors in order to arrange the characters to advantage. Individual characters frequently come "downstage" to AS, particularly in corner foreground positions—for instance, in the opening scene, setting Britannicus apart from Nero being crowned by Agrippine and, in the next, setting Narcisse apart from Britannicus and his friends, on whom he is spying for Nero.

This "theatrical" mode of representation in *Britannicus*, however, is framed within a narrative construction somewhat similar to that of *Notre Dame de Paris*. The action divides into three relatively equal parts, which apparently correspond to reel breaks; not only is the dramatic conflict reworked from one part to another, but various structural parallels enhance the film's requisite unity and coherence. Part one, for instance, is constructed largely in terms of alternating spaces—the throne room and the chamber of the "conspirators"—with, first, Britannicus and, then, Narcisse moving between them. It culminates, after he has shown Britannicus's letter (meant for Agrippine) to Nero, in Narcisse's false report back to Britannicus—conveyed through a dissolve to him delivering the letter to Agrippine, who promptly tears it up. Part two varies this pattern, once Nero has had his soldiers seize Junie, by intercutting three separate spaces, and then elliptically repeating them in sequence. In the first, Nero, Britannicus, and

Junie are brought together in her "prison" room, where she threatens to commit suicide. Immediately thereafter, a letter from Agrippine to Britannicus (in an economical cut from one space to another, she literally replaces her own female messenger in the foreground) brings both mother and son to the prison room, where she now protects the couple from Nero and Narcisse. Part three briefly alternates spaces again, through the circulation of Nero's deceptive letter (inviting the couple to the wedding feast), culminating in a final LS of the banquet hall—where Narcisse has already tested the poison on an old woman. At the crucial moment, a cut-in FS (the only one in the film) now isolates Nero preparing the poisoned wine cup. Finally, once Britannicus has drunk the wine and collapsed in the foreground, followed by Junie (who chooses to die with him), the other characters come forward to frame the dead lovers in a concluding frieze composition: Nero on one side, Agrippine on the other, and Narcisse in the center, admiring his devious handiwork.[43]

Respect for an iconic tradition still weighed on French biblical films as well, but without demanding anywhere near such a strict adherence to the tableau style. The fragment that survives from Gaumont's *Androclès* (1912), for instance, begins and ends with what look like "before" and "after" shots—in one, Androclès is being whipped by his cruel master and, in the other, the two men happily join Nero in patting a very sedate lion. Between these conventional FS/LS tableaux, however, are two interrelated shots that display some spectacular lighting effects.[44] In the first, a strong sidelight defines a half-dozen despondent figures scattered around a dungeon floor, one of whom is Androclès who gets up and goes to the background, pulls aside a curtain in the darkness to reveal a lit area beyond, and exits in silhouette. In the next, he enters another dark area, more faintly sidelit, and moves toward a strongly lit arched stairway in the background, where he has to fight his way past a guard. Pathé's *Le Mort de Saül* (1912), by contrast, eschews such selectively directed artificial lighting to suggest its central character's psychological as well as physical condition by other, more conventional means.[45] This film begins with a half-dozen FS/LSs alternating between adjacent spaces on two sides of a city wall, much as in *Moïse sauvé des eaux*, as King Saul, in search of David, besieges Keilah with an army. And it ends with the Philistines, with whom David has aligned himself, routing that army in battle, killing one of the king's sons, after which Saul commits suicide. Although this climactic battle is handled quite summarily, Saul's journey to the Witch of Endor to seek the prophetic outcome of the battle is given considerable attention. And this middle section of the film reworks some of the strategies of *Caïn et Abel*. A pan, for instance, follows Saul and two soldiers across a mountainous rock ledge, and then he goes off alone into the witch's cave, where she magically produces a supernatural figure to deliver the bad news. What is interesting here is that the soldiers waiting outside the cave can quickly move inside when they hear the king cry out, but Saul's journey is represented in a special "bridge" shot—a MS/FS of him crawling anxiously forward in a narrow rock cleft—as if to emphasize his increasing sense of paranoia and entrapment.

Pathé's new version of *La Vie et la Passion de Notre Seigneur Jésus-Christ*

319

(1914), directed by Maître, also generally adheres to the tableau style; yet, while extending the 1907 film in some ways, it also offers several distinctive changes.[46] Although still divided into four parts, Maître's film is more than double the length of the earlier version, comprising no less than seventy-five tableaux. Those tableaux consist mostly of LSs, FS/LSs, and a few AS/LSs—with the exception, again, of cut-in MSs of Jesus (presented to the people by Pilate) and the Saint Veronica icon. They are shot in studio decors as well as on location, the latter of which often include painted-flat palm trees and cacti that blend in surprisingly well, once Pathé's stencil color is added to the image. Dissolves and superimpositions continue to produce the frequent supernatural effects—from the angel appearing to Mary (sporting the same film-reel halo as before) to Jesus' transfiguration and ascension as a figure encircled by painted-flat clouds and golden rays. And pans occasionally follow characters from one space to another, as in Joseph and Mary's initial journey through the streets of Bethlehem. One notable difference in this version, however, lies in its greater claim to verisimilitude. The acting overall is unusually restrained, compared not only to the earlier version but to historical films such as *Britannicus*—for instance, the poignantly slow reawakening of Jaire's daughter. Certain sections also expand into a sequence of shots that matchcut a character's movement smoothly through several spaces—as, in the opening scene, where Mary journeys to and from a well. And some tableaux seem to extend into an actualité deep space—for instance, the interior of Joseph and Mary's house where, through the background doorway and window, several woodsmen pass among the trees. Yet another difference stems from the film's effort to produce a heightened sense of spectacle.[47] This is most obvious in the long-take LSs of literally hundreds of people trekking down a hillside, among whom are the magi and shepherds. But the most impressive achievement comes in the three LS tableaux illustrating the "Flight into Egypt," where the small figures of Joseph and Mary (again matchcut) cross a flat, empty stretch of sand, pass two giant pyramids in the desert, and come to rest against a huge painted flat of the sphinx. A similar sense of expansive space then recurs in Jesus' journey to Golgotha, where several HA LSs of the procession up a desert hillside culminate in a reverse-angle LS of a bare, sandy ridge with two empy crosses standing left and right, as Jesus, dragging his own cross forward, is driven up and over the crest with flailing whips.

As these biblical films suggest, not every French historical film produced after 1911 was trapped within the tableau system of representation. A fine example is Gaumont's *La Fille du Margrave* (1912), which narrates the attempt by two lovers, Geneviève (Andreyor) and Christian (Jean Ayme), to elope, after her father, the Margrave of Hess, has refused his request for her hand in marriage. Directed by Feuillade, this two-reel film is remarkable, first of all, for its relative lack of intertitles—there are only four to accompany the surviving first reel's seventeen shots.[48] Instead, like many other Gaumont films, this one calls attention—duly noted by *Moving Picture World*[49]—to the pictorial quality of its images. In the second shot of a garden, for instance, Geneviève approaches from background to foreground, in near silhouette, for her clandestine meeting with

Christian. Later, in a LS of the chateau exterior, as if to accentuate her despair, she sits reading in a high window, her small figure reflected on the water of the moat below. The couple's flight, however, is narrated in an extended sequence of a dozen shots (without intertitles), within which an alternating series of exterior and interior shots sets up their eventual capture. In Geneviève's room are two maids (she herself is absent), whose reaction to a sound offscreen prompts a cut to the LS chateau exterior, where Christian wades across a shallow dam toward a background window. In the subsequent shots, the women intercept the note he tosses in, he crosses back over the dam and, unaware of the betrayal to come, blows a kiss toward the window, and the women, after reading the note, leave it on a table for Geneviève to find. In order to sustain suspense, the next four shots keep the characters at so great a distance that it is difficult to distinguish the woman who signals with a handkerchief from a chateau window, and then comes out of a background doorway, from the one who, standing beside another more centered arch, signals to a background group of soldiers to disperse. Only when two figures meet in silhouette at the open grillework of a gate and come forward, sculpted by a strong sidelight, is it certain that the lovers are indeed acting on their plan to elope. And, in the very next shot, on the bridge leading over the moat, the tipped-off soldiers close in, cutting off their escape.

The most accomplished prewar French historical film was also the longest and most ambitious of the 1912–1913 season, *Les Misérables* (1912). And it was highly successful not only in France, where it opened in December, but across the world, including the United States, where it toured the following spring.[50] The length of this SCAGL blockbuster was phenomenal—nearly 3,500 meters or four hours of screen time—even when that was cut by one-fourth in the American version. Essentially, Capellani adapted Hugo's sprawling 1862 novel into a much admired miniseries format of four, more or less equal parts or episodes, each of which was released in France as a one-hour "feature" over four consecutive weeks.[51] Part one covers the early years of Jean Valjean (Henry Krauss) as a petty thief in southern France, where he first encounters Javert (Etiévant) as a jailor at the Toulon prison before escaping in 1817. Part two takes up his successful life as a businessman named Madeleine in the northern town of Montreuil-sur-mer, where he rescues Fantine (Marie Venture) from destitution and imprisonment in a confrontation with Javert who is now the district prosecutor. After he is forced to leave town and Fantine dies, part three focuses on her young daughter, Cosette (Marie Fromet), whom Madeleine has promised to raise and protect—which he does first by paying for her keep with the Thénardiers (Milo and Nau), who turn out to be a pair of unscrupulous Paris innkeepers, but then, when Javert tracks him down again, by rescuing her and placing her in a convent, whose gardener's name, Fauchevelant, he takes as his own. Part four is situated during the 1832 rebellion in Paris, which serves as a context for a love triangle plot involving Cosette, a young student radical named Marius (Gabriel de Gravone), and the older Thénardier daughter, Eponine (Mistinguett). This time Fauchevelant saves Javert from being killed as a spy, rescues the wounded Marius from the barricades—where Eponine sacrifices her life,

100. *Les Misérables*, 1912 (Marie Ventura, Henry Krauss)

along with an orphan boy named Gavroche—and eludes both Javert and Thénardier in the underground sewers, after which his nemesis, finally stricken with
remorse, commits suicide. At the end, the young couple are reunited and the
old man discloses his real identity, just before dying in peace.

According to SCAGL correspondence, the production budget for *Les Misérables* was indeed quite low. It cost a mere 50,000 francs to make, which averaged out to about fifteen francs per meter of negative, and one reason for that
may have been the huge permission fee (180,000 francs) SCAGL had to pay the
Hugo estate.[52] Yet this budget constraint seems not to have compromised
Capellani all that much, especially in the first two or three episodes of the film.
The filmmaker and his crew, headed by cameraman Louis Forestier, apparently
aimed for a strong sense of verisimilitude, which is conspicuous in certain early
scenes—for instance, the detailed studio decors and props for the cabin Valjean
shares with his ailing mother, the Toulon prison cell, or the priest's spartan
quarters where he seeks refuge after his prison escape. And it characterizes as
well the scenes where Madeleine discovers little Cosette on the outskirts of
Paris—struggling to carry a water bucket up a long hill and showing him her
straw-strewn "cell" of a room at the Thénardiers. This sometimes combines
with poignant moments of restrained acting—as in Krauss's subtle registers of
desire and doubt when Valjean goes to steal the silverware of the priest who has
befriended him, in Ventura's despair at having to cut and sell her hair so that

Fantine and her daughter can survive, or in Fromet's fascinated gaze (as Cosette lays down the oversized broom she is using to sweep the inn interior and rests her head in her hand on a table) at the doll the young Eponine is playing with. Yet there also are moments when they fail, moments that a low budget does not entirely explain. Etiévant's makeup toward the end, for instance, almost turns Javert into a simian, subhuman grotesque. Painted flats are still used extensively, and they sometimes jar in the shift from exteriors shot on location to studio interiors—as in the obviously painted trees visible through Javert's prison office window. And, although mammoth and multiplaned, these studio decors tend to "flatten" the climactic barricade scene at the end—for the site of the street battle, the rue Saint-Antoine, was reconstructed in Vincennes in the open air.[53]

What is most remarkable about *Les Misérables*, however, is the way it recovers the representational flexibility of Capellani's earlier *Le Courrier de Lyon*. Part one demonstrates just how wide-ranging, and perhaps also how necessary, the film's strategies are, given that its three reels include only a dozen intertitles. The theft that sends Valjean to prison, for instance, is narrated elliptically in a sequence of four shots: a LS of a bakery in front of which he stops and comes to the foreground to look around, a cut-in MS of him breaking the window and reaching in, a ninety-degree shift to another MS of the interior as his hand grabs a loaf of bread, and an AS of the owner inside (who happens to be black) noticing the theft in an eyeline match. His escape from prison, likewise, is represented through several different changes in framing. In a FS/LS of their crowded cell, Valjean and four others determine by lot who it is that will break out, and a cut-in MCU reveals the small piece of wire concealed in a coin that he uses (as the camera tilts down) to sever the chain of his leg irons. An alternation between him silhouetted at the cell window bars in MS and the guards marching through the prison gate in LS then precedes a sequence that matchcuts his movement through several spaces, one of which cuts from a HA LS of him using a rope to scale down the wall near the gate to an AS as he reaches the ground. Finally, the scene at the priest's residence deploys a slightly different pattern of frame changes. A pan traces Valjean and the priest through one bedroom to another room where the escaped convict is to sleep, establishing the adjacent spaces needed to narrate his theft later that night. For that, the sequence begins in AS as he awakens in the single-source lighting from a background window and cuts out to LS as he gets up; in the priest's bedroom, the pattern is reversed in a cut-in from LS to AS as Valjean opens the cupboard where the silver is stored. Back in the other room in LS, he stuffs the booty into a rucksack and, in a 180-degree reverse-angle cut to an exterior FS, climbs out the window and flees. Once he is caught by gendarmes and returned to the priest, the latter forgives him and insists that he keep what he has taken in several long-take tableaux, which allow Krauss to register Valjean's astonishment and gratitude—for the stolen silver will provide the basis for his later business success.

The rest of the film's episodes extend and vary the representational strategies invoked in the first, much as in Capellani's earlier films. Part two, for instance, comes to a climax in the famous "Tempest" scene that prompts Madeleine to

101. *Les Misérables*, 1912 (production photo: Henry Krauss)

confess his criminal identity in court and leave Montreuil-sur-mer for Paris. That scene, at least according to Pierre Trimbach, who served as an assistant to Forestier, culminated in a special clou of subjective intensity—a CU of Madeleine's agonized face with a matted-in image of his earlier trial embedded within and filling the space of his forehead.[54] The subsequent court scene includes an external variant of that internal image, in the cut-in MCU of whiplash scars on the ex-convict's bared upper arm. Part three, by contrast, uses several patterns of alternation to reach its conclusion. When Javert tracks Madeleine down to the old Marais district of Paris, he takes a room directly above that of his prey, which is revealed through a sequence of intercutting prompted by the sound cue of a knocked-over stool. This leads then to a sustained sequence of parallel editing as Madeleine and Cosette are pursued through the narrow streets by Javert and several policemen and into a dead-end alley that requires the former convict to draw on his scaling skills again. In a loose POV-shot sequence that neatly reverses the power of surveillance, he now watches from above as the police press on with their ineffectual search. Part four repeats certain patterns from before—most notably in the pans that follow Eponine from the Thénardiers' new quarters to Marius's room next door, and back, and the 180-degree reverse-angle cuts from his room to the balcony outside, where she slowly paces in LS, after discovering that Marius loves Cosette and not her. If this final section relies more extensively than before on long-take LSs and tends to drag somewhat—only the flight through the sewers picks up the pace, yet surprisingly without the aid of any special lighting effects—*Les Misérables* concludes with aptly contrasting emblems for its two central antagonists. Although Javert's suicidal plunge into the Seine ends in the near empty shot of a circle widening on the surface of the water, Valjean dies in the company of Cosette and Marius and in conjunction with the background dream vision of the old priest blessing the reciprocated generosity and sacrifice that have marked the life of his "disciple." If Capellani's adaptation of Hugo rearticulates the latter's republican ideology, it does so by almost resacralizing the construction of the good bourgeois family and couple.

At this juncture in the writing of early cinema history, *Les Misérables* can be seen as the culmination of the early French historical film. For one thing, it caps a long line of work that stretches—to single out only Capellani titles—from *Un Drame à Venise* through *Jeanne d'Arc* and *La Mort du Duc d'Enghien* to *Le Courrier de Lyon* and *Notre Dame de Paris*. Moreover, it deploys nearly the full spectrum of available representational strategies in what was considered at the time a model of narrative construction for the feature-length film. And, in its adapation of Hugo's famous novel, it exploits the cultural capital of the French literary heritage in a highly exportable commodity on the world cinema market. A quite different tradition within the genre, however, is evident in *La Dame aux camélias*, *Queen Elizabeth*, or *Britannicus*. Much more restricted in their mode of representation, these films tend to privilege the spectacle of richly detailed set decors and costumes as well as the finely choreographed performances of individual actors or stars, within long-take LS tableaux.[55] And they often do so within the tightly unified format of the well-made play with its catastrophe finale. Perhaps the epitome of this tradition, which reached back at least to *Epopée napoléonienne* and *Faust et Marguerite*, came in Pathé's *Néron et Aggripine* (1914), whose celebration of the Greco-Roman heritage to which France saw itself as sole heir, was mounted in just "four sumptuous studio decors"[56]—the action of its six episodes choreographed according to a specially arranged score.[57] It is this tradition, which hardly escaped harsh criticism at the time, rather than that summed up in *Les Misérables*, which mistakenly has come down to us as representative of early French cinema. That so many French historical films have not survived, however, makes even this attempt to counter received history a hypothesis in need of further evidence and argument.[58] Perhaps that will come in the discovery of lost films such as Pathé's *Les Mystères de Paris* (1912), Les Grands Films Populaires' *Le Bossu* (1913), or Film d'Art's *Les Trois Mousquetaires* (1913) as well as in the restoration of Gaumont titles like *L'Agonie de Byzance* (1913) and *L'Aiglon* (1914).[59] Yet, whatever the case, during the two years prior to the Great War, it is clear from the weekly listings of French releases that the future of the French cinema did not necessarily lie in the historical film genre. Even within the feature-length format, the French cinema increasingly favored contemporary subjects.

Life As It Is: In and Out of Fashion

During this three-year period before the war, French films with contemporary melodrama subjects differed from their historical film counterparts in several ways. First, they ranged quite widely across the spectrum of representational modes, tending much more readily, in fact, to exploit a mixture of mise-en-scène, framing, and editing strategies. Second, they played an equally important role in the emergence of the multiple-reel film, but with narrative structures less reliant on the division and trajectory of the well-made play. Yet large numbers of films, perhaps following the practice of the American cinema industry, continued to be produced in the single-reel format. Third, both Gaumont and Pathé seized on the marketing strategy of the series, initially developed for the single-reel comic and detective films, in order to further standardize the production and distribution of these films. Finally, differences in the choice of subjects grew more pronounced and, in some sense, divided along class lines. That is perhaps most sharply drawn if one compares Gaumont's initial films in the *Scènes de la vie telle qu'elle est* series or the various adaptations of Zola novels to Pathé's *Scènes de la vie cruelle* series or de Morlhon's distinctly bourgeois melodramas. Conclusions about these contemporary melodrama films, however, have to be as qualified as those about the historical films. Again, the survival rate of film prints is low, and uneven as well. There is almost nothing still extant from Film d'Art and Eclipse, and only a few titles remain from Eclair.[60] Not unexpectedly, a greater number of Pathé titles survive, but there are even more from Gaumont, so that evaluating Feuillade's and Perret's work for the company can be done with some degree of certainty.

As before, the French cinema industry continued to produce a few films that either remained firmly committed to the tableau mode of representation or repeated what was pretty much standard practice, although with some variation. Perhaps the most surprising of these films is Pathé's *Victimes de l'alcool* (1911), directed by Bourgeois, which was released in three reels shortly after *Le Courrier de Lyon*. Essentially, this film, like its 1902 predecessor, is an adaptation of the moralizing nineteenth-century melodramas chronicling the disastrous consequences of a family man who falls prey to the vice of alcoholism. And it relies, even more than does the 1909 *L'Assomoir*, on a restricted number of studio decors, enframing the action consistently in long-take tableaux, many of them introduced by intertitles. The steady downward trajectory of this well-known story is mapped according to four class-specific spaces, beginning with the emblematic bourgeois dining room, where the contented family is seated around the table and served by a maid. Six months later, they are living in a smaller apartment, where several formerly segregated actions now occur in one central room—for instance, the mother does put-out work on a sewing machine at the table while a child sleeps in a nearby bed. Eight years later, their living space has become a decrepit garret room, where the mother and child (who has contracted tuberculosis) commit suicide, which, in the final tableau, sends the father, raving mad, to the straw-strewn cell of an asylum.

Other representational and narrative choices, however, turn *Victimes de l'alcool* into something more than either an "old-fashioned" melodrama or a misguided "high art" film emulating the historical drama.[61] The actors are drawn, for instance, not from Pathé's regular stable of stars (out of the Paris theaters), but from the faubourg theaters—in an attempt presumably to give the characters a degree of authenticity.[62] And the waist-level camera is positioned slightly closer than usual to the action (perhaps in imitation of Vitagraph films) so that the characters are constantly moving into MS, which tends to make the interior spaces all that more claustrophobic and to accentuate the violence within the family once the father begins drinking. In an interesting ideological move, the film also makes the father a white-collar worker rather than an industrial worker or artisan, shifting the locus of what the French press usually described as a working-class social problem.[63] Instead, it is the drunken man's sober, hardworking brother-in-law who is the proletarian and who does what little he can to shore up his sister's family's condition. And, in a blatant pun, Bourgeois gives his own name to the doctor who prescribes some medicine for the sick child. In the end, then, *Victimes de l'alcool* endorses the social order by aligning the bourgeois with the proletariat and congratulating both for their moral behavior, while at the same time exploiting the "fear of falling" of the newly emergent white-collar class.

A range of single-reel films also narrate familiar melodrama stories, some of whose characters succeed in overcoming their disabilities. Eclipse's *The Tie That Binds* (1911), for instance, makes its alcoholic father an artisan who sinks to stealing the little money given to his wife by the Children's Aid Society, after which he reforms and resumes his role as the requisite foundation of his family. This moralistic story is recounted in just a dozen FS/LS tableaux, with two exceptions—the MS/FS that emphasizes his dedication to a new job in a small machine shop, and the conventional emblematic tableau of the restored family. Eclair's *Le Coeur et les yeux* (1911) tells the story of a widow and her young daughter who are threatened with destitution after the mother's accidental blinding; by coincidence, they meet a doctor who performs an operation to restore the woman's sight and then marries her. Directed probably by Chautard, this film is much more varied in its strategies of representation. A cut-in MS in the opening scene, for instance, accentuates the blinding from a benzine bottle, and a later, matching HA MCU (framed in an iris mask) presents a condensed version of the restorative operation. The final long-take AS/LS, which returns to the very room where the blinding occurred, then uses the device of a background mirror to unite the couple—for the doctor behaves so shyly that only the reflection of his blown kiss, as he is about to exit, lets the woman literally see his intentions.

Other single-reel melodramas are less sanguine. Bourgeois's *Le Démon du jeu* (1911) focuses on the vice of gambling, within a strictly bourgeois milieu. Here, a young dandy is forced to steal from his own family to cover his gambling debts, loses the money he has stolen, and is refused forgiveness at the bedside of his dying father. Much like *Victimes de l'alcool*, this Pathé film traces a steady, inexorable descent to catastrophe, within a limited number of AS/LS interiors. Yet Bourgeois also makes some effort to heighten the young man's emotional state. The deep-space spectacle of the gambling den—which stretches into a raised adjacent room in the background, with a painted perspective ceiling—gives it an attractive atmosphere not only for the young gambler but for the spectator as well. And the desperate, climactic robbery in his father's office is intensified by single-source arc lighting from a side window. Finally, Gaumont's *L'Amour qui tue* (1911), directed by Perret, traces the physical decline of a Mlle Gréville (Andreyor) whose love for an adventurer named Pierre-Jacques (Perret) is thwarted by her parents because of his illegitimate origins. This story is narrated in just three scenes and is confined to a half-dozen bourgeois interiors (supposedly near Nice), consistently recorded in FS/LS or AS/LS. The scene in which the young woman, now suffering from tuberculosis, discovers that her former suitor will be attending a local ball and persuades her parents to let her accompany them there culminates, however, in a MCU of her alone before a mirror—in which her pretense of recovery is exposed in a desperately drawn, pale face. The ball scene then climaxes in another kind of pretense after she suddenly collapses and dies in a stunned Pierre-Jacques's arms. In a moment of grand guignol irony, he "graciously" greets the smiling dancers (including the Grévilles) coming out of the background ballroom and exiting frame right, all the while shielding her body (frame left) from their sight.

Roughly at the same time that Pathé was releasing *Le Courrier de Lyon* and *Victimes de l'alcool*, Gaumont was announcing a new series of films to be scripted and directed by Feuillade and organized not around a single character or star but around an ensemble of actors playing different roles from film to film. The general title of the series—perhaps modeled on Vitagraph's *Scènes de la vie réelle*[64]—was simply *Scènes de la vie telle qu'elle est.*

> These scenes are intended to be slices of life. If they are interesting, even compelling, it is because of the quality of virtue which emerges from and inspires them. They eschew all fantasy and represent people and things as they are and not as they should be. And by treating only those subjects which can be viewed by anyone, they will prove more elevated and more significant as expressions of morality than can those falsely tragic or stupidly sentimental tales which leave no more trace in the memory than they do on the projection screen.[65]

This polemic itself is interesting, not least of all for the way it makes explicit the aesthetic that had governed many of Pathé's earlier "dramatic and realist" films. The intention to present "slices of life" and to "represent people and things as they are," of course, invokes the French tradition of a faits divers or even grand guignol aesthetic as well as the nineteenth-century obsession with producing a simulacrum of reality. Yet other phrases—"the quality of virtue" and "expressions of morality"—obviously refer to the more conventional tradition of French melodrama. In the convergence between these two traditions, the "realist" aesthetic tends to predominate, at least in the series' initial films.

Drawn from original scenarios, these "thesis plays" (to cite Gaumont's publicity language again) recount stories of traumatic losses or humiliating shifts downward in social position and focus particularly on single women and mothers. Instead of resorting to coincidence, criminal threats, and other kinds of violence to determine dramatic plot turns, they focus on the more mundane, but deeply engrained social antagonisms of class, gender, and generation. And, while narrating with a moral rather than an ironic voice, they seem to call in question the melodrama's ideological project of restoring and confirming the family and respectable bourgeois society as the locus of virtue. The impetus for this new series, as Fescourt attests, may well have been partly economic—Gaumont's need, in 1911, to produce films at a cost of no more than eight francs per meter of negative.[66] But a low budget compromised Feuillade, his new set designer Robert Jules Garnier, and his new cameraman Guérin, no more than it did Capellani in making *Les Misérables*, for the *Scènes de la vie telle qu'elle est* series were as compelling as the Vitagraph films Jasset would praise so highly later in the year.

Les Vipères (1911), Feuillade's first film for the series, is representative in that its faits divers story is set in a provincial town and focuses on the plight of a single "insignificant" character. A young widow (Marie Dorly) is evicted from a run-down dwelling and then is hired as a domestic servant by the local gendarme to care for his invalid wife and their baby son.[67] The townspeople refuse to have anything to do with the woman and spread rumors about her and the gendarme, until finally the wife, believing them, angrily turns her out into the street again. In the recurring dimly lit central room of the gendarme's home, recorded consistently in waist-level AS/LS,[68] the position and movement of the characters establish a "staging in depth" paradigm for much of the film. The invalid wife usually occupies a chair in the left foreground, characters enter and exit through a door to the exterior in the right background, and, while the woman ranges around the room and even seems to displace the wife at one point, she alone can occupy the right foreground—where she once arranges a white vase of flowers. The recurring central room and pattern of character position and movement create a tightly unified, almost mechanistic structure, even more so than in *Victimes de l'alcool*, and these formal patterns seem to overdetermine the "fatalism" of the story. As the rumors pass through several social sites of hostility (the school, the grocer's shop, the café), and the young woman is expelled from each in turn, they reach the crucial site of contested possession, the family home, from which two women friends and finally the mayor persuade the wife to "evict" her as well. The final shots of *Les Vipères* resolve this story in an economical, symbolic farewell to the social space of the domestic which is worthy of Griffith. First, the young woman takes her leave of the baby, in a room not described until now and lit only by arc lighting through a window (frame right). Then, in the darkness of the central room (lit dimly from the baby's room, frame right), she moves slowly in an arc from right foreground to right background, where she pauses momentarily in the doorway, in silhouette. Her decentered position in the frame, together with the dark, empty space of

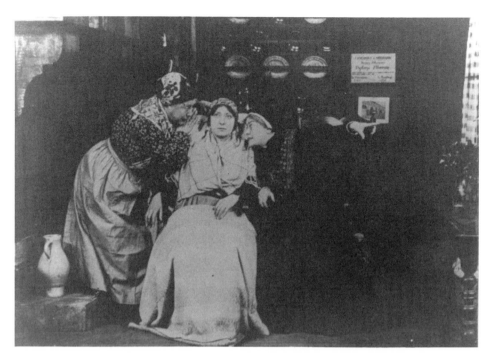

102. *Les Vipères*, 1911 (production photo)

the room, conspire to evacuate the home as a social site of value and meaning.

The subject of *Le Roi Lear au village* (1911) is also a marginal provincial character, an unwanted aging father. This story loosely follows the Shakespeare play (reviewed in a copy of *Le Figaro* read to the old man in the opening scene), but here the characters are all peasants, the old man's daughters simply find him a burden, and there is no Cordelia figure to promise any kind of reconciliation or redemptive ending.[69] As in *Les Vipères*, the action keeps returning to one interior, the central room of the elder daughter (Carl), with "excursions" to a lawyer's office (where his property is transferred), the younger daughter's house, the village café, and a nearby canal. In other words, with one exception, the story unfolds in something like ten long-take AS/LS tableaux. This draws attention to the relatively detailed decors of the elder daughter's room, to her everyday life (she is washing sheets in one scene), and, inadvertently, to the painted-flat countryside visible through the background door. But it also allows Feuillade to choreograph changes in the old man's status there, for his chair first is situated in the center foreground and then is moved next to a window (frame right), from which he twice unsuccessfully tries to resume "center stage"—only to be shunted aside when the daughter, pinching pennies, lets her part-time servant go and when he comes forward to ask for a bowl of coffee and drops it. The climactic moment comes when the old man leaves his younger daughter's house one evening and goes to the canal (according to an intertitle) to drown himself. There, in a deep-space AS/LS of a bridge over the canal, shot from a slightly high angle, he meets the servant who persuades him not to. What is remarkable about this tableau is the way it combines the evocation of a milieu and a moment of suspense. For the pan that traces the old man's movement along the bridge, until the servant climbs up from the canal path with a laundry basket, continues on in order to reveal a "gossip" coming up to spy on them from the left background as well as a distant barge drifting slowly, inexorably, like fate itself toward the bridge. In the end, the old man is forcibly returned to the interior of his elder daughter's house but set in a right foreground chair (and in a slightly closer shot, as if to give it an added sense of claustrophobia), from which he must again either escape or be banished, since nothing in this family relationship has changed.

Several other French melodramas released about this time share the aesthetic of the Gaumont series. One of these, *Les Chalands* (1911), may be the only extant title of Lacroix's work for Gaumont. Its slight story is little more than a faits divers that happens to end happily. The young daughter of a canal barge couple runs away one night to be with her lover, and his mother returns with them the next day to convince her parents to accept their marriage. *Les Chalands* is unusual, however, in several ways. Although hardly any of the film's tableaux are free of intertitles, most of them, at least according to the scenario, are lines of dialogue[70]—and they focus on the father's anxiety over his daughter (as well as the barge). Indeed, that anxiety extends through several early morning tableaux as he wanders alone along a canal and asks several villagers if they have seen her. Yet, most remarkable is the location shooting on an actual barge, especially in the opening and closing scenes—for the last shot, the camera is mounted on the back of the barge as it glides into Paris. In its "documentary" recording of a barge family's everyday life, *Les Chalands* looks very much like a prototype for later French films such as Antoine's *L'Hirondelle et la mésange* (1921),[71] Jean Epstein's *La Belle Nivernaise* (1924), and Jean Vigo's *L'Atalante* (1933). Another of these melodramas, Eclair's *L'Inutile Sacrifice* (1911), recounts the story of two peasant women, Blanche and Mariette, who are rivals for the love of a young man named Pierre. This film, too, uses location shooting for its "realism" (apparently in the Pyrenees), most strikingly perhaps in the scene where Blanche's father begs Mariette to sacrifice her love so that Pierre can marry his daughter—which takes place as she is washing clothes in a stream that curves through the village. Even more interesting, however, is the graphic match between Mariette, in AS/LS, writing her note of renunciation and Blanche seated exactly in the same position—an editing strategy in which the two women's despair is mirrored with poignant irony. For Blanche runs off to commit suicide (by leaping off a cliff), and, when her father returns with Mariette's letter, he finds only his daughter's shawl draped over the empty chair.[72]

As for Gaumont's *La Vie telle qu'elle est* series itself, several shifts soon were underway, as is evident in *La Tare* (1911). First of all, this was probably the first Gaumont film to be released in three reels, and it became the feature attraction of the program inaugurating the Gaumont-Palace cinema, on 1 October 1911. Second, it clearly begins to abandon the provinces for an urban bourgeois professional milieu. Third, it recuperates from earlier melodramas the rhetorical device of the CU photograph, but this time, because the subject is female, it seems to elicit rather than resolve the anxieties associated with modern urban life. For *La Tare* tells the story of a single woman's rise and fall, this time circumscribed almost exclusively by men. The woman is Anna Moulin (Carl), a barmaid in a Paris café, who accepts an offer from a doctor friend to leave her job—as well as her gentleman lover, Alphonse Marnier (Ayme)—to become the chief nurse in an orphanage in the south of France. When the doctor dies, she takes over his administrative duties at the orphanage, but Marnier tracks her down and, failing to renew their relationship, provokes her dismissal by informing the orphanage trustees of her "disreputable" past. As befits a psychological study, this film unfolds slowly in perhaps no more than two dozen shots, most of them recorded in AS/LS, with at least a half-dozen involving long-takes of up to five minutes each—as in the deep-space opening scene recorded on location in a café. One effect of this long-take strategy is a sense of verisimilitude, and other strategies help sustain this—for instance, the actualité sequence of five shots which narrates Anna and the doctor's train journey to the orphanage. The multiple-reel structure of *La Tare* is significant for at least one other reason as well. Each of the first two reels concludes not on a narrative climax but on a moment of suspense: the first, with the doctor suddenly falling ill, the second, with Alphonse back in the Paris café discovering Anna's whereabouts. Each of the last two reels then opens with a resolution of the suspense and a new dramatic situation: after the doctor's elided death, Anna is appointed the orphanage's new administrator, and Alphonse suddenly shows up at her office.

In conjunction with this calculated use of the reel break, *La Tare* also narrates its story through a variation of the "staging in depth" paradigm from *Les Vipères*. This is especially characteristic of scenes in the orphanage office, dormitory, and boardroom—where a right background door again regularizes most entrances and exits, while the left foreground position serves as a kind of "anchor" or point of rest for Anna—at least until the final reel. In contrast to the earlier films, however, several scenes also include cut-in shots, as in the MS of Anna and the doctor talking over his offer in the café. The most important of these, of course, is the CU of Anna's photograph that circulates in the film's narrative and symbolic economy. This first appears in Anna's office, as a sign of her new status and success, and then turns up in Alphonse's hands back in Paris, inadvertently disclosed by a former patient. Once Anna spurns his advances, he arranges for it to reappear in a salacious newspaper story disclosing her past, which is read by the "scandalized" orphanage trustees. Unlike the truthful photographs in earlier melodramas, this one fixes Anna irrevocably as morally tainted—at least to the men through whose hands it passes as part of the public discourse they control. In their anxiety over this French version of the "new woman," they subject her body to "misrecognition," in a deliberate misreading that represses her newly constructed professional identity and "re-rights" her position in the socioeconomic order. The injustice of that positioning is then extended in the film's final shots.[73] In an employment office, a pan follows Anna from the waiting room to the office and back (she is chastised for not waiting her turn), in an economical emblem of how her freedom of movement has been circumscribed and constricted. Then, in one final variation on the "staging in depth" paradigm, in a dark, bare attic room, Anna goes to a right background window (looking out on a real cityscape) and seems about to jump off its ledge to her death. But she pauses, backs away, and sits in misery in the left foreground, barely illuminated by single-source lighting from the right.[74] The shot holds on her decentered position in the frame, not to emphasize any gestures (there are none), but to provide a centered empty space in which her emotional state of distress can reverberate, and ultimately echo out into the audience. That this concluding "portrait" of Anna invites a reading quite at odds with that imposed on her published photograph strongly suggests that the film also assumed a differently gendered audience from that of its reviewers, most of whom dismissed such a woman's story as "completely devoid of . . . interest."[75]

Les Destin des mères (1912) continues the series' shift to a bourgeois milieu but confines its central women characters more "properly" to domestic roles. As Sadoul argues, this may be one sign that Feuillade was bringing the series more in line with the morality tales published by the Catholic La Bonne Presse or even the more popular stories in *Le Petit Echo de la mode*.[76] And it may be further evidence that Gaumont was aiming the series primarily at a female audience. For this time Carl plays a widow, Mme Herbelin, whose daughter Suzanne (Grandais) falls in love with and, against her mother's wishes, marries an unscrupulous young man, Herbert de Saint-Gilles (Navarre). When her husband is threatened with ruin, Suzanne appeals to her mother who suppresses the information she has on his financial dealings and literally underwrites her daughter's "happiness" by sacrificing her own savings. Although only two reels in length, this film is composed of just sixteen AS/LSs, most of them located in the drawing room and dining room of the mother's house. Again, the sets are quite detailed, but here deliberately old-fashioned in their choice of dark wallpaper, curtains, and furniture. And these rooms take on added significance because the film's story is articulated as a gradual invasion of the mother's space, whose consequence is the forced separation of mother and daughter.

After an opening scene in the drawing room, which defines Mme Herbelin's indulgent attitude toward her daughter, Hubert is introduced obliquely in a cut-in MS/LS of the mother looking out a window in the same room (after turning off the light) to see Suzanne getting out of his car outside. Later, the maid brings him into the drawing room while the two women are elsewhere so that he already is in her space when she enters and is introduced to him. Once the couple has married, the mother's fears are condensed (and partly doubled in a background mirror) in a confrontational dining room scene: Suzanne asks Hubert to wait for her mother to appear before they begin to eat, and then, irritated at her interest in talking with her mother, he drags her off to an evening engagement. This long-take scene concludes the first reel, after which the mother, in looking over the family accounts, has to deal with Hubert's disrespectful butler, who seems to displace her own maid (she is marginalized to the hallway, crying, at one point). Hubert's dominance is summed up in a long-take scene in the study, where he initially sits with his back to the camera (right foreground) and then lounges in a chair partly offscreen (frame left), before the mother confronts him with mismanaging their accounts. Although he exits in anger, Suzanne defends him to her mother so that he can return, after the older woman leaves, to resume his position of authority. The final long-take scene in the drawing room then returns to the beginning as Suzanne, in a smart new outfit, appeals to her mother one last time, and, after a subtly worked-out series of gestures, receives the check that will sustain her marriage. In the end, much like Anna Moulin, the mother is left alone in the left foreground, after tearing up the letter that would expose Hubert—not only as a conventional emblem of maternal sacrifice and suffering, but as the victim of a morally bankrupt younger generation.

By 1912, the socioeconomic milieu of the middle and even high bourgeoisie dominated French contemporary melodramas, not only in Gaumont's *La Vie telle qu'elle est* series but in Pathé's productions as well. The construction of new luxury cinemas such as the Pathé-Palace, the Electric-Palace, and the Tivoli, along with the renovation of the Gaumont-Palace and the Omnia-Pathé, put the industry in direct competition with the Paris boulevard theaters. As a consequence, contemporary melodrama films, in striking parallel with the boulevard plays of Henry Bernstein, Henry Bataille, and Paul Hervieu, turned increasingly to stories of lurid intrigue and violence, often predicated on the "eternal love triangle" or the threat of mésalliance between individuals of different social classes.[77] As Mistinguett already had done in *L'Epouvante*, actresses such as Napierkowska, Robinne, and Grandais began to display the latest fashions in playing seductive figures, sometimes associated with the theater. This double appeal to conspicuous consumption and titillating deviance, however, only served to raise and more firmly answer the question of a man or woman's commitment to a specific regime of family relations or to a particular social practice of marriage. In contrast to the earlier Gaumont films, the consequence was a clear affirmation of the patriarchal bourgeois family as the locus of moral and spiritual value and, hence, social stability. This was particularly true of the Pathé series, *Scènes de la vie cruelle*, which began to compete with the Gaumont series in early 1912.

Pathé's *La Pipe d'opium* (1912), the earliest surviving film directed by Leprince, for instance, has a young man, René de Kernadec (Castillan), torn between his love for Suzanne Vermont (Napierkowska) and loyalty to his father (there is no mother to complicate matters). This conflict between male desire and duty is pushed to the extreme, however, by making Suzanne an opium addict (her room is further stereotyped with "oriental" decors) and the father a French admiral in command of his own ship, the Triton. When the Triton is sunk in an accidental explosion, and the father is reported missing, René rejects Suzanne and, in penance, exiles himself to the navy as an enlisted seaman. The father survives, of course, to recognize and confront René five years later on another ship, but his knowledge of René's earlier "decadent" liaison blocks the expected father-son reconciliation (and the only extant film print breaks off before their relationship can be restored). Not only does *Le Pipe d'opium* subordinate the "feminine" (or "East") to the "masculine" (or "West"), but it does so by closely aligning the patriarchal family with the state, specifically with the military as a source of regeneration for the modern prodigal son. Feuillade's *Le Nain* (1912) explores a similar, yet more explicitly oedipal infatuation. This son is a newly hailed playwright, Paul Dancourt (Delphin), in love with his leading actress, Lina Béryl (Grandais)—but he has kept his identity secret because he is a dwarf. Moreover, he is closely linked to a mother (Carl) rather than a father (there is none)—once he even climbs into her lap as a literal "mama's boy." Put simply, the son's task is to find a substitute figure for the mother, which he does surreptitiously by turning Lina into "La Vierge de Corinthe" (the title of his play). Unlike *La Pipe d'opium*, which scarcely deviates from the standard AS/LS tableau, this film makes some intriguing choices in representation. Dancourt's love becomes public, for instance, during a telephone call that Lina makes to him, presented initially in triptych and then in alternating MSs of the two. The sequence concludes, however, with an MS/AS of several telephone operators, joined by their supervisor, listening in on the conversation. Although the surviving print of *Le Nain* also is incomplete, its resolution seems to have the actress search him out and (once she realizes his "abnormality") laugh in his face, so that the disillusioned son rushes back into his mother's arms.

One other extant title from the Pathé series, *La Coupable* (1912), apparently also directed by Leprince, is especially noteworthy for what it achieves within less than a single full reel.[78] The story is hardly unusual: a woman (Massart) married to a successful businessman (Henry Krauss) is involved in an affair with a younger man. Her sister Lucile (Napierkowska) learns of this at a party one evening and gets her to promise to break off the affair; the husband, warned of his wife's infidelity in an anonymous letter, however, mistakes the lovers' last meeting for a rendezvous, and only Lucile can stop him from shooting his wife. *La Coupable* condenses this story into a few hours and a half-dozen spaces in and around this bourgeois family's very modern home (the drawing room, for instance, has art nouveau wall decors). Yet, in contrast to a similar suspense film like *L'Epouvante*, this one is composed of just nine shots, three of them long-take AS/LSs. Within these deep-space tableaux, the actors perform intricately choreographed moves—as in the pas de deux of confrontation between the sisters or in the precisely timed exits and entrances (using two doors and a window) of all four characters in the final drawing room scene.[79] In addition, the initial tableau of the study not only opens onto a second room of dancing couples but includes a background mirror in which Lucile, along with the spectator, can see the adulterous couple kiss briefly offscreen (frame right).[80] The suspense in *La Coupable* is generated, however, by the sequence following the sisters' meeting which intercuts three separate spaces simultaneously, according to a sound cue. First Lucile responds in her bedroom, and then the husband goes to a window in the study (where he is reading the letter), followed by a cut-in MS of him staring off in profile. Next comes an exterior LS of the house (with the foreground area dark and two floor-length background windows opening onto fully lit rooms) as the wife steps out of one window and comes forward (faintly lit) while Lucile opens the other to watch. After an intertitle, the husband enters the same space to look into his wife's empty room and exits; then Lucile opens the other window (her room is now dark) and steps out to exit in the other direction—so she can warn the couple and hide her sister before the husband bursts in with a gun. Intriguingly, this deadly serious game of hide-and-seek, enhanced by chiaroscuro, continues into the final scene, for it is Lucile who persuades the husband to reconcile with his wife—and only then does the latter emerge from hiding behind a background door, not to join him in the foreground, but to blow a kiss before making an ambiguous exit.

After *La Coupable* or, even more tellingly, *L'Epouvante*, the one SCAGL literary adaptation of feature length which survives from this period, Monca's *Le Petit Chose* (1912), looks quite pedestrian.[81] Probably based on a stage adaptation of Alphonse Daudet's novel, Monca's four-reel film tells the story of the title character as a "prodigal son" (Pierre Pradier) who is tempted away from his bourgeois family in Lyon by the libertine world of the Paris theater. The young man fails initially as a lycée teacher (he cannot instill discipline) and, through his older brother Jacques (Henry Bosc), becomes secretary to a marquis in the capital, who introduces him to the theater—and he falls in love with an actress, Irma Borel (Robinne). In the end, on his deathbed, Jacques gets his brother to give up the actress and marry Camille Pierrotte (Andrée Pascal), whom the family originally had chosen as his fiancée.[82] Much like *La Pipe d'Opium* as well as certain historical films, *Le Petit Chose* consistently relies on AS/LS tableaux, and, with the exception of several location shots, most scenes take place in rather standard studio decors. Occasionally, there are deviations from this—the teachers once stand in a shadowed foreground area looking out onto the lycée courtyard where the boys are playing, Jacques spots his brother, in a side view, coming offstage as an extra—but overall the film seems dully consistent in style, whether describing the temptations of modern Paris or the safe comforts of traditional bourgeois life. Yet there are two points of some interest. In the back-to-back scenes in his Paris apartment, where first Camille and then Irma come to appeal to him, "Le Petit Chose" is placed in the same left foreground position and acts in a similarly fickle, petulant fashion toward both women. Moreover, a photograph of Irma serves the symbolic economy of the scenes. Initially, he tears it into pieces, which Camille notices when she arrives; but the photograph reappears, in a CU insert, "magically" restored (perhaps shot through gauze), before Irma returns to win him back one last time. Finally, although the film's last two reel breaks mark major divisions in the narrative, the conclusion to the lycée scenes comes not at the end of the first reel but at the beginning of the second. Somewhat like *Le Siege de Calais* and *La Tare*, *Le Petit Chose* seems to experiment with overriding the reel break in structuring its narrative.

Feature-length "modern dramas," all from original scenarios, also figured prominently in de Morlhon's productions for his own company, Valetta. Of those recently rediscovered and restored, the earliest, *La Broyeuse des coeurs* (1913), reworks the subject of *Le Petit Chose*—but with a more risqué love triangle. This hero, Pierre de Brézeux (Pierre Magnier), is a prosperous Paris busi-

103. *La Broyeuse des coeurs*, 1913 (production photo: Léontine Massart)

nessman who abandons his fiancée Marthe (Suzanne Delvé) to go off to the Pyrenees with a famous dancer, Ida Bianca (Massart), only to be abandoned in turn when she draws the fervent attention of a Spanish bullfighter. Although much of this film, too, is comprised of AS/LS tableaux, several choreograph the characters' movement in long-takes reminiscent of *La Coupable*. In her dressing room, for instance, Ida is introduced with her back to the camera, giving her an aura of mystery; then she and Pierre perform a nuanced "courtship" of thinly veiled desire and mock resistance. The film's overall strategies of representation, however, are relatively varied. The opening scene, in which Pierre leaves Marthe for his office, smoothly matchcuts the direction of their looks from interior to exterior. The theater scenes of Ida's performance include cut-in FSs of the stage (after an establishing FS/LS looking over the heads of the audience), and Marthe's "inconsolable" state, after Pierre abandons her, is conveyed through a LA FS of her standing alone on a balcony. Actualité footage also is blended in at several points—in the automobile trip through the Pyrenees and in the bullfight where Ida's new admirer is badly gored—to let spectators share the couple's indulgence in the new sport of tourism. Perhaps most inventive in *La Broyeuse des coeurs* is the repeated circulation of letters (a melodramatic convention), whose variation helps structure its three reels, for what initially gets Pierre in trouble is the pair of letters written to the two women, each of which is delivered to the wrong one. Another of his letters to Ida then figures in their reconciliation: in his presence, she lights a match as if to burn it, pauses, and tucks it in her bosom. Finally, Pierre intercepts a love letter from the toreador so that, when Ida appears at the bullfight without the requisite corsage of violets, he tries to commit suicide in the ring. As a consequence, the two concluding AS/LSs neatly juxtapose Pierre's abandonment (after Ida finds the letter and angrily exits) and his return to Marthe, begging her forgiveness, by shifting the woman's position, respectively, from the right foreground in one tableau to the left foreground in the other. And the couple's reconciliation, as well as the double standard of sexual behavior it assumes, is abetted and blessed by none other than Marthe's own mother.

As these films suggest, most contemporary melodramas located in an urban bourgeois milieu took an ambivalent attitude toward the "modern" and, in recuperating the traditional patriarchal family, even expressed resistance to one of its emblems: the "new woman." Those that told stories set in the provinces and depicting an artisan or working-class milieu sometimes were no less ambivalent, but in a different way, and usually were limited to the single-reel format. The most paradoxical of these films is Pathé's *L'Ame des moulins* (1912), directed by Machin for Hollandesche Film. Its anachronistic villain, for instance, is a tramp who is refused food or money by a Dutch miller and his family; he retaliates that night, in a fit of melodramatic hyperbole, by setting fire to the miller's isolated windmill. As if that were not enough, he prepares for his revenge by smashing the toy windmill that the miller's son constructs in the opening scene. If this story seems disappointing, compared to his earlier *Nuit de Noël* or *Le Moulin maudit*, Machin nearly compensates for that in his framing strategies and use of color processes. The first half of the film's fifteen tableaux often are framed in LA, as if approximating the perspective of the miller's son; and they are all imbued with stencil color. Once night falls, however, the film shifts to tinting and then toning—and once holds on a AS/LS of the tramp, on a foreground canal bridge, staring at the distant windmill. The climax, of course, comes in the grand guignol spectacle of the fire, but its culmination is a LS/ELS, vividly toned blue and tinted red, as the family huddles in the foreground watching the huge windmill in the background, completely engulfed in flames.[83] If the windmill serves as a metaphorical emblem for the family (and perhaps, nostalgically, for a vanishing way of life), there is a peculiarly ironic twist in making them the spectators of their own destruction.

In contrast to *L'Ame des moulins*, Riche's scenario for Pathé's *Le Signalement* (1912) sounds more lurid than it actually is: an escaped madman and child-killer named Maxim (Jean Kemm) threatens the French village of an old shoemaker (Duhar) and his granddaughter (Fromet). Although a good deal of this film is shot on location—tracing the shoemaker's daily trip to the local café as well as Maxim's journey to and from the village—the crucial scenes occur in the studio decor of the shoemaker's house. This is an unusually deep-space interior, cluttered with roughhewn props, within whose spatial coordinates Maxim and the

104. *Le Signalement*, 1912 (Jean Kemm, Marie Fromet)

girl engage in a suspenseful confrontation, accentuated by backlighting from the door and window.[84] In a long-take FS/LS, she offers him food, gets him to comfort her doll, and finally breaks open her piggy bank to give him some money—her "innocent nature" serving to tame this Frankenstein monster and "cure" him of his deviance. What is especially interesting about *Le Signalement*, however, is its undermining of conventional authority through an ironic voice that controls the flow of narrative information (using just a few intertitles and two notes). The initial sign of this comes in the opening scene when a gendarme ordering a new pair of boots tries to pass a false coin. More important is the note reporting Maxim's escape, which comes to him after the girl has gone out on an errand, so that later, unlike the spectator, she does not realize how dangerous is the stranger she shelters—until the moment when he takes a brief nap and she, too, finds the note. By now, however, a discrepancy has become evident between her experience of Maxim and the earlier official report, which now seems as counterfeit as the gendarme's coin. The outcome of Maxim's escape then is delayed until the final tableau, when a second note arrives at the shoe-maker's—another signed, official report that "Maxim, the maniac is dead." And this cruelly ironic twist only widens the gap opened up between government documentation on an individual and the "true" experience a spectator can have through the eyes of a child.

Two Gaumont films from the summer of 1912, both directed by Perret (with cameraman Georges Specht and set designer Jean Perrier now part of his regular crew), are just as fascinating in how they position a spectator vis-à-vis the central characters. *Le Coeur et l'argent* returns to a provincial milieu very like that in *Le Vertige* for its story of a young woman who falls victim to social forces beyond her control.[85] The daughter of a country innkeeper, Mme Mauguiot (Carl), Grandais is forced to sacrifice her love for a young man named Raymond (Paul Manson) and marry an older, wealthy landowner, M. Vernier. When Vernier dies suddenly on a business trip, however, Suzanne returns to the stream where she used to meet Raymond, only to be spurned—and she drowns herself in despair. Much of this film, too, is shot on location, but its strategies of representation are quite varied and organized in distinctive spatial patterns within a two-part narrative structure. It opens, for instance, with a LS of Suzanne and Raymond drifting in a boat and jumpcuts to a MS of the two gathering flowers on the bank of a stream. A brief alternation then links the couple (through a sound cue) to Mme Mauguiot standing by a foreground tree, in AS/LS, calling out over the water, and, when the AS/LS returns, the boat is approaching her from the background. Following an intertitle (the mother disapproves of this "idyll"), the last shot of the sequence repositions all three characters by the tree (now in the background) and has them come forward across the inn's back terrace. Here, the Eden-like world of the couple gives way to the more restricted social space of the mother, setting in motion a narrative trajectory that repeatedly will repress "natural impulses." The next sequence confirms the mother's control over her daughter when Vernier comes to propose, in a cut-in AS/LS of the inn's front terrace—Suzanne's response is to slowly move off to a shadowed background door. After another intertitle, the mother replaces her in the frame, confers with Vernier, and goes after Suzanne. A reverse-angle cut to the back of the inn then shows Suzanne, in AS, standing in the doorway (presumably gazing off toward the stream), as her mother comes out of the dark interior to browbeat her into submission. In the next shot, she brings Suzanne back to Vernier—a literal go-between in this highly condensed "love and money" transaction.

This juxtaposition of spaces and characters introduces several other patterns of resonant repetition and a kind of return of the repressed in *Le Coeur et l'argent*. The white flowers the couple gathers, for instance, circulate throughout as an increasingly ironic sign of their love. They are prominent on a centered table when Vernier first arrives, Suzanne is associated with flowers in the Vernier house, both before and after he dies, and she drowns somewhere close to the bank where she first picked them with Raymond. The couple's relationship also is privileged by the two MSs in that opening sequence, but there is no close framing in their final encounter. Instead, Perret inserts a MS as part of the emblematic crosscut in the middle of the film.[86] There, a LS of Raymond alone in the boat is followed by a MS of Suzanne holding a bouquet of flowers and looking sadly at the camera (in an unusually direct appeal for spectator identification). As mediated by the spectator, this produces a kind of communion across space—their "inconsolable" condition is doubly shared—and sets up the film's climax, for the anticipated reunion of the lovers founders on a different kind of juxtaposition. In the FS/LS that follows the MS of Suzanne with the flowers, she sits in the left foreground while the initial LS image of the couple in the boat dissolves in and out on the right half of the frame. This subjective image of remembered happiness (again repressed by the mother's entrance) is then countered at the end by Raymond's own contrasting subjective image. Now, while Suzanne pleads with him in the boat in the right foreground, a FS/LS of Vernier kissing Suzanne in a garden dissolves in and out on the left half of the frame. Unlike the other, this memory—of a powerful rival, a world of money, and a "sullied" woman—is one that the spectator, now firmly aligned with Suzanne, simply cannot share. Consequently, if Raymond's memory serves to erase hers and turn the stream world into a site of unbearable loss, the spectator implicitly is invited to hold the two juxtaposed images in suspension and view his rejection, much like the mother's repression, as an act of perverse moral cruelty. And the final image of Suzanne's body drifting in the stream enacts a further form of erasure, in a sentimental "realization" of the drowned Ophelia, as painted by Millet.

Released just one week after *Le Coeur et l'argent*, Perret's *Sur les rails* recounts the tragic outcome of another love triangle, but within a working-class railyard milieu resembling that of Lux's *Un Drame sur une locomotive*. Here, an engineer named Jacques is so jealous of his friend Pierre's plans to marry Augustine, a local café owner, that he tries to kill him; when that fails, he is so shamed he commits suicide.[87] Although shot almost entirely on location, *Sur les rails* is most interesting for the way it exploits lighting effects and changes in framing to position the spectator somewhat ambiguously in relation to its grand guignol violence. The opening shot, for instance, describes the café exterior, with several engineers at a foreground table toasting Augustine before she goes to sit in a background window and Pierre walks over to talk with her. Then comes what Fescourt has singled out as a trademark of Perret's style: a cut-in MS shows him handing her a small flower from his shirt pocket, and a reverse-angle AS silhouettes the couple in the window, as Jacques suddenly appears in the background to see them kiss.[88] After Jacques harasses Augustine in the next exterior shot, another cut-in MS shows her in the window again, worriedly writing Pierre a note accepting his marriage offer. Jacques's "vengeance" (so says one of only four intertitles) is to get Pierre drunk and then strangle him in the railyard, but he is constrained, much like Raymond was in the earlier film, by a subjective image dissolving in and out in the right half of the frame—a delayed FS of his perspective on the lovers kissing. Instead, he simply drags his drunken friend onto the tracks, where the latter comes out of his stupor just in time to flatten himself between the rails as an express train roars over him. The film's climax comes in a confrontation back at the now shuttered café after Pierre returns to tell the story to Augustine who takes him inside. There, in the faint light of an AS, he watches at the door's peephole, and a cut-in POV shot shows Jacques coming along the road in front of the café. When Jacques knocks at the door, he is stunned to have it open on his friend, and a cut-in MS of their profiled faces accentuates Jacques's horror at Pierre's angry accusation. A ninety-degree shift in camera position then opens up a deep background space outside the café door into which Jacques rushes off. As he runs onto a bridge over the railyard, the camera distance increases from LS to ELS so that, when he jumps to his death in the final shot, he is reduced to a tiny, vulnerable figure within a virtually empty frame.[89]

Perret's representational choices—deep-space tableaux, reverse-angle cutting, silhouetted figures, cut-in close shots, emblematic crosscuts, and subjective images within the frame—all serve to render his films' stories more intimate and psychological and to implicate the spectator in their sometimes ambiguous shifts in narration. Durand's *Le Railway de la mort* (1912) demonstrates a different kind of versatility in its grim adventure tale, supposedly set in the American West (but shot on location in the Camargue), by piling one action sequence on top of another.[90] Borrowing liberally from Jack London, this "lust for gold" story turns two friends, Tom Burke (Dhartigny) and Joe Baker (Hamman), into fierce antagonists in their frantic search for the rich claim of a dying miner. After two concise scenes establish this premise, the next shows Tom, in LS, leaping onto the back of a passing train, quickly pursued by Joe on horseback, and, in a reverse-angle cut, the two men trade gunshots.[91] When Joe fails to catch the train, he races ahead to a signal pole from which, in LS, he can drop onto the top of one of the passing train's cars. There, in an AS/LS (looking ahead past the engine), Joe has to fight another man and toss him off the car, after which, in a LA LS, he climbs over the engine cab roof, shoots the engineer, and uncouples the cars. Now stranded, Tom rushes off, pulls himself across a river in a skiff, borrows a truck at "Fort Williams," and reaches a point far enough ahead that he can drag a heavy timber onto the rails. In a stunning LS, the engine hits the timber and flips over on its side, and a cut-in closer shot shows Joe crawling out of the cab window, barely alive. In the final sequence, sometime later, Joe discovers the mining claim that Tom is now working. Softly silhouetted through some gingham curtains, he stealthily approaches Tom's shack of explosives, opens the curtained window, and tosses several sticks of dynamite inside. When the smoke of the explosion clears, the whole site is in ruins, and a cut-in FS reveals the two dying men still grappling desperately over the claim document. *Le Railway de la mort* sustains this narrative drive with such confidence, despite any logical discrepancies in its handling of space and time, that the film won special praise from *Moving Picture World*—just as Gaumont was poised to increase its distribution of multiple-reel films in the United States.[92]

One of Fescourt's earliest surviving films for Gaumont, a nifty one-reeler entitled *Jeux d'enfants* (1913), takes a slightly different tack by exploiting the strategy of parallel editing in a Griffith-like story of last-minute rescue suitable for both adults and children. This film is set in a provincial French mill town, where the mill owner's daughter Juliette, playing with her cousins one Sunday afternoon, is saved from being crushed in a hydraulic lift by a working-class boy. The opening scene quickly defines Juliette as a spoiled brat—in the bedroom and garden, she torments her maid, with her mother's permission. A short alternation of shots then brings Juliette and the boy together in the street: she slaps him for returning her errant ball, and a mill foreman orders him to look after the mill on Sunday, as punishment. When her three cousins visit, Juliette takes them off to play in the mill yard (the parents have gone off in their car, the maid is distracted by a man, and an insert shot of the boy places him somewhere nearby). The dilemma on which the rest of the film pivots is set up plausibly and economically: the kids, at Juliette's insistence, of course, will play "ladies paying a visit," using a door they come to rest against after briefly running about. As Juliette opens the door, in FS, she points to a button alongside it, and, in a ninety-degree shift in camera position, also in FS, she enters a tiny boxlike space, with a greased pole in the center. As the cousins primp in preparation for their "visit," the older of the girls puts her hand to the button, and a cut in MCU reveals a sign over the button: unknowingly, she has just turned on a hydraulic lift. Inside, Juliette primps in turn and notices the pole sliding downward. A game of social manners abruptly has turned deadly serious, in an excess of displaced vengeance against her earlier "improper" behavior.

The rest of *Jeux d'enfants* uses this simple alternation between inside and outside to sustain an extended sequence of parallel editing, with several variations. The first of just three intertitles establishes that it takes the hydraulic weights eight minutes to descend—a precise temporal deadline that turns out to equate screen time with real time, raising the level of suspense. And, to emphasize the threat, there is a cut to a shot of heavy rocks piled on top of a slowly descending platform. After further intercutting shows the cousins unable to open the door in response to Juliette's cries, the older girl races off to find the maid. When they return, she reads the sign and now realizes the danger. They run off together to fetch a couple (apparently caretakers) from an office and meet the boy (responding to their offscreen shouts for help), who exits in the opposite direction from them, his movement accentuated by a pan. At its climax, the film intercuts the action in three spaces: a half-dozen people outside struggling at the door, Juliette inside crouching and then fainting as the platform descends above her, and the boy racing to the top of the mill's dam and turning its sluice levers (precisely what he is doing is deliberately left unclear). Suddenly the platform stops and begins to ascend, the door is torn open, and Juliette is carried out. Instead of explaining how the boy's action apparently reversed the hydraulic lift, the film inserts an elliptical sequence—a brief intertitle and a MCU of the mill owner at a wall telephone—in order to get Juliette's family back to the house. The explanation does not come, in fact, until the final scene in the family's spacious drawing room, where Juliette awakens and gratefully apologizes to the boy, who reports that he overheard workmen once say that opening the dam's sluices would stop all the lifts. This sets up a concluding emblematic AS of Juliette watching the boy, "a future engineer," studying a book under the light of a lamp. *Jeux d'enfants* resolves class differences in melodramatic fashion by humbling one rich child and propelling another poor one up the social ladder, all within a properly restored gender hierarchy.

Perhaps the best way to summarize the range and achievement of the prewar French contemporary melodrama is to take up several pairs of feature-length films. Both Eclair and Pathé, for instance, released adaptations of Zola's *Germinal* (1885), a work whose ambivalent attitude toward violence as a means of improving industrial labor conditions may have seemed relatively safe for the screen now that the syndicalists and their general strike strategy were on the decline. Jasset's adaptation, *Au pays de ténèbrès* (1912), was part of a series of so-called social dramas that Eclair began to produce in late 1911. This two-part film updated Zola's story to the present and condensed it into the rivalry of two miners, Charles Mercourt (Charles Krauss) and Louis Drouard (Marcel Vibert), over an orphan girl, Claire Lenoir (Cécile Guyon), who is torn between them and her own attraction to a young engineer, Roger Joris (Liabel). There is some truth to Sadoul's charge that this film reduces the working-class milieu of the northern coal fields to an exotic backdrop for romantic intrigue, "in which princes [still] marry shepherdesses." [93] But Jasset's work does have considerable merit, as Sadoul himself acknowledged. For one thing, Eclair's publicity drew attention to the location shooting in Belgium, which is especially notable in the first reel where the two miners walk with Claire along a country canal and Claire later persuades Charles not to drown himself. [94] For another, the studio decors for the mine interiors are quite detailed, and the acting of the principals is consistently restrained.

This sense of verisimilitude, accentuated by certain patterns of editing, is especially evident in the second reel after a fight between Charles and Louis sparks a gas explosion in the mine. A sequence of four shots which describes a trapped group of begrimed men struggling to escape the water flooding the mine shafts catches the danger of their predicament with stunning veracity—and for French spectators, as Sadoul reminds us, this scene would have recalled the 1906 Courrières mine disaster that claimed more than 1,100 lives. The rescue operation Roger designs then leads to a sustained sequence of alternation between the miners digging at the rubble in one shaft and the two rivals trapped on a bit of dry ground, where they belatedly reconcile as comrades. As the rescuers get closer to the trapped men, the alternation includes closer and closer shots to increase the suspense; listening at the crevice they are digging, they seem to hear a response. But Charles collapses and dies of asphyxiation, and Louis soon follows, so that, when the rescuers eventually break through, they find their bodies "united in death." The final sequence begins in a simple corridor whose central doors open to reveal a background room full of corpses and mourners, and then a 180-degree reverse-angle cut focuses on Claire, backlit, kneeling before Charles and Louis, until Roger comes forward to take her hand. If *Au pays de ténèbrès* locates social conflict within the working class as much as between the classes, its "happy ending" can hardly erase the terrible costs of that conflict.

Before taking up the SCAGL adaptation of Zola's novel, there is one other Eclair "social drama" that can be paired with *Au pays des ténèbrès*. *Gerval, maître des forges* (1912) also shifts the cause of its factory strike to personal rivalries. Here, the principals include Durville (André Dubosc), a "bad capitalist" intent on buying out Gerval (Gilbert Dalleu), a "good capitalist" whose precision-tool factory happens to share the same Epiney-sur-Seine site as Eclair itself. When Gerval refuses to sell, Durville hires Bertrand (Mévisto), a disgruntled worker who is jealous of the factory's chief foreman, Hubert (Louis Gauthier), to falsely foment a strike that will prove costly to Gerval. The pivotal characters responsible for resolving these conflicts, however, are a faithful old worker, Père Morin (Duquesne), who in a drunken stupor agrees to side with Bertrand, and Gerval's daughter, Germaine (Yvonne Pascal), who finally persuades Morin to oppose him. And who should he enlist, along with Hubert, to end the strike but the workers' own wives, whose presence in the final confrontation in Gerval's gardens—where Germaine is injured by Bertrand—exposes the strike's threat to the social order as a threat to properly gendered family relations. And, in the re-righting of that order, Gerval turns over his factory to Hubert, the man who has proved a "good son," and blesses Germaine's love for him with a concluding wedding celebration. This complicated, if conventionally resolved, narrative may have encouraged a greater flexibility in this film's strategies of representation. The opening scene, for instance, begins with the two capitalists, in MCU, at a window looking out at the factory and then shifts to a FS/LS of what turns out to be Gerval's office. His response to Durville's offer is delayed as the latter keeps upping the figure in repeated CUs of his checkbook. A similar MS/LS later frames Germaine and Morin, almost silhouetted before the distant factory, when she begs for his help, while HA LSs are used to describe the strikers' initial showdown in Gerval's office as well as the final confrontation. Most remarkable, however, is the location shooting—in a LS exterior of the workers' living quarters, where the women pour down a rough cobblestone street, and especially in what probably were Eclair's own laboratory interiors, where the low-key lighting partially masks Bertrand's initial attempt to sabotage a machine. Such "actualité" scenes were precisely what Louis Delluc would later praise in Henry Roussel's *L'Ame du bronze* (1918), one of the last important films to be released by the company.[95]

With Capellani's *Germinal* (1913), Pathé may have hoped to repeat the success of *Les Misérables* the previous year. Although hardly a failure, the film seems not entirely to have fulfilled those hopes. The reasons were several: by the fall of 1913, blockbuster feature-length films were being released almost weekly in Paris, a study of class conflict in the coal mines may have seemed "unfashionable" for the lengthy format of a dozen or more reels,[96] and the American version seems to have been reduced in length and then exhibited with relatively little notice. One thing is certain, however: Capellani's adaptation put much of Zola's story onto the screen. It begins, in fact, with an added scene, as Etienne Lantier (Henry Krauss) is let go from a factory job—for trying to help a family being evicted from their quarters—and seeks work in the coal fields.[97] There, where Zola's novel opens, he finds shelter with old Maheu (Mévisto) and his family, joins them in working at the Montsou mine, and starts to take an interest in their eldest daughter, Catherine (Sylvie), who labors alongside him. However, she is claimed by and soon becomes the mistress of another miner, Chaval (Jacquinet), who secretly agrees to act as a stool pigeon for the mine company owner, Grégoire. The manager, Hennebeau (Albert Bras), reluctantly goes along with the deceit, for he wants to marry Grégoire's daughter, Cécile (Guyon). When the company changes its system of wages (to reduce costs) and ignores the miners' negotiating efforts (led by Lantier), Chaval deceptively spurs some workers to shut the mine down, a tactic that soon turns into a riot and climaxes in a bloody confrontation with soldiers in front of the Grégoire house—among the dead are Cécile (struck by a stray bullet) and old Maheu. With collective action an apparent failure, a lone anarchist figure, Souvarine (Dharsay), commits an act of sabotage, but the water storage tank he breaches only floods the mine shafts, trapping and killing more people, including Chaval (in a fight with Lantier), Catherine, and Souvarine himself. Hennebeau organizes a rescue operation that saves Lantier and some others, but the devastation is so great that, in the end, Lantier is lucky to be able to go off in search of work elsewhere.

Whether *Germinal* adopts the five-act structure of Busnach's 1888 stage version of Zola's novel, which lasted only seventeen performances,[98] or is drawn from the original's seven-part structure is unclear. Capellani's adaptation does, however, seem to condense the middle sections of the novel narrating the progress of the strike action and retain more of the beginning and ending. The first part, in fact, which lasts several reels, functions almost like a documentary on the everyday life of workers in the coal mining industry. As in Jasset's earlier film, much of this section is shot on location. Lantier's arrival in the mining area is presented in LSs, extended by pans, of him walking by a rail siding, past the distant mine entrance tower, and over hills of slag—an appropriate place for him to meet a discarded old miner like Maheu. Later the film follows Lantier, old Maheu, Catherine, and others as they enter the mine, crouch in the "bucket" trains that carry them underground, descend in an elevator (in an approximation of a boom shot), fan out into different shafts (again conveyed through pans), shovel coal into horse-drawn carts, and break to eat lunch close to where they have been working. This whole section can be said to rework the opening tableaux of *Au pays noir* from eight years earlier—at much greater length and with a heightened degree of verisimilitude—for, although Lantier and other characters sometimes come forward into AS or even MS, the emphasis throughout is on the harsh conditions of their physical environment. And it is only after this working-class milieu is well established that the contrasting bourgeois world of Grégoire and Hennebeau is introduced and a narrative conflict develops. In a sense, *Germinal* adheres to the aesthetic supposedly underlying the *Scènes de la vie qu'elle est* series, but it also anticipates what Delluc and others would argue that French films should be doing after the war—for its story emerges gradually (albeit melodramatically), as one of several possible events or incidents, out of a specific, thoroughly described natural or social milieu.[99]

Although somewhat limited in its strategies of representation, *Germinal* does more than simply sustain a high level of verisimilitude. As the conflict over wages erupts, Capellani uses an emblematic crosscut reminiscent of Griffith's *A Corner in Wheat* (although it comes right out of Zola's novel), contrasting Grégoire's well-laden dinner table, where Hennebeau proposes to Cécile, with the much more meager one in Maheu's all-purpose room, where the miners draw up their demands. Out of the long-take AS/LS confrontation in Grégoire's drawing room, where Lantier takes over for the ineffectual Maheu, come the increasingly suspenseful scenes that circle back to Grégoire's house for the climactic confrontation. There, the film deploys cut-in MSs of Grégoire on the telephone calling in army reinforcements for the local police. While Lantier escapes into the now empty mines (the police pursue him as the instigator of the riot), the soldiers arrive to face off against the miners in 180-degree reverse-angle cuts. After the bloodbath, crosscutting returns, but now linked by a dissolve, to equate the two families and classes—as Grégoire and Hennebeau mourn Cécile, and the Maheus mourn their father. In the final section of the film, Souvarine shifts from being a detached, ironic observer, often positioned in the left or right foreground of the frame, to acting as the misguided saboteur. Once he breaks the water tank open (in one shot, the water literally engulfs his pinned body), an extended sequence of alternation links the action in different spaces: the trapped miners underground and their families clustered at the mine entrance, and Lantier, Catherine, Chaval, and several others in a partially flooded chamber and the rescue team digging to reach them. Like Jasset, Capellani includes closer and closer shots of the rescuers, but also returns to the surface to exploit the spectacular effect of their dynamiting—as smoke and debris pour out of the entrance tower—and concludes the sequence with a LS of Lantier brought out on one stretcher, followed by Catherine dead on another. The final scenes return to the documentary mode of the beginning as pans trace Lantier's movement to and from the Maheu house, where he bids farewell to what remains of the family. Then he sets out on the open road once more, breathing the fresh country air (as Zola has him do), but the last LS contradicts his gesture of hope by holding on what he is leaving behind—an empty landscape devoid of everything but slag piles.

If *Germinal* takes the spectator on an extended tour of the northern coal fields, condemning both miners and mine owners in its fatalistic vision of class conflict, de Morlhon's surviving bourgeois melodramas, following the model of *La Broyeuse des coeurs*, offer a very different kind of tour to the south. *La Fleuriste de Toneso* (1913) pits the unsavory bourgeois world of Paris, in the character of Georges de Passamont (Jean Dax), against the healthy exoticism of a peasant village in Italy (though shot in the Pyrenees), in the person of a simple flower-seller, Malvina (Massart). Ignorant of her origins, the latter has been left a fortune by a dying uncle, and Georges, as a distant cousin, conspires to take control of her money—first by having her bandit lover, Stello (Paul Guidé), arrested and then by forcing her to marry him instead. The uncle's lawyer hires a detective to search for Malvina and finally links up with Stello (once the charges against him are exposed) to capture the villain and save Malvina from suicide. Each of this film's three reels is constructed as separate, yet they are linked by specific patterns of repetition. After the initial scenes establish the particulars of the uncle's will and Georges's plotting, the detective's journey to Toneso to locate Malvina is then repeated by Georges. While the first journey establishes a crucial HA AS/LS looking down the alley steps that lead up to Malvina's room and includes a cut-in MCU of the tiny moles on her ear which identify her, Georges's journey is depicted deceptively as that of a leisurely tourist. He poses on the village hillside against a lake, sits idly at a café table, follows Malvina through a silhouetted arcade, and surprises her with his attention (and gift of a pearl necklace). The second reel repeats this shift from Paris to Toneso, through some of the same spaces, but now Georges persuades Malvina to go off with him to Nice (a faked letter from Stello seems to dismiss her) before the detective can return with the lawyer. The third reel then traces Stello's return to the alley where Malvina once lived, after which he, too, passes through several pictur-esque tableaux—but as the prelude to a suicide attempt, which the detective, who has been following him, forestalls. A sequence of alternation in Nice—Georges goes to a casino, while Malvina gathers wild flowers—sets up the melo-dramatic climax, for which she fills her villa bedroom with flowers before col-lapsing in bed (from the effects of a drug). In the final long-take AS/LS of that room, however, she revives to join Stello in a foreground embrace, as the lawyer and detective shake hands in the background—the rightful couple restored, their "natural" state confirmed by the abundance of flowers, but backed invisibly now by equally abundant financial resources.

Sacrifice surhumain (1914) quite literally reworks the risqué love triangle of *La Broyeuse des coeurs*, with Massart now playing the part of the wronged woman, Yvonne de Grécourt. Her husband, Marcel (Dax), is so infatuated with a dancer, Blanche Mireille (Delvé), that he follows her to Annecy in the French Alps and gambles away nearly all his money in trying to support her expensive tastes. Without his knowledge, Yvonne offers some of her own money to Blanche in order to ensure Marcel's happiness—hence the film's title—which finally shames him into ending the affair.[100] This film opens with an automobile tour of the Savoie region, where the de Grécourts just happen to rescue Blanche from a stalled car. And the location shooting provides an appropriately picturesque background, especially around the lake at Annecy, for their later affair. The narrative's real interest, however, lies not in the illicit couple but in Yvonne's response to Marcel's infatuation. She knows about it from the beginning: after discovering the special invitation Blanche has slipped him earlier, she sits silently in the right foreground of their bedroom and notices Marcel surreptitiously take it up from a frame left table. At the party after Blanche's star performance, he comes to the foreground to present her with a pearl necklace, which again Yvonne notices, but from the distant background. This layering of looks has the effect of "staging" Marcel's liaison with Blanche and aligning the spectator squarely with Yvonne's moral position of disapproval. And it culminates in a later scene, after Marcel has lost most of his money, where a background mirror allows Yvonne to see her husband take a revolver from his study and bring him to a halt, in an exchange of looks. The result is a silent confrontation in which a cut-in MCU reveals that he has already tried (and failed) to commit suicide by slitting his wrist.

As in *La Broyeuse des coeurs*, the narrative also turns in *Sacrifice surhumain* on

105. *Sacrifice surhumain*, 1914 (production photo: Jean Dax, Suzanne Delve)

the circulation of letters, especially in the last two of the film's three reels. The second reel builds to a climax through an extended alternation of sequences in which Marcel goes to Blanche's villa and is refused entrance at the gate while Yvonne finds the crumpled letter Blanche has written rejecting him. This doubled realization is followed by the suicide scene (where Marcel thinks his real motive is still secret), which leads Yvonne to write her letter to Blanche in a state of near collapse (her left foreground position in an otherwise empty frame reminiscent of Feuillade's earlier films). However, the subject of that letter is delayed until the beginning of the third reel, when Blanche reads it and, puzzled yet pleased, sends for Marcel. After the couple tours the Annecy countryside once more, this time on horseback, the film concludes in two long-take AS/LSs. In Blanche's drawing room, Marcel discovers Yvonne's letter and recognizes the extent of her suffering and sacrifice as well as his own selfish indulgence and unknowing cruelty. Drawn back to his wife's drawing room (where she sits knitting in the right foreground), as if in acknowledgment of the moral voice (or thread) that so explicitly organizes this text through both letters and looks,

Marcel confesses his remorse and receives Yvonne's blessing (if not the contemporary spectator's) in a restored domestic tableau that condenses the mother and daughter of *La Broyeuse des coeurs* into a single, martyrlike madonna figure.

At least two films from Gaumont explore melodramatic subjects whose narrative dilemma and resolution once again turn on the revelatory power of the recorded image. This time, however, perhaps in response to a disruptive summer of censored films in France (among them Gaumont's own *Main de fer*), it is the cinema image itself that becomes the locus of truth. The title of Feuillade's two-reel *L'Erreur tragique* (1913),[101] refers to the nearly fatal consequences of a husband's "misrecognition" of his wife. The husband is René de Romiguières (Navarre), an aristocratic businessman from the remote southern region of Cévennes, who suspects his wife Suzanne (Grandais) of having an affair. On a visit to Paris, where he chances to go into a cinema, René undergoes a specific kind of modern urban "shock" when suddenly he sees his wife arm in arm with another man among the passersby in a Gaumont comic film entitled *Onésime vagabond*. Returning home, his suspicion deepens when Suzanne receives a letter (the contents of which she keeps from him) and mysteriously prepares to meet someone named Roger at the local train station—to the point where René tries to sabotage her carriage. Too late he discovers that the suspected rival is her own brother (she simply wished to surprise him), and he rushes off to find Suzanne in the carriage wreckage, luckily unharmed.

As with Feuillade's previous work, this film exhibits a number of noteworthy features, integrating a systematic pattern of "staging in depth" with an unusually flexible use of camera movement, reverse-angle cutting, and parallel editing, especially near the end of the first of the film's two reels, in René's sabotage of the carriage and the suspense of its careening journey. The crucial feature of *L'Erreur tragique*, of course, is the explicit use of the cinema and the cinematic image within the narrative. Here, René's misreading of Suzanne, which is shared by the spectator, is articulated through a repeated image from the *Onésime* film which comes under his possessive control. First of all, the authenticity of what René sees is suggested by the cut-in, from a LS of the darkened Paris cinema hall, to a FS of the screen image as Suzanne appears with the unidentified man. That seems confirmed when René buys a copy of the film print and examines it more closely in his hotel room—for a cut-in CU of three frames "fixes" Suzanne's image to produce the illusion of incriminating evidence. Intriguingly, the darkness of the cinema hall, where a comic fantasy of the male vagabond turns into a "nightmare" of the "wandering" woman, then carries over into the following night scene when René returns home unannounced. Entering her darkened bedroom, René hovers threateningly over Suzanne sleeping in a softly lit area (left foreground), and this radically different, almost angelic, glowing image of her seems to stay him from doing any immediate harm. Unable to find further evidence of his wife's infidelity in a search of the house, he returns to the *Onésime* print in his study, and another cut-in CU of the film frames renews his obsessive suspicions. When Roger's letter arrives the next day, René stages a kind of revenge counterscene to what he believes he witnessed in the cinema, and the cut-in close shots of his sabotage (he weakens a strap of horse's bridle, succinctly echoing those of the supposed cause) continue to align the spectator with his perspective—that is, until the final shots of the first reel place the spectator along with Suzanne in the carriage and the reel break leaves her fate suspended.

Roger's actual arrival (he has come by an earlier train) transforms René's reading of his wife, but the film continues, much like *La Tare*, to circumscribe her figure in relation to men. The final CU of the "fixed" film image now is "framed" by a note identifying the brother to the husband and then by an intertitle that registers René's shock of recognition, both of which resecure Suzanne within the signs of kinship "proper" to such a woman. What René had read initially as a scene of immorality proves perfectly moral after all, and the process of his "comeuppance" seems to justify the cinema against its detractors—and all those like-minded "bad readers" in the audience—as a legitimate form of wholesome family entertainment. Yet that legitimation is not without one troubling qualification: nothing in the final tableau suggests that René has confessed to or apologized for either his misreading of Suzanne or his unsuccessful act of revenge against her. In other words, what continues to "haunt" this film's resolution is the male anxiety and its mechanism of projection which governs the specter of the sexual female body escaping a husband's "rightful possession."

Released just two months before Feuillade's film, as the first of four feature-length adventure melodramas specially marketed by Gaumont that fall,[102] *Le Mystère des Roches de Kador* (1912), directed by Perret, puts the cinema to even more remarkable use: as a kind of psychoanalytic cure. And the "sick subject" requiring this cure, of course, is not a man—such as René in *L'Erreur tragique*— but a woman.[103] Perret divides this scenario of traumatic loss and restoration into three distinct, yet interrelated parts that closely correspond to the film's three full reels. Part one begins with Fernand de Keramic (Perret himself) appointed as guardian to Suzanne de Lormel (Grandais again), the underage heir to an immense fortune. As Suzanne approaches the age of inheritance, she falls in love with a Captain Jean d'Erguy (Emile Keppens), but Fernand hopes to marry her in order to elude the threat of blackmail over his own heavy debts. All this is sketched in quickly so that most of the first reel can work out (with a minimum of intertitles) an elaborate plot concocted by her guardian, after Suzanne rejects his marriage proposal.[104] Using a forged letter and the pretense of a hunting trip, Fernand draws the two lovers together on the beach beneath the Kador Cliffs, drugs Suzanne, shoots Jean, and abandons them so that, when wakened, Suzanne will go mad with grief (for the inheritance goes to him should she die or go insane).

Repeatedly calling attention to the act of viewing, Perret deliberately, almost maliciously, shares almost all the details of Fernand's plot with the spectator, beginning with his steady gaze at the camera before reading the blackmail letter and his skilled forgery of Suzanne's signature on the letter inviting Jean to the cliffs. During the preparatory lunch scene, a cut-in CU shows him putting a sleeping potion in Suzanne's coffee (she is busy testing a pair of binoculars); once she drinks it down and exits with her rifle, he gazes at the camera again, then at her empty cup, and calmly sips at his own. The elliptical linear sequence of the setup on the beach (once Suzanne has collapsed at a cliff cave entrance) includes not only a POV shot (Fernand looks off through the binoculars, followed by an iris-masked LS of Jean approaching in a rowboat) but 180-degree reverse-angle cutting (first Jean waves toward the shore from the foreground rowboat, then Fernand shoots at him twice from the foreground as the boat reaches the beach). Miraculously, however, Jean survives in sequences of which Fernand, now separated from the spectator, has no knowledge: in several HA shots, Jean finds Suzanne, carries her to the boat, and sets off rowing, only to collapse himself. When Suzanne finally does awaken, a HA FS shows her staring down at her unconscious, wounded lover; Fernand's plot, though bungled, succeeds in convincing her that her own gun is the guilty weapon, and so traumatizes her into catatonic silence.

Part two of *Le Mystère des Roches de Kador* delays any attempt to prove Fernand guilty, even though a letter from Suzanne's doctor, a Professor Williams, suggests that he must be the culprit. Instead, Perret devotes the second full reel to Williams's experiment in curing Suzanne: he will use the cinema as psychotherapy, inducing "a state of hypnotism which [will] lend itself admirably to suggestion." His initial plan, in striking parallel to Fernand's, is to film a reenactment of the crime (this comes in the last intertitle until the end of the reel), which is presented in one long-take FS/LS of the same beach area—with Williams and a cameraman in the foreground, Jean acting out his part in the background, and a double performing Suzanne's role. Next, a projection space is set up in Williams's laboratory, in another long-take FS/LS, with the screen raised in the background and Suzanne brought in to sit in the foreground, as the privileged spectator of filmic address. As the reenactment begins, the sequence intercuts Suzanne now in silhouette before the screen image and an MS of her, isolated and spotlit in the dark (mismatching the direction of her look), as she becomes increasingly agitated at what she sees. At the end, in another long-take, Suzanne rises and moves as if sleepwalking toward the screen, but, when the lights suddenly are flicked on, she staggers back and faints. Quickly Williams places Jean between her and the screen so that, when she revives, Suzanne recognizes him (recovering a sense of herself as subject to him) and is released from her catatonic state. Although highly reductive, this amazing scene of *mise-en-abyme* is suggestive in its articulation of the imaginary and the symbolic stages of subject construction through doubling and role-playing. Not only does it literalize the cinema's value as a therapeutic "dream screen" but it serves to legitimize the commercial cinema as a thoroughly moral entertainment. The patient-spectator who has to be made normal again, of course, is a "sick woman" (as were the hysteria patients of Charcot and Freud), and her "cure" repositions her as the willing object of her fiancé's embrace—in what will turn out to be another, no less passive state.

Returning to the suspended plot line involving Fernand, part three focuses on Jean as the active agent of the film's resolution. In repeated CUs that equate

106. *Le Mystère des Roches de Kador,* 1912

the spectator's knowledge with his, Jean detects "proof" of guilt in a comparison of letters and then, in conjunction with the police, sets up his own plan to expose Fernand at a "fancy dress ball" the latter has been invited to attend. There, Jean stages his own "theatrical" hunt with Fernand as the unknowing prey. After an intricate choreography of maneuverings through several rooms, Fernand finds himself alone with an alluring masked female figure who, when he goes to unmask and kiss her, turns out to be Suzanne—and Jean steps in from offscreen as the real stage manager of the revelation. Within the triangulated mise-en-scène that Jean (in one foreground corner) and Suzanne (in the other) map out, with disguised policemen blocking the curtains, Fernand has no choice but to accede to their demand that he write and sign a letter confirming his guilt. In the end, one last tableau (perhaps in imitation of a Bonnard or Vlaminck painting) recapitulates and fixes the strongly gendered positions of this now "happily married" couple: with Jean as the active male subject on horseback cantering through a distant gate into the background garden, and Suzanne as the complementary subordinate female subject standing in near silhouette on a foreground balcony, restored to the condition of satisfied spectator once again.

No one film can summarize the French contemporary melodramas during this period before the war, for their pattern of development is far from uniform. Although Gaumont's *Scènes de la vie telle qu'elle est* may mark another stage in the genre's negotiation between the aesthetics of realism and melodrama, the terms of that negotiation shift during the course of the series—a shift that gives increasing attention to the milieu of the urban bourgeoisie and to romantic intrigue, and which is evident in Pathé's *Scènes de la vie cruelle* as well. Many of these films, especially those released by Pathé, reaffirm the patriarchal bourgeois family, sometimes now aligned with the military, as the locus of social value and stability. Yet a good number, especially from Gaumont, focus on figures on the margins of that institution, such as single women, or victims of its excesses or abuses, such as wives and mothers. That these families and figures range across the French class system suggests that the contemporary melodramas continue to address a cross-class audience, just as do their invitations to tour various sites of spectacle, from the lower depths of mine fields to the heights of mountain resorts. Yet the number of stories privileging female characters—from *Les Vipères, La Tare*, and *Le Destin des mères* to *La Coupable, Le Coeur et l'argent*, and *Sacrifice surhumain*—seems to assume a high percentage of women in certain French cinema audiences. Unlike the historical films, the contemporary melodramas continue to appear within the single-reel format, sometimes reaching a high level of achievement and integrating a variety of representational strategies—as in *La Coupable, Sur les rails*, or *Jeux d'enfants*. But they also constitute a growing proportion of titles in the emerging multiple-reel format. Again, in contrast to the historical films, a distinct pattern emerges here in the function of the reel break, partly because of the genre's tendency to rely on original scenarios. Although most films structure their narratives into segments according to reel breaks, both Feuillade and de Morlhon begin to use the end of the reel as a means of creating suspense that is not resolved until the beginning of the subsequent reel. And both Monca and Perret seem to experiment with carrying over a scene—in *Le Mystère des Roches de Kador*, this includes the added feature of suspense—from one reel to the next. Together with the crime plots that steadily infiltrate the contemporary melodramas once more, this strategy would become a staple of the newly specialized genre of detective and crime films.

Crime Pays: Detectives Versus Criminals

By this time, another group of French films initially marketed in the series format could be said to have coalesced into a subgenre of the contemporary melodrama. All of these films were produced in single reels and were released on an irregular basis, and they recounted what could be called adventure stories involving a central male character or hero. The most popular series—Eclair's *Nick Carter* and Pathé's tongue-in-cheek *Nick Winter*—focused on the detective as an independent urban professional upholding the Third Republic's bourgeois social order. Others singled out more "exotic" characters such as the western cowboy—Eclair's *Riffle Bill* or Lux's *Arizona Bill*, starring Hamman, a series then revived by Eclipse—or the provincial outlaw, as in Eclair's *Meskal le contrebandier*.[105] Even though the landscapes of the latter series offered one more opportunity for imaginary touring in the cinema, the exploits of their heroes probably appealed to the French spirit of anarchist individualism. In 1911–1912, the male adventure film series underwent a double-edged transformation. In parallel with

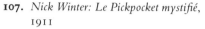

107. *Nick Winter: Le Pickpocket mystifié,* 1911

108. *Nick Winter: Le Pickpocket mystifié,* 1911

the historical film and the domestic melodrama, it, too, began to take up subjects and stories that could be shaped into the newly emerging multiple-reel format. With these stories came a change in the nature of the male hero, as the professional detective gave way to the master criminal of the modern city or, more topically, the criminal gang. Contingent with this was a sharp increase in the level of thrills and sensational violence, so that the genre almost became a specialized form of grand guignol. These changes would have consequences for the French cinema industry in the summer of 1912.

Detective heroes do not disappear, of course, as the *Nick Winter* films attest. First released in June 1910, the Pathé series located its mystery stories in Paris and, much as in the earlier *Nick Carter* films, in a consistently bourgeois milieu. As played by Georges Winter, Pathé's detective shared the same stocky build with Nick Carter, but his thick hair, bushy black eyebrows, and mustache gave Winter a rather comical appearance, which writer Garbagni would soon exploit in parodic scenarios. The earliest extant film, *Le Pickpocket mystifié* (1911), exemplifies the narrative pattern that the series generally follows. The detective identifies a criminal near the film's beginning, disguises himself to observe and trap the man in a crime, and then has to prove to the police that the suspect indeed is the culprit. In this case, the criminal is a pickpocket who follows a businessman into a bank, in front of which Nick Winter just happens to be standing. As the detective consults his slim booklet of known criminals, a cut-in CU of a photograph and short "rap sheet" quickly confirms his suspicions, which he shares with a glance at the camera.[106] While the pickpocket and his prey enter the cashiers office inside, Winter ducks behind a pillar and returns disguised as a simple workman. From his foreground vantage point, in a FS/LS of the office, he then watches the pickpocket and his special cane in action at the cashiers counter. Another cut-in CU reveals the "magical" theft: in stop motion, the knob end of the cane unscrews and a hook emerges to open the businessman's satchel, pull out a wad of bank notes, and substitute a false set. When Winter tries surreptitiously to rectify the situation, however, he is seized and

109. *Nick Winter: Le Pickpocket mystifié*, 1911

arrested as the thief. The film then delays his explanation of the crime by showing everyone involved marching off to the police station, in a spectacular long-
take backward dolly shot, which begins near a small park, moves down the
street and around a corner, passes through a courtyard entrance, and ends in
silhouette as the doors are closed.[107] An unusual strategy for 1911, this vehicle-
mounted dolly shot serves a double function: it celebrates the actor with a tongue-
in-cheek actualité parade (he is handcuffed all the way) and thus diverts attention
from the detective's inexplicable withholding of information. Finally, in the police station, Winter drops his disguise, reasserting his identity in a cut-in ECU
of his business card, which matches the earlier CU photograph of the pickpocket. What distinguishes the "good guys" from the "bad guys," this film
implies, is simple documentation.

That the Pathé series seems to settle into an increasingly parodic formula is
evident in several titles released in the fall of 1911.[108] *Nick Winter et le rapt de Mlle
Werner*, for instance, opens with two well-dressed thieves seizing a young woman
in her own bedroom and dropping a thirty thousand francs ransom note before
carrying her off. The parents (in a gratuitous MCU) immediately telephone the
detective, who takes the call in his pajamas (in AS) and then goes into a "thinking" pose, puffing on his Holmes-like pipe. In disguise, Winter tries to thwart
the kidnappers at the rendezvous site, but is captured instead and taken to an

aristocratic sitting room. There, in a long-take AS/LS, the gentleman heading up this gang discovers Winter's calling card (along with a couple of guns and a case of cigars), orders him bound, and hands around the cigars to smoke in celebration—which, because they are drugged, put them all right to sleep. The kidnapped woman turns out to be hidden in a small space behind one of the room's tapestry panels, so the film can go on to conclude in a conventional tableau of the restored bourgeois family. Winter displays another Holmes-like gesture—refusing the father's offer of money—just as he earlier restrained himself from returning the gentleman's condescending slap in the face. *Nick Winter et le vol de la Jocande* exploits the topical theft of the Mona Lisa from the Louvre in an even more parodic story. Here, Winter has so much trouble dressing in the opening shot that he finally leaves on his nightshirt under his suit—but a cut-in CU of one shoe that is missing a button primes him for the clue that supposedly solves the mystery. For his investigation in the gallery quickly turns up another button on the floor (in a matching CU). Then, in a sequence of just two exterior shots, he assumes the disguise of a shoeshine man he meets and, under the pretense of shining shoes, discovers his suspect in a respectable-looking old man sitting at an outside café table. In the concluding AS/LS of the gallery, Winter makes his arrest when the old man comes looking for and recognizes the button the detective holds out to him. But there is a final twist after their exit, for the real thief returns to replace the Mona Lisa (now probably a fake), smile at the camera, and then make off with another da Vinci painting. When Winter himself returns, he is stunned by the changed configuration of the gallery's artwork—the victim of his own narrow vision and someone even better than he is at "faking it."

Les Exploits de Nat Pinkerton, which Eclipse began to release in 1911, adopts a serious attitude toward its subject, by contrast, and explicitly addresses an American as well as French audience. Its detective hero, after all, takes his name from the famous American agency, although he usually works alone and avoids disguises, and he seems to operate in a generic city somewhere in the United States. By 1912, the *Nat Pinkerton* films were being released in two reels, as was the case with *Le Cheveu d'or*, perhaps the series' only extant title. In this film, an inventor named James Parker accuses his secretary-assistant Robert of stealing the designs for a new machine—after his daughter Lucy naively has given them to a family friend and "admirer," Frank Bronson. Chagrined at her action, Lucy engages Nat Pinkerton (Bressol) to get Bronson to confess and return the designs, exonerating Robert and raising his prospects as a suitor for her hand. Since there is nothing unusual about this plot, any interest must be generated elsewhere—as in the way the film varies the representation of its two principal spaces: Parker's office and then Bronson's. In the initial scene, Parker's wood-paneled office is described in FS/LS as a dark, enclosed space; in the second, that space expands (or is breached) because the background door through which Bronson enters to visit remains open onto another room. For the third scene, "later that evening," the camera is positioned to the right and closer, in order to reveal a window (frame right) and to focus on Lucy, at the foreground desk, rereading Bronson's letter requesting a look at the designs (the only light comes from the window and a left foreground lamp). A cut-in MCU shows her opening a desk drawer to get out the designs, and a ninety-degree shift in camera position shows Bronson on the balcony outside the window taking them from her (and kissing her hand). Only in the second reel does Pinkerton appear, and the surviving print has so deteriorated that exactly what he does to persuade Bronson is unclear—but their confrontation seems to climax in several MSs, after which the former friend signs a letter of confession. Finally, *Le Cheveu d'or* ends in a conventional emblematic shot: a MCU of Pinkerton's hand (not Parker's) covering Lucy and Robert's joined hands in a kind of "professionalized" blessing of the romantic couple.

Neither Nick Winter nor Nat Pinkerton generally had much trouble securing the bourgeois family or its larger social order in their combats with criminals.[109] That was hardly the case in Eclair's *Zigomar*, which radically transformed the adventure film series almost single-handedly in September 1911. Dureau pinpointed one of these changes on the very eve of the film's premiere.

> As the *series* film returns in a multiple-reel format, remember that it still must be screened all at once, one reel after another. Just as the *Nick Carter* films worked as a *series*, in that each episode was shown separately, so, too, will *Zigomar* have its greatest impact as one, continuous film within a single program.[110]

It was *Zigomar*—along with Pathé's *Notre Dame de Paris*, Film d'Art's *Madame Sans-Gêne*, and Gaumont's *La Tare*—which successfully established the production and marketing format of the multiple-reel film that would be screened in its entirety on a cinema program. In the person of Zigomar (Arquillière), it also elevated the criminal to a status equal to, if not surpassing, that of the detective—in this case, the Paris chief of police, Paulin Broquet (Liabel). Jasset's three-reel film was based loosely on Sazie's popular serial novel that had appeared as a weekly feuilleton in *Le Matin*, from 7 December 1909 to 22 June 1910.[111] According to Eclair's own publicity,[112] Jasset condensed Sazie's narrative into a series of confrontations between Zigomar and Broquet in a select number of spaces chosen for the clous of spectacle they could evoke. But he retained and even strengthened Sazie's conception of Zigomar as evil reincarnate in the modern dress of a bourgeois gentleman: "clever, reckless, and thoroughly immoral in his lust for lucre."[113] In a sense, Méliès's earlier satanic hero had returned to sally forth from a masquerade "cathedral" to his own glory and frolic in a continually renewed, but always coolly restrained guise (except for his distinctive red hood)—a capitalist entrepreneur pushed to the point of excess and completely at ease anywhere he happened to appear in contemporary society.

The only extant archive print of this first *Zigomar* film is incomplete, but some traces of its appeal do remain, along with the descriptive commentary Eclair provided, one month before its release, in *Ciné-Journal*. The first reel, for instance, juxtaposes the empty nave and crypt of a deserted cathedral (aptly named Saint Magloire), where Zigomar's black-clad gang regularly meet in secret ceremony (like Satan's minions in Méliès), to the richly stocked studio of a high fashion designer, from which a charming young worker, Riri-la-Jolie, is plucked for Zigomar's pleasure. And when Broquet tries to trap the Z gang in the cathedral (cleverly hiding himself behind a stone knight topping a sarcophagus), he is quickly ensnared in a mechanized iron cage, dropped into a coffin, and then trucked off into the countryside where he is saved only by coincidence—as several gendarmes pass by checking for contraband. The second reel compresses the antagonism between Zigomar and Broquet into three emblematic spaces: a famous Montmartre restaurant (for a costume party, the two men, respectively, take on medieval and *ancien régime* disguises), an express train (after eluding Broquet on the station platform, Zigomar terrorizes the passengers), and a Swiss alpine resort (where the Z gang nightly plunders the hotel guests, and Broquet, lured onto a glacier, barely escapes falling to his death). The last reel returns to Paris for two set pieces of spectacular action. Zigomar seems safely ensconced at the Moulin Rose, watching the dancer Esmée perform in the style of Loïe Fuller (this sequence was tinted and toned and accompanied by a specially composed score),[114] when his nemesis arrives unexpectedly—and he sets the music hall on fire to cover his escape, but not before collecting the jewelry of several unconscious "slumming" bourgeois revelers. Finally, Broquet tracks Zigomar down to the subterranean depths of Saint-Magloire, but again the satanic figure eludes him by blowing up what had been the infernal center of his farflung criminal operations.

As this summary suggests, Jasset organizes the action in *Zigomar* so that each reel acts as a quasi-autonomous episode, much like the company's earlier series one-reelers. But he seems to adopt a strategy similiar to that of the original newspaper feuilleton by concluding each reel with a moment of anticipation or suspense, much as does Feuillade in *La Tare*. At the end of the first episode, Broquet gets a lead from one of his captors on where Zigomar will materialize next; at the end of the second, he is found on the glacier, but his survival remains in doubt. Zigomar also shares something else with *La Tare*. That is a commitment, at least according to the company's publicity, to a "realist" aesthetic: "The cinema . . . must be comprehensible by means of a simple representation of events, and never be overinsistent, for the spectator is seated in front of a film like a street corner observer before a *faits divers*."[115] And that commitment is perhaps most evident in the detailed decors of the dressmakers' studio and in the deep spaces of the streets through which the cart bearing Broquet's coffin rolls unnoticed. In other words, with *Zigomar*, Jasset seems to have been experimenting with a format that could combine the sensational shocks of grand guignol and the mass spectacle of the historical film with a "realist" representation of everyday life—or "the complete illusion of reality" that he so admired in American Vitagraph films.[116] The experiment paid off, for, within another six months, Eclair had a second Zigomar title ready for release.

Zigomar contre Nick Carter (1912) made explicit the connection Dureau already had drawn, bringing together the famous detective of one of the first films en series with the master criminal of one of the first multiple-reel films. In the very beginning of this four-reel film, the Z gang badly wounds Paulin Broquet in his office (they smuggle in explosives with the wood for his fireplace) so that Nick Carter, one of his top detectives (now played by Charles Krauss), has to take over the pursuit of Zigomar (Arquillière again).[117] Carter is perhaps even more obsessed than was Broquet at ridding the world of Zigomar, and he black-mails a former Z associate, Olga Liontef (Domidoff), into aiding him in his endeavors, which repeatedly turn futile despite his skill at disguises. Acting on Olga's tip, he first takes on the role of a servant in order to disrupt the chic gambling casino (its interior decors done all in white) which Zigomar now is running in Paris. Next he is tricked into following the master criminal's double to a gala hotel reception in the capital, while the real Zigomar is robbing a prominent jeweler's mansion in Marseille. And, when the detective does arrive in the southern port city, to thwart a kidnapping scheme perpetrated by the Z gang, he is seized (again in disguise) and has to be rescued by Olga from being crushed by a suspended stone slab. Later, he tracks Zigomar to a dockside cabaret cum opium den in Toulon, only to be chased by boat across the harbor, and, when he and Olga don the guise of sportsmen to protect an isolated chateau from the Z gang, both fall into their hands. Finally, after a partly botched es-cape, Olga is tortured by her archrival, Rosaria (Josette Andriot)—culminating in her being dragged behind a lashed horse racing across the countryside—and Carter vows revenge. A newspaper story deceptively reports the detective's death (ironically, from falling off a horse), and, when Zigomar and his gang celebrate their victory at a banquet, Carter and his agents take them all by surprise. But Zigomar pulls off one last trick: in court, Rosaria slips him a drug and he col-lapses, apparently poisoned.

In terms of narrative structure, *Zigomar contre Nick Carter* follows the earlier film closely, in that each of its four reels concludes with a moment of suspense. The first, for instance, breaks off after Carter fires at Zigomar as he is disap-pearing through a secret casino door. The second ends with Olga threatening to light a barrel of gunpowder as she confronts the Z gang in a grotto. And the third concludes with both Carter and Olga surrounded by Zigomar and Rosaria in a rough peasant cabin. In terms of its strategies of representation, however, the film seems rather conventional in its consistent reliance on FSs and LSs, along with relatively frequent intertitles. Yet, if Jasset eschews cut-in close shots[118]— there is only one, a CU photograph of Zigomar taken surreptitiously during the Marseille robbery, which reveals his whereabouts to Carter—he does often make use of alternation for suspense. A good example comes in the first reel, when four members of the Z gang, disguised as piano movers, toss Carter into the stairwell of Broquet's apartment building: alternating shots reveal Carter cling-ing to a lower railing, the Z gang dropping the piano into the stairwell, and the piano falling through the lower space, with Carter now safely looking on from the background. Similar sequences of alternation occur at the Paris gambling casino and the Toulon cabaret, as well as in the subsequent boat chase.

The film's principal interest, however, lies in its unique blend of the realistic, the fantastic, and the melodramatic—in what *Bioscope* described as an "orgy of sensationalism."[119] Eclair's commitment to "realism," for instance, is quite evident in the location shooting around Marseille and Toulon, whether in the mountains where the gang kidnaps a couple of wealthy tourists or in the desolate dock area where the cabaret is located. Along with this strong sense of verisimilitude comes an unexpected array of truc effects taken over wholesale from Méliès and Pathé's earlier trick films and féeries. Not only are disguises rampant throughout—at a mountain inn, Carter disappears behind a stack of boxes and, seconds later, emerges as an old peasant—but Zigomar's power literally becomes magical. Through stop-motion filming, the gambling casino is transformed into a recital hall, complete with a small ensemble of musicians. At the hotel reception, his double performs as a magician—producing a table and matching candelabra, servants, and a greyhound, all out of thin air—while Zigomar himself, at the end of his heist, plays the acrobat by pushing away from the mansion on an upright ladder and dropping into a passing getaway car. Finally, in the opium den, a man lying full length on the floor dreams of geishas with parasols who dance above him in superimposition and eventually close in around him. But this turns out to be a ruse, for the spectator as well as Carter, when the detective creeps in to attack—for behind the back wall tapestry lurks Zigomar poised to seize his prey. Together with all the melodramatic coincidence and violence, this conjunction of fantastical acts and demonstrably real spaces creates a fascinatingly schizoid vision of the world as simultaneously normal and abnormal, as marvelous as it is disorienting.

With the *Zigomar* films, Eclair succeeded in making the transition to the multiple-reel format by establishing a clear difference between its productions and those of its French rivals. One of those differences, again according to the company's own publicity, was that its male adventure stories focusing on criminal activity sought to explore "the strange and the fantastic within the very real fabric of modern life."[120] As a corollary, they encouraged the reinvention of something like a bricolage model of film construction, in which heterogeneous genre elements could be cobbled together into a feature-length format—and Jasset had just surveyed all those genres in a series of articles on cinema history in *Ciné-Journal*.[121] As a consequence, within a single film, the black-clad characters ranged freely through the French social system, from top to bottom, as well as toured its geographical regions—in a game of mock social mobility and control, in which victory went to the more resourceful, perhaps more devious performer. Finally, in contrast to Gaumont's *Scènes de la vie telle qu'elle est* or Pathé's *Scènes de la vie cruelle*, these Eclair films circulated the criminal hero, whether a superhuman individual or a professional *equipe*, not only outside the law but well outside the bounds of the family, in blatant repudiation of the latter's centrality as an institution to the French social order.

Certain of these features are evident in other extant Eclair films from early 1912. Advertised as one of the company's "social dramas," for instance, *Redemption* achieves an acute sense of veracity in re-creating the rank atmosphere of the vice-ridden streets and cabarets around the Saint-Lazare station, where Manette Aumont, under the tutelage of Comte de Aubiers, sinks into debauchery.[122]

110. *Zigomar contre Nick Carter*, 1912

111. *Zigomar contre Nick Carter*, 1912 (Josette Andriot, Alexandre Arquillière, Charles Krauss)

Le Cercueil de verre, by contrast, emphasizes the fantastic in its tale of two aristocrats in love with a Hindu princess, a "sleeping beauty" who has been awakened after centuries from her newly discovered glass coffin. After first trying to force himself on this exotic figure (and being thwarted), Guillaume de Noirmont has her abducted and hidden away in a second-rate fairground circus. Once rescued, with the help of the circus clown and his wife, the princess pleads to be returned to her former lifeless state in the coffin, and a Brahman priest accommodates her wish. The tale ends with the other aristocrat, Comte de Noyen, repressing this entire adventure as a dream—rather than a nightmare in which Noirmont acts as a perverse double for his own desire—or even a male fantasy of escape, before his upcoming marriage. *Le Cercueil de verre* sometimes makes use of a deep-space mise-en-scène within its otherwise conventional FSs and LSs, and this also is true of the fragment that remains of *Tom Butler*. Again, a single woman is the object of male attraction and vengeance: but, here, the woman is an actress, Miss Hampton (Andriot), and there is only one man, her former husband and escaped convict, Tom Butler (Arquillière), who threatens and assails her repeatedly—driving her at one point to attempt suicide by jumping out a window. In one spectacular scene, Butler barely eludes capture when he appears in the audience at the Folies Bergères where Hampton is performing. In the concluding trial scene, accentuated by a tilting camera movement, a superimposition of one attempt on her life—an admirer's bouquet is laced with chloroform—appears above and behind the unrepentant Butler moments after he shakes his fist at Hampton and just before he attacks a guard and tries to escape once more. Leaping out of a window, however, he plunges to his death—in an ironic form of poetic justice that nonetheless succeeds in circumventing the law.

Although directed by Chautard for ACAD, *Le Mystère de Pont Notre Dame* (1912) also can be loosely grouped with Jasset's crime films.[123] Its three-part narrative, sharply divided by reel breaks, turns on several coincidences and doublings by which a man is mistakenly accused of robbery and murder as well as infidelity. He is Claude Duval (Roger Karl), whose dire financial straits lead him to break off his engagement to Germaine Darlot (Dermoz)—provoking her father's wrath—and to consider drowning himself one night in the Seine. By chance, Claude interrupts another man about to dump the body of a gentleman he has robbed into the river, and he carries the victim back to his lodgings, only to have him die—a circumstance he cannot fully explain to Germaine, who has left her family to join him. Later, after Claude's finances improve and another woman begins flirting with him, Germaine, in a fit of anger, denounces him to the police. Despite her remorseful pleas in the courtroom, Claude is sentenced to twenty years in prison, where another convict, Rosquin (Duquesne), recognizes him and tries to kill him in a quarry explosion—but only succeeds in badly wounding himself. On his deathbed, Rosquin confesses to Germaine (who is exorcising her own guilt as a prison nurse) that it was he who committed the Pont Notre Dame crime, which finally exonerates Claude, for her as well as the law, and prompts his release.

Comparatively restrained in its melding of the melodramatic and the realistic, Chautard's film also tends to use rather austere studio decors (with the exception of the deep-space trial scene) and favors presenting its characters in AS/LS. More intriguing is its narrative structure, for each reel makes a different character and his or her double the focus of narration or accumulating narrative information. Although this deftly delays solving the mystery of the film's title until the very end, it also—unlike *Le Mystère des Roches de Kador*—deflects the spectator from a position of involvement with the romantic couple to one of almost ironic detachment. The crucial night scene near the Pont Notre Dame, for instance, is comprised of ten uninterrupted shots that alternate between Rosquin's and Claude's trajectory toward the Seine, bringing the two together just once when Claude looks off over the bridge wall and then surprises Rosquin over the body and momentarily gets knocked unconscious. Although Claude is always visible in AS, Rosquin remains at a distance, and unidentifiable, especially in the HA LSs that show him descending and then ascending the river bank stairs. If the spectator clearly is positioned to empathize with Claude here, that is not the case in the second reel. His own attitude toward the flirtatious woman seems ambiguous, for Germaine now takes over as the focal point of narration or even investigation—spotting the lady traveling by carriage to his lodgings, and discovering her letter requesting a rendezvous. As a consequence, her own letter to the police denouncing him (and implicitly herself) becomes almost plausible. In the third reel, it is Rosquin who finally comes to the fore, but his actions and identity remain mysterious until the deathbed confession. Although this "truth"—unexpectedly emanating from the mouth of the real criminal—allows the couple to reconcile, its even more important consequence comes in the concluding tableau, which circles back to resolve the family break between father and daughter. As in *Le Cercueil de verre*, the "adventure" into which Claude and Germaine are plunged—and in which they confront "unlawful" doubles of themselves—turns into a bad dream to be suppressed beneath the conventions of proper social behavior.

The most notorious of Eclair's crime films apparently were *L'Auto grise* (April 1912) and *Hors la loi* (May 1912), part of a short-lived series entitled *Bandits en automobile*. They restaged in fictional form the well-publicized exploits of the anarchist Bonnot gang that had terrorized Paris that past winter and whose leader had been executed by guillotine.[124] Mayors and provincial prefects across France, but especially in the south, banned these two films—along with others such as Pathé's *Charley Colms* and *Le Collier de la danseuse* and Gaumont's *Main de fer*—during the summer of 1912. The Radical politician and mayor of Lyons, Edouard Herriot (who would become prime minister fourteen years later), was one of the leaders of this campaign. In celebrating criminal figures, Herriot argued, such "scandalous and demoralizing spectacles" threatened the public order, especially by setting bad examples for children and adolescents who comprised up to a quarter of the overall cinema audience in France.[125] These bannings—along with the court case involving *Tom Butler*—produced an extensive debate in both the mass-circulation dailies and the trade press, with Eclair supporters such as Dureau at *Ciné-Journal* leading a spirited defense of the cinema, pointing to the moral position not only of the newsreels of Bonnot's execution but of films like *L'Auto grise*. In a sense, Dureau and others sought to enfold even these films within the dominant "reformist" discourse that spanned the French political spectrum and even attracted literary critics such as Doumic—a discourse that consistently extolled the salutory "educational" effects of news-reels, travelogues, and documentaries.[126] The French cinema industry's response to this official outcry was interesting. Gaumont, for instance, immediately set out to produce films like *Le Mystère des Roches de Kador* and *L'Erreur tragique*, which demonstrated the instrinsic social value of the cinema—and implicitly blamed spectators for misreading. Although neither Pathé nor Eclair dropped crime films completely from their releases, they did call less attention to them than before. But Eclair was back publicizing more titles by early 1913, and among them was perhaps the best of Jasset's *Zigomar* films.

In preparation for Zigomar's return, Jasset turned to Sazie's fellow serial writer at *Le Matin*, Gaston Leroux, for a somewhat different adaptation, *Balaoo* (1913). This two-reel film locates the fantastic quite specifically in the story of a monkey who is transformed into a man and named Balaoo (Lucien Bataille), in a variation on Mary Shelley's *Frankenstein*. His "creator" is a Doctor Coriolis (Camille Bardou), who lets him roam freely around the countryside outside Milan, where he is tormented by peasants and rescued by a fearsome poacher named Hubert (Henri Gugot). Learning all sorts of vengeful tricks from Hubert, Balaoo leaves one master for another, and the two head for the Swiss border, where Hubert gets his "servant" to commit a murder. Drawn to Lugano by reports of a strange creature "terrorizing" the people, Coriolis joins the pursuit for him, but Hubert kidnaps the doctor's niece, Madeleine (who has accompa-nied him), and Balaoo has to turn on his new master to free her. Surprisingly, the only distinctive feature of the film's first reel is the extensive camera move-ment, sometimes along with barely perceptible fast-motion, used to accentuate Balaoo's unusual physical attributes, especially around Lake Lugano. The one truly sensational moment comes early on in the second reel, in the murder scene. Beginning with a LA LS of Balaoo crawling upside down across a ceiling, the scene cuts to a sidelit MS of the drunken victim asleep on a billiard table, as two hands suddenly reach down toward his throat. Finally, a shift in camera position reveals not only the strangulation but, framed in a background window leading to the kitchen, the stunned, staring face of a woman—like a mirror image of the startled spectator. Perhaps the most interesting thing about *Balaoo*, however, is its reworking of the Frankenstein story into a psychoanalytic tale similar to that in *Le Cercueil de verre*. Hubert, rather than Coriolis, is set up as Balaoo's double, especially in that both desire Madeleine, and, in thwarting Hubert's lust, Balaoo demonstrates the sacrificial purity of his love. Moreover, the film exonerates Coriolis completely of any responsibility for Balaoo's actions, shifting that in-stead onto the anachronistic poacher. Indeed, *Balaoo* consistently privileges the bourgeois urban professional at the expense of the provincial peasant—while touring the spectacular landscape of Lugano—which is very suggestive of the audience it aims to address.

Released soon after *Balaoo*, *Zigomar, peau d'anguille* (1913) serves as a capstone to Jasset's series of crime films. Beginning in Paris, with Zigomar's resurrection after the apparent suicide in the courtroom, its narrative moves outward, like that of *Zigomar contre Nick Carter*, touring the empty tracts on the city's outskirts and then the mountains and lakes of northern Italy. In the process, it also shifts abruptly from one social site to another—from Zigomar's underground "control center" to the fairground tents and wagons of the Grand African circus (already explored in *Le Cercueil de verre*) and finally to the *haut bourgeois* mansion of an Italian banker. This time, however, along with the perpetually renewed, consistently black-clad *Z* gang, Zigomar (Arquillière) has a partner of equal status in Rosaria (Andriot) for his criminal enterprise. And Paulin Broquet (Liabel) returns as their chief antagonist, so marked by his previous encounters that he seems to have taken on some of Zigomar's callousness: in the opening scene, for instance, he asks the doctor in charge of the "corpse" to peel the skin off its arm for a memento card case. Furthermore, this film adds to the series' usual array of melodramatic weapons of seizure, torture, and death several that would soon prove themselves effective as new technologies of war.

In contrast to the other Zigomar films, each of this title's three reels constitutes a self-contained narrative episode, with a more or less certain conclusion. And each constructs its action so as to produce two or three major climaxes of increasing magnitude. In the first reel, Zigomar drops a huge net to ensnare Broquet in his lair and, much as he did in the original *Zigomar*, then suspends him in an iron cage—to let the detective ponder his bribery offer of one million francs, at least until one of Broquet's trusted lieutenants arrives to rescue him. In the second, Zigomar and Rosaria disguise themselves as circus performers in order to steal another million francs that the circus manager has won in a lottery. Here they use a midget and an elephant to make off with his safe, only to lose it in the mud of the sewer and barely escape Broquet (who infiltrates the circus in the guise of a clown) by again using the elephant to pin him to the ground. Finally, they themselves assume the guise of gypsies in a nearby camp, where, in a deftly ironic touch, Zigomar boldly and successfully begs a coin from the detective. In the third reel, Zigomar and Rosaria spot Broquet in the Italian alps and plant dynamite in a cable car to dispense with him, but, warned of the plot, he flees in a power boat across a mountain lake, only to have the pair drop bombs on him from an airplane. Under the cover of a festive ball, Zigomar and Rosaria lead the *Z* gang into the Italian banker's cellar (where he has secreted his safe), unaware that their nemesis has been rescued from the lake. Now it is they who fall into Broquet's trap as the banker suddenly floods the cellar—and Zigomar and Rosaria are lifted out of the water through a trapdoor, in chains.

If, in the previous film, Zigomar's power bordered on the magical, literalized in all those truc effects, here it is scaled down to the "natural" (hence the nickname, "eelskin") and is perhaps even more symptomatic. He can exercise uncanny control over everything from an animal straight out of the French colonies to the very latest invention in modern technology. Yet, paradoxically, where he loses control now is underground—in the sewer near the circus site and then in the banker's cellar. Correspondingly, the film's mode of representation tends toward the "realistic" when he is on top—the elephant performs its own "tricks" in lifting the safe and pinning the detective, and, except for the bombing run on the boat, the takeoff, flight, and landing of the plane is right out of an actualité—and toward the opposite when he is not, as in the stylized set decor of the sewer cross-section. Whatever the case, Jasset's representational strategies are much more flexible than before. When Rosaria comes to revive Zigomar, for instance, a cut-in MCU registers his awakening surprise as she cradles his head. Their escape is then described in a sequence that alternates shots of the window they leap from and the tautly stretched tarp they fall into below. When Broquet is rescued, by contrast, twice he and his lieutenant come forward into FS, only to whirl and fire their revolvers into the background, once into a dark void out of which several Z gang members stumble and sprawl. Finally, the climactic scene at the banker's mansion includes two POV shots that underscore Broquet's reassertion of control: first, he and the banker spot the Z gang creeping through the garden, then they use a surveillance telescope to view Zigomar and the gang, in HA LS, attacking the safe in the cellar. Rather than align the spectator with Broquet in his mise-en-scène of poetic justice, this strategy seems to create an ironic disjunction, for it is a foreign capitalist he is in league with—and the very one who throws the switch releasing the flood that engulfs Zigomar. The final courtroom tableau suggests that this may not yet be the end of Zigomar and Rosaria—nor should the spectator wish it to be—as she smiles and casts a sly wink at the camera.

Yet the Zigomar films did come to an end here, partly because Sazie sued Eclair for letting Jasset take too many liberties with the character he had created. Reportedly, he was particularly incensed by the elephant episode in *Zigomar, peau d'anguille*—although Deslandes suggests that he simply wanted out of his agreement with Eclair in order to write scenarios for other companies.[127] To replace his master criminal, Jasset invented a new character for the first of a planned series of feature-length adventure films—revamping Andriot's character of Rosaria into a spy named Protéa, of ambiguous political affiliation, who uncannily resembled the later Mata Hari. Although no print of *Protéa* (1913) seems to survive, it is clear from the trade press descriptions of its espionage plot aboard the Orient Express on its passage through the Balkans that Jasset was recycling more than a character from the earlier films: Protéa (Andriot) is protected by a lion at one point, for instance, and her partner is a monkey-man named Anguille (Bataille). Perhaps for reasons of economy, as Deslandes argues, that recycling even included set decors from the *Zigomar* films.[128] But most significant here was the decision to make a woman the active agent of the adventure narrative, in a fantasy display of female prowess (and imperilment) that underlined the genre's aversion to domesticity. Alone among French films, *Protéa* thus seems aligned with such American serial-queen melodramas as Edison's *What Happened to Mary* (1912–1913), Selig's *The Adventures of Dolly* (1913–1914), and, of course, Pathé-Eclectic's *The Perils of Pauline* (1914).[129] Although *Protéa* proved to be one of Jasset's last films (he died suddenly in late June 1913), Eclair would produce three more adventure films under that title from 1914 to 1917.[130] Yet even before *Protéa*'s release, the torch of notoriety already had passed from Zigomar to another master criminal, the even more famous Fantômas, and that passing required a belated shift from one side of the law to the other at Gaumont.

Along with his historical and biblical films as well as the *Scènes de la vie telle qu'elle est*, in 1912–1913, Feuillade produced several multiple-reel films featuring a detective hero, Jean Dervieux (Navarre). Several of these titles—*Le Proscrit* (1912) and *L'Ecrin de Radjah* (1913)—resemble Jasset's at Eclair in their attention to exotic characters and places. If the first seems to anticipate the Balkan adventure of *Protéa*, the second, more tellingly, takes over the "fantastic realism" of Jasset's adventure films—with its elemental combat on a desert island and its black-clad bandits freely circulating through the streets and salons of Paris.[131] The only one that seems to survive, *L'Oubliette* (1912), takes Dervieux to an isolated chateau that Jacques de Montalban has just bought for his wife Hélène and where she mysteriously vanishes.[132] Unlike the other two longer films, this economical two-reeler is confined almost exclusively to the half-dozen spaces that the couple explores within the chateau and sometimes looks like an exercise in continuity editing. The first crucial moment comes when Hélène gets up in the night, apparently to tease Jacques, and hides in a chest sitting along one wall of the foyer. Suddenly, the floor of the chest gives way (in MS) and Hélène falls into a void (in LS). Now Jacques gets up and searches for her, and an insert FS of Hélène shows her coming forward into a lit area underground, calling out (without response) and then calmly lying down. After his fruitless search, Jacques goes off in the car, and the first reel ends ambiguously on a FS of the seemingly abandoned Hélène. He returns, of course, with Dervieux, and they explore the chateau much as the couple did when they first arrived. Only now it is the detective alone who goes back to examine the chest and, after finding a bobby pin inside (in MCU), falls through exactly as Hélène did. In the brief alternating sequence that follows, Dervieux awakens Hélène, Jacques finds the chest bottom open, the detective fires his revolver, and the servants throw down a rope ladder for the "victims" below. Hélène emerges first to cheerfully embrace Jacques, and, after they exit, Dervieux crawls out and nonchalantly lights a cigarette— the thoroughly modern, almost blasé bourgeois couple matched by an inadvertently successful, yet no less assured, detective hero.

Along with Feuillade, Perret also produced at least three multiple-reel detective films in the controversial *Main de fer* series (1912–1913), apparently all drawn from original scenarios. These films, however, more closely resemble the *Zigomar* films, at least in their staging of repeated, inconclusive showdowns between police inspector Necker (Keppens), nicknamed "The Iron Hand," and several nefarious villains (all played by Perret).[133] For the first film in the series, released in August, Perret appears as Rizzio, the leader of a spy ring intent on stealing secret documents from the south coast villa of an Admiral Nyard and his daughter Yvette (Grandais). The versatility of Perret's cameraman, Specht, already is on display in the initial confrontation, for it is prefaced by a double oval mask of each man, back to back, in AS, dressing for an embassy reception. Because Necker has assumed a disguise, it is one of Rizzio's spies who gets to play detective at the reception, spotting a metro ticket and a name label, in ECU, in the inspector's coat. Although Necker is quickly captured (he is roped and blindfolded while being driven away in the spies' car), he escapes a "tied-to-the-rails" scenario, and the film's tongue-in-cheek attitude toward such plot conventions continues with the spies eventually racing off in a speedboat while Necker, for his transportation, has to settle for a bicycle. Yet, in the final scene, Rizzio and his men are surprised during their search of the villa, when Yvette (with the aid of a police radio) signals a naval vessel offshore, and, after the ship begins firing one of its big guns, the speedboat in which the spies attempt to flee once more, explodes in flames. Rizzio's devious desires may be enhanced by certain new technologies of mobility, but he ultimately proves no match for the military power of the French state—and Yvette and her naval officer fiancé receive its blessing in the final tableau.

Released one month later, *Main de fer contre la Bande aux "Gants Blancs"* has Perret return as a dapper gang leader in the guise of a wealthy Egyptian preying—much like his earlier SCAGL counterpart—on haut bourgeois women. In the opening scene at a musical soiree, for instance, he chloroforms a woman he has taken aside and deftly lifts her jewelry. The film sticks closely to the capital, where Necker this time is captured in an ordinary apartment building with the help of the gang leader's mistress, Ninie (Grandais). This scene includes its own deft maneuvering, for the "normal" activity in the central room is juxtaposed to the gang's chloroforming of Necker in an adjacent one (frame left), alternately disclosed and concealed by a pan through the wall separating the two. Yet Ninie proves to be ambiguous in her loyalties and allows Necker to escape from the cellar of a cabaret the gang controls. Then, when a police raid on the cabaret nearly results in her own arrest, she switches back to helping the gang leader in his attempt to reach the Belgian border. Necker, however, has put a tap on her apartment phone so that, when she calls her lover, now a reverse pan to the other adjacent room (frame right) reveals him listening in on their conversation. A nifty variation on the triptych device then concludes this sequence—with the gang leader and Ninie, on opposite sides of the frame, oblivious to Necker sneaking out her apartment door in the central panel. But the film seems to end with the gang leader's capture in doubt, setting up the expectation of another sequel.

The censorship problems that *Main de fer* encountered probably kept Gaumont from fulfilling that expectation in the fall and pushed Perret to make films such as *Le Mystère des Roches de Kador*, in which the "good guys" triumphed with much more certainty. By early 1913, however, Perret resumed the series with *L'Evasion de Forçat de Croze*, whose release nearly coincided with that of *Zigomar, peau d'anguille*. This film is linked closely to its predecessor in that de Croze (Perret again) is a former leader of the "Gants Blancs" gang now using a Paris bank as a cover for his criminal operations. This time Necker wines and dines a young secretary in the bank (Petit) and, when she passes out, successfully cases her office to find traces of de Croze's presence. An ECU of a locket photo, however, reveals that she is in love with de Croze, and, when Necker and his men raid the bank and discover how de Croze plans to flee the country by boat, she uses her lover's secret passageway to escape their dragnet. Now it is she who, in MCU, dons the disguise of a prim, proper woman—her hair pulled back in a bun, her eyes reshaped by rimless glasses, and her face half-concealed by a hat and veil—and deftly eludes the police in several public places before taking the train to Marseille. The local police there have spotted de Croze, however, and Necker joins them in time for a most unusual chase. The sequence begins with reverse-angle dolly shots of the motoring pursuers and pursued, into which is inserted (at the point where Necker looks through his binoculars) a shot that encompasses three separate masked images (all in motion)—separate MCUs of de Croze and the woman and a LS of their car. Despite this skill at "synthesized" surveillance, Necker's car breaks down briefly so that the other can get far enough ahead to reach the coast. Yet the climax of the sequence comes in an even more unconventional shot that includes three discrete masked images, fading in and out in succession across the frame, which trace the woman stepping out of the car (upper left), getting into a speedboat (center right), and then gliding off across the water (lower left). No longer framed by Necker's binoculars, this shot escapes surveillance altogether and turns the narrative suspense into a smoothly choreographed spectacle of special effects. For its conclusion, the film then re-capitulates the spectacular moment from the finale of the first title in the series. A police boat traps de Croze on the sailing ship he has bought, and, once he is certain that his young companion has been taken off unharmed by Necker, he "choreographs" his own sensational end by setting fire to the ship and disappearing with its burning hulk into the sea. Or so we are led to believe.

Shortly after this final *Main de fer* film, René Navarre returned in Feuillade's *Fantômas* series (1913–1914), but now on the other side of the law, as an even more formidable figure than either de Croze or Zigomar. These five films—all feature-length at four to six reels each—were based on a phenomenally popular series of novels written by Marcel Allain and Pierre Souvestre which Arthème Fayard first began to publish in September 1911. Over the course of the next two years, the pair wrote a staggering total of thirty-two volumes, each of which (averaging four hundred pages in length) sold up to 600,000 copies.[134] What fascinated readers was Fantômas's paradoxical criminal nature as both an-archist and bourgeois gentleman, captured vividly in the first book cover illus-tration (by Gino Starace): a gigantic masked man in formal dress literally brood-ing over Paris, with one foot testing the strength of a bridge over the Seine and his right hand clenching a barely concealed dagger. And there were even more lurid covers: a group of gendarmes laying hands on a woman in a bridal gown and a black mask, two men stripping the gold from the dome of the Invalides, and a bloody hand clutching a casino roulette wheel.[135] But the novels' popu-larity also stemmed, as the poet John Ashbery suggests, from the characters' constant movement, by every available means of modern locomotion, through a rich variety of actual landscapes and social milieus, particularly in and around

Paris, whose atmosphere was "brushed with remarkable sensitivity."[136] Indeed, so popular was the archcriminal that Apollinaire and his circle of literati at *Les Soirées de Paris* (1912–1914) even formed a special club in his honor, "Société des Amis de Fantômas."[137]

Early in 1913, according to Lacassin, both Pathé and Gaumont approached the writers to secure permission to adapt *Fantômas* for the screen, and Gaumont won out by a sizable sum.[138] So it was Feuillade and his cameraman Guérin who got the chance to make the first *Fantômas* film, released in April 1913 (with a special score composed by Paul Fosse),[139] and four other titles that followed like sequels at two- or three-month intervals, beginning that next September.[140] Since he never seems to have wavered from the conservative Catholic views of his southern provincial upbringing, what was it that attracted Feuillade to the Fantômas adventures? Perhaps he was like those who twenty years earlier had been drawn to Léo Taxil's scandalous books, widely circulated under the pseudonym of Dr. Bataille and by a reputable Catholic publisher at that, which purported to expose the nefarious schemes of the Freemasons and other "satanic" secret societies.[141] Perhaps he saw in Allain and Souvestre's adventure novels an opportunity to achieve something that might outperform both the *Zigomar* and *Main de fer* films. Whatever the case, Gaumont promoted *Fantômas* with a poster that duplicated the initial book cover, only the figure looming over Paris now seemed less threatening—slightly smaller, more crisply outlined, and with the dagger removed from his clenched fist.

Fantômas introduces René Navarre immediately in MCU, in the three guises he will take on throughout its three episodes: a Dr. Chaleck, a hotel bellhop, and a bourgeois gentleman named Gurn. This device quickly sketches one of the resources Fantômas must draw on in his profession, but it also places the spectator in a privileged position vis-à-vis all the other characters because Navarre never appears except in these disguises until the very end of the film. The first episode, running the full length of the first reel, skillfully establishes the "fantastic realism" that so characterizes the series—in which the mundane, reassuringly sober facade of daily life masks incredible, sometimes bloody exploits. A dozen shots ranging from LS to AS describe the arrival one evening of Princess Danidoff (Jane Faber) at the Royal Palace Hotel in Paris. In a meticulous model of continuity editing, the sequence traces her movement through a series of contiguous spaces—the hotel exterior, the foyer, the lobby, the elevator, the fourth-floor corridor, and her spacious room. Later, apparently after an intertitle,[142] Dr. Chaleck is introduced in MS, followed by a LS that suddenly situates him alone in the same room, where he opens the drawer of a foreground secretary desk and then, in response to an offscreen sound, hides behind the background window curtains. After the princess returns in her nightgown, Chaleck calmly steps out to confront her. His smooth demeanor mesmerizes her into silence, and he tops that with the presentation of a blank card (which she gazes at in HA MS and ECU). All the while, of course, he is emptying the desk of her money and jewels. Only after he has blown her a kiss and exited does she telephone the hotel front desk, where the night manager sends a bellhop off to

112. *Fantômas*, 1913 (René Navarre)

the elevator. But Chaleck seizes him in the fourth-floor corridor, and, after a series of shots that reverse the elevator's earlier ascent past each floor, the thief steps out into the lobby in the guise of the bellhop. He shrugs at the night manager, gets the key to the front door, lets himself out, and, silhouetted in MS in the opaque glass, relocks the door and, in a final exterior shot, strides off in triumph. Now the film cuts back to the princess who examines the blank card once more—and, in ECU, the name of Fantômas dissolves in, in sharp block letters.

After this display of Fantômas's singular prowess, the other two episodes introduce police inspector Juve (Bréon) and crime reporter Fandor (Georges Melchior), who are investigating the disappearance of Lord Beltham. In episode two, Fantômas, now disguised as Gurn, is arrested after Juve discovers Beltham's corpse stuffed into a steamship trunk in Gurn's apartment. In the third, however, Lady Beltham (Carl), who has become his mistress, bribes a prison guard Nibet (Naudier) and concocts a plan by which Fantômas is replaced by an actor named Valgrand (Volbert) and is freed to resume his ruthless career. This section of the film at several points depends on long-take tableaux—for instance, in the sunny, deep-space drawing room of Lady Beltham's suburban villa (with its light-colored wallpaper and floor-length windows overlooking a garden) and in Gurn's smaller, darker bourgeois apartment. Yet both of these also include cut-in CUs—as Juve picks up a clue to Gurn's identity and address through the manufacturer's name on the hat he has left behind and later finds a packet of blank cards in Gurn's apartment. These two episodes also differ from the first in that their action covers not two but three reels and, consequently, carries over through the reel breaks, much as did not only the earlier *Zigomar* films but also Feuillade's own films from *La Tare* to *L'Erreur tragique*. Reel two ends, for instance, with Lady Beltham approaching Nibet in the paddy wagon so that reel three can begin with a MS of her passing money to him. Reel three then ends with the alternating sequence of Valgrand disguised as Fantômas (at her request) approaching her villa and Fantômas himself being taken out of his prison cell by Nibet for one last visit to her. This increases the suspense for reel four, which opens with the scene of substitution.

Perhaps most intriguing in *Fantômas* are these scenes with Valgrand, who just happens to be playing Fantômas in a successful new drama about the arch-criminal's life and death. In an ironic comment on the genre's conventions, it is he who is shown backstage putting on his "disguise" (for a circle of admirers) and then performing on stage, with Lady Beltham in the audience. She and Fantômas then exploit this theatrical representation in a deceptive mise-en-scène of their own, privately at her villa. In another long-take tableau, Valgrand sneaks into her sitting room, is drugged into semiconsciousness, and is substituted for Fantômas, whom Nibet has "tactfully" allowed to remain alone with his mistress (and who, at the crucial moment, hides behind some curtains). This sets up the next-to-last scene where Valgrand barely escapes being guillotined, in a literal "realization" of his death scene on stage (Juve recognizes him at the last moment), while Fantômas and Lady Beltham watch from the window of a nearby apartment. This latter shot is interesting because it focuses on the difference between the two—in silhouette, with his back to the camera, Fantômas draws the reluctant Lady Beltham to the window, from which she recoils in horror. If this final episode, like the first, encourages the spectator to admire Fantômas's savoir faire in manipulating others, the shifting figure of Lady Beltham, much more than the ineffectual Juve, suggests another more conventional reading position of moral outrage. Consequently, in the final tableau, the mocking specter of Fantômas (replicating the poster) which dissolves in before Juve in his office and holds out his crossed hands (as if to be handcuffed) may provoke some sense of ambivalence in the spectator—all the while, of course, planting the seeds of anticipation for the next film.

Gaumont itself may not have expected the full measure of success *Fantômas* enjoyed that spring—Navarre reportedly drew crowds whenever he appeared in public.[143] But the company exploited its opportunity for the 1913–1914 cinema season, publicizing *Juve contre Fantômas* as one of its "big films" for September and October.[144] True to its title, this sequel focuses on the personal antagonism between Fantômas and Juve, opening with close shots of both Navarre and Bréon, each in the disguises he will take on during its four episodes.[145] But this time, instead of operating alone or with just a single partner, for one major heist Fantômas has an apache gang, which includes a young streetwalker named Josephine (Andreyor). The film's narrative divides into more or less equal halves, with the division marked by a clear reel break. Although each half is further subdivided into two episodes, the action in both seems to carry across the other two reel breaks. In the first episode, disguised as the gangster Loupart, Fantômas plots the robbery of a wealthy wine merchant, Martielle, using Josephine to lure him onto the last car of an express train bound for Switzerland, hiring the gang to uncouple the car in the mountains, and, after the theft, letting the detached car be smashed by the Simplon-Express. In the second, Loupart composes a fake letter to lure Juve and Fandor at night to Martielle's warehouse on the Quai de Bercy (on the southeastern edge of Paris) for a gun battle with his gang and then has to devise a clever means of escaping the two, when they force Josephine to reveal where he is seated, disguised again as Chaleck, in the luxurious Crocodile restaurant. Lady Beltham returns in the third episode (the film opened with a disfigured body, thought to be hers, found in Chaleck's apartment) to be drawn away from the convent where she has secreted herself and back to her villa at night, under Fantômas's spell. Juve and Fandor reconnoiter the empty villa during the day and follow Lady Beltham there one evening to overhear Fantômas plotting the inspector's death—and, despite their precautions, a boa constrictor unloosed in his apartment the next night nearly strangles him in bed. The final episode pits Fantômas (now all in black, including a hood) versus Juve, Fandor, and a team of policemen in the villa one night. After eluding them by submerging himself in a cellar cistern and then by decoying them into thinking he can be smoked out through an air vent (the boa surprises Juve again), Fantômas destroys the villa with dynamite. The film ends with the famous apocalyptic tableau of his lone figure in silhouette at the villa's gate, his arms raised in triumph before the background smoke and debris.

Rather than simply repeat the earlier film's formula, *Juve contre Fantômas* increases the number of climactic action scenes as well as the level of grand guignol violence. Some of these scenes are highly synthetic in their construction. The train accident, for instance, stitches together a shot of Fandor and Martielle clinging to the side of the rolling, detached car (Fandor looks up in horror), an actualité shot of an express train rushing forward, and a shot of a papier-maché mountain set and model train cars for the collision. Others, while filmed entirely at one location site, also involve a good deal of editing. The twelve-shot night sequence on the Quai de Bercy, for instance, includes cut-in closer shots of the gun battle among the rows of wine casks and then a linked series of shots as Fantômas's gang rolls a cask full of gunpowder (the fuse is lit) toward Juve and Fandor, who have to leap into the Seine. Although this scene now looks almost comical because no one seems to be hit in the close-range firing, the blue tinting in the original positive prints would have masked the distance between antagonists and thrown into relief the fire and smoke of the explosions.

Yet it is not the action and violence that remain so remarkable about this film. Instead, it is the acute sense of verisimilitude in certain scenes which "naturalizes" Fantômas's exploits, rendering them even more terrifyingly marvelous. This is especially evident in the deep-space location shooting around the Place

113. *Juve contre Fantômas*, 1913

114. *Juve contre Fantômas*, 1913 (René Navarre, Yvette Andreyor)

Pigalle and Boulevard de La Chapelle—where Josephine nonchalantly slips Loupart a note in passing, Fandor follows her into the darkness of one metro station entrance and out of another, and Juve's taxi pursuing Loupart is immobilized when a gang member slashes its tires (while an old shoemaker silently watches from his shop). It even extends to Robert Jules Garnier's unusually detailed studio decors of the spacious Crocodile restaurant, in a scene that includes cut-in shots of the second background room, where the unperturbed Chaleck is dining (the coat he picks up in the foyer turns out to have fake arms so he can easily slip out of Juve's grasp). And it culminates in the scenes at Lady Beltham's empty villa. As Juve and his colleagues circulate through the richly decorated rooms, what could be promotional displays of haut bourgeois interior design instead assume a museumlike or even funereal air. If not literally haunted, as the watchman claims, they evidence, in microcosm, how completely under Fantômas's spell is the whole world in this film. Moreover, inserted throughout these scenes of combat between Juve and Fantômas, which also include some alternation for suspense, are an unusual number of close shots. Although serving a narrative function—Juve examines a quill pen still wet with ink, the watchman opens the air vent grate, Fantômas breaks a wine bottle off at the bottom (which he uses for breathing in the cistern)—these close shots give added weight and significance to the ordinary objects of everyday life. They, too, are circumscribed by Fantômas's power, symptoms not of the moral truth that Pathé's earlier melodramas sought to reveal through intensification but its grand guignol opposite—the criminal, the mad, and the perverse.

The six episodes of the next sequel, *Le Mort qui tue* (November 1913), make it one of the longest in the series, and, in reprising characters and situations from the earlier films, it is even more grisly in its violence. After Juve and Fandor escape the destruction of Lady Beltham's villa (not without injury), it is the journalist who now pursues the archcriminal, but with no more success than Juve had. As before, Fantômas's exploits take him and his pursuer through several different levels of French society. In the first episode, Fantômas chloroforms a painter named Jacques Dollon (André Luguet) in order to set him up for the murder of a wealthy baron he has killed. In the second, Nibet stabs Dollon in prison, and Fantômas takes away the body in order to remove the skin of its right hand—for a human glove. Here, Juve (disguised as a clochard) has to rescue Fandor who has followed Fantômas to a Seine sewer inlet (where Dollon's body is dumped). Princess Danidoff returns in the third episode, to give a party for her fiancé Thomery (Luitz-Morat), a sugar plantation owner, and promptly is robbed of her jewels again by Fantômas, disguised as a banker named Nanteuil—but on her neck (she has been rendered unconscious) is a fingerprint that turns out to be Dollon's. Lady Beltham then returns in the next episode, to deliver a ransom note for the jewels to Thomery, who is lured to an empty apartment and garroted by Fantômas's gang. In the fifth episode, Fantômas searches the pension Bourrat, where Elizabeth Dollon (Fabienne Fabrèges) is staying, trying to recover an enigmatic list she found earlier in her brother's cell, and Fandor arrives just in time to save her from being asphyxiated—and sends her to a convent for protection. Then, hidden in a packing basket of her belongings which Fantômas has requisitioned, he is transported to the gang's hideout and discovers Thomery's body. Finally, Fandor links up again with Juve, and they confront Nanteuil, thinking they have Fantômas at last—but he vanishes before their eyes (and guns) through a secret wall panel door.

From this narrative summary, the six episodes of *Le Mort qui tue* would seem to correspond closely to the film's six reels. According to the National Film Archive's print, however, which covers only the last three episodes and has Czech intertitles, this film, too, either carried the action across at least some of the reel breaks or else used the reel break to heighten suspense near the end of an episode.[146] One break in the NFA print, for instance, comes just after Fantômas exits from Elizabeth's room at the pension, after having drugged her coffee and turned on the gas; the next opens with Fandor breaking into the room to turn off the gas and open a window.[147] Yet, if *Le Mort qui tue* resembles its predecessors in this use of reel breaks, its mode of representation is slightly different. Most of the scenes, for instance, are shot in studio decors, and frequent intertitles either link or interrupt the AS/LS or FS/LS tableaux. Some of the decors, especially the ones with less depth, are quite spare, but this is used to good effect for moments like the garroting—where Thomery steps from a background painted-flat hallway into an empty room, through a central doorway on either side of which two hooded figures stand poised. One of the film's more interesting features, however, is the greater number of cut-in CUs and ECUs of objects, which prove more deceptive than revealing. In episode three, for instance, the CU photograph of the fingerprint lifted from the princess's neck baffles her guests, and the ECU of the pearls that Lady Beltham shows Thomery deceives him into believing the ransom exchange is genuine—in both cases, by contrast, the spectator can conclude this is Fantômas's handiwork. Curiously, another cut-in close shot briefly positions the spectator as superior to Fantômas— when Elizabeth stuffs the list into the back of a blotter, which he later overlooks in his search of her room. Yet, a cut-in CU of his hand turning the gas lever then threatens to take revenge on her for the sleight of hand, as well as on any spectator tempted to identify with her. These CUs culminate in the last scene as Juve rips the glove of human skin from Fantômas's hand—only to have him disappear through the wall, secreted beneath one more fake exterior.

Fantômas contre Fantômas (February 1914) shows some signs of exhaustion in its recirculation of situations from the earlier films. Once more Lady Beltham returns, but now married to a prince, so that, when she throws a masked ball, this time it is her jewels that are stolen. Again, Fandor is carried off to the gang's hideout, this time in a barrel (where he has overheard Fantômas's plans), so he can coach Juve (who has been abducted from his office by fake masons) into pretending he is their leader in disguise. And Fantômas himself initially appears in a "lower class" guise, this time as the slum landlord and usurer, Père Moche, in a Paris *banlieue*. This latter figure dominates the first and perhaps most interesting of the film's four episodes, whose self-contained story, minimal intertitles, and plain, shabby decors are reminiscent of the early *Scènes de la vie telle*

115. *Le Mort qui tue*, 1913 (Luitz-Morat)

qu'elle est. It focuses on Père Moche's upstairs neighbors, a young couple named Nestor and Nini Paulet, who murder a tax collector who has just taken his money out of the usurer's safe (his killing is handled much like Thomery's in the previous film). After a MS insert of Père Moche responding to the sound of the body's fall, he goes upstairs and opens the couple's door, sees them washing their hands in a side room, and steals the dead man's satchel left laying on a nearby chair. Soon Nestor (Morlas) saunters down to Père Moche's room and threatens him with a knife, but the older man easily subdues him and then black-mails him into his service.

The other interesting thing about *Fantômas contre Fantômas* is the return of the initial film's explicit playacting in a game of mise-en-abyme—with Fantômas at one point disguised as a detective, and both Juve and Fandor assuming the guise of the criminal. In the second episode, Fantômas shows up as Tom Bob, an American detective (this name sounds peculiarly southern), to quickly solve the case of the missing tax collector. In the Paulet's former room, which is being replastered, he simply pounds a nail into one wall and stands back to let the new landlady watch blood pour out in a stream. In the third episode, at Lady

Beltham's ball, Fandor and a policeman disguise themselves as hooded, black-clad gang members and confront Fantômas in the same costume—which provokes a duel and chase, resulting in the policeman's death in the garden. Meanwhile, Juve has been detained in prison for incompetence—rumors even circulate that he may *be* Fantômas. The morning after the ball, he wakes up to find his right arm slashed and bloody (Fandor reports he wounded Fantômas precisely that way), but the blame for this deception is soon pinned on the old guard Nibet. Although both Fandor and Juve finally make good on playing Fantômas–Père Moche—they do arrest most of the gang in their hideout—Fantômas himself, as always, escapes. In one last, clever twist, he takes with him all the money Lady Beltham collected as a reward for his capture.

In what would be the last film in the series, *Le Faux Magistrat* (May 1914), Feuillade abandoned Paris as the central site of Fantômas's exploits and turned to the provinces southwest of the capital, specifically to the town of Saint-Calais near Le Mans. This film's story introduces a new set of characters around the three principals, and it has Fantômas and his gang pervert not only the French legal system but, for good measure, the Catholic Church as well.[148] The film begins with an elliptical episode in which the Marquis de Tergell (Mesnery) sells his wife's jewelry for 250,000 francs, only to have the jeweler accuse him of substituting an empty box for the one with the gems. A stolen cassock found along the town's railroad tracks, however, points to a "priest" Tergell bumped into leaving his hotel as the real culprit. Then, on the way home to his country estate, Tergell is waylaid and robbed of the money. Meanwhile, in Belgium, Fantômas is escaping from prison, with the help of none other than Juve (in disguise), who plans to follow his trail back to France and arrest his whole gang (Belgian law does not permit his extradition). Fantômas gives Juve the slip on the train, however, when an old judge arrives late at the rail station and has to get into the baggage car, where he is promptly killed so that the escapee can assume his identity (although his clothes are a bit big for him). The judge just happens to be en route to Saint-Calais, where Fantômas can rejoin his gang, including Nestor (their hideout is an abandoned rail car), and enjoy the profits of the jewel theft it turns out he planned. Taking up the judge's role, he resumes his criminal activity—asphyxiating Tergell and blackmailing his wife with compromising letters—until Fandor, who is in town to investigate the jewel theft, notices his strangely padded clothing. When Nestor and Ribonard (Martial) go to retrieve the jewels they have hidden in the town church tower, Fantômas suspects the latter of betrayal and leaves him suspended from a huge bell clapper—only to discover that he, too, has been deceived (again, the jewel box is empty). Consequently, when the church bells are rung at Tergell's funeral the next day, in the words of Maurice Raynal, "there is this sublime spectacle of blood, pearls, and gold raining down on the faithful mourners."[149] Finally, Fantômas is trapped when Fandor discovers that the Tergell's maid Rosa (Suzanne Le Bret) is Nestor's accomplice, and Juve arrives (once more disguised as Fantômas) to testify at the Tergell trial and to expose the "false judge." Yet the film ends on a note of suspense—can Fantômas escape or not?—which suggests that

116. *Le Faux Magistrat,* 1914 (René Navarre)

Feuillade himself may have been planning yet another sequel for the series, until the war intervened later that summer.

If Feuillade's *Fantômas* films remain one of the high points of Gaumont's production during the 1913–1914 season, Perret's two blockbusters, *L'Enfant de Paris* and *Le Roman d'un mousse,* certainly constitute another. Both were "super-productions" of eight reels or more, putting them in the same category as Pathé's *Germinal* and Film d'Art's *Les Trois Mousquetaires.* And both were exhibited as *exclusivités* on cinema programs, divided into two more or less equal parts by an interval, in a successful attempt to equate them with the theatrical performance of a play.[150] In their choice of subjects, these films combine criminal and detective features of the *Zigomar, Main de fer,* and *Fantômas* series with others having to do with the bourgeois family of the contemporary melodrama. On the one hand, consequently, they offer excursions through a variety of social and geographical sites, from passing tours of the haut bourgeois playgrounds to "slumming" experiences of the "down and out" margins. On the other, they reintroduce the story of the "lost child" that threatens the very continuance of the bourgeois family as the locus of social value and order. And this re-merging of the two recently divergent genres takes its most explicit shape, especially in the first film, in the character of the adolescent boy who is at first the criminals' victim and then their nemesis as the detective hero.

L'Enfant de Paris (1913) essentially reformulates and updates the child kidnapping and child detective narratives of Pathé's earlier melodrama films. It begins with what was, in 1911, a very topical situation: Lieutenant Pierre Valen (Keppens), of a well-to-do Parisian family, is commissioned to lead an infantry company in Morocco, as part of the French move to occupy the ancient capital of Fez, the last stage in the long colonial process of securing the country as a protectorate.[151] After receiving news that he is missing and presumed dead in a counterattack against his fort, his wife (Jean-Marie Laurent) sickens and soon dies, leaving their only child, a young girl named Marie Laure (Suzanne Prévat), in the care of her uncle. He, too, is called to military service, in Indochina, and the girl is sent to an orphanage on the city's outskirts, where her despair only deepens—and one night she steals away. The family having been destroyed by one kind of external threat—those opposing French colonialization (and the dispute over Morocco came close to provoking war with Germany)—Marie Laure now falls into the hands of an apache gang led by Edmond le Bachelier (Louis Leubas) and is turned over to an old shoemaker, Piron (Marc Gérard), for safekeeping, where she is befriended by his assistant, le Bosco (Maurice Lagrenée). When Valen escapes from a POW camp and returns a war hero, the gang offers to ransom the girl in the back room of a café. Le Bosco alerts the police, and most of the gang is caught, but not before they trick Valen into doubling the ransom. Edmond escapes with Marie Laure, however, and, in disguise, takes her by train to the empty Villa Carmen in Nice. Le Bosco follows their trail to the south and, after donning a new suit of clothes and taking a hotel room (a wealthy couple takes pity on him one day in the park), sends a telegram to Valen in Paris, before going off to rescue the girl himself when the apache leaves her alone one night. Only then does the boy contact the local gendarmes and help apprehend the apache on his return, and it is he who brings Valen to his hotel room for the reunion with his long-lost daughter. *L'Enfant de Paris* concludes, therefore, with a reconstituted bourgeois family to which le Bosco now belongs as an older brother, having successfully passed muster in his own "war" against crime. Marie Laure becomes an object of exchange in restoring the family as even more fully patriarchal and patriotic, the mother having been replaced by the more highly valued adopted son.

The chauvinism marking Perret's melodramatic scenario—and already evident in the initial *Main de fer*—closely aligns *L'Enfant de Paris* with the nationalism then rampant in France. Yet, as Sadoul remarked, on viewing a newly rediscovered print at the Cinémathèque française in 1951, the film still comes as a stunning revelation.[152] Somewhat like Griffith, in the slightly later *Birth of a Nation*, Perret deploys an audacious range of representational strategies in an unusually supple "syntax" (considerably aided by cameraman Specht and set designer Perrier), which makes the most of an ideologically regressive subject (although hardly one as controversial as Griffith's). Certain scenes, for instance, depend on deep-space interior decors, whether well lighted—as in the café in-

117. *L'Enfant de Paris*, 1913 (Jean-Marie Laurent, Suzanne Prévet, Emile Keppens)

terior whose background opens onto the slightly raised front room and the street beyond—or very selectively lighted by arc lamps—as in the orphanage dormitory the night Marie Laure makes her escape. Some use background mirrors (as in the girl's Paris bedroom) or repeated short pans (as in the shoemaker's room and adjacent garret space, where the girl is hidden)—to extend the playing area beyond the initial limits of the frame. Others present figures from a high angle—as when Valen speaks briefly, after his return, from an apartment balcony to a crowd cheering and waving flags. Still others shade foreground figures and door or window frames in silhouette—especially during le Bosco's exploration of Nice (its shops and hotels as well as its surrounding hills)—in picturesque images accentuated by tinting and toning. The overall effect is a "pictorial" style of composition similar to that associated with Danish and Swedish filmmakers at the time or with that of Tourneur slightly later.

At the same time, Perret also exploits a variety of editing patterns. Certain sequences involving Edmond and the kidnapped girl—as he takes her through the trapdoor in the gang's hideout and to a banlieue shed, where he assumes the guise of a beggar and carries her off in a basket—or le Bosco in pursuit of them both sustain a clear sense of linear continuity through matching the direction of character movement from shot to shot, including exits and entrances, and through 180-degree reverse-angle cutting. A good number of scenes use alternation in the form of POV shots, focusing on le Bosco's discovery and accu-

118. *L'Enfant de Paris*, 1913 (Maurice Lagrenée)

mulation of information—especially in Paris, where he follows the gang to the café and discovers the Villa Carmen address in Edmond's abandoned clothes in the shed. And scene after scene, even more often than in the *Fantômas* films, includes cut-in close shots, from MSs to ECUs. Sometimes these single out significant objects—such as the girl's locket containing a photograph of her parents, the lock of hair the boy finds by the trapdoor, or the wealthy couple's gift of a coin that so stuns him that he tries to return it (and is rewarded with even more). At other times, however, they serve to privilege facial expressions—such as Marie Laure's in response to the orphanage environment and personnel or even Edmond's in his desperate efforts to evade the police in Paris. The explicit attention to characterization manifest in these latter cut-in close shots makes *L'Enfant de Paris* one of the few French films to share in a development just then getting underway in the American cinema.[153]

To an extent, all of these discursive features coalesce into an attraction of their own in *L'Enfant de Paris*, something that has come to be known as the Perret "style." And to maximize their appeal, they are distributed with a good deal of variety across the film's eight reels. Likewise, Perret seems to vary the function of the reel break in relation to the film's narrative structure. The first reel, for instance, closes the initial episode on a note of suspense, as the second commission letter arrives: having lost her father and mother, Marie Laure is about to lose her uncle as well. The third reel ends, however, after Valen has spoken from the balcony to the crowd, in an emblematic series of shots that juxtaposes his private grief to the continuing public applause and then concludes with a CU photograph of the lost girl and a note offering a reward of 25,000 francs for her recovery. The fourth nearly wraps up the narrative with the rescue of Valen and the capture of the apache gang, except that Marie Laure remains missing—in order for the second half of the film to shift to Nice. By contrast, the last reel break comes near the beginning of le Bosco's penetration into the empty Villa Carmen, so that the suspense of his possible rescue carries over and actually increases from one reel to the other.

This pattern of repetition and variation provides one means of coherence for a lengthy film like *L'Enfant de Paris*. Another, intriguingly, comes in the circulation of significant props associated with Marie Laure—as in the locket with her parents' photograph, by which the apaches recognize and exploit her identity. One of the more intriguing of these appears in the Paris drawing room, following a flashback sequence that visualizes a newspaper report on the battle in Morocco (which leaves Valen's survival in doubt). From the background, a ball bounces into the room where the uncle is reading, and the girl comes running after it to briefly play with him. Moments later, following the same trajectory, the telegram arrives announcing Valen's apparent death—so that the ball serves uncannily to designate the uncle as her father's possible replacement. The most widely circulated of these props, however, is Marie Laure's doll, whose recurrence takes on an increasingly symbolic function.[154] The doll first appears just after the mother dies, and the uncle helps Marie Laure to put a pair of socks on its feet as he tells her of his commission. At the orphanage, one of the first things the manageress does is take the doll away from the girl, leaving the locket as the sole link to her past life. Later, le Bosco takes time out from his shoe repair work to make Marie Laure another doll, and this turns their friendship into a quasi-family relationship. As a consequence, when he first explores Nice, the boy pauses before a doll shop, which prompts a dream vision (dissolving in and out on the right half of the frame) of the two children comforting one another earlier in the tiny garret space. The doll thus serves as a kind of displaced lost object of desire, for not only the girl but the boy as well, condensing the concept of generation, both past and future, into a single concrete figure. And the doll returns in the end, as an integral part of the final family portrait, its exchange value having linked each child with the film's title, in succession, and now extending out to encompass all the children of Paris in a comforting patriarchal narrative of recovery and social mobility.

In *Le Roman d'un mousse* (1914), Perret locates the story of the "lost child" within a haut bourgeois world of criminal intrigue reminiscent of *Le Mystère des Roches de Kador*. Instead of a matching detective plot, however, Perret counters that intrigue with an exciting adventure story off the coast of Brittany, in a kind of "return to one's roots" in the simple life of the French provinces. Still, the overall narrative of this eight-reel film divides into episodes that use the reel break in a variety of ways, much like *L'Enfant de Paris*. The first episode begins in the resort of Biarritz with an "international swindler" named Werb (Maurice

Luguet) blackmailing the heavily indebted Marquis de Luscky (Leubas) into marrying a wealthy widow, the Countess de Ker Amor (Mlle Lerida), so they can snatch from her son, Charles-Henri (Adrien Petit), the substantial inheritance of his dead American father. Through the second reel, at least, their diabolic plot seems to be succeeding—after the marriage, Luscky and the countess go off to Italy, and Werb takes Charles-Henri on an educational tour of Brittany, where he persuades him to undergo the test of shipping off as a cabin boy on a fishing vessel. However, after returning to Paris in the fourth reel, Luscky tries to poison his wife and inadvertently kills himself instead—so that the second half of the film begins with the countess's arrest for murder. Meanwhile, an old sailor named Paimpol (A. Dutertre) befriends Charles-Henri and gets wind of a pact between Werb and the ship's captain, Dick (Emile André), to lose the boy at sea. In the fifth and sixth reels, the two escape in a small boat one night and, after drifting for days and surviving a terrible storm, are picked up by a passing cargo ship and returned to Le Havre, where they learn of Dick's death and confession as well as the countess's upcoming trial. In a classic courtroom scene of revelation at the end, Charles-Henri and Paimpol burst in to accuse Werb and exonerate the countess; then papers are discovered in the swindler's private safe which confirm his guilt. So this film, too, ends with a restored family, but in an interestingly gendered tableau that "marries" the modern and the traditional: for at its center are a wealthy mother and son (now dressed in chic white outfits), supported by the grandfatherly figure of Paimpol (still in his sailor's garb), a nostalgic patriarchal figure of old French values. Moreover, this gendering is complicated by the "foreign" interests that generate as well as threaten the countess's money (Werb's name links him with Germany), the overall effect of which is to point up the bankruptcy of the French haut bourgeoisie.

Perret's handling of mise-en-scène, framing, and editing is perhaps even more deft here than in the earlier film. Werb is introduced, for instance, in HA LSs of his modern mansion interior one evening, moving at ease among a group of his fellow financiers, who are drawn to a newspaper story about the Countess de Ker Amor. In the final shot of the scene, Perret has him look coldly at the camera (in a familiar tactic), before sitting down to write the note that will draw the unfortunate Luscky into his web. Later, Werb concludes the pact with Luscky, in MS, before a Renaissance tapestry of a forest, as if to situate his plotting within a long history of preying on others' blood and money. And the spectator's knowledge of that plotting casts an ironic pall over the picturesque images of Luscky and the countess's courtship and honeymoon, which often silhouette the couple in doors and windows against a seascape. By contrast, the deep-space interior of the countess's Paris apartment (overlooking the Champs du Mars) is so selectively lit that its inhospitable darkness perfectly mirrors Charles-Henri's agony over his mother's marriage. In the scene where the countess and Luscky depart for Italy, he is left alone in the same interior—its cold emptiness accentuated now by the sheets obliterating all the furniture—standing estranged in the left foreground, much like the despairing heroines of Feuillade's earlier films. By this point, Charles-Henri clearly is being positioned to attract the spectator's empathy, for he is the only character, other than the villains, even half-cognizant of what seems an overwhelming threat to his family.

These representational strategies combine with specific patterns of editing to produce two extended set pieces in the first half of the film. The first narrates the abduction of Charles-Henri one night from the peninsular ramparts of Saint-Malo. It begins with a LS of Werb and his ward sitting in silhouette before the sea and then, in a 180-degree reverse-angle shift, cuts in to a MS of the boy being given a drugged cigarette, which quickly renders him unconscious. A ninety-degree shift to LS lays out an area beyond the two where a guard passes unawares, and then Dick comes forward to carry the boy off in one direction while Werb walks off in the other. In a sequence of four silhouetted LSs, the captain follows the sharp angles of the wall down to a plank walkway at the water's edge—in one LA LS, Werb even comes forward through an arched gate while Dick and the boy pass behind him overhead. When Charles-Henri awakens the next morning aboard the ship, literally transported into another world, a similar sequence matchcuts his movement forward through several spaces—from his cabin bed, in MCU, to the ship deck, in FS/LS, where he confronts Dick and then meets his protector, Paimpol. The other set piece concludes the first half of the film in a concisely repeated pattern of editing which focuses on just two rooms in the countess's Paris apartment. First, in a FS/LS of her bedroom, Luscky puts on gloves to pour a vial of poison into the water pitcher by his wife's bed. Next, in a similar shot of the drawing room, a nurse takes the countess off to the left while Luscky passes unseen in the opposite direction in the background. The brief sequence in which he meets Werb at the Palais de Tango then cuts in from HA LS to HA MS as the two conspirators celebrate their apparent success. Similarly, the following simultaneous sequence, in which the nurse puts the countess to bed, cuts in from LS to FS as a friend keeps her from drinking a glass of water. Instead, she gives the water pitcher to one of the servants, who places it on a left foreground table in the drawing room. It is there that Luscky returns much later, only to exit and, in MS/LS, open the door to the bedroom just a crack so as to gaze in at the still figure of the countess. Returning to the drawing room, in FS, he sits by the table, unthinkingly pours a drink from the water pitcher, then goes to a right foreground chair to rest in contentment, suddenly gasps and collapses—an image that neatly echoes that of Charles-Henri all alone earlier in the very same room. The smooth efficiency and quietly bitter irony with which this poisoning is carried out make these sequences nothing less than a subtly refined version of a de Lorde play for the Grand Guignol.

The second half of *Le Roman d'un mousse* begins with both mother and son in a vulnerable position—the one incarcerated in prison, the other performing dangerous tasks on the ship (to facilitate his "disappearance"). Two shots linked by a dissolve concisely equate their "martyrdom": a MS of the countess, in which the strong sidelighting casts diagonal bar shadows across her face and arms, and a LS of the boy praying at the ship's prow. In order to transform these conditions, Charles-Henri, seconded by Paimpol, now becomes the active character in at least two more set pieces of sustained action. One, of course, involves their escape in a small boat and subsequent voyage, much of which is shot on location. This elliptical sequence is succinct in its details: initially, the two raise a makeshift sail and carve up a big round of stolen bread, but, after the storm, the sail is gone, and the boy eats the last bread scrap. It also includes a brief "dream vision" that defines Paimpol's role as a father substitute—a HA FS of the boy asleep in his arms dissolves into a MS of him in his own mother's arms. Moreover, the tempest sequence culminates in the spectacular truc effect of a horizontally split screen, with the sea waves roiling in reverse motion. Charles-Henri takes over completely in the final episode, for Paimpol has never been on a train before, let alone visited Paris. Here, crosscutting prepares for the court-room climax as Werb testifies against the countess, while the two travelers arrive at the Gare Saint-Lazare. Two reverse-angle HA LSs establish the courtroom space, with the judges lined up in either the background or foreground. Into this space rushes the boy just as the prosecutor, in AS, is beginning his final statement, and a MS of him and Paimpol immediately precedes his outburst defending his mother. The judges' interrogation of Charles-Henri, Werb, and the old sailor (who recalls seeing Werb on board the ship) then is articulated according to a system of editing which itself recalls and extends that of the earlier abduction. That system includes 180-degree reverse-angle cuts, ninety-degree shifts to the side, and cut-in MSs, focusing first on the mother and son, then on Paimpol and Werb, and finally on the chief judge. In sum, *Le Roman d'un mousse* offers a clearcut alternative here to the continuity system—defined by the eyeline match and shot–reverse shot, using the 180-degree line rule—just then emerging in the American cinema.[155]

The feature-length crime melodrama owes its development as a partially autonomous genre in the French cinema to two companies in particular, Eclair and Gaumont. Under the direction of Jasset, Perret, and Feuillade, the genre proved profitable in calling attention to as well as differentiating the "product lines" of both companies—which Pathé may well then have exploited in De-nola's now lost *Rocambole* series (1914). First of all, they established the crime melodrama as a series in which individual feature-length titles followed one an-other like sequels and, by the time of *Fantômas*, on an increasingly regular basis. In doing so, they extended the strategy of using the reel break, not only to divide a lengthy narrative into segments, but to create suspense or anticipation, and sometimes they simply ignored the break so as to sustain an action from one reel to the next.[156] In the *Zigomar, Main de fer*, and *Fantômas* films, the three filmmakers also developed a particular aesthetic—then, as now, labeled "fantas-tic realism"—that explored the fantastic, diabolical powers surging beneath the surface and charging the most ordinary objects of modern life. Yet the films themselves were ambivalent or even contradictory in their ideological position-ing, encouraging a multiplicity of readings, perhaps as a way of attracting more than a single audience. Their almost exclusively male heroes could be read as displaced satanic figures, rebellious anarchists, or either renegade or model capi-talists; and, however fascinating they might be in their subversive mockery, the films nearly always constructed the possibility of a conventionally moral reading. Indeed, Perret's two big films imbued the latter perspective with a very topical chauvinism, suggesting that French society was in need of moral regeneration—through the traditional "testing" of young French men. Other differences between individual films and filmmakers emerged, especially in terms of modes of representation. While Jasset, for instance, sometimes fell back on an anachronistic tableau style, Feuillade used a variety of strategies of spatial-temporal continuity with ease and flexibility. Perret, however, showed himself more "advanced" than either, even to the point of working out an alternative system of analytical editing to that which, in the American cinema, would later be called "classical." This unique "style" would serve equally well his many comic films.

The Comic Series in Full Swing

Of the various genres that the French cinema industry had developed over the previous half-dozen years, only the comic series did not play some kind of role in the emergence of the feature-length film. Most of these series—especially those from Eclipse and Eclair—continued to be produced in split reels, sometimes running little more, or even less, than one hundred meters in length. Those with more prestige—such as the *Max* series from Pathé or the *Léonce* series from Gaumont—generally came in full single reels of about three hundred meters. Whatever the length, their popularity was evident in the sheer number of comic series circulating through the cinemas before the war—there were well over two dozen, and among the best new ones were Gaumont's *Onésime* and *Léonce*. It was also apparent in their presence as a regular component of each company's weekly programs (with the exception of Film d'Art). At Pathé, in fact, short comic films often made up a quarter to a third of the weekly release titles, whereas at Gaumont, at least one title in the new *Bout-de-zan* series was released as the week's "grand film artistique." The more successful comics tended to stay with a single company, developing their characters over the course of several years and through scores of films; some of the lesser comics, however, circulated from one company to another. Eclair was particularly adept at exploiting this—picking up Bertho from Lux, Bataille from Gaumont, and Duhamel, the first important female comic (Robinson calls her a "Gallic Marie Dressler"[157]), from Comica. Although many series—especially at Lux, Eclipse, Eclair, and Comica—got by on loosely structured scenarios and miniscule budgets, some like *Max, Rigadin,* and *Léonce* came up with well-crafted, tightly organized stories and sometimes had budgets close to the median level of feature-length films. Indeed, just before the war, there is evidence—notably, Eclair's *Gaîtés de l'escadron* (1913), Gaumont's *La Vie drole* series (1913–1914), and Aubert's *Champignol malgré lui* (1914)—that the industry was gearing up to produce and market feature-length comic films.

Not all of the short comic films came in series, of course, and several extant

Pathé titles give some sense of what those were like. If they generally have the look of the company's films from five years before, their comic action is concise, assured, and tightly structured. *Une Maison bien lavée* (1912), for instance, uses ten separate studio decors to "construct" a four-story bourgeois apartment building with two rooms to a floor, a stairway, and a courtyard exterior.[158] In an elaborate reworking of Lumière's *Arroseur et arrosé*, this film begins outside with a boy seizing a water fire hose and, at his sister's suggestion, directing its powerful spray into a second-floor window. Essentially, the film traces the destructive trajectory of the water through the entire building as it goes up one side and down the other. First, the water punches up through a kitchen, a dining room (where a couple sit glumly under an umbrella), and a bedroom to shoot out a hole in the roof; then it miraculously falls back through a chimney to flood out of a study fireplace, pour out of an office wall, and finally rush down the stairs like a waterfall, rolling all the residents out into the courtyard—where the concierge gets blamed for the mess. Having a kid "send up the bourgeoisie" this way may be amusing enough, but doing it with such symmetrical concision certainly doubles the pleasure. Similarly, *Vengéance de concierge* (1912) uses the ubiquitous Pathé stairway to "anchor" another four-story apartment building with rooms for three white-collar couples, a garret for a struggling artist and his mistress, an office for the concierge, and an exterior doorway. After receiving an angry letter from the landlord, this concierge climbs the stairs to sweep the piles of paper and straw cluttering each floor—and, in the process, sweeps all three couples coming out of their apartments, one after the other, down into the street. To top his revenge, he then writes letters to all the residents. Because the letters throw blame on the garret couple, the other three confront and thrash them, tossing them down the stairs and outside—where all, in turn, pile into the trash heaped in front of the doorway and, in the climactic gag, get hosed by the waiting concierge. In a sense, the concierge bests both the artist and his betters in a "class action" of his own artful design.

La Saucisse mystérieuse (1913), by contrast, pursues a different trajectory through a succession of, for the most part, actual provincial locations.[159] It begins outside a small town charcuterie, in an AS/LS, as a fishmonger sets up her cart in the right foreground and a boy sidles in to take down a pig's head hanging over a table next to the shop door and toss it about like a balloon. The shop owner comes out to chase him off, but he returns to swipe an eel from the fishmonger's cart and drop it on a plate of sausages on the table—and a cut-in CU shows the eel (in stop motion) wriggling into one of the sausages. Next, a country bumpkin stops to buy the sausage, in a closer shot of the table and doorway, and then sits on a park bench to eat it as part of his basket lunch. This economical premise, augmented by realistic detailing, sets up a bizarre chase when the sausage leaps out of the basket and slithers off down the street. The astonished peasant pursues the errant sausage through a sequence of eight shots, repeatedly traversing the frame from background to foreground. As he passes through a barbershop (bumping the barber, who accidentally cuts the head off the man he is shaving!), dives down a sewer manhole, stumbles through a wine cellar, and trips across the stone block of an open air laundry, the pace of the editing quickens. The sausage ends up leaping into the sentry box of the local army garrison, which the peasant topples over (with a hapless soldier inside) and from which he finally extracts his wily prey. But that is not the end, of course, for when the peasant tries to bite into the sausage, back on the park bench, the still hidden eel latches onto his nose. In the final MCU, the peasant turns into a grotesque figure of carnivorous consumption or simply "bad table manners"— the butt of two passing bourgeois men's laughter.

The comic series, of course, shared certain features with these films. They, too, tended to rely on the structuring principle of repeated gags, either within a limited number of recurring spaces or in an open-ended succession of new ones. Many stuck to a broad, slapstick style of physical comedy, putting their actors through pratfalls, pummelings, and pursuits. Eclipse's *Polyte esclave de la consigne* (1912), for instance, makes its unidentified comic into a raw army recruit ordered to take a message from a barracks officer to a general out on maneuvers. Although small and clumsy, Polyte is single-minded in his mission: when he is thrown from his horse (after much bouncing) and into a group of washerwomen, he expropriates a dog cart and finally a pig in order to get to his destination. The pig runs into the general and dumps its rider, scattering the officers, but the concluding HA FS has Polyte kiss it in gratitude and wipe the tears from his eyes with its ears. Another Eclipse series, *Arthème Dupin* (with Servaes) follows a similar pattern, but its comedy is much more slick. *Arthème Dupin echappe encore* (1912), for instance, reworks the magical appearances and disappearances of Pathé's earlier *Jim le glisseur*. It begins with Dupin trying to bribe his way out of a speeding ticket; when that fails, he simply makes his car vanish (through the first of many invisible cuts), lights a cigarette, and calmly walks off. In a succession of escapes, he lures two cops to a drawing room door (by blowing smoke through a crack) and smashes them into paper cutouts, then constructs a working bicycle out of spare parts, and finally lets himself be caught, only to leap (in reverse motion) out of a sack the cops have thrown into a river and back onto a bridge—where a cut-in AS shows him nonchalantly leaning on the railing to smoke one more cigarette. In the end, like Jim, Dupin locks two cops in a jail cell and, dissolving through the bars, saunters off, the trademark cigarette dangling from his lips.

With their focus on a single recurring character, however, the comic series were also different in that they could more easily exploit topical events or issues for their stories or situations and take advantage of entertaining locations or seasonal activities, for both actors and audiences. The two Eclair series, *Gavroche* and *Petronille*, illustrate this especially well. In *Gavroche au Luna-Park* (1912), for instance, the quick, compact Bertho plays a white-collar womanizer, decked out in a boater and puffing on a cigarette, who follows a young woman from the provinces into the popular Paris amusement park. Gavroche takes the place of a palm reader in order to impress himself on the woman, but she slaps him and pursues him, along with a cop, through the park. Outmaneuvering them over such obstacles as a moving staircase, a bump car arena, and a rollercoaster, he finally assumes the role of the park band conductor and sends both of his pursuers into a fit of dancing and acrobatics. If he cannot control the future or spark a woman's desire, at least he can master, if only briefly, the amazing machines of the modern amusement park and make people move to their mechanical rhythms. In *Petronille gagne le Grand Steeple* (1912), Duhamel gets a tip from a jockey on which horse is favored to win the steeplechase and is so desperate (her shabby room suggests gambling has nearly ruined her) that she pawns an antique clock to place her sure bet. At the Longchamps racetrack, however, her horse and rider fall into a water hazard, and soon the hefty Petronille is changing her old-fashioned dress for an ample jockey's outfit and mounting the horse herself. Quickly taking the lead, she draws all the other horses off the course—to race a train, gallop along a canal, and rush over a railway bridge—then returns to cross the finish line well ahead of her exhausted rivals. When she weighs in at one hundred kilos, the other jockeys break out crying, but, surrounded by admirers, in a closing MS, Petronille simply sticks out her tongue at the camera. Not only does she win instant fame and fortune, but her impromptu performance reduces the upper-class status of horse racing to no more than a pretense.

Similar demonstrations of performative skill, or its lack, marked other series at Gaumont and Pathé's affiliate, Comica. Gaumont seems to have used the *Zigoto* series, starring Bataille, to belittle the crime series of its rivals, specifically Eclair's *Zigomar* and Pathé's *Nick Winter*. In *Zigoto toreador* (1912), for instance, Bataille adopts Nick Winter's look, only to display his incompetence at handling a bull loosely tethered in a corral—for he comes equipped with a cane instead of a sword. The bull breaks loose to run rampant through a small town, and, retelling his "exploits" at the end, Zigoto repeats the destruction within the space of a café. The *Little Moritz* and *Rosalie* series, usually directed by Bosetti, illustrate how such performances also could play off other kinds of animals as well as technological devices. In *Little Moritz chasse les grands fauves* (1911), directed by Machin, the wiry, bright-eyed music hall acrobat, Schwartz, plays a big game hunter who is chased by a rhino (made out of cloth and papier-mâché) and a leopard, only to finally face down a rabbit, which he captures by accident.[160] To compensate for his lack of courage, Little Moritz buys several cages of leopards and tigers (Comica probably rented them for the day), and this roughly assembled film trumpets his success with an official parade through the streets of Nice. At a concluding banquet, however, one of the cage doors is opened, and the leopard gets to star in the final MS—licking its paws contentedly among scattered hats and coats. In *Rosalie et sa phono* (1911), by contrast, Duhamel demonstrates the magic of a phonograph she has just purchased and had delivered (stingily, she avoids tipping the deliveryman).[161] When she and her maid test the machine, everything in the dining room, including the two of them, goes into a quick-step dance, by means of stop motion (probably accentuated by up-tempo musical accompaniment). Delighted, Rosalie takes the phonograph from room to room, using it to rearrange the furniture and tire out her father, and finally displays her multipurpose acquisition at a neighborhood café. Not only does this film serve to market Duhamel as a new comic, but it adver-

119. *Rosalie et sa phono,* 1911 (Sarah Duhamel)

tises the conspicuous consumption of new commodities and their "magical" effects—after all, Pathé also sold phonographic equipment. In fact, the only thing lacking in the opening emblematic CU of Rosalie smiling next to her phonograph is a brand name.

As these films suggest, in order to appeal to various segments of the cinema's mass audience, the comic series ranged widely through the French social system, especially in their efforts to single out social types and behavior for ridicule. Lux, for instance, mined both ends of the social scale. In *Cunegonde, femme de mode* (1912), the unidentified comic is a maid who dresses up in her employer's clothes, after the latter has gone off on a trip. In a cut-in MS, Cunegonde adorns herself with a wig, bracelets and rings, powder, and pearls; then, in a return to FS, she discards a white hat for a more vampish, wide-brimmed black one. Promenading in a park, she attracts a suitable young gentleman who invites her to his apartment, where he gallantly props up her feet with a pillow and kneels to propose. Suddenly, the real owner of the apartment appears and breaks this idyll by ordering him back into his butler's uniform—for the "gentleman" is an imposter just like herself. When the two meet in the street the next day, Cunegonde attacks him, but at the police station, she accepts his explanation—and they reconcile, having found "true love" within their proper social level. *Gratitude obsédante* (1912) uses a similar pretense in having Bertho, costumed in a top hat and oversized topcoat and calling himself Filippic Brom, beg among the passersby on a street.[162] When a bourgeois gentleman is tricked into handing over his wallet, Filippic leaps into his arms in gratitude—and the man soon discovers that he cannot get rid of his newfound overweening "friend." Filippic pursues him in an increasingly outrageous manner: following his carriage, he is caught and spun round in the spokes of the back wheel; racing after his train, he arrives at the destined station to leap on him again; pushed over a railing onto some rocks, he rebounds (in reverse motion) to doff his hat and display a huge bump on his head. Finally, the two "friends" are hit by a woman driving a cart, and Filippic's legs are cut off at the knees—at which the man promptly seizes them and runs off. Imagining himself free at last, he rejoins his real friends at a street café, only to go into shock when Filippic happily wheels up in a basket—and the film ends with the comic gratefully kissing the unconscious man's shoe. In so literalizing the fawning behavior of the bourgeois hanger-on, *Gratitude obsédante* prepares the way for the equally absurd extremes of Gaumont's *Onésime*.

Yet the class most frequently sent up in these films clearly was the bourgeoisie, and that send-up increasingly came from within, through masquerade, as is evident in two other series, Eclipse's *Polycarpe* and Eclair's *Gontran*.[163] As Polycarpe, Edouard Pinto is a bit of a loner, with his scrunched sour face and wide slit of a mouth, and an obvious poseur. *Le Trouvaille de Polycarpe* (1913), for instance, begins with him posed as a bourgeois gentleman standing in front of an office building, but a cut-in MCU reveals that his shoe is concealing a coin someone has dropped on the sidewalk—and he waits for a cop to pass before picking it up. This sets in motion a series of purchased services, each of which includes at least one deftly cut-in close shot, beginning with the ECU that exposes the coin as a fake, to both him and the audience. Cut in to a tracking FS of a taxi, for instance, is an ECU of the meter, which prompts Polycarpe to order the driver to halt. His coin is refused by the driver, of course, and then by a shoeshine man (who leaves a blackened hand print, in CU, on his cheek), a pastry seller, and a café waiter, but finally is accepted, with a touch of irony, by a vendor selling the financial paper, *La Presse*. There, Polycarpe reads an ad calling for an assistant to a prince at the Bourse, gestures that he is indeed the man, and begins pulling at his hair until he is nearly bald—where the only extant print breaks off. Whatever topical allusion forms the basis for reading this last scene is now lost, but not Polycarpe's send-up of the financially assured bourgeois consumer.

As played by Grehan, by contrast, Gontran is an anxious, overconfident bourgeois type not unlike Max—and his polished style of performance and facial appearance (large eyes, hair parted in the middle, and thin mustache) do remind one of Linder. In *Gontran doute la fidelité de sa femme* (1912), Gontran is a jealous, insecure husband who suspects his wife of having an affair. After chasing away a bushy-haired admirer in a park and finding what seems to be a coded letter on her desk, he sits stunned, in AS, and then deceives his wife into thinking he is taking a trip, in order to confirm his suspicions. The next day two workmen arrive on schedule to clean the couple's second-floor fireplace, and Gontran is waiting outside with a gun, at the foot of a ladder. In a nicely timed sequence of

120. *Little Moritz aime Rosalie,* 1911

alternation, Gontran appears at the second-floor window just as one workman enters the fireplace with a whisk broom to climb a rope dropped down the chimney by his colleague on the roof. Gontran pulls on the rope and is yanked off his feet (dropping the gun) to be dragged into the fireplace, with his wife momentarily hanging on to his leg. The alternation continues with a LS of the cutaway chimney as first the workman and then Gontran are pulled up on the rope, a MS of the fireplace as the wife looks up into it astonished, and a FS of the roof as the two men pop out of the chimney in succession. Gontran falls off the roof edge, of course, and straight into a tub of dirty water, and comes out black with grime—a mark of the guilt that has settled on him. When he tries to embrace his wife (after hearing the workmen's explanation), she dips out of his grasp and, smiling coyly, eludes him—as if to define herself, however briefly, as separate from his jealous possession.

As some of these series increasingly assumed the look of comedies of manners, they began to distribute their parody of social behavior and convention over several films in succession. In the summer and fall of 1911, for instance, Bosetti and Rollini brought together Comica's two stars, Schwartz and Duhamel, in four films covering the comic stages of their love, courtship, and elopement. This group of films opens with *Little Moritz aime Rosalie* and its introductory "valentine" portrait of the two, in CU, framed within a heart-shaped iris mask. It is love-at-first-sight between this unlikely pair when they meet during a party given by her father, in a long-take FS/LS of the family townhouse salon. And their attraction is worked out in an elaborate dance competition that puts the acrobatic skills of the big woman and little man equally on display. They spin each other around, in between pas de deux routines, he punches her out and lifts her up by the hair, and she retaliates by whirling him about by his legs and tossing him in a corner. Later, Little Moritz comes courting, only to get tangled up in some background curtains, and has to crawl toward Rosalie, considerably dwarfed by an immense bouquet. His real obstacle, however, is her father, who laughs at his declaration of love and picks him up like a suitcase and throws him out into the hall, where he rolls down several flights of stairs and into the cellar. Next, he tries the chimney, emerging into the drawing room through the fireplace, in blackface, and Rosalie leaves off practicing her piano to give his foolhardy persistence her approval. In *Little Moritz demande Rosalie en mariage*, he returns to perform a long pantomime plea, in a cut-in MS, and the father retaliates with his own demand that he prove himself a man—and his pounding fist, in a matchcut to FS/LS, shocks the suitor into backward leaps out the door. Taking up boxing, in another long-take FS/LS, Little Moritz quickly gets punched out by a much bigger opponent, but recovers to leap on him and pound him into the floor, then attack everyone else in the gym like a miniature whirlwind—after which he nonchalantly picks up his coat, hat, and cane and exits in triumph. Yet the only way he can persuade Rosalie's father to believe him is to repeat his performance, which leads him ironically to smash one bourgeois townhouse interior after another. Pushed to the extreme, patriarchal prerogative and masculine performance together end up destroying the social framework for grounding this parodic fable of romantic love, but it skips blithely on just the same into a conventional MCU kiss.[164]

This kind of parody of courtship behavior also was a favorite subject of those few individual films produced outside the comic series, especially at Gaumont. *Eugène amoureux* (1911), for instance, focuses on a lovesick butler attracted to a maid in the townhouse next door. Although the scenario is rather conventional, the direction—probably by Perret—is quite sophisticated.[165] It begins concisely by setting up adjacent spaces with a ninety-degree shift from a drawing room where Eugène is brushing his master's coat to the balcony where he steps out to look directly at the camera. In a highly unusual series of straight-on shot–reverse ASs, he mimes his love to the maid cleaning a rug on the opposite balcony (while another servant works in the room behind her). To accentuate an already remarkable sequence, Eugène uses his clothes brush to blow a kiss, after which the maid has to wipe a speck of dust from her eye (this is the only indication of the distance between them). Eugène's master enters the drawing room to break up this exchange and, before going out, warns his butler about a bottle of poison he has bought—yet a cut-in closer shot reveals it is really brandy, mislabeled to keep it out of the hands of Eugène (who has gone off to practice his courting strategy). The rest of the film works out its gags at the butler's expense in two long-take interior AS/LSs. First, Eugène visits the maid next door, who is sitting with the cook and another servant imbibing a little brandy (which may explain his own master's strategem), and proposes to her in an elaborate routine. Her simple response is to introduce him to her husband (the other butler), who promptly beats him up in a fast-motion fight and throws him out the door. Back in his master's room, the badly disheveled suitor considers suicide. Too frightened to stab himself or jump out the window, he finally decides to drink some of the poison, which turns out to be so unexpectedly delectable that he soon empties the bottle. When the master returns, Eugène not only suffers a second beating but loses his job as well—another lower-class "victim of alcoholism" in comic guise.

In Perret's *Le Leçon d'amour* (1912), by contrast, an even more hapless young man is rewarded for his troubles, but in delightfully tongue-in-cheek fashion.[166] This light comic fantasy decorates its four principal characters in eighteenth-century costumes and looses them in a small chateau and attached garden (and all of these "properties" are enhanced by tinting and toning).[167] For its premise, the Chevalier d'Armençon invites his nephew, the Marquis de Cargouêt, to his chateau, in order to further his daughter Christiane's education, especially in music, and to court her as well. The young man is completely oblivious to this latter task, however, and no wonder: he arrives just after the father has given Christiane a pinch of snuff, and she sneezes in his face—twice. So the maid takes over *his* education, in a long-take interior FS/LS, teaching him all the courtship rituals so well that he becomes positively enamored of her. She manages to deflect this quasi-oedipal awakening of desire and place Christiane in the very same room, where the two adults can observe the young man properly perform his role as a suitor—which, much like parents, intriguingly, they view through a keyhole mask, in a kind of reverse "primal scene." As if to underscore this reversal, the maid then demands that the father court her, which exposes his own problem as a performer: he kneels and promptly sprains his knee. The film's final two tableaux fix the older, "illicit" couple in the position of spectators: in LS, the young lovers stroll in the garden while the adults gaze out through the foreground windows, in silhouette (and then gently erase them); in another LS, the lovers walk along a country canal, now framed by silhouetted foreground trees. With that, this comic oedipal drama comes to a perfectly "naturalized" end.[168]

If turning adults into children was one way of creating situations for ridicule, another was simply to use kids themselves, as Feuillade had done in Gaumont's *Bébé* series. Indeed, the *Bébé* films, with Dary, profilerated throughout 1911–1912, averaging nearly two titles per month. One of the few that survive from this period, *Bébé tire à la cible* (1912), turns the family maid into the target of the boy's bad behavior. An uncle provides the means, the birthday gift of a rifle, and a cut-in CU shows Bébé's father warning him to use blanks and not real cartridges. Surreptitiously, however, the boy takes a box of bullets out of his father's pocket and soon is shooting up the house. This culminates in his firing at a circular target he has attached to the maid's backside, as she bends over to look in the oven. And the parents' laughter at her plight (although they do offer help) seems to approve of Bébé making the maid the literal butt of his joke. *Bébé juge* (1912) turns the ridicule against his own sisters. This film is unusual in being confined to a single tableau, an AS/LS of the bourgeois family sitting room, where the parents (going out for the evening) leave Bébé and two younger sisters in the custody of a maid (who, with good reason, tries to avoid the boy by keeping busy elsewhere). Bébé first torments the girls by sneaking up and blow- · ing a horn in their ears, and when the maid returns to break up their struggle and offer them a tray of pastries, the girls quickly begin fighting over who has the bigger share. In order to resolve this argument, Bébé decides to play judge— wrapping a scarf around his shoulders, slapping a lamp shade on his head, and donning eyeglasses—and has one sister bring up a pair of scales so that he can weigh their plates. His method of adjudication, however, is to equalize the plates by eating a pastry off one and then the other, repeatedly, until he has literally licked both clean. As the two girls go off crying to sulk, Bébé simply snatches another pastry from the tray and winks at the camera—his assertion of male prerogative accomplished through legal chicanery.

Feuillade's own running argument with Bébé or rather with Dary's parents, who kept insisting on more and more money for their son's services,[169] finally led Gaumont to cancel the *Bébé* films by late 1912. But there were other kid series to take up the slack, most notably Eclair's *Willy*, directed by Joseph Faivre, and Gaumont's own *Bout-de-zan*, both of which kept to the established pattern of featuring male actors. Even the short-lived Eclectic production company got into the act by recruiting René Dary (now using his real name, Abélard), for a brief continuation of the *Bébé* series. *Bébé n'aime pas sa concierge* (1913) indicates that this new series might have become successful had Eclectic not folded so soon, probably due to the poor distribution of its product. The object of this film's comic attack is not the bourgeois family but another much less formidable (though still dreaded) figure of authority, the female concierge. Here, Bébé also has a younger sister whom he recruits in his assault, beginning with a maneuver in the apartment building lobby, where the concierge sits on guard, knitting, with her tiny dog. When the postman calls her away for a minute, the kids take the dog behind her chair—in MS, they busy themselves with the knitting needles—then leave the animal decked out in a brightly striped jersey for the horrified concierge to find on her return. Although she complains to the kids' parents, they express only mock indignation, so, when the two indulged troublemakers are put to bed that evening, Bébé comes up with a second battle plan. This is worked out in a skillful sequence of alternation involving three adjacent spaces—the two kids' bedroom, the concierge's bedroom across the hall, and an apartment building exterior that places their bedroom window near the outside door—all accentuated by several cut-in close shots. Now, Bébé climbs out the window to repeatedly pull the bell chain by the door, and, when the exasperated concierge finally gets up in her nightdress and steps outside, he simply sneaks in behind her back and locks the door. To add insult to injury, when she accosts a passing policeman, she is promptly put under arrest and hustled off. Enormously pleased with themselves and their handiwork, in a concluding MS of the window, the two kids mime their desire to sleep (at last) and blow kisses of complicity at the camera.

The *Willy* series, directed by Faivre, also tended to direct its ridicule outside the bourgeois family, if only to have it sometimes circle back to strike within. In fact, this *enfant terrible* was even played by an outsider, an English urchin named Sanders, who had come to Eclair's attention through a 1911 British film.[170] In *Willy et le prestidigitateur* (1912), the boy's target is a magician whom his parents have hired to entertain the guests at a dinner party. Most of this film is comprised of long-take AS/LSs of just two rooms in the family townhouse, with the only interruptions coming from the intertitles and a couple of cut-in MSs of Willy in action. First, he hides under a centered foreground table and (with an arm visible only to the camera) makes a lady's jewelry and his own father's wallet disappear, to the surprise even of the magician, and then sends the table itself dancing about, scattering everyone in fright. When the magician creeps up to pull the cloth off the table, however, Willy has mysteriously vanished—and there is an outburst of applause. Next, Willy dons a villainous oriental mask and scares off both parents and guests so that he can pummel the magician like a puppet buffoon. Finally, he leads the bewildered man into the next room, where they begin to wolf down trays of food and champagne, with the magician demonstrating some real skill at last, stuffing sandwiches into his pockets. But this is only a ruse to trick the poor magician one last time, for Willy simply turns him over to the police when all the other adults come back. In *Les Trois Willy* (1913), his parents join the boy in tricking his own grandfather, who refuses to visit until they have had three children. The setup for this film uses several cut-in MSs and MCUs of Willy and his parents as they respond to the grandfather's letter: to avoid tiring him, they will send all three of their sons to visit, but only one at a time. This provides the occasion for Willy to perform three separate roles: an ill-mannered apache, a snobbish "gentleman" sporting a monocle, and a smiling, sailor-suited boy bearing a gift of flowers (a sentimental figure fit for a Norman Rockwell illustration). When the grandfather accepts this last grandson, the parents step in to expose their fraud—and win his consent to the "modern" one-child family—but, of course, this third Willy is no more real than the other two.

Willy et les Parisiens (1913) ostensibly assumes a different class position and perhaps a different audience as well. Here, Willy takes on the guise of a clever country boy who saves his village from a pair of Parisian relatives on vacation for their health. An opening sequence of just four shots presents the arrival of these Fignolle cousins, with lots of baggage piled on a horse cart, and two cut-in dialogue intertitles reveal that they come unannounced and are oblivious of the villagers' dismay. Quickly, Willy is set up as their potential adversary, and it is the Fignolle woman who bears the brunt of his "accidents": he falls on her from a table (where he has been placed to greet the Parisians), and he stomps on her new hat as if it were a big bug. The next day, the Fignolles further offend the villagers with their odd behavior—pecking holes in fresh eggs to suck out the egg white, drinking milk straight from a cow, and kissing in public before the picturesque image of a mill waterwheel. That night, sitting around the fireplace (the principal source of lighting in this single AS), Willy explains to the villagers how he will get rid of the intruders. A LA MS of him at a barn window pouring pepper into the hole in an egg then serves as the prelude to four LSs of revenge. The Fignolles now spit out the eggs' contents in disgust and do likewise with the bowls of milk laced with plaster, they rest against a haystack only to have whole sheaves topple on them, and retreating to their bedroom, they find it inhabited by a cow, sheep, and chickens. This "staged" version of country life so deviates from their own "tourist" vision that it sends them packing, and Willy gets to shoo them off like bad children with a broom. All the while, of course, this disguised city boy gets to upstage the villagers into whose midst he has dropped—in a subtext reversal of the main plot.

Gaumont, meanwhile, underwent its own "housecleaning" as Feuillade replaced the *Bébé* series with *Bout-de-zan*, beginning in January 1913.[171] This new series featured René Poyen, a dark-haired, clever, versatile kid, who had already appeared in several of Fescourt's one-reelers.[172] To some extent, the subjects and situations for these films followed those of the *Bébé* series, except that Bout-de-zan was an only child of bourgeois parents in Paris and much less tied to his mother. *Bout-de-zan et le lion* (1913), for instance, uses the topical device of an escaped wild animal to work out a favorite theme: the boy's exploitation of the family maid (Marthe Vinot). The film begins with Bout-de-zan and his mother in the drawing room, when news comes that a lion has escaped from a local cinema—an ironically implausible premise that sends the mother into hysterics and the boy off with an idea. Crawling inside the lionskin rug in his father's study, Bout-de-zan returns to the drawing room and so startles his mother that she collapses—and a cut-in CU of the lion's head reveals his grinning face behind its gaping mouth. Next, he frightens the maid into fainting in the kitchen and then revives her, in MCU, with a spray of selzer water. When the father returns home, he finds the mother and several of her friends literally petrified in the salon and has to slap them back to consciousness. Leading them all to the study, he notices the rug is missing and relieves them with his explanation—and they turn in response to a sound offscreen. On this sound bridge, the film cuts back to the kitchen where Bout-de-zan is blowing on a bottle and the maid now, at his suggestion, is crawling around in the lionskin. This sets up the climax as the father and his butler rush in to repeatedly club the lion over the head and finally unmask the poor maid. But she is hardly alone in getting the short end of the stick in this comedy of class violence, for the men get to alternately terrorize and save the women throughout, whatever their class or age.

The family maid provides a recurring target for Bout-de-zan's exploits in this series, in what could be seen as a displaced rebellion against the figure of the mother. A surviving fragment from an unidentified film, for instance, has the boy use hypnotism to make her the butt of a racist joke: mesmerized, she rubs a plate blackened with candle soot systematically all over her face.[173] But the whole family sometimes gets taken in by his tricks. The premise of *Bout-de-zan et le chemineau* (1913) is that a reading of the prestigious daily, *Le Temps*, prompts the boy to invite in a passing tramp and offer him his bed for the night. However, Bout-de-zan gets chilly sleeping on the floor and climbs in bed again—which sets up the film's crucial gag literally equating the two. When the maid comes in the next morning, she finds the boy's head at one end of the bed and two huge feet sticking out from the other, and, when the father appears and pats his son's forehead, the feet wriggle in response. While the two adults rush off for a doctor, Bout-de-zan resumes his class identity and orders the tramp out—his charity extends only so far—and, when the doctor arrives, he is his regular self once more. *Bout-de-zan et le crime au téléphone* (1914) sends up the family by locating the then current fascination with violent crime stories within their circle. Here, the parents and their friends get together for an amateur theatrical reading one night and perform a murder mystery (complete with props), which Bout-de-zan then complicates by surreptitiously taking the telephone off the hook. What follows is a clever sequence of alternation as more and more people overhear what they take to be a real crime in progress—first a telephone operator, who alerts the apartment building concierge and some of her friends, who finally call in a policeman from the street—and several faint away in fright at various stages of suspense. The climax comes in a HA LS of the drawing room as the players all freeze and raise their arms in disbelief when the policeman and others burst in from the background to arrest them—and the concierge now faints at seeing the father with a gun. Bout-de-zan's explanation causes everyone to laugh at the joke, but not before the sacrosanct bourgeois family has been turned into the comic subject of a tabloid scandal.

Despite this influx of new series, the major comics who had established their reputations between 1907 and 1910 continued to thrive. But here, too, a more or less clear difference separated those series that favored a very physical, slapstick comedy from those committed to a comedy of manners. When Pathé, for instance, resumed the *Boireau* series early in 1912 (after Deed's return from a three-year stint in Italy[174]), it was, as before, to exploit Deed's acrobatic skills in highly structured scenarios that often had his character working at some kind of trade or profession.[175] *Boireau domestique* (1912), for instance, deftly stitches together several adjacent spaces inside and outside the building where Boireau has been hired to clean a bourgeois apartment. His initial strategy is to empty several rooms by tossing all the furniture, half of which gets smashed, into others nearby. This sets up not one but two gags at once. A CU of a doorbell being rung, to which Boireau responds by looking up from his sweeping, is followed by a LS of the corridor, which reveals that the ringers are two mischievous kids. To get to the door now, Boireau literally has to crawl over piles of furniture and debris in two successive rooms (his slow passage traced by a pan), and when he does reach the corridor, no one is there. His next strategy is to dump some of the debris he has created out a window, which rains down on a passing couple on the sidewalk. He follows this with a carpet beating, which sends clouds of dust into the dining room of another couple living on the floor below. The payoff for this gag structure comes when the two couples converge on the apart-

121. *Boireau cuirassier*, 1912 (André Deed)

ment door, for what they get, when they now ring the doorbell, is the proverbial bucket of water in the face.

Although less tightly organized, *Boireau cuirassier* (1912) concludes with the destruction of another, somewhat more public bourgeois space. This time Boireau is a low-level army officer invited as a baroness's godson to a salon reception, to which he comes costumed in an oversized uniform of breastplate armor, plumed helmet, and sword. This preening caricature of the heroic soldier constantly threatens to either come apart at the seams (mounting the staircase, he momentarily loses a boot and then his helmet) or else attract all manner of "decorations" (at the door, his spur catches on a carpet, which he drags in with him). The reception is full of haute bourgeoise ladies who, one after another, indecorously fall victim to this swaggering male figure—two are swept over a couch, another has part of her dress ripped off. Finally, the plumed helmet snags the chandelier overhead, and it comes crashing down on all the assembled guests. Depending on a spectator's ideological position, one could read this film as either a send-up of the French military hero so dear to the Nationalist Revival movement or else a critique of the ordinary Frenchman's inability to live up to that heroic ideal.

Boireau, roi de boxe (1912) takes this kind of physical comedy to an extreme, partly through the addition of cinematic trucs, but especially through its reveling in absurd incongruities. It begins with a marvelously disorienting "wake up" sequence, in which Boireau steps out of an armoire, glances at a newspaper and then uses it to wash his face, and pours some water into a paper bag to drink. In his cellar cum gym, he puts out a candle by pulling off the flame with a pair of pliers, leaps into his shoes (in an invisible cut) before adding a tie, shirt, and pants, shakes his coat out of a coal sack, and finally breaks a vase to get his hat. A completely implausible POV shot through a handy telescope (and the gag partly depends on the spatial incongruity) situates a neighborhood boxing hall nearby, and Boireau sits on a lighted keg of gunpowder to blast himself out of a window and enter the hall to view a boxing match. The rest of the film turns him into a victim who then can enjoy taking his revenge over and over again. A couple of bourgeois spectators whom he irritates pummel Boireau at the hall entrance, to the pleasure of the black barker stationed there, and he takes himself off to a boxing "school"—where he learns so quickly that, within five seconds, he has decked the instructor. Returning to the hall, he is bumped by a postman and retaliates by punching him in the nose, which swells up to the size of a melon. At the entrance, he knocks over a lamppost with a passing blow, which sends the black barker fleeing; inside, he clambers over the crowd of spectators and drags off his two initial assailants. Outside, one gets thrown against a wall and flattens into a dummy to be tossed aside, while the other, after one punch, runs off with his whole head swelling up to three times its normal size. This time, in a cartoonlike fantasy of triumph, Boireau's comic "everyman" gets to demonstrate his incongruous competence in both private and public spheres.

In a parallel trajectory at Gaumont, Durand was still writing and directing the *Calino* series, with Migé. Although these films may have appeared less frequently after 1911, they hardly lost any of their inventiveness or gleeful penchant for mayhem. *Calino, courtier en paratonerres* (1912), for instance, costumes the comic in a slightly undersized outfit (somewhat like the later Stan Laurel) and makes him an inventor with the absurd task of selling a sheared-off lamppost as a lightning rod.[176] The lamppost functions more like a lance or spear, however, creating havoc wherever this parodic simpleton of a knight takes it. When a banker refuses to consider buying the device, Calino accidentally punches it into the ceiling; erupting into the room above, the roving spear point upends cabinets and desks that, along with the floorboards, come crashing down into the banker's office. In quick succession, Calino and his lance then rampage through a bourgeois drawing room, a grocery shop, and a café, before a fat couple perhaps even crazier than he is sees its potential for their apartment building. So successful is the device, however, that it attracts every lightning bolt in the next storm, sending all the residents there into convulsive fits. Similarly, *Calino sourcier* (1913) equips the comic with a divining rod that makes water spring out of the most unlikely places. When he is arrested and taken off to the police station, the rod promptly causes jets of water to erupt out of a wall painting, a desk inkwell, and even one cop's ear. In a clever twist at the end, Calino himself magically dissolves away in a jail cell, leaving water spraying from every direction.

122. *Calino sourcier,* 1913 (poster)

Perhaps the most interesting of the *Calino* films, however, continue the carnivalesque parody of civil servant bureaucracy so characteristic of the earlier films. A perfect example is *Calino, chef de gare* (1912), in which Calino is given the job of managing a small provincial rail station. The opening AS establishes the plain office where he quickly dispatches his paperwork and takes a nap, while trains come and go in the matted-in deep space of a background window. As the film runs through one work site after another, Calino's attitude is no less cavalier or at least nonplussed. At the switch box, he pushes and pulls levers while reading *Le Journal*, and, in response, a huge locomotive lurches backward and forward several times. In the baggage room, a woman grabs her suitcase from a pile, and a whole wall of luggage topples over on him. As if in retaliation, in the ticket office he sits smiling, with his feet up on a foreground desk, while customers clamor angrily in the background. Then, on a local passenger train waiting in the station, when one man complains about the dust and junk in his compartment, Calino simply tosses him out the window. For this train is to do double duty: into another compartment, to the astonishment of its three occupants, he stuffs a hay bale, a basket of chickens, and a calf. To top off his task, he uses a third compartment, where two men are sleeping in bunks, to install a full-grown horse. In the end, the new station master forgets to change a rail switch for a passing express train, and it plows right through a cart stalled on the tracks. But, as a dedicated paper pusher, what finally bothers him most, in the concluding MS, is that his pencil breaks—although that still cannot prevent him from taking his customary nap.

What most engaged Durand's interest at Gaumont by the summer of 1912, however, were the *Onésime* films. This new series featured Bourbon, a masterful acrobat, lean and slightly stooped, with an unusually expressive face (highlighted by a "grinning mouth and malicious little eyes"[177]), along with a supporting cast of music hall comics whom Durand had assembled over several years and who took to calling themselves "Les Pouics."[178] With their often frenetic action, offhand reflexivity, and freewheeling invention of perfectly absurd situations, these films arguably constitute the high point of French prewar slapstick comedy. One of the earliest of the series, *Onésime a un duel à l'américaine* (1912), draws attention to its arbitrary premise almost immediately as Onésime and another gentleman reach for the same newspaper in a club room, argue, trade blows, and arrange to duel. It also introduces the duel with a flippant, extended intertitle—"What shall the weapons be? Swords at forty paces? Hot frankfurters stuffed with dynamite? Frying pans, rolling pins, lolly pops, putty blowers, gatling guns, air rifles, or ice cream forks?"—which soon became a trademark of the series. When he and his opponent are given enormous dueling pistols the next morning, however, Onésime is so drunk that he points the pistol at himself and, curious, sniffs the barrel. The duel itself begins with each man hiding behind a tree in an empty park, but once the shooting starts, the film leaps into the fast-motion chase of what *Le cinéma* described as an "abracadabra fantasy."[179] The two opponents dart in and out of the trees, hop onto a bridge (in reverse motion), suddenly crash through a dining room and drawing room, rampage through a creamery shop, and pause briefly in a café. But that is because a cut-in MS shows them caught in a revolving glass door, both pistols firing straight up in the narrow space. Suddenly, they are back in the countryside again, where Onésime does a flip dive off another bridge and swims off downstream, all the while continuing to shoot at his pursuing opponent. When the two finally are seized by gendarmes under another bridge and thrown into a jail cell, their clothes ripped to shreds and faces blackened, they burst out laughing at one another—and that, just as arbitrarily, resolves their differences.

This no-holds-barred parody of narrative conventions is no less evident in several later films. In *Onésime et le chien bienfaisant* (1912), for instance, the woman Onésime loves has been promised by her father to another, more suitable rival, which plunges the comic into a funk. The father's big black poodle is dismayed at the choice, however, and determines to rectify this mistake in patriarchal judgment. First, the poodle saves Onésime from asphyxiating himself—it jumps in one of his windows and carries off several smoking logs. Then, after bearing the brunt of its master's pats and kicks, the poodle has a "dream vision" of the father chatting with Onésime's rival and plots revenge. That plan unfolds in a sequence that moves from CU to FS to LS, as the poodle snatches a woman's boot, trots out of a shop, and races down a street. Variations on these shots are then repeated, with the dog finally swimming across a stream (as in *Rescued by Rover*) and mysteriously entering the rival's apartment. The mystery is resolved in the end when the father visits and discovers, in cut-in MSs, the "illicit" boot in a bookcase and a woman's undergarment on the bed. This ruins the rival's reputation and reinstates the oblivious Onésime, all the result of the poodle's double performance as both "hero" and "good father." This mildly risqué parody gets pushed to an extreme in *Onésime et son âne* (1913). In this film, Onésime has promised his only companion, an ass named Aliboron, that he will share any wealth he comes to possess. One day, in a variation on the féerie fable of the hen that laid the golden egg, the ass literally begins to shit golden coins. As promised, the comic treats Aliboron royally—after all, as a piece of property, the ass has turned into a rentier's "dream machine." Indeed, the comic himself now turns into a servant in a series of repeated gags—bathing and dressing Aliboron, serving him dinner in a restaurant, putting him to sleep in a proper bed (an image that prefigures the cow in Luis Buñuel's *L'Age d'or*). Alas, in the end, the coins prove to be fake, and Onésime reverts to his former state, except for the reversed master-servant relationship that the ass has "earned" and to which he has grown accustomed. The film's final LS has Onésime, still a "slave" to his property, now pulling Aliboron comfortably seated in a cart.

Onésime gentleman détective (1912)[180] not only parodies the popular crime films of the period but uses the genre's conventional plot as a baseline to run off one incongruous riff after another, much like the later Marx Brothers films.[181] Responding to a bourgeois family's call for help in locating some stolen money, Onésime shows up elegantly dressed (in frock coat, gray top hat, white spats and gloves), but refuses to give up his cane and traveling bag while repeatedly shaking everyone's hands. His own living quarters are reminiscent of *Boireau,*

123. *Onésime horloger*, 1912 (Ernest Bourbon)

roi de boxe and look ahead to the Rube Goldberg contraptions of Keaton: the bed slides forward out of the wall when he wants to get up, he somersaults over his clothes neatly laid out on the floor and springs up fully dressed, and, grabbing a pelt off the kitchen wall, he sticks it briefly in the oven and pulls out a little dog. À la *Zigomar*, his investigation moves rapidly through disconnected sites, using up one set of characters after another. Seized and tossed into what looks like a grave, he re-emerges looking like Lewis Carroll's Mad Hatter, with an enormous gray hat and elongated gloved hands. Soon after, he gets into a fight and falls out of a window along with an armoire, only to get up and begin plucking its panels like a harp. Finally, after shinnying up a gutter pipe to crawl into another room, his chief suspect knocks him back out the window with a chair and then tosses out furniture until he is completely buried in debris. But out of that pile, of course, he not only rises again but comes up with the stolen money, in a tidy equation that underscores the absurdity of its exchange value as well as his own circulation.

    As the anarchic, pell-mell spirit of these films attests, the *Onésime* series expropriated cinematic trucs probably more than any other comic series.[182] The best known, and perhaps most accomplished, of these films is *Onésime horloger* (1912), whose premise stipulates that Onésime cannot receive his inheritance from an uncle for twenty years.[183] To overcome this obstacle, he reads an 1859 treatise on timepieces and constructs a special pneumatic clock that can accelerate time in his interest. After a quick test, in which the traffic on a Paris street goes into fast motion, the film launches into a fantasy chronicle of his life over the next twenty years. He joins the dancing craze, passes a bar exam, marries and has a kid, shops at department stores, attends the Opéra, builds a new house, and ends up dining at the Café de la Paix. These emblematic moments of rapid, easy success are accentuated not only by fast motion, as in the LS of the house wall going up, but also by close shots and invisible cuts, as in the AS of the family portrait where the parents quickly "age" while the kid "grows" into a strapping young man. In the end, of course, an old lawyer counts out the inheritance money to an immensely pleased Onésime, who promptly reverses his special clock to twenty years before and prepares to enjoy his wealth all over again. Intriguingly, *Onésime horloger* exploits two very different concepts of "making it" in a paradoxical time loop. Although Onésime makes his way in society through individual initiative, he still believes in the social significance of inherited property. Normally, the one would cancel the other out—his actions over that twenty-year period, for instance, would seem to evacuate the inheritance of any value. But his magical clock, which is as responsible for his success as is any initiative on his part, permits him to tinker with and remake himself and his story—he can have his cake and eat it, too, perhaps repeatedly. And, as the product of another "magical" apparatus, *Onésime horloger* itself epitomizes the cinema's ability to do the same, serving up incompatible ingredients in a fantasy space of pleasurable consumption.[184]

Of the French comic series that tended to eschew slapstick for a less active, "more refined" comedy of manners, certainly Pathé's *Rigadin* series was the most prolific and long-lived. Hardly a week went by, between 1911 and 1914, when a *Rigadin* film (most of them directed apparently by Monca) was not part of Pathé's standard release package. Ten years later, shortly after another reorganization of the company cut short his attempt to resume the series, Prince looked back on the prewar years in amazement: "Every week I had to have a new scenario idea. In 52 weeks I needed 52 scenarios! Complete scenarios with a dominant idea, a premise, a development, a complicated action and a denouement. Actual short plays, you know!"[185] This production pace often showed, not only in the simplicity of the scenarios, but in the frequent use of rather anachronistic painted flats, whether quickly executed or merely recycled. Unfortunately, a smaller percentage of these films also seem to have survived, in comparison to the other major series. But the titles and press descriptions that remain indicate that Prince usually located his character within the social strata of the older petit bourgeoisie or newer white-collar bourgeoisie. Although sometimes working at a trade or profession, more often than not Rigadin was either courting, involved in a love affair, or having marital problems—with one of two comic partners, Germaine Reuver or Gabrielle Lange.

Le Nez de Rigadin (1911) provides a good example of the comic touches that made the series so appealing. It begins with an AS/LS of Rigadin and his dog sitting alone in a one-room apartment, with Amelie (Reuver) working at a sewing machine in her apartment next door (the two neatly linked by a pan). As she goes to her background window to water some plants (Sacre Coeur is visible in the distance), a 180-degree reverse-angle cut frames the two windows as Rigadin appears (looking quite lovesick), chats politely with her, and hands her a note, using a pair of tongs.[186] To his proposal of marriage, she responds with another note of acceptance, on one condition: that he get another nose. Now, Prince's large, turned-up nose was one of his comic assets (Amelie had even laughed at it), so when he goes off to meet a fellow comedian at a sidewalk café, he chooses from among his friend's available disguises the biggest, most Gallic protuberance of all—one that might have made even Cyrano de Bergerac proud. The new nose astonishes the waiter, draws the admiration of several women on a park bench, and wins Amelie's approval as well. However, the dog is not won over, and, when Rigadin goes to sign the marriage contract, it snatches the fake nose right off his face—and Amelie promptly withdraws her assent. Then, just as Rigadin is about to hang himself back in his room (with the noose slipped over his nose, of course), the dog relents and begins barking, which brings Amelie rushing in to accept him at last—unlike the unlucky Cyrano—nose and all.

Two other *Rigadin* films released early in 1912, one after the other, develop this self-conscious, somewhat unassuming character in divergent directions. The later of the two, *Rigadin avale son ocarina*, reworks the courting story of the earlier film, with a different object or body part now linked to crucial shifts in musical accompaniment. Here, Rigadin is in love with Suzette (Reuver), the daughter of a music teacher named Laflute, but has absolutely no knack for playing an instrument—given a clarinet, for instance, he tries to blow in the wrong end. One day, when her father is out, Suzette invites him to visit, and they take turns practicing on an ocarina or "sweet potato." Unfortunately, Rigadin has it in his mouth when Laflute unexpectedly returns, and he is so startled that he swallows it. This leads to an extended sequence of gags as Rigadin goes about Paris, producing tunes just by breathing, and everyone he passes or meets—a policeman, his doctor, and his servant—breaks uncontrollably into dance. When he finally is invited back to Suzette's apartment, Laflute discovers where the missing ocarina is lurking and kicks him in the rear so hard that the ocarina pops back into his mouth again. By this time, however, the comic is such an accomplished player that he quickly wins both Suzette and her father's approval. In *Rigadin et la baguette magique*, by contrast, the comic is a henpecked husband who reluctantly accepts the slaps and kicks of his wife (Reuver) as they prepare to attend a party given by friends. The last straw comes when he asks her to take his hat and coat at the door, like a "good wife," and she storms out of the party. Rigadin is so impressed by a magician hired to entertain the party guests that he visits the man the next day and, after learning how to make a vase vanish, buys one of his wands. Its magic works nicely as he journeys back to his apartment—he makes a ferocious dog disappear and then a crowd of people fighting to get into a taxi. However, when he confronts his angry wife in the dining room and confidently waves the wand, a duplicate of her appears on the opposite side of the frame. The final tableau has him kneeling in anguish, center foreground, vainly trying to appease this doubly threatening figure of the "woman on top."[187]

Perhaps the most intriguing, and disturbing, of these films is *Rigadin, défenseur de la vertu* (1912), which mixes nuanced comic touches with scatological
gags, within a skillfully constructed play of spatial coordinates. André Hugon's
scenario of the film is simple enough: a young milliner who lives down the hall
in Rigadin's apartment building is annoyed by the persistent propositions of an
old rake, and the comic finds a way to drive off this sexual caricature. Before
the old rake is introduced, however, the film maps out several spaces in order to
set up Rigadin's relationship to the milliner and to prepare the first gag. First
comes an establishing LS of the building exterior as the woman enters the doorway (frame left) and Rigadin, at a second-floor window (frame right), blows a
kiss (once she has gone in). After a missing intertitle, she exits the building, in
another LS that centers the doorway, only to turn and wave. A FS of the window
now has Rigadin look down, in a perfect eyeline match, and wave in response.
After the milliner has delivered a hat to a shop, where the old rake accosts and
pursues her, she returns to the apartment building; in another LS before the
door, he pins a note on the empty hatbox she is carrying. In an eyeline-matched
AS, Rigadin notices what is going on and dumps his chamber pot, which, in the
cut back to LS, drenches the old man—who angrily removes his own hat to
reveal his bald head. The note asks for a rendezvous at a restaurant that evening,
and Rigadin takes the milliner there to show the old rake up one more time, in
what turns out to be another obscene gag.

This last sequence uses a long-take AS/LS of the restaurant interior as Rigadin seats the woman among some friends in the background and comes to sit
at a left foreground table, straight across from the old rake seated in the right
foreground. What follows is a fine bit of sustained comic pantomime. Rigadin
stares at the old man, to get his attention, and slowly wipes his prominent nose
with a handkerchief, twice—which the old man nervously repeats, as if something were marring his own nose. When Rigadin wipes his eye, the old man
quickly repeats the gesture, and then each simultaneously puts his handkerchief
in a vest pocket. Unobserved, Rigadin stops a waiter briefly to tamper with the
plate holding the other's bill and then, getting the old man's attention again,
begins slowly wiping his face with his own plate; when the old man, mesmerized, repeats this strange gesture, too, he unknowingly blackens his entire face.
In a nasty turn, everyone in the restaurant now joins in laughing at this stereotypically racist joke, but only Rigadin, the milliner, and the cinema audience
may take pleasure in its scatological resonance. The film ends with both Rigadin
and the woman, like adolescents mocking adults, literally thumbing their noses
at the old man as he is carried out.

Linder's films remained the most popular of Pathé's comic series, of course,
but their numbers were nowhere as prodigious as the *Rigadins*. For one thing,
Linder fell gravely ill with appendicitis in December 1910, and did not resume
making films until six months later. During this period, Pathé parceled out the
films he had been making up to the point of his illness, releasing them at intervals of every four to six weeks instead of the customary one or two. The company also kept his name in the public eye by running ads of support for him

during his convalescence. Although scarcely any titles released during these six months survive, according to press descriptions, they narrated stages in a continuing "love story" (much as in the *Little Moritz* and *Rosalie* films) with Max resisting, wooing, and finally marrying a young woman played by Paulette Lorsy and then suffering abuse at the hands of his new mother-in-law (Lange).[188] When Linder did return to the studio, his production rate was much slower than before; in fact, the *Max* series did not become a regular biweekly attraction in Pathé's programs until March 1912. However, with the assistance of Leprince, he now took over direction of the series' films and sometimes wrote his own scenarios. Linder also took the unusual step of embarking on what would become a series of tours throughout Europe, during which he produced films and also performed onstage. That spring he was in Germany, the following summer he was in Spain, with Napierkowska, and in the winter of 1912–1913, he and his new acting partners, Lucy d'Orbel and Gorby, traveled through Vienna, Warsaw, Saint Petersburg, Moscow, and Odessa.[189] Apparently, it was during these tours that Linder began to realize the full extent of his fame—he and Napierkowska, for instance, were mobbed in Barcelona—and he successfully pressed Pathé into upping his salary from 150,000 francs at the end of 1911 to one million francs by the end of 1912.[190] That made Linder by far the highest paid star anywhere in the prewar cinema.

The *Max* series' titles released by Pathé in the summer and fall of 1911 were calculated to exploit the comic's recent brush with death as well as to display his undiminished skills as a performer. The first film, *Max en convalescence*, reworks Linder's own recuperation by having Max spend the summer at his family's small country estate (with the mother and father played by Linder's own parents).[191] The chief obstacle to his recovery is the family pony, which plays a series of mildly amusing tricks on him, and from which he has to be rescued by the family dog. *Max a un duel*, which returns to the earlier films' subject of courting, is much more inventive and tightly structured. Here, Max's fiancée (Lorsy) will marry him on one condition: he must fight a duel. Intriguingly, Max pumps himself up by practicing, in AS, in front of a portrait of her father—he delivers it a slap, shows it his calling card, and finally pierces the portrait with a sword. The problem is that no one he challenges on the street pays him much attention. He stomps a gentleman's foot and is kicked out of the frame; he uses his cane to stir the wine glass of a man writing at a café table, and the man simply tosses the wine at him. Max finally has his servant (Coquet) play an opponent he can easily defeat, but his fiancée's father (scriptwriter Armand Massard) discovers the ruse when the servant later sneaks up to remind him of their pact—at which the father promptly shoves Max's hat down over his ears. This concluding image, accentuated by a cut-in MS, makes a neat contrast with the opening, where the fiancée scares him in the drawing room by entering with a huge grotesque mask over her head—as if to literalize his fear of the woman as a threat. In the end, with the hat scrunched down over his head, however, it is Max himself who is reduced to the grotesque—and by the father he had sought to eliminate and replace—in a concise image of repression and oedipal revenge.

The slower work pace during 1911 also gave Linder, unlike Prince, more time to prepare his films—an edge that he turned to real advantage in *Victime du quinquina* (1911), one of the best films of his career. Maurice Delamare's scenario has Max get high on an overdose of quinine (prescribed for yet another illness) and suffer its consequences in a cleverly structured series of encounters. Two quick ASs—of Max in a doctor's office and at a café table—set up the premise, with the added ironic touch of a cut-in CU of the Bordeaux souvenir glass that he patiently sips at with a straw. In rapid succession, Max "drunkenly" gets into quarrels with the Minister of War (as they both try to get into the same open carriage) and then with an ambassador as well as the Paris police chief (at a restaurant), each of whom presents a calling card and challenges him to a duel. In another ironic touch, the minister's address is Place de Saint-Placide, and he and Max simultaneously step into the carriage, not once but three times, like automatons. On the street again, Max bumps into a lamppost and leans against it to put on his topcoat; as the result of this vaudeville turn, he is pinned there, unable to walk off in any direction. A cop comes up to help and, picking out one of the cards Max has collected, takes the dazed, puppetlike figure for his own boss and escorts him home—in the first of a repeated set of encounters, but in reverse order. The police chief is so frightened by the knock at his door that he hides under the dining room table, but he leaps up when Max sits down to eat, wraps him in the tablecloth, and tosses him into the street—where he rolls into another cop. This cop takes him to the ambassador's residence, from which he is ejected once again, and a third cop carries him off to the home of the war minister—like an expensive piece of luggage. Here, in what turns out to be a clever variation on the earlier repetition at the carriage, Max goes straight to bed with the minister's wife, who simply ignores him. When the minister returns, he angrily throws Max out; but the cop is still nearby and respectfully sends him back in, so that, while the minister and his wife argue in another room, Max climbs sleepily back into their bed. Now, when the minister returns to the bedroom, he lays down on top of Max and then, thoroughly enraged, picks him up like a bag of laundry and tosses him out the second-story window. In a neatly condensed conclusion, Max lands on top of all three cops who have been so deferential to him, and they simultaneously snap to attention. Once they recognize his cards, however, the hapless Max gets yet another beating. Not only is the remedy much worse than the illness in this film, but the obsessively repeated situations add up to an economical satire of inflated social status, and especially of the behaviorial latitude accorded French authority figures.

A number of titles released early in 1912, all from his own scenarios, explore the troubles Max encounters as a newly married bourgeois, with his partner in these films now played by Jane Renouard. *Max reprend sa liberté*, for instance, begins with Max elated to see his wife Anastasie go back to her mother, leaving him free to live on his own.[192] Within a day, however, his "housekeeping skills" have nearly demolished the domestic space of the apartment, and he reluctantly solicits her return. Then, before she can respond, he receives word of an unexpected inheritance, and, when she does reappear, ready to start over, Max has reverted to his old self—now that he can pay others to support him in proper bourgeois style. *Max et son chien Dick* resorts to a different kind of parody to get rid of a wife. In the opening AS/LS, Jane draws lots to determine whom she will marry, Max or William, but in the second, shortly after his honeymoon, Max discovers her writing a love letter to his rival. While he goes off to his office the next day, Max orders his own dog to play detective and spy on Jane in order to confirm his suspicions. Sure enough, William comes to visit and, when Jane takes him into the next room, the dog dashes to the telephone. In a short sequence of alternating MSs and CUs, reminiscent of *Medor au téléphone*, the dog barks out his information to Max, and the sequence is capped by a triptych tableau of the two separated by a Paris boulevard. Rushing home, Max surprises the couple kissing on the drawing room sofa and, rather than threaten them, nonchalantly pulls a cigarette case from his pocket. The dog signals his next move by dragging in a trunk for Jane to pack her things, and the film concludes in a parodic MS of Max sitting down to dinner, with his "best friend" replacing his unfaithful wife—as the dog, with a napkin securely tied around its neck, demonstrates its skill in drinking from a cup.

During the summer of 1912, surviving titles suggest that the *Max* series played off a variety of earlier or concurrent films. Massard's scenario for *Max Linder contre Nick Winter*, for instance, has the comic easily outwit Pathé's premiere detective, even with Bressol as the "guest star."[193] Cinematic trucs consistently aid him in his deceptions: in one scene, he passes through a locked, mirrored cabinet, as a superimposition, in another, he blacks out the gallery where the Mona Lisa is on display, in order to steal through a window in silhouette—and, when the lights come up after a struggle, Nick Winter has tied up his own assistant and the painting is gone. In the end, he sets up another Max as a decoy and then, disguising himself as Winter, has the astonished detective arrested as an imposter. Rollini's scenario for *L'Ane jaloux* reworks Max's encounters the previous summer with the family pony. Here, Joë Dawson takes on the guise of a donkey in order to harrass the comic, who is trying to court Mlle Lilli (Lorsy). When Max and Lilli sit on a park bench, the donkey follows close behind; rubbing its backside against the suitor, it stomps on his foot, before finally threatening him outright—and the comic takes to flight. This produces a delightfully absurd chase through an apartment building, with the donkey imitating Max at one point (pausing to peer over the staircase railing), standing up on its hind legs to ring a doorbell, and resting briefly on top of a man in bed before crawling into the fireplace in pursuit of its victim. Far more subdued or "refined," Linder's scenario for *Peintre par amour* relies on his own performance within just three studio decors. Here, Mlle Cabaneilles (Napierkowska), whom Max is courting on the sly, suggests that he make himself out to be a painter and do a portrait of her mother (Lange) so that she will assent to their engagement. Max's initial strategy, however, is to use his easel as a screen to keep the mother from seeing the couple kissing, but the mother exposes him as a fraud when she discovers the childish caricature he has drawn. His next strategy is to take on the guise of Léonard de Vincennes and portray the mother as a "Mona Lisa," which he produces by tearing off the canvas's top layer to reveal (in an in-joke reference) a copy of the famous painting stolen from the Louvre. The problem now is to reproduce the plumed hat the mother insists on wearing, and his witty solution is to clip off several feathers and stick them directly onto the copy, in a very up-to-date form of collage.

Throughout the next year and a half, most of the extant titles in the *Max* series focused on the troubles Linder's character has as either a lover or a married man. One of the more inventive of these is *Max veut grandir* (1912), for which he himself contributed the scenario. It begins with Max as a frustrated suitor for the hand of Mlle Giacordy (Renouard), apparently because her father finds him too short. One solution after another fails him (until the end), in a series of structurally parallel sequences.[194] First, he tries stilts, on which he practices briefly in his own apartment, but he gets no further than the Giacordy dining room—where he has to hang and then swing on the chandelier, sending both him and it, along with a sideboard, crashing down on the central table. Next, Max tries an inventor's special machine that is supposed to lengthen anyone within its range. Here the truc depends on a distorting lens, perhaps even an early anamorphic lens, because the image distorts and returns to normal within the shot rather than across a cut.[195] When he shows up to challenge M. Giacordy once more, however, the machine balks and then shortens both of them—and the father again runs him off. Now, Max's friend suggests that they dress as one person in an elongated costume, with the comic inside sitting on his shoulders. Practicing this technique destroys Max's apartment, but it convinces M. Giacordy—until he surprises Max revealing the trick to his daughter in the next room. Persistent to the end, Max tries yet another invention that sends a surge of electricity through him, with the result that he slowly rises in height—and gains such confidence that he walks off without paying the inventor. This finally satisfies M. Giacordy, who checks Max's shoes and legs, in CU, to make sure they belong to him, before granting his daughter's engagement—but now the disproportionate couple have trouble embracing. Eventually, however, size apparently poses no problem, for the concluding LS, in a clever twist, shows Max and his wife years later followed by several kids on hidden stilts, the last of whom is a good twelve feet tall!

In *Max n'aime pas les chats* (1913), Linder's scenario works a peculiarly whimsical variation on the subject of a suspected rival for a woman's love. Here, the rival is a cat that, in an initial cut-in MS, Max's wife (d'Orbel) places between them when he tries to kiss her on a drawing room couch. Her concern for the cat is such that, one day when he is out, she believes it to be ill and puts a thermometer under its paws, a gesture singled out in CU. Max returns to find his wife playing the piano for the cat, neatly coiffed in a towel and lounging comfortably on a chair. Exasperated, Max later tries sneaking up on the cat (when his wife is out) and throwing it out the window—but reverse motion simply sends it back in. When his wife is invited to visit a relative, Max conspires with his servant (Gorby) to make it disappear. As the wife circulates in and out of the drawing room, collecting her bags, the servant quickly shifts the cat from its traveling case into the grand piano—and she reluctantly goes off without it. A short sequence "bridge" sets up the final gag: as the servant dusts the piano, a CU insert reveals the cat inside with kittens. When the wife returns from her trip, she and Max celebrate by having him sit down at the piano to accompany her singing, but the notes he produces are so off-key that he raises the piano top to peer inside. In astonishment, he pulls cat after cat out of the piano, like rabbits out of a magician's hat, and a CU insert reveals that the piano is still swarming with them. This trick of multiplication seems to push Max over the edge for, in the last sequence, he faces a cat already smashed against a wall and fires at it with a revolver (at which it vanishes), then turns to advance menacingly into a CU that goes into soft focus.[196] In what looks like a nightmare sequence of obsessive vengeance, Max's fearful anger is pushed far past whimsy to the point of hysteria, perhaps glancing past the cat to the real character it may figure, his own wife, and, rather than her love for a "rival," her own threatening powers of reproduction.

In *Max et la doctoresse* (1914), Linder also relies on reproduction to resolve his scenario's comic dilemma of reversed gender roles. Here, Max is in love with a "new woman," a doctor (d'Orbel), whom he conspires to meet by visiting her office for an examination. This sets up a relatively long-take AS/LS in which the doctor plays "straight man" to his comic "courtship." He has to partially undress and submit to probings (at which he becomes ticklish)—his emotional anxiety increasingly manifest in his exposed physical vulnerability. In a sense, the examination serves as a test, and, once his proposal of marriage is accepted, the film moves quickly to their first night together. Her profession now presents an obstacle to block and frustrate Max's desire as their servant (Gorby) calls her away from the bedroom, not once but three times, in response to emergencies. Throughout this series of sequences, the doctor remains dressed in her bridal outfit (Max gets no further than taking off her veil), so that her actions continually belie the significance of her costume—and the patients she attends are all married men. Max also sticks to his role—first throwing a tantrum, then falling asleep, but reviving to toss a pillow at the servant's third entrance. The final sequence reworks the beginning, with a half-dozen men waiting in the doctor's office while she examines a seventh in the next room—and, when she asks the latter to undress, in AS, he smiles at the camera. Now it is Max who interrupts this scene to disperse all these rival patients (any economic threat is subordinated to the sexual), but he does not come alone—instead, he is carrying a baby. This surprise introduction of the child sustains the pattern of reversed gender roles, making him and not her seem its apparent creator or "mother."[197] Even human reproduction, it turns out, cannot completely resolve this dilemma, and the film has to resort to a concluding fantasy tableau borrowed from the family melodrama. There, the couple return to their "normal" roles—at least in the space of the home—as the wife sits cradling the baby in their bedroom, while Max smokes contentedly beside them.

Although Linder's scenario for *Max pédicure* (1914) is hardly unfamiliar, this late film exhibits a highly nuanced sense of comic invention and execution, exactly of the kind that Chaplin would be exploiting in another year or two. Here, Max is a typical bourgeois dandy seeking an affair with a married woman (d'Orbel) he meets one day in the park. When he calls on her later, they are surprised by her husband's return, and Max assumes the guise of the pedicurist (Gorby) who is there for a scheduled appointment. One of the film's pleasures lies in the performances of all four principal characters and in the keenly observed moments scattered like grace notes throughout. Max meets the woman in the park, for instance, after two boys steal the dog she is walking, but she is so absorbed in her reading that for several seconds she does not notice it is missing. He then uses the dog (which he retrieves) to get close to her: when she kisses it, he does, too (trying to kiss her as well); he picks it up to make sure he can accompany her home; and, in front of her apartment building, he gazes soulfully at the dog and kisses its paw.

But these moments are distributed within a filmic structure that makes very economical use of three adjacent spaces: a corridor stairway, a deep-space drawing room, and a dining room—where the real pedicurist is sent to cool his heels, only to run into the family maid. Once secreted in the drawing room, the would-be lovers give a slow, suspicious look offscreen (after a cut to the husband approaching in the corridor), and Max goes into a panic, racing around the room like a caged animal, until the woman tells him to take up the pedicurist's tools. When the husband enters, Max is busy with her foot, but handling his tiny file like a chisel. In a nicely timed sequence of alternation, the maid drops a plate when she surprises the pedicurist in the dining room, Max shoves him through the background door when he tries to enter the drawing room, the pedicurist falls back into the maid who now drops a stack of plates, and the woman tells the men she will take care of whatever is going on in the dining room and ends up sitting down among the broken plates to have her feet done properly. Unable to leave, in a long-take FS/LS, Max now confronts the unexpected challenge of treating the husband's feet. Donning gloves, he tries to pull off one shoe and eventually has to take the rivets out of a buckle to get it off. The foot he faces is so disagreeable that he puts on another glove and gingerly works at getting off the dirty sock. Staring at the bare foot at last, he slaps at a louse, slams the shoe against the stool, and wipes the heel with the sock. In a cut-in AS, Max now picks up a huge pair of scissors and goes to cut off the man's toes; when the husband complains, he tries a smaller pair to trim any stray hairs, which sends the man into ticklish convulsions. Finally, Max slavers the toes in shaving cream and, while the man stares, begins shaving his foot and wiping the razor on his trouser leg. In a cut back to FS/LS, the husband angrily orders him out, and, stealing a gag from *La Chausette*, Max discovers that he is mopping his own brow with the offensive sock. After Max exits, however, the

124. *Max pédicure*, 1914 (Max Linder)

husband finds the pedicurist's hat on a chair and, confronting him in the dining room, takes him for a fake—and promptly tosses him out a background window. He falls, of course, on Max (coming out of the building), who momentarily is scrunched into a beetlelike position before rebounding to shake hands with his "accomplice." In this final gag, the *Max* series circles back to the myth of its own origins, reprising a key moment from *Les Debuts de Max Linder au cinématographe*.

One of the last extant films in the series, *Mari jaloux* (1914), recapitulates Linder's career even more thoroughly, in a cleverly deceptive scenario. In skeletal outline, it has a M. and Mme Bourgeois invite Max, who is performing at the Alhambra Theatre, to join them one afternoon for tea. After the husband's fears that his wife is having an affair with the comic are allayed (at his own expense), the couple asks to visit Max at his film studio—and their experience turns out to be far more than they bargained for. The initial scenes are a tip-off to this film's deft sleight-of-hand. An intertitle announces Max's sketch at the Alhambra, but a long-take FS/LS offers two look-alike male dancers performing in perfect synchrony, like Siamese twins. The following intertitle announces his sketch as a triumph, and the comic takes three bows—seemingly having done nothing. The middle section of the film works out a more conventional twist on narrative expectation, one that harkens back to the earlier comedies of "bad taste." Provided with Molière's dictum that "ridicule kills love," the husband laces Max's tea cup with a purgative whose effect, a CU label warns, is immediate. Another long-take AS/LS focuses on the polite behavior of this social ritual, in order to delay the inevitable: all three characters defer to one another repeatedly before sitting down, the husband draws Max's attention to a background painting, and, when the wife takes him off, the husband has to bring them back (with another painting). In clearing the table, while they are gone, however, the maid shifts the serving tray, and it is the husband, of course, who gets the "doctored" tea. While he rushes off in anguish and returns, repeatedly, Max glances in bewilderment at the camera, and the wife reveals her real interest—acting in the cinema.

The final scene then stages a variation on the opening, but focuses on the work that goes into what seems an effortless film performance, with one last deceptive twist. A FS/LS presents Linder's crew setting up a shot: the cameraman, for instance, steps off the distance between foreground camera and background interior decors and draws a chalk line on the floor for the actors.[198] A FS of the decors frames the rehearsal process for a script that ironically replays the afternoon tea scene, but now the Bourgeoises are the illicit couple and Max the irate husband who is to kill both of them and himself. The comic briefly acts out all the roles, and the disastrous "take" begins. After M. Bourgeois is shot, Max's revolver misfires, and he has to improvise—throwing Mme Bourgeois about like a sack, dumping flour on her, thrashing both of his victims—with the result that the two guest "actors" (although "dead") frantically drag themselves off the set. Even though Linder has a last laugh at this literal send-up of the bourgeoisie—which also debunks anyone else seeking their cinema debut—the film itself extends the joke with a final LS of the couple's escape down a nearby street, in fast motion.

If Gaumont consistently produced the most outrageous of the slapstick comedies in the *Onésime* series, the company also was responsible for the most sophisticated—Perret's *Léonce* series. Perret seems to have tried out several formulas long before the series became a regular component of Gaumont's programs, in late 1912.[199] A pair of films in 1911, for instance, experiments with one drawn from the tongue-in-cheek titles used in caricature illustrations. *Comment on les prend* has a young woman (Andreyor) take on the "exotic" guise of a gypsy flower seller to attract the attention of an eligible bachelor (Perret). Shot largely on location on the south coast, the film steers its actors like bourgeois tourists through several picturesque tableaux—a small village market, a field of flowers, an observation point overlooking the sea—only to reveal that Yvette has been acting in collusion with the Perret character's mother. The final tableau stages this revelation for Perret himself, sitting with his mother on an enclosed veranda, as Yvette, framed in a background window, steals up to tickle his ears with a bouquet of flowers. Shot exclusively in chic studio interiors, *Comment on les garde* focuses on the same couple, presumably, with Yvette now trying to combat Perret's interest in other "exotic" women outside their marriage. The first scene provides each of them with privileged information: a cut-in CU of a note (she only gets to sniff its odor of perfume) confirms his rendezvous with an admirer at a masked ball that night, and a keyhole-masked POV shot lets her

417

see him writing a response in the adjacent study. Yvette's initial tactic in "keeping her husband" is to play the "good wife" so she sets the dining room table, prepares dinner, lays out his nightclothes (all with the help of a maid), and then dresses in her nightgown (slyly pulling a screen in front of the camera). However, Perret barely notices all this and, as planned, goes out for the evening. Eliding Yvette's next move, the film shifts to the masked ball where Perret is drawn to a veiled figure, and as he is about to be taken off in a taxi, he accepts being blindfolded. This sets up a final deep-space tableau, through which the veiled woman leads Perret still blindfolded, from background to foreground, turning on the lights in three rooms in succession. The last, as expected, turns out to be the couple's own dining room, in which she now asks him to kneel, lets him unblindfold himself and then lift her veil—and Yvette lets out a laugh at his surprised chagrin. Still, Yvette's control of the narrative as well as the mise-en-scène[200] turns out to be more apparent than real, for this comedy of delayed exposure and recognition remains securely grounded in the social norms of gender relations.

By the time of *L'Express matrimonial* (1912), certain elements of the *Léonce* series were firmly in place. This film, too, begins with Perret as the central character, who notices two women (the younger played by Petit) boarding a train he is taking to Paris. The deep, narrow space of the train car corridor (lit principally from the left, through the windows)[201] establishes the location of two adjacent first-class compartments, as Perret amiably persuades the conductor to change his seating, politely greets Petit, and then saunters up and down the corridor, smoking a cigarette. A sequence of alternation then links the two spaces, framing each through the exterior window, as Petit laughs at a newspaper she is reading, and Perret tries to listen through the wall, but actually primps and admires himself in a cut-in CU of a mirror. They next meet in the dining car, where the waiter (already bribed) seats Perret in the right foreground, opposite the two women at the same table. This space, too, seems illuminated by available light, with the added "realistic" details of a landscape passing in the background windows and a very slight, slow shaking of the image. A cut-in MS of the two women serves to set up the film's only gag, but its principal effect is to turn Perret into an offscreen reflection in a mirror behind them—as if to literalize his image as a poseur. The gag is a reworking of the old train tunnel kiss and exposes Perret kissing the older woman (they have switched seats), which sends Petit into laughter again. After the train reaches Paris, the topper to this extended comedy of manners—as in *Comment on les prend*—comes in a long-take FS/LS of the family terrace where Perret and his father are sitting comfortably. Who should arrive but the two women from the train, with Petit introduced as the father's prospective fiancée for his son. In a deft, deceptive maneuver, the earlier expectation of illicit sexuality is transformed into romance (as Petit seems to accept Perret's explanation), which in turn is transformed into a conventionally arranged marriage (that Perret and Petit were actually married throws an interesting spin on this resolution). And the train becomes a legitimate site of love in the concluding MCU of yet another exterior window frame, with the couple now leaving together and kissing in a shared compartment.

As *L'Express matrimonial* suggests, Perret's character in the *Léonce* series is a very solid, assured bourgeois type, completely modern in his habits, and more agile and quick-witted than his slightly heavyset body and large open face might suggest. The comedy depends almost exclusively on situations in which he is involved with a young woman, sometimes clearly a French variation of the "new woman." And the distinctive versatility of Perret's "style" is no less evident here than in his other films. *Le Homard* (1912) introduces a crucial change that would remain characteristic of the series: Perret is a married man (using his own first name), whose comic battle for dominance with his wife (now played by Grandais) is unimpeded by children. For this film, the couple—introduced in oval-masked CUs, chatting with one another—are honeymooning on the Brittany coast.[202] Venturing out among the fishermen on a pier one day, Suzanne tells Léonce that she wants a lobster for dinner, but he refuses (they are too expensive). The ensuing argument carries over into the next scene back at their inn that evening, where Léonce finally gives in and promises to catch one for her. When he reaches the pier again, however, a POV shot shows the surf pounding the rocks below, and he soon is negotiating with an old fisherman to buy one. The following sequence frames Suzanne's growing concern for him (alternating shots of a storm lashing the coast and of her pacing anxiously at a bedroom window) with a LS of Léonce joining the crowd at a local fête foraine, which just happens to be showing Gaumont films. And it is capped by a concise triptych of Suzanne kneeling in prayer, the roiling surf, and Léonce laughing among the fair's cinema audience. When he later returns dripping wet in a slicker, with two lobsters, she gratefully tucks him into bed but soon discovers the truth as the old man comes to collect his rented slicker and hands her the full bill. The next morning, while he is happily shaving, she simply shows him the bill, lathers his whole face, and throws a pitcher of water at him. An extended POV-shot sequence works out the obligatory reconciliation scene as Suzanne runs out into the now calmed surf, and Léonce, obviously dismayed, watches her through binoculars. Suddenly, she cries out in pain, and he splashes out fully dressed to her side—and finds, in a cut-in CU, a lobster attached to the backside of her bathing suit. Reunited at last, Léonce carries Suzanne on his shoulders back to the beach, while she waves the lobster high over their heads. In the final MS, as they dine on the offending lobster, and he turns to wink at the camera, she warns him not to make too much of his "triumph."

Les Epingles (1913) carries this battle of wits back to the couple's comfortable apartment in Paris, staged in just three studio decors.[203] The premise for this film has Léonce and Suzanne already at odds, which explains the opening AS/LS as he sneaks into the drawing room to give her a small present. Their temporary reconciliation is signaled by a kiss, and, when he asks for another, she has him hold up a desk mat to screen this one from the camera. Although a prelude of what is to come, this coy playacting is quickly deflated when Suzanne discovers, in a cut-in CU of the tiny box in his hand, that the gift is a large hatpin, which he whimsically tries to attach to her knitting needle. Such a "petty annoyance" (the title's secondary meaning) causes their argument to flare up once more and carry over into the next sequence: that evening, when she gets ready to go out, he tries to put the pin into her hat, and she angrily pokes him in the eye. Léonce goes into his own bit of playacting here, pretending to be injured, which requires Suzanne to swathe his head in a bandage, mobilizes several maids, and brings in a doctor, who takes him into the bedroom for an examination. Surprised to find the bedroom door locked, Suzanne peers at the keyhole, and a POV shot reveals the two men sharing a laugh at Léonce's trick (at her expense). In retaliation, Suzanne stages a fake accident to her leg in the dining room and, once she has the doctor alone, stands unaided to accuse the astonished man and force him to go along with her ruse. Léonce now caters to her needs— massaging her foot, carrying her into the drawing room—until she calmly rises, yells at him, and tears the bandage from his head. After an initial standoff (the tone is quite different here from *Comment les on garde*), she forces him to kneel and beg forgiveness—and finally he has to kiss her "injured" foot before she will agree to kiss his "injured" eye. In this clever rewriting of Kate's famous speech to Petruchio at the end of *The Taming of the Shrew*, marital harmony is restored, even if momentarily, on *her* terms.

In *Léonce flirte* and *Léonce pot au feu* (both 1913), Suzanne has to cope with Léonce's attraction to a second woman, in two different variations on the illicit rendezvous scene. The first film has the couple residing in a large white stone house on the Mediterannean coast, from whose balcony Suzanne (in binocular POV shots) spots Léonce making advances to a woman as they approach in a motorboat. She angrily takes off in their car, only to have it break down within a few miles, and a local innkeeper stops to offer her a ride to the place he and his wife run. When Léonce discovers she is gone, he follows on a bicycle and arrives at the inn in time for them to argue over a simple dinner in the central room, then before the fireplace, and finally in an upstairs bedroom. There, in a long-take AS/LS, after she rejects his moves to appease her, he divides the room in half—much as Clark Gable will do later in Capra's *It Happened One Night* (1934)—by setting up a screen between the bed (for her) and the upholstered chair (for him). Suzanne eventually relents and folds back one screen panel, to ask Léonce to help undo her hair, but then discreetly unfolds it again to block the camera from their reconciliation in bed. The second film locates the couple in their Paris apartment and involves a more explicit form of substitution that recapitulates the earlier *Comment les on garde*. Here, Léonce's interest in another woman is figured by means of a bedroom wall mirror—where he first notices his growing paunch and slightly flabby cheeks and then, as if to confirm his own appeal, conjures up the superimposition of an available "other woman." After he arranges a private dinner with this woman (who turns out to be his wife's friend), Suzanne disguises herself in a hood and veil to take her friend's place in the darkened rendezvous room.[204] When Léonce tries to kiss this veiled figure, the lights come up, and the sudden revelation transforms his "dream scene" extension of the earlier mirror image into a snapshot exposure. After his gestures of pleading escalate to suicide threats, Suzanne agrees to reconcile, and, like good bourgeois, the couple sits down to eat. A clever series of framings then closes off the film in a tongue-in-cheek fashion. Another screen is placed upside down in front of the camera (above which champagne glasses briefly rise in a toast); finally, against a black curtain, a cupid figure is shown sewing a heart; and the heart shape serves as an iris mask framing the couple's final kiss.

In *Léonce et Toto* (1913), it is Renée, now played by Petit,[205] whose affection turns elsewhere, much like Linder's wife's in the slightly later *Max n'aime pas les chats*. This film's couple is a conventionally happy one, summarized in the opening image of them together playing a piano, occasionally interrupted by kisses. What disrupts their harmony is a birthday present for Renée (apparently from her own family) which, in a cut-in MCU, turns out to be a tiny black dog. This creature, which seems to function like a substitute child, pleases Léonce far less than his wife, and his displeasure turns to anger when she sits the dog on a pillow on the dining room table. After dinner, when Renée leaves the room for a moment, Léonce blows cigarette smoke at the animal; the maid finally becomes so outraged at Renée's insistence that the dog always dine with them that she quits. The couple continues to argue when Renée and her new "friend" go out for a walk, an argument smoothly conveyed through eyeline matches between Léonce at a second-floor window and his wife outside on the sidewalk.[206] Later, when she is invited to visit her family, Léonce snatches the satchel holding the dog out of her car just before it drives off, but, once the dog is back in the apartment, he breaks down and begins playing with it. After a quick shot of him peeking out a window (which implies that his wife is returning), Léonce sets up a dramatic scene for her (and the spectator) by pinning a note to a background drawing room door and then waiting, in MS, on the other side. A POV shot through the keyhole informs him when Renée enters the drawing room, at which point he takes out a revolver, fires it, and runs off—suddenly the door is thrown open, and she stares wildly about. As she searches the bedroom, a cut-in AS shows her cautiously drawing the curtains back from the bed, frightened at finding the revolver under a pillow, relieved at discovering the dog under the blanket, but then anxious again at her husband's absence. At that moment, of course, he leaps out of the background shadows, successful at last in getting her attention and, more important, restoring his own potency. The concluding tableau, which reworks the opening, celebrates his triumph: between the two— one at the piano, the other in a chair sewing—sits a huge black dog (its size a register of gendered power), whose paw he shakes as a sign of their friendship, and shared dominance.

In *Léonce à la campagne* (1913), the struggle between Léonce and Poupette (Petit) plays out in a series of contradictory riffs, which sets them off against several other couples. This Edenic comedy begins with Léonce walking through a country estate garden, growing increasingly affronted by the servants who (at least once in a POV shot) show more interest in kissing than in picking cherries or tending roses. Such excessive prudery, so comically out of character, turns

125. *Léonce à la campagne*, 1913 (Léonce Perret)

126. *Léonce à la campagne*, 1913 (Valentine Petit)

127. *Léonce à la campagne*, 1913 (Léonce Perret, Valentine Petit)

128. *Léonce à la campagne*, 1913 (Léonce Perret)

out to be frustrated desire, of course, when Léonce sits down to write a letter in a spacious conservatory and sadly contemplates himself in a wall-sized mirror. Breaking off a visit to her sick mother in response to her lovesick husband, Poupette arrives at the estate (the property of his uncle and aunt) with enough spunk for both of them. After climbing down from a straw-filled cart and giving the horse a smack, she vaults over a balcony railing to gaze out over the garden and surprises Léonce watering some flowers by jumping on him from behind and then leaping into his arms, provocatively wrapping her legs around him. Later in the day, she assumes a much more demure pose when they water a huge flowering shrub together—her watering can is positively miniscule compared to his. That evening, however, after a boring dinner with his relatives' four invited guests, it is Poupette who leads Léonce surreptitiously out through the silhou-etted terrace glass doors and into the garden for a little lovemaking under the trees. Suddenly, a second couple "escapes" across the terrace, and, in a sequence of 180-degree reverse-angle cuts, including MSs of Léonce and Poupette hiding in some leafy branches, the latter startle this couple with offscreen sounds and chase them out of the garden. A third, older couple then follows the same route into the garden, surprising Léonce and Poupette, who give them exactly the same treatment and then add a parodic riff on their frightened behavior. This playful comedy of indulged and frustrated desire does have its ironically moral consequences, however, for both couples, according to the last intertitle, leave the estate engaged to be married. All of which leaves Léonce and Poupette happily embracing on the silhouetted balcony and then coming forward and off, but not before he smiles knowingly at the camera, in a reverse-angle MS, and discreetly closes the shutters. Continually threatening to run loose in the garden, desire is neatly contained by the film's end, within the conventional confines of a good bourgeois marriage.

Of the film titles surviving from the *Léonce* series, perhaps the most intriguing is *Léonce cinématographiste* (1913). For one thing, much like *Les Debuts de Max Linder au cinématographe* and *Mari jaloux*, the film is incredibly self-referential. Léonce, for instance, plays a noted filmmaker at Gaumont; one sequence includes a production scene at the studio, with Bout-de-zan watching the filmmaking process and Onésime handing Léonce a note. In the apartment he shares with Poupette (Petit), a poster for *Léonce flirte* hangs in the front hallway; at the cinema they later attend separately, there is another one for *Eugène amoureux*. Although the storyline returns to the earlier subject of Léonce's attraction to a second woman, the climactic rendezvous scene is quite clever in how it withholds information and stages its revelations. Poupette's suspicions are aroused one evening when she finds several unfamiliar hairs on her husband's coat and jacket (the poster only adds to her worry) and discovers an unopened note from an admirer in his wallet which suggests a rendezvous. Her tactic is to substitute another note, one that arranges a meeting at the Gaumont-Palace (with specific seat numbers one row apart), and then to go to the cinema herself to expose Léonce, much as Suzanne did in *Léonce pot au feu*.

For this scene, two 180-degree reverse-angle FS/LSs establish the cinema interior, with the camera in front of and then behind an audience largely comprised of families (with children) and couples laughing at a slapstick comedy.[207] In the first, Poupette is ushered to a next-to-the-last row seat in the left background; in the second, the same usherette stops a couple from necking in the back row opposite—and as the man turns around, he can be recognized as Léonce. Cut-in close shots now focus on a man's hand reaching forward to clasp a woman's and his foot caressing hers. Then in FS/LS, a man leans down to Poupette in the audience, and a cut-in AS reveals her shock at realizing that he is not Léonce. Springing up to slap the man, she now becomes the spectacle toward which the audience turns—and a cop is called in to hustle her out. When she finally returns home, much chagrined, Léonce is comfortably seated in a drawing room chair, reading his paper and smoking his pipe, and she has to make a spectacle of herself again—kneeling to beg forgiveness for her "scandal-

129. *Léonce cinématographiste*, 1913 (production photo: Georges Specht, Léonce Perret, Bout-de-zan)

ous" behavior at the cinema. Exploiting the fiction of her infidelity to mask his own, Léonce deceptively reasserts his power and prerogative over Poupette. That he can enjoy the benefits of this double standard at the cinema is doubly provocative, for it challenges all those Gaumont films made six months to a year earlier which were so intent on demonstrating the cinema's moral worth. In a deftly constructed mise-en-abyme, Perret literally invites the audience to join in mocking its own self-righteousness as well as his own—from the secure framework (at least here) of a benevolent patriarchal authority.

Appropriate as it might be to conclude this section with the *Onésime, Max,* and *Léonce* series, which mark the high point of the one-reel French comedy, there was, just before the war, another move underway within the industry that deserves notice. Essentially, this was an attempt to transfer popular vaudeville sketches and short plays to the screen, in films of more than one reel in length. That it followed by several years the largely successful effort to adapt everything from classic dramas to recent boulevard melodramas testifies both to the privileged status of "serious" or "sensational" subjects for early feature-length films and the continued profitability of one-reel and split-reel comedies on cinema programs everywhere. Gaumont seems to have initiated this strategy with a half-dozen films directed by Feuillade and marketed in a series entitled *La Vie drole*—figuratively, and perhaps literally, replacing *La Vie telle qu'elle est*.[208] These films were relatively easy to produce because their two- and three-reel format seems to have imitated the two- and three-act structure of their vaudeville sources.[209] They also introduced a new set of boulevard actors to the cinema—for instance, Madeleine Guitty in *Les Millions de la bonne* (1913), Marcel Levesque in *L'Hôtel de la gare* (1914), and Charles Lamy in *L'Illustre Machefer* (1914). Although their provincial stories of mismatched couples and bureaucratic snafus may have had a wide appeal in France (*L'Hôtel de la gare* was quite successful),[210] the culturally determined humor of those stories, however, tended to make the films somewhat less suitable for export—which may have been another reason for the delay in their production.

Gaumont was not the only company producing these comedies, of course, as is evident from Aubert's *Champignol malgré lui* (1914), which draws on the military barracks comedy so common to French vaudeville.[211] An adaptation of Georges Feydeau and Georges Desvaillières's immensely popular play (first staged in 1893), this film's story is so complicated that at least half its length is used up in establishing the premises. A painter by profession, Champignol is ordered to report for a short period of army training at the same time that he receives word from a wealthy client that one of his paintings is in need of immediate repair. The restoration work leads to a seaside escapade with the client, a Mistress Connecticut; taking advantage of his absence, a local aristocrat named Saint-Florimond, moves into Champignol's house and assumes his identity, with the eager consent of Mme Champignol and the unknowing support of a substitute servant. Meanwhile, Captain Camaret, the military garrison commander, whose niece is about to be engaged to Saint-Florimond, decides to have Champignol do his portrait—and orders the painter found and brought in to perform his service. Hardly a willing recruit, but unable to resume his real identity, Saint-Florimond is seized and put into uniform, which sets up a series of comic confrontations and misrecognitions when the real Champignol himself arrives (and promptly has his head shaved). Everything finally is resolved at a soiree for the niece, with husband and wife coming to an agreement by which Saint-Florimond is trapped in the role of Champignol—and has to forfeit both the niece and Mme Champignol—while the painter gets to assume a new identity, leave the garrison, and go off with his ex-wife. Much like the earlier comic series, of course, *Champignol malgré lui* relies on the skill of its performers (which is competent, at best), especially in long-take tableaux such as the climactic soiree scene. At least two things are strikingly different, however. The film abso-

130. *Champignol malgré lui*, 1914 (production photo)

lutely needs all of its many intertitles to explain what is going on, so that the visual tableaux often come close to illustrating a primarily verbal text. Furthermore, it depends on a limited range of representational strategies, generally eschewing cut-in close shots, sequences of alternating shots, and certainly any eyeline matches or POV shots. As a result, Aubert's vaudeville comedy does not look all that different from the more regressive of Pathé, Film d'Art, and Eclipse's "serious" historical dramas and literary adaptations.

Eclair's *Gaités de l'escadron* (1913), however, is another matter entirely. This film is adapted from a Courteline play and directed by Tourneur, making it his earliest extant film. Although little more than a military barracks revue, the film features an ensemble of characters offering a wide range of comic performances. There is a M. Adalbert de la Valmombrée, an effete city bourgeois recruit who, after being dragged by a horse, straightens the crease in his trousers and the carnation in his lapel—and later waters the stones of the latrine like a flowerbed. There is Poitrin, looking like a French version of Fatty Arbuckle and possessing a similar agility, who prefers performing in a nearby café to soldiering. And there is the Mutt and Jeff team of Laplote and Fricot, whose craving for head cheese and antics with a wheelbarrow keep getting them tossed in the brig. Tourneur's own ability to construct some of the film's comedy through choices in framing and editing—and with a minimum of intertitles—is no more apparent than in the opening scene, in which Flick (Henri Gouget) lets the latter two comics circumvent the strict orders of Captain Hurleuret (Duquesne) against smoking in the barracks yard. This is done through a deft distribution of cut-in CUs and MSs, along with an establishing LS, as Flick covers one dropped cigarette with his boot and slips another into one comic's hands behind his back—without Hurleuret noticing a thing. Similar strategies of representation, along with a sequence of alternation, mark the film's final scenes, where a general (Roussel) arrives unannounced to support Flick's attitude toward the recruits—his only ambition is to be loved by his men—rather than Hurleuret's. That such an attitude best motivates a soldier is then articulated in a superimposed "dream vision" battle scene above the heads of the "prisoners" the general is inspecting.[212] And this "dream vision" curiously echoes an earlier scene in the café, when the old woman who owns it calls up for another officer a superimposed memory image of their love affair many years before. Rapping his cane on a table, the officer simply dismisses the memory, pays for the stolen head cheese, and walks off; but the scene unexpectedly lingers, in LS, on the woman holding the coins in her hand, dropping them on the table, leaning forward on one arm, and wiping a tear from her hardened face. This moment does as much as anything else in the film to call in question all the so-called masculine virtues of military discipline that so many other French films had long been espousing.

Cinema historians generally have acknowledged and even celebrated the achievement of the French prewar comic series, but they have tended to focus, and with good reason, either on individual performers or on the series' use value to the slightly later American comic films.[213] This chapter claims, however, that the significance of these films extends far beyond that. First of all, as a textual practice, they offered a model of economy and efficiency in constructing patterns of accumulating comic effects. Some titles were particularly effective for their well-honed structures of repetition and variation—for instance, *Onésime horloger*, *Victime du quinquina*, or *Léonce et Toto*. Others were accomplished in dissecting scenes into parts, so as to play with unexpected parallels, juxtapositions, and causal relations between the characters' actions within two or more adjacent spaces—for instance, *Rigadin, défenseur de la vertu*, *Max pédicure*, or *Léonce à la campagne*. And nearly all were consistently inventive, from the wildly absurd gags of *Boireau, roi du boxe*, *Calino, chef de gare*, or *Onésime gentleman détective* to the embarrassing or surprising social situations of *L'Express matrimonial* or *Mari jaloux*. Second, as ideological constructions, the comic series constituted an unusually frank appraisal of the French social order. Although a good number of films ultimately reaffirmed the status quo, just as many interrogated the accepted social relations of difference, locating that interrogation at a variety of sites clearly marked by class—from the female domestic (Cunegonde) to the white-collar worker or civil servant (Boireau, Calino, Rigadin) to the rentier dandy and the bourgeois married man (Gontran, Max, Léonce). These provided the basis for singling out a wide range of social types and behavior for ridicule, but more often than not they served to send up the bourgeoisie—but without calling the French class system into serious question. Instead, what the *Max* and

Léonce series principally interrogated were gender relations, as is evident in the contradictory positions articulated in such films as *Max n'aime pas les chats* and *Max et la doctoresse* or *Les Epingles* and *Léonce cinématographiste*. Much like other French genres, then, the comic series engaged with the modern figure of the "new woman," whether she seemed to exhibit so-called American attributes or to represent a threatened shift in gender relations within France itself.

Afterword

IN THIS BOOK, I have sought to rewrite the history of French cinema between 1896 and 1914, particularly during those years when Pathé-Frères, the first major corporation in the new industry, led the world in film production and distribution. That rewriting shatters long-standing preconceptions about the so-called primitive cinema, reinstates French films at the center of early cinema history (even in the United States), and recovers their contribution to the cinema's development as a major mass culture industry. The French cinema, I argue, is especially crucial to what may be called a paradigm shift from a cinema of attractions, which dominated the period of 1896–1904, to a narrative cinema, not only during the transitional period of 1904–1907, but during the standardization of the single-reel story film, between 1907 and 1911, and then during the prewar emergence of the feature-length film. One of my chief aims, of course, has been to reconstruct the systems of representation and narration which governed the production of early French films and their reception. But I have also tried to show how the representational strategies of particular film genres were mapped according to a referential body of French social relations or hierarchies of difference—class, gender, generation, race, and region. In the end, I conclude, the historical specificity of early French cinema created a partially overlapping, yet distinctly alternative model of film representation and narration to that which ultimately would become dominant in the American cinema.

Since specific components of these historical arguments already are concisely articulated at the ends of section chapters, rather than rehearse them further, let me offer, as I did in an earlier book, a kind of blueprint for future work on early French cinema. There are several areas of activity and sets of questions, all concerning the first twenty years of French cinema, which demand consideration as the subject of further research and analysis.

Some of that work will be determined by particular conferences, expositions, and programs of screenings that are, at this writing, being organized for the approaching centenary celebrations of the cinema and which extend the archaeological work begun at least fifteen years ago. These include the week-long Domitor conferences scheduled in New York (1994) and Paris (1996), the special expositions devoted to Pathé-Frères in Paris (1994) and to Lumière in Lyon (1995), and the week-long, full-day screenings, each October, at the Pordenone Silent Film Festival. All these gatherings will depend, of course, on the restoration work that currently is underway at FIAF archives around the world. But they also raise a question that is especially pertinent to the study of early French cinema: the availability of film prints for teaching as well as research purposes. It is difficult enough to have the time and financial resources requisite for archive research (once one has discovered where specific film titles are preserved and accessible for viewing), but in the United States it is virtually impossible to find more than a handful of early French films available for pedagogical use (the Museum of Modern Art and Em Gee Film Library are almost the only distributors).[1] This dearth of primary texts has had the effect of promulgating some very misleading notions about early cinema history, both inside and outside the classroom. One way to begin to fill this void and counter such notions would be to make a representative selection of films available for sale or rental, as Leyda and Musser did for the six programs of the "Before Hollywood" exhibition sponsored by the American Federation of the Arts. One possible source for such a selection would be the special film programs surveying the Gaumont Company's history, programs that are to tour the United States in 1994.

One area that certainly demands further research is the industrial organization and technological base of early French cinema. That research has been hampered severely up to now by the unavailability of company documents. Very little seems to have survived from such companies as Eclair, Eclipse, Film d'Art, Lux, Aubert, and AGC, and Gaumont and Pathé have begun only recently to open their records for cataloging and research. A great number of questions might be answered, or at least addressed more thoroughly, by such research. What kinds of production units, schedules, and practices were standard in France? How were they different from company to company, how did they change over time, and how did they compare to the American system of production, as outlined for instance, by Staiger and Musser? How extensive were the economic alliances between the cinema and other segments of the culture industry in France, and what was their relation to the network established by specific personnel as they circulated between the cinema and the theater, the music hall, the circus, and other cultural institutions? What changes occurred in the design and function of film studios (especially in set decoration, lighting techniques, and shooting methods) and in editing practices? More specifically, how did Pathé develop and deploy its various color film processes, and how extensively were they used? How significant to the industry's overall position within the international market were the array of apparatuses produced and sold by various companies, from commercial cameras and projectors to equipment for the home? Finally, as revealed by internal documents, how did the French companies respond to emerging developments in the American cinema industry—from Edison's patent suits and Eastman's near monopoly on film stock production to the institution of the MPPC and the rise of the "independents"—and what were their strategies of coping with those?

Similar questions can be asked of the distribution and exhibition segments of the industry. What was the full range of distribution patterns in France? How were they different from company to company, from region to region, even from country to country, and how did they change over time, especially as film sales gave way to film rentals and fête foraine cinemas were superseded by permanent urban cinemas? What was the full range of exhibition practices? How were they different from venue to venue, how did they change over time, and how were they affected by the emergence of different publicity practices? What kinds of cinemas employed bonisseurs or commentators, and for how long were they an important component of exhibition? How standardized was the practice of musical accompaniment and sound effects, what local variations were permitted or encouraged, and how extensive was the composition of original music scores?

A specific area of research now wide open for investigation is the French practice of writing scenarios and scripts. Nearly all of the Pathé and Gaumont scenarios deposited at the Bibliothèque nationale (between 1908 and 1914), for instance, now have been cataloged by Toulet and her staff at the Bibliothèque de l'Arsenal. Supplementing them are several boxes of Lux scenarios. The Pathé scenarios are especially interesting because they consist of two kinds: one can be described as a summary of the story and includes a strip or two from a positive film print, and the other is closer to a script or découpage, commonly divided into scenes or even tableaux and interspersed with intertitles. As for the Gaumont scenarios, they, too, generally follow this second format.[2] These scenarios are valuable for several reasons. First of all, they provide an extensive resource, for not only are there no extant archive prints for at least half of the film titles, but there are no publicity descriptions for a good number of those that are lost. Second, they add another kind of text—along with surviving film prints, publicity descriptions, posters, and "reviews"—to the discursive framework around individual films and sets of films. Third, they constitute a base from which to compare French scenario practices with those of the American cinema, as worked out, for instance, by Staiger and Thompson.

The single most neglected area of research in early French cinema, as I wrote in the Preface, has to do with cinema audiences or spectators and the historical reception of films. Who actually went to the cinema, and for what reasons, and what use-value did the overall cinema experience as well as individual films have for them? Although French historians such as Deslandes, Toulet, and others have done very valuable research on the sites and practices of film exhibition, there is nothing like the extensive work done by American historians— from Robert C. Allen, Musser, and Staiger to Hansen, Lynne Kirby, and Mary Carbine—on early American cinema audiences and spectatorship. And there is some evidence that French scholars such as Michèle Lagny are becoming keenly aware of this lacuna.[3] Addressing this lack calls for a series of interrelated research projects, some of which already may be underway in France. Certainly there is a need for further empirical research into local government documents, film company records, newspaper and magazine articles, and even individual memoirs. But such research has to be put in the service of unpacking and explaining the historical conditions for the interrelations between actual spectators and films. In other words, the sense that a French spectator made of the cinema, as a particular social subject, and the pleasure she or he experienced needs to be seen as shaped by and also shaping the social construction of identity or subjectivity at the time of the Third Republic. What did "going to the cinema" mean for the French, say, in 1899, as compared to 1903–1904, or 1907–1908, or

1912–1913? How did that differ from one social site to another, from one social group to another? What would a history of early French cinema look like if written predominately from the perspective of film reception?

Once some of this work has been accomplished and these questions have been addressed more thoroughly, we can be more assured in taking up several lines of research which extend beyond early French cinema itself or the period before the Great War. We should be able to situate the production, distribution, and exhibition practices of early French cinema more precisely vis-à-vis other national cinemas, and especially the American cinema. We can be more certain in investigating the continuities and discontinuities between the prewar cinema and that of the war period as well as that of the twenties—to what extent did the latter actually represent a break with the earlier cinema? Moreover, we may be able to explore the trajectories of exiled French film personnel such as Tourneur, Perret, Capellani, and others within the American cinema industry during the war, and so trace their reciprocal impact on one another. Finally, and more broadly, we will be able to better understand how it was that French cultural identity was constructed—as a more or less distinct form of the dominant, yet conflicted, Eurocentric identity—and, perhaps even more important, how a "new" American cultural identity was set off as different from the French[4] through what film spectators shared and did not share, as the ciné went to town in one country after another, in the decade before 1914.

Filmography

This filmography includes all titles viewed and discussed in this history. They are listed year by year, company by company (alphabetically) within each year, and chronologically for each company within any one year. Each title is given in French or English, and often both, along with the print's archive location (see acronyms below), specific film stock gauge, and length (in meters or feet).

Release dates for France and/or England or the United States are drawn from the trade press, newspapers, and catalogs (the acronyms below also are used in the Notes). When available, a film title's original catalog number and length is provided in brackets.

Archives and Collections

AF	Archives du Film, Bois d'Arcy	GP	Garth Pedlar, London
AGM	Les Amis de George Méliès, Paris	LOC	Library of Congress, Washington
CF	Cinémathèque Française, Paris		
CG	Cinémathèque Gaumont, Paris	MOMA	Museum of Modern Art, New York
CM	Cinema Museum, London		
CQ	Cinémathèque Québécois, Montréal	NFA	National Film Archive, London
CSL	Cinémathèque Suisse, Lausanne	NFC	National Film Center, Tokyo
DKB	Deutsche Kinematek, Berlin	NFM	Netherlands Film Museum, Amsterdam
EG	Em Gee Library, Los Angeles		
GEH	George Eastman House, Rochester	RFAB	Royal Film Archive of Belgium, Brussels

Journals and Catalogs

APC	*Argus-Phono-Cinéma*	KLW	*Kinematograph and Lantern Weekly*
BH	*Bulletin Hebdomadaire Pathé-Frères*		
Bio	*Bioscope*	MPW	*Moving Picture World*
Cin	*Le Cinéma et l'Echo du cinéma*	Nic	*Nickelodeon*
CJ	*Cinéma-Journal*	NYC	*New York Clipper*
Com	*Comoedia*	PC	*Pathé Catalogue*
Fas	*Le Fascinateur*	PCG	*Phono-Ciné-Gazette*
Film	*Le Film*	PJ	*Pathé-Journal*
FR	*Film-Revue*	PWB	*Pathé Weekly Bulletin*
GP	*Gaumont Palace Programme*	Var	*Variety*
IF	*L'Industriel Forain*	VFI	*Views and Film Index,* then *Film Index*
Jour	*Le Journal*		

For some films I depend on other sources: for the early Méliès films, I use the Star-Film catalogs reprinted in Sadoul's *Lumière et Méliès* (as revised by Eisenschitz); for several of the earliest Pathé titles, I use Bousquet and Redi's *Pathé-Frères;* for several later

Pathé titles, I use Bousquet's *Catalogue Pathé*; for Eclair's *Journée de la grève*, I rely on Cherchi Usai's checklist of Eclair films; for two of Gaumont's *Bébé* titles, I accept the dates in Lacassin's *Louis Feuillade*; and for Gaumont's *Comment on les prends*, I accept the date in d'Hugues and Muller's *Gaumont, 90 ans de cinéma*.

1896
Méliès   *Le Manoir du diable*. AGM, 35mm. [#78–80, 75 meters]

1897
Lumière   *Mort de Marat*. NFA, 16mm, 19 feet. [#746]
Méliès   *Combat naval en Grèce*. AGM, 35mm. [#110]
           L'Auberge ensorcelée. AGM, 35mm. [#122–123]

1898
Méliès   *Visite sous-marine du "Maine."* AGM, 35mm. [#147]
           Guillaume Tell. LOC, 35mm, 59 feet. [#159]
           La Lune à un mètre or *Astronomer's Dream*. AGM, 35mm. EG, 16mm.
             [#160–162]
           Tentation de Saint-Antoine. AGM, 35mm. [#169]

1899
Méliès   *Le Diable au couvent*. LOC, 35mm, 196 feet. [#185–187]
           L'Affaire Dreyfus. NFA, 35mm, 738 feet. [#206–217, 240 meters]
           Cendrillon or *Cinderella*. NFA, 35mm, 375 feet. [#219–224, 120 meters]
           Le Chevalier mystère. GEH, 35mm, 93 feet. [#226–227]

1900
Méliès   *L'Homme-orchestre*. NFA, 35mm, 92 feet. [#262–263]
           Rêve de Noël. NFA, 35mm, 264 feet. [#298–305, 160 meters]
Pathé   *The Artist*. NFA, 35mm, 49 feet. PC (Paris, 1900).
           Une Dispute or *Some Argument*. NFA, 35mm, 50 feet. PC (Paris, 1900).
             [20 meters]
           The Dancers. NFA, 35mm, 88 feet. PC (Paris, 1900).

1901
Méliès   *Barbe-bleue* or *Bluebeard*. NFA, 35mm, 650 feet. [#361–370, 210 meters]
Pathé   *Ce que l'on voit de mon sixième* or *Scenes from My Balcony*. NFA, 35mm,
             75 feet. PC (London, May 1903), 21. [#267, 130 feet]
           Histoire d'un crime or *The Story of a Crime*. AF, 35mm, 106 meters. CF,
             35mm. PC (London, May 1903), 80. [#358, 350 feet]
           Rêve et réalité or *Dream and Reality*. NFA, 35mm, 42 feet. PC (London,
             1903), 21. [#365, 50 feet]
           An Intelligent Waiter. NFA, 35mm, 50 feet. PC (London, May 1903), 38.
             [#369, 80 feet]
           Un Drame au fond de la mer or *A Drama at the Bottom of the Sea*. NFA, 35mm,
             53 feet. PC (Paris, October–December 1901). PC (London, May 1903),
             81. [#372, 65 feet]

Par le trou de la serrure or *Peeping Tom*. NFA, 35mm. PC (London, May 1903), 32. [#380, 115 feet]

Chez le dentiste. LOC, 35mm, 50 feet. PC (Paris, October–December 1901). [20 meters]

1902

Méliès   *L'Homme à la tête de caoutchouc.* NFA, 35mm, 150 feet. [#382]

Le Voyage dans la lune or *A Trip to the Moon*. MOMA, EG, and LOC, 16mm. NYC (4 October 1902), 712. [#399–411, 260 meters]

Le Sacre d'Edouard VII or *The Coronation of Edward VII*. NFA, 35mm, 318 feet. NYC (23 August 1902), 570, 572.

Les Trésors de Satan. NFA, 35mm, 160 feet. [#413–414]

L'Homme-mouche. NFA, 35mm, 133 feet. [#415–416]

Equilibre impossible or *Marvelous Suspension and Evolution*. LOC, 35mm, 129 feet. [#419]

Une Indigestion, ou chirurgie fin-de-siècle. GEH, 35mm, 254 feet. [#422–425, 80 meters]

Pathé   *Victimes de l'alcoolisme.* NFA, 35mm, 334 feet. PC (London, May 1902). PC (London, May 1903), 116. [#396, 450 feet]

Ali Baba et les quarante voleurs. NFA, 35mm, 557 feet. PC (London, August 1902). IF (30 August 1902). [#400, 615 feet]

Baignade impossible or *Impossible to Get a Plunge*. AF, 35mm, 47 meters. PC (London, May 1903), 39. [#601, 130 feet]

Pêche miraculeuse or *Extraordinary Fishing*. NFA, 35mm, 70 feet. PC (London, May 1903), 40. [#603, 80 feet]

The Wonderful Hair Restorer. NFA, 35mm, 62 feet. PC (London, May 1903), 41. [#611, 65 feet]

Le Chien et la pipe or *The Dog and the Pipe*. NFA, 35mm, 117 feet. PC (London, May 1903), 30–31. [#635, 130 feet]

Repas infernal or *A Diabolical Dinner*. NFA, 35mm, 33 feet. PC (London, May 1903), 47. [#681, 65 feet]

La Fée des roches noires or *The Fairy of the Black Rock*. AF, 35mm, 47 meters. PC (London, May 1903), 85–86. [#686, 150 feet]

Les Sept Chateaux du diable. NFA, 35mm, 795 feet. MOMA, 35mm, 841 feet. PC (London, May 1903), 86–87. [#688, 930 feet]

La Fée printemps or *The Fairy of Spring*. LOC, 35mm, 76 meters. GEH, 35mm. PC (London, May 1903), 88–89. [#699, 180 feet]

1903

Méliès   *Un Maleur n'arrive pas jamais seule* or *Misfortune Never Comes Alone*. LOC, 16mm, 70 feet. [#451–452]

Le Cake-Walk infernal. LOC, 16mm, 121 feet. NYC (13 June 1903), 388. [#453–457]

Le Mélomane or *The Melomaniac*. LOC, 16mm, 70 feet. NYC (15 August 1903), 596. [#479–480]

Le Monstre or *The Monster*. LOC, 16mm, 74 feet. NYC (15 August 1903), 596. [#481–482]

Le Royaume des fées or *The Kingdom of the Fairies*. NFA, 35mm, 1045 feet.
   EG, 16mm. NYC (12 September 1903), 692. [#483–498, 335 meters]
Le Chaudron infernal. AF, 35mm, 43 meters. EG, 16mm. NYC (17 October
   1903), 820. [#499–500]
Le Tonnerre de Jupiter or *Jupiter's Thunderbolts*. MOMA and EG, 16mm.
   [#503–505]
Le Parapluie fantastique or *Ten Ladies in One Umbrella*. LOC, 16mm, 75 feet.
   MOMA, 16mm. NYC (7 November 1903), 896. [#506–507]
Tom Tight et Dumm Dumm. LOC, 16mm, 65 feet. EG, 16mm. [#508–509]
Illusions funambulesques. GEH, 16mm, 54 feet. [#512–513]
La Lanterne magique or *The Magic Lantern*. LOC, 35mm. EG, 16mm. NYC
   (19 December 1903), 1040. [#520–524]
Damnation de Docteur Faust. LOC, 16mm, 170 feet. EG, 16mm. NYC
   (12 December 1903), 1016. [#527–533, 150 meters]
Le Rêve du maître de ballet or *The Ballet-Master's Dream*. LOC, 16mm, 68
   feet. MOMA and EG, 16mm. NYC (19 December 1903), 1040.
   [#525–526]

Pathé   *Le Cake-Walk chez les nains* or *Dwarfs' Cakewalk*. NFA, 35mm, 144 feet. PC
   (Paris, August 1904), 62. [#715, 45 meters]
Peinture animée or *The Animated Painting*. GEH, 35mm, 63 feet. PC
   (London, May 1903), 50. [#716, 82 feet]
Le Marchand de statues or *The Statue Dealer*. NFA, 35mm, 107 feet. PC
   (Paris, August 1904), 62. [#717, 35 meters]
Les Mésaventures d'un artiste or *Painter's Misfortune*. NFA, 35mm, 45 feet. PC
   (Paris, August 1904), 63. [#721, 15 meters]
Don Quichotte. CF, 35mm. PC (London, August 1903). IF (10 October
   1903). 36–37. [#722, 430 meters]
Une Bonne Histoire or *The Funny Story*. NFA, 35mm, 80 feet. PC (Paris,
   August 1904), 58. [#727, 25 meters]
Ma Tante or *Auntie*. NFA, 35mm, 76 feet. PC (London, November 1903), 6.
   [#738, 80 feet]
Le Chat botté or *Puss-in-Boots*. NFA, 35mm, 529 feet. PC (London,
   November 1903), 15. PC (Paris, August 1904), 129. [#739, 582 feet]
Ramoneur et patissier or *Chimney Sweep and Pastry Cook*. AF, 35mm,
   22 meters. PC (September–October 1903), 7. [#753, 20 meters]
Peintre et Modèle. NFA, 35mm, 37 feet. PC (Paris, August 1904), 99. [#812,
   20 meters]
Borgia s'amuse. NFA, 35mm, 16 feet. PC (Paris, August 1904), 99. [#816,
   30 meters]
La Soubrette ingénieuse or *Magic Picture Hanging*. NFA, 35mm, 144 feet. PC
   (London, May 1903), 52. [#893, 130 feet]
Samson et Delila. NFA, 35mm, 248 feet. PC (London, May 1903), 92.
   [#884, 450 feet]
La Vie et la Passion de Jésus-Christ. AF, 35mm, 1425 meters. NFA, 35mm.
   MOMA, 35mm, 873 feet. PC (London, May 1903), 93–95. PC (Paris,
   August 1904), 132–134. NYC (15 October 1904), 784. NYC (4 February
   1905), 1172. NYC (2 December 1905), 1060. [#851–866, 871–872,
   939–954: available in versions of 32, 20, and 12 tableaux]

Epopée napoléonienne or *Life of Napoleon*. LOC, 35mm, 988 feet. NYC
(7 November 1903), 896. PC (Paris, August 1904), 90–91. [#982, 160
meters; #983, 270 meters]

Valse excentrique or *Eccentric Waltz*. NFA, 35mm, 118 feet. PC (Paris, August
1904), 110. [#981, 40 meters]

1904

Méliès   *Le Bourreau turc* or *The Terrible Turkish Executioner*. LOC, 16mm, 62 feet.
EG, 16mm. NYC (9 January 1904), 1113. [#534–535]

Au clair de la lune or *Moonlight Serenade*. LOC, 16mm, 62 feet. NYC
(6 February 1904), 1208. [#538–539]

Le Roi du maquillage or *The Untamable Whiskers*. LOC, 16 mm, 60 feet. EG,
16mm. NYC (12 March 1904), 67. [#552–553]

Le Rêve de l'horloger or *The Clockmaker's Dream*. LOC, 16mm, 66 feet. EG,
16mm. NYC (12 March 1904), 67. [#554–555]

Faust et Marguerite. LOC and NFA, 16mm, 143 feet. NYC (2 April 1904),
140. [#562–574, 270 meters]

Le Merveuilleux Eventail vivant. LOC, 35mm, 295 feet. NYC (11 June 1904),
380. [#581–584]

La Sirène or *The Siren*. LOC, 16mm, 95 feet. EG, 16mm. NYC (2 July
1904), 430. [#593–595]

Le Voyage à travers l'impossible or *The Impossible Voyage*. NFA, 35mm,
1185 feet. EG, 16mm. NYC (28 October 1904), 848. [#641–659, 380
meters]

Pathé   *Metamorphoses du roi du pique* or *Metamorphosis of the King of Spades*. GEH,
35mm, 85 feet. PC (Paris, August 1904), 69 [#1024, 30 meters]

Un Coup d'oeil par étage or *Scenes at Every Floor*. LOC, 35mm, 375 feet. PC
(London, January 1904), 13–14. NYC (24 September 1904), 718. [#1030,
395 feet]

Paravent mystérieux or *Mysterious Screen*. NFA, 35mm, 126 feet. PC (Paris,
August 1904), 69–70. [#1042, 40 meters]

Le Mitron. NFA, 35mm, 58 feet. PC (Paris, August 1904), 45. [#1052,
20 meters]

La Purge or *The Bad Remedy*. NFA, 35mm, 64 feet. PC (Paris, August 1904),
45. [#1063, 25 meters]

Metamorphose du papillon or *A Butterfly's Metamorphosis*. LOC, 35mm. PC
(London, May–June 1904), 5. PC (Paris, August 1904), 71. NYC
(1 October 1904), 741. [#1065, 115 feet]

Danse des Apaches or *Apache Dance*. NFA, 35mm, 104 feet. PC (Paris,
August 1904), 112. [#1071, 40 meters]

Indiens et cow-boys. LOC, 35mm, 558 feet. PC (Paris, August 1904), 121.
NYC (3 September 1904), 644. [#1052, 180 meters]

Erreur de porte or *Wrong Door*. NFA, 35mm, 106 feet. PC (Paris, August
1904), 46. [#1076, 35 meters]

Les Dénicheurs d'oiseaux or *Nest Robbers*. NFA, 35mm, 160 feet. NYC
(27 August 1904), 613. PC (New York, 1906), 11. [#1077, 164 feet]

La Grève or *The Strike*. LOC, 35mm, 205 feet. PC (Paris, August 1904),
120–121. NYC (3 September 1904), 644. [#1096, 135 meters]

Le Bain des dames de la cour or Ladies in Court Bathing. NFA, 35mm, 74 feet.
PC (Paris, August 1904), 105. [#1104, 25 meters]

Un Drame dans les airs or Drama in the Air. AF, 35mm, 55 meters. PC
(London, August 1904), 3. NYC (1 October 1904), 741. [#1106, 200 feet]

Le Regne de Louis XIV. NFA, 35mm, 324 feet. NYC (24 December 1904),
1024. IF (31 December 1904), 4. PC (Paris, 1907), 156–157. [#1143,
260 meters]

1905

Méliès   Les Cartes vivantes or The Living Playing Cards. LOC, 35mm, 165 feet. NYC
(8 April 1905), 181. [#678–679]

La Palais des milles et une nuits or The Palace of the Arabian Nights. NFA,
35mm, 1300 feet. MOMA and EG, 16mm. NYC (24 June 1905), 464.
[#705–726, 460 meters]

La Chaise à porteurs enchantés or The Enchanted Sedan Chair. LOC, 16mm,
76 feet. [#728–730]

Le Raid Paris-Monte Carlo en deux heures. NFA, 35mm. EG, 16mm.
[#740–749, 200 meters]

L'Ile de Calypso: Ulysse et Polyphème. LOC, 16mm, 89 feet. [#750–752]

Rip van Winkle or Rip's Dream. GEH, 35mm, 910 feet. [#756–775,
310 meters]

Pathé   The Strong Arm of the Law. NFA, 35mm, 261 feet.

Ruche merveilleuse or Wonderful Beehive. NFA, 35mm, 235 feet. IF (4 March
1905), 4. PC (Paris, 1907), 109–110. [#1132, 75 meters]

L'Assassinat du Grand Duc Serge. GEH, 35mm, 101 feet. NYC (25 March
1905), 134. [114 feet]

Rêve de Dranem. NFA, 35mm, 53 feet. PC (Paris, 1907), 110. [#1173,
20 meters]

Le Melon enchanté or The Enchanted Melon. GEH, 35mm, 80 feet. PC (Paris,
1907), 26. [#1175, 25 meters]

L'Amoureux ensorcelé or The Bewitched Lover. GEH, 35mm, 136 feet. PC
(Paris, 1907), 111. [#1177, 45 meters]

L'Incendiaire or The Incendiary. NFA, 35mm, 550 feet. PC (Paris, April
1905), 16–17. IF (8 April 1905), 4. NYC (8 April 1905), 181. [#1189,
195 meters]

La Fée au fleurs. AF, 35mm, 42 meters. PC (Paris, April 1905), 11. IF (8
April 1905), 4. PC (Paris, 1907), 113. [#1195, 25 meters]

Dix Femmes pour un mari or Ten Women for One Husband. NFA, 35mm,
230 feet. EG, 16mm. PC (Paris, April 1905), 8. IF (8 April 1905), 4.
[#1200, 75 meters]

Créations renversantes or Stunning Creations. NFA, 35mm, 93 feet. PC (New
York, 1906), 16. PC (Paris, 1907), 115. [#1212, 30 meters]

Le Rêve à la lune or The Moon-Lover or Drunkard's Dream. AF, 35mm,
120 meters. PC (Paris, May 1905), 14. IF (20 May 1905), 4. NYC (13 May
1905), 316. [#1207, 140 meters]

Honneur d'un père or A Father's Honor. MOMA, 16mm. PC (Paris, May
1905), 16. IF (20 May 1905), 4. NYC (27 May 1905), 364. [#1214,
115 meters]

Au pays noir or *In the Mining District*. NFA, 35mm, 785 and 600 feet. PC
   (Paris, May 1905), 17. IF (10 June 1905), 4. NYC (10 June 1905), 400.
   [#1213, 250 meters]
Automobile et le cul-de-jatte. NFA, 35mm, 122 feet. PC (Paris, May 1905), 7.
   [#1216, 40 meters]
Les Martyrs chrétiens. NFA, 35mm, 423 feet. PC (Paris, May 1905), 18–21.
   NYC (24 June 1905), 457. PC (Paris, 1907), 174–177. [#1228, 135 meters]
Opération chirigucale or *Surgical Operation*. NFA, 35mm, 168 feet. PC (New
   York, 1906), 12. PC (Paris, 1907), 32–33. [#1238, 55 meters]
La Perruque or *The Wig*. NFA, 35mm, 111 feet. PC (New York, 1906), 13.
   PC (Paris, 1907), 33. [#1240, 35 meters]
Vot' permis? Viens l'chercher! LOC, 35mm, 240 feet. IF (8 July 1905), 4. PC
   (Paris, 1907), 33–34. [#1241, 105 meters]
Le Dejeuner du savant. AF, 35mm, 37 meters. PC (Paris, July 1905), 7. IF
   (8 July 1905), 4. [#1243, 40 meters]
Par le trou de la serrure. AF, 35mm, 32 meters. PC (Paris, July 1905), 8.
   [#1244, 40 meters]
Les Petits Vagabonds or *Young Tramps*. GEH, 35mm, 527 feet. NYC (22 July
   1905), 556. IF (5 August 1905), 4. PC (Paris, 1907), 177–178. [#1245,
   175 meters]
La Révolution en Russie or *Mutiny on a Man-of-War in Odessa* or *Revolution in
   Odessa*. MOMA, 35mm, 253 feet. MOMA, 16mm. PC (Paris, July 1905),
   16. NYC (5 August 1905), 600. NYC (25 November 1905), 1085. [#1249,
   80 meters]
Brigandage moderne or *Highway Robbery Modern Style*. NFA, 35mm, 490 feet.
   PC (Paris, July 1905), 17–18. NYC (19 August 1905), 664. [#1250, 160
   meters]
Joyeuses lavendières or *Gay Washerwomen*. LOC, 35mm, 94 feet. PC (Paris,
   July 1905), 9. PC (New York, April 1906), 9. [#1251, 30 meters]
Les Cartes lumineuses. DKB, 35mm, 55 meters. PC (Paris, 1907), 166–167.
   [#1161, 55 meters]
L'Album merveilleux or *The Wonderful Album*. NFA, 35mm, 221 feet. PC
   (Paris, July 1905), 14. IF (12 August 1905), 3. PC (Paris, 1907), 116–117.
   [#1264, 80 meters]
D'Ou vient-il? or *Whence Does He Come?* MOMA, 16mm. PC (Paris,
   August 1905), 13. [#1257, 35 meters]
Vendetta! LOC, 35mm. IF (12 August 1905), 3. NYC (26 August 1905), 668.
   [#1267, 155 meters]
La Chaussette or *The Sock*. NFA, 35mm, 127 feet. PC (New York, 1906), 12.
   PC (Paris, 1907), 38. [#1269, 40 meters]
La Vie de Moïse or *Life of Moses*. NFA, 35mm, 478 feet. PC (Paris, 1907),
   243. NYC (15 September 1905), 752. [#1276, 160 meters]
Le Remords or *Remorse*. NFA, 35mm, 176 feet. PCG (1 October 1905), 208.
   PC (New York, 1906), 23. PC (Paris, 1907), 181. [#1287, 65 meters]
Cache-toi dans la malle. NFA, 35mm, 263 feet. PCG (1 October 1905), 208.
   IF (7 October 1905), 3. PC (Paris, 1907), 42–43. [#1286, 100 meters]
Voyage irréalisable or *Impractical Journey*. NFA, 35mm, 230 feet. EG, 16mm.
   PC (Paris, 1907), 120. [#1299, 75 meters]

Les Farces de Toto gâte-sauce or *The Pastry Cook's Practical Jokes*. LOC, 35mm,
76 meters. IF (14 October 1905), 4. NYC (11 November 1905), 997. PC
(Paris, 1907), 46. [#1303, 80 meters]

L'Inquisition. NFA, 35mm, 631 feet. IF (11 November 1905), 4. [210 meters]

La Poule aux oeufs d'or or *The Hen with the Golden Eggs*. NFA, 35mm, 960
and 830 feet. PC (Paris, November 1905), 14–20. IF (9 December 1905),
5. NYC (9 December 1905), 1069. PCG (1 January 1906), 327–328.
[#1311, 280 meters]

Miracle de Noël or *Christmas Miracle*. MOMA, 35mm, 291 feet. NYC
(16 December 1905), 1116. PC (Paris, 1907), 243–244. [#1315, 85 meters]

Cascades de feu or *Fireworks*. LOC, 35mm, 40 meters. PC (November 1905),
23. [#1319, 40 meters]

1906

Gaumont   *La Vie du Christ* or *The Life of Christ*. AF, 35mm, 320 meters. NFA, 35mm,
1048 feet. IF (24 March 1906), 5. PCG (1 April 1906), 131. MPW (18 May
1907), 172. [680 meters]

Le Matelas alcoolique or *Drunken Mattress*. AF, 35mm, 213 meters. NYC
(29 December 1906), 1180. [727 feet]

Méliès   *Le Tripot clandestin* or *The Scheming Gamblers' Paradise*. LOC, 35mm,
188 feet. NYC (3 February 1906), 1283. [#784–785]

Le Maestro Do-Mi-Sol-Do or *The Luny Musician*. LOC, 16mm, 89 feet. EG,
16mm. PCG (1 May 1906), 179. [#807–809]

Les Affiches en goguettes or *The Hilarious Posters*. LOC, 35mm, 202 feet. PCG
(1 May 1906), 179. MPW (30 March 1907), 62. [#821–823]

L'Hôtel des voyageurs de commerce or *The Roadside Inn*. LOC, 16mm, 92 feet.
[#844–845]

Bulles de savon vivantes or *Soap Bubbles*. NFM, 35mm, 70 meters. NYC
(6 October 1906), 886. [#846–848]

Les Quatre Cent Farces du diable or *The Merry Frolics of Satan*. NFA, 35mm,
1040 feet. MOMA, 35mm, 1059 feet. PCG (1 September 1906), 332. IF
(3 November 1906), 5. MPW (30 March 1907), 62. [#849–870, 300
meters]

L'Alchimiste Parafaragamus. LOC, 16mm, 79 feet. IF (3 November 1906), 5.
PCG (15 November 1906), 439. [#874–876]

La Fée carabosse or *The Witch*. NFM, 35mm, 232 meters. PCG (15 November 1906), 439. NYC (15 December 1906), 1151. [#877–887, 250 meters]

Pathé   *Au bagne* or *Life of a Convict*. MOMA, 16mm. PC (Paris, December 1905),
11–12. NYC (13 January 1906), 1207. PC (Paris, 1907), 185. [#1329,
280 meters]

The Strong Arm of the Law or *Tramp*. NFA, 35mm, 261 feet. NYC
(13 January 1906), 1207. [360 feet]

Le Déserteur. AF, 16mm, 44 meters. NYC (27 January 1906), 1264. IF
(3 February 1906), 5. PCG (15 February 1906), 76. [#1335, 165 meters]

Le Nihiliste or *Socialism and Nihilism*. NFA, 35mm, 530 feet. NYC
(3 February 1906), 1268. PCG (1 April 1906), 131. PC (Paris, 1907), 159.
[#1336, 170 meters]

La Peine du talion or *Tit for Tat*. NFA, 35mm, 312 feet. MOMA, 16mm. IF
(17 February 1906), 4. PCG (1 March 1906), 96. PC (New York, 1906),
24. [100 meters]

Un Drame en express or *Tragedy in a Train*. NFA, 35mm, 307 feet. NYC
(10 February 1906), 1294. PCG (1 April 1906), 131. [#1344, 110 meters]

Les Effets de l'orage or *Victims of the Storm*. AF, 35mm, 70 meters. NYC
(24 February 1906), 35. PCG (1 April 1906), 131. PC (Paris, 1907),
120–121. [#1346, 75 meters]

J'ai perdu mon l'orgnon or *I've Lost My Eyeglasses*. LOC, 35mm, 92 meters. IF
(10 March 1906), 4. NYC (17 March 1906), 123. PCG (1 April 1906),
131. [#1359, 85 meters]

Le Théâtre du Petit Bob. PCG (1 April 1906), 131. [105 meters]

Histoire d'un pantaloon. NFA, 35mm, 343 feet. PC (Paris, March 1906), 8.
NYC (14 April 1906), 218. PC (Paris, 1907), 59–60. [#1371, 110 meters]

Les Invisibles or *The Invisible Men*. EG, 16mm. PC (Paris, March 1906), 13.
NYC (14 April 1906), 218. PCG (15 May 1906), 191. [#1372, 200 meters]

Ecole buissonnière or *Playing Truant*. NFA, 35mm, 580 feet. PC (Paris, March
1906), 9. [#1374, 185 meters]

Nuit de carnaval or *Carnival Night*. LOC, 35mm, 48 meters. PC (Paris,
March 1906), 17–18. NYC (14 April 1906), 218. [#1375, 85 meters]

La Loi du pardon or *Law of Pardon*. NFA, 35mm, 460 feet. PC (Paris, April–
May 1906), 29–30. NYC (5 May 1906), 318. PCG (15 August 1906),
313–314. [#1381, 145 meters]

Richesse d'un jour or *Ephemeral Wealth*. NFA, 35mm, 480 feet. PC (Paris,
April–May 1906), 14–15. PCG (15 May 1906), 191. NYC (2 June 1906),
421. [#1394, 145 meters]

La Course à la perruque or *The Wig Chase*. AF, 35mm, 83 meters. PC (Paris,
April–May 1906), 6–7. NYC (19 May 1906), 371. PCG (15 August
1906), 314. [#1384, 130 meters]

Mariage enfantine or *A Childish Match*. LOC, 16mm, 190 feet. PC (Paris,
April–May 1906), 15–16. NYC (19 May 1906), 371. [#1397, 160 meters]

Pitou amoureux or *The Amorous Soldier*. LOC, 35mm, 248 feet. PCG (15
May 1906), 191. PC (Paris, 1907), 73. [#1413, 75 meters]

Le Fils du diable à Paris. MOMA, 35mm. PCG (1 June 1906), 211. PC (Paris,
September 1906), 27–29. IF (3 November 1906), 4. [#1403, 350 meters]

Le Détective. NFA, 35mm, 460 feet. PC (Paris, April–May 1906), 32–33.
PCG (1 June 1906), 211. [#1406, 140 meters]

Automobile à vendre or *Motor Car for Sale*. LOC, 35mm, 300 feet. PC (Paris,
1907), 76–77. [#1418, 115 meters]

Chien de garde or *Wanting a Watch Dog*. NFM, 35mm, 86 meters. PCG (1
June 1906), 211. PC (Paris, 1907), 78–79. [#1424, 95 meters]

En Vacances or *The Holiday*. GEH, 35mm, 536 feet. PC (Paris, April–May
1906), 22–23. NYC (16 June 1906), 474. [#1435, 170 meters]

Le Concierge bat son tapis or *The Danger of Carpet Beating*. NFA, 35mm,
192 feet. PC (Paris, 1907), 80. [#1426, 65 meters]

Un Tour du monde d'un policier or *Detective's Tour of the World*. MOMA,
35mm, 1148 feet. MOMA, 16mm. PC (Paris, April–May 1906), 32–33.

NYC (16 June 1906), 474. PCG (15 August 1906), 314. [#1443, 350 meters]

Le Sorcier arabe or *An Arabian Magician*. LOC, 35mm. PC (Paris, 1907), 126. [#1446, 55 meters]

Fée aux pigeons. NFM, 35mm, 34.5 meters. PC (Paris, 1907), 128–129. [#1456, 45 meters]

Les Chiens contrebandiers. NFA, 35mm, 440 feet. AF, 35mm, 111 meters. PCG (1 May 1906). PC (Paris, 1907), 203–205. [#1459, 185 meters]

L'Obsession d'or. NFM, 35mm, 64.5 meters. PCG (15 August 1906). PC (Paris, 1907), 239–240. [#1466, 135 meters]

Bobby et sa famille or *Bobby and His Family*. GEH, 35mm, 125 feet. AF, 35mm, 35 meters. PCG (15 October 1906), 393. [#1445, 40 meters]

Voyage autour d'une étoile. NFA, 35mm, 458 feet. PCG (1 September 1906), 334. PC (Paris, 1907), 127–128. [#1463, 145 meters]

Le Braconnier. NFA, 35mm, 375 feet. PC (Paris, 1907), 211–212. [#1495, 145 meters]

Pauvre Mère! NFA, 35mm, 350 feet. PC (Paris, September 1906), 25–26. PCG (15 October 1906), 393. [#1525, 115 meters]

La Grève des bonnes. AF, 35mm, 115 meters. PCG (15 October 1906), 392. IF (3 November 1906), 4. [#1538, 140 meters]

Vengéance de nègre. NFA, 35mm, 162 feet. PC (Paris, November 1906), 8–9. [#1505, 55 meters]

Le Chercheur d'aventures. LOC, 35mm. PCG (1 December 1906), 454. PC (Paris 1907), 212–213. [#1498, 165 meters]

L'Antre de la sorcière or *The Bewitched Shepherd*. NFA, 35mm, 353 feet. PCG (1 December 1906), 454. PC (Paris, 1907), 131–132. [#1519, 115 meters]

1907

Eclipse *The Short-Sighted Cyclist*. NFA, 35mm, 319 feet. KLW (16 May 1907), 14. VFI (29 June 1907), 5. [334 feet]

Gaumont *Un Coup de vent* or *A Gust of Wind*. NFA, 35mm, 305 feet. NYC (2 February 1907), 1332. [367 feet]

The Stepmother. NFA, 35mm, 560 feet. NYC (2 February 1907), 1320. [584 feet]

Le Thé chez le concierge or *The Housekeeper's Tea Party*. AF, 35mm, 190 meters. KLW (6 June 1907), 62. [#1588, 435 feet]

The Inlaid Floor Polisher or *Polishing Day*. NFA, 35mm, 221 feet. KLW (11 July 1907), 136. VFI (7 December 1907), 9. [#1649, 230 feet]

L'Homme aimanté or *The Magnetized Man*. CF, 35mm, 135 meters. KLW (4 July 1907), 124. PCG (1 August 1907), 291. MPW (10 August 1907), 366. [#1646, 467 feet]

In the Hands of the Enemy. NFA, 35mm, 625 feet. KLW (15 August 1907), 216. [#1653, 734 feet]

The Glue Pot or *Glue for Birds*. LOC, 35mm, 350 feet. NFA, 35mm, 378 feet. KLW (29 August 1907), 248. MPW (26 October 1907), 533. [#1666, 467 feet]

La Barricade. CG, 35mm, 84 meters. PCG (15 October 1907), 369.

The Bomb. LOC, 35mm, 300 feet. MPW (2 November 1907), 569. [314 feet]

Nuit agitée. AF, 35mm, 243 meters. PCG (1 December 1907), 420.

Méliès — Le Tunnel sous la manche. MOMA, 16mm. PCG (1 July 1907), 259. MPW (27 July 1907), 331–332. [#936–950, 1000 feet]

Satan en prison. LOC, 16mm, 112 feet. MPW (23 November 1907), 622. [#1010–2113, 310 feet]

Pathé — Les Debuts d'un chauffeur or The Inexperienced Chauffeur. AF, 35mm, 85 meters. PC (Paris, 1907), 255–256. VFI (5 January 1907), 9. PCG (15 January 1907), 34. [#1490, 60 meters]

Les Mésaventures d'un tonneau or Travels of a Barrel. GEH, 35mm, 199 feet. EG, 16mm. VFI (5 January 1907), 9. PCG (15 January 1907), 33. PC (Paris, 1907), 256. [#1492, 70 meters]

Bain forcé or Unforeseen Bathing. GEH, 35mm, 166 feet. PC (Paris, 1907), 99–100. [#1524, 55 meters]

L'Accordéon. LOC, 35mm, 318 feet. PC (Paris, 1907), 100–101. [#1527, 100 meters]

La Jeteuse de sorts or The Witch's Curse. LOC, 35mm, 410 feet. GEH, 35mm, 440 feet. VFI (5 January 1907), 9. PC (Paris, 1907), 266–267. PCG (15 January 1907), 34. [#1509, 150 meters]

Un Jour de paye or Payday. EG, 16mm. PC (Paris, 1907), 260–261. [#1535, 90 meters]

L'Espionne or The Female Spy. NFA, 35mm, 420 feet. PC (Paris, 1907), 269–270. NYC (15 December 1906), 1145. PCG (15 January 1907), 34. [#1556, 130 meters]

Les Roses magiques or Magic Roses. LOC, 35mm, 60 meters. VFI (5 January 1907), 9. PC (Paris, 1907), 265. [#1560, 60 meters]

La Revanche de l'enfant or Child's Revenge. GEH, 35mm, 125 feet. PC (Paris, 1907), 270–271. VFI (5 January 1907), 9. [#1561, 105 meters]

Une Drame à Venise or A Venetian Tragedy. MOMA, 35mm. NFA, 35mm, 525 feet. VFI (5 January 1907), 9. PC (Paris, 1907), 272–273. MPW (28 November 1908), 422. [#1577, 180 meters]

Aladdin ou la lampe merveilleuse. AF, 35mm, 236 meters. NFA, 35mm, 788 feet. EG, 16mm. PC (Paris, 1907), 274–275. PCG (1 January 1907), 16. VFI (5 January 1907), 9. [#1506, 250 meters]

Lèvres collées. NFA, 35mm, 148 feet. PC (Paris, November 1906), 14. [#1584, 50 meters]

Le Charmeur or The Magician and the Butterfly. NFA, 35mm, 285 feet. PC (Paris, 1907), 294. PCG (1 February 1907), 54. VFI (9 February 1907), 2. [#1579, 90 meters]

La Petite Aveugle or Little Blind Girl. LOC, 35mm, 417 feet. PC (Paris, 1907), 298. VFI (19 January 1907), 12. [#1558, 135 meters]

Un Attentat sur la voie ferrée or Crime on the Railroad. AF, 35mm. VFI (19 January 1907), 12. PCG (16 March 1907), 113. PC (Paris, 1907), 300. [#1570, 160 meters]

Les Mésaventures d'une mission négre à Paris. NFA, 35mm, 220 feet. PC (Paris, 1907), 287–288. PCG (1 February 1907), 54. [#1588, 105 meters]

Medor au téléphone or *Spot at the 'Phone*. NFM, 35mm, 47 meters. PC (Paris, January 1907), 14. VFI (9 February 1907), 2. [#1624, 50 meters]

La Course de sergents de ville or *The Policemen's Little Run*. AF, 35mm, 102 meters. PC (Paris, January 1907), 13–14. PCG (15 January 1907), 33. VFI (9 February 1907), 2. [#1611, 155 meters]

Mauvaise Mère. AF, 35mm, 152 meters. PCG (15 February 1907), 74. PC (Paris, 1907), 304. [#1616, 155 meters]

Difficult Arrest. LOC, 35mm, 382 feet. VFI (16 February 1907), 11. [393 feet]

Cendrillon or *Cinderella*. NFA, 35mm, 925 feet. PC (Paris, January 1907), 32–33. VFI (16 March 1907), 11. [#1557, 295 meters]

La Vie et la Passion de N. S. J. C. NFA, 35mm, 610 feet. NFM, 35mm. PC (Paris, 1907), 244–245. VFI (16 March 1907), 11. PCG (1 April 1907), 133–134. [#1604–1608, 950 meters]

Le Bailleur or *The Yawner*. LOC, 35mm, 250 feet. PC (Paris, January 1907), 16–17. VFI (16 March 1907), 11. [#1626, 85 meters]

Jalousie et folie or *From Jealousy to Madness*. LOC, 35mm. PC (Paris, February–March 1907), 26–27. VFI (20 April 1907), 5. [#1614, 180 meters]

Le Scarabée d'or or *The Golden Beetle*. LOC, 35mm. PC (Paris, February–March 1907), 19. VFI (20 April 1907), 2. [#1571, 55 meters]

Jules, the Sandwich Man. LOC, 35mm, 124 meters. VFI (4 May 1907), 2. [442 feet]

The Lawyer Enjoys Himself. GEH, 35mm, 496 feet. VFI (4 May 1907), 2. [524 feet]

Pour un collier! or *All for a Necklace*. GEH, 35mm, 345 feet. PC (Paris, February–March 1907), 25. VFI (11 May 1907), 11. [#1597, 110 meters]

Les Debuts d'un patineur or *Skater's Debut* or *An Unskillful Skater*. MOMA and EG, 16mm. VFI (11 May 1907), 11. PCG (15 May 1907), 185. [410 feet]

Ruse de mari or *Artful Husband*. NFA, 35mm, 240 feet. PC (Paris, February–March 1907), 10. VFI (18 May 1907), 5. [#1653, 85 meters]

Distress. LOC, 35mm, 370 feet. VFI (18 May 1907), 5. MPW (1 June 1907), 206. [606 feet]

Amour d'esclave or *A Slave's Love*. LOC, 35mm, 518 feet. EG, 16mm. PC (Paris, May 1907), 22–24. PCG (15 May 1907), 185. KLW (6 June 1907), 49. VFI (8 June 1907), 12. [#1688, 210 meters]

Toto fait de la peinture or *Charley Paints*. GEH, 35mm, 338 feet. PC (Paris, May 1907), 6–7. PCG (15 May 1907), 194. KLW (16 May 1907), 1. VFI (15 June 1907), 2. [#1654, 110 meters]

La Course des belles-mères or *The Mother-in-Laws' Race*. LOC, 35mm, 234 feet. PC (Paris, May 1907), 12–13. KLW (16 May 1907), 17. VFI (22 June 1907), 11. [#1738, 95 meters]

A Hooligan Idea. GEH, 35mm, 295 feet. KLW (16 May 1907), 13. VFI (22 June 1907), 11. [360 feet]

La Fille du Corse or *A Corsican's Daughter*. GEH, 35mm, 523 feet. KLW (16 May 1907), 1. VFI (1 June 1907), 2. [#1707, 175 meters]

Les Deux Soeurs or *Two Sisters*. NFA, 35mm, 720 feet. VFI (1 June 1907), 2. [#1681, 228 meters]

Lutte pour la vie or *Struggle for Life*. NFM, 35mm, 275 meter. KLW (23 May

1907), 17. PCG (1 June 1907), 213. VFI (22 June 1907), 11. [#1760, 300 meters]

Les Chiens de police or *Police Dogs*. NFA, 35mm, 710 feet. EG, 16mm. PC (Paris, May 1907), 29–30. KLW (23 May 1907), 17. PCG (1 June 1907), 214. VFI (22 June 1907), 11. [#1771, 250 meters]

Les Apprentissages de Boireau or *Jim's Apprenticeship*. NFA, 35mm, 435 feet. PC (Paris, May 1907), 10–12. KLW (30 May 1907), 33. VFI (29 June 1907), 12. [#1730, 205 meters]

Le Chien récalcitrant or *The Obstinate Dog*. NFA, 35mm, 273 feet. KLW (13 June 1907), 77. PCG (15 June 1907), 235–236. [#1772, 90 meters]

La Légende de Polichinelle or *Harlequin's Story*. NFA, 35mm, 1100 feet. EG, 16mm. PCG (15 June 1907), 234. KLW (4 July 1907), 123. MPW (20 July 1907), 317. [#1783, 410 meters]

The Red Spectre. LOC, 35mm, 610 feet. GEH, 35mm, 602 feet. EG, 16mm. KLW (4 July 1907), 123. MPW (17 August 1907), 381. [623 feet]

Le Bon Grand-père or *Good Grandfather*. NFA, 35mm, 728 feet. PC (Paris, July 1907), 36–38. KLW (11 July 1907), 139. VFI (3 August 1907), 11. [#1766, 240 meters]

Le Nettoyeur de devantures or *The Window Cleaner*. LOC, 35mm, 229 feet. PC (Paris, July 1907), 13–14. KLW (11 July 1907), 139. VFI (27 July 1907), 2. [#1761, 70 meters]

Geneviève de Brabant. GEH, 35mm, 530 feet. PC (Paris, July 1907), 43–44. KLW (11 July 1907), 139. VFI (27 July 1907), 2. [#1756, 200 meters]

Le Diabolo. NFA, 35mm, 163 feet. PCG (1 July 1907), 256. VFI (27 July 1907), 2. [#1801, 60 meters]

Les Debuts d'un aeronaute or *His First Air Trip*. NFA, 35mm, 374 feet. PC (Paris, July 1907), 16–18. KLW (25 July 1907), 173. [#1793, 165 meters]

Les Chrysanthèmes or *Chrysanthemums*. GEH, 35mm, 210 feet. PC (Paris, July 1907), 31. KLW (1 August 1907), 189. VFI (17 August 1907), 2. [#1762, 70 meters]

Le Bagne de gosses or *Children's Reformatory*. LOC, 35mm, 82 meters. PC (Paris, July 1907), 38–39. KLW (22 August 1907), 239. VFI (31 August 1907), 11. [#1778, 230 meters]

Vues d'espagne en cartes postales. NFA, 35mm, 332 feet. PC (Paris, July 1907). [#1805, 140 meters]

Vengéance du forgeron or *The Blacksmith's Revenge*. NFM, 35mm, 135 meters. KLW (12 September 1907), 285. VFI (21 September 1907), 11. [#1751, 150 meters]

La Course au parasol. LOC, 35mm, 250 feet. PC (Paris, July 1907), 27–28. [#1833, 90 meters]

Enchanted Glasses. LOC, 35mm. KLW (19 September 1907), 311. [330 feet]

Poor Pig. LOC, 35mm, 194 feet. KLW (19 September 1907), 311. MPW (28 September 1907), 477. [196 feet]

Le Fils prodigue or *The Prodigal Son*. NFA, 35mm, 605 feet. KLW (26 September 1907), 349. [708 feet]

Tommy in Society. NFA, 35mm, 192 feet. VFI (2 November 1907), 11. [196 feet]

La Planche or *The Plank*. GEH, 35mm, 155 feet. MPW (23 November 1907), 620, 622. [229 feet]

Ali-Baba and the Forty Thieves. GP, 9.5mm. PC (Berlin, November 1907), 40–41. MPW (23 November 1907), 622. [#1725, 330 meters]

The Pirates or *Die Seeräuber.* GEH, 35mm, 351 feet. PC (Berlin, November 1907), 31–33. MPW (23 November 1907), 618, 620. [#1869, 541 feet]

Economical Trip or *Traveling on the Cheap.* NFA, 35mm, 234 feet. VFI (30 November 1907), 16. MPW (7 March 1908), 193. [278 feet]

The Clockmaker's Secret. LOC, 35mm, 216 meters. PC (Berlin, November 1907), 25–27. MPW (30 November 1907), 636, 638. [#1940, 245 meters]

Bathers Race. LOC, 16mm, 99 feet. VFI (7 December 1907), 2. [278 feet]

Adventures of a Madman or *Erlebnisse eines narren.* NFA, 35mm, 398 feet. PC (Berlin, November 1907), 19–20. [#1895, 130 meters]

Le Pêcheur des perles or *Down in the Deep.* LOC, 35mm, 452 feet. EG, 16mm. MPW (7 December 1907), 652. Var (21 Dec 1907). [#1918, 160 meters]

Le Contremaître incendiaire or *Incendiary Foreman.* LOC, 35mm, 1169 feet. MPW (15 February 1908), 123–124, 126. [#1987, 270 meters]

Théophile Pathé   *Governess Wanted.* GEH, 35mm, 415 feet. VFI (1 June 1907), 9. MPW (18 January 1908), 50. [517 feet]

1908

Eclair   *Nick Carter: Le Guet-Apens* or *The Doctor's Rescue.* NFA, 35mm, 546 feet. CJ (8 September 1908), 11. APC (12 September 1908), 17. KLW (17 September 1908), 424. [185 meters]

Film d'Art   *L'Assassinat du Duc de Guise.* AF, 35mm. CSL, 35mm, 324 meters. MOMA, 16mm. CJ (19 November 1908), 1–2. Bio (27 November 1908), 4. MPW (13 February 1909), 184. [340 meters]

Gaumont   *Buying a Cow.* LOC, 35mm, 450 feet. MPW (18 January 1908), 50. [517 feet]

La Course aux poitrins or *The Pumpkin Race.* NFA, 35mm, 427 feet. MOMA, 16mm. APC (15 February 1908), 17. KLW (20 February 1908), 265. PCG (1 March 1908), 516.

Le Bon Invalide et les enfants. AF, 35mm, 105 meters. PCG (15 March 1908), 533.

Une Dame vraiment bien or *A Truly Fine Lady.* MOMA, 16mm. CJ (15 August 1908), 8. [75 meters]

Fantasmagorie. MOMA, 16mm. CJ (25 August 1908), 11. PCG (1 September 1908), 712. [36 meters]

L'Hôtel du silence or *Silent Hotel.* CF, 35mm. KLW (8 October 1908), 502. CJ (13 October 1908), 11. APC (17 October 1908), 19. PCG (1 November 1908), 778. MPW (7 November 1908), 370. [226 meters]

Un Drame chez les fantoches. NFA, 35mm, 225 feet. MOMA, 16mm. CJ (12 November 1908), 11. MPW (19 December 1908), 505. [72 meters]

Le Lion   *Eine Kleine Mutter.* NFA, 35mm, 366 feet.

Méliès   *François 1ᵉʳ et Triboulet.* NFA, 35mm, 330 feet. MPW (25 January 1908), 63. APC (15 February 1908), 16. [#1040–1143, 321 feet]

The Genii of Fire. LOC, 16mm, 130 feet. MPW (14 March 1908), 214. [#1069–1072, 310 feet]

Why That Actor Was Late. LOC, 16mm, 150 feet. VFI (28 May 1908), 4. [590 feet]

L'Avare or *The Miser*. LOC, 16mm, 119 feet. APC (6 June 1908), 14. MPW (13 June 1908), 518. CJ (25 August 1908), 13. [#1146–1158, 270 meters]

His First Job. LOC, 16mm, 128 feet. VFI (18 July 1908), 14. [320 feet]

The Mischances of a Photographer. LOC, 16mm, 77 feet. VFI (8 August 1908), 12. [205 feet]

French Cops Learning English. LOC, 16mm, 182 feet. VFI (12 September 1908), 7. [463 feet]

Not Guilty. LOC, 16mm, 261 feet. VFI (26 September 1908), 12. [645 feet]

La Bonne Bergère et la méchante princesse. LOC, 35mm, 860 feet. CJ (24 November 1908), 13. [#1429–1441, 280 meters]

Pathé   *The Wonderful Mirror*. LOC, 35mm, 131 meters. NFM, 35mm, 136 meters. VFI (28 December 1907), 2. MPW (18 January 1908), 50. [442 feet]

Le Pied du mouton or *The Talisman*. AF, 35mm, 259 meters. NFA, 35mm, 500 feet. VFI (28 December 1907), 8. [#1960, 300 meters]

The Black Witch. NFA, 35mm, 307 feet. VFI (4 January 1908), 7. MPW (18 January 1908), 50. [328 feet]

A Prince's Idea. LOC, 35mm, 398 feet. VFI (11 January 1908), 2. [459 feet]

His First Cigar. LOC, 16mm, 150 feet. EG, 16mm. VFI (11 January 1908), 2. [393 feet]

The Man Who Walked on Water. LOC, 16mm, 88 feet. VFI (18 January 1908), 16. [196 feet]

The Adventures of an Overcoat. LOC, 16mm, 125 feet. VFI (18 January 1908), 16. [311 feet]

La Vestale. AF, 35mm, 212 meters. MOMA, 35mm, 736 feet. Com (17 January 1908), 3. PCG (1 February 1908), 483–484. MPW (21 March 1908), 247. [#1922, 225 meters]

Nuit de Noël or *Christmas Eve Tragedy*. NFM, 35mm, 205 meters. Com (17 January 1908), 3. VFI (18 April 1908), 7, 9–10. [#2017, 220 meters]

Le Cheval emballé or *The Runaway Horse*. NFA, 35mm, 402 feet. MOMA, 16mm. PCG (1 February 1908), 483. VFI (8 February 1908), 2. [#2027, 135 meters]

Artistic Rag-Pickers. LOC, 35mm, 468 feet. MPW (8 February 1908), 104. KLW (30 April 1908), 426. [492 feet]

A Cabman's Delusion. GEH, 35mm, 88 feet. MPW (15 February 1908), 124.

The Little Cripple. NFM, 35mm, 225 meters. MPW (22 February 1908), 145–146. VFI (22 February 1908), 2. [885 feet]

Rêve des marmitons or *Scullion's Dream*. MOMA, 16mm. MPW (22 February 1908), 146–147. [541 feet]

Cruel Joke. NFM, 35mm, 176 meters. VFI (22 February 1908), 2. [606 feet]

The Old Fool or *Unlucky Old Flirt*. NFA, 35mm, 425 feet. VFI (29 February 1908), 16. [459 feet]

The Mattress. LOC, 35mm, 125 meters. MPW (7 March 1908), 190, 194. KLW (23 April 1908), 410. [475 feet]

Toula's Dream. GEH, 35mm, 312 feet. MPW (14 March 1908), 214, 217. [328 feet]

The Idler. GEH, 35mm, 214 feet. MPW (28 March 1908), 270. [557 feet]

The Waif. NFA, 35mm, 365 feet. MPW (28 March 1908), 268, 269. Var
(19 December 1908). [459 feet]

L'Apprenti architecte or *Jim Gets a New Job.* NFA, 35mm, 396 feet. MPW
(28 March 1908), 270. KLW (16 April 1908), 394. [#2041, 125 meters]

A Narrow Escape or *The Physician in the Castle.* NFA, 35mm, 360 feet. MPW
(28 March 1908), 268. KLW (7 May 1908), 446. [426 feet]

The Would-Be Juggler or *Amateur Acrobat.* NFA, 35mm, 470 feet. MPW
(4 April 1908), 296. Var (4 April 1908). [541 feet]

Falsely Condemned or *Harry, the Country Postman.* NFA, 35mm, 535 feet.
MPW (25 April 1908), 374. KLW (4 June 1908), 62, 77. [639 feet]

Le Roman d'un malheureux or *A Poor Man's Romance.* NFA, 35mm, 582 feet.
MPW (25 April 1908), 374. Var (25 April 1908). [#2061, 210 meters]

The Little Chimney Sweep or *A Cruel Revenge.* NFA, 35mm, 415 feet. KLW
(30 April 1908), 426. VFI (16 May 1908), 7, 11. [459 feet]

The Hanging Lamp. NFA, 35mm, 81 feet. VFI (2 May 1908), 7, 10. [295 feet]

The False Coin. NFA, 35mm, 398 feet. MPW (9 May 1908), 425. [410 feet]

Tormented by His Mother-in-law. GEH, 35mm, 166 feet. KLW (7 May 1908),
446. VFI (6 June 1908), 13. [344 feet]

Don Juan. GEH, 35mm, 745 feet. KLW (4 June 1908), 2. VFI (6 June 1908),
13. [#2140, 330 meters]

Hurry Up Please. CM, 35mm. KLW (11 June 1908), 82. VFI (14 November
1908), 9. [442 feet]

The Dreyfus Affair. AF, 35mm, 338 meters. KLW (18 June 1908), 102. VFI
(4 July 1908), 13. MPW (4 July 1908), 11. [1213 feet]

Cuisine magnétique or *Unusual Cooking.* GEH, 16mm, 79 feet. KLW (2 July
1908), 142. VFI (19 September 1908), 13. [196 feet]

The Runaway Mother-in-law. GEH, 35mm, 125 feet. VFI (18 July 1908), 15.
KLW (6 August 1908), 274. [328 feet]

L'Aspirateur or *The Vacuum Cleaner.* AF, 35mm, 85 meters. GEH, 35mm,
236 feet. MPW (1 August 1908), 91. KLW (20 August 1908), 314. [393 feet]

Samson or *Samson and Delilah.* NFA, 35mm, 1010 feet. APC (12 September
1908), 3. VFI (29 August 1908), 13. [1082 feet]

Rêves d'argent or *The Policemen's Vision.* MOMA, 16mm. MPW (19 September 1908), 222–223. [623 feet]

Cabman's Wife or *Women Chauffeurs.* LOC, 35mm, 480 feet. KLW (1 October 1908), 484. [528 feet]

Les Reflects vivants or *A Living Reflection.* NFA, 35mm, 183 feet. Bio (30 October 1908), 8. [#2400, 155 meters]

Electric Hotel. CF, 35mm. PC (Berlin, November 1908). VFI (19 December
1908), 13. [#2510, 150 meters]

L'Homme aux gants blancs or *The Man with White Gloves.* GEH, 35mm, 232 feet.
PC (Berlin, December 1908). VFI (17 April 1909), 8, 13. [#2588, 310 meters]

1909

Eclair   *Fleur empoisonnée* or *The Poisoned Flower.* AF, 35mm, 206 meters. CJ
(23 April 1909), 12. KLW (6 May 1909), 1541. MPW (26 June 1909), 885.
[216 meters]

Journée de grève. NFA, 35mm, 485 feet. [167 meters]

Nick Carter: Le Club des suicides. NFA, 35mm, 534 feet. CJ (20 September 1909), 17. [200 meters]

Film d'Art Le Retour d'Ulysse. AF, 16mm, 90 meters. Com (23 January 1909), 4. VFI (20 March 1909), 5. [320 meters]

La Tosca. NFA, 35mm, 1146 feet. Com (14 March 1909), 4. Bio (11 March 1909), 22–23. VFI (15 June 1909), 16. [380 meters]

Macbeth. CF, 35mm, 300 meters. Bio (2 December 1909), 13. Com (7 December 1909), 4. MPW (4 June 1910), 915. [325 meters]

Gaumont L'Aveugle de Jérusalem. NFA, 35mm, 688 feet. KLW (1 April 1909), 1348. CJ (3 April 1909), 12. [200 meters]

Joyeux Microbes. CF, 35mm. CJ (10 April 1909), 12. [102 meters]

Clair de lune espagnol or The Man in the Moon. LOC, 35mm, 370 feet. EG, 16mm. CJ (24 April 1909), 12. MPW (17 July 1909), 106. [98 meters]

Un Monsieur qui a mangé un taureau. NFA, 35mm, 575 feet. CJ (13 May 1909), 13. [181 meters]

Le Déraciné ou artiste or The Actor's Mother. NFA, 35mm, 720 feet. MPW (8 May 1909), 584. Nic (June 1909), 170. [743 feet]

Judith et Holophernes. NFA, 35mm, 270 feet. CJ (5 June 1909), 13. MPW (30 April 1910), 699, 701. [89 meters]

Les Trois Mannequins or The Tricky Dummies. NFA, 35mm, 319 feet. CJ (18 July 1909), 13. VFI (18 Sept 1909), 8, 15. [112 meters]

La Possession de l'enfant. AF, 35mm, 220 meters. CJ (26 July 1909), 13. [235 meters]

Cocher, à l'heure. CF, 35mm. CJ (16 August 1909), 13. [117 meters]

La Légende des phares. CG, 35mm, 211 meters. CF (23 August 1909), 13. MPW (25 September 1909), 432. [232 meters]

Le Dernier Requiem de Mozart or La Mort du Mozart or Mozart's Last Requiem. NFA, 35mm, 800 feet. CJ (2 August 1909), 13. MPW (11 September 1909), 351. Var (18 Sept 1909). [264 meters]

Le Huguenot. NFA, 35mm, 971 feet. CJ (13 September 1909), 13. Bio (16 September 1909), 33. [310 meters]

The Old Woodcutter. NFA, 35mm, 588 feet. Bio (21 October 1909), 37, 58. [560 feet]

A Mix Up at Court. LOC, 35mm, 500 feet. MPW (27 November 1909), 769. [590 feet]

Idylle corinthienne or The White Slave or The Greek Slave's Passion. NFA, 35mm, 1080 feet. CJ (6 December 1909), 19. Bio (23 December 1909), 41. VFI (25 December 1909), 11. [1052 feet]

Le Lion Der Instinkt des blinder. NFA, 35mm, 486 feet. Bio (29 July 1909), 23.

Lux Le Retour de Columbine. NFA, 35mm, 390 feet. CJ (13 May 1909), 13. Bio (27 May 1909), 33. MPW (24 July 1909), 141. [485 feet]

How a Dog Saved the Flag. NFA, 35mm, 549 feet. Bio (4 November 1909), 43.

Pathé L'Assommoir or Drink. NFM, 35mm, 319 meters. Bio (11 March 1909), 22–23. MPW (23 October 1909), 557, 581, 583. VFI (23 Oct 1909), 7, 10. [#2815, 740 meters]

La Part du pauvre. PC (Milan, June 1909), 35–36. [#2813, 155 meters]

Jeanne d'Arc. NFA, 35mm, 586 feet. MOMA, 35mm, 852 feet. Bio (10 June 1909), 12. MPW (19 June 1909), 852. [#2957, 270 meters]

Dog Detective. NFA, 35mm, 605 feet. MPW (12 June 1909), 803. [659 feet]

Voyage au planete Jupiter or *A Trip to Jupiter.* EG, 16mm. NFM, 35mm, 166 meters. Bio (17 June 1909), 39. VFI (14 August 1909), 133. [#2863, 195 meters]

La Petite Policière or *The Girl Detective.* NFA, 35mm, 348 feet. VFI (10 July 1909), 12. Bio (15 July 1909), 37. [#2870, 250 meters]

Un match enragé or *A Game of Chess.* NFA, 35mm, 550 feet. VFI (2 October 1909), 8, 10. [#2954, 175 meters]

Three Neighbors or *The Miser and His Daughter.* EG, 16mm. Bio (2 September 1909), 19, 50. VFI (27 November 1909), 15. [445 feet]

Le Petit Poucet or *Tom Thumb.* NFA, 35mm, 720 feet. VFI (11 September 1909), 11. [1016 feet]

Une Conquête or *A Conquest.* NFA, 35mm, 379 feet. Bio (23 September 1909), 33. Com (27 October 1909), 4. Var (2 April 1910). [#3116, 130 meters]

Le Mort du Duc d'Enghien or *The Death of the Duke d'Enghien.* NFA, 35mm, 523 feet. Bio (28 October 1909), 37. Com (27 November 1909), 4. VFI (18 December 1909), 13. [#3154, 310 meters]

Oncle Burton or *Young Rascal.* NFA, 35mm, 585 feet. Bio (4 November 1909), 39, 41. [#3170, 205 meters]

La Petite Rosse or *The Little Vixen.* LOC, 35mm, 450 feet. Com (7 November 1909), 4. VFI (2 April 1910), 12. [#3095, 165 meters]

Joseph vendu par ses frères or *Joseph Sold by His Brethren.* NFA, 35mm, 643 feet. Bio (11 November 1909), 12. Com (12 December 1909), 4. VFI (5 March 1910), 14. [#3148, 240 meters]

Othello. LOC, 35mm, 1038 feet. Bio (11 November 1909), 45. Com (12 December 1909), 4. MPW (23 April 1910), 662. Var (30 April 1910). [#3178, 335 meters]

Roméo se fait Bandit or *Romeo Turns Bandit.* LOC, 16mm, 155 feet. Bio (25 November 1909), 13. Com (22 December 1909), 4. MPW (28 May 1910), 900. [#3161, 165 meters]

Satyre de bois-joli or *Adonis Robbed of His Clothes.* LOC, 16mm, 156 feet. EG, 16mm. VFI (20 November 1909), 16. [#2965, 135 meters]

Le Moulin maudit or *The Mill.* AF, 35mm, 130 meters. Bio (9 December 1909), 13, 39. [#3215, 190 meters]

Le Roman de l'écuyère or *A Story of Circus Life.* LOC, 35mm, 755 feet. Bio (23 December 1909), 41. Com (18 January 1910), 4. VFI (22 January 1910), 24. [#3264, 245 meters]

Théâtro-
Film   *Mathéo Driani.* NFA, 35mm, 550 feet. CJ (27 September 1909), 19. [173 meters]

1910

Eclair   *Eugènie Grandet.* AF, 35mm, 238 meters. CJ (21 May 1910), 23, 24. MPW (4 June 1910), 940. [295 meters]

Le Musée des souverains. GEH, 35mm, 172 feet. CJ (8 October 1910), 27. [124 meters]

L'Elixir de bravoure or *The Elixir of Bravery*. LOC, 35mm, 369 feet. CJ
(3 December 1910), 27. MPW (11 February 1911), 323. [130 meters]

Balandard est en grève or *Mr. Fiddleway Is on Strike*. LOC, 35mm. CJ (17 December 1910), 27. [162 meters]

Film   *L'Arrestation de la Duchesse de Berry*. GEH, 35mm, 410 feet. Com (19 Feb-
d'Art   ruary 1910), 4. MPW (12 March 1910), 395.

Rival de son fils or *Don Carlos*. NFA, 35mm, 760 feet. CJ (27 March 1910),
21. MPW (14 May 1910), 787. [283 meters]

Werther. CF, 35mm. CJ (2 April 1910), 7–8, 14. Com (23 April 1910), 4.
Bio (12 May 1910), 12. MPW (14 May 1910), 808. Var (22 Oct 1910).
[290 meters]

Héliogabale or *Vitellius and Heliogabalus*. NFA, 35mm, 483 feet. CJ (9 April
1910), 14–15. Com (23 April 1910), 4. MPW (28 May 1910), 912.
[190 meters]

Carmen. NFA, 35mm, 1001 feet. CJ (30 July 1910), 18. MPW (13 August
1910), 336. [302 meters]

Gaumont *Calino a peur du feu* or *Calino's Fire Extinguisher*. NFA, 35mm, 335 feet. CJ
(3 January 1910), 19. Bio (13 January 1910), 16. [107 meters]

Le Binettoscope. AF, 35mm, 102 meters. CJ (10 January 1910), 19. [113
meters]

Getting Square with the Inventor. GEH, 35mm, 375 feet. VFI (22 January
1910), 13. [393 feet]

André Chenier or *Poet of the Revolution*. AF, 35mm, 241 meters. CJ (30 January 1910), 19. MPW (5 March 1910), 356. [349 meters]

Le Festin de Balthazar. NFA, 35mm, 896 feet. CJ (13 February 1910), 19. Bio
(17 February 1910), 6. Var (2 April 1910). [290 meters]

Christophe Colomb. NFA, 35mm, 820 feet. CJ (2 April 1910), 25. Bio
(14 April 1910), 37. MPW (14 May 1910), 788. [333 meters]

The Princess and the Fishbone. LOC, 35mm, 424 feet. Bio (28 April 1910), 52.
MPW (30 July 1910), 259. [585 feet]

Le Mobilier fidèle. CG, 35mm, 132 meters. CJ (30 April 1910), 27.
[132 meters]

Le Vertige or *In's leven's maalstroom*. NFM, 35mm, 265 meters.

Le Peintre néo-impressionannate. AF, 35mm, 111 meters. MOMA, 16mm. CJ
(11 June 1910), 25. [143 meters]

Les Sept Péchès capitaux. MOMA, 35mm, 2424 feet. CJ (3 September 1910),
29. Bio (8 September 1910), 25.

La Vie de Molière or *The Life of Molière*. CG, 35mm, 302 meters. CJ (10 September 1910), 29. VFI (29 October 1910), 14. [380 meters]

Calino achête un chien de garde or *Calino Buys a House Dog*. LOC, 16mm,
115 feet. CJ (10 September 1910), 29. Bio (15 September 1910), 31. MPW
(17 June 1911), 1400. [101 meters]

Mater Dolorosa. NFM, 35mm, 174.5 meters. CJ (8 October 1910), 27.
[184 meters]

La Guépe or *Mind the Wasps!* NFA, 35mm, 300 feet. CJ (22 October 1910),
27. Bio (3 November 1910), 21. [105 meters]

Le Gardien de la camargue. CG, 35mm, 270 meters. CJ (29 October 1910), 27.

Bébé apache. NFA, 35mm, 473 feet. CJ (24 December 1910), 27. [198 meters]

Lux   *A Young Aviator's Dream.* NFA, 35mm. MPW (16 April 1910), 622.
[367 feet]

Bill as a Boxer. LOC, 35mm, 279 feet. Bio (27 October 1910), 52. MPW
(12 November 1910), 1092. [327 feet]

Les Lavendières or *The Truth Revealed.* LOC, 35mm, 497 feet. Bio (3 November 1910), 25. CJ (5 November 1910), 28. MPW (12 November 1910),
1092. [649 feet]

Patouillard amoureux or *Bill as a Lover.* NFM, 35mm, 106 meters. CJ (26 November 1910), 28. MPW (19 November 1910), 1194. [155 meters]

Un drame sur une locomotive or *The Rival Engine Drivers.* NFA, 35mm,
290 feet. Bio (15 December 1910), 31. CJ (17 December 1910), 28. MPW
(7 January 1911), 6. [112 meters]

Pathé   *Timidité vainçu* or *A Cure for Cowardice.* NFA, 35mm, 335 feet. Bio
(27 January 1910), 53–54. MPW (12 March 1910), 395. [460 feet]

Cléopatre. NFA, 35mm, 868 feet. Bio (27 January 1910), 53. Com (27 February 1910), 4. MPW (7 May 1910), 721. [1170 feet]

Le Bon Patron or *The Kind-Hearted Employer.* LOC, 35mm, 82 meters. Bio
(6 January 1910), 13. Com (6 February 1910), 4. MPW (9 April 1910),
574. [725 feet]

Grand-père or *The Grandsire.* NFM, 35mm, 253 meters. Bio (10 February
1910), 55. [1088 feet]

Une Excursion incohérente or *A Panicky Picnic.* CQ, 35mm, 568 feet. VFI
(19 February 1910), 11. [672 feet]

L'Enlèvement des Sabines or *The Rape of the Sabines.* NFM, 35mm, 331 meters.
Bio (24 February 1910), 66. [1304 feet]

Tout est bien qui finit bien or *Perseverance Rewarded.* GEH, 35mm, 206 feet. CJ
(21 May 1910), 24. PWB (20 June 1910). [443 feet]

Cagliostro. NFA, 35mm, 945 feet. AF, 35mm, 379 meters. Bio (5 May 1910),
12. MPW (6 August 1910), 313. [1000 feet]

Duel de M. Myope or *A Short-Sighted Duellist.* CQ, 35mm. Bio (26 May
1910), 29. CJ (25 June 1910), 26. MPW (5 November 1910), 1067.
[130 meters]

Rêve du détective or *Detective's Dream.* NFA, 35mm, 505 feet. CJ (4 June 1910),
26. MPW (30 July 1910), 262. [180 meters]

La Petite Bergère or *The Little Shepherdess.* NFA, 35mm, 503 feet. CJ (11 June
1910), 26. [180 meters]

Le Petit Blanche-Neige or *Little Snowdrop.* NFA, 35mm, 349 feet. CJ (18 June
1910), 30. MPW (17 December 1910), 1429. [335 meters]

Mariée du chateau maudit or *The Missing Bride.* NFM, 35mm, 220 meters. CJ
(16 July 1910), 26. MPW (11 February 1911), 326. [255 meters]

Fouquet, l'homme au masque de fer. GP, 17.5mm. Bio (16 June 1910), 45. CJ
(3 September 1910), 26. [1006 feet]

Max se trompe d'étage or *The Wrong Floor.* CQ, 35mm. Bio (18 August 1910),
27. CJ (24 September 1910), 30. [150 meters]

Une Belle-mère collante or *The Crocodile.* GEH, 35mm, 195 feet. CJ (3 September 1910), 26. [115 meters]

Athalie. Bio (25 August 1910), 29. GEH, 35mm, 90 feet. CJ (1 October
1910), 28. MPW (15 April 1911), 817. [410 meters]

Les Timidités de Rigadin. NFC, 35mm, 162 meters. CJ (15 October 1910), 28.
    [175 meters]
Le Negre blanc or *The White Nigger* or *How Jack Won a Wife*. CF, 35mm,
    161 meters. MPW (10 September 1910), 574. Bio (15 September 1910),
    29. CJ (22 October 1910), 28. [165 meters]
L'Inventeur or *The Inventor's Rights*. LOC, 35mm, 732 feet. Bio (29 Sep-
    tember 1910), 27. CJ (29 October 1910), 27. MPW (18 March 1911), 606.
    [906 feet]
Les Débuts de Max Linder au cinématographe. NFA, 35mm, 490 feet. Bio
    (13 October 1910), 27. PWB (17 October 1910). CJ (19 November 1910),
    28. [185 meters]
Jim le glisseur or *Slippery Jim*. MOMA, 16mm. MPW (15 October 1910),
    822. PWB (17 October 1910). [531 feet]
Nick Winter connut les courses or *Why Nick Winter Went to the Races*. NFA,
    35mm, 552 feet. CJ (15 October 1910), 28. [220 meters]
Max fait du patinage aroulettes or *One on Max*. NFA, 35mm, 298 feet. VFI
    (22 October 1910), 15. [531 feet]
Tom Pouce suit une femme or *Tommy Short and Mary Long*. GEH, 35mm, 362
    feet. CJ (22 October 1910), 28. MPW (22 April 1911), 912. [125 meters]
Qui est l'assassin? NFA and LOC, 35mm, 637 feet. Bio (27 October 1910),
    49. CJ (3 December 1910), 28. MPW (25 February 1911), 435. [215
    meters]
Max prend son bain or *By the Doctor's Orders* or *Max Embarrassed*. CF, 35mm.
    Bio (3 November 1910), 23. CJ (24 December 1910), 28. MPW (11 March
    1911), 544–545. [210 meters]
When the Shoe Pinches or *The Joys of Tight Boots*. GEH, 35mm, 411 feet. Bio
    (10 November 1910), 27. MPW (18 March 1911), 612. [510 feet]
Family Football. NFA, 35mm, 315 feet. Bio (17 November 1910), 28.
Grandeur d'âme. NFM, 35mm, 191 meters. CJ (19 November 1910), 28.
    [195 meters].
Max hypnotise or *Max Hypnotized*. LOC, 35mm, 408 feet. Bio (1 December
    1910), 27. CJ (14 January 1910), 32. [160 meters]
King Lear. NFA, 35mm, 966 feet. Bio (8 December 1910), 25. CJ (21 Janu-
    ary 1911), 32. [1072 feet]
Evadé des Tuileries. NFA, 35mm. CJ (10 December 1910), 17. MPW (11 Feb-
    ruary 1911), 316. [320 meters]
Sémiramis. AF, 35mm, 311 meters. NFM, 35mm, 277 meters. CJ (24 Decem-
    ber 1910), 12. MPW (27 May 1911), 1212. [330 meters]

1911

Eclair *Tommy étrenne son cor de chasse* or *Tommy Gets a Trumpet*. EG, 16mm. CJ
    (18 March 1911), 33. Bio (23 March 1911), 52. MPW (10 June 1911),
    1334. [127 meters]
La Parabole de l'enfant prodigue. NFA, 35mm, 798 feet. CJ (20 May 1911), 43.
    Bio (25 May 1911), xvii. MPW (24 June 1911), 1415. [995 feet]
L'Inutile Sacrifice. AF, 35mm, 215 meters. CJ (29 July 1911), 39. [240 meters]
Zigomar. GEH, 35mm. CJ (9 September 1911), 51. [935 meters]
Eclipse *La Mégère Apprivoisée* or *The Taming of the Shrew*. LOC, 35mm, 1000 feet.

MPW (1 July 1911), 1540. CJ (23 September 1911), 5, 51. Bio (28 September 1911), ix. [328 meters]

The Tie That Binds. LOC, 35mm, 727 feet. MPW (15 July 1911), 60.

Film d'Art

Idylle florentine. AF, 35mm, 269 meters. CJ (25 February 1911), 14. [290 meters]

Madame Sans-Gêne. CF, 35mm. MOMA, 16mm. CJ (4 November 1911), 50. CJ (11 November 1911), 52. MPW (10 February 1912), 468. [940 meters]

Gaumont

Bébé fait visiter Marseille. NFA, 35mm, 443 feet. CJ (28 January 1911), 31. [145 meters]

Calino pompier or *Calino as a Fireman.* NFA, 35mm, 330 feet. CJ (18 February 1911), 31. Bio (23 March 1911), 33. [124 meters]

Eugène amoureux or *Eugene in Love* or *Romance of a Valet.* NFA, 35mm, 470 feet. CJ (25 February 1911), 35. Bio (30 March 1911), 29. MPW (29 April 1911), 972. [145 meters]

Rembrandt de la rue Lepic. NFA, 35mm, 297 feet. CJ (11 March 1911), 39. [114 meters]

Bébé marchand des quatre saisons. AF, 35mm, 203 meters. [217 meters]

Les Vipères or *Village Gossip.* CF, 35mm, 338 meters. CJ (22 April 1911), 39. Bio (1 June 1911), xiii. MPW (1 July 1911), 1540. [360 meters]

Le Roi Lear au village or *A Village King Lear.* CF, 35mm, 330 meters. LOC, 16mm, 399 feet. CJ (13 May 1911), 39. Bio (15 June 1911), xiii. MPW (8 July 1911), 1624. [360 meters]

Calino donne une chasse à courre. NFA, 35mm, 415 feet. CJ (1 July 1911), 39. Bio (13 July 1911), vii. [200 meters]

Comment on les prend. AF, 35mm, 238 meters.

Comment on les garde. AF, 35mm, 240 meters. CJ (8 July 1911), 35. [260 meters]

Un mariage au revolver. AF, 35mm, 193 meters. CJ (26 August 1911), 44. [210 meters]

La Tare. CF, 35mm, 803 meters. CJ (19 August 1911), 43. Bio (7 September 1911), xiii. [900 meters]

Les Chalands. CG, 35mm, 230 meters. CJ (16 September 1911), 51. [230 meters]

L'Amour qui tue or *The Drawn Curtain.* AF, 35mm, 178 meters. CJ (16 December 1911), 68. MPW (3 June 1911), 1272. [324 meters]

Lux

That Horse Did Run. NFA, 35mm. MPW (11 February 1911), 326. [272 feet]

Patouillard paie ses dettes or *Bill Pays His Debts.* NFA, 35mm, 121 feet. CJ (30 September 1911), 52. [135 meters]

Pathé

Max cherche une femme or *Max Is Almost Married.* CQ, 35mm. CJ (7 January 1911), 28. VFI (14 January 1911), 21–22. [200 meters]

Moïse sauvé des eaux. LOC, 35mm, 557 feet. Bio (12 January 1911), 27. CJ (25 February 1911), 36. [260 meters]

Amour de page or *De Liefde van den page.* NFM, 35mm, 235 meters. CJ (11 March 1911), 40. [255 meters]

La Poudre de valse or *The Dancing Powder.* NFA, 35mm, 450 feet. BH, 13 (1911), 9. Bio (16 March 1911), 29. [140 meters]

Madame Tallien. NFM, 35mm, 200 meters. Bio (16 February 1911), 42. CJ (1 April 1911), 36. [210 meters]

Le Retapeur de cervelles or *Brains Repaired*. NFA, 35mm. Bio (16 February
   1911), 41. CJ (1 April 1911), 36. [130 meters]
The Merchant of Venice. NFA, 35mm, 568 feet. BH, 10 (1911), 3. Bio
   (23 February 1911), 39. CJ (8 April 1911), 40. [270 meters]
Caïn et Abel. NFA, 35mm, 474 feet. BH, 9 (1911), 3. CJ (1 April 1911), 36.
   [170 meters]
L'Intrigante. NFM, 35mm, 162 meters. BH, 9 (1911), 6. CJ (1 April 1911),
   36. [175 meters]
La Doctoresse. AF, 35mm, 129 meters. BH, 11 (1911), 6. [160 meters]
L'Epouvante or *Terror-Stricken*. NFM, 35mm, 180 meters. BH, 14 (1911), 4.
   Bio (23 March 1911), 31. CJ (6 May 1911), 40. [235 meters]
Le Courrier de Lyon or *The Mail Coach of Orleans*. NFA, 35mm, 2150 feet.
   BH, 9 (1911), 11. CJ (25 March 1911), 2, 10–11. Bio (27 April 1911), 144.
   MPW (25 May 1912), 710–711. [2580 feet]
Boniface VIII. LOC, 35mm, 1000 feet. Bio (27 April 1911), v. CJ (10 June
   1911), 36. [290 meters]
Les Victimes de l'alcool or *In the Grip of Alcohol*. CF, 35mm. BH, 18 (1911), 3.
   CJ (20 May 1911), 2. Bio (20 July 1911), 109, 111, 112. [795 meters]
Nick Winter: Le Pickpocket mystifié. GEH, 35mm, 366 feet. BH, 22 (1911),
   10. CJ (1 July 1911), 40. [120 meters]
Little Moritz aime Rosalie. GEH, 35mm, 430 feet. BH, 23 (1911), 9. CJ
   (15 July 1911), 2, 40. [210 meters]
Rosalie et ses meubles fidèles. NFM, 35mm, 99 meters. CJ (19 August 1911),
   44. [120 meters]
Max en convalescence. CQ, 35mm. BH, 37 (1911), 7. Bio (31 August 1911),
   iii, v. MPW (18 May 1912), 658. [245 meters]
Nick Winter, la voleuse et la somnambule or *Nick Winter and the Somnambulist
   Thief*. LOC, 35mm, 614 feet. BH, 36 (1911), 10. Bio (24 August 1911),
   iii. CJ (21 October 1911), 52. [210 meters]
Nick Winter et le rapt de Mlle Werner or *Nick Winter and the Kidnapping of Mlle
   Werner*. GEH, 35mm, 450 feet. BH, 34 (1911), 4. CJ (23 September 1911),
   52. [205 meters]
Max à un duel or *Max and His Duel*. CQ, 35mm. BH, 41 (1911), 5. Bio
   (28 September 1911), v. CJ (18 November 1911), 56. [235 meters]
Little Moritz demande Rosalie en mariage. GEH, 35mm, 401 feet. BH, 35
   (1911), 7. CJ (30 September 1911), 52. [150 meters]
La Rivale de Richelieu. NFA, 35mm, 863 feet. BH, 35 (1911), 3. CJ (30 Sep-
   tember 1911), 52. MPW (24 August 1912), 776. [750 meters]
Le Démon du jeu. CF, 35mm. BH, 37 (1911), 3. CJ (21 October 1911), 60.
   [450 meters]
Notre Dame de Paris. NFA, 35mm, 2092 feet. LOC, 35mm, 1657 feet. BH,
   39 (1911), 3. Bio (21 September 1911), 635, 637. CJ (4 November 1911).
   MPW (16 December 1911), 884–885. [810 meters]
Nick Winter et le vol de "La Jocande" or *Nick Winter and the Theft of the Mona
   Lisa*. CF, 35mm. BH, 34 (1911), 11. Bio (12 October 1911), iii. [595 feet]
Le Cauchemar de Pierrot or *Pierrot's Nightmare*. AF, 35mm, 330 meters. NFM,
   35mm, 337 meters. BH, 42 (1911), 3. Bio (12 October 1911), iii. CJ (25 No-
   vember 1911), 52. [365 meters]

Le Siège de Calais. NFA, 35mm, 1703 feet. BH, 45 (1911), 2. Bio (12 October 1911), 80. CJ (16 December 1911), 68. MPW (23 March 1912), 1063. [620 meters]

Le Nez du Rigadin. NFA, 35mm, 510 feet. BH, 45 (1911), 9. Bio (26 October 1911), iii. CJ (16 December 1911), 68. [185 meters]

Little Moritz chasse les grands fauves or *Little Moritz Shoots Big Game.* CQ, 35mm. BH, 46 (1911), 4. Bio (2 November 1911), iii. CJ (23 December 1911), 52. [265 meters]

Rosalie et son phono. NFM, 35mm, 82 meters. BH, 40 (1911), 6. CJ (11 November 1911), 52. [115 meters]

Victime du quinquina or *Max Takes Tonics.* CF, 35mm. EG, 16mm. BH, 46 (1911), 10. CJ (9 December 1911), 52. Bio (4 January 1912), vi. MPW (13 July 1912), 157. [375 meters]

1912

Eclair   *Au Pays des Ténèbres* or *The Great Mine Disaster.* LOC, 35mm, 803 feet. NFM, 35mm, 516 meters. Bio (11 January 1912), xx. CJ (13 January 1912), 59. [705 meters]

Le Cercueil de verre. LOC, 35mm, 1036 feet. Bio (25 January 1912), viii. CJ (24 February 1912), 67. [730 meters]

Zigomar contre Nick Carter. LOC, 35mm, 1577 feet. NFM, 35mm, 920 meters. Bio (8 February 1912), 399. Cin (1 March 1912), 3. CJ (9 March 1912). [1050 meters]

Amour et Science. NFM, 35mm, 287 meters. CJ (25 May 1912), 67. [309 meters]

Le Mystère du Pont Notre-Dame. NFM, 35mm, 639 meters. Bio (18 April 1912), viii. Cin (19 April 1912), 3. CJ (20 April 1912), 78. [752 meters]

Gontran doute de la fidelité de sa femme. NFM, 35mm, 125 meters. Cin (3 May 1912), 3. Bio (9 May 1912), ix, xi. CJ (11 May 1912), 69. [150 meters]

Tom Butler. LOC, 35mm, 377 feet. Cin (10 May 1912), 3. Bio (16 May 1912), xvii. CJ (18 May 1912), 67. MPW (31 August 1912), 899. [765 meters]

Gerval, le maître de forges. AF, 35mm, 456 meters. CJ (5 October 1912), 90. [565 meters]

Willie et le prestidigitateur or *Willie and the Conjurer.* GEH, 35mm, 482 feet. CJ (12 October 1912), 85. [184 meters]

Petronille gagne le Grand Steeple. NFM, 35mm, 134 meters. Cin (25 October 1912), 3. [167 meters]

Gavroche à Luna-Park. NFM, 35mm, 126 meters. CJ (21 December 1912), 93. [154 meters]

L'Escarpin de Gontran. NFM, 35mm, 200 meters. CJ (28 December 1912), 89. [214 meters]

Eclectic   *Bébé n'aime pas sa concierge.* GEH, 35mm, 466 feet. CJ (28 December 1912), 20.

Eclipse   *Nat Pinkerton: Le Cheveu d'or* or *The Golden Curl.* LOC, 35mm, 1000 feet. Cin (14 June 1912), 3, 4. CJ (15 June 1912), 71. [450 meters]

Arthème Dupin echappe encore. NFM, 35mm, 145 meters. CJ (27 July 1912), 71. [185 meters]

Polyte esclave de consigne. NFM, 35mm, 95 meters. CJ (31 August 1912), 79. [103 meters]

Queen Elizabeth. MOMA, 16mm. NFA, 35mm, 3138 feet. MPW (27 July 1912), 311. CJ (3 August 1912), 13, 47. [1100 meters]

Film d'Art   *La Dame aux camelias.* RFAB, 35mm. CF, 35mm. MOMA, 16mm. MPW (10 February 1912), 468. CJ (24 February 1912), 40–41. Cin (1 March 1912), 1, 3. [700 meters]

Gaumont   *Le Destin des mères.* CF, 35mm, 515 meters. CJ (13 January 1912), 60. [633 meters]

Bébé tire à la cible. AF, 35mm, 222 meters.

La Fille du Margrave or *The Margrave's Daughter.* LOC, 35mm, 596 feet. CJ (27 January 1912), 62. Bio (15 February 1912), ix. MPW (9 March 1912), 875–876. [400 meters]

Calino, courtier en paratonneres or *Calino's New Invention.* NFM, 35mm, 92 meters. Cin (1 March 1912), 3. CJ (9 March 1912), 74. Bio (21 March 1912), vii. [115 meters]

L'Enlèvement de Bonaparte or *The Kidnapping of Bonaparte.* NFA, 35mm. CJ (30 March 1912), 69. Bio (11 April 1912), vii. [400 meters]

Androclès. LOC, 35mm, 149 feet. CJ (6 April 1912), 71. MPW (3 August 1912), 488. [300 meters]

Bébé juge. NFM, 35mm, 74 meters. CJ (11 May 1912), 69. Cin (17 May 1912), 3. Bio (30 May 1912), xi. [78 meters]

Le Railway de la mort. CG, 35mm, 446 meters. CJ (25 May 1912), 67. Bio (13 June 1912), xiii. MPW (27 July 1912), 345. [470 meters]

Main de fer. CG, 35mm. CJ (3 August 1912), 65. [776 meters]

Main de fer contre la Bande aux "Gants Blancs." CG, 35mm. CJ (14 September 1912), 84. [705 meters]

Onésime a un duel à l'Américaine. GEH, 35mm, 346 feet. CF (3 August 1912), 65. [140 meters]

Le Coeur et l'argent. AF, 35mm, 366 meters. CJ (10 August 1912), 13, 71. Bio (5 September 1912), xv, xvii. [382 meters]

Sur les rails or *4:40 Express.* NFA, 35mm, 850 feet. CJ (17 August 1912), 75. [280 meters]

L'Express matrimonial. NFM, 35mm, 229 meters. CJ (31 August 1912), 79. [290 meters]

Le Nain. CF, 35mm, 229 meters. CJ (31 August 1912), 79. [415 meters]

Onésime aux enfer. GEH, 35mm, 413 feet. CJ (14 September 1912), 84. [164 meters]

Onésime et le chien bienfaisant. MOMA, 16mm. CJ (21 September 1912), 90. GP (4 October 1912). [155 meters]

Calino, chef du gare. NFA, 35mm, 405 feet. CJ (28 September 1912), 86. [144 meters]

Onésime horloger. MOMA, 16mm. CJ (19 October 1912), 81. [140 meters]

L'Oubliette. CF, 35mm, 412 meters. CJ (26 October 1912), 78. [449 meters]

Onésime contre Onésime. AF, 35mm. CJ (9 November 1912), 85. [177 meters]

Onésime gentleman détective. CF, 35mm. CJ (16 November 1912), 89. [214 meters]

Le Mystère des Roches de Kador. NFA, 35mm. CJ (16 November 1912), 89.
GP (29 November 1912). [900 meters]

Les Rivales. CG, 35mm, 142 meters. CJ (23 November 1912), 99. [300 meters]

Le Leçon d'amour. NFM, 35mm, 221 meters. CJ (30 November 1912), 103.
[300 meters]

Sous la griffe or *The Panther's Prey*. NFA, 35mm, 1758 feet. CJ (7 December
1912), 89. [600 meters]

Le Homard. CG, 35mm, 272 meters. CJ (28 December 1912), 89. [300
meters]

Lux   *Cunegonde, femme du monde*. NFM, 35mm, 136 meters. Cin (26 April 1912),
3. CJ (27 April 1912), 64. [140 meters]

Gratitude obsédante. NFM, 35mm, 145 meters. CJ (23 November 1912), 100.
[150 meters]

Pathé   *Un Intrigue à la cour d'Henry VIII d'Angleterre*. LOC, 35mm, 566 feet. BH,
47 (1911), 6–7. CJ (30 December 1911), 60. [800 meters]

La Pipe d'opium. NFM, 35mm, 349 meters. BH, 48 (1911), 7. CJ (6 January
1912), 2, 52. [375 meters]

Vengéance de concierge. NFM, 35mm, 138 meters. CJ (20 January 1912), 64.
[140 meters]

Une maison bien lavée or *The Well-Washed House*. NFA, 35mm, 311 feet. Bio
(11 January 1912), v. Cin (1 March 1912), 3. CJ (15 June 1912), 72.
[105 meters]

La Coupable or *The Anonymous Letter*. CF, 35mm, 188 meters. BH, 52
(1911), 4. CJ (3 February 1912), 62. MPW (13 April 1912), 150, 162.
[215 meters]

Rigadin et la baguette magique. CQ, 35mm. Cin (1 March 1912), 3. CJ
(2 March 1912), 64. [165 meters]

Rigadin avale son ocarina. CF, 35mm. BH, 5 (1912), 6. Bio (25 January 1912),
vii. Cin (15 March 1912), 3. CJ (16 March 1912), 68. [170 meters]

La Mort de Saül. LOC, 35mm, 737 feet. Bio (15 February 1912), 471. CJ
(13 April 1912), 68. MPW (29 June 1912), 1260. [305 meters]

Rigadin défenseur de la vertu. NFA, 35mm, 458 feet. Bio (22 February 1912),
iii. Cin (29 March 1912), 5. CJ (30 March 1912), 70. [170 meters]

Max et son chien Dick. MOMA and EG, 16mm. Bio (22 February 1912), v.
Cin (5 April 1912), 3. CJ (6 April 1912), 72. [195 meters]

L'Or qui brule. NFM, 16mm, 151 meters. BH, 9 (1912), 8–9. Cin (5 April
1912), 3. [515 meters]

A la conquête du pôle or *The Conquest of the Pole*. MOMA, 16mm. Bio
(14 March 1912), iii. Cin (26 April 1912), 3, 6. CJ (27 April 1912), 64.
[650 meters]

L'Ame des Moulins or *The Mills in Joy and Sorrow*. NFM, 35mm, 130 meters.
Bio (4 April 1912), v. Cin (17 May 1912), 3. [180 meters]

Max Linder contre Nick Winter. NFA, 35mm, 741 feet. Bio (11 April 1912), v.
Cin (24 May 1912), 3. CJ (25 May 1912), 68. [420 meters]

L'ane jaloux. NFA, 35mm, 350 feet. Bio (16 May 1912), iii. Cin (21 June
1912), 3. CJ (29 June 1912), 2, 72. [170 meters]

Le Miracle des fleurs. CF, 35mm, 260 meters. Bio (16 May 1912), iii. Cin
(21 June 1912), 3. CJ (29 June 1912), 2, 72. [285 meters]

L'Idylle à la ferme. NFC, 35mm, 197 meters. CJ (10 August 1912), 72. [240 meters]

Boireau domestique. CF, 35mm, 153 meters. CJ (14 September 1912), 85. [165 meters]

Le Petit Chose. CF, 35mm. BH, 38 (1912), 8–9. CJ (19 October 1912), 82. [795 meters]

Boireau, roi de la boxe. CQ, 35mm. CJ (9 November 1912), 86. [180 meters]

Le Signalement or *The Marked Man*. LOC, 35mm, 877 feet. Cin (15 November 1912), 4. CJ (16 November 1912), 90. [310 meters]

Max veut grandir. CQ, 35mm. CJ (23 November 1912), 100. [405 meters]

Les Misérables. CF, 35mm. CJ (30 November 1912), 105. CJ (7 December 1912), 90. CJ (14 December 1912), 94. CJ (21 December 1912), 94. MPW (5 July 1913), 50. [3400 meters]

Boireau cuirassier. CQ, 35mm. CJ (7 December 1912), 90. [140 meters]

Britannicus. AF, 35mm, 492 meters. Cin (13 December 1912). CJ (14 December 1912), 94. [700 meters]

1913

Eclair   *Balaoo*. LOC, 35mm, 852 feet. AF, 35mm, 504 meters. CJ (22 February 1913), 89. [652 meters]

Zigomar, peau d'anguille. NFA, 35mm, 2825 feet. CF, 35mm. CJ (15 March 1913), 94. [995 meters]

Les Trois Willy or *Willy Plays a Part*. NFA, 35mm, 485 feet. Bio (3 July 1913), x. CJ (5 July 1913), 85. [162 meters]

La Bergère d'Ivry. NFM, 35mm, 532 meters. CJ (19 July 1913), 89. [595 meters]

Jack. NFM, 35mm, 1063 meters. CJ (13 September 1913), 97. [1250 meters]

Willy et les Parisiens. LOC, 16mm, 220 feet. CJ (23 August 1913), 101. [170 meters]

Les Gaités de l'escadron. AF, 35mm, 854 meters. CJ (18 November 1913), 113. [920 meters]

La Gueuse. NFM, 35mm. CJ (29 November 1913), 121. [940 meters]

Eclipse   *Shylock*. GEH, 16mm, 1068 feet. CJ (22 February 1913), 89. [642 meters]

La Trouvaille de Polycarpe. NFM, 35mm, 114 meters. CJ (30 August 1913), 101. [129 meters]

Gaumont   *L'Erreur tragique*. AF, 35mm, 475 meters. CJ (11 January 1913), 93. GP (24 January 1913). [530 meters]

Main de fer: l'evasion du forçat de Croze. CG, 35mm. CJ (22 February 1913), 89. [1055 meters]

Les Epingles. NFM, 35mm, 249 meters. CJ (8 February 1913), 89. [275 meters]

Léonce flirte. NFM, 35mm, 305 meters. CJ (8 March 1913), 93. [320 meters]

Léonce en ménage. CF, 35mm. CJ (29 March 1913), 89. [225 meters]

Onésime et son âne. NFM, 35mm, 140 meters. CJ (12 April 1913), 89. [175 meters]

Le Gui. NFM, 35mm, 287 meters. CJ (19 April 1913), 93. [297 meters]

Fantômas. AF, 35mm, 1007 meters. CJ (26 April 1913), 81. [1115 meters]

Léonce pot au feu. CF, 35mm. CJ (24 May 1913), 89. [312 meters]

Onésime début au théâtre. NFM, 35mm, 120 meters. CJ (31 May 1913), 85. [208 meters]

Jeux d'enfants or *Snatched from Death.* NFA, 35mm, 900 feet. CJ (14 June 1913), 105. MPW (18 October 1913), 310, 312. [285 meters]

Le Disaparition d'Onésime. NFA, 35mm, 550 feet. CJ (28 June 1913), 89. [187 meters]

Loup dans la bergèrie. NFM, 35mm, 194 meters. CJ (28 June 1913), 89. [298 meters]

Léonce et Toto. NFM, 35mm, 192 meters. CJ (19 July 1913), 89. [214 meters]

Léonce as a cinematographist. NFA, 35mm, 950 feet. CJ (26 July 1913), 89. [289 meters]

Juve contre Fantômas. MOMA, 16mm. AF, 35mm, 1222 meters. CJ (6 September 1913), 109. [1288 meters]

L'Enfant de Paris or *In the Clutch of the Paris Apaches.* CF, 35mm, 2169 meters. Cin (19 September 1913), 3. CJ (27 September 1913), 66. Com (3 October 1913), 4. MPW (18 October 1913), 246. [2325 meters]

Bout-de-zan et le chemineau. NFA, 35mm, 530 feet. CJ (11 October 1913), 114. GP (24 October 1913). [117 meters]

Léonce à la campagne. GEH, 35mm, 784 feet. CJ (11 October 1913), 114. GP (24 October 1913). [268 meters]

L'Obsession du souvenir. NFM, 260 meters. Cin (17 October 1913), 4. [300 meters]

Bout-de-zan et le lion. NFA, 35mm, 415 feet. CJ (8 November 1913), 94. [140 meters]

Fantômas, Le Mort qui tue. NFA, 35mm. AF, 35mm, 1804 meters. CJ (15 November 1913), 117. [1945 meters]

Calino sourcier. NFM, 35mm, 82 meters. CJ (22 November 1913), 110. [121 meters]

Le Restaurant de l'impasse Canin. CG, 35mm, 138 meters.

Pathé *Max Jockey par amour.* AF, 16mm, 164 meters. CJ (8 March 1913), 94. [365 meters]

La Saucisse mystérieuse. GEH, 35mm, 199 feet. CJ (12 April 1913), 90. [80 meters]

La Broyeuse de coeurs or *A Thief of Hearts.* CF, 35mm. CJ (19 April 1913), 94. Cin (25 April 1913), 8. MPW (10 January 1914), 183. [850 meters]

Max n'aime pas les chats. CQ, 35mm, 129 meters. PJ, 33 (1913). CJ (30 August 1913), 101. [295 meters]

La Fleuriste de Toneso. CF, 35mm. PJ, 30 (1913), 10–11. CJ (11 October 1913), 114. Com (24 October 1913), 4. [1050 meters]

Germinal. CF, 35mm. PJ, 35 (1913), 1–2. Cin (26 September 1913), 3, 8. CJ (27 September 1913), 2, 30–31, 82–83. Com (5 October 1913), 4. CJ (11 October 1913), 85. [3020 meters]

1914

Aubert *Champignol malgré lui.* NFM, 35mm, 266 meters. CJ (7 March 1914), 121. Film (13 March 1914), 28. [1059 meters]

Eclair   *Les Enfants du Capitaine Grant.* NFM, 35mm, 1425 meters. Cin (24 March
         1914). [1770 meters]
         Le Corso rouge. AF, 35mm, 800 meters. FR (8 June 1914), 19. [870 meters]
         Le Roman d'un caissier. NFM, 35mm, 848 meters. Cin (11 July 1914).
         [840 meters]
Eclipse *Anne Boleyn.* LOC, 16mm, 600 feet. CJ (14 January 1914), 101. MPW
         (28 March 1914), 1696. [950 meters]
Gaumont *Bout-de-zan et le crime au téléphone.* NFM, 35mm, 137 meters. CJ (3 January
         1914), 101. GP (16 January 1914). [150 meters]
         Le Roman d'un mousse. RFAB, 35mm. Jour (13 February 1914), 7. GP
         (13 February 1914). CJ (14 February 1914), 92. [c. 2000 meters]
         Fantômas contre Fantômas. NFA, 35mm, 1290 feet. AF, 35mm, 1238 meters.
         CJ (21 February 1914), 121. Var (27 March 1914). [1274 meters]
         Fantômas, le faux magistrat. AF, 35mm, 1153 meters. Jour (8 May 1914), 8.
         GP (8 May 1914). Var (17 July 1914). [1881 meters]
Pathé   *Sacrifice surhumain.* CF, 35mm. PJ, 49 (1913), 6–7. CJ (3 January 1914), 102.
         [875 meters]
         La Lutte pour la vie. NFC, 35mm, 896 meters. PJ, 2 (1914), 8–13. CJ
         (7 February 1914), 122. [1455 meters]
         La Vie et la Passion de Notre Seigneur Jésus Christ. MOMA, 35mm. PJ, 8
         (1914), 9–12. MPW (11 April 1914), 188. [2090 meters]
         Max pédicure. NFA, 35mm, 1075 feet. PJ, 11 (1914). CJ (11 April 1914), 130.
         [335 meters]
         Maudite soit la guerre. NFM-RFAB, 35mm, 850 meters. CJ (16 May 1914),
         134. PJ, 15 (1914), 10–11. Film (3 July 1914), 23. [1050 meters]
         Mari jaloux. AF, 35mm, 378 meters. PJ, 19 (1914). [330 meters]
         Max et la doctoresse. CQ, 35mm. PJ, 22 (1914). CJ (27 June 1914), 110.
         [350 meters]
         Bigorno et le parachute. CQ, 35mm. CJ (18 July 1914), 98. [205 meters]

Notes

Preface

1. Founded in 1987, Domitor is the largest and most important of several groups of scholars and researchers dedicated to the study of early cinema; another is the Association Française de Recherche sur l'Histoire du Cinéma (1985).

2. This is especially evident in several recent books that are otherwise extraordinary—Charles Musser's *Before the Nickelodeon*, Tom Gunning's *D. W. Griffith*, Miriam Hansen's *Babel and Babylon*, and Eileen Bowser's *Transformation of Cinema*. Noël Burch's *Life to those Shadows* is a lone exception to this silence, but his analysis is somewhat sketchy, partly because it is based on a relatively small sampling of films.

3. Fredric Jameson, *The Political Unconscious: Narrative as a Socially Symbolic Act* (Ithaca: Cornell University Press, 1981), 106.

4. Surviving Pathé film prints are supplemented by a great number of scenarios (many of which include a short strip of film) desposited at the Bibliothèque nationale, probably in compliance with a 1907 directive on photographs from the French Minister of Interior—see "Ciné-Nouvelles," *PCG* 45 (1 February 1907), 53. For a brief survey of these deposits, see Emmanuelle Toulet, "Une année de l'édition cinématographique Pathé: 1909," in Guibbert, *Les Premiers Ans du cinéma français*, 133–134.

5. As Paolo Cherchi Usai argues, any film title "restored" by an archive and available for viewing is already a metatext, in that it differs significantly from the master nitrate negative or initial nitrate positive print. Cherchi Usai, "The Film It Might Have Been, or The Analysis of Lacunae as an Exact Science," Society for Cinema Studies Conference, Los Angeles, 25 May 1991.

6. Raymond Williams, *Problems in Materialism and Culture* (London: Verso, 1980), 48.

7. I borrow these terms, respectively, from Michel de Certeau, *The Practice of Everyday Life*, trans. Steven Rendall (Berkeley: University of California Press, 1984), xi–xxiv; and Tony Bennett and Janet Woollacott, *Bond and Beyond: The Political Career of a Popular Hero* (London: Macmillan, 1987), 60.

1: Turn-of-the-Century France

1. E. Brocherioux, ed., *Guide-boussle: Exposition et Paris* (Paris: Paul Ollendorff, 1900); as quoted in Toulet, "Le Cinéma à l'Exposition Universelle de 1900," 179.

2. Maurice Talmeyr, "L'Ecole du Trocadéro," *La Revue des deux mondes* 162 (1 November 1900); quoted in Williams, *Dream Worlds*, 63. See, also, Paul Greenhalgh, *Ephemeral Vistas: The Expositions Universelles, Great Exhibitions and Worlds Fairs, 1851–1939* (Manchester: Manchester University Press, 1988), 83–85.

3. Rearick, *Pleasures of the Belle Epoque*, 132.

4. Material for this and the following paragraphs, unless otherwise indicated, is drawn principally from Mayeur and Rebérioux, *Third Republic*, and from Hobsbawm, *Age of Empire*.

5. "The twelve hundred motor cars which made French roads so hazardous in 1898 were built in sixty factories, of which the largest produced no more than three cars per week." Romein, *Watershed of Two Eras*, 317.

6. MacMillan, *Housewife or Harlot*, 39.

7. The metaphor of cement to describe social cohesion comes from Emile Durkheim, *Les Règles de la méthode sociologique* (Paris: Alcan, 1895).

8. For a thorough analysis of late nineteenth-century female education in France, see Clark, *Schooling the Daughters of Marianne*, 5–80.

9. One of the founding organizers of the universités populaires was the lycée teacher and Radical party "philosopher," Alain. H. Stuart Hughes, *Consciousness and Society: The Reorientation of European Social Thought, 1890–1930* (London: MacGibbon and Kee, 1959), 235.

10. For a brief guide to the major Paris theaters, see A.-P. De Lannoy, *Les Plaisirs de Paris* (Paris: L. Borel, 1900), 51–68.

11. See, for instance, the influence of anarchism on Camille Mauclair, in Williams, *Dream Worlds*, 155–156. French anarchists gained a good deal of notoriety and disapproval with a series of bombings and assassination attempts between 1892 and 1894. See Romein, *Watershed of Two Eras*, 146, and Weber, *France, Fin de Siècle*, 115–118.

12. Guy Debord, *La Société du spectacle* (Paris: Champs libre, 1971), 22. Vanessa Schwartz has done some fascinating research on the daily spectacle offered by the Paris morgue, research first presented in "The Public Taste for Reality: The Morgue, Wax Museums and Early Mass Culture in Fin-de-Siècle Paris," Society for Cinema Studies Conference, New Orleans, 13 February 1993.

13. For a brief guide to Paris café-concerts and music halls, see De Lannoy, *Les Plaisirs de Paris*, 74–78.

14. Berlanstein, *Working People of Paris*, 122, 148–150.

15. Michel Foucault, "Of Other Spaces," *diacritics* 16 (Spring 1986), 22–27. Hansen uses this concept to analyze the historical specificity of the American nickelodeon, in *Babel and Babylon*, 107.

16. As John Higham has argued, immigrant minorities to the United States tended to fight to become part of the nation—see, for instance, Higham's recent work, "The Cumulative Mobilization of Urban Immigrants, 1850–1940," presented to the Seminar in Political History, National Humanities Center, 14 December 1988.

17. Rearick, *Pleasures of the Belle Epoque*, 93.

18. Georges d'Avenal, *Les Mécanismes de la vie moderne*, vol. 1 (Paris: Flammarion, 1902); quoted in Nord, *Paris Shopkeepers*, 149, and Weber, *France, Fin de Siècle*, 71. See, also, Georges d'Avenal, *Le Nivellement des jouissances* (Paris: Flammarion, 1913), 302–303. For an analysis of d'Avenal's writings, see Williams, *Dream Worlds*, 94–106.

19. The term comes from Gabriel Tarde, *L'Opinion et la foule*, 2d ed. (Paris: Félix Alcan, 1904); quoted in Rearick, *Pleasures of the Belle Epoque*, 188. For an analysis of Tarde's writings, see Williams, *Dream Worlds*, 342–384.

20. Sartre, *The Words*, 118–119.

21. The "woman by the hearth" ideal also contrasted with the fact that women actually comprised 37 percent of the French work force in the early 1900s. Mayeur and Rebérioux, *Third Republic*, 340. For the French attitude toward this kind of woman, see Shapiro, "Love Stories," 45–68, and Clark, *Schooling the Daughters of Marianne*, 19. For a particularly fine study of the "new woman" in turn-of-the-century American culture, see Singer, "Female Power," 107–115.

2: The French Cinema Industry, 1896-1914

1. Alan Williams, "The Lumière Organization and 'Documentary Realism'," in Fell, *Film Before Griffith*, 153–161. Recently, Marie and Jacques André suggested that Lumière initially considered developing its lightweight camera-projector for amateurs and tourists, as a corollary to the popular Kodak still camera. "La Prospective internationale de la Cinématographe Lumière: son évolution, son ambiguités (1894–1900)," Deuxième Colloque International de Domitor, Lausanne, 30 June 1992.

2. See the testimony of his brother, Auguste Lumière, cited in Sadoul, *Histoire générale du cinéma*, 1: 210.

3. The first demonstration, on 22 March 1895, was for the Société d'encouragement à l'industrie national. For the inventor's own description of the cinématographe, see Louis Lumière, "The Lumière Cinématographe," in Fielding, *Technological History*, 49–51. For a personal account of one of the first Lumière screenings, see Jeanne, *Cinéma 1900*, 7–14. Antoine Lumière, who arranged the Grand Café presentation, had championed another neologism, *Domitor*, to designate the new apparatus, one that the recently established International Association to Promote the Study of Early Cinema has taken as its name.

4. See, for instance, Paul Genard, "Les opérateurs de la Société Lumière dans le monde," in FIAF, *Le Cinéma français muet dans le monde*, 47–56; Philippe Jacquier, "Un opérateur de la maison Lumière, Gabriel Veyre," in FIAF, *Le Cinéma français muet dans le monde*, 57–60; and Jean-Paul Seguin-Vergara, "La légende Promio (1868–1926)," *1895* 11 (1992), 94–100.

5. Dureau, "Un Point d'Histoire: quelles ont été les premières vues projetées," *CJ* 244 (26 April 1913), 4–5. For an extensive study of the documents surrounding this film, and its several versions, see Bernard Chardère, "1895 . . . ou 1894?" *1895* 11 (1992), 3–18. For a thorough analysis of the Lumière company's early experience in the United States, see Musser, *Emergence of Cinema*, 135–145.

6. Toulet, "Le Cinéma à l'Exposition Universelle de 1900," 186–188.

7. Alan Williams suggests that Lumière's interest in the cinema may have declined because the company lost out to Edison, as a result of the latter's economic pressure and intimidation, in the American market. Citing Mesguich's own testimony, Musser suggests that legal difficulties were partly responsible for Lumière's abandonment of the American market. Musser, *Emergence of Cinema*, 177.

8. Guy Olivo, "La Production Gaumont éditée au début du siècle en cartes postales," *1895* 2 (1987), 15–18.

9. See the Gaumont ad in *NYC* (27 December 1902), 985. See, also, "Who's Who: L. Gaumont & Co.," *KLW* 1 (16 May 1907), 7; Michael Chanan, "Economic Conditions of Early Cinema," in Elsaesser, *Early Cinema*, 182; and Musser, *Emergence of Cinema*, 489.

10. The Phono-Cinéma-Théâtre had lost nearly 150,000 francs after two months of exhibition, probably because of the poor quality of both its image and sound. Toulet, "Le Cinéma à l'Exposition Universelle de 1900," 198–200.

11. See Léon Gaumont, "Gaumont Chronochrome Process Described by the Inventor," in Fielding, *Technological History*, 65–67.

12. Jehanne d'Alcy, Méliès's second wife, lists some of these publicity films in "Transcripts of the Round-table on Georges Méliès Held at the Cinémathèque Française (Paris, June 17, 1944)," in Cherchi Usai, *A Trip to the Movies*, 151.

13. See the Lubin and Edison ads in *NYC*, from May 1902 through February 1903, and the first Star-Film ad in *NYC* (6 June 1903), 368. See, also, Musser, *Emergence of Cinema*, 277, 364.

14. The information in this paragraph, unless otherwise noted, comes from Binet and Hausser, *Les Sociétés de cinématographe*; Pathé, *De Pathé-Frères à Pathé-Cinéma*; Sadoul, *Histoire générale du cinéma*, 2; and Pathé-Frères's annual stockholder meeting reports (1900, 1902, 1903, 1904). Carton 1, Pathé-Archives.

15. The Pathé and Méliès versions of the eruption of Mont Pélé in Martinique may have sold as many as one thousand copies throughout the world. Leclerc, *Le Cinéma, temoin de son temps*, 20.

16. "Faria," *Cin* (20 September 1912), 1.

17. Both Méliès and Gaumont had produced a total of seven thousand meters of negative film stock each by 1902; Pathé's production outpaced them exponentially in just one year.

18. The information in this and the next paragraph, unless otherwise noted, is drawn from Deslandes, *Le Boulevard du cinéma*; and Deslandes and Richard, *Histoire comparée du cinéma*, 2.

19. Schwartz and Meusy, "Le Musée Grévin et le Cinématographe," 20.

20. Reynaud had given nearly thirteen thousand performances to a half-million spectators at the Musée Grévin by 1900. Liesegang, *Dates and Sources*, 52-53. See Pierre Bracquemond, "Emile Reynaud: peintre de films," *La Cinémathèque française* 12 (August 1986), 8-10; Glenn Myrent, "Emile Reynaud: First Motion Picture Cartoonist," *Film History* 3.3 (1989), 191-202; and Schwartz and Meusy, "Le Musée Grévin et le Cinématographe," 26-27.

21. The thirty-minute program of Lumière films at the Café de Paris, for instance, cost one franc. Leclerc, *Le Cinéma, temoin de son temps*, 11; and Gili, "Les Débuts du spectacle cinématographique en France," 23-24.

22. This view was first expressed in Francis Mair, "Les Etablissements Pathé," *Phono-Gazette* 4 (15 May 1905), 57.

23. Thierry Lefebvre, "Le cas étrange du Dr Doyen," *Archives* 29 (February 1990), 3. Doyen also arranged for Ambroise-François Parnaland to record several operations with a very different camera.

24. Jean-Jacques Meusy, "L'Enigme du Cinéorama de l'Exposition Universelle de 1900," *Archives* 37 (January 1991).

25. The committee that selected the Exposition exhibits in the photography category included only two men associated with the cinema—Louis Lumière and Etienne Jules Marey.

26. The Berlin office was run by Théophile Pathé, the estranged brother of Charles and Emile Pathé.

27. Just one tableau for the *Damnation du Docteur Faust* took eight days to prepare and shoot and cost 3,200 francs. By contrast, the entire cost of *Le Voyage dans la lune*, two years earlier, had been 10,000 francs. Malthête-Méliès, *Méliès l'enchanteur*, 268.

28. Lucien Astaix, one of Méliès's cameramen, speaks of how specialized Méliès had become during this period and of how overextended he himself also felt, having to do all the projections at the theaters and music halls. "Transcript of the Round-table on Georges Méliès," 153, 155.

29. It is worth noting that Gaumont did not abandon the technological side of the

industry—in fact, beginning in September 1905, the company's ads in *PCG*, rather than advertise film titles, consistently promoted the apparatuses it manufactured.

30. The term, "glass cathedral," comes from Kress, *Conférences sur la cinématographie*, 34. For further information on the early use of artificial lighting, see Salt, *Film Style and Technology*, 73, 76.

31. During this period, Gaumont films were distributed in the United States chiefly through Star-Films as well as American Mutoscope and Biograph.

32. [Edmond Benoît-Lévy], "A nos lecteurs," *PCG* 13 (1 October 1905), 197.

33. Binet and Hausser, *Les Sociétés de cinématographe*, 17–18.

34. Sadoul, *Histoire générale du cinéma*, 2: 261–262.

35. See the Pathé ad in *PCG* 13 (1 October 1905), 209; and Sadoul, *Histoire générale du cinéma*, 2: 225, 259, 263.

36. See *PCG* 40 (15 November 1906) and the Pathé ad in *NYC* (24 November 1906), 1070.

37. Another report, from the same period, put the number of Pathé employees at 3,000. "Who's Who: Pathé-Frères," *KLW* 2 (23 May 1907), 22. Méliès himself employed up to 220 women for coloring prints, under the supervision of Mme Thullier and Mme Chaumont. Malthête-Méliès, Quévrain, and Malthête, *Essai du reconstitution*, 10.

38. The subject of the labor union movement's involvement in the early cinema industry in France is yet to be examined.

39. Staiger identified four stages in the development of American film production: cameraman (1896–1907), director (1907–1909), director-unit (1909–1914), and central producer (1914–1931). Staiger, "The Director System: Management in the First Years," in Bordwell et al., *Classical Hollywood Cinema*, 116–141. Musser has challenged this schema by arguing that, between 1907 and 1909, American film production moved rapidly from a collaborative system (involving cameraman and stage manager) to a central producer system. Musser, "Pre-Classical American Cinema: Its Changing Modes of Production," *Persistence of Vision* 9 (1991), 46–65. In France, according to these categories, each company initially worked under a different system: Lumière (cameraman), Gaumont (collaborative), Méliès and Pathé (collaborative, but with an emphasis on the director). Pathé instituted a "director-unit" system of production around 1904–1905, but Zecca's supervisory role never approached that of a central producer.

40. Sadoul, *Histoire générale du cinéma*, 2: 223–225.

41. Robert Allen locates this change from actualités to story films in the United States between 1905 and 1906. Allen, *Vaudeville and Film*, 218. Musser and Hansen locate it in 1904. Musser, *Before the Nickelodeon*, 276–277, 284; Hansen, *Babel and Babylon*, 44. The Kleine Optical catalog (November 1905), reprinted in Pratt, *Spellbound in Darkness*, 41—tends to support Musser and Hansen.

42. The journal began as *Phono-Gazette* (1 April 1905), devoted exclusively to the phonograph business, but, in six months, it changed to *Phono-Ciné-Gazette* (1 October 1905), in order to include the cinema as well. The journal's new objectives were to provide information about patents, legal decisions, technological innovations, industry changes, and new film titles; to defend and encourage the industry as a whole; and to initiate the public into the many pleasures of the cinema. "Extension de notre but," *PCG* 13 (1 October 1905), 197.

43. France exported more automobiles than any other country before 1914. See Caron, *An Economic History of Modern France*, 107, 108.

44. [Benoît-Lévy], "A nos lecteurs," 197.

45. "Informations financières: Pathé-Frères," *PCG* 78 (15 June 1908), 631. Gaumont quickly followed Pathé in opening agencies in many of these cities. Binet and Hausser, *Les Sociétés de cinématographe*, 33.

46. See the 1 July letter from Pathé-Frères to Edison, the 21 July letter from Frank Dyer to W. E. Gilmore, and the 1 November McCoy Report of the Edison Legal Department, in the 1904 Motion Pictures Folder, ENHS.

47. Musser, *Before the Nickelodeon*, 279.

48. Between November 1902 and March 1905, Edison brought nearly thirty patent suits against its competitors. See the 1905 Motion Pictures Folder, ENHS.

49. Musser, *Emergence of Cinema*, 412.

50. See the Edison ad in *NYC* (12 July 1902), 444, as well as the contrasting Edison and Pathé ads in *NYC* (5 August 1905), 612; and (30 September 1905), 800. See, also, William E. Swanson's testimony in *United States vs. MPPC*, vol. 1 (1914), 322.

51. See, for instance, *Billboard* (13 October 1906), 21; the Pathé ads in *PCG* 40 (15 November 1906), n.p., and *NYC* (24 November 1906), 1070; and "Editorial: What Does It Mean?" *MPW* 1 (26 October 1907), 536. By contrast, Vitagraph was releasing just one "headliner" film per week. Musser, *Before the Nickelodeon*, 334. Pathé also was aided by George Kleine Optical of Chicago, another major distributor of its films—see the Kleine purchases, from 1904 to 1907, reprinted in Musser, *Before the Nickelodeon*, 482–483.

52. Edward Wagenknecht, *The Movies in the Age of Innocence* (Norman: University of Oklahoma, 1962), 12. See, for instance, "The Nickelodeon," *MPW* 1 (4 May 1907) 140; "Trade Notes," *MPW* 1 (11 May 1907), 152–153; and "The Nickel Madness," *Harpers Weekly* (24 August 1907)—reprinted in *MPW* 1 (5 October 1907), 484–485.

53. *PC* (Paris, 1907), 3. "Notes from Manufacturers: Pathé," *MPW* 7 (16 July 1910), 165.

54. See the article from *Le Petit Parisien* reprinted in *PCG* 19 (1 June 1906), 214.

55. The best studies of the French fairground cinemas can be found in Deslandes and Richard, *Histoire comparée du cinéma*, 2: 135–249; and Sadoul, *Histoire générale du cinéma*, 2: 335–346. At least one writer singled out the De Dion electric generator as a principal reason for the French fairground cinemas' success. "Strolling Notes in France," *KLW* 12 (1 August 1907), 183.

56. Berneau, "Les Débuts du spectacle cinématographique à Bordeaux," 18–32.

57. Although the first nickelodeon opened in Pittsburgh, in June 1905, their numbers multiplied greatly, especially in the Midwest, between March and October, 1906. See Allen, *Vaudeville and Film*, 201; Musser, *Before the Nickelodeon*, 325–329; and Gomery, *Shared Pleasures*, 18–33. The nickelodeon boom produced its own trade paper, *Views and Film Index*, initially sponsored by Vitagraph and Pathé, and first published on 25 April 1906. Musser, *Emergence of Cinema*, 424. That Pathé could list fifty-eight new and recent film titles for sale, compared to fifteen for Vitagraph, nine for Edison, and six for Biograph, in January 1907, was one clear sign of its success in the nickelodeon market. "Popular Films," *VFI* (5 January 1907), 9.

58. On 15 August, 1905, Pathé ads suddenly began to take up one quarter of a tabloid-size page in *L'Industriel forain*.

59. In the spring of 1907, one major Paris fair housed as many as twenty-eight

cinemas, nearly all of which were showing Pathé films, but without using the company's name. "Ciné-Nouvelles," *PCG* 50 (15 April 1907), 153.

60. See "Ciné-Nouvelles," *PCG* 21 (1 February 1906), 56; "Le Cinématographe officiel," *PCG* 30 (15 June 1906), 233; and Guido Convents, "Documentaries and Propaganda Before 1914," *Framework* 35 (1988), 107.

61. Maxime Leproust, "Le Théâtre-Cinéma," *PCG* 43 (1 January 1907), 13–14. "Trade Notes from France," *KLW* 1 (16 May 1907), 2. Rémy de Gourmont, "Epilogues: Cinématographe," *Mercure de France* (1 September 1907), reprinted in Abel, *French Film Theory and Criticism*, 1: 47–50. Marcel Baudoin, "Le Cinématographe au théâtre," *PCG* 65 (1 December 1907), 418. André Maurel, "Le Suicide du théâtre," *Gil Blas*, reprinted in *PCG* 76 (15 May 1908), 595.

62. Quoted in "Les Comédiens et le cinéma," *APC* 62 (7 March 1908), 6.

63. François Valleiry, "Les Cinématographes de Paris," *PCG* 49 (1 April 1907), 131. J. B., "Le Cinématographe," *L'Ochestre* (12 July 1907). "Le Cinéma Pathé," *Com* (1 February 1908), 4. Louis Schneider, "Les Théâtres de Paris," *Etoile Belge*, reprinted in *PCG* 82 (15 August 1908), 693–694.

64. E. Benoît-Lévy, "Causerie sur le cinématographe," *PCG* 63 (1 November 1907), 382.

65. Georges Prud'homme, "Trop de . . . Pathé," *Paris Moderne* (3 August 1908), quoted in Crafton, *Emile Cohl*, 99. The final line in this limerick puns on pâté, alluding to Pathé's origins in a family of butchers.

66. Hunnings, *Film Censors and the Law*, 332–333; and Léglise, *Histoire de la Politique du cinéma française*, 29.

67. Jeanne and Ford, *Histoire encyclopédique du cinéma*, 1: 78.

68. Georges Dureau, "La Guillotine devant le cinématographe," *CJ* 22 (14 January 1909), 3–4.

69. Quoted in Edelman, *Ownership of the Image*, 48.

70. "Les Sujets de cinématographe," *Fas* 46 (1 October 1906), 328–329. For a thorough appraisal of this "crisis," see Sadoul, *Histoire générale du cinéma*, 2: 439–447.

71. As late as November 1904, a Pau court rejected the claim of a local banker that he could be the author of a short documentary on the miracles at Lourdes. Maugras and Guegan, *Le Cinématographe devant le droit*, 100–105.

72. Maugras and Guegan, *Le Cinématographe devant le droit*, 105–110.

73. Fernand Divoire, "Le Cinématographe et les auteurs," *PCG* 44 (15 January 1907), 32–33; "Ciné-Nouvelles," *PCG* 52 (15 May 1907), 190; Pierre Le Roux, "Chronique judiciaire," *APC* 74 (30 May 1908), 8; "Chronique judiciaire: Le Cinématographe et les droits d'auteur," *APC* 78 (27 June 1908), 5–6; "French News," *VFI* (25 July 1908), 9; "Les Auteurs et le cinématographe," *PCG* 81 (1 August 1908), 679; and "Procès des auteurs contre le cinématographe," *PCG* 84 (15 September 1908), 726–727.

74. Maugras and Guegan, *Le Cinématographe devant le droit*, 115–118.

75. Mair, "A la compagnie Pathé: la nouvelle situation," *PCG* 56 (15 July 1907), 270. Benoît-Lévy often wrote under the pseudonym of Francis Mair as well as François Vaillery.

76. Benoît-Lévy, "Le Droit d'auteur cinématographique," *PCG* 62 (15 October 1907), 365. See, also, "Propriété littéraire," *PCG* 79 (1 July 1908), 645.

77. Maugras and Guégan, *Le Cinématographe devant le droit*, 25–28.

78. "Jurisprudence photographique," *CJ* 25 (4 February 1909), 7–9. See especially

Article 14 in the Berlin Commission's revision, reprinted in "Jurisprudence photographique," *CJ* 35 (17 April 1909), 9. See, also, Maugras and Guegan, *Le Cinématographe devant le droit*, 2–33, 127–139.

79. Paul Franz, "L'Art populaire," *Phono-Gazette* 1 (1 April 1905), 14–15; "Ciné-Nouvelles," *PCG* 24 (15 March 1906), 111; Benoît-Lévy, "Communication sur le cinématographe et l'instruction publique," *PCG* 86 (15 October 1908), 757–758. For a biographical sketch of Benoît-Lévy, see Jeanne, *Cinéma 1900*, 97–105. Beginning in 1908, W. Stephen Bush would play a similar role as reviewer and then editor of *MPW* in the United States. See Stromgren, "Moving Picture World," 15.

80. Valleiry, "Au pays du cinématographe: La Chine," *PCG* 18 (15 December 1905), 305–306; Valleiry, "Les Cinématographes de Paris," 131.

81. Valleiry, "Notre festival phono-cinématographique au Trocadéro," *PCG* 27 (1 May 1906), 105–106; "Programme de la fête cinématographique et phonographique," *PCG* 28 (15 May 1906), 191.

82. Valleiry, "Le Première fête cinématographique," *PCG* 29 (1 June 1906), 210–211; Mair, "La Deuxième Soirée du Trocadéro," *PCG* 30 (15 June 1906), 229–230.

83. "Ciné-Nouvelles: Grand Fête de *Phono-Ciné*," *PCG* 51 (1 May 1907), 172; Charles Delac, "Grand Fête du *Phono-Ciné*," *PCG* 52 (15 May 1907), 185. Benoît-Lévy also briefly set up what he called a *ciné-club* or information center in the spring of 1907. "Le Ciné-Club," *PCG* 50 (15 April 1907), 145.

84. Benoît-Lévy, "Le Droit d'auteur cinématographique," *PCG* 62 (15 October 1907), 365–366. Maugras and Guegan, *Le Cinématographe devant le droit*, 19–20.

85. See "Cinéma et Théâtre," *PCG* 44 (15 January 1907), 32; Fernand Divoire, "Le Cinématographe et les auteurs," *PCG* 44 (15 January 1907), 32–33; and "Les Auteurs cinématographiques," *PCG* 83 (1 September 1908), 709. In the New York–Philadelphia area of the United States, Bush adopted the strategy of lecturing on film adaptations of literary classics. Stromgren, "Moving Picture World," 17.

86. "Ciné-Nouvelles," *PCG* 52 (15 May 1907), 190; and 53 (1 June 1907), 211; and Valleiry, "Théâtre des Variétés," *PCG* 56 (15 July 1907), 270–271.

87. Pathé's "monopoly" strategy was rather unusual within the context of French industry at the time for powerful cartels only existed in the chemical and aluminum industries. For further information on the general structure of French industry before the war, see Caron, *An Economic History of Modern France*, 167–171.

88. Benoît-Lévy's own associates included Charles Dussaud, Maurice Guegan, and E. Maugras. See "Société pour exploiter le Cinématographe Pathé-Frères," *PCG* 46 (15 February 1907), 74, and "Documents financières," *PCG* 54 (15 June 1907), 230.

89. "Ciné-Nouvelles," *PCG* 41 (1 December 1906), 453; and 42 (15 December 1906), 474.

90. "Ciné-Nouvelles," *PCG* 42 (15 December 1906), 474; "Nouveaux Cinémas," *PCG* 44 (15 January 1907), 33; Valleiry, "Les Cinémas de Paris," *PCG* 53 (1 June 1907), 210.

91. The number of spectators visiting the Paris morgue annually ran as high as one million. Schwartz, "The Public Taste for Reality."

92. See the Théâtre Pathé ad reproduced in *PCG* 41 (1 December 1906), 456; Valleiry, "Les Cinémas de Paris," *PCG* 53 (1 June 1907), 210; "Trade Notes from France," *KLW* 4 (6 June 1907), 80; and "Ciné-Nouvelles," *PCG* 55 (1 July 1907), 253.

93. This poster is reproduced in Toulet, "Les Spectacles cinématographiques à Paris de 1895 à 1914," 558–559.

94. C. C., "Une Première au Cinéma-Palace," *APC* 86 (22 August 1908), 4–5. See, also, Berneau, "Les Débuts du spectacle cinématographique à Bordeaux," 26–31.

95. "Ciné-Nouvelles," *PCG* 51 (1 May 1907), 172; Louis Morénas, "Compagnie des Cinéma-Halls," *PCG* 57 (1 August 1907), 288.

96. "Recettes des Théâtres de Paris en 1909," *Com* (17 June 1910), 4.

97. "Ciné-Nouvelles," *PCG* 65 (1 December 1907), 418; and 67 (1 January 1908), 452.

98. See "Picture Shows in Paris," *Bio* 188 (19 May 1910), 5–7; and Charles Mendel, fils, "The French Cinematograph Trade," *Bio* 263 (26 October 1911), 219, 221.

99. See "Le Gaumont-Palace à l'Hippodrome de Paris," *CJ* 161 (23 September 1911), 19, and "Comment l'Hippodrome devient le 'Gaumont-Palace'," *CJ* 163 (7 October 1911), 9, 11.

100. In the summer of 1908, for instance, the annual fair in Lille was reported to have thirty cinema shows. "Facts from France," *KLW* 71 (17 September 1908), 421.

101. "Appeal aux exploitants," *APC* 59 (15 February 1908), 3–6; "Revue financière: Société générale des cinématographes forains," *APC* 71 (9 May 1908), 13; E. Chabot, "Un Congrès d'exploitants de cinématographe," *APC* 75 (6 June 1908), 7–9; "L'Ecole foraine," *CJ* 4 (8 September 1908), 3. Compare the argument in favor of permanent cinemas, in Valleiry, "La Location des vues," *PCG* 70 (15 February 1908), 497.

102. Dureau, "Notre dernière campagne," *CJ* 19 (24 December 1908), 5–6; Berneau, "Les Débuts du spectacle cinémtographique à Bordeaux," 26–31.

103. Schneider, "Les Théâtres de Paris," 693; Rearick, *Pleasures of the Belle Epoque*, 95.

104. "Ciné-Nouvelles," *PCG* 46 (15 February 1907), 71; and "Picture Shows in Paris," *Bio* 188 (19 May 1910), 5.

105. Berlanstein, *Working People of Paris*, 130–131.

106. "Nos Recettes," *Cin* (3 May 1912), 2.

107. "Ciné-Nouvelles," *PCG* 64 (15 November 1907), 402; and "La location des films aux Etats-Unis," *CJ* 1 (15 August 1908), 7. One of the best descriptions of the American nickelodeon can be found in Joseph Medill Patterson, "The Nickelodeons, The Poor Man's Elementary Course in Drama," *Saturday Evening Post* 180 (23 November 1907), 10–11, 88, reprinted in Pratt, *Spellbound in Darkness*, 46, 48–52.

108. In Bordeaux, one cinema had a Monday matinee, another added a Thursday morning program, and tickets were either free or sharply reduced for all children who attended accompanied by parents. Berneau, "Les débuts du spectacle cinématographique à Bordeaux," 24, 26–27. Thursday matinees for children could be found in Paris as early as 1907, and children's matinees were popular in both the United States and England as well. See, for instance, "French Notes," *MPW* 1 (9 November 1907), 576; "Revue financière: Compagnie des Cinéma-Halls," *APC* 65 (29 March 1908), 14; and "Topics of the Week: Special Pictures for Children," *Bio* 162 (18 November 1909), 4.

109. Toulet, "Les Spectacles cinématographiques à Paris de 1895 à 1914," 410; Berlanstein, *Working People of Paris*, 125–127, 130–131.

110. See the Grands Magazins Dufayel ad in *Com* (5 January 1909), 6; Miller, *Bon Marché*, 178; and Berlanstein, *Working People of Paris*, 133.

111. See the excerpt from a front-page article in *Le Petit Parisien*, reprinted in *PCG* 29 (1 June 1906), 214–215; "Ciné-Nouvelles," *PCG* 46 (15 February 1907), 71; and "Picture Shows in Paris," *Bio* 188 (19 May 1910), 5. These matinee screenings differed from

the special evening screenings of Georges Méliès féeries such as *Les Quatre Cent Farces du Diable* at the Châtelet.

112. G. de Pawlowski, "Le Spectacle court," *Com* (13 January 1910), 1; and "Music Halls," *Com* (27 April 1910), 5. The American Biograph cinema was owned by Raleigh & Robert. "Echos," *CJ* 87 (23 April 1910), 4.

113. Dureau, "La Triomphe du cinématographe," *CJ* 149 (1 July 1911), 3–4. The Omnia-Pathé had succeeded in attracting such a public as early as 1910. "Music Halls: Omnia-Pathé," *Com* (3 June 1910), 4.

114. Mair, "A la Compagnie Pathé: la nouvelle situation," 270. The decision also was announced in "Trade Notes," *MPW* 1 (9 November 1907), 576–577. For further information on how this system worked, see "Un Document," *APC* 82 (25 July 1908), 4–5. Rental exchanges for used films, of course, were already operating in the United States, with the Miles Brothers being perhaps the earliest. See Albert E. Smith's testimony in *United States vs. MPPC*, vol. 3 (1914), 1702–1703.

115. See the announcement of the first of these, the Cinéma-Omnia, in "Information financières," *PCG* 58 (15 August 1907), 304–305.

116. Pathé-Frères ad, *PCG* 74 (15 April 1908), 564. See, also, Binet and Hausser, *Les Sociétés de cinématographe*, 20.

117. Leproust, "Le Théâtre-Cinéma," 14. François Valleiry, "Le cinématographe au Salon de l'Automobile," *PCG* 67 (1 January 1908), 449–451. Edison's rather unreliable spy in France, F. Desbrière, reported that Pathé was considering such an automobile service as early as 1905; at first skeptical of the idea, he was convinced of its success by the summer of 1907. See his 31 March 1905 and 5 September 1907 letters to Edison's British agent, Croydon-Marks, in the 1905 and 1907 Motion Picture Folders, ENHS.

118. "Concessions à perpétuité: le *Monopole* est en caoutchouc," *APC* 65 (29 March 1908), 5–6; G. F., "Révolution? . . . Non. Evolution? . . . Oui!," *APC* 67 (11 April 1908), 3–5.

119. See, for instance, "Notes from Paris," *KLW* 13 (8 August 1907), 201.

120. See, for instance, Marette, "Les Procédés de coloriage mécanique," 3–4; Patterson, "The Nickelodeon," 49; and Binet and Hausser, *Les Sociétés de cinématographe*, 81–82.

121. See, for instance, the Pathé ad in *MPW* 4 (3 April 1909), 350; and "Pathé Machines on United States Warships," *MPW* 6 (28 May 1910), 885. For a good description of the Pathé studio camera, see Salt, *Film Style and Technology*, 68.

122. See the Pathé ad in *Filma* 10 (December 1908) and in *CJ* 37 (29 April 1909).

123. See the Pathé ad in *CJ* 98 (9 July 1910), 2.

124. "Items of Interest," *Bio* 133 (29 April 1909), 7; "Pathé Notes," *MPW* 6 (26 March 1910), 469; and the first Pathé ad in *CJ* 90 (14 May 1910), 17.

125. "Nos Auteurs et le cinéma: M. Daniel Riche," *Cin* (7 June 1912), 1.

126. See, especially, "Max Linder, The Inimitable," *VFI* (16 July 1910), 3; Georges Fagot, "Max Linder," *CJ* 101 (30 July 1910), 17; and the Pathé ad for both Linder and Prince, in *CJ* 107 (10 September 1910), 2.

127. See the Pathé ad for the Comica series in *CJ* 121 (7 December 1910), 2; and "Comica," *Cin* (14 June 1912), 4.

128. Fagot, "La Cinématographie des microbes," *CJ* 96 (25 June 1910), 17. One of Pathé's chief engineers, Labrély, also was working on slow-motion cinematography.

129. Fagot, "*Pathé-Journal*," *CJ* 93 (4 June 1910), 19. Initially, the newsreel was titled *Pathé Faits Divers*, but that was changed in March 1909.

130. See the Kleine Optical ads in *NYC* (2 February 1907), 1320, 1332. The earliest

issues of *MPW*—for instance, March through June 1907—also give prominent attention to Gaumont films being distributed by George Kleine Optical and imply that the distribution arrangement went back several months.

131. Binet and Hausser, *Les Sociétés de cinématographe*, 35.

132. One indication of Alice Guy's eclipse—which certainly stems, at least in part, from the cultural refusal to consider women as artists—is the almost complete absence of any reference to her in early French film histories. See Guy's own comment on this eclipse, in an interview in the *New York Dramatic Mirror* (6 November 1912), reprinted in Victor Bachy, "Alice Guy, les raisons d'un effacement," in Guibbert, *Les Premiers Ans du cinéma français*, 27.

133. Selected letters are reprinted in Lacassin, *Pour un Contre Histoire du cinéma*, 59–63.

134. Arnaud and Cohl's animation films were the subject of a survey of filmmaking practices at the Gaumont studio, in Gustave Babin, "Les Coulisses du cinématographe," *L'Illustration* (28 March and 4 April 1908), summarized in "A Travers la presse," *PCG* 74 (15 April 1908), 565.

135. The first *Gaumont-Actualités* was released on 21 October 1910. See the Gaumont ad in *CJ* 113 (22 October 1910), 24. See, also, the reviews of Gaumont's films of the Shackleton and Pointing polar expeditions, respectively, in "Notes d'Italie," *CJ* 75 (23 January 1910), 7; and "My View of Things," *Bio* 263 (26 October 1911), 201.

136. See "French Films on the American Market," *MPW* 6 (12 February 1910), 203; and "The Qualitative Picture: Influence of the French School of Picture Making," *MPW* 6 (25 June 1910), 1089–1090.

137. See the first Comptoir Ciné-Location ad in *CJ* 38 (6 May 1909), 8.

138. "Chronique financière: Gaumont," *CJ* 42 (5 June 1909), 9–10.

139. See the rebuttal to Méliès's attack on the industrialization of the cinema, in Valleiry, "Doit-on le dire? Reponse à M. Méliès," *PCG* 78 (15 June 1908), 628. By late 1906, in contrast to Pathé's mass production, Méliès was calling attention to his own creative individualism, insisting on having composed the scenario, trick effects, and decors, for instance, in *Les Quat' Cents Farces du Diable*. See the Méliès ad in *PCG* 38 (15 October 1906), 399. See, also, the testimony of cameraman Lucien Astaix in "Transcripts of the Round-table on Georges Méliès," 157.

140. Until recently, it was mistakenly believed that this second studio was erected in 1905. Malthête, "Le second studio de Georges Méliès à Montreuil-sous-Bois," 67–72.

141. "Burglars Break In and Steal," *MPW* 1 (25 May 1907), 188. For more information on Gaston Méliès, see McInroy, "The American Méliès," 250–254; and Jacques Malthête, "Biographie de Gaston Méliès," *1895* 7 (1990), 85–90.

142. For more information on Gaston Méliès's apparent deception of his brother, see Bowser, *Transformation of Cinema*, 30. Jehanne d'Alcy speaks bitterly about Gaston Méliès's deceit in "Transcripts of the Round-table on Georges Méliès," 151, 165.

143. Ads for Méliès's films disappear from *PCG* even earlier, around November 1908.

144. Both Jehanne d'Alcy and Lucien Astaix bitterly denounce Pathé and Zecca's "sabotage" of Méliès's last films in "Transcripts of the Round-table on Georges Méliès," 159.

145. Binet and Hausser, *Les Sociétés de cinématographe*, 41. The earliest reference to Eclipse film titles came in *PCG* 39 (1 November 1906), 413.

146. Binet and Hausser, *Les Sociétés de cinématographe*, 44–45.

147. The figure comes from "Revue financière: Eclipse," *APC* 60 (22 February 1908), 13.

148. "Société générale des cinématographes 'Eclipse'," *CJ* 2 (25 August 1908), 7–9.

149. See the George Kleine ad in *MPW* 4 (16 January 1909), 54. No less than sixteen films, most of them comic shorts and actualités, were released by Eclipse in the first week of January 1910. "Nouveautés," *CJ* 72 (3 January 1910), 19.

150. Another small production company, Le Soleil, made a number of short films in Marseille during this period.

151. "Ciné-Nouvelles," *PCG* 51 (1 May 1907), 171–172. See, also, Binet and Hausser, *Les Sociétés de cinématographe*, 57–63.

152. Promio assumed outright control of the company within six months. "French and American Tall Talk," *KLW* 13 (8 August 1907), 196. This was probably due to the court case that pitted Théophile versus his brothers over the use of the Pathé name. "Trade Notes from France," *KLW* 3 (30 May 1907), 44. In any case, the company only produced films for another two years and was finally dissolved in 1910. "Echos," *CJ* 97 (2 July 1910), 4.

153. "Ciné-Nouvelles," *PCG* 52 (15 May 1907), 190; "Informations financières," *PCG* 52 (15 May 1907), 195. See, also, Binet and Hausser, *Les Sociétés de cinématographe*, 53–54.

154. See "Ciné-Nouvelles," *PCG* 84 (15 September 1908), 728; "News from America," *Bio* 163 (25 November 1909), 23; and "The Lux Films," *MPW* 6 (8 January 1910), 20–21.

155. See the Lux ad in *CJ* 27 (18 February 1910), 11.

156. See "Informations financières," *PCG* 76 (15 May 1908), 600–601; "Compagnie des cinématographes 'Le Lion'," *CJ* 8 (6 October 1908), 7–8; and Binet and Hausser, *Les Sociétés de cinématographe*, 70–71. *Ciné-Journal* provided a measure of support to Le Lion by letting the company advertise on its front covers throughout 1909 and 1910.

157. See "Incendie des usines de la maison Raleigh et Robert," *CJ* 36 (23 April 1909), 2–3; and "Raleigh & Robert Burned Out," *MPW* 4 (15 May 1909), 631.

158. "Informations financières," *PCG* 56 (15 July 1907), 272–274; Binet and Hausser, *Les Sociétés de cinématographe*, 64–65; and Benedicte Salomon, "La Société française des films et cinématographes Eclair, de 1907 à 1918," Université de Paris, 1987. For information on Eclair, see the dossier collected by Henri Bousquet and Laurent Mannoni in *1895* 12 (October 1992) and the essays edited by Richard Abel and Lorenzo Codelli in *Griffithiana* 47 (May 1993).

159. Binet and Hausser, *Les Sociétés de cinématographe*, 65. Eclair's studio measured thirty-five meters in length and twelve meters in height. Deslandes, "Victorin-Hippolyte Jasset," 251. See, also, Crafton, *Emile Cohl*, 158.

160. Binet and Hausser, *Les Sociétés de cinématographe*, 44–45.

161. Deslandes, "Victorin-Hippolyte Jasset," 249–251.

162. Deslandes, "Victorin-Hippolyte Jasset," 251–252.

163. Dureau, for instance, included the first *Nick Carter* films among his list of models for French film production. "Le Cinéma et le théâtre," *CJ* 5 (15 September 1908), 2.

164. Some measure of this Eclair film series success can be gathered from "Latest from Paris," *KLW* 78 (5 November 1908), 627; and "Avant *Nick Carter*," *Com* (2 November 1909), 2. See, also, "Pierre Bressol," *Cin* (17 January 1913), 1.

165. Dureau first attributed the origins of the films en séries to Eclair. See Dureau, "Les Films en séries," *CJ* 159 (9 September 1911), 3–4.

166. Coissac, *Histoire du cinématographe*, 503; and Salomon, "La Société française des films et cinématographes Eclair," n.p.

167. Eclair announced the formation of the ACAD *séries d'art* in "Echos," *CJ* 64 (8 November 1909), 4; but the first film titles were not advertised until four months later, in *CJ* 82 (13 March 1910). Salomon, "La Société française des films et cinématographes Eclair."

168. Deslandes, "Victorin-Hippolyte Jasset," 261. Sadoul, *Histoire générale du cinéma*, 4: 221.

169. Deslandes, "Victorin-Hippolyte Jasset," 261.

170. "L'A.C.A.D. en marche vers le succès!" *CJ* 117 (19 November 1910), 8-10; and "Échos," *CJ* 135 (25 March 1911), 4. See, also, Sadoul, *Histoire générale du cinéma*, 3: 52.

171. See, for instance, the Eclair ads in *CJ* 63 (1 November 1909), 16; and 243 (19 April 1913), 76.

172. See "Le Film Eclair en Italie," *APC* 78 (27 June 1908), 7; the Eclair ads in *KLW* beginning in March 1909; "French Films on the American Market," *MPW* 6 (12 February 1910), 203; and Bowser, "Eclair en Amérique," in FIAF, *Le Cinéma français muet dans le monde*, 182.

173. Covielle, "L'Illustre Cinéma," *Le Matin*, reprinted in *PCG* 71 (1 March 1908), 514-515; "Future Pathé Films," *VFI* (11 April 1908), 3; "Informations financières," *PCG* 75 (1 May 1908), 583; "Informations financières," *PCG* 78 (15 June 1908), 631; and Binet and Hausser, *Les Sociétés de cinématographe*, 66-67. Paul Lafitte apparently was no relation to the Lafitte brothers who owned and managed the Paris press empire, including such magazines as *Je Sais Tout, La Vie au grand air, Fermes et chateaux*, and *Femina*. He also was involved in an early advertising film company, Société La Publicité animée. "Informations financières," *PCG* 75 (1 May 1908), 583.

174. See E. B.-L., "Une Première sensationelle," *PCG* 89 (1 December 1908), 804; and Adolphe Brisson's review of the film in "Chronique théâtral: *L'Assassinat du Duc de Guise*," *Le Temps* (22 November 1908), 3-4, reprinted in Abel, *French Film Theory and Criticism*, 1: 50-53.

175. *L'Illustration* also published the scenarios of *L'Assassinat du Duc de Guise* (21 November 1908) and *Le Baiser de Judas* (28 December 1908). Jeanne and Ford, *Le Cinéma et la presse*, 39-40. See, also, Edouard Helsey's "Les Films Artistiques," in *Comoedia*, reprinted in *CJ* 12 (3 November 1908), 6-7.

176. Lavedan alone was paid eight thousand francs for acting in *L'Assassinat du Duc de Guise*.

177. See the conflation of Film d'Art and SCAGL in "The Pathé Film d'Art," *Bio* 126 (11 March 1909), 22-23; and the Pathé ad in *Bio* 134 (6 May 1909), 12.

178. Here Pathé may have also looked to the automobile and textile industries, both of which concentrated on producing luxury goods for a growing urban market within France as well as for foreign export. Caron, *An Economic History of Modern France*, 106, 144-145.

179. The writer Eugène Gugenheim, a close colleague of Decourcelle, seems to have been the link between the two men, for Gugenheim was the titular head of Cinéma-Exploitation, Pathé's new distribution company covering Paris and eastern France.

180. "Informations financières," *PCG* 81 (1 August 1908), 680.

181. "Albert Capellani," *BH* 5 (1912), 15.

182. Mair, "Cinématographe: un art nouveau: *L'Arlésienne*," *PCG* 85 (1 October

1908), 741. Fagot singled out *L'Arlésienne* and *L'Assomoir* for particular praise in his survey of the company in "La SCAGL," *CJ* 95 (18 June 1910), 23.

183. Gaumont put up the initial money for Maurice de Féraudy's company. "Le Théâtro-Film," *CJ* 46 (4 July 1909), 5–6. See, also, "Le Film des auteurs," *CJ* 84 (2 April 1910), 5.

184. Initially, Pathé tried to release both reels of *L'Assomoir* or *Drink* at once in the United States, but encountered so much resistance that it fell back on the usual practice of releasing the reels in consecutive weeks. Bowser, *Transformation of Cinema*, 197.

185. Provoked by these French films as well as others from Italy and Denmark, some American writers began advocating the production of multiple-reel films in early 1911. See H. F. Hoffman, "The Moving Picture Play," *MPW* 8 (25 February 1911), 418; and Perry Vekroff, "The Passing of the Nickel Show," *VFI* (4 March 1911), 1, 3.

186. Dureau, "Propos de fin d'année," *CJ* 20 (31 December 1908), 1–2.

187. Dureau, "Le Splendide Isolement de Pathé-Frères," *CJ* 15 (26 November 1908), 1–2; Charles Pathé, "La Crise du cinéma," *PCG* 89 (1 December 1908), 806; Charles Pathé, "Etat actuel de l'industrie cinématographique," *CJ* 16 (3 December 1908), 2–4.

188. See the Pathé advertisement in *CJ* 142 (13 May 1911), 22–23.

189. This figure comes from Rosen, *Le Cinématographe*, 81.

190. See "Le Film d'Art: Interview de M. P. Gavault," *CJ* 79 (20 February 1910), 4–5; and the Film d'Art–Monofilm ad in *CJ* 79 (20 February 1910), 10.

191. See Monofilm's two-page advertisement for *L'Enfer*, in *CJ* 136 (1 April 1911). In 1907, Charles Delac had served briefly as Benoît-Lévy's assistant in editing *PCG*.

192. Aubert first announced his intent to distribute foreign films in France, in *CJ* 46 (4 July 1909), 7; his first ad, for Vesuvio Films, appeared in *CJ* 60 (4 October 1909), 15.

193. See the Aubert advertisement on its successful films of the previous year, in *CJ* 175 (30 December 1911), 24–25.

194. See "Echos," *CJ* 85 (9 April 1910), 5; and the insert AGC ad in *CJ* 87 (23 April 1910). By 1911, AGC was releasing four thousand meters of film per week. See the AGC ad in *CJ* 143 (20 May 1911), 8–9.

195. "Foreign Trade Prospects," *Bio* 145 (22 July 1909), 3. Edison and Gaumont, however, seem to have come to an agreement by which Edison's films were printed and sold by Gaumont in France, beginning in January 1910: see the exchange of letters between Frank Dyer and Léon Gaumont, in October 1909, as well as various drafts of the agreement. Gaumont folder, Motion Picture Patents Company Box no. 4, ENHS.

196. "Ciné-Nouvelles," *PCG* 46 (15 February 1907), 71.

197. "La Vitagraph Cᵒ s'installe à Paris," *APC* 59 (15 February 1908), 10; "Foreign News and Notes," *MPW* 2 (7 March 1908), 186–187.

198. See the Vitagraph advertisement in *CJ* 124 (7 January 1911).

199. "Les Images sans pareilles," *Fas* 7 (1 July 1903), 197–198; "A nos lecteurs," *Fas* 7 (July 1903), 198. The Augustinian order that ran La Bonne Presse had initiated this "learning by means of images" project at least as early as 1894. Jacques and Marie André, "Le rôle des projections lumineuses fixes et animées dans la pastorale catholique française de 1895 à 1914," in Cosandey, et al., *Une Invention di diable?* 44–59.

200. La Bonne Presse ad, *Fas* 36 (1 December 1905), 381. See, also, "Ciné-Nouvelles," *PCG* 24 (15 March 1906), 111; and Coissac, *Histoire du cinématographe*, 385–387. La Bonne Presse also produced and distributed, with little success, its own

film version of the life of Christ, probably directed by Léar in association with le Frère Basile.

201. La Bonne Presse had established film projection groups in fifty-four dioceses by late 1907. "Ciné-Nouvelles," *PCG* 65 (1 December 1907), 419.

202. La Bonne Presse ad, *Fas* 43 (1 July 1906).

203. Benoît-Lévy, "L'Education sociale par le cinématographe," *PCG* 87 (1 November 1908), 774-775; "Echos," *CJ* 40 (21 May 1909), 11; and "La Cinématographe et les universités populaires," *CJ* 113 (22 October 1910), 8.

204. Pathé had distribution agencies in at least twenty-six major cities across the world. See Petitioner's Exhibit No. 139 in *United States vs. MPPC*, vol. 2 (1914), 689.

205. Jay Leyda, *Kino: A History of the Russian and Soviet Cinema, from 1896 to the Present* (Princeton: Princeton University Press, 1960), 24-30.

206. The 1907 figures for foreign profits, as of 28 February 1908, were 289,838 francs from the United States, 129,661 francs from Russia, and 106,373 francs from England, Germany, and Austria combined. "Informations financières," *PCG* 78 (15 June 1908), 629.

207. "Le Film russe," *Cin* (31 May 1912), 4. See, also, Cherchi Usai and Tsivian, *Silent Witnesses*, 50, 52, 56, 58, 574; and Leyda, *Kino*, 37-38.

208. According to a contemporary reviewer, *Peter the Great* became the first Russian film to outsell any of the imported "quality" films and was brought back "for a second run in the best provincial theaters in response to public demand." Cherchi Usai and Tsivian, *Silent Witnesses*, 74, 76. All three films also were released in France, England, and the United States.

209. "Alfred Machin," *PJ* 43 (1913). Pathé also may have sent a production team to Japan, in 1910, which led to such films as *Le Châtement du samouri*, starring Udagawa and Kawamoura of the Imperial Theater in Tokyo. See the Pathé ad in *CJ* 105 (27 August 1910), 2. However, most of its "Japanese Films," such as the recently restored *La Trahison du Daimon* (1912), were shot in Vincennes, using French actors.

210. For further information on the early Italian cinema industry, see Aldo Bernardini, "La Pathé Frères contre le cinéma italien," in Guibbert, *Le Premiers Ans du cinéma française*, 88-98; and Bernardini, "Le Cinéma muet, étapes et tendances," 33-45.

211. See, for instance, "The Makers in Paris," *KLW* 102 (22 April 1909), 1445, 1447; and Jean Gili, "Les Rapports entre la France et l'Italie de 1896 à la fin des années 20," in FIAF, *Le Cinéma français muet dans le monde*, 105.

212. "Film d'Arte Italiana," *Cin* (10 May 1912), 4.

213. This figure comes from *MPW* 2 (18 April 1908), 344. Over one year later, Dureau raised the figure to ten thousand cinemas. See *CJ* 68 (6 December 1909), 5. However, six months later, the figure was put at 7,500 cinemas. See *CJ* 99 (16 July 1910), 8. For concise, accurate histories of the nickelodeon, see Bowser, *Transformation of Cinema*, 1-20; and Gomery, *Shared Pleasures*, 18-33.

214. See "Arthur Roussel," *MPW* 20 (11 April 1914), 197; "Kinematography in the United States," *MPW* 21 (11 July 1914), 176; Frank L. Dyer's testimony in *United States vs. MPPC*, vol. 3 (1914), 1504; Thompson, *Exporting Entertainment*, 12; and Musser, *Before the Nickelodeon*, 334-335, 378. In Rollin Lynde Hartt's 1909 survey of nickelodeons, nearly all of the films he cites are French (and recognizably Pathé). Hartt, *People at Play* (Boston: Houghton Mifflin, 1909), 115-152. By 1910, according to Dureau, for every five French film prints distributed in France, forty were reserved for the rest of Europe and 150 were shipped to the United States. "Le Point de vue national," *CJ* 73

(10 January 1910), 3–4. Sadoul misdates this article as October 1908. Sadoul, *Histoire générale du cinéma*, 2: 333.

215. In an exchange of letters, between March and May 1907, Pathé sought, without success, to resolve its differences with Edison, which used the threat of litigation to try to bring the French company's selection of imported films under its control. 1907 Motion Picture Folders: Film and Pathé, ENHS. See, also, Thompson, *Exporting Entertainment*, 4–10; and Bowser, *Transformation of Cinema*, 22–23, 26.

216. See the 11 February 1908 letter from J. A. Berst to George Eastman—MPPC Box no. 5, ENHS—and J. A. Berst's testimony in *United States vs. MPPC*, vol. 3 (1914), 1768–1770. The Film Service Association may have been agreed to as early as November 1907. "Le Cinéma aux Etats-Unis," *PCG* 72 (15 March 1908), 529. For an overview of the development of the Film Service Association, the MPPC, and the General Film Company, see Thompson, *Exporting Entertainment*, 10–19.

217. Pathé also insisted on paying only one-half of the royalty fee that Edison charged the other members. Musser, *Before the Nickelodeon*, 377. Eclipse, for instance, was forced to close its newly opened branch office in New York and restrict its releases to actualités for a while. "Edison Roi du Cinématographe aux Etats-Unis," *APC* 60 (22 February 1908), 7–8; "Derniers films communiqués," *APC* 63 (14 March 1908), 16. The French quickly realized that the Film Service Association was dominated by the Americans rather than being a joint American-French venture. "Le Trust Edison Pathé et le rire américain," *APC* 71 (1 May 1908), 5–6.

218. Of the 515 film titles McCoy viewed in June 1908, 458 were from "licensed" manufacturers (grouped in the FSA), with most of the remaining 57 titles coming from Biograph and "independent" distributors of foreign imports. Of those 458 "licensed" films, 14 came from Méliès, 26 from Selig, 32 from Kalem, 40 from Lubin, 42 from Essanay, 45 from Edison, 82 from Vitagraph, and 177 from Pathé. McCoy's survey is reprinted in Musser, *Before the Nickelodeon*, 417.

219. See "Pathé's Position," *VFI* (13 June 1908), 4; "Pathé Will Not Invade Rental Field," *MPW* 2 (12 September 1908), 192; and "Pathé Announcement," *VFI* (19 September 1908), 3. See, also, Bowser, *Transformation of Cinema*, 28–29.

220. See the testimony of J. A. Berst in *United States vs. MPPC*, vol. 1 (1914), 1778.

221. See H. N. Marvin's testimony in *United States vs. MPPC*, vol. 1 (1914), 26; Frank L. Dyer's testimony in *United States vs. MPPC*, vol. 3 (1914), 1519; and Bowser, *Transformation of Cinema*, 28.

222. These figures come from Rosen, *Le Cinématographe*, 92–93. See, also, Dureau, "L'Industrie Européenne du film et les Etats-Unis d'Amérique," *CJ* 131 (25 February 1911), 3–4. Pathé-Frères was said to have a standing order of 160 prints for every film title distributed in the American market as late as 1911. "Montagu Talks Early Days," *MPW* (7 April 1917), 101.

223. See Petitioner's Exhibit nos. 131 and 132, in *United States vs. MPPC*, vol. 1 (1914), n.p. One sign of the independents' strength was the demonstrated ability of IMP, Reliance, and American Film Company to raid the licensed companies of actors and technicians. Bowser, *Transformation of Cinema*, 79. Pathé himself later pointed to 1910 as the date when the American cinema industry began its move to supersede the French. Pathé, *De Pathé-Frères à Pathé-Cinéma*, 61. For a thumbnail sketch of the rise of the independent producers and distributors, see "Appendix B," in Bordwell et al., *Classical Hollywood Cinema*, 397–398.

224. For further information on Jules Brulatour, see "Lettre d'Amérique," *CJ* 126 (21 January 1911), 8; Kevin Brownlow, "Notes on Jules Brulatour," *Griffithiana* 32–33 (September 1988), 237–242; and Bowser, "Eclair en Amérique," 185.

225. See the Sales Company ad in *MPW* 6 (21 May 1910), 838. For further information on the Sales Company and its distribution of foreign films in the United States, see Bowser, *Transformation of Cinema*, 80–81; and Mottram, "The Great Northern Film Company," 77–78. In 1911, the court decisions breaking up the American Tobacco Company and the Standard Oil Company also set unfavorable precedents for the MPPC. Although effectively in retreat by 1912 (the date of the government's suit against it), the MPPC was finally declared in violation of antitrust laws in 1915. See the government brief of the case, recently reprinted in full in *Film History* 1.3 (1987).

226. See the Associated Independent Film Manufacturers ad in *MPW* 6 (4 June 1910), 971.

227. See, for instance, the *Variety* film reviews of 17 October 1907, 10 April 1908, and 2 October 1908; as well as James D. Law, "Better Scenarios Demanded," *MPW* 3 (29 August 1908), 153–154. Some sense of these attacks was reported in France. John Collier, "Autre Lettre d'Amérique," *PCG* 77 (1 June 1908), 613.

228. T. B., "News from America," *Bio* (24 June 1909), 25. See, also, the letter from a Boston exhibitor who argues that only Biograph films have attained the standard of quality set by Pathé films, in *MPW* 4 (29 May 1909), 716.

229. See the weekly reports of John Collier, from 30 March 1909 to 14 June 1910, on the Board of Censorship decisions. 1909 and 1910 Motion Picture Folders: Censorship, ENHS. See, also, H. N. Marvin's testimony in *United States vs. MPPC*, vol. 1 (1914), 222; and W. Stephen Bush, "National Traits in Films," *MPW* 20 (25 April 1914), 488.

230. See the range of Pathé ads in *Bio* for instance, from December 1909 to August 1910. See, also, Roy Armes, *A Critical History of British Cinema* (London: Secker and Warburg, 1978), 27. It is possible that Pathé used its extensive weekly program in England, whose release often coincided with that of the same program in France, as the basis for selecting a limited number of films for later release in the American market.

231. See especially "Pathé Notes," *VFI* (20 November 1909), 2; and the advertising campaign for *Cleopatra*, in "Pathé Pointers," *VFI* (26 March 1910), 6.

232. According to a New York Child Welfare survey in late 1910, young boys who were frequent filmgoers preferred "Indian and Cowboy" pictures above all others. See "Pictures that Children Like," *VFI* (21 January 1911), 3.

233. The first film released was a western, *The Girl from Arizona. PWB* 133 (16 May 1910). Pathé's success can be gathered from "News from America," *Bio* 191 (9 June 1910), 29; and "Topics of the Week: The Popularity of Western Films," *Bio* 201 (18 August 1910), 4–5. Although announced during the spring, Pathé's studio was not completed until December. "Pathé American Studio Announced by Mr. Berst," *VFI* (9 April 1910), 1, 3; "New Pathé Studio," *VFI* (6 August 1910), 3; "Berst Returns," *VFI* (8 October 1910), 2.

234. "Notes from Manufacturers," *MPW* 7 (16 July 1910), 165.

235. The following paragraph draws on Vincent Pinel, "Pathé contre Eastman (1907–1912)," in FIAF, *Le Cinéma français muet dans le monde*, 193–206.

236. Dureau, "De quoi demain sera-t-il fait?" *CJ* 13 (12 November 1908), 1–2.

237. See Dureau's sudden praise of Eastman Kodak for refusing to back the MPPC, to the exclusion of all other film producers. Dureau, "La Marché reste ouvert," *CJ* 25 (4 February 1909), 3.

238. Dureau, "Le Congrès des fabricants," *CJ* 21 (7 January 1909), 2–4. Gaumont and others attempted (unsuccessfully it turned out) to lay the groundwork for a counter-organization to the Edison Trust, in Europe, in February 1908. "Les Fabricants de Ciné-matographe et de Films Français et Etrangers forment une section dans la Chambre Syndicale de la Photographie," *APC* 61 (29 February 1908), 3–5. See, also, Bowser, *Transformation of Cinema*, 28.

239. See the 15 June letter from Berst to Dyer. MPPC Box no. 5, ENHS. William Selig refers to this cutoff of negative film stock in his 4 November 1909 letter to the MPPC, summarizing his recent trip to Europe. George Kleine Collection, LOC Manuscript Division. That letter is printed in *VFI* (1 January 1910), 1, 3.

240. See the 20 September letter from G. F. Smith (Edison) to E. A. Ivatts (Pathé), questioning this process of recycling film stock. 1909 Motion Picture Folder-Film, ENHS. In an oblique attack on Pathé, Eastman Kodak placed ads refusing any responsibility for reconstituted film stock. *CJ* 62 (25 October 1909), 17.

241. A good number of Pathé titles, dating from 1905 to 1908, were rereleased in the United States during the summer and fall of 1909. See, also, the sudden appearance of Lumière ads, beginning in *Bio* 126 (11 March 1909), 30. Jules Brulatour, Lumière's American agent, also signed a big contract with the independents in September 1909. Bowser, *Transformation of Cinema*, 74. Carlos Bustamante has found documents that indicate AGFA also was selling a large quantity of film stock to French producers as early as 1908. Bustamante, "Nos sincéres salutations: Eclair-AGFA," *Griffithiana* 47 (May 1993), 157.

242. "Charles Pathé—World Promoter of the Photoplay," *VFI* (21 January 1911), 1. Pathé, *De Pathé-Frères à Pathé-Cinéma*, 77–78. Recently, Bustamante has discovered correspondence between Eastman Kodak and AGFA which suggests that Pathé actually may have worked out an agreement whereby the American company helped to operate its film stock factory.

243. Pathé argued that this decline resulted from selling off the phonograph branch of the American company, at a loss. Pathé, *De Pathé-Frères à Pathé Cinéma*, 78–79.

244. "Echos de partout," *CJ* 183 (24 February 1912), 34–36.

245. These figures are from Sadoul, *Histoire générale du cinéma*, 3: 24. See, also, Bowser, *Transformation of Cinema*, 232; and Jean-Pierre Jeancolas, "Le Marché français entre la production nationale et les productions étrangères, 1910–1920," in FIAF, *Le Cinéma français muet dans le monde*, 18–19.

246. Pathé was reported, for instance, to have exported 462 film titles to the Eastern European country of Romania, in 1913, and Gaumont was not far behind with 393 titles. "Le Cinéma en Roumanie," *FR* 51 (1 December 1913), 12.

247. This example comes from Sadoul, *Histoire générale du cinéma*, 3: 27.

248. W. Stephen Bush, "Charles Pathé's Views," *MPW* 19 (24 January 1914), 390–391. See, also, Thompson, *Exporting Entertainment*, 57–59. Pathé may also have been experiencing the tension in French capitalism "between forces tending toward concentration in large enterprises and forces tending to maintain a system of divided and small enterprises." Caron, *An Economic History of Modern France*, 167.

249. "Charles Pathé," *VFI* (21 January 1911), 1. Cher, "Parisian Notes," *Bio* 287 (11 April 1912), 111. Pathé, *De Pathé-Frères de Pathé-Cinéma*, 79–80. French film

distributors called themselves *éditeurs*, a term that previously had been reserved for publishers.

250. E. Ventujol, "La Cinématographie en couleurs par le procédé L. Gaumont," *CJ* 222 (23 November 1912), 17, 21; L. Gaumont, "La Cinématographie en couleurs," *CJ* 230 (18 January 1913), 20–21; and Jacques Ducom, "Le Nouveau Cinématographe en couleurs naturelles de M. Gaumont," *CJ* 231 (25 January 1913), 7–8. The Kinemacolor process developed by George Albert Smith in England, at the time, was even more commercially successful in Europe. See Trimbach, *Quand on tournait la manivelle*, 98–99; and Salt, *Film Style and Technology*, 102–103.

251. See the insert Debrie ad as well as "Une Invention sensationnelle," *CJ* 54 (30 August 1909), 5–6; and "Nouvel Appareil de prise de vues," *CJ* 59 (4 October 1909), 6–8, 10–11. Ads for the Parvo camera began appearing in England, in *Bio* 156 (7 October 1909), 64. For a good description of the Debrie Parvo camera, see Salt, *Film Style and Technology*, 84.

252. "Agrandissements de la Maison J. Debrie," *CJ* 157 (26 August 1911), 6.

253. See the 6 July 1908 letter from J. A. Berst to Frank Dyer—MPPC Box no. 5, ENHS—and "Arthur Roussel," *MPW* 20 (11 April 1914), 197.

254. See the 1913 catalog of Pathé's KOK films collected at the Bibliothèque de l'Arsenal in Paris; and Singer, "Early Home Cinema," 44–46.

255. See, for instance, "The Pathescope Home Cinematography," *British Journal of Photography* 60 (1913), 216–217; and "The Pathescope," *MPW* 20 (13 June 1914), 1524.

256. "An advertisement in the Sunday *New York Times* of 9 August 1914, claims 8,000 [KOK] units to be in use." Singer, "Early Home Cinema," 45.

257. See the Eclair ad in *FR* (7 November 1913); Cher, "Paris Notes," *MPW* 18 (22 November 1913), 872; the Eclair ad in *MPW* 19 (24 January 1914), 455; and George Blaisdell, "Jourjon Outlines Plans," *MPW* 20 (11 April 1914), 217.

258. See the Pathé ads in *Bio* 227 (16 February 1911), 12; and 228 (23 February 1911), 20. See, also, the extensive Pathé scenario deposits at the Bibliothèque de l'Arsenal in Paris.

259. E. L Fouquet, "Les Metteurs-en-scène," *Cin* (15 March 1912), 1; G.-Michel Coissac, "Le Cinématographe," *Annuaire de la cinématographie* (Paris: Ciné-Journal, 1918), 493–494; Fescourt, *La Foi et les montagnes*, 77; and Trimbach, *Quand on tournait la manivelle*, 75. Dureau also argued that the name of the filmmaker or scenario writer should be included in the credits of each film. Dureau, "Le Droit de signer appartient-il aux auteurs de scénarios?" *CJ* 232 (1 February 1913), 3–4.

260. W. Stephen Bush, "The Film in France," *MPW* 17 (12 July 1913), 180.

261. See the Le Film Français ad in *Cin* (1 March 1912), 5. See, also, Roger Icart, *Abel Gance ou Le Prométhée foudroyé* (Lausanne: L'Age d'homme, 1983), 48–50, 442–443.

262. "Une Nouvelle Firme," *CJ* 206 (3 August 1912), 12–13.

263. See "Films Azur," *CJ* 248 (24 May 1913), 84.

264. See "Sur les grands boulevards," *CJ* 156 (19 August 1911), 5; S. Fleury, "*Le Bossu*," *Cin* (5 April 1912), 1; the Aubert ad in *CJ* 261 (23 August 1913); the Grands Films Populaires ad in *CJ* 268 (11 October 1913); Cher, "Paris Letter," *MPW* 21 (4 July 1914), 52; and Coissac, "Le Cinématographe," 493.

265. Cher, "Parisian Notes," *Bio* 268 (30 November 1911), 649; Cher, "Paris Letter," *MPW* 17 (27 September 1913), 1382; "Les Nouvelles Firmes cinématographiques," *CJ* 272 (8 November 1913), 25; and, "Paris Letter," *MPW* 18 (13 December 1913), 1269.

266. See the Filma ad in *CJ* 267 (4 October 1913), 72; Cher, "Paris Letter," *MPW*

18 (25 October 1913), 369; the Exclusif Agency ad in *Le Film* 8 (17 April 1914), 34; and the R. Plaissetty ad in *Le Film* 12 (15 May 1914), 15.

267. See the Les Films Suzanne Grandais ad in *CJ* 245 (3 May 1913), 56; and the Géo Janin ad for Yvette Andreyor in *CJ* 267 (4 October 1913), 26–27.

268. See the Aubert-Les Grands Films Populaires ad in *CJ* 246 (10 May 1913), 56.

269. In June 1914, SCAGL also announced that the famous theater director André Antoine would soon be making films. André Heuzé, "A André Antoine," *Le Film* 15 (5 June 1914), 6.

270. Trimbach, *Quand on tournait le manivelle*, 24–25.

271. "Le Film Valetta," *Cin* (11 October 1912), 4.

272. "Le Film biblique," *Cin* (21 June 1912), 4.

273. "Hollandsche Film," *Cin* (17 May 1912), 4.

274. According to Pathé's list of weekly releases in *Ciné-Journal*, both Linder and Prince also were running their own production companies by May 1914.

275. Pathé's strategy coincided to some extent with that advocated by *MPW*, which argued that production companies should specialize in particular kinds of films. "Separate Producers for Drama and Comedy," *MPW* 8 (8 April 1911), 755–756. It also corresponded with the views of Jourjon as well as Laemmle and Selig that short films would continue to be in high demand in Europe. Blaisdell, "Jourjon Outlines Plans," 216; William N. Selig, "Present Day Trends in Film Lengths," *MPW* 20 (11 July 1914), 181; and Carl Laemmle, "Doom of Long Features Predicted," *MPW* 20 (11 July 1914), 185.

276. See the Gaumont ad in *CJ* 187 (23 March 1912), 5.

277. "Items of Interest," *Bio* 272 (4 January 1912), 17.

278. Lenny Borger, "Louis Nalpas, un seigneur du ciné-roman," *La Cinémathèque française* 23 (July 1987), 10–11. See, also, "Nouveaux concessionnaires," *CJ* 172 (9 December 1911), 5.

279. See the Film d'Art ad in *CJ* 287 (21 February 1914). For a "capsule" history of Film d'Art's first ten years of production, see A. R., "Le Film d'Art," *Film* (2 April 1918), 42.

280. "*La Reine Elizabeth*, un grand film de 'L'Histrionic'," *CJ* 206 (3 August 1912), 47. See, also, Sadoul, *Histoire générale du cinéma*, 3: 343–344, and Kenneth MacGowan, *Behind the Screen: The History and Techniques of the Motion Picture* (New York: Dell, 1965), 155–170.

281. See, for instance, André de Reusse, "Du cinéma scolaire (suite): une intéressante visite," *FR* 23 (16 May 1913), 13–14; Blaisell, "Jourjon Outlines Plans," 216; and Thierry Lefebvre, "The Scientific Production," *Griffithiana* 47 (May 1993), 137–155.

282. See the Eclair ad in *CJ* 202 (6 July 1912), 6.

283. Jean Mitry, "Maurice Tourneur," *Anthologie du cinéma,* vol. 4 (Paris: L'Avant-Scène Cinéma, 1968), 269.

284. As many as eighty prints of *Zigomar contre Nick Carter* had been ordered four weeks prior to its release. "Items of Interest," *Bio* 281 (29 February 1912), 571.

285. See Salomon, "La Société française de films cinématographiques Eclair," n.p.; and Jourjon, "Concerning Eclair Enterprises," 207. John Cher seemed especially impressed by Eclair, but that may have been a function of his deliberate coolness toward the French giant, Pathé. "Paris Letter," *MPW* 17 (12 (12 July 1913), 179–180; and 18 (25 October 1913), 370.

286. See the Gaumont Chronophone ad in *MPW* 1 (14 September 1907), 443; and Bowser, *Transformation of Cinema*, 79–80.

287. The first ad for Solax appeared in *MPW* 7 (8 October 1910), 812. New factory facilities were added in 1912. Louis Reeves Harrison, "Studio Saunterings: Solax," *MPW* 12 (15 June 1912), 1007–1011.

288. Kleine soon picked up the feature releases of Cinès, to compensate for the loss of Gaumont, and eventually also those of Eclipse. "Kleine to Release Cines Pictures," *MPW* 11 (6 January 1912), 26; and the Georges Kleine ad in *MPW* 17 (9 August 1913), 599. Herbert Blaché left Gaumont to help his wife run Solax just as Exclusive began distributing Gaumont's films. "Independent Film Stories," *MPW* 17 (12 July 1913), 244, 246; and "F. G. Bradford to Manage Gaumont," *MPW* 17 (19 July 1913), 322.

289. See "Pathé American Studio Announced by Mr. Berst," *VFI* (9 April 1910), 1, 3; and "Berst Returns," *VFI* (8 October 1910), 2.

290. See Richard V. Spencer, "Notes of the Los Angeles Studios," *MPW* 8 (11 February 1911), 302; "James Young Deer," *MPW* 8 (6 May 1911), 999; and the Pathé ad in *MPW* 9 (22 July 1911), 95.

291. See the Pathé ad in *MPW* 9 (15 July 1911), 7; "Reviews of Notable Films: The Pathé Journal," *MPW* 9 (12 August 1911), 359–360; W. Stephen Bush, "The Overproduction of 'Western Pictures'," *MPW* 10 (21 October 1911), 189–190; C. H. Claudy, "Modern Melodrama," *MPW* 11 (13 January 1912), 113; and Louis Reeves Harrison, "Studio Saunterings: Pathé-Frères," *MPW* 11 (16 March 1912), 945.

292. "Reviews of Notable Films: *In the Grip of Alcohol*," *MPW* 10 (2 December 1911), 706–707.

293. See the Pathé ad in *MPW* 17 (5 July 1913), 18; and "Pathé Putting Out News Daily," *MPW* 20 (13 June 1914), 1524.

294. "What Pathé Is Doing," *MPW* 8 (24 June 1911), 1434–1435; "The Dangers of the Foreign Market," *MPW* 10 (16 December 1911), 877–878; "Notre Humour est bestial, disent les Américains!" *CJ* 176 (6 January 1912), 21; and "Eclectic to increase output," *MPW* 18 (22 November 1913), 874. An exception to this strategy was *Germinal*, which was cut from ten to five reels and distributed by General Film. See the General Film ad in *MPW* 19 (24 January 1914), 443. See also Bowser, *Transformation of Cinema*, 218.

295. See "Boosting Pathé Pictures," *MPW* 19 (14 March 1914), 1392–1393; and the Eclectic ads in *MPW* 19 (21 March 1914), 1546–1547, and 20 (16 May 1914), 1001. Instead of the usual twenty-five to thirty prints, 147 prints of *Perils of Pauline* were released the first week. "Expediting Service," *MPW* 21 (11 July 1914), 284.

296. Thompson, *Exporting Entertainment*, 57–60.

297. The company's production was singled out for praise almost immediately. See, for instance, "Eclair Films," *MPW* 6 (28 May 1910), 891, 893.

298. "Lettre d'Amérique," *CJ* 140 (29 April 1911), 19; "Eclair factory nearing completion," *MPW* 8 (1 July 1911), 1500; "American Eclair Studio," *MPW* 10 (7 October 1911), 24–25; "Eclair d'Amérique," *CJ* 168 (11 November 1911), 45.

299. "M. Arnaud Arrives," *MPW* 11 (20 January 1912), 210; Louis Reeves Harrison, "Studio Saunterings: Eclair," *MPW* 11 (2 March 1912), 758; and Bowser, "Eclair en Amérique," 184.

300. For further information on the Eclair staff at Fort Lee, see Spehr, *The Movies Begin*, 74, 76.

301. "An Eclair Weekly," *MPW* 13 (27 July 1912), 334; and "Eclair Notes," *MPW* 13 (17 August 1912), 643.

302. Initially, Eclair was undecided as to which faction of the Sales Company it

would follow. See "The Independent Situation," *MPW* 12 (15 June 1912), 1016. For its later distribution arrangements, see the Universal ad in *MPW* 13 (3 August 1912), 409; the World Special ad for *Protéa* in *MPW* 18 (8 November 1913), 641; and Bowser, "Eclair en Amérique," 187.

303. "Eclair's Fort Lee Factory Burned," *MPW* 19 (28 March 1914), 1699; and "Eclair Factory Fire," *MPW* 20 (4 April 1914), 45.

304. Jourjon announced this reconstruction at Fort Lee, as well as a possible relocation of production to Arizona, within weeks of the fire. Blaisdell, "Jourjon Outlines Plans," 216. See, also, "La Société Eclair en Amérique," *FR* 52 (8 December 1913), 19; and "Western Eclair Company," *MPW* 20 (11 April 1914), 225.

305. See "Lettre d'Amérique," *CJ* 126 (21 January 1911), 8; Brownlow, "Notes on Jules Brulatour," 237–242; and Bowser, "Eclair en Amérique," 189.

306. For further information on Maurice Tourneur and the Eclair studio at Fort Lee, see Abel, "Maurice Tourneur's *The Wishing Ring* (1914)," in Paolo Cherchi Usai and Lorenzo Codelli, ed., *Sulla via di Hollywood, 1911–1920* (Pordenone-Edizioni Biblioteca dell'Immagine, 1988), 318–341.

307. See Cher, "Parisian Notes," *Bio* 287 (11 April 1912), 111; and the Pathé ad in *Bio* 288 (18 April 1912), 163.

308. See the Pathé ad in *CJ* 118 (26 November 1910), 2; as well as *BH* 41–45 (1911). *Film Index* began printing photographs of Kalem and Vitagraph actors as early as January 1910, and *Moving Picture World* published "star" shots of Pearl White, Maurice Costello, and Mary Pickford the following December. This practice finally reached the daily newspapers, in February 1911, when the *New York Telegraph* introduced a motion picture section in its Sunday edition. Musser, "The Changing Status of the Actor," in Leyda and Musser, *Before Hollywood*, 60.

309. See the Pathé ad in *Cin* (1 March 1912), 4.

310. See the AGC ads in *CJ* 133 (11 March 1911), 24–25; *CJ* 150 (8 July 1911), 20–21; and *CJ* 167 (4 November 1911), 50.

311. See "Echos," *CJ* 212 (14 September 1912), 13; the AGC ad in *CJ* 219 (2 November 1912); "Interview de l'A.G.C.: M. P. Kastor," *CJ* 225 (14 December 1912), 5, 8; and the AGC ad in *CJ* 262 (30 August 1913), 78–79.

312. "Interview de M. Louis Aubert," *CJ* 224 (7 December 1912), 11, 14.

313. "Echos," *CJ* 240 (29 March 1913), 5; and "Le Triomphe de *Quo Vadis?*" *CJ* 248 (24 May 1913), 10. Aubert was still distributing *Quo Vadis?* one year later, in Belgium, Holland, and the colonies. See the Aubert ad in *CJ* 288 (28 February 1914).

314. See the Aubert ads in *CJ* 244 (26 April 1913) and 261 (23 August 1913), as well as "Concerts et spectacles," *Le Journal* (14 November 1913), 8.

315. This was encouraged by the Chambre syndicale français de la cinématographie banquet at the Salles des Fêtes in Paris, in June 1913, which the daily newspapers covered in unprecedented front-page stories. Bush, "The Film in France," 179.

316. See the Aubert ad in *CJ* 256 (19 July 1913); the AGC and Pathé-Frères ads in *CJ* 257 (26 July 1913); and the Gaumont ad in *CJ* 262 (30 August 1913). Pathé and Gaumont each advertised the second half of its season in *CJ* 279 (27 December 1913) and 283 (24 January 1914), respectively.

317. Cher, "Parisian Notes," *Bio* 268 (30 November 1911), 649; Cher, "Paris Letter,"*MPW* 18 (13 December 1913), 1269; and "Cinémas," *Le Journal* (27 February 1914), 7.

318. See the M. P. Sales Agency ad in *CJ* 139 (22 April 1911), 10; and "American

Films Abroad," *MPW* 10 (4 November 1911), 357. As the distributor of the most popular American films in France, Vitagraph expanded its facilities again in 1913. Cher, "Paris Letter," *MPW* 18 (25 October 1913), 369; and 18 (8 November 1913), 602.

319. See "Echos," *CJ* 285 (7 February 1914), 8, and the Western Import ads in *CJ* 286 (14 February 1914) and 287 (21 February 1914). Western Imports had exclusive distribution rights to Mutual's Kay Bee, Broncho, and Keystone films.

320. "Nouveautés de la semaine," *Le Film* 10 (1 May 1914), 35. For more information on how well *Queen Elizabeth* did in the United States, see Thompson, *Exporting Entertainment*, 26.

321. "Les Agrandissements de l'Omnia-Pathé," *CJ* 227 (28 December 1912), 9.

322. Cher, "Paris Letter," *MPW* 18 (22 November 1913), 872; and "Concerts et spectacles," *Le Journal* (15 May 1914), 8.

323. "Les Recettes des Théâtres à Paris en 1913," *CJ* (9 May 1914), 125–126. See, also, Adolphe Brisson, "Chronique théâtral," *Le Temps*, reprinted in *Le Film* 13 (22 May 1914), 25–26; and Coissac, "Le Cinématographe," 504.

324. Trimbach, *Quand on tournait la manivelle*, 92. W. Stephen Bush considered these two cinemas as the best in Paris, in 1913. Bush, "The Film in France," 179.

325. In 1912, the average ticket costs were as follows: the cinema, 0.75 francs; the music hall, 3 francs; the café-concert, 4 francs; and the theater, 5 francs. "Nos recettes," *Cin* (3 May 1912), 2.

326. Adolphe Brisson, "Le Cinéma et le Théâtre en province," *Le Temps*, reprinted in *Le Film* 10 (1 May 1914), 27–28.

327. The Pathé-Journal cinema cost only twenty-five centimes. Cher, "Paris Letter," *MPW* 17 (27 September 1913), 1382.

328. Cher, "Parisian Notes," *Bio* 271 (21 December 1911), 849; Cher, "Parisian Notes," *Bio* 278 (8 February 1912), 399; and "Programmes des cinématographes," *Cin* 2 (8 March 1912), 6.

329. Compare the three or four "classes" of cinema which existed in the United States during this period. W. Stephen Bush, "Gradations in Service," *MPW* 20 (2 May 1914), 645; and William Fox's testimony in *United States vs. MPPC*, vol. 2 (1914), 697–698.

330. See, also, "La Longeur des films," *Cin* (26 April 1912), 1. Only in late 1913 did Dureau admit that people now came to the cinema not just to experience "going to the cinema" but to see certain feature-length films. Dureau, "La Valeur d'un programme influence-t-elle les recettes," *CJ* 275 (29 November 1913), 3–4. For more on this debate over film length, see Abel, *French Film Theory and Criticism*, 1: 16–17. In the United States, the *MPW* reviewer and editor, W. Stephen Bush, also resisted the move to feature-length films, viewing the one-reel film as the backbone of the industry. See Stromgren, "Moving Picture World," 15.

331. Several Film d'Art productions—*L'Assassinat du Duc de Guise* (1908) and *Madame Sans-Gêne* (1911)—had received special premieres before their general release, but they remained exceptions to the rule.

332. One of these big features, Capellani's *La Glu* (1913), was perhaps the first French film released on nonflammable film stock, in response to the Paris police prefect's order, in November 1913, that Paris cinemas be required to show only nonflammable films. Cher, "Paris Letter," *MPW* 18 (6 December 1913), 1160.

333. Cher, "Paris Letter," *MPW* 18 (13 December 1913), 1268.

334. Dureau, "Le Cinéma tel que le juge la grande presse," *CJ* 199 (14 June 1912),

3-4; "La Liberté des spectacles menacés," *CJ* 200 (22 June 1912), 3-4; "Lettre ouverte à M. Herriot, maire de Lyon et à ses imitateurs," *CJ* 201 (29 June 1912), 3-5; and "La Censure devant les syndicats," *CJ* 203 (13 July 1912), 5-11.

335. The last film of the *Fantômas* series was playing almost everywhere in Paris. "Concerts et spectacles," *Le Journal* (8 May 1914), 8.

336. Cher, "Paris Letter," *MPW* 20 (16 May 1914), 958.

337. Louis Haugmard, "L'Esthétique' du cinématographe," *Le Correspondant* (25 May 1913), 762-771; and René Doumic, "Revue dramatique: L'Age du cinéma," *Le Revue des deux mondes* 133 (15 August 1913), 919-930, both reprinted in Abel, *French Film Theory and Criticism*, 1: 77-89. Moreover, Pathé, Gaumont, Eclair, and Eclipse all had special educational or scientific film divisions, whose work consistently won the praise of French and American reviewers. Charles Mendel fils, "The French Cinematograph Trade," *Bio* 263 (26 October 1911), 219, 221; Eclipse ad, *CJ* 186 (16 March 1912), 38; W. Stephen Bush, "Theories vs. Facts," *MPW* 19 (28 March 1914), 1652; and Blaisdell, "Jourjon Outlines Plans," 216.

338. André Chalopin, "Le Cinéma dans l'enseignement," *Le Journal* (24 October 1913), 7. For more on this subject, see Abel, *French Film Theory and Criticism*, 1: 10-11.

339. These included *Ciné-Journal* (Georges Dureau), *Le Courrier cinématographique* (Charles Le Frapper), *Filma* (A. Millo), *Cinéma-Revue* (Charles Mendel), *Le Cinéma* (E. L. Fouquet) which soon merged with *L'Echo du cinéma* (Georges Lordier), and *Le Film* (André Heuzé and then Henri Diamant-Berger).

340. "Echos," *Le Film* 16 (12 June 1914), 13; Cher, "Paris Letter," *MPW* 21 (4 July 1914), 52.

341. For the "story" of that resistance, see Richard Abel, *French Cinema: The First Wave, 1915-1929* (Princeton: Princeton University Press, 1984).

3: The Cinema of Attractions, 1896-1904

1. Hansen, *Babel and Babylon*, 29.

2. The Lumière catalogs are reprinted in Sadoul, *Lumière et Méliès*, 126-145.

3. Méliès produced four kinds of films: actualités, scientific films, mise-en-scène films, and transformation films (trick films and féeries). See Méliès, "Les Vues cinématographiques," (1907), reprinted in English translation in Abel, *French Film Theory and Criticism*, 1: 30-31.

4. Kress, *Conférences sur la cinématographie*, 14.

5. My principal sources here are the photocopies of Pathé catalogs collected by Paolo Cherchi Usai. See, also, Guillaudeau, "Les Productions Pathé et Méliès en 1905-1906," 39; Emmanuelle Toulet, "Une Année de l'édition cinématographique Pathé: 1909," in Guibbert, *Les Premiers Ans du cinéma français*, 138; and Bousquet and Redi, *Pathé-frères*.

6. See Toulet, "Une Année de l'édition cinématographique Pathé," 137-139.

7. Burch, "Primitivism and the Avant-Gardes," 486.

8. See, especially, Gunning, "The Cinema of Attraction," 63-70; and Gunning, "'Primitive' Cinema," 3-12. Until recently, others who have contributed greatly to our understanding of early cinema have tended to use the label "primitive cinema" to designate this period. See, for instance, Burch, "Porter or Ambivalence," 91-105; Burch,

"Un Mode de représentation primitif?" 113–122; and Kristin Thompson, "From Primitive to Classical," in Bordwell et al., *Classical Hollywood Cinema*, 157–173.

9. Burch takes over this concept as crucial to early cinema, in "Narrative/Diegesis—Thresholds, Limits," *Screen* 23 (July–August 1982), 21–22.

10. Hansen, *Babel and Babylon*, 34.

11. Burch, "Primitivism and the Avant-Gardes," 486. Gunning singles out this point as an important insight for any consideration of the cinema of attractions. Gunning, "'Primitive' Cinema," 7.

12. André Gaudreault, "Temporality and Narrativity in Early Cinema, 1895–1908" in Fell, *Film Before Griffith*, 322.

13. Gunning, "'Primitive' Cinema," 10.

14. Burch, "Primitivism and the Avant-Gardes," 487.

15. Thomas Elsaesser, "Comparative Style Analysis for European Films, 1910–1918," Deuxième Colloque International de Domitor, Lausanne, 1 July 1992.

16. This catalog of practices is drawn principally from Vincent Pinel, "La Restauration des films," *La Cinémathèque française* 4 (December 1985), 8–14; and Malthête, "Les Bandes cinématographiques en couleurs artificielles," 3–4. See, also, Paolo Cherchi Usai, "The Unfortunate Spectator," *Sight and Sound* 56 (Summer 1987), 170–173.

17. Musser, "The Eden Musée," 73–83, and "The Nickelodeon Era Begins," 4–11. See, also, Musser's reworking of this argument in *Before the Nickelodeon*, 103–156.

18. Gunning, "Attractions and Narrative Integration," Society for Cinema Studies Conference, Los Angeles, 23 May 1991.

19. See, for instance, the Star Films ads in *PCG*, beginning on 1 October 1905. Méliès mentions his preference for "fantastical scenes" in "Les Vues cinématographiques," (1907), reprinted in Abel, *French Film Theory and Criticism*, 1: 38.

20. This information as well as the following is drawn from Méliès, "Importance du scénario," *Cinéa-Ciné* 28 (April 1932), reprinted in Sadoul, *Lumière et Méliès*, 220. Méliès is much less insistent on this point, admittedly, in the earlier essay, "Les Vues cinématographiques," 40.

21. The following catalog of cinematic devices is drawn from Frazer, *Artificially Arranged Scenes*, 59–76. See, also, Méliès, "Les Vues cinématographiques," 44–45. For an analysis of trick films produced by the British Brighton School about the same time, see David Francis, "Films à trucs (1896–1901)," in Guibbert, *Les Premiers Ans du cinéma français*, 143–146.

22. Williams, "Film Body," 29.

23. Méliès himself refers to the difficulty he encountered in producing this film, in "Les Vues cinématographiques," 45.

24. Jacques Malthête was one of the first to rediscover Méliès's cutting, while preparing the original negatives for reprinting so that Les Amis de Georges Méliès could project positive prints for the Méliès colloquium at Cérisy, in August 1981. Malthête, "Les Collages dans les 'Star' films," 145–155. For a more systematic analysis of Méliès's cutting, see Pierre Jenn, "Le Cinéma selon Georges Méliès," in Malthête-Méliès, *Méliès et la naissance du spectacle cinématographique*, 143–146. Méliès himself seems to allude to the trick of simple cutting, in "Les Vues cinématographiques," 45.

25. This point is crucial to Gunning's argument in "'Primitive' Cinema," 6–7.

26. For a shot-by-shot analysis of *Le Mélomane*, see Malthête, "Les Collages dans

les 'Star' films," 149, 151–155. This film probably draws on the perception of telegraph lines as seen from an express train, perhaps best articulated in Verlaine's poem cycle, *La Bonne Chanson* ("Whose wires look strangely like a music-score"), quoted in Schivelbusch, *Railway Journey*, 40.

27. Only one other silent film is perhaps more accomplished in its use of this many multiple exposures—Buster Keaton's *The Playhouse* (1921).

28. Frazer, *Artificially Arranged Scenes*, 7–8.

29. For a more complete analysis of how turn-of-the century French society is represented in Méliès's films, see Hélène Puiseux, "Un Voyage à travers l'histoire: Une Lecture sociale des films de Méliès," in Malthête-Méliès, *Méliès et la naissance du spectacle cinématographique*, 23–35.

30. This film would seem to exemplify Lucy Fischer's argument that the principal function of women's bodies in Méliès's films is to disappear, but Linda Williams rightly calls attention to the fact that, generally, "there are probably an equal number of magical appearances and disappearances of men in these films." See Fischer, "The Lady Vanishes," 32–33; and Williams, "Film Body," 31.

31. Similar jokes occur in *Illusions funambulesques* (1903), where a magician twice is startled to see that the young woman he has "created" has turned into a cook, and in *Le Rêve de l'horloger* (1904), where a sleeping man awakes to find that the dancing women he has envisioned are no more than clocks in his workroom.

32. *Le Tonnerre de Jupiter* (1903) parodies this kind of classical Greek figure: Jupiter sends off his thunderbolts for repairs, and, when they are returned, he loses control over them as they produce fires and explosions all over the studio set.

33. Williams, "Film Body," 33.

34. Fischer, "The Lady Vanishes," 30.

35. Williams, "Film Body," 33.

36. Williams, "Film Body," 33.

37. Lubin was offering a dupe of this film as late as May 1902. See *NYC* (31 May 1902), 324. Other early Méliès féeries also had women's stories as their subjects: *Jeanne d'Arc* (1900) and *Le Petit Chaperon rouge* (1901).

38. Lubin was selling a dupe of this film as late as May 1902. See *NYC* (3 May 1902), 236.

39. For a series of suggestive connections between Méliès, Charcot, and Freud, see Anne-Marie Quévrain and Marie-George Charconnet-Méliès, "Méliès et Freud: Un Avenir pour les marchands d'illusions?" in Malthête-Méliès, *Méliès et la naissance du spectacle cinématographique*, 221–239.

40. Félix Mesguich, *Tours de manivelle: souvenirs d'un chasseur d'images* (1932), quoted in Sadoul, *Histoire générale du cinéma*, 2: 207. *Cendrillon* also did quite well in both French and British music halls. Sadoul, *Histoire générale du cinéma*, 2: 111.

41. Weber, *Peasants into Frenchmen*, 455–456.

42. "New Pieces in Paris," *The Era Almanack* (London, 1900), 80. Frazer, *Artificially Arranged Scenes*, 7, 220. See, also, Vardac, *Stage to Screen*, 152–164; and Katherine Singer Kovács, "Georges Méliès and the *Féerie*," in Fell, *Film Before Griffith*, 244–257.

43. Sadoul, *Lumière et Méliès*, 171.

44. Frazer, *Artificially Arranged Scenes*, 6–7. Jenn, "Le Cinéma selon Georges Méliès," 137. Another version of *Blue Beard*, by Arthur Donville, was popular in England. See, for instance, *The Era Almanack* (London, 1900), 66.

45. Mesguich, *Tours de manivelle*, as quoted in Sadoul, *Histoire générale du cinéma*, 2: 207. Musical accompaniment certainly determined the rhythm of later féeries such as *Faust aux enfers* (1903) and *La Damnation de Faust* (1904). See, for instance, Frazer, *Artificially Arranged Scenes*, 133.

46. I borrow this term from Bann, *Clothing of Clio*, 134. See, also, Meisel, *Realizations*, 33, 61–63; and Jenn, "Le Cinéma selon Georges Méliès," 135–136.

47. Méliès, "Les Vues cinématographiques," 40–41. Méliès may have been the first to appreciate the significance of painting decors exclusively in black and white as well as shades of gray, in order to control his compositional effects on orthochromatic film.

48. Puiseux, "Un Voyage à travers l'histoire," 27–28.

49. Salt was the first to notice this slight change in decors. *Film Style and Technology*, 44.

50. Frazer, *Artificially Arranged Scenes*, 89–90. Frazer mistakenly reads the second of these as "parallel intercut action," ignoring Bluebeard and his bride in the foreground of the tower ramparts shot-scene and focusing on the woman (upper background) whose look and cry announces the coming of the knight and his army. See, also, Salt, *Film Style and Technology*, 58.

51. Salt, *Film Style and Technology*, 45.

52. See, for instance, the 1900 Palais de l'Electricité program, which makes all twenty shot-scenes of *Cendrillon* (1899) its major attraction. Deslandes and Richard, *Histoire comparée du cinéma*, 2: 163.

53. Pierre Jenn's découpage of the film is published in *L'Avant-Scène Cinéma* 334 (November 1984), 29–37. Edison and Lubin were both selling dupes of this film in October 1902. See *NYC* (4 October 1902), 712; and (11 October 1902), 733. American Mutoscope and Biograph at least advertised their print as a Méliès film. See *NYC* (4 October 1902), 712.

54. Brewster briefly mentions this early representation of "deep space" in "Deep Staging in French Films, 1900–1914," in Elsaesser, *Early Cinema*, 45.

55. Frazer, *Artificially Arranged Scenes*, 97.

56. Salt credits Méliès with realizing "fairly quickly the importance of 'correct' directions of entrances and exits for the smoothness of film continuity." *Film Style and Technology*, 56.

57. Quévrain, "A la redécouverte de Méliès," 163; Jenn, *Georges Méliès cinéaste*, 51.

58. Quévrain, "A la redécouverte de Méliès," 163–164; Jenn, *Georges Méliès cinéaste*, 52–53, 60–61.

59. Quévrain, "A la redécouverte de Méliès," 165.

60. Frazer, *Artificially Arranged Scenes*, 98.

61. André Gaudreault, "'Théâtricalité' et 'narrativité' dans l'oeuvre de Georges Méliès," in Malthête-Méliès, *Méliès et la naissance du spectacle cinématographique*, 213–214; Quévrain, "A la redécouverte de Méliès," 164.

62. Even Salt, who is no fan of Méliès, concedes that "the combined effect of color and flat scenery quite transforms a film like *Le Royaume des fées* (1903), giving it the look of a series of popular 19th-century block-colored wood-cuts which have been animated." *Film Style and Technology*, 79.

63. Frazer, *Artificially Arranged Scenes*, 7, 118.

64. Several hand-colored frame stills from this scene are reproduced in Toulet, *Cinématographe, invention du siècle*, 66–67.

65. Frazer, *Artificially Arranged Scenes*, 118.

66. Gaudreault, "'Théâtricalité' et 'narrativité' dans l'oeuvre de Georges Méliès," 217–218.

67. Malthête-Méliès et al., *Essai de reconstitution*, 170, 171. There were British versions of both titles that Méliès may also have drawn on. See *The Era Almanack* (London, 1900), 69; and *The Era Almanack* (London, 1903), 54.

68. This film cost Méliès 37,500 francs to produce—see Frazer, *Artificially Arranged Scenes*, 148—but ninety-five prints were sold in the United States in the first five days. See the Star Film ad in *NYC* (12 November 1904), 885. All of the several signs in this film are in three languages—French, German, and English.

69. Frazer, *Artificially Arranged Scenes*, 6, 145.

70. Frazer, *Artificially Arranged Scenes*, 146. There actually was an important late nineteenth-century group of French artists called the Incoherents, among whom was the caricaturist and future animation filmmaker, Emile Cohl. Crafton, *Emile Cohl*, 29–34, 47–51.

71. Francis Lacassin, "Filmographie d'Alice Guy," in Guy, *Autobiographie d'une pionnière du cinéma*, 173–177.

72. A complete description of this film is provided in Gaudreault, *Ce que je vois de mon ciné . . .*, 147–149.

73. The NFA print presents certain problems because it may be a copy of Pathé's 1907 reissue of the film, with stencil color and brief intertitles added. The NFA print is further complicated in that its single dialogue intertitle, "Sésame, ouvre-toi!," is placed right after the film's title rather than before either one of the two openings of the secret cave mouth. Edison, Lubin, and Vitagraph all sold dupes of this film. See *NYC* (1 November 1902), 808; (28 February 1903), 36; and (21 March 1903), 108.

74. See the special Pathé catalog supplement, August 1902, for a list of the film's tableaux. Decorations are attributed to Albert Collas; costumes, to L. Granier.

75. A similar beheading appeared in Lubin's *Beheading the Chinese Prisoner* (1900), which was included in Program I of *Before Hollywood* (1987), a film exhibition organized by Leyda and Musser for the American Federation of Arts. Méliès would quadruple this trick in *Le Bourreau turc* (1904).

76. See the introductory note, "A Nos Clients," *PC* (Paris, August 1904), 3. Pathé also may have drawn on the set designs of Saint-Saëns's 1877 opera of the same title.

77. *Samson et Delila* may also be the earliest Pathé film that survives with traces of color, which, as in Méliès's films, was applied by hand.

78. The frame stills reproduced in the 1904 Pathé catalog differ slightly from the film prints preserved at LOC and GEH (only the GEH print has tinting and stencil color). This means that the surviving prints probably are of the 1907 Pathé remake (further evidence is the Pathé rooster trademark attached to the background interior wall). Yet the remake may have resembled the earlier version closely for each runs the same length.

79. *Don Quichotte* was first advertised as having fifteen tableaux and running 430 meters in length. A shorter version of 255 meters was offered a year later. The film usually is attributed to Lucien Nonguet. Another adaptation, by Jacques Lorrain, was performed the following year at the Théâtre Victor Hugo. "New Pieces in Paris," *The Era Almanack* (London, 1904), 73.

80. *Ali Baba et les quarante voleurs* also includes intertitles, but they probably were inserted in the 1907 reissue of the film.

81. Edison was selling a dupe of *Le Chat botté* in early 1904. See *NYC* (16 January 1904), 1136. This film usually is attributed to Zecca and Nonguet.

82. See, for instance, the J. Hickory Wood version at the Garrick Theatre in London. *The Era Almanack* (London, 1901), 57.

83. In the set-up rescue of Puss-in-boot's master by the marquis, the film also seems to use the same decor from *Baignade impossible*, only this time a miniature carriage (the marquis's) passes in the background.

84. Crafton, *Emile Cohl*, 249–256. See, also, Crafton, *Before Mickey*, 37–38.

85. Sadoul, *Histoire générale du cinéma*, 2: 192.

86. Sadoul, *Lumière et Méliès*, 254, 255.

87. Lacassin, "Filmographie d'Alice Guy," 171, 175, 177, 179. See, also, the reference to *Clown en sac* (1904), in Olivo, "La Production Gaumont éditée au début du siècle en cartes postales," 16.

88. Sadoul, *Lumière et Méliès*, 136, 137, 139, 140, 142.

89. *PC* (Paris, August 1904), 25 30, 74–75. See, also, Sadoul, *Histoire générale du cinéma*, 2: 192.

90. Emile Reynaud produced a "film" version of Galipaux's act for his Théâtre Optique, in 1896–1897. Deslandes and Richard, *Histoire comparée du cinéma*, 1: 297–298.

91. Near the end of his life, Dranem appeared in such early French sound films as *Ciboulette* (1933) and *Le Malade imaginaire* (1934).

92. Méliès's version of *Arroseur et arrosé* was only the sixth film he produced. Sadoul, *Lumière et Méliès*, 251.

93. For a thematic analysis of early Méliès and Pathé comic films, which unfortunately takes up over two dozen films without dating more than a couple of them specifically, see Guillaudeau, "La Production comique," 31–35.

94. These examples come from the Lumière catalogs reprinted in Sadoul, *Lumière et Méliès*, 126–145.

95. Tom Gunning, "'The World Within Your Reach': Early Cinema and the World Tour," Deuxième Colloque International de Domitor, Lausanne, 2 July 1992.

96. Sadoul, *Lumière et Méliès*, 138–139, 143. These two series of vues were included in a special retrospective of Lumière films at the Cinémathèque française, in 1986. Lumière also presented four consecutive vues of a fire brigade rescue, in January 1896; and, similarly, Warwick Trading Company offered three consecutive views of a Madrid procession, in its 1897–1898 catalog. Bottomore, "Shots in the Dark," 201–202.

97. Sadoul, *Lumière et Méliès*, 137, 140.

98. See, for instance, Francis Doublier's account of using stock actualité footage to produce a four-shot film supposedly about Alfred Dreyfus, for Russian audiences, in 1898, reported in the *New York World Telegram* (23 October 1935), and reprinted, with commentary, in Bottomore, "Dreyfus and Documentary," 290.

99. See, for instance, Roland Barthes's notion of the photograph's principal function as "having been there," in Barthes, *Image, Music, Text*, trans. Stephen Heath (New York: Hill and Wang, 1977), 44.

100. A Pathé version of *L'Affaire Dreyfus* (in eight tableaux), made slightly after Méliès's film, apparently has not survived. *PC* (Paris, March 1902), 17–18.

101. Sadoul, *Lumière et Méliès*, 257.

102. For a family account of Méliès's political postion during this period, see Maltête-Méliès, *Méliès, l'enchanteur*, 214–215.

103. See the Star Film catalog entries reprinted in Sadoul, *Lumière et Méliès*, 257;

and a comparison of the British, American, and French catalogs in Malthête, "Les Actualités reconstitutées de Georges Méliès," 5. Neither the NFA print nor the CF print is complete (two of the eleven tableaux are missing), and neither has those tableaux in the proper chronological order. Both, however, have about sixteen frames of black film between each shot, which was standard practice in actualités of the early period. Bottomore, "Shots in the Dark," 200.

104. Sadoul, *Lumière et Méliès*, 165; Frazer, *Artificially Arranged Scenes*, 78; Malthête-Méliès, *Méliès, l'enchanteur*, 220.

105. Sadoul, *Lumière et Méliès*, 257. Bottomore reproduces a frame still of Méliès's courtroom scene, along with a photograph of the actual room where the trial took place in a Rennes schoolhouse (from *Black and White*, 12 August 1899). Bottomore, "Dreyfus and Documentary," 291.

106. Dreyfus, for instance, was played by an ironworker who happened to look like the man. Bottomore, "Dreyfus and Documentary," 292.

107. Both Frazer and Salt refer to the second of these shot-scenes, and Salt to the first as well. Frazer, *Artificially Arranged Scenes*, 79; Salt, *Film Style and Technology*, 44.

108. Malthête-Méliès et al., *Essai de reconstitution*, 6.

109. Apparently, *Jeanne d'Arc* (1900) uses entrances from both right and left foreground in at least one shot-scene, according to Jenn, *Georges Méliès cinéaste*, 35–41.

110. The production information provided in this paragraph comes from Sadoul, *Lumière et Méliès*, 178–179, 260; Frazer, *Artificially Arranged Scenes*, 100–101; and Malthête, "Les Actualités reconstituées de Georges Méliès," 9–10.

111. Paolo Cherchi Usai has found a letter from Charles Urban documenting this point.

112. At least one journalist, reporting in *Le Petit Bleu*, did not share this attitude and condemned the film as a "trick" on the British people. Reprinted in Frazer, *Artificially Arranged Scenes*, 101–102.

113. Edison offered an exact dupe of *Epopée napoléonienne* as *Life of Napoleon*—see the Edison ads in *NYC* (7 November 1903), 896; and (14 November 1903), 920—listing it as an import, but without, of course, divulging Pathé's name.

114. Stage versions of the "national epic" of Napoleon's life were performed in Paris in 1899 and 1904. "New Pieces in Paris," *The Era Almanack* (London, 1900), 80; and "New Pieces in Paris," *The Era Almanack* (London, 1904), 72.

115. *PC* (Paris, August 1904), 92–95.

116. See, for instance, the Pathé program for Ville d'Aubervilliers, 24–26 June 1905, reprinted on page 26. In the United States, this film was the feature attraction on Lyman Howe's roadshow program during the 1903–1904 season. Musser, *High-Class Moving Pictures*, 137–138.

117. Edison's dupe of *Epopée napoléonienne* (with slight changes in the title and intertitles) could be purchased either as an integral unit or as separate tableaux. "Grand Spectacular and Historical Film: *The Rise and Fall of Napoleon the Great*," *Edison Films*, no. 200 supplement (January 1904), 7–9.

118. The LOC print, part of the Taylor Collection (from Australia), is incomplete (missing tableaux 12 and 15, for instance) and rearranged (shot 8 is inserted between shots 10 and 11). An even less complete MOMA print includes only shots 11 through 14.

119. See, for instance, Charles Musser, "Screen Presentations of the Passion Play in the United States (1880–1900)," and Isabelle Raynauld, "Les Scénarios de la Vie de Jésus (Pathé, 1902–1914)," in Cosandey et al., *Une Invention du Diable?* 131–141.

120. *PC* (London, May 1903), 93–95, and (Paris, August 1904), 132–136. At least three versions of 1,410 feet, 2,000 feet (27 tableaux), and 2,122 feet (29 tableaux), however, were released in the United States. See the Pathé ads, respectively, in *NYC* (15 October 1904), 784; (4 February 1905), 1172; and (2 December 1905), 1060.

121. Ricardo Redi, for instance, has viewed four separate Italian archive prints of the film. Redi, "La Passion Pathé de Zecca, problèmes de datation," in Guibbert, *Les Premiers Ans du cinéma français*, 167–171.

122. Sadoul, *Histoire générale du cinéma*, 2: 196–197. For further information on the influence of Saint Sulpice iconography on the early French cinema, see Joseph Marty, "Quelques Problèmes de représentation religieuse soulevés par de films biblique, primitifs Pathé," in Guibbert, *Les Premiers Ans du cinéma français*, 172–180.

123. Meisel, *Realizations*, 204. For an analysis of Paul Delaroche's famous historical paintings of this same period, see Bann, *Clothing of Clio*, 71–75.

124. Meisel, *Realizations*, 30.

125. Meisel, *Realizations*, 216–217.

126. I borrow the terms of this question from Bann, *Clothing of Clio*, 62–63.

127. Napoleon was one of the principal subjects of popular nineteenth-century engravings. See Weber, *Peasants into Frenchmen*, 109. Illustrations began to supplement the narrative of major French histories at least as early as Augustin Thierry's *Histoire de la conquête* (1838) and *Ducs de Bourgogne* (1842). Bann, *Clothing of Clio*, 45–47.

128. Pierre Guibbert, "Les Clichés scolaires dans le 'film d'art'," in Guibbert, *Les Premiers Ans du cinéma français*, 162–166.

129. *PC* (Paris, 1900), 26.

130. Michael R. Booth, *English Melodrama* (London: Herbert Jenkins, 1965), 175. Several photographs of the ship's sinking, which leads up to this underwater sensation scene, are displayed in the Theatre Museum in London.

131. See, especially, Booth, *English Melodrama*, 165–176.

132. The Pathé catalog supplement for *Alcohol and Its Victims* (May 1902) refers specifically to "the success gained by the STORY OF A CRIME" the previous year.

133. Sadoul, *Histoire générale du cinéma*, 2: 187. Edison's *Execution of Czolgosz, with Panorama of Auburn Prison* (November 1901), by contrast, reenacted the execution of the man who had assassinated President McKinley. Musser, *Before the Nickelodeon*, 187–190.

134. Although the Pathé catalog lists six scenes, the last is divided into two tableaux. As Alan Williams suggests, the only tableau not reproduced from the Musée Grévin is the court trial, probably so as to limit the film's cost. Williams, *Republic of Images*, 46.

135. Vardac, *From Stage to Screen*, 171.

136. Sadoul, *Histoire générale du cinéma*, 2: 188. See, for instance, such British examples as "The Bottle" (1847) and "The Drunkard's Children" (1848). Meisel, *Realizations*, 124–141.

137. The earliest surviving American film to have intertitles is Edison's *The European Rest Cure* (September 1904), which was included in Program I of *Before Hollywood*. Long ago, Kemp Niver concluded that the earliest American film with an intertitle was Edison's *Uncle Tom's Cabin* (September 1903). Niver, *The First Twenty Years*, 34, 80, 91, 98, 101.

138. See "Very Important Notice," *PC* (London, May 1903), 12; and "Avis Très Important," *PC* (Paris, August 1904), 12.

139. Sadoul, *Histoire générale du cinéma*, 2: 311.

140. See *PC* (London, May–June 1904), 11, as well as the special 1904 supplement for *Annie's Love Story*, the film's title in England. Pathé is reported to have sold one thousand copies of this film. Sadoul, *Histoire générale du cinéma*, 2: 312–313.

141. Sadoul, *Histoire générale du cinéma*, 2: 311. Although Burch resists this temptation to see the system of representation in these films "as an authentically working-class system," he sometimes still tends to conflate the terms *proletarian* and *popular*, resisting the notion that anything like a popular culture was being redefined as a mass culture, certainly by the end of the nineteenth century. Burch, "Films's Institutional Mode of Representation and the Soviet Response," 77.

4: The Transition to a Narrative Cinema, 1904-1907

1. Gunning, *D. W. Griffith*, 17–18. Gunning's work on early film narrative or narrativization depends, as does my own (although much less explicitly), on both the theoretical formulations and specific textual analyses of such structuralist critics as Roland Barthes, Tzvetan Todorov, and Gérard Genette.

2. Gunning, *D. W. Griffith*, 66.

3. Musser, *Before the Nickelodeon*, 207.

4. Burch's phrase for this is "linearization of the iconic signifier." See, for instance, Elsaesser, "Introduction: Early Film Form," in *Early Cinema*, 21–22.

5. Gunning, *D. W. Griffith*, 18. Stephen Heath, *Questions of Cinema* (Bloomington: Indiana University Press, 1981), 109, 122.

6. Gunning, *D. W. Griffith*, 17, 93.

7. Elsaesser, "Introduction: The Institution Cinema," in *Early Cinema*, 153.

8. Elsaesser, "Introduction: The Continuity System," in *Early Cinema*, 299.

9. Edwin S. Porter, the principal early filmmaker for Edison, presents an analogous case, but Porter moved further than Méliès did toward a narrativized cinema, even though he, too, resisted any further change after about 1905. For an excellent analysis of Porter's work in early cinema, see Musser, *Before the Nickelodeon*, especially where he makes an explicit connection between Porter and the French filmmaker and documents his commitment to a prenickelodeon mode of representation, pp. 209, 403–407.

10. I borrow the concept of narrative "voice" from Gérard Genette, *Narrative Discourse: An Essay in Method*, trans. Jane Lewin (Ithaca: Cornell University Press, 1980), 31–32, 255–256. Gunning, for instance, attributes a moralizing voice to what he calls Griffith's specific approach to storytelling, or "narrator system." Gunning, *D. W. Griffith*, 25–28, 93–94.

11. My formulation here assumes a cultural materialist framework and is indebted specifically to Robert A. Nye, who has researched nineteenth-century French cultural perceptions of deviance in *Crime, Madness, and Politics in Modern France*.

12. Judith Mayne examines the cross-class composition of the early American cinema audience in "The Two Spheres of Early Cinema," in *Private Novels, Public Films*, 68–81. Although she writes that the "development of more sophisticated 'story films' in early motion pictures occurred only when film exhibitors were eager to attract a middle-class audience," her analysis of specific films suggests that it took place even earlier.

13. Another possible term for this model would be what Miles Orvell calls the "omnibus form" of nineteenth-century popular culture, a structure of variable size and

shape capable of containing an expandable number of parts. Orvell, *The Real Thing: Imitation and Authenticity in American Culture, 1880–1940* (Chapel Hill: University of North Carolina Press, 1989), 18, 28.

14. Musser, "The Travel Genre in 1903–1904," 47–59. For the release dates of these films, see the Edison ads in *NYC* (15 August 1903), 596, and (3 September 1904), 644.

15. Musser also argues that this hybrid format originated in the exhibitor-constructed programs, following suggestions like those of William Selig in his company's 1902 catalog. Musser, *Before the Nickelodeon*, 249. The variety principle continued to operate later in Hale's Tours, for which nearly every American production company was advertising films in the spring of 1906. See, for instance, the Biograph, Lubin, Miles Service, and Edison ads, respectively, in *NYC* (14 April 1906), 231, 240, (21 April 1906), 259, and (28 April 1906), 281.

16. Hansen, "Reinventing the Nickelodeon," 192, and *Babel and Babylon*, 29, 47–48. As a critical term describing textual heterogeneity, *bricolage* derives from Claude Levi-Strauss.

17. Gunning, "Heard over the Phone," 185–186. Such air disasters were popular *fait divers* at the time. See, for instance, the depiction of an early airplane crash in *Le Petit Journal: Supplement Illustré* 601 (25 May 1902), 168.

18. See, for instance, Weber, *Peasants into Frenchmen*, 62–65; and Wright, *Between the Guillotine and Liberty*, 145, 154, 160. In the United States, by contrast, the tramp or vagrant seems more often to have been represented as a comic figure in comic strips, plays, and films. Musser, *Before the Nickelodeon*, 311.

19. *PC* (Paris, April 1905), 16–17.

20. Lant, "The Curse of the Pharoah," 98.

21. For this ideological analysis of *Un Tour du monde d'un policier*, I borrow several points from Rosen, "Disjunction and Ideology in a Pre-Classical Narrative."

22. Tom Gunning discusses such "free-floating images"—the best example being the close shot of the revolver-wielding outlaw in Edison's *The Great Train Robbery* (1903)—as a carryover from the early cinema of attractions, in "The Non-Continuous Style of Early Film," in Holman, *Cinema 1900–1906*, 227.

23. A similar radical shift in reading position occurs in Edison's *The 'Teddy' Bears* (1907), where a fairy tale of Goldilocks's integration into the bears' world turns into a literal destruction of that world (a hunter kills the parent bears) and appropriation of its remains as commodities (the baby bear and his "teddy" bears). Hansen, *Babel and Babylon*, 49–57. For that film's release date, see the Edison ad in *MPW* 1 (16 March 1907), 18.

24. Nor was the bricolage model any more viable for the American cinema, despite such intriguing novelties as Edison's *The 'Teddy' Bears* (1907), which combined féerie studio decors, animation, and location snowscapes for a chase.

25. Musser, "The Nickelodeon Era Begins," 5–6.

26. Gunning, *D. W. Griffith*, 67.

27. Jasset, "Etude sur le mise-en-scène en cinématographie," *CJ* 166 (28 October 1911), 33. One of the earliest references to the popularity of the chase film comes in the Kleine Optical catalog (November 1905), reprinted in Pratt, *Spellbound in Darkness*, 41.

28. For the release dates of these films, see the Edison ad in *NYC* (4 July 1903), 452; the Biograph ad in *NYC* (10 September 1904), 668; and the Lubin ad in *NYC* (26 November 1904), 948.

29. In a polemical argument that the cinema should become more like the theater, Dureau criticized Pathé specifically for specializing in comic chase films for so long. Dureau, "Le Cinéma et le Théâtre," *CJ* 5 (15 September 1908), 1–2.

30. *L'Incendiaire*, which also was released in April 1905, contained a chase as well, but there it did not constitute the entire film.

31. Georges Sadoul attributes the scenarios for nearly all of these early chase films to André Heuzé. Sadoul, *Histoire générale du cinéma*, 2: 318–319.

32. Biograph's *Hold Up of the Rocky Mountain Express* (1906) used several long-take dolly shots, taken from the front of a locomotive, for narrative purposes as well as those of spectacle attraction.

33. Francis Lacassin attributes this film to Etienne Arnaud and Louis Feuillade. See Lacassin, *Louis Feuillade*, 165.

34. Gunning, "The Cinema of Attraction," 68.

35. Doug Riblet, "Chase Films and Narrativity, 1904–1906," Society for Cinema Studies Conference, Los Angeles, 23 May 1991.

36. Burch, *Life to those Shadows*, 149–150.

37. Gunning, "Non-Continuity, Continuity, Discontinuity," 108–109.

38. Pathé was not the only company making comic films about "delinquent kids" during this period. See Musser, *Before the Nickelodeon*, 344.

39. For an introduction to the "melodramatic" dangers of modern city traffic, see Ben Singer, "'A New and Urgent Need for Stimuli': Sensational Melodrama and Urban Modernity," BFI Melodrama Conference, London, 6 July 1992.

40. Salt, *Film Style and Technology*, 55–56; and Burch, *Life to those Shadows*, 193.

41. See, for instance, the "Scènes grivoises d'un caractère piquant" in Pathé's earliest surviving film catalog (Paris, 1900), 50–52.

42. For a thorough description and analysis of the standard POV-shot system, see Edward Branigan, *Point of View in the Cinema: A Theory of Narrativity and Subjectivity in the Classical Cinema* (New York: Mouton, 1984), 103–121.

43. Gunning, "What I Saw from the Rear Window of the Hôtel des Folies-Dramatiques," in Gaudreault, *Ce que je vois de mon ciné . . .*, 37–38. Gunning takes over this distinction between *ocularization* and *focalization*, with some modification, from François Jost, *L'Oeil-Caméra: Entre film et roman* (Lyon: Presses Universitaires de Lyon, 1987).

44. Elena Dagrada, "Through the Keyhole: Spectators and Matte Shots in Early Cinema," *Iris* 11 (1990), 100.

45. Brewster, "A Scene at the Movies," 7.

46. Apter, *Feminizing the Fetish*, 42. Exactly where these films were shown remains unclear, although they were called "scenes for smoking concerts" in England. *PC* (London, May 1903), 69–78. Emmanuelle Toulet, for instance, dates the earliest pornographic cinemas in Paris from 1906. "Le Spectacle cinématographique à Paris de 1895 à 1914," 519–521.

47. It is worth noting, however, that the predominantly male gaze of the spectacle erotic film did not become a crucial feature of the early narrative cinema paradigm, in either France or the United States.

48. In shot 2, the man is looking toward the left background, whereas in shot 4, he already is turned and looking toward the right background.

49. One exception to this is the female voyeur in *La Fille de bain indiscrète* (1902).

50. Burch, *Life to those Shadows*, 233, n.24.

51. These terms are drawn from Michel Foucault's analysis of Jeremy Bentham's Panoptican, in *Discipline and Punish: The Birth of the Prison*, trans. Alan Sheridan (New York: Pantheon, 1978), 195–208.

52. Burch, "How We Got into Pictures," 36; Gunning, "What I Saw from the Rear Window," 38.

53. These images uncannily reenact Villiers de l'Isle-Adam's feminized description of the cinema prior to its existence, in *L'Eve future* (1888): "La vision, chair transparente, miraculeusement photochromée, dansait, en costume pailleté, une sorte de danse mexicaine populaire. Les mouvements s'accusaient avec le fondu de la Vie elle-même." Villiers de l'Isle-Adam, *L'Eve future* (Paris: Jean-Jacques Pauvert, 1960), 202.

54. It is possible that one further tableau originally followed this last one in the NFA print. The frame still accompanying the film's description in the 1907 Pathé catalog shows an older man standing in the foreground of the room, but it is more likely that this figure originally appeared as part of the opening tableau, in order to designate this as the boy's father's study and to provide a model for his initiation.

55. Gunning argues that, because the observers in Biograph's *A Search for Evidence* (1903) were moving from one view to another in order to solve a narrative enigma, this earlier film already was leading "towards the classical point of view shot and a more fully narrativized cinema." Gunning, "What I Saw from the Rear Window," 39–40.

56. Authoritative documentation on this film can be found in Alain Lacasse, Sonia Lemelin, and André Michaud, "*La Révolution en Russie*: Fiche signalétique/Découpage technique," in Guibbert, *Les Premiers Ans du cinéma français*, 259–266.

57. Burch, by contrast, sees *La Révolution en Russie* as unambiguous in its sympathy for "the oppressed and rebellious masses." Burch, *Life to those Shadows*, 65.

58. Vitagraph's *The 100 to 1 Shot* (August 1906) includes several shots at a racecourse, which are loosely linked to a watching spectator, but without the aid of binoculars.

59. Mayne, "The Two Spheres of Early Cinema," 83. Mayne's argument relies on the specific analysis of selected American films — *Uncle Josh at the Moving Picture Show* (1902), *Grandpa's Reading Glass* (1902), *A Search for Evidence* (1903), and *The Story the Biograph Told* (1904) — as well as on the work of Burch. See, for instance, "How We Got into Pictures."

60. See, for instance, Booth, *English Melodrama*, 136–138; and Daniel Gerould, "Melodrama and Revolution," BFI Melodrama Conference, London, 8 July 1992.

61. The surviving LOC print contains only the first two of the film's five tableaux. According to a Kleine Optical catalog (November 1905), Pathé's *The Strike* was one of the more popular 1904 films in the United States. Reprinted in Pratt, *Spellbound in Darkness*, 41.

62. Similar pans and cut-ins can be found in Pathé *actualités* such as *Pélerinage à Lourdes* (1904), a copy of which has been found at LOC.

63. A columnist for *Le Journal*, Arthur Dupin, first used the word *apache* to describe several street gangs of the working-class Paris suburbs, in 1902. The term circulated so widely that Robert Nye concludes that "bourgeois and crime" constituted the "true binary opposition" of the period. Nye, *Crime, Madness, and Politics in Modern France*, 182–184. See, also, Wright, *Between the Guillotine and Liberty*, 171; and Berlanstein, *Working People of Paris*, 148.

64. The twelve-page booklet describing this "startling dramatic film depicting American Cow-Boy Life" (collected at the National Film Archive) lists the chief actors

as Capt. W. Robert Peterson's Cowboys and calls the stagecoach the Central Pacific stage.

65. *Brigandage moderne*'s release coincided closely with that of Hepworth's more famous *Rescued by Rover* (July–August 1905). See, for instance, *PC* (Paris, July 1905), 17–18, and the Pathé-Frères ad in *NYC* (19 August 1905), 664. The film was popular enough to be rescreened in the second "festival" of Pathé films which Benoît-Lévy organized on 27 May 1906.

66. It is worth recalling Bottomore's argument that a precedent for this matching action or movement across several shots can be found in early actualité films. Bottomore, "Shots in the Dark," 200–204. Gunning also reminds me that matchcutting occurs even earlier in Edison's *Maniac Chase* and Biograph's *Escaped Lunatic* (both 1904).

67. A similar cut-in MS, serving a narrative function, occurs at the beginning of Vitagraph's *Foul Play*, but that film was not released until January 1907.

68. Burch calls attention to the use of offscreen space in *Brigandage moderne* —in *Life to those Shadows*, 173.

69. *Au pays noir* may have been inspired by a British-Gaumont documentary on mining, *L'Explosion de grisou* (1904). Sadoul, *Histoire générale du cinéma*, 2: 312.

70. *Au pays noir* was advertised for two full months in *L'Industriel forain*, from June to August 1905.

71. Burch, *Life to those Shadows*, 170.

72. Salt was perhaps the first to mention this feature of 1905–1906 Pathé films. Salt, *Film Style and Technology*, 78.

73. The two surviving prints at the National Film Archive include very different actualité footage. One of the prints has French intertitles, but includes the trademarks of two different Belgian fairground distributors or exhibitors; the other has German intertitles, one of which includes the trademark of Raleigh & Robert.

74. One of the surviving prints has an actualité shot of a funeral cortege appended to this concluding tableau. The other contains an initial, unintegrated MS of a coal miner on his back picking at a coal seam just above him—an example of the "emblematic shot" that was sometimes used to open or close a film during this period.

75. Although the film could have been used for strike purposes, most strikes were centered in Paris rather than in the northeast region of the coal and steel industries during this period. Nye, *Crime, Madness, and Politics in Modern France*, 200.

76. For a comparative analysis of these two films, see André Gaudreault, "Récit singulatif, récit itératif: *Au bagne* (Pathé, 1905)," in Guibbert, *Les Premiers Ans du cinéma français*, 233–241. See, also, Haggar's *The Life of Charles Pearce* (1906), made some months later.

77. The film is coded contradictorily in terms of costumes: initially, the men wear contemporary clothes, but the prisoners' shackles are those of an earlier period in nineteenth-century France. I am indebted to Patricia O'Brien for this observation.

78. Gaudreault analyzes this shift in the film, following Genette's theoretical work on narrative, as a shift from the *iterative* to the *singulative*. Gaudreault, "Récit singulatif, récit itératif," 238–240.

79. Earlier British films had employed similar reverse-angle cuts, but usually for comic purposes—see, for example, Bamforth's *Ladies' Skirts Nailed to a Fence* (1900), Collins's *The Runaway Match* (1903), and *The Other Side of the Hedge* (1905). Brewster, "A Scene at the Movies," 7–9; and Salt, *Film Style and Technology*, 65. One might also recall the reverse-angle shift at the end of Pathé's own earlier *Les Petits Vagabonds* (1905).

80. *Le Déserteur* (1906), which was released the same month as *Au bagne*, also includes reverse-angle matchcuts of a soldier entering and exiting a window (to steal an army payroll) as well as a pan that reveals an obstacle (marching soldiers) to his escape.

81. In *Le Déserteur*, the captured soldier is stripped of his military insignia in a public ceremony and then given a revolver with which to shoot himself in his cell.

82. See, for instance, Wright, *Between the Guillotine and Liberty*, 150–151.

83. See, for instance, Nye, *Crime, Madness, and Politics in Modern France*, 189–190, 214–226, 265–309. Wright traces the doctrine of "social defense" to an eminent nineteenth-century jurist at the Collège de France, Adolphe Franck. Wright, *Between the Guillotine and Liberty*, 115.

84. Rémy de Gourmont, "Epilogues: Cinématographe," *Mercure de France* 69 (1 September 1907), 125. This essay is reprinted in English translation in Abel, *French Film Theory and Criticism*, 1: 47–50.

85. See, for instance, the graphic threats to children depicted in *Le Petit Journal: Supplement Illustré* (2 February 1902), (23 March 1902), and (14 December 1902).

86. See, for instance, Weber, *Peasants into Frenchmen*, 178; and Berlanstein, *Working People of Paris*, 148.

87. My use of the opposition between public and private space here is indebted to Judith Mayne, "The Two Spheres of Early Cinema," 69–88.

88. Gledhill, "The Melodramatic Field: An Investigation," in *Home Is Where the Heart Is*, 36.

89. See, also, Barthélemy Amengual, "Propos pédants sur le mélodrame d'hier et le faux mélo d'aujourd'hui," *Les Cahiers de la cinémathèque* 28 (1979), 12–15; Jacques Goimard, "Le 'Mélodrame': Le Mot et la chose," *Les Cahiers de la cinémathèque* 28 (1979), 17–65; and Roger Icart, "Le Mélodrame dans le cinéma muet français," *Les Cahiers de la cinémathèque* 28 (1979), 191–200.

90. Brooks, *Melodramatic Imagination*, 15.

91. Brooks, *Melodramatic Imagination*, 4, 32. See, also, Catherine Bodard Silver, "Salon, Foyer, Bureau: Women and the Professions in France," in *Clio's Consciousness Raised*, ed. Mary Hartman and Lois W. Banner (New York: Harper and Row, 1974), 78–82; Zeldin, *France 1848–1945: Ambition and Love*, 11–22; and, especially, MacMillan, *Housewife or Harlot*, 11–12.

92. Brooks, *Melodramatic Imagination*, 14, 15. See, also, Meisel, *Realizations*, 38–51.

93. Brooks, *Melodramatic Imagination*, 47, 48.

94. Nicholas Vardac was one of the first to draw some parallels between stage and film melodrama in *Stage to Screen*, 20–67. For an unusually incisive introduction to film melodrama, see Gledhill, "The Melodramatic Field," 5–39.

95. Brooks, *Melodramatic Imagination*, 2. Both Gunning and Turim express a similar idea in different contexts. See Gunning, "What I Saw from the Rear Window," 41; and Turim, "French Melodrama," 312.

96. This first shot, in the NFA print, is introduced by an enigmatic dialogue intertitle, "The path is clear," which, because the print seems relatively complete, may not have originally belonged to the film. In a number of films between 1906 and 1908, Vitagraph used split sets to allow a character to overhear something in an unseen, but adjacent space. Brewster, "Frammenti Vitagraph alla Library of Congress," in Cherchi Usai, *Vitagraph Co. of America*, 292.

97. Pathé's *Nuit de carnaval* (1906) follows an opposite tact by focusing, not on two men who go off to fight a duel, but on the woman who has provoked it, as she stealthily

moves along a stream and through a wood, to intervene in the duel and, at least according to the catalog description, get herself killed (the surviving GEH print is incomplete).

98. Both de Gourmont and Jasset make much of these films, and Jasset specifically
singles out *Les Chiens contrebandiers*. See de Gourmont, "Epilogues: Cinématographe,"
48; and Jasset, "Etude sur le mise-en-scène en cinématographie," *CJ* 166 (28 October
1911), 35.

99. Vitagraph's *The 100-to-1 Shot* (August 1906) has a short sequence of crosscutting,
but it was released several months after *Les Chiens contrebandiers*. See Salt, *Film Style and
Technology*, 67. Gaumont's *Le Matelas alcoolique* also opens with a short sequence of
crosscutting, but it, too, was released months later. Burch singles out *Les Chiens contrebandiers* as an early instance of crosscutting, but misdates the film in *Life to those Shadows*, 158.

100. One year later, and consistent with its move to more overtly law-abiding films,
Pathé released *Les Chiens de police* (1907), in which a mixed band of dogs serves as track-
ers for the police. Although less tightly constructed than the earlier film, this one is no
less complicated in its cutting, especially in an economical sequence of reverse-angle
cutting between two different exteriors and interiors, when the dogs break into a cellar
and surprise some thieves who are trying to rob a house.

101. A similar letter insert also occurs near the beginning of Biograph's *The Black
Hand* (March-April 1906).

102. An alternating sequence of exterior and interior shots does not appear in Vitagraph's films until *The Mill Girl*, which was released in September 1907.

103. Cf. Burch's notion of a concluding "ideological point," which he attributes to
the "institutional cinema" of a decade later, in *Life to those Shadows*, 196.

104. That the train compartment was perceived as a potential scene of crime, in
France, dated at least from the 1860 murder of Chief Justice Poinsot on a train bound for
Paris. Schivelbusch, *Railway Journey*, 84–88. See, also, Kirby, "Male Hysteria and Early
Cinema," 116, 120; and Gunning, "Heard over the phone," 185–186. Another Pathé
film, *Un Attentat sur la voie ferrée* or *Crime on the Railroad* (1906), stages a different kind
of threat, the head-on crash of two locomotives, caused by a disgruntled railway employee, in simulated actualité footage. See also Edison's *Train-Wreckers* (1906), in which
the villains tie the heroine to the rails and then, escaping on a handcar, are pursued by
the hero in a locomotive. Vardac, *Stage to Screen*, 184. The earliest stage versions of this
melodramatic convention occur in Boucicault's *After Dark* and Daly's *Under the Gaslight*
(both 1867). Vardac, *Stage to Screen*, 48–50.

105. Jasset's reference to *La Loi du pardon* came in "Etude sur le mise-en-scène en
cinématographie," *CJ* 166 (28 October 1911), 35. The film usually is attributed to Albert
Capellani.

106. The principal feature defining it as modern is the light-colored wallpaper,
which had been pioneered by the late nineteenth-century bourgeois spas and resorts.

107. A POV shot (but of a note offering a tip on a horse race) is used similarly, at
one point, to motivate the narrative action in Vitagraph's *The 100-to-1-Shot* (August
1906). See Thompson, "The Continuity System," in Bordwell et al., *Classical Hollywood
Cinema*, 199.

108. I am indebted to E. Ann Kaplan for this formulation. See Kaplan, "Mothering,
Feminism and Representation: The Maternal in Melodrama and the Woman's Film,
1910–1940," in Gledhill, *Home Is Where the Heart Is*, 116–120.

109. Several writers comment on the mixed composition of the French cinema

audience, including women and children. See, for instance, Maxime Leproust, "Le Théâtre-Cinéma," *PCG* 43 (1 January 1907), 13–14; and François Vaillery, "Les Cinémas de Paris," *PCG* 53 (1 June 1907), 210. Russell Merritt was one of the first to raise the question of women and children in early cinema audiences, in "Nickelodeon Theaters 1905–1914: Building an Audience for the Movies," in Balio, *American Film Industry*, 73.

110. This perspective on the mother was suggested to me by Kaplan's brief analysis of mother-daughter relations in nineteenth-century American fiction. Kaplan, "Mothering, Feminism and Representation," 116.

111. One alleged distinction—that Pathé films were shot in the studio, while Gaumont films were shot on location—simply does not hold up, as more and more film archive prints become available for viewing.

112. Vitagraph also began using a standardized waist-level camera position about the time of *Foul Play* (December 1906). Brewster, "Frammenti Vitagraph alla Library of Congress," 300.

113. These logo "brands," together with logo changes in the intertitles and changes in the filmstrip edge coding, can be used to help identify and date early Pathé films. Suzanne Richards, "Pathé, marque de fabrique," *1895* 10 (October 1991), 13–27; and Paolo Cherchi Usai, 22 January 1990 letter to the author.

114. A slightly later Pathé film, *The Lawyer Enjoys Himself* (1907), makes an interesting contrast here, for, when the lawyer steals away from his wife one night to drink champagne with two women at a Paris café, there is a cut-in MS that serves no other narrative purpose than to confirm his drunkenness (which the women later exploit).

115. Pathé released at least one other film with this character, *Pitou, bonne d'enfants*. See "Nouveautés Pathé," *PCG* 57 (1 August 1907), 289.

116. Edison already had used this gimmick in *The Little Train Robbery* (1905).

117. Vitagraph begins to use this room-to-room cutting in slightly later films such as *The Boy, the Bust, and the Bath* (July 1907). Brewster, "Frammenti Vitagraph alla Library of Congress," 294. Pathé's *Difficult Arrest* (1907) even has several policeman pursue two thieves through a single building in what looks like a parody of editing together supposedly adjacent spaces. The first floor seems to lead directly to the garret and roof, rooftop windows offer entrances into a corridor as well as a garret room, and the fourth floor includes a bathroom where a woman is bathing, a dentist's office, and an empty dining room.

118. This film has been attributed to Alice Guy, Roméo Bosetti, and Etienne Arnaud. See, respectively, Guy, *Autobiographie d'une pionnière du cinéma*, 187; Jean Mitry, *Filmographie universelle* XXIII (Bois d'Arcy: CNC, 1981), 28; and Emmanuelle Toulet, ed., *Cinémémoire* (Arras: Cituation & Ensemble, 1991), 148. An earlier Méliès film, *Les Cardeuse de matelas* (April 1906), has a similar gag, but does not develop it into a chase.

119. Another brief seqence of alternation occurs at the end of Gaumont's *The Saucy Magazine* (c. 1906–1907)—a print of which can be found at the NFA—but its date of production remains uncertain. Méliès even adopted the strategy of alternation in a short sequence of three tableaux in *Le Mariage de Victorine* or *How Bridget's Lover Escaped* (1907), and capped the film with an emblematic MS of the cook embracing her fireman fiancé. An unedited 16mm print of this film can be found at LOC.

120. Gaumont films were recorded consistently by a camera positioned at close to eye level in 1906–1907—one of the features that distinguished them from Pathé films as well as those of Vitagraph.

121. A similar gag involving a baby falling off a bridge and into the arms of a man on a tourist riverboat appears in Gaumont's *Distractions of a Nurse* (c. 1906–1907). I have not included this film because, not only are the surviving prints incomplete, but its release date remains uncertain. A print is available from EG.

122. Frederick Taylor explains in some detail how the tricks in *The Magnetized Man* were executed. Taylor, *Moving Pictures*, 210–211. A shot-by-shot description of the film (attributed to Bosetti, from a scenario by Feuillade) is printed in *L'Avant-Scène Cinéma* 334 (November 1984), 40–41.

123. This convention also was characteristic of "documentary" films such as Pathé's *The Dog and His Various Merits* (1907–1908), which concludes with a MS of a man holding up his favorite terrier and a fox it has killed.

124. G.-Michel Coissac reports on Lucien Nonguet shooting this film, in "Variétés: Le Cinématographe et l'actualité," *Le Fascinateur* 33 (1 September 1905), n.p.

125. I thank Tom Gunning for sharing his notes on the complete 35mm print of this film at MOMA. The film is attributed to Capellani in "Albert Capellani," *BH* 5 (1912), 15.

126. There is no CU insert of the letter here, just as there is none earlier when the woman first writes it; nor is there any sign that one might have been spliced in.

127. This climactic sequence may echo the horseback ride staged in the often revived equestrian melodrama, *Mazeppa* (1831). Booth, *English Melodrama*, 98–99.

128. The best introduction to the history of grand guignol theater is Gordon, *Grand Guignol*, 4–34. See, also, Turim, "French Melodrama," 309; and Tom Gunning, "The Horror of Opacity: The Melodrama of Sensation in the Plays of André de Lorde," BFI Melodrama Conference, London, 6 July 1992. Although Turim's principal concern is with French films of the 1920s, her essay makes a good argument for the historical specificity of French film melodrama.

129. A particularly graphic example of the rosse play is Auguste Linert's *A Christmas Story* (1890), in which a peasant girl, unable to find someone to take her in, kills the child she has just borne and throws its dismembered body to a farmer's pigs, while, in the distance, a group of neighboring peasants sing Christmas carols on their way to midnight Mass.

130. André de Lorde, "Fear in Literature [1927]," trans. Daniel Gerould, in Gordon, *Grand Guignol*, 112–117.

131. *Terrible Angoisse*, which apparently does not survive, was only seventy-five meters in length. *PC* (Paris 1907), 195–196.

132. Gunning, "Heard over the Phone," 185–186, 190–192.

133. A similar effort to convey a husband's emotional state occurs in *Jalousie et folie* (1907), where an old man discovers that his young wife is deceiving him, and goes crazy, ending up in a local asylum. There, a sequence describing his treatment concludes in an unusual HA LS of his cell, where he is reduced to catching and eating rats, in a scene of sinister horror, says the Pathé catalog, worthy of Poe or Conan Doyle.

134. Gaumont's *The Stepmother* (1907) recounts almost exactly the same story, but in even fewer LS tableaux.

135. This distinction between ex-convicts circulated widely in France during the time. See Nye, *Crime, Madness, and Politics in Modern France*, 174.

136. A similar story is illustrated on the back cover of *Le Petit Journal: Supplement illustré* 619 (28 September 1902).

137. The dark wallpaper in the bourgeois family's rooms marks the old couple as rather traditionally bourgeois.

138. A similar reconciliation among generations, which pivots on the presence of a grandchild, concludes Edison's *The Miller's Daughter* (1905).

139. *Views and Film Index* (1 June 1907) describes the elder sister as the man's wife, but there is little in the intertitles or images to confirm this.

140. After the two sisters exit, the shot holds briefly on a suggestive detail: the maid now sits at the dressing table to dab some powder on her face.

141. *Views and Film Index* (1 June 1907) calls attention to the mise-en-scène detail of the empty chair.

142. Burch, *Life to those Shadows*, 155.

143. Schlüpmann, "Cinema as Anti-Theater: Actresses and Female Audiences in Wilhelminian Germany," *Iris* 11 (Summer 1990), 77–93.

144. *Le Raid Paris-Monte Carlo en deux heures* was specially commissioned to be part of a Folies-Bergère revue that enjoyed more than three hundred performances. Sadoul, *Lumière et Méliès*, 184, 263.

145. For this film's sources, see Frazer, *Artificially Arranged Scenes*, 5–6, 157. According to Sadoul, a shorter version of 160 meters was released to the fairground cinemas. Sadoul, *Lumière et Méliès*, 263.

146. Frazer, *Artificially Arranged Scenes*, 156.

147. Frazer, by contrast, sees this film as one of Méliès's greatest achievements. Frazer, *Artificially Arranged Scenes*, 172, 175.

148. Sadoul, *Lumière et Méliès*, 264.

149. See, for instance, Malthête-Méliès, *Méliès, l'enchanteur*, 300.

150. Malthête, "Le second studio de Georges Méliès à Montreuil-sous-Bois," 67–72.

151. Frazer, *Artificially Arranged Scenes*, 133.

152. According to Malthête, a piano score of the Gounod opera themes was sold along with *Faust et Marguerite*. Malthête, "Méphisto-Méliès et les thèmes religieux chers à Pathé," in Cosandey et al., *Une Invention du Diable?* 223–229.

153. Sadoul suggests this in his brief discussion of the *Faust* films, in Sadoul, *Histoire générale du cinéma*, 2: 151.

154. It is also possible that Méliès, rather than trying to convey the drunk's perception of an object (none of the others is "magnified"), is parodying the penchant for cut-in close shots in Pathé films such as *La Rêve à la lune* (1905).

155. The seemingly awkward rhythm of this film also may have depended on a discordant, unsyncopated musical accompaniment.

156. I have not been able to view *Les Incendiaires*, which, from the catalog description, seems to be a reworking of Pathé's earlier *L'Incendiaire* and *Au bagne*.

157. The choice of the boy's name suggests that the film was made primarily for an American and British audience.

158. Pathé's stencil color process would have rendered these cardboard figures less obtrusive, as it would have the painted flat tents and cannons in one tableau from *Le Regne de Louis XIV*.

159. When this recently restored film was shown at the Deuxième Colloque International de Domitor, the musical accompanist produced sound effects for breaking ligaments and bones when, in the next tableau, another man was stretched upon a rack.

160. In either the British or American print of Gaumont's film, one narrative intertitle was turned into a dialogue intertitle—"La Veillée" becoming "Simon, sleepest thou?"

161. Lacassin, "Filmographie d'Alice Guy," in Guy, *Autobiographie d'une pionnière du cinéma*, 185. Recently, Herbert Reynolds demonstrated that Tissot's illustrations provided the principal basis for Kalem's *From the Manger to the Cross* (1912). Reynolds, "From the Palette to the Screen: The Tissot Bible as Sourcebook for *From the Manger to the Cross*," in Cosandey et al., *Une Invention du Diable?* 275–310.

162. See, for instance, *PC* (Paris, 1907), 244–245, and "Nouveautés Pathé," *PCG* (1 April 1907), 133–134.

163. The full Pathé version circulating in the United States had thirty-nine tableaux and ran 3,114 feet. It was advertised at least five times in *Views and Film Index*, from 2 March to 28 September 1907, and Pathé published a forty-four page booklet to aid exhibitors in their screenings. See "Trade Notes," *VFI* (17 August 1907), 4. See, also, "Trade Notes," *MPW* 1 (11 May 1907), 152–153; "Correspondence," *MPW* 1 (26 October 1907), 541; Joseph Medill Patterson's article in *The Saturday Evening Post* (23 November 1907), reprinted in Pratt, *Spellbound in Darkness*, 51; and Wagenknecht, *Movies in the Age of Innocence*, 14–15.

164. Lacassin, "Filmographie d'Alice Guy," 185–186.

165. Tom Gunning has analyzed a particularly fine example of this in Gunning, "Passion Play as Palimpsest: The Nature of the Text in the History of Early Cinema," in Cosandey et al., *Une Invention du diable?* 102–111.

166. This revival "essentially began in France with the work of Jean-Léon Gérôme and his circle of 'Neo-Grecs' in the 1840s and traveled to England in the 1860s, with Frederic Leighton, Edward Poynter, and Lawrence Alma-Tadema." Caroline Dunant, "Olympian Dreamers: Canvas to Screen," BFI Melodrama Conference, London, 7 July 1992.

167. Gaumont's *Sur la barricade* (1907) provides another point of contrast. Here (the date is probably 1830), a young boy who has been sent off by his mother to fetch some milk gets caught at a street barricade and, in a HA LS, is nearly killed by victorious soldiers. The film ends with a peculiar recapitulation as the boy returns to the barricade and has to be rescued by his mother. Lacassin attributes this film to Guy. Lacassin, "Filmographie d'Alice Guy," 187.

168. David Mayer, "Toga Plays into Toga Films," BFI Melodrama Conference, London, 7 July 1992.

169. Shortly before making *Les Invisibles*, Chomón experimented with silhouette effects in *La Maison hantée* (1906). His later silhouette films would include *La Silhouette anime* (1907) and *Les Ombres chinoises* (1908). Tharrats, *Los 500 Films de Segundo de Chomón*, 104, 114, 119.

170. This film usually is attributed to either Velle or Zecca.

171. The corridor set here is the same one used in *Par le trou de la serrure* (1905).

172. A similar trip through the sky provides the spectacle centerpiece of Edison's *The Dream of a Rarebit Fiend* (1906).

173. This film has been attributed to either Velle or Capellani.

174. The NFA's black-and-white print includes an intertitle, "La Loterie. Mathieu gagne *une belle poule blanche* . . ." to break the opening tableau into two shots. The sentence is then completed in the intertitle " . . . qui prend place au poulailler," which then serves to introduce the second section of the film. The number of intertitles in this

print (sixteen in all) suggests that they may have been added to a later reissue or remake of the film. In fact, there is some evidence that the film was remade in 1913. See the ad for a 345-meter version of *La Poule aux oeufs d'or* in *PJ* 36 (1913); and Michele Canosa and Elena Dagrada, "Due Galline dalle uova d'oro," *Immagine* 12 (Autumn 1989), 6–15.

175. Julienne Mathieu plays the "star" dancer in this group. Tharrats, *Los 500 Films de Segundo de Chomón*, 102.

176. The NFA's black-and-white print breaks this section into five shots, which exactly correspond to the description in "Nouveautés Pathé," *PCG* 19 (1 January 1906), 326.

177. This CU reproduces the "Great Devil Money" in the Image d'Epinal tradition. See Weber, *Peasants into Frenchmen*, 458. This particular shot is absent from the NFA's black-and-white print; instead, a CU of a hen on a nest of eggs is tacked on to the beginning of the film, just after the first intertitle.

178. The NFA's black-and-white print includes a dialogue intertitle, "Tu as tué! Redeviens pauvre!," at this point—another indication of its probable later release.

179. According to Tharrats, this film was directed by Lépine and young Satan was played by André Deed. Tharrats, *Los 500 Films de Segundo de Chomón*, 105.

180. This tableau stands in marked contrast to the studio decor for the "Fête d'été à la Malmaison" in *Epopée napoléonienne* (1903), or even the Versailles garden tableau in *Le Regne de Louis XIV* (1905).

181. This point is somewhat complicated by the fact that the film probably contained more than the four intertitles that survive in the NFA print.

5: The Pre-Feature, Single-Reel Story Film, 1907-1911

1. See, for instance, W. Stephen Bush, "The Single Reel," *MPW* 20 (27 June 1914), 1800.

2. Gunning, *D. W. Griffith*, 26–27, 161–162.

3. Eric de Kuyper has begun to raise questions about the nature and function of the intertitles in early cinema, suggesting that they may have been read like chapter headings in nineteenth-century novels. Kuyper, "Le Cinéma de la seconde époque," *Cinémathèque* 1 (May 1992), 31–35.

4. Martin Marks has raised intriguing questions about how early film music could create narrative coherence, significance, and even subjectivity (through such practices as repetition and the incorporation of familiar melodies and lyrics) as well as how musical choices might determine the cultural specificity of a national cinema. Marks, "Rethinking the History of Film Music: Walter Cleveland Simon's Scores for Kalem Films, 1911–1913," Society for Cinema Studies Conference, Los Angeles, 25 May 1991.

5. Carl Anderson is praising D. W. Griffith's Biograph films, in *MPW* 5 (31 July 1909), 165.

6. This paragraph benefits greatly from Kristin Thompson's discussion of how the short story, novel, and drama offered models of narrative construction for the American cinema during this period. See Thompson, "From Primitive to Classical," in Bordwell et al., *Classical Hollywood Cinema*, 163–173. The term *pre-feature* is beginning to circulate more widely in discussions of the single-reel story film which dominated production and exhibition between, say, 1907 and 1917.

7. George Rockhill Crow sketched both of these models of narrative construction,

especially for "building a tragedy," in "The Technique of the Picture Play-Structure," *MPW* 8 (28 January 1911), 178–180.

8. Jasset, "Etude sur le mise-en-scène en cinématographie," *CJ* 170 (25 November 1911), 26, reprinted in English translation in Abel, *French Film Theory and Criticism*, 1: 57. For an example of American reviewing that criticized the "sad endings" of French films, see *MPW* 4 (22 May 1909), 671.

9. A similar strategy was undertaken by Vitagraph in the United States during this period, a strategy that was promoted, indirectly but with missionary zeal, by W. Stephen Bush. See especially Bush, "The Film of the Future," *MPW* 3 (5 September 1908), 172–173.

10. For a quick summary of these court decisions, see "Items of Interest: Films and Plays," *Bio* 136 (20 May 1909), 7.

11. I borrow the term *cultural capital* from Pierre Bourdieu and Jean-Claude Passeron, *Reproduction, Education, Society and Culture*, trans. Richard Nice (London: Sage Publications, 1977). See, also, Michael Budd, "The National Board of Review and the Early Art Cinema in New York: *The Cabinet of Dr. Caligari* as Affirmative Culture," *Cinema Journal* 26 (Fall 1986), 6.

12. Dureau, "Films d'Art et 'Film d'Art'," *CJ* 94 (11 June 1910), 3.

13. Brewster, "Deep Staging in French Films, 1900–1914," in Elsaesser, *Early Cinema*, 45–55; and Burch, *Life to those Shadows*, 173. Along with Brewster, Salt was among the first to emphasize this feature of the French narrative cinema as somewhat different from the American cinema. See Salt, *Film Style and Technology*, 113, 116.

14. Mary Layoun, "Fictional Formations and Deformations," *South Atlantic Quarterly* 87 (Winter 1988), 60.

15. For further information on both the Classical Renaissance and the Nationalist Revival, see André Billy, *L'Epoque contemporaine, 1905–1930* (Paris: Jules Tallandier, 1956), 22–32; Weber, *Nationalist Revival*; and Hobsbawm, *Age of Empire*, 142–164.

16. Mayeur and Rebérioux, *Third Republic*, 286–287.

17. From a 1902 speech to the Chamber of Deputies, quoted in Mayeur and Rebérioux, *Third Republic*, 287.

18. Jasset, "Etude sur la mise-en-scène en cinématographie," *CJ* 166 (28 October 1911), 35.

19. Jasset's survey was to have continued beyond its fifth installment, published on 25 November 1911, but nothing further appeared—nor was any explanation given.

20. John Frazer suggests that Méliès may not have been responsible for directing this film. See Frazer, *Artificially Arranged Scenes*, 205–206.

21. Although this technique imitates nineteenth-century stagecraft and resembles the imaginary recollections in Edison's *Fireside Reminiscences* (1908), its function also is quite similar to that in Pathé's *Histoire d'une crime* (1901). For more on the Edison film, see Musser, *Before the Nickelodeon*, 411–412.

22. *Falsely Condemned* (1908) has one double coincidence lead to the arrest of a rural postman for murder, and then another (his efforts to save a wounded prison guard are compensated by a confession letter from two vagrants) leads to his release.

23. In *A Little Mother* (c. 1908), one of Le Lion's only surviving films, it is the older daughter, after the mother dies in their garret room, who saves her drunken father from being robbed on the street and restores him as a responsible parent. In the concluding tableau of an overgrown cemetery, a "dream vision" of the mother then appears to bless the newly restored family.

24. This film, among others, contradicts Albert E. Smith's later self-serving criti-

cism of the repeated "goings and comings" in Pathé films—quoted from Smith's *Two Reels and a Crank* (1952), in Salt, "Vitagraph, un tocco di classe," in Cherchi Usai, *Vitagraph Co. of America*, 179.

25. *The Pirates* was still receiving excellent notices in the United States one year after its initial release. See *Variety* (21 November 1908).

26. One possible source for this film is a play called *The Factory Fire*, which was playing in London, in November 1905. *The Era Almanack* (London, 1906), 61. Another slightly later, apparently lost Pathé film, *Hate Between Races* (March 1909), takes on the subject of race conflict in the southern United States.

27. Mayer, "Toga Plays into Toga Films."

28. This reference is made explicit in *MPW* 2 (15 February 1908), 123.

29. Although pardoned on 19 September 1899, Dreyfus was not fully exonerated until 12 July 1906. According to the surviving archive print, *L'Affaire Dreyfus* was directed by Nonguet, from a scenario by Rollini.

30. The NFA viewing copy of *The Physician of the Castle* was compiled by Elaine Burrows from English, German, and Spanish prints. Salt reproduces ten of the film's thirty-one shots, and briefly describes the others, in *"The Physician of the Castle,"* 284–285.

31. Shelley Stamp Lindsay argues that, in the gendered nature of the characters' mobility and sight in these spaces, Griffith's very similar melodrama films are symptomatic of a larger male anxiety over the control of a changing public space. Lindsay, "Gender and Narrative Space in Early Griffith Biographs," Society for Cinema Studies Conference, Los Angeles, 23 May 1991.

32. As Gunning argues in some detail, Griffith clearly used this film as a model for *The Lonely Villa* (1909), yet, while extending the alternation to the very end of his film, in a frenzy of agonized delay, inexplicably he did not use the cut-in close shots. Gunning, *D. W. Griffith*, 195–204. Salt was perhaps the first to draw this parallel between the Pathé and Biograph films. See Salt, *Film Style and Technology*, 111.

33. Gunning argues that this kind of contrast edit was crucial to the development of a moral discourse in Griffith's films—for instance, *The Drunkard's Reformation* (June 1909), *Pippa Passes* (August 1909), and *A Corner in Wheat* (November 1909). Gunning, *D. W. Griffith*, 165, 178–179, 240–252.

34. Yet, based on Pathé as well as Gaumont titles described in both *Moving Picture World* and *Bioscope* (between 1908 and 1910), a good number of French films did tell stories that focused on women or girls, even if they generally assumed the norm of patriarchal family relations, as in Gaumont's *The Sentimental Wife* (1909), and of class relations, as in Pathé's *In the Mirror* (1910). That almost none of these films survives raises questions about how those that have did, particularly since many of the latter come from the Joye Collection at the National Film Archive—a collection whose chief purpose, Roland Cosandey has shown, originally was to instruct and entertain children, most of them boys, in a Catholic diocese in Switzerland. Cosandey, "L'abbé Joye—Une collection, une pratique: premières approches," in Cosandey et al., *Une Invention du Diable?* 60–70.

35. The best study of these "pamphlet novels" or "cheap stories" is Michael Denning's *Mechanic Accents: Dime Novels and Working-Class Culture in America* (London: Verso, 1987).

36. Denning, *Mechanic Accents*, 204–206; Deslandes, "Victorin-Hippolyte Jasset," 251–252.

37. Lacassin, *Pour une contre histoire du cinéma*, 116.

38. The other titles in this first series were *L'Affaire des bijoux* (22 September), *Les Faux Monnayeurs* (6 October), *Les Dévaliseurs de banque* (20 October), *Les Empreintes* (27 October), and *Les Bandits en noir* (15 November).

39. Denning, *Mechanic Accents*, 204–205.

40. The *Nick Carter* series was particularly popular in England. See, for instance, *Bio* 113 (10 December 1908), 7. The popularity of the series even produced a stage version of *Nick Carter* in Paris. See "Avant *Nick Carter*," *Com* (2 November 1909), 2.

41. Eclair, "Nick Carter, Roi des détectives," *CJ* 5 (15 September 1908), 4.

42. The other titles in this second series were *En Danger* (25 February), *Le Sosie* (5 March), and *Les Dragées soporifiques* (27 September).

43. The play is André Mouëzy-Eon and Armont's *Night at the Hampton Club* (1908), which was inspired by Robert Louis Stevenson's short story, "The Suicide Club." Gordon, *Grand Guignol*, 76.

44. During this period, Pathé was still promoting its specialty in dog films. See the Pathé ads in *Bio* (29 July 1909), 12; and *Bio* (21 April 1910), 12. Lux also was exploiting this kind of film in *How a Dog Saved the Flag* (1909).

45. In Le Lion's *The Blind Detective* (1909), an old blind man helps exonerate a man falsely accused of attacking a provincial offical, when he identifies the voices of the apaches who had stopped near him to tally up the money from the official's stolen wallet.

46. De Lorde's play was entitled *The Dead Rat, Room #6* or *A Pair of White Gloves*, which climaxed with a young Russian woman revenging the torture and death of her revolutionary sister by accepting a czarist general's invitation to a private dinner and then strangling him with her long white gloves.

47. Henri Desfontaines talks briefly about his acting work on this film in an interview with René Jeanne, in *Cinémagazine* (March 1930), reprinted as "Débuts de la SCAGL," in Lapierre, *Anthologie du cinéma*, 67.

48. *Moving Picture World* refers to the Charles Reade adaptation, which suggests that SCAGL may have been using the English version, or at least that Pathé was publicizing that version, as a strategy for marketing the film in the United States. "Coming Headliner," *MPW* 5 (16 October 1909), 531.

49. Capellani's film seems to differ from Zola's novel on two key points: it demonizes Virginie into an outright villainess, and it focuses more attention on Coupeau than on Gervaise toward the end.

50. The NFM nitrate print has several original intertitles tinted in either red or blue-green, while the images are all in black and white, without a trace of stencil color.

51. An incomplete print of SCAGL's *La Part du pauvre* (June 1909), however, tends to support this generalization.

52. Pathé's *Va petite mousse* (1907), though incomplete, uses a similar Breton landscape for its story of a young boy who leaves his grandmother to go to sea.

53. This kind of "empty" emblematic shot, full of emotional resonance, is characteristic of later Griffith films such as *The Country Doctor* (1909) and *Lines of White on a Sullen Sea* (1909). Gunning, *D. W. Griffith*, 214–218, 233–235.

54. In Auguste Linert's *A Christmas Story* (1890), a peasant girl, unable to find someone to take her in, kills the child she has just borne and throws the dismembered body to a farmer's pigs, while, in the distance, a group of neighboring peasants sing Christmas carols on their way to midnight Mass.

55. See, for instance, the review in *Variety* (18 April 1908).

56. See John Collier's letters, 1 and 9 February 1910, on the National Censorship Board to the Manufacturers of Motion Pictures. Motion Picture: Censorship Folder no. 1, ENHS.

57. "Alfred Machin," *PJ* 42 (1913). *Le Moulin maudit*'s production also may have been stimulated by Film d'Art's *Mireille* (1909), which, based on Mistral's Provençal epic poem, told another tragic love story among peasants in the Camargue. See Carmen and Vicens Armendares Pacreu, "Popularité de *Mireille: Mireille* et le cinéma (II)," *France-Latine* 106 (1988), 152–173.

58. Lacassin, *Louis Feuillade*, 167.

59. Mitry attributes this film to Léonce Perret and says the ranger is played by Joë Hamman. Mitry, *Filmographie universelle* 23 (1981), 67.

60. This text by the melodrama playwright, Owen Davis, first appeared in Montrose J. Moses, *The American Dramatist* (1911). Quoted in Booth, *English Melodrama*, 15.

61. "Chas. Pathé Makes a Statement," *VFI* (16 May 1908), 4.

62. Booth, *English Melodrama*, 49–50.

63. Nye, *Crime, Madness, and Politics in Modern France*, 171–226. See, also, Shapiro, "Love Stories," 45–68; and Harris, *Murders and Madness*, 208–242, 285–320.

64. Nye, *Crime, Madness, and Politics in Modern France*, 194–196.

65. See, for instance, Benjamin F. Martin, *The Hypocrisy of Justice in the Belle Epoque* (Baton Rouge: Louisiana State University Press, 1984), 15–78; and Shapiro, "Love Stories," 45–68. There is even evidence that a film was made of the "Steinheil Affair," in which a mob lynched the acquitted woman at the end. "The Latest from Paris," *KLW* 83 (10 December 1908), 777.

66. Gordon, *Grand Guignol*, 23.

67. In examining the Pathé scenarios collected at the Bibliothèque de l'Arsenal, Toulet has found at least one, *Le Bon Quinquina*, from 1909, which warns against having several characters drink from the same wine bottle, in order to make the film marketable in the United States. Toulet, "Une année de l'édition cinématographique Pathé: 1909," in *Les Premiers Ans du cinéma français*, 141–142.

68. Gaumont's *La Possession de l'enfant* (1909) uses a similar deep-space playing area at one point to tell its story of an unfaithful wife who is forced out of her bourgeois home and into a small apartment, where she does put-out work for a clothing store, and whose young daughter finally persuades her father to reconcile with her.

69. Pathé's *Three Neighbors* (1909) experiments with a different structural rhyme, involving several tilting shots, all within just four adjacent interior decors, in order to provide a happy ending to its threatened "fairy tale" urban romance. Recurrent spaces, of which two especially are emotionally resonant, also can be found in a Pathé film that the NFA tentatively has entitled *Mistakenly Accused of Murder* (c. 1909–1910).

70. My discussion here is indebted to Gunning, "'The World Tour Within Our Reach'."

71. CU photographs also can be found in American films, such as Essanay's *The Ranchman's Raid* (1909), but they seem to have been more frequent in French films during this period. Alan Trachtenberg, "Photograph/Cinematography," in Leyda and Musser, *Before Hollywood*, 73–79.

72. Henri Matisse letter to Alfred Stieglitz, *Camera Work* 24 (1908), quoted in Beaumont Newhall, *The History of Photography*, rev. ed. (New York: Museum of Modern Art, 1964), 137. My analysis of the following films benefits from some of Mary Ann

Doane's remarks on photography and early cinema, in "Technology's Body," Modern Language Association Convention, San Francisco, 29 December 1991.

73. Walter Benjamin, "On Some Motifs in Baudelaire," *Illuminations*, trans. Harry Zohn (New York: Schocken, 1969), 175.

74. Roland Barthes, *Camera Lucida: Reflections on Photography*, trans. Richard Howard (New York: Hill and Wang, 1981), 77, 87.

75. André Bazin, "The Ontology of the Photographic Image," *What Is Cinema?*, vol. 1, trans. Hugh Gray (Berkeley: University of California Press, 1967), 14.

76. For the purposes of comparison, see also Pathé's *Cruel Joke* (1908), in which a father doubts his own child's legitimacy when another man lays claim to the baby's portrait, and he is only assured (his own wife proves powerless to persuade him) when the man admits that his claim was a trick. Several 1908–1909 Vitagraph films, by contrast, incorporate either the filmmaking or film viewing process into their stories. Brewster, "Frammenti Vitagraph alla Library of Congress," 302–303.

77. Except in its ending, this story is quite similar to that of Pathé's *Mater Dolorosa* (1909). See, for instance, *Bio* 137 (27 May 1909), 34–35.

78. Gaumont's *Mater Dolorosa* (1910) uses a photograph in the beginning to guide a bourgeois couple searching for their lost daughter, but it ends with a long-take tableau that focuses on Renée Carl's performance as a gypsy woman who has raised the girl and to whom the mother sacrifices her blood ties once she recognizes the love that binds the two.

79. The American review of the film called particular attention to this lesson. See "Notable Film of the Week: *The Actor's Mother*," *MPW* 4 (22 May 1909), 671.

80. Susan Sontag, *On Photography* (New York: Dell, 1977), 155. Vitagraph's *A Tin-Type Romance* (December 1910) parallels shots of the hero and heroine each putting a tintype portrait in a locket, along with cut-in closer shots.

81. *Bioscope* took special note of the detailed "realism" of the location shooting in *Les Lavendières*, which probably was directed by Gérard Bourgeois.

82. SCAGL's *L'Inventeur* (1910), written and directed by Carré, also conforms closely to the tableau style in telling a similar story, but in a more modern milieu. Here, an inventor foolishly sells his patent on a puncture-proof automobile tire to a company whose owner announces the invention as his own. Their dispute is settled in court when the owner's daughter exposes his deceit—he collapses and dies in the courtroom—and later she rewards the inventor with a large sum from her father's estate. Carré is careful to make his villain a "bad" capitalist (who "naturally" dies when his true character is revealed) and his hero a family man who, by the end, is in the enviable position, especially for the French, of becoming an independent entrepreneur.

83. When I viewed the LOC print of *Le Bon Patron*, it consisted of fragments that were very much out of order. My narrative summary and analysis is based on the most probable rearrangement of those fragments.

84. This film, too, probably was directed by Bourgeois; the principal actors, according to the NFA print, were Servas, Vibert, and Goidsen.

85. Schivelbusch, *Railway Journey*, 131–145.

86. This change in the direction of the train's movement almost suggests that a second train is heading toward the runaway one. That the filmstrip was not reversed in editing suggests that creating a more or less continuous direction of movement across a sequence of shots still was not a standardized procedure in film construction.

87. In 1991, I identified this NFM print as *Le Vertige*. The Gaumont scenarios at the

Bibliothèque de l'Arsenal reveal that is incorrect; although not yet identified, Perret's film probably dates from 1911–1912.

88. "Mistinguett," *Cin* (12 April 1912), 1. Jean Mitry attributes the direction of *L'Epouvante* to Georges Monca, but misdates the film as 1910.

89. See, for instance, the Pathé ad promoting their comic films for people of all ages, in *Bio* 174 (10 February 1910), 12.

90. Lacassin, *Pour une contre histoire du cinéma*, 76–78.

91. Toulet, "Le Cinéma comique de la Belle Epoque (1908–1914)," 3, 4.

92. An exception might be made for Pathé's *Betty* series, which was first released in England in May 1910, but it seems not to correspond with either the *Léontine* or the *Rosalie* series produced slightly later by Comica in southern France and may have been made in England. See, for instance, "Four Fine Films," *Bio* 185 (28 April 1910), 7.

93. See, for instance, the Pathé ad describing Max Linder as a "sure draw," in *Bio* 183 (14 April 1910), 50; as well as "Pathé Notes," *MPW* 6 (26 March 1910), 469, 471; and "Notes from the Manufacturers: Pathé," *MPW*, 7 (9 July 1910), 113.

94. Frazer suggests that Méliès may not have been directly responsible for this film. See Frazer, *Artificially Arranged Scenes*, 202.

95. Crafton attributes this film to Roméo Bosetti and scriptwriter Louis Feuillade. Crafton, *Emile Cohl*, 116.

96. Gaumont's later *Getting Square with the Inventor* (1910) uses a "magical" device to create similar gags of fast motion; that device also is turned against its perpetrator.

97. This film was important enough to premiere as part of Edmond Benoît-Lévy's second Paris film festival in 1907. See Charles Delac, "Grande Fête du *Phono-Ciné*," *PCG* 52 (15 May 1907), 185. Sadoul attributes this film, like all of Linder's early comic films, to Louis Gasnier. See Sadoul, *Histoire générale du cinéma*, 2: 321. Linder also appears as a workman in an incomplete NFA Pathé print, *La Suspension* (1908).

98. *Une Dame vraiment bien* is attributed to Bosetti, from a scenario by Feuillade.

99. This film provides a perfect example for Constance Balides's argument that many early films involved a gendered struggle over the definition and use of public space, especially in terms of whether a woman was shown engaged in the actions of everyday life or was viewed as a sexual spectacle. Balides, "Scenarios of Exposure in the Practice of Everyday Life: Women in the Cinema of Attractions," *Screen* 34 (Spring 1993), 19–37.

100. *The Adventures of an Overcoat* (1907–1908), by contrast, creates a schematic comedy of commodity exchange, as a stolen overcoat circulates through the hands and over the backs of three different men, together with a stolen watch—whose taking is singled out in a cut-in MCU.

101. Given the descriptions in Pathé's catalogs, this print probably is an extended version of *Première Sortie* (110 meters in length), which Pathé released in July 1905. See the Pathé ad in *IF* 833 (22 July 1905), 4. The date and authenticity of this print are complicated, however, by the listing of similar titles, probably reedited for rerelease, in the Pathé KOK film catalog (Paris, 1913) and the Pathéscope film catalog (New York, 1920).

102. The film is attributed to Gasnier. See "Pathé Progress," *MPW* 6 (9 April 1910), 557; and "Notes d'Amérique et d'Outre-Manche," *CJ* 87 (23 April 1910), 4.

103. In Gaumont's *Cocher, à l'heure* (1909), a carriage driver picks up a passenger and goes on a series of his own errands, leading to a fight and a fast-motion race of destruction, which leaves his horse dead of exhaustion.

104. Crafton tells me that a similar use of actualité footage, of rooftop chimneys, occurs in Gaumont's *Le Ski* (1908), which I have not seen.

105. A number of French comic films did hinge on the consumption of some unexpected bit of food or drink. See, for instance, Pathé's *The Man Who Ate Horse Meat* (1908) and an as-yet-unidentified Pathé film (c. 1908) in which a man drinks coffee laced with a laxative and then adventures through the Paris streets to the disgust of those he encounters. An as-yet-unidentified Gaumont film (c. 1910) also probably would have offended American viewers with its wildly inventive parody of Paris newlyweds who fall into a sewer, live in harmony with rats, use the carcass of a dead dog to divert a flood of water, and pop out of a gutter opening, one year later, with no less than four kids!

106. Occasionally, a Gaumont comic film would deviate from the chase format: in *A Mix Up at Court* (1909), for instance, a simple musician who admires the ancien regime court life hits on the idea of disguising himself as a minister to the king and successfully takes his place. This film sets up parallel lines of action in two consecutive sequences, while also moving smoothly between location and studio LSs, and it concludes with two cut-in MCUs that confound an old nurse called in to distinguish the real man from the imposter—for each one has a patch of hair on the same knee.

107. Eclair's *Balandard est en grève* (1910) also falls within this group: after he gets worked to death by his wife at home, a strike leader persuades his fellow workers to return to their jobs.

108. *Satyre de bois-joli* (1909) develops parallel lines of action to reach a very different conclusion, also in a police station, and, in the process, comically inverts the disruptive display marking *Une Dame vraiment bien*.

109. Pathé's *The Old Fool* (1908) also ends with a MCU of an old man (now toupee-less) sleeping in a garden chair, surrounded by his doting servants, after a futile day of seeking bathing beauties at the beach.

110. See, also, Pathé's *Repos impossible* or *Impossible to Get Sleep* (1909), which deploys pans, tilts, ninety-degree shifts in camera position, and cut-in close shots to take a man (played by Max Linder) trying vainly to get some sleep through one interruption after another.

111. The editing in *Oncle Burton* is much more complex than that in Pathé's *Noisy Neighbors* (1908), which intercuts the room where a boarder is trying to rest with one where a Scottish band of bagpipers is practicing as well as with another further away where the concierge and his wife are sleeping. The Pathé film itself is a remake of Gaumont's earlier *Une Nuit agitée* (1907).

112. Pathé had used similar tilting camera shots two months earlier in *Three Neighbors*.

113. The NFA print of *The Would-Be Juggler* differs from Pathé's *The Maniac Juggler* (1907), at least as the latter is described in *MPW* 1 (28 September 1907), 477.

114. Sadoul, *Histoire générale du cinéma*, 2: 319–321.

115. Robinson, "Rise and Fall of the Clowns," 198.

116. The earliest Deed film, *Boireau démenagé* (1906), seems not to have survived. See *PCG* 39 (1 November 1906), 416. Another Deed film, *Débuts d'un canotier* (1907–1908), survives only in a fragment (at GEH), but it seems to follow the loose structure of Linder's earlier *Les Débuts d'un patineur* or *Les Débuts d'un aéronaute*.

117. *Jules the Sandwichman* (1907) also seems to be part of the *Boireau* series: here, a wine merchant hires the comic to strap on a sandwich board advertising his shop, and its unwieldiness sets up one destructive gag after another.

118. A portion of this letter is reprinted in "Le Cinéma selon Léon Gaumont, a travers ses lettres à Louis Feuillade," in Lacassin, *Pour une contre histoire du cinéma*, 59.

119. See, for instance, A. B., "M. Calino," *Cin* (5 December 1913), 2; and Robinson, "Rise and Fall of the Clowns," 200–201.

120. I borrow this point from Fredric Jameson, who sees this increasing division of labor as a framework for the naturalist narrative material of the late nineteenth century. Jameson, *The Political Unconscious*, 190.

121. E. F., "M. Bertho," *Cin* (1 March 1912), 2.

122. In England, for instance, see "A Popular Comedian: Paul Bertho as Bill," *Bio* 241 (25 May 1911), 371.

123. See, for instance, Hugues and Marmin, *Le Cinéma français: le muet*, 50, 52.

124. The judgment comes from Robinson, "Rise and Fall of the Clowns," 200. But see, also, Sadoul, *Histoire générale du cinéma*, 3: 151–152; and Mitry, *Histoire du cinéma*, 2: 47–48.

125. See, for instance, "Nouveautés de SCAGL," *PCG* 86 (15 October 1908), 760; Jeanne and Ford, *Histoire encyclopédique du cinéma*, 1: 93–94; and Hugues and Marmin, *Le Cinéma français: le muet*, 54.

126. Fagot, "Les Comédiens du cinématographe: Prince," *CJ* 100 (23 June 1910), 17.

127. Still the best introduction to the turn-of-the-century bourgeois drama of *amour* is Clifford H. Bissell, *Les Conventions du théâtre bourgeois contemporain en France, 1887–1914* (Paris: Les Presses universitaires de France, 1930), 60–92.

128. Robinson, "Rise and Fall of the Clowns," 200.

129. The film's British title, *The White Nigger*, certainly blunts any notion of a satire on racial prejudice, while the American title, *How Jack Won a Wife*, suggests that part of the final tableau was cut, implying that Prince may have accepted the father's offered engagement.

130. See, for instance, *BH* 42 (1911), 11.

131. See, for instance, *L'Homme au chapeau de soie* or *The Man in the Silk Hat* (1983).

132. Mitry, "Max Linder," 294; Hugues and Marmin, *Le Cinéma français: le muet*, 57.

133. Weber, *France, Fin de Siècle*, 18.

134. Mitry, *Histoire du cinéma*, 2: 41–43; and Mitry, "Max Linder," 298.

135. For the advance publicity, noting that Linder was already well known to Parisians, see "Music Halls," *Com* (22 June 1909), 4. In the United States, Linder was first referred to by name as one of the best film comedians for his role in *The Servant's Good Joke*. See *MPW* 5 (25 September 1909), 425.

136. The *New York Dramatic Mirror* review of this film (4 June 1910) is reprinted in Pratt, *Spellbound in Darkness*, 115.

137. *La Petite Rosse*, mistitled as *A Tantalizing Young Lady*, is included in a recent LOC nitrate film test series for stencil color. Its scenario is attributed to de Morlhon.

138. Another Linder film, tentatively identified as *Max Maitresse de piano* (1910), also has the comic perform as a suitor, this time on a drawing room piano that he systematically dismantles, in order to disguise his lack of playing ability.

139. See the Pathé ad, *VFI* (2 April 1910), 12.

140. See the Pathé ad, *VFI* (25 June 1910), 13.

141. This may also be in response to the American criticism of early Linder comedies such as *The Servant's Good Joke* (1909), which focused on the unexpected addition of castor oil to a bourgeois family salad. See *MPW* 5 (9 October 1909), 491.

142. Sadoul, *Histoire générale du cinéma*, 3: 142–143.

143. See Fagot's informative publicity piece, "Max Linder," *CJ* 101 (30 July 1910), 17. According to Jean Mitry, the early films in the *Max* series were directed, not by Gasnier, but by Lucien Nonguet. See Mitry, "Max Linder," 344.

144. In *The Joy of Tight Boots* (1910), cut-in CUs stage a mini-comedy hidden under a table at which Linder is one of several dinner guests. First he slips a pinching boot purchased earlier off his foot, next the family dog carries it off, then the foot taps about "looking" for the vanished boot.

145. One American reviewer found this film successful only as a roughhouse comedy and unworthy of any other interest. See *MPW* 8 (11 March 1911), 542.

146. This film reverses the master-servant relationship of at least two earlier Linder films, *The Servant's Good Joke* (1909) and *Servants and Masters* (1910).

147. This sequence makes an interesting contrast to the eyeline-matched shots at the end of *Calino achète un chien de garde*. Here, the waist-level LS of the tub obstructs the spectator's view of Max (once he has ducked underwater), which seems to stand in for the passing women's inability to see him.

148. Robinson uses this image as a perfect example of Max's incredible sangfroid. See Robinson, "Rise and Fall of the Clowns," 200.

149. Jasset, "Etude sur le mise-en-scène en cinématographie," *CJ* 169 (11 November 1911), reprinted in English translation in Abel, *French Film Theory and Criticism*, 1: 56.

150. E. B. L., "Une Première sensationelle," *PCG* 89 (1 December 1908), 804.

151. At least one other historical film may have played a significant role in France—Vitagraph's *Francesca da Rimini*, which was released as "a masterpiece of cinematographic art" in late February 1908. The release was timely for, not only were theatrical versions of Dante's story quite popular in France (Sarah Bernhardt's being one of the latest), but it coincided with the first announcements of Film d'Art's inception.

152. Pathé's *Don Juan* (1908) condemns a very different passion, in several episodes drawn from the life of the legendary Spanish lover, yet in a dozen similar LS tableaux. This film's appeal also stems from the stencil color—which sets Don Juan off in a broad, bright yellow hat—and from the truc effects in the concluding cemetery scene: here, he disappears miraculously, at the Commodore's command, in a burst of flame.

153. At least one feature differentiates *Samson* from most other Pathé films at the time—a consistent eye-level camera position. Another somewhat unusual feature is the painted light and shadow design in the room where Delilah seduces Samson.

154. Recently, film historians have been calling this film *La Mort du Duc de Guise*, presumably because the surviving negative used in the Archives du Film restoration had "La Mort" on its title card footage. Every source I have checked from 1908 and 1909, however, refers to the release title as *L'Assassinat du Duc de Guise*. One explanation for the discrepancy is that, for the film's rerelease in 1912 (and, again, in 1916), when it was sometimes called *La Mort du Duc de Guise*, a new title card may have been recorded (perhaps along with new intertitles) in order to bring it in line with other French films entitled *La Mort . . .* , and perhaps to deflect attention from de Guise's death as an assassination.

155. The film was directed by André Calmettes and Le Bargy; other actors included Berthe Bovy, Raphaël Duflos, Albert Dieudonné, and Huguette Duflos. A special musical score was composed by Camille Saint-Saëns. Shortly after the Paris premiere, the *Duke de Guise* was screened privately, along with *L'Arlésienne*, to an enthusiastic audience in London. See *Bio* 111 (27 November 1908), 4. The film received a generally cool recep-

tion, however, when it was released in the United States in February 1909, partly because few people seem to have understood the story. See, for instance, *MPW* 4 (13 February 1909), 184; *MPW* 4 (20 February 1909), 200; and *MPW* 4 (27 February 1909), 236.

156. Adolphe Brisson was perhaps the first to take note of this difference in film acting, in "Chronique théâtral: *L'Assassinat du Duc de Guise*," *Le Temps* (22 November 1908), reprinted in Abel, *French Film Theory and Criticism*, 1: 50–52. See, also, Rollin Summers, "The Moving Picture Drama and the Acted Drama," *MPW* 3 (19 September 1908), 211–213.

157. This extension of the frame space into a second background area also can be found in Vitagraph films such as *A Spanish Romance* (October 1908). Brewster, "Frammenti Vitagraph alla Library of Congress," 301.

158. Salt makes this supposition in *Film Style and Technology*, 106.

159. Dialogue intertitles did not appear with any consistency until around 1909–1910, and then usually preceded the shot rather than being cut in at the moment of utterance. See Salt, *Film Style and Technology*, 67; and Thompson, "The Formulation of the Classical Style," in Bordwell et al., *Classical Hollywood Cinema*, 184. See, also, "Latest Films," *MPW* 4 (13 February 1909), 184; and the British pamphlet published to coincide with the film's release, in the NFA collection.

160. See, for instance, "Films of the Week," *VFI* (20 February 1909), 4; and "Reviews of New Films," *New York Dramatic Mirror* (27 February 1909), 13. Reprinted in Pratt, *Spellbound in Darkness*, 114.

161. Billy, *L'Epoque contemporaine, 1905–1930*, 24.

162. SCAGL also followed Film d'Art in this turn to "high art" adaptations such as *Mireille* (1909), which was based on Gounod's opera, whose text Michel Carré had drawn from Mistral's Provençal epic poem.

163. Dureau, "Films d'Art et 'Film d'Art'," *CJ* 94 (11 June 1910), 3.

164. "Notable Film of the Week: *La Tosca*," *MPW* 4 (19 June 1909), 832. See, also, the *New York Dramatic Mirror* review (19 June 1909), reprinted in Stanley Kauffmann, ed., *American Film Criticism: From the Beginnings to Citizen Kane* (New York: Liveright, 1972), 32–33.

165. *La Tosca* was mentioned as one of Film d'Art's best films, in "Le Film d'Art: Interview de M. P. Gauvault," *CJ* 79 (20 February 1910), 4–5. The film apparently was directed by Calmettes, perhaps with the assistance of Zecca.

166. No actors approach, however, as close as the "nine-foot line," which was then becoming characteristic of Vitagraph films. See Salt, *Film Style and Technology*, 106.

167. Cathérine Clément, *Opera or the Undoing of Women*, trans. Betsy Wing (Minneapolis: University of Minnesota Press, 1988), 41.

168. Because the NFA print is incomplete, it is not clear whether Tosca herself also dies in the end; the description of the American release print indicates that she does, but the description of the British release print suggests that she does not.

169. See, for instance, Vitagraph's *A Friendly Marriage* (1911). Salt, *Film Style and Technology*, 106; and Thompson, "Formulation of the Classical Style," 215—and Biograph's *Swords and Hearts* (1911). Gunning, *D. W. Griffith*, 263. Salt revises his opinion to take into account a brief moment in *Duc de Guise*. Salt, "Vitagraph, un tocco di classe," 182.

170. The only surviving print of *Le Retour d'Ulysse* was reedited for the Pathé-Baby system in the 1920s (by Mlle G. Jousset) and included many added dialogue intertitles.

171. Adapted from Prosper Mérimée's novel, probably by way of Bizet's popular

opera, *Carmen* (1910) opts for a similar mode of representation. Almost every tableaux is filled with crowds of people, whose mass movements seem as significant as those of the main characters, Don Jose (Max Dearly) and Carmen (Régina Badet), and sometimes even obscure them. None of the mise-en-scène, framing, or editing features so characteristic of the earlier Film d'Art productions are in evidence here. In fact, the narrative significance of each shot is so closely tied to a prior expository intertitle (there is only one letter, from Carmen to Don Jose) that the overall effect of the tableaux's broad spectacle is merely to illustrate an essentially verbal text. For further analyses of the Carmen story in different media, see Jeremy Tambling, *Opera, Ideology, and Film* (New York: Taylor and Francis, 1987); and Susan McClary, *Georges Bizet Carmen* (Cambridge: Cambridge University Press, 1992).

172. Film d'Arte Italiana's *L'Enlèvement des Sabines* (1910) also makes a companion piece to *Héliogabale*, but it was shot on location rather than in a studio. The newly restored archive print reveals a stunning use of sidelighting, enhanced by Pathé's stencil color.

173. This scene may "realize," in part, one of Alma-Tadama's paintings, "The Roses of Heligobablus." Dunant, "Olympian Painters: Canvas to Screen."

174. Antonia Lant first drew my attention to this conflict and the shift in Europe's conception of Egypt (and the Orient), which preconditioned that conflict: once taken to be the foundation of Europe, by the turn of the century, Egypt had become the epitome of the magical, the mysterious, the primitive, and the perversely sexual. Lant, "The Curse of the Pharaoh," 87–112.

175. Another point of interest is the relative lack of "toga plays" (and their conflict between Romans and Christians) in the French cinema vis-à-vis either the American or Italian cinemas, where such titles as *The Last Days of Pompeii, Ben Hur*, and *The Sign of the Cross* were prominent. Mayer, "Toga Plays into Toga Films."

176. Gaumont's films were particularly praised for their lighting effects in this period, but these effects began appearing even earlier in such American films as Vitagraph's *After Midnight* (1908) and Biograph's *A Drunkard's Reformation* (1909) as well as *The Cricket on the Hearth* (1909). Salt, *Film Style and Technology*, 89, 98; and Gunning, *D. W. Griffith*, 170–171, 176–177. Feuillade's production team for *Judith et Holphernes* included Ménessier as set designer and Sorgius as cameraman.

177. *BH* 4 (1911), 3, 11.

178. Antonia Lant, "Egypt in the Cinema," Deuxième Colloque International de Domitor, Lausanne, 2 July 1992.

179. Pathé undertook an extensive ad campaign for *Cléopatre* in several major American metropolitan newspapers and was rewarded with reviews that extolled the film's spectacle. "Pathé Pointers," *VFI* (26 March 1910), 6; "Comments on the Films," *MPW* 16 (21 May 1910), 833–834; and *PWB* 135 (30 May 1910).

180. *VFI* (26 March 1910), 13–14. *Moving Picture World* described *The Fall of Babylon*, its American release title, as an "important, sumptuous film." See *MPW* 6 (16 April 1910), 597.

181. Despite its contradictions as a moral lesson, *Le Festin de Balthazar*, which was released in a completely tinted and toned print, served as a preliminary showcase for the company's *films esthétiques* series. See, for instance, "Le Film Esthétique," *CJ* 92 (28 May 1910), 16. As part of that series, *Les Sept Péchès capitaux* (1910) exhibited an even stronger pictorial tendency, perhaps because each of its seven segments was relatively short and could stand alone.

182. Other "oriental" films from 1910 include Pathé's *Isis, The Egyptian Maid, Salomé*, and *Au Temps des Pharons*, along with Film d'Art's *Tragédie de Byzance* (1910), none of which seem to have survived.

183. "*Semiramis* a Pathé feature," *VFI* (20 May 1911), 7.

184. *PWB* (10 October 1910).

185. Massenet's opera opens and closes with scenes set at Christmas, but in the latter Charlotte comes to the dying Werther in his apartment, where the voices of children celebrating Christmas can be heard faintly offstage. Vitagraph's *Clancey, Romance of a Policeman* (December 1910) contains a similar moment that crosscuts Clancey being beaten up by a gang he had arrested several years before and his wife decorating the family Christmas tree.

186. Henri Lavedan's scenario for *Le Baiser de Judas*, first published in *L'Illustration* (26 December 1908), is reprinted in Lapierre, *Anthologie du cinéma*, 60–65.

187. Gaumont's *L'Aveugle de Jérusalem* (1909) also relies exclusively on long-take LS tableaux. The two tableaux that survive from Carré's *Athaliah* (1910) suggest that it, too, may have relied exclusively on this older style.

188. Pathé rereleased *Le Fils prodigue* in conjunction with *Joseph vendu par ses frères*, in the fall of 1909.

189. Other Gaumont titles included *La Légende de Daphne, Amphytrion, L'Idéal d'Arias*, and *Le Roi de Thulé*, all from 1910. British audiences apparently were not taken with *Idylle Corinthienne*. See *Bio* 167 (23 December 1909), 66.

190. Jasset's *Dans les ruines de Carthage* (1910), a related archaeological adventure film (composed exclusively of LS tableaux), may survive in a tinted, untitled 35mm print at the Cinémathèque francaise. See Deslandes, "Victorin Jasset," 293. Eclair also released its own version of *Caïn* (December 1910).

191. This tableau uses the setting for Tissot's painting of Mary and Joseph departing from Bethlehem for Egypt—Herbert Reynolds showed a slide of this painting during his presentation, "From the Canvas to the Screen: Sources and Motives in *From the Manger to the Cross*," First International Domitor Conference, Québec, 10 June 1990.

192. Ball, *Shakespeare on Silent Film*, 38–134.

193. Shakespeare's status in France at the time is suggested by *Comoedia*'s front-page coverage of the opening of the theater season in Stratford-upon-Avon. "Les Fêtes du Shakespeare," *Com* (20 April 1909), 1.

194. Pearson and Uricchio, "How Many Times Shall Caesar Bleed in Sport," 243–261.

195. Ball, *Shakespeare on Silent Film*, 38–60. Apparently, *Romeo and Juliet* and *King Lear* are the only ones of these titles to have survived, other than those in incomplete paper prints at LOC. Ball, *Shakespeare on Silent Film*, 310–313.

196. See, for instance, W. Stephen Bush, "The Film of the Future," *MPW* 3 (5 September 1908), 172–173; and "Shakespeare in Moving Pictures," *MPW* 3 (5 December 1908), 446–447.

197. *Bioscope* described 1909 as a memorable year for film productions of Shakespeare. See "Looking Backward," *Bio* 167 (23 December 1909), 3.

198. See, for instance, the reviews in *Variety*, from 28 November 1908 to 19 May 1910.

199. For a slightly different description of the film and further information on various surviving prints, see Ball, *Shakespeare on Silent Film*, 91–95, 324–325.

200. I am indebted to Barbara Hodgdon for several points of description and analysis, in a section that was cut from her "Kiss Me Deadly; or, The Des/Demonizing Spectacle," *Othello: New Perspectives*, ed. Virginia M. Vaughan and Kent Cartwright (Rutherford: Farleigh Dickinson University Press, 1991), 214–255. For reports of the location shooting in Venice, see *MPW* 6 (19 March 1910), 429; and Ball, *Shakespeare on Silent Film*, 103.

201. The film is attributed to Henri Desfontaines. Earlier Eclipse adaptations of Shakespeare no longer extant included *Hamlet* (1910) and *Falstaff, or The Merry Wives of Windsor* (1911). At least two other French film adaptations of Shakespeare have not survived—Le Lion's *Midsummer Night's Dream* (1909) and Lux's *Hamlet* (1910). See *Bio* 168 (30 December 1909), 51; and *Bio* 170 (13 January 1910), 7. Other Shakespeare adaptations released during this period, which coincided with the English coronation of George V, included Will Barker and Beerbohm Tree's *Henry VIII* (February 1911), F. R. Benson's *Julius Caesar* and *Macbeth* (both March 1911), and Nordisk's *Hamlet* (March 1911).

202. For the French release of Vitagraph's *Napoleon*, see *CJ* 40 (21 May 1909), 13.

203. Fagot, "La S.C.A.G.L.," *CJ* 95 (18 June 1910), 23. Outside France, Talbot was one of the first to praise Pathé, and SCAGL (by extension), for developing the genre of the historical film, especially with subjects drawn from the revolutionary period. Talbot, *Moving Pictures*, 169–170.

204. For a brief consideration of what the beatification of Jeanne d'Arc meant in France, see Weber, *Nationalist Revival in France*, 69–71.

205. Gunning drew my attention to this "empty" frame, partly because it reminded him of similar images in Griffith's films of the same period.

206. This scene was especially criticized in *MPW* 5 (3 July 1909), 14.

207. Similarly, the film's intertitles carefully refrain from even mentioning that the soldiers Jeanne is fighting are English, which accords with the 1904 Entente Cordiale France had signed with Great Britain, allying the two nations against Germany.

208. In French literature, Jeanne d'Arc had received acclaim from both royalists and republicans as early as the Second Empire. See, for instance, Janine R. Dakyns, *The Middle Ages in French Literature, 1851–1900* (Oxford: Oxford University Press, 1973), 170, 202–203.

209. Léon Hennique's play, on which this film was based, provided André Antoine with one of his first successes at the Théâtre Libre. See, for instance, Bettina Knapp, *The Reign of the Theatrical Director: French Theatre, 1887–1924* (Troy, N.Y.: Whitson, 1988), 25–26.

210. One of the few surviving prints from Pathé's Russian affiliate, *Princess Tarakanova* (1910), concludes with a similar sequence of crosscutting between the relatively static figure of a jealous Catherine the Great in her palace and the more mobile figure of the Princess, the effect of which is to accentuate the one's control over the other's descent from court to dungeon. For more on Pathé's *films russes*, see Abel, "Pathé's Stake in Early Russian Cinema," *Griffithiana* 38/39 (October 1990), 242–247.

211. This film usually is attributed to Capellani; the impetus for its production perhaps came from Itala's *The Man in the Iron Mask* (1909). See *Bio* 138 (3 June 1909), 35.

212. A similar use of location shooting distinguishes the earliest surviving ACAD film, *Eugènie Grandet* (1910).

213. Martin Meisel, "Scattered Chiaroscuro," BFI Melodrama Conference, London, 9 July 1992.

214. Earlier examples of a single cut-in CU serving a narrative function can be found Griffith's *Golden Louis* and *At the Altar* (both February 1909) as well as SCAGL's *L'Homme aux gants blancs* (December 1908) and Gaumont's *Le Déraciné ou artiste* (May 1909).

215. The *Variety* review of this film was particularly severe. See *Variety* (18 September 1909). Maurice de Féraudy's *Mathéo Driani* (1909), apparently the only Théâtro-Film production still extant, is quite similar to *Le Dernier Requiem de Mozart* in its reliance on autonomous LS tableaux, each of which is introduced by an intertitle.

216. Similar "dream visions" occur in Gaumont's *André Chenier* (1910), one of which inspires the young composer to write "La Marseillaise," while another, of the revolutionaires going to the guillotine, horrifies Danton. One also appears in Eclair's *Eugènie Grandet*, in which a young man "sees" his father in such financial despair that the older man is close to suicide—and from which he gets to rescue him at the last moment, with the aid of an inheritance from a generous cousin (Germaine Dermoz).

217. This film's strategy contrasts with that of Vitagraph's slightly earlier *Napoleon: Man of Destiny* (1909), which shows Napoleon sitting in his palace in 1815, after the battle of Waterloo, remembering his past life. Alternating with this LS framing tableau are scenes from "history," each of which is cut in after a superimposed title naming the event to come has appeared over Napoleon's head.

218. At least one other French film took up this subject, but has not survived, Eclipse's *The Assassination of Admiral Coligny* (1910). Christian Belaygue drew my attention to this possible connection to the Meyerbeer opera.

219. Feuillade's production team for this film included Ménessier as set designer and Sorgius as cameraman.

220. Pathé's *Grandeur d'âme* (1910), which anchors its Restoration-era melodrama in a single FS/LS interior, makes an interesting comparison here. In a new strategy of mise-en-scène, Joubert constructs the detailed decors of solid wood rather than of light painted flats, giving the long, narrow domestic space added weight and depth.

221. *Madame Tallien* (1911), de Morlhon's adaptation of a Sardou play, recounts a similar story of escape but focuses on the deceptive tactics (a fake letter, a gypsy costume) the title character, played by Berthe Bovy, uses to free her friend, Madame de Lansac. It also stages her figure as spectacle—cloaked in bright yellow in the Concergerie dungeon or, in the end, descending the wide steps of her own chateau garden, being congratulated at her "restoration."

222. Jasset, "Etude sur le mise-en-scène en cinématographie," *CJ* 166 (28 October 1911), 33.

223. Fagot, "La *Féerie* au cinéma," *CJ* 109 (24 September 1910), 21.

224. Carlo Montanaro, "The Strange Case of *Le Théâtre du Petit Bob*," *Griffithiana* 32/33 (September 1988), 278–280. I have been unable to view either of the film's two versions.

225. Donald Crafton, "On the Track of *Bob's Electric Theatre*," Pordenone Colloquium, 14 October 1990.

226. *PCG* 50 (15 April 1907), 154. For the American release date, see *MPW* 1 (30 March 1907), 62. Edison's *The "Teddy" Bears*, which also included a sequence of stop-motion animation (with eight performing toy bears) was released even earlier in the United States, but apparently never was shown in France. See the Edison ad in *MPW* 1 (16 March 1907), 18.

227. Crafton, *Before Mickey*, 14.

228. Charles Delac, "Grande Fête du *Phono-Ciné*," *PCG* 52 (15 May 1907), 185.

Jasset, "Etude sur la mise-en-scène en cinématographie," 35–37. Crafton, *Before Mickey*, 16–17.

229. Talbot, *Moving Pictures*, 242.

230. Gustave Babin, "Les Coulisses du cinématographe," *L'Illustration* (28 March and 4 April 1908), reprinted in summary form in *PCG* 74 (15 April 1908), 565. Crafton suggests quite rightly that these articles were probably a Gaumont "plant." Crafton, *Before Mickey*, 17–18, 30.

231. As Crafton indicates, several British and American films—for instance, Walter Booth's *Haunted Bedroom* (July 1907) and *The Sorcerer's Scissors* (October 1907)—did quickly pick up on the stop-motion technique. Crafton, *Before Mickey*, 25–26.

232. This film, under different titles, exists in several different incomplete prints, for instance, at the Library of Congress, the National Film Archive, and the Nederlands Filmmuseum. Bousquet gives its release date as December, 1907. Bousquet, *Catalogue Pathé*, 56.

233. This film's scenario was written by Emile Cohl; its direction has been attributed to both Etienne Arnaud and Louis Feuillade. Later Gaumont films such as *Le Mobilier fidèle* (1910) eventually would exploit these animation techniques.

234. *Lightning Sketches* was released in France as *Croquis au grand galop*, at the same time as *The Haunted Hotel*. See Crafton, *Before Mickey*, 21, 23, 26, 28.

235. Another Pathé film, entitled *Diabolical Pickpocket* in the surviving GEH print (c. 1908), uses similar truc effects to let a thief elude several policemen.

236. In *Le Voleur invisible* (1909), an enterprising fellow uses the formula from H. G. Wells's *The Invisible Man* to turn himself into a successful thief (also aided by stop motion and black-on-black shooting).

237. *Enchanted Glasses* (1907) includes a similar trick in which Mathieu pours dark wine into six glasses on a table (in CU) while, simultaneously, a miniature woman dissolves into each glass. After testing the wine with her finger, she commands the six women to revolve in place, as if in display windows, and concludes by dissolving in MCU "portraits" of their faces.

238. *Metempsychose* (1907) also exemplifies this pattern, in reworking the earlier *La Fée aux fleurs* and ending with Mathieu producing babies out of a red rose and a green *choufleur* (a French emblem of fertility).

239. Another Chomón film starring Mathieu, *Sculpteurs modernes* (1908), uses a magic picture frame to create several *tableau vivants* and transform tiny sculpted clay figures. See Crafton, *Before Mickey*, 25.

240. One of the marvels of this trick process of creating miniature human figures, of course, is Vitagraph's slightly later *Princess Nicotine* (August 1909).

241. Crafton, *Emile Cohl*, 121, 138–139.

242. Crafton, *Emile Cohl*, 258–266.

243. For the French release date of *Le Cauchemar du fantoche*, see *APC* 90 (19 September 1908), 5.

244. "Comments on Film Subjects," *MPW* 3 (19 December 1908), 505.

245. Crafton, *Emile Cohl*, 140–141.

246. Crafton, *Emile Cohl*, 271–273.

247. Crafton, *Emile Cohl*, 148.

248. Crafton reprints the 1896 cartoon in *Emile Cohl*, 286. The target of Cohl's satire was probably not Jean Comandon, who was beginning to experiment in filming

through a microscope in Pathé's laboratory, but rather the publicity-loving surgeon Doyen, who had been the butt of caricaturist's jokes for ten years. Crafton, *Emile Cohl*, 289–290.

249. Crafton, *Emile Cohl*, 150–151.

250. By contrast, see Eclair's *La Museé des Soverains* (1910), which turns the kings and emperors of Europe into CU caricatures of sculpted clay faces.

251. For further information on this film, see Crafton, *Emile Cohl*, 298–300.

252. Crafton reprints the illustration from *Le Charivari*, along with frame stills from *Le Peintre néo-impressioniste*, in *Emile Cohl*, 292, 295.

253. A frame-by-frame description of this film, mistakenly titled *Traveler's Nightmares* and dated as 1905, can be found in Gaudreault, *Ce que je voie de mon ciné*, 163–174.

254. See, for instance, the deprecating review of *The Pearl Fisher* in *Var* (21 December 1907).

255. Another medieval fairy tale, *Le Pied du mouton* (1907), is comprised of eleven LS, painted-flat studio decors, each of which is preceded by a brief intertitle.

256. Despite *Variety*'s negative review, the film was still being shown over a year later. See *MPW* 4 (9 January 1909), 38. Although Georges Bizet wrote an 1863 opera by this title, its story differs greatly from the Pathé film. Gaumont's *La Légende de la fileuse* (1908) recounts another journey to the bottom of the sea, but it ends with a contest in which Apollo judges Arachne's weaving best and Minerva, in a jealous rage, transforms her into a giant spider in a web.

257. In Lux's *A Young Artist's Dream* (1910), a young boy constructs a model airplane that serves as the vehicle for a more successful dream flight over Paris. The French title and release date of the film, however, remain uncertain.

258. A Pathé film presented by the Film Society, in the 1920s, as *Trip to Davey Jones Locker* seems to date from this period, although neither its French title nor its release date has been documented. Yet its story of a prince, a devil, and an amazon queen doing battle as they all journey through hell and under the sea serves as a pretext for an amazing variety of spectacle.

259. Linder also played Polichinelle at a Christmas party organized by Mme Pathé for seven hundred children of the company's employees in late 1907. See *PCG* 67 (1 January 1908), 453.

260. Other titles that have not survived include Pathé's *Pierrot's Desertion* (1909), Le Lion's *Pierrot-Artist* (1910), Pathé's *Pierrot's Punishment* (1910), and *Pierrot mystifié* (1911).

261. *BH* 42 (1911), 3. Séverin was a favorite of the Paris literary elite, especially the Symbolists. Louise E. Jones, *Sad Clowns and Pale Pierrots: Literature and the Popular Comic Arts in Nineteenth-Century France* (Lexington: French Forum, 1984), 171–172.

262. That this form of pantomime allowed the public display of cross-dressing so characteristic of French lesbian groups at the time was unusual; just five years before, Colette was "nearly arrested for enacting a scene of lesbian love in a pantomime skit at the Moulin Rouge." Shari Benstock, *Women of the Left Bank: Paris, 1900–1940* (Austin: University of Texas Press, 1986), 47–49, 177–182. See also Jennifer Waelti-Walters, *Feminist Novelists of the Belle Epoque* (Bloomington: Indiana University Press, 1990), 19–30.

263. Frazer, *Artificially Arranged Scenes*, 181–183.

264. This film apparently is still lost. For a description, see Sadoul, *Lumière et Méliès*, 266. For its French release date, see *APC* 59 (15 February 1908), 16.

6: The Rise of the Feature Film, 1911-1914

1. This assumes that the 300-meter reel of film was standard for purposes of production and exhibition in France, as was the 1,000-foot reel in the United States. However, differences between trade press descriptions of films as well as the evidence of wear and tear in surviving film prints suggest that this assumption may not be ironclad, at least in Europe.

2. Brewster, "*Traffic in Souls*," 37–56.

3. Thompson, "The Formulation of the Classical Style," in Bordwell et al., *Classical Hollywood Cinema*, 166, 440 n.32.

4. Staiger, "The Hollywood Mode of Production to 1930," in Bordwell et al., *Classical Hollywood Cinema*, 138. One of the few indications of French scriptwriting practice comes from Frederick Talbot, who says that the French tended to write out the dialogue for every scene, in order to let the actors memorize their lines and then improvise their interpretation of the roles in rehearsal. Talbot, *Moving Pictures*, 147–148.

5. Thompson, "Formulation of the Classical Style," 198–212.

6. Brewster, "Deep Staging in French Films, 1900–1914," in Elsaesser, *Early Cinema*, 45–55. See, also, Salt, *Film Style and Technology*, 113, 116.

7. E. L. Fouquet, "Les Metteurs-en-scène," *Cin* (15 March 1912), 1. Fragments from de Morlhon's *Une conspiration sous Henri III* (May 1911), in the collection of Paolo Cherchi Usai, include the filmmaker's name on the title card. Two years later, Les Grands Films Populaires named Andréani as the director of *Le Fils de Lagardère* (1913) in its ads. *CJ* (11 October 1913), 65.

8. "The Progress of Cinematography," *Bio* 232 (23 March 1911), 7.

9. "*Scènes de la vie telle qu'elle est* ," *CJ* 139 (22 April 1911), reprinted in Abel, *French Film Theory and Criticism*, 1: 54.

10. Here I borrow several terms from Brooks, *Reading for the Plot*, 158.

11. For further information on this "moral reform" debate, see Abel, *French Film Theory and Criticism*, 1: 12–13.

12. *Le Courrier de Lyon* was advertised at the same time as the five-reel *Dante's Inferno*, but the Italian film was showcased as an exclusive "feature" at a single cinema in Paris, whereas the shorter French film apparently was released for general exhibition. At least two Danish films of two or three reels in length, *The White Slave Trade* and *The Abyss* (starring Asta Nielsen), also were released that spring. See *CJ* 135 (25 March 1911), 37; and *CJ* 139 (22 April 1911), 14.

13. The stage version of *Le Courrier de Lyon* was written by Paul Siraudin in 1850, and starred Paulin Ménier, who continually revived the play up until his death in 1898. See, also, "*The Courier of Lyon*, Pathé-Frères Reproduction of a Famous Melodrama," *Bio* 238 (4 May 1911), 185, 187.

14. Brewster, "*Traffic in Souls*," 37–41. This analysis of *Le Courrier de Lyon* is not without problems. I have not yet found documentation on how the film was screened in France. In the United States, in 1912, clearly it was exhibited in three reels, but in England, given the evidence of *Bioscope*'s review as well as worn and missing footage at the middle of the NFA print, it may have been shown in two parts. See *Bio* 238 (4 May 1911), 185, 187, and *MPW* 12 (25 May 1912), 710–711, 745.

15. Precisely where the reel break occurs is not clear from the surviving NFA print—which inexplicably repeats several earlier shots during the court scene, skips forward to the execution scene, and lacks several hundred feet at the end.

16. Pathé-SCAGL ad, *CJ* 135 (25 March 1911), 10–11.

17. For some sense of the film's success in England, see "Interview with Mr. L. Solenne, English Historical Films," *Bio* 263 (26 October 1911), 213. For an unusually laudatory review of the film in the United States, see Louis Reeves Harrison, "Reviews of Notable Films: *Notre Dame de Paris*," *MPW* 10 (16 December 1911), 884–885.

18. There is some question, however, about he relationship between reel breaks and divisions in the film's narrative structure, largely because a big chunk of part two as well as the ending of part three are missing from the NFA and LOC prints.

19. For a brief description of this scene, in production, see Trimbach, *Quand on tournait la manivelle . . .*, 52.

20. The last reel of the film condenses a good deal of the novel's action, eliminating one of its major setpieces—Frollo's manipulation of the street people to storm the cathedral and take Esméralda away from Quasimodo—as well as the revelation and death of Esméralda's mother.

21. Again, the American release was delayed, for it was first announced in *MPW* 11 (23 March 1912), 1063. Yet it seems to have been retitled *The Queen's Pity* and then not released until five months later. See *MPW* 13 (17 August 1912), 660.

22. See, for instance, the Pathé ad in *CJ* 173 (16 December 1911), 42–43.

23. The NFA print is missing about 350 feet, most of which comes at what was probably the reel break—between the waiting Calais townspeople and Edward III's dispatch of his terms of surrender.

24. A small-scale version of this sequence occurs in Pathé's earlier *Boniface VIII* (1911), which reenacts a 1303 confrontation between Philippe IV (Paul Guidé) and Pope Boniface VIII (Charles Krauss). In the three concluding shots of the only surviving print, Philippe's army, led by William de Negaret, consistently moves into the depths of the frame from either the left or right foreground, finally entering a cathedral interior to find the pope and his priests cowering against a background wall.

25. Burch, *Life to those Shadows*, 58.

26. The apparent loss of Film d'Art's *Camille Desmoulins* (directed by Pouctal), which received high praise following its release on 14 July 1911, is especially unfortunate when one is trying to draw conclusions about the company's films. The single-reel *Idylle Floretine* (1911), however, provides further evidence of the tableau style. Its story of a Renaissance sculptor in search of a perfect model of female beauty (which borrows its ending from *A Winter's Tale*) takes place in just three studio decors, and each of its seven LS tableaux is introduced by an intertitle. Yet one of these decors is a marvelous construction, with a centered bridge connecting foreground and background streets before several painted flats of city buildings.

27. Four different posters for *Madame Sans-Gêne* are reproduced in *CJ* 167 (4 November 1911), 39–42.

28. Dureau, "Une grande première: *Madame Sans-Gêne*," *CJ* 165 (21 October 1911), 3–4.

29. For reasons that are unclear, Film d'Art rereleased several of its initial productions in the spring of 1912, including *La Tosca* and *L'Assassinat du Duc de Guise*. Gaumont also rereleased *La Mort de Mozart* in June 1912.

30. Marvin Carlson, *The French Stage in the Nineteenth Century* (Metuchen: Scarecrow Press, 1972), 120–122, 192–193.

31. From an interview with Michel Georges-Michel of *Gil Blas*, quoted in Sadoul, *Histoire générale du cinéma*, 3: 39. Bernhardt's strategy makes a striking contrast with that of Réjane.

32. For an even more detailed description of this moment as Bernhardt developed it through a series of theatrical productions, see Gerda Taranow, *Sarah Bernhardt: The Art Within the Legend* (Princeton: Princeton University Press, 1972), 92–95.

33. *La Dame aux camelias* played in nearly all the major Paris cinemas during its opening week. *Cin* (8 March 1912), 6.

34. Sadoul, *Histoire générale du cinéma*, 3: 40, 343–344.

35. See, for instance, W. Stephen Bush's rave review in *MPW* 13 (3 August 1912), 428–429.

36. The film opened in London, as *Queen Beth*, at the Palace Theatre, 16 August 1912. It was first announced in France in a Histrionic Film ad in *CJ* 206 (3 August 1912), 13

37. Taranow, *Sarah Bernhardt*, 127.

38. *Queen Elizabeth* also includes the rare instance of an encore tableau, with Bernhardt sitting on the throne, fully robed and smiling at the camera.

39. Eclipse's *Anne Boleyn* (1914) is slightly "freer" in its mode of representation, mixing numerous studio decors and locations (with fewer intertitles) and occasionally including changes in framing. Yet this film, too, ultimately defines Anne Boleyn as a "martyr to a brave woman's loyalty to the man she loved" and blithely lets Henry go on to "another episode in the life of the Merrie Monarch."

40. Ball indicates that there are differences—principally in the number of intertitles—between the British release print, preserved at NFA, and the American release print, preserved at LOC and GEH. Ball, *Shakespeare on Silent Film*, 180–183, 348. Although the film originally was listed at 642 meters in length, it seems to have been released in three separate reels, as the GEH print clearly indicates.

41. Ball points to this rather anachronistic characteristic of the film, reminiscent of early Méliès and Pathé stagings, in *Shakespeare on Silent Film*, 183.

42. When I viewed the surviving Cinémathèque française print, it lacked intertitles, so that their number, location, and function were uncertain.

43. In Racine's play, Junie escapes to become a vestal virgin, Narcisse is killed by a mob, and Aggripine delivers a final invective speech, prophesying Nero's evil future.

44. Lacassin identifies the cameraman on this film as Albert Sorgius, and the director as Feuillade. Lacassin, *Louis Feuillade*, 170.

45. The *Bioscope* reviewer found *La Mort de Saül* of "educational" rather than "dramatic" value. *Bio* 279 (15 February 1912), 471.

46. For a detailed description of this film, see the 1913 découpage, printed in *Immagine* 9 (January–March 1985) and reprinted in "La Passion Pathé 1913, Eglise-Saint-Roch" souvenir program (Québec, 1990), 7–15. See, also, Emmanuelle Toulet, "Les Ecritures," in the same souvenir program, 5.

47. This sense of spectacle was certainly evident in the special projection of a 35mm, color print, accompanied by an organ, in the Eglise-Saint-Roch, during the First International Domitor Conference, Québec City, 10 June 1990.

48. The surviving first reel of Gaumont's *L'Enlèvement de Bonaparte* (1912), by contrast, relies on frequent intertitles and is limited to only a few studio decors—at least until the kidnapping attempt, when Napoleon's carriage repeatedly moves forward, in the same direction, through several exterior LSs.

49. "*The Margrave's Daughter*," *MPW* 11 (9 March 1912), 875–876.

50. *Les Misérables* was not shown in New York, however, until the fall. *MPW* 18 (1 November 1913), 503. Yet its continuing popularity is evident in the publication

of a specially arranged score for a screening in Indianapolis. *MPW* 21 (25 July 1914), 560.

51. See, for instance, Dureau, "Les Films de long métrage," *CJ* 264 (13 September 1913), 3-4. The specific lengths of *Les Misérables*'s four parts, respectively, were 805, 800, 730, and 1110 meters. Parts one and two covered the first section of Hugo's novel, part three covered the second section, and part four condensed the last three sections into one.

52. Sadoul, *Histoire générale du cinéma*, 3: 26-27.

53. For an account of this barricade reconstruction, see Trimbach, *Quand on tournait la manivelle . . .* , 62.

54. This shot is not included in the "Tempest" sequence, however, in the restored Cinémathèque française print of *Les Misérables*. Trimbach, *Quand on tournait la manivelle . . .* , 57. See, also, Yhcam's more conventional suggestion for conveying the subjectivity of this scene in "La Cinématographie," *CJ* 194 (11 May 1912), reprinted in Abel, *French Film Theory and Criticism*, 1: 75.

55. It was just this kind of emphasis on the choreography of the whole body that was singled out as typical in early attempts to distinguish the French from the American cinema. See, for instance, Hoffman, "Cutting Off the Feet," *MPW* 12 (6 April 1912), 53.

56. Henri Diamant-Berger, "*Néron et Aggripine*," *Film* 17 (19 June 1914), 7. According to Diamant-Berger, this film cost 60,000 to 80,000 francs.

57. Lelièvre arranged eighteen fragments of already existing music for this score, the cue sheet for which is inserted in *PJ* 22 (1914).

58. One crucial point that needs to be examined is the impact, vis-à-vis the French films, of Italian superproductions such as Cinès's *Quo Vadis?* (1913) and *Mark Anthony and Cleopatra* (1913), both in France and the United States.

59. For its premiere at the Gaumont-Palace, *L'Agonie de Byzance* also had a special orchestral and choral accompaniment, arranged by Henri Fevrier and Léon Moreau. Cher, "Paris Notes," *MPW* 18 (22 November 1913), 872. *L'Aiglon*, which was based on Edmond Rostand's famous 1900 play, received unusually high praise in Diamant-Berger, "*L'Aiglon* au Châtelet," *Film* 17 (19 June 1914), 19.

60. Our knowledge of Eclair films has increased with the 1992 Pordenone Silent Film Festival's retrospective of the company. See, for instance, Cherchi Usai, "Société française des films et cinématographes eclair," 28-29.

61. The contrast between American and British reviews of the film are revealing: *Moving Picture World* condemned the film's subject yet praised its acting, while *Bioscope* saw the film as evidence that the cinema was reaching the level of high art. Claudy, "Modern Melodrama," *MPW* 11 (13 January 1912), 112; *Bio* 249 (20 July 1911), 109, 111.

62. Sadoul, *Histoire générale du cinéma*, 3: 268. The cast included Jacques Normand as the alcoholic, Mme Barthe as his wife, and Hauterive as her brother-in-law.

63. Sadoul quotes a letter from a Dr. Legrain praising Pathé for not locating the social problem of alcoholism exclusively in the working class, but Sadoul also misidentifies the main character as petit-bourgeois, in the sense that he is a white-collar employee and not a small shop owner. Sadoul, *Histoire générale du cinéma*, 3: 267.

64. Vitagraph began releasing some of its films under this series title as early as May 1908. Sadoul, *Histoire générale du cinéma*, 3: 78.

65. "*Scènes de la vie telle qu'elle est*," *CJ* 139 (22 April 1911), 19, reprinted in Abel, *French Film Theory and Criticism*, 1: 54.

66. Fescourt, *La Foie et les montagnes*, 77, 85-86. Feuillade even bragged that he could do the *Scènes de la vie telle qu'elle est* series at six francs per meter of negative.

67. When I viewed the CF print of *Les Vipères*, its intertitles were missing; certain specifics of the story thus come from reviews.

68. All the early film titles that I have viewed from the *La Vie telle qu'elle est* series adopt this waist-level camera position, which had long been characteristic of Pathé, Film d'Art, and Vitagraph productions, but not Gaumont's.

69. When I viewed the CF print of *Le Roi Lear au village*, its intertitles were missing and the first two shots were appended to the end of the reel. The LOC print includes nine English intertitles and its shots are in order; however, it is missing the final two shots.

70. When I viewed *Les Chalands* at the Cinémathèque Gaumont, its intertitles had not yet been restored.

71. *L'Hirondelle et la mésange* was not released, of course, until 1983, when Henri Colpi edited the surviving rushes for the Cinémathèque française.

72. In its framing and editing strategies, *L'Inutile Sacrifice* bears some resemblance to concurrent Vitagraph and Biograph films. The fragment of *Les Rivales* (1912), one of Fescourt's earliest films for Gaumont, looks even more like an American film.

73. Gaumont's own publicity for *La Tare* emphasizes this injustice, not from a feminist perspective, of course, but from that of Christian morality. *CJ* 155 (12 August 1911), 15.

74. Richard Roud first called attention to this final tableau, in "Maker of Melodrama: Louis Feuillade," *Film Comment* 12 (November–December 1976), 9.

75. See, for instance, *CC* 5 (11 August 1911), 3–4.

76. Sadoul, *Histoire générale du cinéma*, 3: 249–250. Although distributed in the United States, the *Vie telle qu'elle est* series apparently did not enjoy the same success as did Gaumont's historical, biblical, and crime films.

77. See, for instance, Bardèche and Brasillach, *Histoire du cinéma*, 49, 51; Mitry, *Histoire du cinéma*, 1: 280; MacMillan, *Housewife or Harlot*, 25–26, 30; and Michel Lebrun, "Les 'Figures imposées' du melo," *Les Cahiers de la cinémathèque* 28 (1979), 90–93.

78. When I viewed the Cinémathèque française's newly discovered print of *La Coupable*, its intertitles were missing. The story is summarized in *BH* 52 (1912), 4. Krauss and Napierkowska are named in the Pathé publicity in *MPW*; Massart has been identified by Eric LeRoy.

79. The *Moving Picture World* reviewer described this as "conventional French pantomime acting" that, although "somewhat stilted," was admirably intelligent. *MPW* 12 (27 April 1912), 328.

80. Several of Asta Nielsen's early Danish films—*The Black Dream* and *The Ballet Dancer* (both 1911)—used mirrors to extend the space within the screen and to create suspense. Ronald Mottram, *The Danish Cinema* (Ann Arbor: University Microfilms International, 1980), 143, 145. However, that strategy had appeared in Pathé films as early as *In the Mirror* (1910).

81. Another recently rediscovered SCAGL feature film, *La Lutte pour la vie* (1914), proves to be a remake of the 1907 film of the same title. It is perhaps most interesting for giving its "tramp" figure a past history: unjustly let go from a white-collar job at the Nantes Steel Works, Morin is forced to become a seasonal laborer and finally a vagrant before reascending the socioeconomic ladder to success in Paris. In its lovingly photographed images of rich farmland and a local festival (probably recorded on location in the Beauce region), this film looks ahead to Antoine's *La Terre* (1920).

82. Eclair's recently rediscovered *Jack* (1913) narrates a darker version of this "male

adventure" story (from another Daudet novel) in which a young boy goes from adolescence to early manhood, through several different social milieux, as an "orphan" repeatedly rejected by his widowed mother (at the insistence of her lover), who characteristically arrives too late at his deathbed to be absolved of her accumulated guilt.

83. Machin's *L'Or qui brûle* (1912) also includes the spectacle of a large fishing vessel set afire at sea (with at least one man in flames leaping overboard). But it concludes more conventionally with the well-known Dutch actor, Louis Bouwmeester (the old sailor who has committed arson for the ship owner), getting to perform, in his shack interior, a slow, drunken "dance of death."

84. Trimbach briefly describes the production of this film, which he mistitles *Le Vieux Sauvetier* in *Quand on tournait la manivelle . . .* , 34–35.

85. In a letter castigating Perret for suggesting that he directed most of her films, Suzanne Grandais attributes *Le Coeur et l'argent* to Feuillade, but its "style" is much more like that of Perret's films of the period. "Lettre de Suzanne Grandais," *CJ* 247 (17 May 1913), 9.

86. Fescourt speaks of such close shots as characteristic of Perret's style. Fescourt, *La Foi et les montagnes*, 101. Yet a similar MS appears in Leprince's earlier film, *La Coupable.*

87. Mitry lists René Navarre and Emile Keppens as the principal actors in this film, but I have not yet seen documentation confirming his identification as accurate.

88. Fescourt, *La Foi et les montagnes*, 102. This reverse-angle cutting around doors and windows, often silhouetting characters in the foreground, is indeed characteristic of Perret. See, also, the incomplete prints of *The Gambler's Ruin* (1913), *Obsession du souvenir* (1913), and *La Belle aux cheveux d'or* (1914), recently restored, respectively, at LOC, NFM, and CF.

89. Griffith's *The Failure* (December 1911) uses a similar ELS of a single figure in a nearly empty frame, but near the film's beginning in order to convey the central character's despair as he leaves town after the collapse of his business. Gunning, *D. W. Griffith*, 270.

90. Joë Hamman talks about the stunt work in making *Le Railway de la mort*, in *Du Far-West à Montmartre*, 97–98.

91. The train passes the same abandoned windmill that was on prominent display in *Gardien de la Camargue* (which also starred Joë Hamman).

92. See Gaumont's ad in *MPW* 13 (20 July 1912), 234; and Blaisdell's review of the film in *MPW* 13 (10 August 1912), 535.

93. Sadoul, *Histoire générale du cinéma*, 3: 260.

94. Eclair's publicity is reprinted in Deslandes, "Victorin Jasset," 277.

95. Louis Delluc, "Notes pour moi," *Film* 98 (28 January 1918), 16.

96. However, at least one other feature-length film represented work in the coal mines—Pathé's *Sans Famille* (December 1913), adapted from a Hector Malot novel.

97. This establishes Lantier as a responsible worker concerned for others' welfare, in contrast to Zola's character who initially is prone to alcoholism and violence, as the illegitimate offspring of Gervaise from *L'Assommoir*.

98. Zola, *Les Rougon-Macquart*, vol. 3 (Paris: Gallimard, 1964), 1810.

99. Abel, *French Film Theory and Criticism*, 1: 105–106, 202–203.

100. Eclair's *Le Corso rouge* (1914), which Maurice Tourneur adapted from a Pierre Sales novel, tells a double story of deception and betrayal in which the Comtesse de St-Erment (Maryse Dauvray) dies in grief over the kidnapping of her daughter, Maïna,

and then, twenty years later, Maïna herself (now a circus artiste, also played by Dauvray) is threatened with death, but eventually is reunited with her father.

101. Only Sadoul includes this title in the *Scènes de la vie telle qu'elle est* series. Sadoul, *Histoire générale du cinéma*, 3: 248. Neither Lacassin, who counts sixteen films in the series, and Mitry, who counts twenty, include *L'Erreur tragique*. Lacassin, *Louis Feuillade*, 44; Mitry, *Histoire du cinéma*, 1: 417.

102. In Durand's *Sous le griffe* or *The Panther's Prey* (1912), which was another of Gaumont's fall features, several men (including Gaston Modot) struggle over a gold mine in Rhodesia as well as the owner's young widow, who is threatened by a panther.

103. Eclair's recently rediscovered *Amour et science* (1912) produces a similar cure through insert and split-screen images, but in a comic mode. For this traumatized subject is an engineer whose latest invention, a televisual telephone, leads him to "misrecognize" his fiancée with another man (actually she has disguised a female friend to play a trick on him).

104. The first tableau is interesting in its construction of offscreen space: in order to comfort Suzanne, the lawyer goes around his desk and offscreen momentarily before coming in to stand before her (center foreground).

105. *Un Mariage au revolver* (1911), perhaps the only surviving title in the *Arizona Bill* series, however, presents several problems. The archive print title card lists Gaumont as the producer, Jean Durand as the director, and several Gaumont actors in the cast, but *Ciné-Journal* lists it under the titles released by Pathé, in August 1911. Furthermore, the film comes close to parody—Joë Hamman demonstrates his prowess in steer wrestling (to the chagrin of a half-dozen gentlemen courting Berthe Dagmar), then he kidnaps Berthe from the train carrying her (reluctantly) to her wedding, and finally he lassos a clergyman and forces him to marry the "outlaw" couple at gunpoint.

106. This conspiratorial glance at the camera-spectator is one clear sign that the *Nick Winter* series was conceived and marketed as a comic series, in conjunction with the *Max* and *Rigadin* series for Pathé. I discuss the series here because of its intermediate position between the *Nick Carter* series and the *Zigomar* films, and because of its focus on crime.

107. With a similar degree of obsession, *Why Nick Winter Went to the Races* (1910) repeatedly uses POV shots of horses racing and jumping at Longchamps to animate a group of women while completely exhausting the detective, who has been sent off by several husbands to explain "the extraordinary behavior" of their wives.

108. In *Nick Winter, la voleuse, et la somnambule*, the case involves the repeated disappearance of money from the Richmann's home safe. The detective's initial investigation quickly lays out the spatial arrangement of the house so that he can trap the real culprit by placing a dummy in the bed he occupies that night and then by taking on the disguise of Richmann's daughter, whom the maid has hypnotized into acting as the "somnambulist thief." Although efficiently narrated, this film defines the criminal threat to the bourgeois family as a domestic—in a female version of "the butler did it."

109. Both the *Nick Winter* and *Nat Pinkerton* series continued to be released on an irregular basis up to the war.

110. Dureau, "Les Films en série," 3–4.

111. Deslandes, "Victorin Jasset," 263.

112. "Zigomar ou Paulin Broquet?" *CJ* 154 (5 August 1911), 18–20.

113. "*Zigomar contre Nick Carter,*" *CJ* 185 (9 March 1912), 57.

114. "Zigomar ou Paulin Broquet?" 20. Sadoul, *Histoire générale du cinéma*, 3: 408.

115. "Zigomar ou Paulin Broquet?" 18.

116. Jasset, "Etude sur le mise-en-scène en cinématographie," *CJ* 170 (25 November 1911), reprinted in Abel, *French Film Theory and Criticism*, 1: 57–58.

117. The American release title was *The Phantom Bandit* or *Zigomar vs. Le Roquin*. *MPW* 13 (7 September 1912), 1001. Eclair changed Nick Carter's name either to avoid copyright problems or to distinguish its French from its American productions. The surviving LOC print was distributed by the Consolidated Feature Film Company, Davenport, Iowa.

118. This lack of close shots is notable, given Felix Lorioux's cover design for the Eclair booklet publicizing the film: a MCU of a hooded figure with a hand suspended above and about to seize its head or pull off the hood. Eclair folder, Bibliothèque de l'Arsenal.

119. "The Pick of the Programs," *Bio* 278 (8 February 1912), 399.

120. "*Le Cercueil de verre*," *CJ* 181 (10 February 1912), 56.

121. Jasset's essay, "Etude sur le mise-en-scène en cinématographie," appeared in five consecutive issues of *Ciné-Journal*, from 21 October to 25 November 1911.

122. "*Redemption*," *CJ* 178 (20 January 1912), 63–64.

123. Deslandes is probably right in attributing the direction of *Redemption, Le Cercueil de verre*, and *Tom Butler* to Jasset, because of their subject matter and cast of actors. Deslandes, "Victorin Jasset," 294. But *Le Mystère de Pont Notre Dame* was clearly identified as an ACAD film when released in April 1912. In another recently rediscovered ACAD feature directed by Chautard, *Le Roman d'un caissier* (1914), a banker's son steals some money from his father, and the blame for the missing money falls on an old trusted cashier whose daughter is "ruined" by his consequent loss of position and then is physically attacked by the culprit (who is searching for what he believes to be a "blackmail" letter). Although the son finally confesses and the two fathers reconcile, the old cashier remains cool to the young man, especially when the latter (despite his earlier abuse) becomes the daughter's fiancé. This film is marked by unusually restrained acting and by the strategic use of CU details that both conceal and expose the theft of money.

124. According to Deslandes, these films also used relatively unknown actors instead of Eclair's usual performers, perhaps in imitation of Pathé's earlier *Victimes de l'alcoolisme*. Deslandes, "Victorin Jasset," 273.

125. Herriot's decree was published in *Le Music-Hall illustré* (1 September 1912), quoted in Deslandes, "Victorin Jasset," 273. For further information on these bannings, see Leglise, *Le Cinéma et la IIIe République*, 30–32.

126. For more information on this public debate over the cinema, see Abel, *French Film Theory and Criticism*, 1: 11–13.

127. Deslandes, "Victorin Jasset," 283.

128. Deslandes, "Victorin Jasset," 284.

129. For an excellent study of the serial-queen melodrama of the teens, see Singer, "Female Power in the Serial-Queen Melodrama," 91–129.

130. Eclair produced at least one other adventure film, the recently rediscovered *Les Enfants du Capitaine Grant* (1914), adapted from a Jules Verne novel. This amazingly elliptical tale sends a group of explorers across the world—from Scotland to South America, Australia, New Zealand, and back—where they barely escape an avalanche, one son is captured by a giant eagle, half of them are threatened by rampaging bulls, and

nearly all are stranded on a barren island. This strange film "reads" like a "Tour de France" extrapolated onto the globe or like a parody of exploration as it turns into tourism.

131. Lacassin describes all this as Feuillade's invention, without any reference to Jasset. Lacassin, *Louis Feuillade*, 49–50.

132. When I viewed the CF print of *L'Oubliette*, it still had no intertitles.

133. When I viewed the CG prints of *Main de fer*, they had not yet been put in proper order and were missing intertitles; the second title also seemed to be missing scenes at the end. For this reason, my descriptions and analyses are less thorough and precise than I would have wanted.

134. Société des Amis de la Bibliothèque Nationale, *1913*, 68. Sadoul, *Histoire générale du cinéma*, 3: 412.

135. John Ashbery, "Introduction to Fantômas," *Fantômas* (New York: Ballantine, 1986), 6.

136. Ashbery, "Introduction to Fantômas," 7.

137. Richard Abel, "American Film and the French Literary Avant-Garde, 1914–1924," *Contemporary Literature* 17 (Winter 1976), 87–88.

138. Lacassin, *Louis Feuillade*, 50.

139. Lacassin, *Louis Feuillade*, 176.

140. The *Fantômas* series, as well as the *Zigomar* films, differed from the later American serials in that they were feature-length and released at irregular intervals of several months. The latter, by contrast, were made up of two-reel episodes released weekly over a period of several months.

141. For a biographical sketch of Léo Taxil, see Gordon Wright, *Notable or Notorious? A Gallery of Parisians* (Stanford: Standford Alumni Association, 1989), 87–95.

142. The only surviving copies of *Fantômas* that I have viewed have no intertitles. The full découpage of the film is published in *L'Avant-Scène Cinéma* 271/272 (July 1981), 27–46.

143. Sadoul, *Histoire générale du cinéma*, 3: 413.

144. Gaumont ad, *CJ* 262 (30 August 1913), 75.

145. The full découpage of *Juve contre Fantômas* is published in *L'Avant-Scène Cinéma* 271/272 (July 1981), 47–70. This second film contains nearly 150 shots, almost twice as many as the first *Fantômas* film.

146. I have not viewed the more complete print preserved at the Archives du Film. Only a summary synopsis of *Le Mort qui tue* is published in *L'Avant-Scène Cinéma* 271/272 (July 1981), 71–73.

147. The NFA print of *Le Mort qui tue*, like that of *Le Courrier de Lyon*, does raise the question of how long reels could be in exhibition, for it survives in two 35mm reels of 1,465 feet and 1,290 feet.

148. Only a summary synopsis of *Le Faux Magistrat* is published in *L'Avant-Scène Cinéma* 271/272 (July 1981), 87–89.

149. Maurice Raynal, "Chronique cinématographique," *Les Soirées de Paris* 26–27 (July–August 1914), reprinted in Abel, *French Film Theory and Criticism*, 1: 89.

150. "Cinématographes," *Com* (3 October 1913), 4.

151. Mayeur and Rebérioux, *Third Republic*, 292–295. At the time I viewed the CF print of *L'Enfant de Paris*, it still lacked intertitles.

152. Sadoul, *Histoire générale du cinéma*, 3: 257.

153. Thompson, "The Continuity System," in Bordwell et al., *Classical Hollywood Cinema*, 200–201.

154. One of the posters for *L'Enfant de Paris* shows Marie Laure standing on an empty street corner with her doll. NFM Poster Collection. A girl's doll serves a similar function in the second half of Vitagraph's one-reeler, *Lulu's Doctor* (June 1912). Ben Brewster analyzes the unique way, in the one-reel format, that a single object can sustain the narrative without taking on symbolic significance, specifically in Vitagraph's *An Official Appointment* (November 1912). "A Bunch of Violets," Society for Cinema Studies Conference, Los Angeles, 23 May 1991.

155. Thompson, "The Continuity System," 207–210.

156. The practice of carrying narrative action over from one reel to another may assume that at least the major urban cinemas had two projectors operating in alternation. Precisely when this became standard practice has not yet, to my knowledge, been determined.

157. Robinson, "Rise and Fall of the Clowns," 201.

158. Long ago, a PBS series, "The Amazing Years of Cinema," gave a release date of 1906 for *Une Maison bien lavée* or *The Well-Washed House*. For years, this kind of mistaken guess at release dates has been common for Pathé films from the prewar period.

159. The full découpage of *La Saucisse mystérieuse* is printed in *L'Avant-Scène Cinéma* (November 1984), 43–44. Although undated, it appears erroneously along with several films from 1907–1908.

160. *BH* 46 (1911), 4.

161. *Rosalie et ses meubles fidèles* (1911) very expertly uses the technique of split-screen double exposure to let the furniture she has been forced to sell follow Duhamel through the streets and back to her apartment.

162. Because Bertho was working for Eclair well before *Gratitude obsédante* was released, this comic may be someone else entirely, although he looks much like Bertho.

163. An unidentified film in Eclipse's *Arthème* series, tentatively labeled *Dupin's Happy Lot* by the National Film Archive, also could be included here. It satirizes the family melodrama by having Arthème fail at committing suicide, fall in love with the woman who drags him out of a river, marry her and produce a record number of ten children in ten years, and finally reconcile with the father he had abandoned in the opening.

164. In *Little Moritz enlève Rosalie*, the recalcitrant father chases the pair around the rooftops of Nice, until Rosalie's skirt turns into a balloon that carries them away, only to let them crash through the apartment building roof and right into her bedroom. Sadoul, *Histoire générale du cinéma*, 3: 153.

165. Mitry attributes this film to Perret, but makes the title character female and lists cast members (Perret, Grandais, and Andreyor) who clearly are not in the film. Mitry, *Filmographie universelle*, 23: 68.

166. Mitry's cast list for this film (Grandais, Luguet, Andreyor) seems wrong.

167. Gaumont continued to turn out similar one-reel comedies, as in *La Loup dans la bergerie* (1913).

168. Another Gaumont comedy, *Le Gui* (1913), tests two old, corpulent military officers as suitors to a young woman in the provinces—they must collect a sprig of mistletoe from high up in a tree—but then reveals that she is engaged to a dapper young gentleman who arrives dressed in a tuxedo.

169. Lacassin, *Louis Feuillade*, 40–41.

170. "Willy," *Cin* (18 October 1912), 2. Robinson, "Rise and Fall of the Clowns," 203.

171. The first film to feature Bout-de-zan alone, *Bout-de-zan revient du cirque*, seems to have been a trial balloon. *CJ* 223 (30 November 1912), 103. An NFA print bears this title, but it is not much different from the compilation print entitled *Bout-de-zan et le chemineau*.

172. Lacassin, *Louis Feuillade*, 41. Robinson, "Rise and Fall of the Clowns," 203.

173. This fragment is one of several attached at the beginning of the NFA print of *Bout-de-zan et le chemineau*.

174. A good introduction to Deed's work in Italy, as a character named Cretinetti or Gribouille, chiefly for Itala Film, can be found in David Robinson, "The Italian Comedy," *Sight and Sound* 55 (Spring 1986), 106–107.

175. The first title in the new series was straightforward, *Gribouille redevient Boireau* (10 February 1912).

176. The only extant print of *Calino, courtier en paratonerres* is missing its opening shot and intertitle, which renders the premise even more absurd.

177. Robinson, "Rise and Fall of the Clowns," 202.

178. Among the group of "Les Pouics" (a derivative of *le pou* or lice) were Gaston Modot (the only nonprofessional), Edouard Grisollet, Albert Fouché, Océana de la Platta, Aimos, Lonys, Polos, Beauvais, Berthe Dagmar, and Hector Gendres. For further information on Durand, Bourbon, and "Les Pouics," see Sadoul, *Histoire générale du cinéma*, 3: 158–165; and Hugues and Muller, *Gaumont: 90 ans du cinéma*, 69–72.

179. "Les Meilleurs Films," *Cin* (9 August 1912), 3.

180. When I viewed the CF print, it was erroneously titled *Onésime et le coeur de tzigane*.

181. In sending up Sherlock Holmes stories (among other things), *Le Disaparition d'Onésime* (1913) continues to mine this parodic vein, with more tongue-in-cheek intertitles, but with Gaston Modot, Berthe Dagmar, and other members of "Les Pouics" now assuming the principal roles.

182. One of the early films, *Onésime aux enfers* (1912) literalizes this penchant for trucs when Mephistopheles appears out of nowhere in the Paris café where Onésime is drinking himself silly and tricks him into signing a pact that quickly sends the comic to hell where he endures all kinds of magical temptations and tortures. *Onésime contre Onésime* (1912) consistently uses the technique of double exposure to juxtapose a "good" and "bad" Onésime, whose courtship of a young woman turns into a chase, at the end of which the one finally dismembers the other. *Onésime début au théâtre* (1913) includes even better tricks—several doctors, one after another, climb out of a writing desk, to examine the comic for the strenuous role of a musketeer—and more public abuses: on stage, he is pelted by pillows, chairs, and even a bass drum; then, trying to escape, he does a back flip into and sticks against a painted-flat window.

183. *Onésime horloger* probably is best known because it was remembered, in the 1930s, as a precursor of René Clair's *Paris qui dort* (1924). See, for instance, Bardèche and Brasillach, *Histoire du cinéma*, 67.

184. One last film from the *Onésime* series deserves mention, but neither the title on the CF print, *L'Extraordinaire aventure d'Onésime*, nor the story description seems to correspond to any released during the 1912–1914 period. It could be significant, how-

ever, because nearly half of its approximately sixty shots are either eyeline-matched MSs and MCUs or else POV shots. If this print does turn out to be a copy of *Triste aventure d'Onésime* (1913), for instance, its mode of representation could be read as an excess of imitation, sending up a crucial—but what the French found "unnatural"—component of the emerging American continuity system.

185. Quoted in Robinson, "Rise and Fall of the Clowns," 200.

186. *Bigorno parachutiste* (1914), from a later Bosetti series for Comica, uses a similar strategy of 180-degree reverse-angle LSs, accentuated by cut-in MSs and LAFSs, in a balcony scene of exchanged notes, which sets up a series of performative "tests" for the lovesick comic who leaps from greater and greater heights.

187. In an earlier Rigadin film, *La Doctoresse* (1911), the comic's wife is a doctor (Mistinguett) who has little time for him until a circus barbell falls on his foot. In a stunning reversal, occasioned by her examination of him, she rips up her diploma and falls on her knees, and Rigadin celebrates by smashing her plaster bust of Hippocrates.

188. One of these, *Max Is Almost Married* (January 1911), reverts to the earlier chase film format. Another, *Max et sa belle-mère* (May 1911), has long been thought to be the title of a film collected at several archives, among them CF and CQ. The découpage of this quite intriguing film is printed in *L'Avant-Scène du cinéma* 334 (November 1984), 75-83. However, the plot summary of *Max et sa belle-mère* published in the press is very different from that in this archive film print.

189. Mitry, "Max Linder," 304.

190. Mitry, "Max Linder," 302.

191. *BH* 37 (1911), 7.

192. MOMA has an incomplete print of this film under the title, *Troubles of a Grass Widower*. Pathé did release a film with this latter title four years earlier, and its synopsis, in *Views and Film Index* (29 February 1908), bears a close resemblance to the 1912 film—but whether Linder performed in the earlier film is unclear.

193. According to Mitry, Abel Gance also appears in *Max Linder contre Nick Winter* in a small role.

194. *Max Jockey par amour* (1912) presents the comic with a similar problem. After several attempts to lose weight, so he can enter a steeplechase race, Max succeeds and wins—only to discover that his fiancée (Napierkowska) will not marry a "thin" man. Now he is forced to consume heaping plates of pasta and pastries and huge glasses of wine, which turn him into a "blimp"—and she changes her mind, saying she prefers him "svelte."

195. Abel Gance's first film made during the war, *La Folie du Docteur Tube* (1915), often has been credited with using an anamorphic lens, but, as Kevin Brownlow argues, that film's effects more likely are produced by distorting mirrors.

196. Griffith had used this technique of having the actor come forward into CU, without going out of focus, but for its threatening and suspenseful effects—as in *Conscience* (1910), *The Muskateers of Pig Alley* (1912), and *The House of Darkness* (1913). Gunning, *D. W. Griffith*, 275.

197. The lack of intertitles in the CQ print of *Max et la doctoresse*, of course, may draw undue attention to this image of Max and the baby.

198. *Mari jaloux* provides one of the few "records" of French film production before the war and is notable for its two waist-level Pathé cameras and chalk line placed about twelve feet from the cameras.

199. Apparently the first film with Léonce in the title was *Léonce fait des gaffes*. *CJ* 217 (19 October 1912), 82.

200. In this film as well as the later *Léonce* series, Perret's collaborators again included Specht as cameraman and Perrier as set designer.

201. According to Fescourt, the train sequences were shot in actual train cars, on a siding of the Paris–Niort line. Fescourt, *La Foi et les montagnes*, 102.

202. The Gaumont scenario, at the Bibliothèque de l'Arsenal, sets the story on the New England seacoast.

203. Similarly, Fescourt's *Le Restaurant de l'impasse Canin* (1913) uses just three studio decors of a long, narrow restaurant interior, a kitchen, and an exterior to narrate its story of a desperate restauranteur who invites people in off the street to pack his empty establishment in order to impress a visiting uncle—and then finds himself unable to pay the bills that quickly come due.

204. When I viewed the CF print of *Léonce pot au feu*, it lacked intertitles and still had a good number of shots out of order at this point in the film. The CF print of *Léonce en menage* (1913) was even less complete, so I have not included it in this analysis of the *Léonce* series.

205. Suzanne Grandais left Gaumont, in the spring of 1913, to form her own production company, whose films would be released by Géo Janin. See, for instance, the ad in *CJ* 245 (3 May 1913), 56. That same month, she and Perret exchanged rather acrimonious letters in *Ciné-Journal* over who was responsible for her star status.

206. Here, in *Léonce et Toto*, Perret replicates the system of eyeline-matched shots from the earlier *Rigadin, défenseur de la vertu*.

207. Reducing the huge Gaumont-Palace interior to a small space encompassing little more than one hundred seats is another one of the more recognizable in-jokes in *Léonce cinématographiste*.

208. See, for instance, Lacassin, *Louis Feuillade*, 55–56.

209. Marcel Levesque, however, claims that Feuillade transformed the stage vaudeville into an entirely new cinematic formula, but does not explain how. "De 1913 à 1918, cinq ans à la maison Gaumont avec Louis Feuillade, souvenirs personnels de Marcel Levesque," *Archives* 8 (1987), n.p.

210. "De 1913 à 1918," n.p. Both the Cinémathèque Gaumont and the Archives du Film have copies of *L'Hôtel de la gare*, but neither has yet been restored or printed for viewing purposes.

211. Only the last of *Champignol malgré lui*'s three reels remains extant.

212. This kind of incitement to military heroism would be quite unacceptable within less than a year, after the outbreak of the Great War.

213. Precisely what effect the French comic series may have had on American comic films also depends on the extent of their availability in the United States between 1911 and 1914—something that has yet to be fully documented.

Afterword

1. See also volumes 8 (Lumière and Méliès) and 10 (Pathé) in the 1979 Granada Television series, *Camera: Early Photography and Moving Pictures*, available on videocassette.

2. A preliminary study of the Gaumont scenarios can be found in Valeria Ciezar, "Bibliothèque Nationale: Les Scenarios Gaumont (1906–1924)," *Cinémathèque* 2 (November 1992), 130–135.

3. Michèle Lagny, "Cinéma et histoire culturelle," *Cinémathèque* 1 (May 1992), 14–15.

4. See my initial exploration of what the presence of Pathé films in the nickelodeon market meant for the construction of an American national identity between 1906 and 1910, in "The Perils of Ignoring Pathé: Problems in Rewriting Early American Cinema History," Society for Cinema Studies Conference, New Orleans, 11 February 1993.

Bibliography

General Reference: Turn-of-the-Century France

Apter, Emily. *Feminizing the Fetish: Psychoanalysis and Narrative Obsession in Turn-of-the-Century France.* Ithaca: Cornell University Press, 1991.

Bann, Stephen. *The Clothing of Clio: A Study of the Representation of History in Nineteenth-Century Britain and France.* Cambridge: Cambridge University Press, 1984.

Bellanger, Claude, Jacques Godechot, Pierre Guiral, and Fernand Terrou. *Histoire générale de la presse française, vol. 3, de 1871 à 1940.* Paris: Presses universitaires de France, 1972.

Berlanstein, Lenard R. *The Working People of Paris, 1871–1914.* Baltimore: Johns Hopkins University Press, 1984.

Brooks, Peter. *The Melodramatic Imagination: Balzac, James, Melodrama and the Mode of Excess.* New Haven: Yale University Press, 1976.

———. *Reading for the Plot: Design and Intention in Narrative.* New York: Knopf, 1984.

Cabaud, Michel, and Ronald Hubscher. *1900: La Française au quotidien.* Paris: Armand Colin, 1985.

Caron, François. *An Economic History of Modern France.* Trans. Barbara Bray. New York: Columbia University Press, 1979.

Clark, T. J. *The Painting of Modern Life: Paris in the Art of Manet and His Followers.* Princeton: Princeton University Press, 1984.

Debray, Regis. *Teachers, Writers, Celebrities.* Trans. David Macey. London: Verso, 1981.

El Nouty, Hassan. *Théâtre et pré-cinéma: essai sur la problématique du spectacle au 19è siècle.* Paris, 1978.

Gordon, Mel. *The Grand Guignol: Theatre of Fear and Terror.* New York: Amok Press, 1988.

Harris, Ruth. *Murders and Madness: Medicine, Law, and Society in the Fin de Siècle.* Oxford: Clarendon Press, 1989.

Herbert, Robert. *Impressionism: Art, Leisure, and Parisian Society.* New Haven: Yale University Press, 1988.

Hobsbawm, Eric. *The Age of Empire, 1875–1914.* New York: Pantheon, 1987.

Kuisel, Richard F. *Capitalism and the State in Modern France.* Cambridge: Cambridge University Press, 1981.

Lowe, Lisa. *Critical Terrains: French and British Orientalisms.* Ithaca: Cornell University Press, 1991.

MacMillan, James. *Housewife or Harlot: The Place of Women in French Society, 1879–1940.* New York: St. Martin's Press, 1981.

Magraw, Roger. *France, 1815–1914: The Bourgeois Century.* London: Fontana, 1983.

Mayeur, Jean-Marie, and Madeleine Rebérioux. *The Third Republic from Its Origins to the Great War, 1871–1914.* Trans. J. R. Foster. Cambridge: Cambridge University Press, 1984.

Meisel, Martin. *Realizations: Narrative, Pictorial, and Theatrical Arts in Nineteenth-Century England.* Princeton: Princeton University Press, 1983.

Miller, Michael B. *The Bon Marché: Bourgeois Culture and the Department Store, 1869–1920.* Princeton: Princeton University Press, 1981.

Nord, Philip G. *Paris Shopkeepers and the Politics of Resentment.* Princeton: Princeton University Press, 1984.

Nye, Robert A. *Crime, Madness, and Politics in Modern France.* Princeton: Princeton University Press, 1984.

Ory, Pascal, and Jean-François Sirinelli. *Les Intellectuels en France, de l'Affaire Dreyfus à nos jours.* Paris: Armand Colin, 1986.

Rabinow, Paul. *French Modern: Norms and Forms of the Social Environment.* Cambridge: MIT Press, 1989.

Rearick, Charles. *Pleasures of the Belle Epoque: Entertainment and Festivity in Turn-of-the-Century France.* New Haven: Yale University Press, 1985.

Romein, Jan. *The Watershed of Two Eras: Europe in 1900.* Trans. Arnold Pomerans. Middletown: Wesleyan University Press, 1979.

Schivelbusch, Wolfgang. *The Railway Journey: Trains and Travel in the Nineteenth Century.* New York: Urizen Books, 1980.

Schor, Naomi. "*Cartes Postales*: Representing Paris 1900." *Critical Inquiry* 18 (Winter 1992): 188–244.

Shapiro, Ann-Louise. "Love Stories: Female Crimes of Passion in Fin-de-siècle Paris." *differences* 3.3 (Fall 1991): 45–68.

Silberman, Deborah L. *Art Nouveau in Fin-de-Siècle France: Politics, Psychology, and Style.* Berkeley: University of California Press, 1989.

Weber, Eugen. *France, Fin de Siècle.* Cambridge: Harvard University Press, 1986.

———. *The Nationalist Revival in France, 1905–1914.* Berkeley: University of California Press, 1968.

———. *Peasants into Frenchmen: The Modernization of Rural France, 1870–1914.* Stanford: Stanford University Press, 1976.

Williams, Rosalind. *Dream Worlds: Mass Consumption in Late Nineteenth-Century France.* Berkeley: University of California Press, 1982.

Wright, Gordon. *Between the Guillotine and Liberty: Two Centuries of the Crime Problem in France.* New York: Oxford University Press, 1983.

———. *France in Modern Times.* 3rd ed. New York: Norton, 1981.

Zeldin, Theodore. *France, 1848–1945.* 5 vols. Oxford: Oxford University Press, 1979–31981.

General Reference: Early Cinema

Allen, Robert C. "Motion Picture Exhibition in Manhattan, 1906–1912: Beyond the Nickelodeon." *Cinema Journal* 18 (Spring 1979): 2–15.

———. *Vaudeville and Film, 1895–1915: A Study in Media Interaction.* New York: Arno Press, 1980.

Altman, Rick. "Dickens, Griffith, and Film Theory Today." *South Atlantic Quarterly* 88 (Spring 1989): 321–359.

Balides, Constance. "Scenarios of Exposure in the Practice of Everyday Life: Women in the Cinema of Attractions." *Screen* 34 (Spring 1993), 19–37.

Ball, Robert Hamilton. *Shakespeare on Silent Film: A Strange Eventful History.* London: George Allen and Unwin, 1968.

Bardèche, Maurice, and Robert Brasillach. *Histoire du cinéma*. 2d ed. Paris: Denoël, 1943.

Bernardini, Aldo. "Le Cinéma muet, étapes et tendances." In *Le Cinéma italien, 1905–1945*. Ed. Aldo Bernardini and Jean Gli, 33–45. Paris: Edition du Centre Pompidou, 1986.

Birett, Herbert. *Das Filmangebot in Deutschland, 1895–1911*. Munich: Filmbuchverlag Winerberg, 1991.

Bordwell, David, Janet Staiger, and Kristin Thompson. *The Classical Hollywood Cinema: Film Style and Mode of Production to 1960*. New York: Columbia University Press, 1985.

Bottomore, Stephen. "Dreyfus and Documentary." *Sight and Sound* 53 (Autumn 1984): 290–293.

———. "Shots in the Dark: The Real Origins of Film Editing." *Sight and Sound* 57 (Summer 1988): 200–204.

Bowser, Eileen. *A History of the American Cinema, II: The Transformation of Cinema, 1908–1915*. New York: Scribner's, 1991.

———, ed. *The Slapstick Symposium*. Brussels: FIAF, 1987.

Brewster, Ben. "A Scene at the Movies." *Screen* 23 (July–August 1982): 4–15.

———. "*Traffic in Souls*: An Experiment in Feature-Length Narrative Construction." *Cinema Journal* 31 (Fall 1991): 37–56.

Burch, Noël. "Film's Institutional Mode of Representation and the Soviet Response." *October* 11 (Winter 1979): 77–96.

———. "How We Got into Pictures: Notes Accompanying *Correction Please*." *Afterimage* 8/9 (1981): 24–38.

———. *Life to those Shadows*. Berkeley: University of California Press, 1990.

———. "Un Mode de représentation primitif?" *Iris* 2.1 (1984): 113–122.

———. "Porter or Ambivalence." *Screen* 19 (Winter 1978–1979): 91–105.

———. "Primitivism and the Avant-Gardes: A Dialectical Approach." In *Narrative, Apparatus, Ideology: A Film Theory Reader*. Ed. Philip Rosen, 483–506. New York: Columbia University Press, 1986.

Burch, Noël, and Jorge Dana. "Propositions." *Afterimage* 5 (1974): 40–66.

Chanan, Michael. *The Dream That Kicks*. London: Routledge and Kegan Paul, 1980.

Cherchi Usai, Paolo. "The Color of Nitrate." *Image* 34 (Summer 1991): 29–38.

———, ed. *Vitagraph Co. of America*. Pordenone: Edizioni Biblioteca dell'Immagine, 1987.

Cherchi Usai, Paolo, and Yuri Tsivian, ed. *Silent Witnesses: Russian Films, 1908–1919*. London: BFI, 1989.

Cosandey, Roland, André Gaudreault, and Tom Gunning, ed. *Une Invention du diable? Cinéma des premiers temps et religion*. Lausanne: Editions Payet, 1992.

Crafton, Donald. *Before Mickey: The Animated Film, 1898–1928*. Cambridge: MIT Press, 1982.

———, ed. *Iris* 11 (Summer 1990)—special issue devoted to early cinema audiences.

deCordova, Richard. *Picture Personalities: The Emergence of the Star System in America, 1907–1922*. Urbana: University of Illinois Press, 1990.

Doane, Mary Ann. "Melodrama, Temporality, Recognition: American and Russian Silent Cinema." *Cinefocus* 2 (Fall 1991): 13–26.

Elsaesser, Thomas, ed. *Early Cinema: Space, Frame, Narrative*. London: BFI, 1990.

Fell, John, ed. *Film Before Griffith*. Berkeley: University of California Press, 1983.

Fielding, Raymond. *A Technological History of Motion Pictures and Television*. Berkeley: University of California Press, 1967.

Fischer, Lucy. "The Lady Vanishes: Women, Magic, and the Movies." *Film Quarterly* 22 (Fall 1979): 30–40.

Gaines, Jane. "From Elephants to Lux Soap: The Programming and 'Flow' of Early Motion Picture Exploitation." *Velvet Light Trap* 25 (Spring 1990): 29–43.

Gartenberg, Jon. "The Brighton Project: The Archives and Research." *Iris* 2.1 (1984): 5–16.

———. "Camera Movement in Edison and Biograph Films, 1900–1906." *Cinema Journal* 19 (Spring 1980): 1–16.

———. "Vitagraph before Griffith: Forging Ahead in the Nickelodeon Era." *Studies in Visual Communication* 10.4 (1984): 7–23.

Gaudreault, André. "Detours in Film Narrative: Cross-Cutting." *Cinema Journal* 19 (Fall 1979): 39–59.

———, ed. *Ce que je vois de mon ciné . . . .* Paris: Meridiens Klincksieck, 1988.

Gledhill, Christine, ed. *Home Is Where the Heart Is: Studies in Melodrama and the Women's Film*. London: BFI, 1987.

Gomery, Douglas. *Shared Pleasures: A History of Movie Presentation in the United States*. Madison: University of Wisconsin, 1992.

Gunning, Tom. "An Aesthetic of Astonishment: Early Film and the (In)credulous Spectator." *Art & Text* 34 (Spring 1989), 31–45.

———. "The Cinema of Attraction: Early Film, Its Spectator and the Avant-Garde." *Wide Angle* 8.3/4 (1986): 63–70.

———. *D. W. Griffith and the Origins of American Narrative Film*. Urbana: University of Illinois Press, 1991.

———. "Heard over the Phone: *The Lonely Villa* and the de Lorde Tradition of the Terrors of Technology." *Screen* 32 (Summer 1991): 184–196.

———. "Non-Continuity, Continuity, Discontinuity: A Theory of Genres in Early Film." *Iris* 2.1 (1984): 100–112.

———. "'Primitive' Cinema—A Frame Up? or The Trick's on Us." *Cinema Journal* 28 (Winter 1989): 3–12.

———, ed. *Persistence of Vision* 9 (1991)—special issue devoted to early cinema.

Hansen, Miriam. "Adventures of Goldilocks: Spectatorship, Consumerism and Public Life." *camera obscura* 22 (1990): 51–71.

———. *Babel and Babylon: Spectatorship in American Silent Film*. Cambridge: Harvard University Press, 1991.

———. "Early Silent Cinema: Whose Public Sphere?" *New German Critique* 29 (Spring–Summer 1983): 147–184.

———. "Reinventing the Nickelodeon: Notes on Kluge and Early Cinema." *October* 46 (Fall 1988): 179–198.

Higgins, Steven. "American Eclair, 1911–1915: A Filmographic Chronology." *Griffithiana* 44/45 (September 1992): 89–129.

Holman, Roger, ed. *Cinema 1900–1906: An Analytical Study*. 2 vols. Brussels: FIAF, 1982.

Keil, Charlie. "Reframing *The Italian*: Questions of Audience Address in Early Cinema." *Journal of Film and Video* 42 (Spring 1990), 36–48.

Kirby, Lynne. "Gender and Advertising in American Silent Film: From Early Cinema to the Crowd." *Discourse* 13 (Spring–Summer 1991): 3–20.

———. "Male Hysteria and the Early Cinema." *camera obscura* 17 (1988): 113–131.

Lant, Antonia. "The Curse of the Pharaoh, or How Cinema Contracted Egyptomania." *October* 59 (Winter 1992): 87–112.

Leyda, Jay, and Charles Musser, ed. *Before Hollywood: Turn-of-the-Century Film from American Archives*. New York: American Federation of the Arts, 1986.

Liesegang, Franz Paul. *Dates and Sources: A Contribution to the History of the Art of Projection and to Cinematography*. Trans. Hermann Hecht. London: The Magic Lantern Society, 1986.

Mast, Gerald, ed. *The Movies in Our Midst: Documents in the Cultural History of Film in America*. Chicago: University of Chicago Press, 1982.

May, Lary. *Screening Out the Past: The Birth of Mass Culture and the Motion Picture Industry*. New York: Oxford University Press, 1980.

Mayne, Judith. *Private Novels, Public Films*. Athens: University of Georgia Press, 1988.

Musser, Charles. "Another Look at the Chaser Theory." *Studies in Visual Communication* 10.4 (1984): 24–44.

———. *Before the Nickelodeon: Edwin S. Porter and the Edison Manufacturing Company*. Berkeley: University of California Press, 1991.

———. "The Eden Musée: Exhibitor as Creator." *Film and History* 11 (December 1981): 73–83.

———. *The History of the American Cinema, I: The Emergence of Cinema to 1907*. New York: Scribners, 1991.

———. "The Nickelodeon Era Begins: Establishing the Framework for Hollywood's Mode of Representation." *Framework* 22/23 (Autumn 1983): 4–11.

———. "The Travel Genre in 1903–1904: Moving Toward Fictional Narrative." *Iris* 2.1 (1984): 47–59.

Musser, Charles, and Carol Nelson. *High-Class Moving Pictures: Lyman H. Howe and the Forgotten Era of Traveling Exhibition, 1880–1920*. Princeton: Princeton University Press, 1991.

Nielsen, Michael C. "Labor Power and Organization in the Early U.S. Motion Picture Industry." *Film History* 2.2 (1988): 121–131.

Niver, Kemp. *The First Twenty Years*. Los Angeles: Artisan Press, 1968.

Pearson, Roberta. "Cultivated Folks and the Better Classes: Class Conflict and Representation in Early American Film." *Journal of Popular Film and Television* 15 (Fall 1987): 120–128.

———. *Eloquent Gestures: The Transformation of Performance Style in Griffith Biograph Films*. Berkeley: University of California Press, 1992.

Pearson, Roberta, and William Uricchio. "'Films of Quality,' 'High Art Films,' and 'Films De Luxe': Intertextuality and Reading Positions in the Vitagraph Films." *Journal of Film and Video*, 41 (Winter 1989), 15–31.

———. "How Many Times Shall Caesar Bleed in Sport: Shakespeare and the Cultural Debate about Moving Pictures." *Screen* 31 (Autumn 1990): 243–261.

Peiss, Kathy. *Cheap Amusements: Working Women and Leisure in Turn-of-the-Century New York*. Philadelphia: Temple University Press, 1986.

———. "Making Faces: The Cosmetics Industry and the Cultural Construction of Gender, 1890–1930." *Genders* 7 (Spring 1990): 143–169.

Pratt, George C. *Spellbound in Darkness: A History of the Silent Film*. Greenwich: New York Graphic Society, 1973.

Rabinovitz, Lauren. "Temptations of Pleasure: Nickelodeons, Amusement Parks, and the Sights of Female Sexuality." *camera obscura* 23 (1990): 71–88.

Ramsaye, Terry. *A Million and One Nights.* New York: Simon and Schuster, 1926.

Robinson, David. "Music of the Shadows: The Use of Musical Accompaniment with Silent Films, 1896–1936." Supplement to *Griffithiana* 38/39 (1990).

Rosen, Phil. "Disjunction and Ideology in a Preclassical Film: *A Policeman's Tour of the World.*" *Wide Angle* 12.3 (1990): 20–36.

Rosenbloom, Nancy. "Progressive Reform, Censorship, and the Motion Picture Industry, 1909–1917," in Ronald Edsforth and Larry Bennett, ed. *Popular Culture and Political Change in Modern America* (Buffalo: State University of New York, 1991), 41–59.

Rosenzweig, Roy. *Eight Hours for What We Will: Workers and Leisure in an Industrial City, 1870–1920.* Cambridge: Cambridge University Press, 1983.

Salt, Barry. "The Early Development of Film Form." *Film Form* 1 (1976): 91–106.

———. *Film Style and Technology: History and Analysis.* London: Starword, 1983.

Singer, Ben. "Early Home Cinema and the Edison Home Projecting Kinetoscope." *Film History* 2.1 (1988): 37–69.

———. "Female Power in the Serial-Queen Melodrama: The Etiology of an Anomaly." *camera obscura* 22 (1990): 91–129.

Spehr, Paul. *The Movies Begin: Making Movies in New Jersey, 1887–1920.* Newark: Newark Museum, 1977.

Staiger, Janet. "Combination and Litigation: Structures of US Film Distribution, 1896–1917." *Cinema Journal* 23 (Winter 1984): 41–71.

———. "The Eyes Are Really the Focus: Photoplay Acting and Film Form and Style." *Wide Angle* 6.4 (1983): 14–23.

———. "'The Handmaiden of Villainy': Methods and Problems in Studying the Historical Reception of a Film." *Wide Angle* 8.1 (1986): 19–27.

———. *Interpreting Films: Studies in the Historical Reception of American Cinema.* Princeton: Princeton University Press, 1992.

Stromgren, Richard L. "The Moving Picture World of W. Stephen Bush." *Film History* 2.1 (1988): 13–22.

Swartz, Mark. "An Overview of Cinema on the Fairgrounds." *Journal of Popular Film and Television* 15 (Fall 1987): 102–119.

Thompson, Kristin. *Exporting Entertainment: America in the World Film Market, 1907–1934.* London: BFI, 1985.

Vardac, A. Nichols. *Stage to Screen, Theatrical Origins of Early Film: David Garrick to D. W. Griffith.* Cambridge: Harvard University Press, 1949.

Waller, Gregory. "Situating Motion Pictures in the Prenickelodeon Period: Lexington, Kentucky, 1897–1906." *Velvet Light Trap* 25 (Spring 1990): 12–28.

Williams, Linda. "Film Body: An Implantation of Perversions." *Ciné-Tracts* 12 (1981): 19–35.

General Reference: Early French Cinema

Abel, Richard. "1907–1914: Before the Canon." *French Film Theory and Criticism, I, 1907–1929,* 5–92. Princeton: Princeton University Press, 1988.

————. "Before *Fantômas*: Louis Feuillade and the Development of Early French Cinema." *Post Script* 7.1 (1987): 4–26.

————. "Booming the Film Business: The Historical Specificity of Early French Cinema." *French Cultural Studies* 1 (1990): 79–94.

————. "Eclair: The Other Film Company." *Griffithiana* 44/45 (September 1992): 5–14.

————. "Pathé's Stake in Early Russian Cinema." *Griffithiana* 38/39 (1990): 242–247.

————. "Scenes from Domestic Life in Early French Cinema." *Screen* 30 (Summer 1989): 4–28.

Abel, Richard, and Lorenzo Codelli, ed. *Griffithiana* 47 (May 1993)—special issue devoted to the Eclair Film Company.

Baldizzone, José. "L'Incendie du Bazar de la Charité." *Archives* 12 (March 1988).

Berneau, Pierre. "Les Débuts du spectacle cinématographique à Bordeaux." *1895* 4 (1988): 18–32.

Berneau, Pierre, and Jeanne Berneau. *Le Spectacle cinématographique à Limoges, de 1896 à 1945.* Paris: Editions A.F.R.H.C., 1992.

Bousquet, Henri. *Catalogue Pathé des années 1896 à 1914: 1907-1908-1909.* Paris: Henri Bousquet, 1993.

Bousquet, Henri, and Laurent Mannoni, ed. *1895* 12 (October 1992)—special issue devoted to the Eclair Film Company.

Bousquet, Henri, and Vittorio Martinelli. "La Bella Stasia." *Immagine* 8 (1988): 1–24.

Bousquet, Henri, and Riccardo Redi, ed. *Pathé-Frères: Les Films de la Production Pathé (1896–1907).* Florence: Quarderni di Cinema, 1992.

Cahiers de la cinémathèque 48 (1987)—special issue devoted to Louis Feuillade.

Chardère, Bernard, and Guyad Marjorie Borgé. *Les Lumières.* Lausanne: Payot, 1985.

Cherchi Usai, Paolo. "Le Miracle du Chronochrome." *Cinémathèque* 3 (1993): 83–91.

————. "Société Française des Films et Cinématographes Eclair (1907–1919): A Checklist," *Griffithiana* 44/45 (September 1992): 28–88.

————, ed. *A Trip to the Movies: Georges Méliès, Filmmaker and Magician (1861–1938).* Rochester: International Museum of Photography at the George Eastman House, 1991.

Chirat, Raymond, and Eric LeRoy, ed. *Le Cinéma française, 1911–1920.* Paris: Cinémathèque française, 1993.

Coissac, G.-Michel. *Histoire du cinématographe: De ses origines jusqu'à nos jours.* Paris: Cinéopse, 1925.

Cosandey, Roland. "Cinéma 1908, films à trucs et Film d'Art: une campagne de *l'Illustration*." *Cinémathèque* 3 (1993), 58–71.

Crafton, Donald. *Emile Cohl, Caricature, and Film.* Princeton: Princeton University Press, 1990.

Deslandes, Jacques. *Le Boulevard du cinéma à l'époque de Georges Méliès.* Paris: Cerf, 1963.

————. "Victorin-Hippolyte Jasset." *L'Avant-Scène Cinéma* 163 (November 1975): 241–296.

Deslandes, Jacques, and Jacques Richard. *Histoire comparée du cinéma, II: Du cinématographe au cinéma.* Paris: Casterman, 1968.

Edelman, Bernard. *Ownership of the Image: Elements for a Marxist Theory of Law.* Trans. Elizabeth Kingdom. London: Routledge and Kegan Paul, 1979.

Fescourt, Henri. *La Foi et les montagnes.* Paris: Paul Montel, 1959.

FIAF. *Le Cinéma français muet dans le monde, influences réciproques.* Perpignan: Institut Jean Vigo, 1989.

Ford, Charles. *Albert Capellani, précurseur méconnu.* Bois d'Arcy: Service des Archives du Film, 1984.

Frazer, John. *Artificially Arranged Scenes: The Films of Georges Méliès.* Boston: G. K. Hall, 1979.

Garnier, Jacques. "Cinémas." In *Forains d'hier et d'aujourd'hui,* 318–338. Orléans: Jacques Garnier, 1968.

Gaudreault, André. "Theatricality, Narrativity, and 'Trickality': Re-evaluating the Cinema of Georges Méliès." *Journal of Popular Film and Television* 15.3 (1987): 110–119.

Gili, Jean A. "Les Débuts du spectacle cinématographique." *1895* 3 (1987): 17–24.

Guibbert, Pierre, ed. *Les Premiers Ans du cinéma français.* Perpignan: Institut Jean Vigo, 1985.

Guillaudeau, Thomas. "La Production comique chez Pathé et Méliès en 1905–1906." *Les Cahiers de la cinémathèque* 41 (1984): 31–35.

———. "Les Productions Pathé et Méliès en 1905–1906 (notes préliminaires)." *Iris* 2.1 (1984): 33–46.

Guy, Alice. *Autobiographie d'une pionnière du cinéma.* Paris: Denoël/Gonthier, 1976.

Hamman, Joë. *Du Far-West à Montmartre.* Paris: Les Editeurs français réunis, 1962.

Hammond, Paul. *Marvelous Méliès.* London: Fraser, 1974.

Hugues, Philippe d', and Michel Martin. *Le Cinéma français: Le Muet.* Paris: Atlas, 1986.

Hugues, Philippe d', and Dominique Muller, ed. *Gaumont: 90 Ans du cinéma.* Paris: Ramsay/La Cinémathèque française, 1986.

Hunnings, Neville March. "France." In *Film Censors and the Law,* 332–360. London: George Allen and Unwin, 1967.

Jeanne, René. *Cinéma 1900.* Paris: Flammarion, 1965.

Jeanne, René, and Charles Ford. *Le Cinéma et la presse, 1895–1960.* Paris: Armand Colin, 1961.

———. *Histoire encyclopédique,* vol. 1. Paris: Robert Laffont, 1947.

Jenn, Pierre. *Georges Méliès cinéaste.* Paris: Albatros, 1984.

Lacassin, Francis. *Louis Feuillade.* Paris: Seghers, 1964.

———. *Pour un contre histoire du cinéma.* Paris: Union générale d'éditions, 1972.

Lapierre, Marcel. *Les Cent Visages du cinéma.* Paris: Grasset, 1948.

———, ed. *Anthologie du cinéma.* Paris: La Nouvelle Edition, 1946.

Leclerc, J. *Le Cinéma, temoin de son temps.* Paris: Nouvelles Editions Debresse, 1970.

Lefebvre, Thierry. "*Les Victimes de l'Alcoolisme* (Pathé, 1902)." *Archives* 50 (May 1992).

Leglise, Paul. *Histoire de la politique du cinéma français: Le Cinéma et la IIIᵉ République.* Paris: Librairie générale de droit et de jurisprudence, 1970.

Leprohon, Pierre. *50 Ans du cinéma français.* Paris: Cerf, 1954.

Le Roy, Eric. "A la rencontre de Camille de Morlhon." *1895* 5–6 (1989), 1–25.

Malthête, Jacques. "Les Actualités reconstituées de Georges Méliès." *Archives* 21 (March 1989).

———. "Les Bandes cinématographiques en couleurs artificielles: un exemple de Georges Méliès coloriés à la main." *1895* 2 (1987): 3–10.

———. "Les Collages dans les 'Star' films." *Les Cahiers de la cinémathèque* 35/36 (1982): 145–155.

———. "Couleurs, coloris et colorants des 'Star' Films." *Les Cahiers de la cinémathèque* 35/36 (Autumn 1982): 156–159.

———. "Le second studio de Georges Méliès à Montreuil-sous-bois." *1895* 7 (1990): 67–72.

Malthête-Méliès, Madeleine. *Méliès l'enchanteur*. Paris: Hachette, 1973.

———, ed. *Méliès et la naissance du spectacle cinématographique*. Paris: Klincksieck, 1984.

Malthête-Méliès, Madeleine, Anne-Marie Quevrain, and Jacques Malthête. *Essai de reconstitution du catalogue français de la Star-Film, suivi d'une analyse catalographique des films de Georges Méliès recensés en France*. Bois d'Arcy: Service des Archives du Film, 1980.

Marette, J. "Les Procédés de coloriage mécanique des films." *Bulletin de l'association française des ingénieurs et techniciens du cinéma* 7 (1950), 3–8.

McInroy, Patrick. "The American Méliès." *Sight and Sound* 48 (Autumn 1979): 250–254.

Mitry, Jean. *Histoire du cinéma, I: 1895–1914*. Paris: Edition universitaires, 1967.

———. "Max Linder." *Anthologie du cinéma* 2 (Paris: L'Avant-Scène Cinéma, 1967): 289–348.

Neveu, Raymond. "Les Appareils de Collection Gaumont, Pathé." *Archives* 36 (December 1990).

Norden, Martin. "The Pathé Frères Company During the Trust Era." *Journal of the University Film Association* 33 (Summer 1981), 15–32.

Pathé, Charles. *De Pathé-Frères à Pathé-Cinéma*. Lyon: SERDOC, 1970.

Quévrain, Anne Marie. "A la redécouverte de Méliès: Le Voyage à la lune." *Les Cahiers de la cinémathèque* 35/36 (1982): 160–165.

Richard, Suzanne. "Pathé, marque de fabrique: vers une nouvelle méthode pour la datation des copies anciennes." *1895* 10 (1991), 13–27.

Robinson, David. "Rise and Fall of the Clowns." *Sight and Sound* 56 (Summer 1987): 198–203.

Sadoul, Georges. *Histoire générale du cinéma, I: Les Pionniers du cinéma*. Paris: Denoël, 1947.

———. *Histoire générale du cinéma, II: Les Pionniers du cinéma, 1897–1908*. Paris: Denoël, 1948.

———. *Histoire générale du cinéma, III: Le Cinéma devient un art, 1909–1920*. Paris: Denoël, 1951.

———. *Lumière et Méliès*. Rev. ed., Bernard Eisenschitz. Paris: Lherminier, 1985.

Salt, Barry. "*The Physician of the Castle*." *Sight and Sound* 54 (Autumn 1985): 284–285.

Sartre, Jean-Paul. *The Words*. Trans. Bernard Frechtman. New York: George Braziller, 1964.

Schwartz, Vanessa, and Jean-Jacques Meusy. "Le Musée Grévin et le Cinématographe: l'histoire d'une recontre." *1895* 11 (1992): 19–48.

Staller, Natasha. "Méliès' 'Fantastic' Cinema and the Origins of Cubism." *Art History* 12 (June 1989): 202–232.

Tharratas, Juan-Gabriel. *Los 500 Films de Segundo de Chomón*. Zaragoza: Universidad de Zaragoza, 1988.

Toulet, Emmanuelle. "Aux sources de l'histoire du cinéma . . . Naissance d'une presse sous influences." In *Restaurations et tirages de la Cinémathèque française* 4 (Paris: La Cinémathèque française, 1989), 14–25.

———. "Le Cinéma à l'Exposition Universelle de 1900." *La Revue d'Histoire moderne et contemporaine* 33 (April–June 1986). Trans. in *Persistence of Vision* 9 (1991): 10–36.

———. *Cinématographe, invention du siècle*. Paris: Gallimard, 1988.

————. "Le Spectacle cinématographique à Paris de 1895 à 1914." Thèse de l'Ecole des Chartes (Paris, 1982).

Trimbach, Pierre. *Quand on tournait la manivelle . . . il y a 60 ans.* Paris: CEFAG, 1970.

Turim, Maureen. "French Melodrama: Theory of a Specific History." *Theater Journal* 39 (October 1987): 307–327.

Williams, Alan. *The Republic of Images: A History of French Filmmaking.* Cambridge: Harvard University Press, 1992.

Specific References from the Period

Binet, R., and G. Hausser. *Les Sociétés de cinématographe: Etudes financières.* Paris: La France Economique et Financière, 1908.

Collier, John. "Cheap Amusements." *Charities and the Commons: A Weekly Journal of Philanthropy and Social Advance* (11 April 1908): 73–76.

Davis, Michael M. *The Exploitation of Pleasure: A Study of Commercial Recreations in New York City.* New York: Russell Sage Foundation, 1911.

Hartt, Rollin Hyde. *The People at Play.* Boston: Houghton Mifflin, 1909.

Jasset, Victorin. "Etude sur le mise-en-scène en cinématographie." *Ciné-Journal* 165 (21 October 1911) to 170 (25 November 1911).

Kress, E. *Conférences sur la cinématographie.* 2 vols. Paris: Cinéma-Revue, 1912.

Maugras, E., and M. Guegan. *Le Cinématographe devant le droit.* Paris: V. Giard et F. Brière, 1908.

Rosen, J. *Le Cinématographe: son passé, son avenir et ses applications.* Paris: Société d'éditions techniques, 1911.

Talbot, Frederick A. *Moving Pictures: How They Are Made and Worked.* New York: Lippincott, 1912.

Index

A la conquête du pôle, 1912, 37, 278
ACAD, 39, 51, 363
Académie des sciences, 35
Accordéon, L', 1906, 138–139
Acting style, 61, 167, 246, 249, 253, 254–255, 277, 314, 318, 320, 400, 404, 415, 419, 525n, 526n
Action française, 4, 5
Adventures of a Madman, 1907, 217
Adventures of an Overcoat, 1907–1908, 511n
Affaire Dreyfus, L', 1899, 13, 92–93, 97, 98, 297
Affiches en goguettes, 1906, 161
AGC, 42, 54, 179, 298, 430
AGFA, 46, 480n
Agnel, 39
Aiglon, L', 1914, 325, 525n
Aladdin, 1880, 157
Alchimiste Parafaragamus, 1906, 157
Alcy, Jehanne d', 68
Alexandre, René, 253, 305
Alhambra music hall, London, 93
Ali Baba, 1907, 175
Allain, Marcel, 370, 371
Ambrosia et cie, 42, 267
   Last Days of Pompeii, 1908, 267
American Biograph cinema, 31, 33, 471n
American Federation of the Arts, 430
American "Independents," 9, 44–45, 51, 54, 478n
American Standard Films (Eclair), 53
Amour à crédit, L', 161
Amour à tous les étages, 1903, 118
Amour et science, 1912, 527n
André Chenier, 1910, 274, 518n
André, Emile, 385
Andréani, André, 35, 40, 41, 48, 49, 308, 522n
   Cléopatre, 1910, 40, 258, 259, 277, 308, 516n
   Napoléon, 1909, 41, 267
   Siège de Calais, 1911, 49, 308–311, 336
Andreyor, Yvette, 49, 50, 320, 328, 374, 375
Andriot, Josette, 51, 360, 362, 363, 366, 367
Androclès, 1912, 319

Anti-clericalism, 65, 88, 204, 255, 308
Anti-Semitism, 140, 193, 318
Antoine, André, 21, 36, 37, 40, 99, 150, 331, 481n, 518n
   Hirondelle et la mésange, L', 1921, 331, 525n
   La Terre, 1920, 526n
Antre de la sorcière, L', 1906, 174
Apaches de Paris, 1905, 127
Apollinaire, Guillaume, 5, 371
Apparatuses, 9, 10–11, 17
   Bonne Presse projector, 42
   Debrie: Parvo camera, 47
   Eclair: Kinéclair projector, 48
   Edison: Home Projecting Kinetoscope, 47
   Gaumont: Chromochrome projector, 47
   Gaumont "Chrono" projector, 11–12
   Gaumont "Chronographie," 11
   Gaumont "Chronophone," 12, 35
   Joly camera-projector, 14
   Lumière cinématographe, 10–11, 13, 14, 62, 465n
   Pathé cameras, 14, 20, 34, 244, 245, 417
   Pathé projectors, 14, 20, 25, 35, 42
   Pathé: KOK projector, 47
Apter, Emily, 117
Argus-Phono-Cinéma, 31
Arnaud, Etienne, 20, 36, 52, 53, 142, 271, 495n, 501n, 520n
   Course aux potirons, 1908, 217
   Dernier Requiem de Mozart, 1909, 271
   Un Coup de vent, 1906, 111, 112
Arquillière, Alexandre, 51, 201, 202, 358, 360, 362, 363, 366
Arrestation de la Duchesse de Berry, L', 1910, 260–261, 277
Arthème series
   Arthème Dupin echappe encore, 1912, 390
Artist, "The," 1900, 88
Artistic-Cinéma, 55
Ashbery, John, 370
Aspirateur, L', 1908, 279
Associated Independent Film Manufacturers, 45
Association française du cinématographe, 32

Association professionnelle de la presse
    cinématographique, 58
Astaix, Lucien, 42, 466n
Au Clair de la lune, 1904, 76–77
Auberge du diable, L', 10
Auberge ensorsélé, L', 1897, 62
Aubert, Louis, 41, 48
Aubert-Palaces, 55
Automobile à vendre, 1906, 113
Avare, L', 1908, 184
Avenal, Charles d', 7
Ayme, Jean, 320, 332

Babin, Gustave, 280
Badet, Regina, 48, 515n
Bagne de gosses, 1907, 185
Baignade impossible, 1902, 26, 79, 87, 490n
Bailleur, Le, 1907, 114, 116
Bain des dames de la cour, 1904, 117
Balandard est en grève, 1910, 512n
Ball, Robert Hamilton, 264
Bandits en automobile series, 57, 364
    Auto grise, L', 1912, 364, 365
    Hors la loi, 1912, 364
Banque Adam et cie, 20
Banque de Merzbach, 40
Banque suisse et française, 20
Barbe-bleue, 1901, 69–70, 71, 72, 83
Bardou, Camille, 365
Barjac, Madeleine, 267
Bartet, Mme, 255
Barthes, Roland, 207
Bataille, Henry, 334
Bataille, Lucien, 50, 51, 365, 367, 388, 391
Bather's Race, 1907, 217
Baudelaire, Charles, 59, 207
Baudry, Jean-Louis, 60
Bauer, Harry, 317, 318
Bayard, André, 51
Bazar de la Charité, 1897, 17, 18
Bazin, André, 207
Bébé n'aime pas sa concierge, 1913, 397–398
Bébé series
    Bébé a la peste, 1911, 231
    Bébé apache, 1910, 231
    Bébé fait visiter Marseille, 1911, 232
    Bébé juge, 1912, 397
    Bébé marchand des quatres saisons, 1911,
        231–232
    Bébé tire à la cible, 1912, 396–397
    Noël de Bébé, 1911, 231
Béguiné, Léonard, 15
Belge-Cinéma, 43

Belle au bois dormant, 1908, 291
Benjamin, Walter, 207
Benoit, Georges, 53
Benoît-Lévy, Edmond, xiii, 23, 28, 29, 30,
    32, 34, 40, 42, 57, 58, 96, 167, 182
Berlanstein, Lenard, 6, 33
Berlin Commission, 1909, 28
Berlioz, Hector, 75, 160
Bernhardt, Sarah, 5, 12, 39, 51, 258, 313–
    317, 514n, 523n
Bernon, Bluette, 69, 73
Bernstein, Henry, 334
Berst, J. A., 23, 44, 205
Bertho, Paul, 38, 51, 216, 232, 233, 301,
    388, 390, 392, 531n
Bertini, Francesca, 43
Betty series, 510n
Bibliothèque de l'Arsenal, 431
Biche au bois, 73
Bigorno series
    Bigorno parachutiste, 1914, 532n
Billy, André, 253
Biograph, 11, 44, 54, 104, 109, 110, 180,
    184, 267, 479n
    1776, 1909, 267
    Personal, 1904, 109, 110
Bioscope, 45, 269, 294–295, 300, 360
Bizet, Georges, 515n, 521n
Blaché, Herbert, 35, 52
Blackton, J. Stuart, 280
    Humorous Phases of Funny Faces, 1906,
        280, 282
    Lightning Sketches, 1907, 282
Blind Detective, 1909, 508n
Blum, Léon, 5
Boireau series, 35, 38, 49, 180, 216, 227–
    229, 232, 234, 237, 301, 400–402, 427
    Apprenti architecte, L', 1908, 228–229
    Apprentissages de Boireau, L', 1907, 228
    Boireau curassier, 1912, 401
    Boireau domestique, 1912, 400–401
    Boireau, roi de boxe, 1912, 401–402, 405–
        406, 427
    Débuts d'un canotier, 1907–1908, 512n
    Jules the Sandwichman, 1907, 512n
Bomb, The, 1907, 144
Bon Grand-père, 1907, 153–154, 184
Bon Invalide et les enfants, 1908, 216–217
Bon Quinquina, 1909, 509n
Bonafé, Pépa, 317
Bond, James, 124, 282
Boniface VIII, 1911, 523n
Bonnard, Pierre, 353

Bonne Bergère et méchante princesse, 1908, 297

Bonne Presse, La, 42, 47, 95, 333, 476n

Bonne Purge, 1904, 88

Bonnot gang, 364, 365

Bordoni, Mlle, 296

Borgia s'amuse, 1902, 117

Bosc, Henri, 336

Bosetti, Roméo, 19, 35, 36, 49, 141, 142, 216, 229, 391, 394, 501n, 511n, 532n

  Bigorno series, 49

  Calino series, 36

  Little Moritz series, 35, 53, 216, 301, 391, 410

  Roméo series, 36, 216, 229

  Rosalie series, 35, 49, 301, 391, 410

  Un Homme aimanté, 1907, 142–144

  Une Dame vraiment bien, 1908, 219–220

Boucicault, Dion, 271

Bourbon, Ernest, 50, 301, 404, 406

Bourgeois, Gérard, 38, 41, 48, 51, 299, 311, 326–328, 510n

  Démon du jeu, Le, 1911, 327–328

  Rivale de Richelieu, 1911, 311

  Roman d'une pauvre fille, 1912, 48

  Un Drame sur une locomotive, 1910, 212–213, 341

  Victimes d'alcool, 1911, 41, 48, 52, 299, 326–327, 328, 329

Bourreau turc, 1904, 63–64

Bout-de-zan series

  Bout-de-zan et le chemineau, 1913, 399–400

  Bout-de-zan et le crime au téléphone, 1914, 400

  Bout-de-zan et le lion, 1913, 399

Bovy, Berthe, 53, 514n, 519n

Braconnier, Le, 1906, 130, 147

Bras, Albert, 346

Bréon, 372

Brésil, Mlle, 199

Bressol, Pierre, 38, 50, 198, 301, 357, 412

Bretteau, 85, 87

Brewster, Ben, 103, 104, 182, 300, 303

Brézillon, Léon, 55

Brisson, Adolphe, 55, 249

British Museum, 316

Brockliss, Frank, 51

Bromhead, A. C., 11, 19

Brookes, Peter, 130

Brulator, Jules, 45, 53

Brulé, André, 261

Brunetière, Fernand, 181

Bulles de savon, 1906, 157

Buñuel, Luis, 405

  Age d'or, L, 1930, 405

Bunzli, 14

Burch, Noël, xiv, 60, 102, 116, 118, 155, 183, 311, 493n

Burguet, Charles, 48, 49

Bush, W. Stephen, 48, 264, 470n, 485n

Busnach, William, 201, 346

Bussy, 39

Buying a Cow, 1907, 219

Cabman's Delusion, 1908, 278

Cabman's Wife, 1908, 224–225

Cache-toi dans la malle, 1905, 113

Caïn et Abel, 1911, 49, 256, 257–258, 319

Cakewalk chez les nains, 1903, 81, 283

Cake-Walk infernal, 1903, 65, 81

Calino series

  Calino a peur de feu, 1910, 230, 245

  Calino achête un chien de garde, 1910, 230–231, 244

  Calino agent, 1910, 229

  Calino bureaucrate, 1909, 229

  Calino, chef de gare, 1912, 404, 427

  Calino, courtier en paratonerres, 1912, 402

  Calino pompier, 1911, 229–230

  Calino sourcier, 1913, 402–403

Calmettes, André, 40, 50, 264, 312, 314, 514n

  Assassinat du Duc de Guise, L', 1908, 39, 246, 248–253, 254, 260, 270, 272, 277, 514n

  Baiser de Judas, 1909, 262

  Carmen, 1910, 40, 515n

  Dame aux camélias, 1912, 313–315, 325

  Macbeth, 1909, 264–265, 266

  Madame Sans-Gêne, 1911, 40, 54, 275, 312–313, 358

  Retour d'Ulysse, 1909, 39, 253, 255, 256, 277, 312

  Rival de son fils, 1910, 40, 253, 254, 256, 277

  Tosca, La, 1909, 39, 253–254, 255, 260, 277

Camby, Alexandre, 24

Capellani, Albert, 21, 37, 40–41, 47, 49, 55, 57, 175, 199, 247–248, 268, 272, 299, 302–308, 321–325, 329, 345, 432, 500n, 504n, 518n

  Aladdin, 1907, 175–176, 291, 293

  Amour d'esclave, 1907, 166–167, 247

  Arlésienne, L', 1908, 40, 267, 514n

Assomoir, L', 1909, 41, 201–202, 210,
    212, 303, 326, 475n
Cendrillon, 1907, 176–178, 293, 297
Courrier de Lyon, 1911, 41, 302–305,
    323, 325, 326, 328, 522n
Germinal, 1913, 47, 57, 345–347, 380,
    483n
Glu, La, 1913, 485n
Homme aux gants blancs, L', 1908, 40,
    199–201, 210, 211, 272
Jeanne d'Arc, 1909, 268, 269, 277, 309,
    325
Loi du pardon, 1906, 21, 134–135, 136,
    148, 154, 206
Marie Stuart, 1908, 305
Misérables, Les, 1912, 49, 55, 299, 302,
    321–325, 329, 345, 524n
Mort du Duc d'Enghien, 1909, 268–270,
    277, 325
Notre Dame de Paris, 1911, 49, 299, 305–
    308, 311, 312, 318, 325, 358
Pauvre Mère, 1906, 135–136, 151, 156
Roi s'amuse, 1909, 305
Samson, 1908, 248
Un Drame à Venise, 1907, 145, 147–148,
    325
Vestale, La, 1908, 40, 247–248
Capellani, Paul, 303
Capra, Frank, 420
    It Happened One Night, 1934, 420
Carl, Renée, 50, 205, 219, 231, 256, 330,
    332, 333, 335, 340, 372
Carlo Rossi et cie, 43
Carré, Benjamin, 20, 53
Carré, Michel, 29, 40, 167, 257, 260, 268,
    305, 510n, 515n, 517n
    Athaliah, 1910, 517n
    Enfant prodigue, L', 1907, 29, 40, 167
    Inventeur, L', 1910, 510n
Carroll, Lewis, 406
Cartes vivantes, 1905, 156–157
Casimir series, 51
Casino de Paris, 16
Castillan, 334
Catholic Church, 3, 42, 57, 95, 136, 268
Ce que l'on voit de mon sixième, 1901, 118
Cendrillon, 1899, 13, 14, 68, 70, 71
Cervantes, 84
CGPC, 52
Chaise à porteurs enchantée, 1905, 156
Chalopin, André, 57
Chambre syndicale francaise de la cinéma-
    tographi, 58, 484n

Champignol malgré lui, 1914, 388, 425–426
Chaplin, Charlie, 415
Charcot, Jean, 10, 70, 352
Charivari, Le, 289
Charley Colms, 1912, 364
Chat botté, Le, 1908, 291
Chaudron infernal, 1903, 65
Chaussette, Le, 1905, 137, 415
Chautard, Emile, 39, 51, 53, 327, 363–364
    Mystère de Pont Notre Dame, 1912, 363–
        364
    Roman d'un caissier, 1914, 529n
Cherchi Usai, Paolo, 463n, 522n
Chevalier mystère, 1899, 62
Chez le dentiste, 1902, 88
Chicot, dentiste américaine, 1897, 87
Chien de garde, 1906, 111
Chien et la pipe, 1902, 88–89
Chien récalcitrant, 1907, 111, 112
Chiens contrebandiers, 1906, 132, 499n
Chiens de police, 1907, 500n
Chiffonniers caricaturistes, 1908, 281–282,
    283, 289
Chirurgie fin-de-siècle, 1902, 90
Chomón, Segundo de, 19, 35, 169–170,
    175, 278, 279–281, 283–286, 289,
    291, 292
    Black Witch, 1908, 283
    Bobby et sa famille, 1906, 283
    Charmeur, Le, 1907, 169, 283
    Chrysanthèmes, Les, 1908, 284, 285
    Cuisine magnétique, 1908, 285
    Démenagement, Le, 1908, 280, 289
    Electric Hotel, 1908, 280–281
    Enchanted Glasses, 1907, 520n
    Invisibles, Les, 1906, 170
    Maison ensorcelé, La, 1907–1908, 280
    Red Spectre, 1907, 283–284, 297
    Rêve des marmitons, 1908, 281
    Roses magiques, 1906, 169
    Scarabée d'or, 1907, 170, 283
    Sculpteurs modernes, 1908, 520n
    Sorcier arabe, 1906, 169
    Théâtre du Petit Bob, 1906, 279–280
    Toula's Dream, 1908, 285–286
    Une Excursion incohérente, 1910, 289–291
    Voyage au planete Jupiter, 1909, 292–293
Christmas Story, A, 1890, 204, 502n
Christophe Colomb, 1904, 94
Ciné-Journal, xiii, 31, 38, 41, 45, 46, 54,
    55, 57, 183, 198, 253, 276, 358, 361,
    364
Cinéma, Le, 404

Cinema audiences, 7, 24, 30–31, 33, 59, 78, 87, 105, 118, 130, 136, 156, 166, 178, 179, 182, 236, 278, 293, 294, 301, 354, 387, 471n, 496n, 500n
Cinema circuits
  Aubert, 55
  Gaumont, 31, 54, 179
  Pathé-Frères, 9, 30–31, 55, 179
Cinéma-Palace, 31
Cinémathèque française, La, 381
Cinématographe Grenier, 16
Cinématographe-Théâtre, 24
Cinès et cie, 35, 42, 43, 54, 299
  Marc Antoine et Cléopatre, 1913, 54
  Quo Vadis?, 1913, 54, 484n
Cirque d'hiver, 31, 33
Civilisation à travers les âges, 1908, 36, 297
Clair, René, 157, 532n
  Entr'Acte, 1924, 157
  Paris qui dort, 1924, 532n
Claretie, Jules, 6
Clockmaker's Secret, 1907, 291
Clowns, Les, 1902, 87
Cocher, à l'heure, 1909, 511n
Coeur et les yeux, 1912, 327
Cohl, Emile, 36, 53, 278, 286–289, 292, 490n, 520n
  Binettoscope, 1910, 289
  Cauchemar du fantoche, 1908, 287
  Clair de lune espagnol, 1909, 288, 292
  Fantasmagorie, 1908, 286, 287
  Garde-Meuble automatique, 1910, 289
  Joyeux Microbes, 1909, 288–289
  Peintre néo-impressioniste, 1910, 289
  Retapeur de cervelles, 1911, 289
  Un Drame chez les fantoches, 1980, 287–288
Coissac, G.-Michel, 42, 96
Colette, 521n
Colisée Cinéma, 55
Collier de la danseuse, 1912, 364
Color film processes, 11–12, 39, 47, 480n
  hand coloring, 13, 19, 73–74, 84, 158, 467n, 490n
  stencil color, 20, 22, 34, 78, 81, 84, 95, 164–165, 167–170, 173, 175–176, 237, 248, 257, 258, 260, 277, 283–284, 291–292, 306, 503n, 516n
  tinting, 84, 128, 165, 168, 201, 202, 210, 289, 291, 338, 359, 374, 382, 396, 508n, 516n
  toning, 167, 338, 359, 382, 396, 516n
Comandon, Dr. Jean, 35

Combat naval en Grèce, 1897, 92
Comédie Française, 39, 41, 49, 182, 264
Comica, 35, 49, 51, 301, 388, 391, 394
Compagnie des Cinéma-Halls, 31, 42
Comptoir Ciné-Location, 36, 53
Concierge bat son tapis, 1906, 139
Continsouza, 14, 34
Continuity editing, development of, xv–xvi, 103–105, 109, 112, 115, 117, 121, 130, 136, 139–141, 145, 147–148, 155, 178, 180–181, 184, 195, 199–201, 202, 208, 210–211, 212–215, 221, 225, 226–227, 231, 238–239, 244, 249, 251, 256–257, 261–262, 271, 272, 273–274, 275, 292–293, 300, 304–305, 323–325, 340–343, 354, 368, 371, 381–383, 385–387, 409, 497n
Contremaître incendiaire, 1908, 190–192, 195, 211
Coquelin, Ernest, 13
Corman, Nelly, 260
Coronation of Edward VII, 1902, 14, 93
Corsican Brothers, 271
Cosmograph films, 48
Costil, Edgar, 31
Course de parasol, 1907, 111
Course de sergents de ville, 1907, 111, 112, 116
Course des belles-meres, 1907, 111
Courteline, Georges, 51, 426
Crafton, Donald, 87, 279, 280, 286, 288
Crédit Lyonnais, 14
Creissel, Eugène, 308
Crisis of film subjects, 27
Crisis of overproduction, 41
Cruel Joke, 1908, 509n
Cullison, Webster, 53
Cunegonde series, 392, 427
  Cunegonde, femme de mode, 1912, 392

Dadaists, 289
Dagmar, Berthe, 528n, 532n
Daguerre, Louis, 70
Dalleu, Gilbert, 344
Dame aux camélias, La, 313–315, 325
Damnation du Docteur Faust, 1904, 19, 75–76, 160
Dancers, The, 1900, 78
Danse des apaches, 1904, 78
Dary, René, 216, 231, 396, 397
Daudet, Alphonse, 336, 526n
Dauvray, Maryse, 39, 527n

David, Louis, 96
Davis, Owen, 205
Dawson, Joë, 412
Dax, Jean, 347, 348, 349
Debord, Guy, 1, 6
Debrie, André, 47
Debrie et fils, 47
Débuts d'un aéronaute, 1907, 219
Débuts d'un chauffeur, 1906, 114
Débuts d'un patineur, 1907, 218–219, 236
Decauville, Paul, 12
Decaux, L.-R., 11, 47
Decourcelle, Pierre, 28, 40, 214, 244
  Deux Gosses, Les, 28
Decroix, Charles, 261
Deed, André, 35, 43, 49, 216, 227–229,
  232, 237, 282, 301, 400, 401, 505n
Degrada, Elena, 117
Dejeuner du savant, Le, 1905, 120, 288
Delac, Charles, 41, 50, 476n
Delamare, Maurice, 411
Delluc, Louis, 345, 346
Delphin, 335
Delvair, Jeanne, 264
Delvé, Suzanne, 337, 348, 349
Demaria, Jules, 114
Demenÿ, Georges, 11
Dennery, Adolphe, 70, 77
Denning, Michael, 198
Denola, Georges, 40, 49, 387
  Rocambole series, 49, 387
Déraciné ou artiste, 1909, 207–208, 272
Dermoz, Germaine, 39, 268, 363, 519n
Déroulade, Paul, 4
Déserteur, Le, 1906, 498n
Desfontaines, Henri, 37, 49, 51, 199, 317,
  517n
  Anne Boleyn, 1914, 51, 524n
  Queen Elizabeth, 1912, 51, 299, 315–
  317, 325, 523n
  Shylock, 1913, 51, 317–318
Deslandes, Jacques, 367, 431
Desvaillières, Georges, 425
Détective, Le, 1906, 132–133, 153, 154
Détresse et charité, 1904, 19
Deux Soeurs, Les, 1907, 154–155, 156, 184
Dharsay, 346
Dhartigny, 342
Diable au couvent, 1899, 13, 65
Diabolo, Le, 1907, 140, 144
Dialogue intertitles, 251, 253, 317, 330,
  404, 504n, 514n, 515n
Diamant-Berger, Henri, 58

Dieudonné, Albert, 303, 514n
Difficult Arrest, 1907, 501n
Distress, 1907, 151–152
Dog and His Various Merits, 1907, 501n
Dog Detective, 1909, 198–199
Domidoff, Olga, 255, 360
Domitor, xiv, 429, 465n
Don Juan, 1908, 514n
Dondini, Cesare, 265
Doré, Gustave, 73
Dorival, Georges, 308, 312, 313
Dorly, Marie, 329
Doublier, Francis, 53, 491n
Doublon, Francis, 11
Doumic, René, 57, 365
Doyen, Dr. Eugène Louis, 17, 27–28, 38,
  90, 109, 520n
Dranem, 88, 89, 119, 491n
Dreyfus, Alfred, 92
Dreyfus Affair, 3, 4, 92–93, 140
Dubosc, André, 344
Duclaux, Emile, 3
Dufayel department store, 15, 33
Duflos, Huguette, 514n
Duflos, Raphaël, 514n
Duhamel, Sarah, 49, 51, 301, 388, 391,
  392, 394
Duhar, 338
Dujardin-Beaumetz, Henri, 183
Dulaar brothers, 16, 24
Dulac, Laurence, 261
Dumas, Alexandre, 51, 313
Dumien, Jules, 37
Dunant, Caroline, 167
Dupin, Arthur, 497n
Duquesne, Edmond, 312, 345, 363, 427
Durand, Jean, 38, 50, 342, 402, 404, 527n,
  528n
  Calino series, 50, 180, 216, 229–231,
  232, 245, 301, 402–404, 427
  Onésime series, 50, 301, 350, 388, 392,
  404–407, 417, 424
  Railway de la mort, 1912, 342
  Sous le griffe, 1912, 527n
  Un Mariage au revolver, 1911, 528n
Dureau, Georges, 33, 41, 55, 57, 182, 312,
  358, 364, 481n, 485n, 495n
Dussaud, Franz, 20
Dutertre, A., 385

Eastman Kodak, 9, 45–46, 430
Eclair, xvii, 9, 38–39, 41, 45, 47, 48, 51,
  52–53, 54, 57, 179, 180, 183, 184,

192, 195–198, 199, 216, 233, 237,
263, 264, 270, 277, 298, 299, 300, 301,
302, 326, 327, 344–345, 354, 358–
368, 387, 388, 390, 393, 397, 398,
426–427, 430, 483n
Eclair-Journal, 51
Eclectic Film Company (Pathé-Frères), 52
Eclectic Films, 48, 397
Eclipse, xvii, 37, 38, 39, 41, 44, 50–51, 54,
113, 179, 216, 233, 267, 299, 300, 301,
302, 315, 316, 326, 327, 354, 357–
358, 388, 390, 393, 426, 430, 478n,
517n
Eclipse-Journal, 37
Ecole buissonnière, L', 1906, 114
Edelman, Bernard, 27
Edison, 9, 10, 13, 14, 15, 23, 36, 44, 54,
105, 110, 116, 367, 430, 476n, 477n
European Rest Cure, 1904, 105
Great Train Robbery, 1903, 116, 123,
495n
How a French Nobleman Got a Wife, 1904,
110
Rube and Mandy at Coney Island, 1903,
105, 116
Teddy Bears, 1907, 495n, 519n
What Happened to Mary, 1912–1913, 367
Whole Dam Family and the Dam Dog,
1905, 280
Eichler, 195–196
Eiffel, Gustave, 10
Eldorado music hall, 16, 78
Electric-Palace, 54, 55, 334
Elsaesser, Thomas, 60, 103, 104
Empire Palace music halls, 93
En Vacances, 1906, 114, 115, 117, 137
Enfants du Capitaine Grant, Les, 1914, 529n
Enlèvement de Bonaparte, L', 1912, 524n
Entente Cordiale 1904, 216, 311
Episode of 1812, An, 1910, 274
Epstein, Jean, 331
Belle Nivernaise, 1924, 331
Equilibre impossible, 1902, 65–66
Erreur de porte, L', 1904, 89–90
Eruption du Mont Pélé, 1902, 14
Eruption volcanique à la Martinique, 1902, 93
Espionne, L', 1907, 43, 148–149
Essanay, 54
Etiévant, Henri, 308, 321, 323
Eugénie Grandet, 1910, 518n
Evadé des Tuileries, L', 1910, 275–276, 277
Excelsior, 58
Exclusif Agency, 54

Exclusive Film Corporation, 52
Exhibition, 9, 15–17, 29–32, 54–57, 59,
61, 105, 302, 305, 321, 358, 380, 471n
café-concerts and music halls, 9, 16–17,
19, 24, 33, 36
fête foraine cinemas, 9, 16–17, 19, 22,
24–25, 31–33, 34, 36, 37, 59, 61, 179,
468n, 471n
nickelodeons, 9, 22, 24, 32, 36, 44, 179,
180, 468n, 471n
palace cinemas, 31, 33, 54–57, 299, 334
urban cinemas, 9, 15–16, 24, 31–33,
179, 530n

Faber, Jane, 371
Fabrèges, Fabienne, 376
Fagot, Georges, 41, 240, 267, 278
Faivre, Joseph, 397, 398
Willy series, 39, 301, 397, 398–399
False Coin, 1908, 186–187
Falsely Condemned, 1908, 506n
Family Football, 1910, 234
Famous Players, 54, 315
Fantastic realism, 360–361, 366–367, 371,
387
Fantômas series
Fantômas, 1913, 371–373, 387
Fantômas contre Fantômas, 1914, 377–379
Faux Magistrat, 1914, 378–379
Juve contre Fantômas, 1913, 373–376
Mort qui tue, Le, 1913, 376–377, 378
Fantômes du Nil, 37
Faria, 15
Fascinateur, Le, 42
Faure, Félix, 91
Faust et Marguerite, 1904, 75–76, 160, 325
Fayard, Arthème, 370
Fée carabosse, 1906, 158
Fée des fleurs, 10
Fée des roches noires, 1907, 175
Fée printemps, 1907, 175, 490n
Féraudy, Maurice de, 41, 518n
Mathéo Driani, 1909, 518n
Ferry, Jules, 4
Fescourt, Henri, 50, 329, 342–343, 399,
533n
Jeux d'enfants, 1913, 342–343, 354
Restaurant de l'impasse Canin, 1913, 533n
Festin de Balthazar, 1910, 258–259, 260,
277, 516n
Feuillade, Louis, 20, 35–36, 41, 50, 57,
142, 205, 229, 231, 256, 271, 273, 300,
301, 320, 326, 328–334, 335, 349,

Feuillade, Louis (*continued*)
  350–351, 354, 368, 370–380, 387,
  388, 396–397, 399–400, 425, 495n,
  511n, 520n, 524n
  Agonie de Byzance, L', 1913, 50, 57, 325,
  525n
  Bébé series, 36, 180, 216, 231–232, 245,
  301, 396–397, 399
  Bout-de-zan series, 50, 301, 388, 397, 399
  Christophe Colomb, 1910, 273–274
  Ecrin de Radjah, L', 1913, 368
  Erreur tragique, L', 1913, 57, 350–351,
  365, 373
  Fantômas series, 50, 57, 299, 370–380,
  387
  Fille du Margrave, 1912, 50, 299, 320–
  321
  Huguenot, Le, 1909, 271–272, 277
  Judith et Holophernes, 1909, 256–257,
  259, 277
  Légende des Phares, 1909, 205
  Oubliette, L', 1912, 368
  Proscrit, Le, 1912, 368
  Scènes de la vie telle qu'elle est series, 50,
  301, 302, 326, 328–334, 346, 353,
  361, 368, 377, 425
  Thé chez le concierge, 1907, 222
Février, Henri, 57
Feydeau, Georges, 425
Figaro, Le, 58, 330
Fille du Corse, 1907, 149–150, 184
Film d'Art, xvii, 31, 39–40, 45, 50, 54, 96,
  179, 182, 183, 246, 248–256, 260–
  262, 264, 271, 276, 277, 302, 312–
  315, 325, 326, 358, 380, 388, 426, 430,
  514n, 508n, 515n, 523n
Film d'Arte Italiana, 43, 179, 183, 237,
  264, 265, 515n
  Enlèvement des Sabines, L', 1910, 515n
  Françoise de Ramini, 1910, 43
  Idylle Florentine, 1911, 523n
  King Lear, 1910–1911, 266
  Merchant of Venice, 1911, 266
  Othello, 1909, 43, 265–266
  Salomé, 1910, 43
Film des auteurs, Le, 41
Film distribution
  AGC, 42, 54
  Aubert, 41–42, 54
  Bonne Presse, La, 42
  Eclair, 39, 51, 53
  Gaumont, 36, 52, 53, 54
  Lux, 38

Pathé-Frères, 9, 22, 23, 33–35, 41, 43–
  44, 47, 52, 53, 54, 477n, 478n, 479n,
  480n
  rental system, 9, 33–34, 36, 179
Film français, Le, 48
Film Index, 238, 239, 468n, 484n
Film production costs, 22–23, 46–47, 311,
  322, 329, 466n, 475n, 489n, 525n
Film production systems
  Eclair, 39, 51, 52–53
  Eclipse, 37, 50
  Film d'Art, 39–40, 50
  Gaumont, 35–36, 50
  Méliès, 13–14, 473n, 486n
  Pathé-Frères, 21–22, 35, 41, 43–44, 45,
  47–49, 52, 482n
  SCAGL, 40, 41, 49
  USA, 467n
Film Service Association, 36, 44, 478n
Film stock negative
  Eastman, 9, 45–46
  Gaumont, 466n
  Lumière, 10–11, 19, 46
  Méliès, 19, 36, 466n
  Pathé-Frères, 14–15, 34, 41, 45–46
Film stock positive
  Gaumont, 20, 35
  Pathé-Frères, 20, 23, 24, 34, 44
  Vitagraph, 42
Film Supply Company, 52
Film within film, 218, 244, 350–353, 417,
  423–424, 527n
Films Valetta, 49, 53, 298, 336
Fils prodigue, Le, 1907, 246–247, 262, 277
Fischer, Lucy, 67, 488n
Folies-Bergère, 16, 19, 31, 72, 160, 228
Fontenay, Catherine, 201
Footit, Tommy, 216, 233
Footit and Chocolat, 87, 233
Forestier, Louis, 322, 324
Fosse, Paul, 371
Foucault, Michel, 6
Fouquet, l'homme au masque de fer, 1910,
  270, 277
France, Anatole, 179
France-Film, 54
François 1er et Triboulet, 1908, 296
Frankenstein, 365
French Colonial Exposition, 1906, 25
French Cops Learning English, 1908, 216
French law and cinema, xiv, 27–29, 34,
  57, 181–182
Freud, Sigmund, 352

Fromet, Marie, 321, 323, 338, 339
Fronde, La, 93
Fuller, Loïe, 359

Gab-Ka cinema, 30
Gable, Clark, 420
Galand, 38
Galipaux, Félix, 88, 220, 221, 491n
Gance, Abel, 48, 533n
Garavaglia, Ferrucio, 265
Garbagni, Paul, 49, 355
Gardien de la Camargue, 1909, 205
Garnier, Philippe, 261
Garnier, Robert Jules, 329, 376
Garry, Claude, 305, 307
Gasnier, Louis, 35, 52, 236, 237, 511n
  At the Cinematograph Theatre, 1910, 244
  Cheval emballé, Le, 1908, 221–222, 227, 233
  Conquête, Le, 1909, 237
  Perils of Pauline, 1914, 52, 367, 483n
  Petite Rosse, 1909, 237–238, 240, 245
  Roméo se fait Bandit, 1909, 237
  Servant's Good Joke, 1909, 513n
  Timidité vaincu, 1910, 239–240
  Tout est bien qui finit bien, 1910, 238–239
Gaudreault, André, xiv, 60, 74, 103
Gaulois, Le, 93
Gaumont, Léon, 10, 11, 13, 17, 19–20, 35, 58, 229
Gaumont et cie, xvii, 9, 11–13, 17, 19–20, 29, 31, 35–36, 37, 41, 44, 47, 48, 49–50, 51, 52, 53, 54, 57, 78, 91, 95, 102, 104, 109, 110, 111, 114, 137, 141–145, 160, 164–166, 179, 180, 184, 185, 188, 193, 195, 205, 206, 207, 213, 215–217, 219, 222–224, 229–232, 256–257, 262, 263, 264, 271–274, 277, 278, 280, 281, 286–289, 294, 298, 300, 301, 302, 319, 320, 325, 326, 328–334, 339, 342, 350–354, 358, 361, 364–365, 368–387, 388, 391, 395–397, 399, 402–407, 417–425, 430, 431, 500n, 501n
Gaumont Ltd, 19
Gaumont-Actualités, 36, 50
Gaumont-Palace, 7, 31, 47, 54, 55, 57, 58, 331, 334, 423
Gauthier, Louis, 345
Gavault, Paul, 39
Gavroche series, 51, 301, 390
  Gavroche au Luna-Park, 1912, 390–391
Gémier, Firmin, 21, 40

General Film Company, 44, 52
Genii of Fire, 1908, 296
Genres, xiv, xvii, 59–60
  actualités, 11, 13, 20, 21, 23, 25, 60, 61, 91–92, 105, 106, 107, 119, 125, 191, 223, 266, 491n, 497n, 498n
  animation films, 36, 278, 279–282, 286–289, 290, 473n
  comic films, 11, 19, 21, 23, 36, 60, 61, 87–91, 104, 109–117, 137–145, 156, 215–227, 234–235, 389–390, 511n
  comic series, 35, 36, 37, 39, 49, 50, 51, 180, 215–216, 227–245, 300–301, 388, 390–428
  crime melodramas, 358–387
  crime series, 50, 51, 298, 299
  dance films, 60, 78
  detective series, 38, 50, 180, 195–198, 354–358
  documentary, 36, 39, 50, 53, 57, 331, 346
  domestic melodramas, 21, 40, 49, 50, 51, 104, 109, 129–136, 151–156, 184–198, 206–211, 257, 298, 301, 326–354, 355
  dramatic and realist films, xiv, 21, 60, 61, 96–101, 104, 121–136, 161–162, 180, 181, 183, 301
  educational films, 35, 51, 57, 486n
  erotic films, 60, 104, 109, 117–119
  féeries, 13–14, 19, 21, 23, 35, 36, 61, 67–78, 81–87, 104, 105, 157–160, 170–178, 181, 278, 291–297, 361
  grand guignol melodramas, 97, 104, 132, 133, 150–151, 180, 184, 199–206, 210–211, 271, 301, 328, 341–342, 355, 359
  historical films, 14, 19, 21, 35, 36, 39–40, 43, 49, 50, 51, 57, 60, 61, 91–96, 105, 145–147, 162, 166–167, 181, 182, 248–256, 260–262, 267–277, 298, 299, 302–325, 355, 359, 518n
  newsreels, 35, 36, 37, 49, 50, 51, 57, 92
  oriental films, 256, 258–260, 277
  plein air films, 60
  publicity films, 13, 15, 16
  religious or biblical films, 36, 49, 57, 60, 61, 95, 162–166, 181, 182, 246–247, 248, 256–258, 262–264, 319–320
  sports films, 60
  synchronized sound films, 19, 47, 60
  trick films, 13–14, 19, 21, 35, 36, 60, 61, 61–67, 70, 78–81, 87, 156–157, 160–161, 167–169, 278–291, 296–297, 361

Genres (*continued*)
    vaudeville comedies, 425–427
    westerns, 37, 45, 50, 51, 180, 354, 479n
George Kleine Optical, 23, 35, 37, 44, 52
Gérard, Marc, 381
Gérôme, Jean-Léon, 271, 504n
Gerval, le maître de forges, 1912, 51, 344–345
Getting Square with the Inventor, 1910, 511n
Geveviève Brabant, 1907, 291
Gironde, La, 24
Glue Pot, 1907, 114, 115
Goethe, Johann Wolfgang von, 261
Gontran series, 39, 216, 301, 393, 427
    Gontran doute la fidelité de sa femme, 1912, 393–394
Gorby, 410, 413, 415
Gouget, Henri, 427
Gounod, Charles, 75, 76, 160, 515n
Gourmont, Rémy de, 129
Governess Wanted, 1907, 218
Grand, Georges, 268, 275
Grand Biorama, 59
Grand Café, 11, 15
Grand-père, 1910, 208–209, 210
Grandais, Suzanne, 49, 50, 333, 334, 335, 340, 350, 351, 368, 369, 419–421, 526n
Grande Bréteche, 1909, 267
Grandeur d'âme, 1910, 519n
Grands Films Artistiques, 41
Grands Films Populaires, 48, 54, 325
Gratitude obsédante, 1912, 392–393
Gravone, Gabriel de, 321
Greco-Roman classicism, 183, 256, 263, 318, 325
Grehan, René, 39, 216, 237, 301, 393
Grétillat, Jacques, 199, 200, 201
Griffith, D. W., 54, 105, 180, 184, 192, 195, 257, 274, 297, 329, 342, 346, 381, 533n
    Battle of Elderbush Gulch, 1913, 54
    Birth of a Nation, 1915, 381
    Cord of Life, 1909, 195
    Corner in Wheat, A, 1909, 192, 346
    Fatal Hour, 1908, 195
    Intolerance, 1916, 297
    Lonely Villa, 1909, 195, 507n
Grimoin-Sanson, Raoul, 17
Grivolas, Claude, 14
Grumbach, Jeanne, 318
Guégan, M., 28
Guêpe, La, 1910, 223

Guérin, 329, 371
Gugenheim, Eugène, 475n
Gugot, Henri, 365
Gui, Le, 1913, 531n
Guibbert, Pierre, 96
Guidé, Paul, 347, 523n
Guilhème, Jacques, 255
Guillaume Tell, 1903, 94
Guissart, René, 53
Guitty, Madeleine, 425
Gunning, Tom, xiv, 60, 91, 103, 104, 106, 109, 112, 117, 118, 150, 180, 195, 236, 494n
Guy, Alice, xvii, 11, 12, 19–20, 35, 52, 78, 87, 95, 141, 165, 166, 472n, 501n, 504n
    Assassinat du courrier de Lyon, 1904, 19
    Bébé embarrassant, 1905, 19
    Danse des saisons, 78
    Esmeralda, 1905, 20
    Guillaume Tell, 1898, 87
    Matelas alcoolique, 1906, 19, 141–142, 143
    Saut humidifié de M. Plick, 1900, 87
    Sur la barricade, 1907, 504n
    Vénus et Adonis, 78
    Vie de Christ, 1899, 95
    Vie du Christ, 1906, 20, 164, 165–166
Guyon, Cécile, 344, 346

Haggar, William, 109
    Desperate Poaching Affray, 1903, 109
Hallucinations du Baron de Münchhausen, 1911, 37, 278
Hamlet, 1907, 264
Hamman, Joë, 37, 50, 342, 354, 508n, 528n
Hansen, Kai, 43
Hansen, Miriam, 59, 60, 105, 431
Hatot, Georges, 11, 21, 37, 38, 39, 87, 91, 95
    Assassinat du Duc de Guise, L', 1897, 91
    Course à la perruque, 1906, 111
    Dix Femmes pour un mari, 1905, 21, 110
    Entrevue de Napoléon et du Pape, 1897, 91
    Execution de Jeanne d'Arc, 1897, 91
    Farces de Toto gâte-sauce, 1905, 114, 116
    Mort de Marat, 1897, 91–92
    Mort de Robespierre, 1897, 91
    Vie et la Passion de Jésus-Christ, 1897, 11, 95
Haugmard, Louis, 57
Hearst newspapers, 52
Heath, Stephen, 103

Héliogabale, 1910, 253, 255–256, 260, 277, 312

Hennique, Léon, 518n

Hepworth, Cecil, 116
   Rescued by Rover, 1905, 116, 497n

Herriot, Edouard, 364

Hervé, Jean, 317, 318

Hervieu, Paul, 334

Hervil, René, 51
   Fred series, 51
   Maud series, 51

Heuzé, André, 21, 35, 48, 49, 153, 495n
   Bossu, Le, 1913, 49, 54, 325

Hippodrome, 11, 20, 31

His First Cigar, 1908, 220–221, 241, 511n

His First Job, 1908, 216

Histoire d'un pantalon, 1906, 113

Historical painting tradition, 95–96, 166–167, 260, 271
   "Neo-Grec" historical painting, 247, 255, 504n

Histrionic Film Company, 51, 315

Hobsbawm, Eric, xiii, 1, 6

Hodel, P., 54

Hollandsche Film, 49, 338

Holmes, Sherlock, 107, 198, 241–242, 532n

Homme à la tête de caoutchouc, L', 1902, 63, 72, 87

Homme-mouche, L', 1902, 63

Homme-orchestre, L', 1900, 62–63

Hooligan Idea, A, 1907, 140–141

Horrors of a Strike, 1909, 193

Hôtel de la gare, 1914, 425

Hôtel des voyageurs de commerce, 1906, 160

Hôtel du silence, 1908, 281

How to Settle a Labor Dispute, 1910, 193

Howe, Lyman, 492n

Hugo, Victor, 49, 153, 299, 305, 308, 321, 322, 325

Hugon, André, 48, 409

Hurry Up Please, 1908, 218

Idler, The, 1908, 281

Idylle corinthienne, 1909, 263, 277

Ile de Calypso, L': Ulysse et Polyphème, 1905, 157

Illusions fantastiques, 1898, 13, 62

Illusions fundambulesques, 1903, 488n

Illustration, L', 6, 39, 91, 92, 280, 475n

Illustre Machefer, L', 1914, 425

In the Hands of the Enemy, 1907, 188, 195

In the Mirror, 1910, 507n, 526n

In the Realm of Terror, 1910, 274

Ince, Thomas, 48, 55
   Battle of Gettysburg, 1914, 55

Incendiaires, Les, 1906, 19, 161

Indiens et cow-boys, 1904, 26, 123–124, 125, 128, 129

Industriel forain, L', 19, 22, 24

Inlaid Floor Polisher, 1907, 144–145

Intelligent Waiter, 1901, 79

International Congress of Film Producers, 1909, 34, 45–46

Intrigante, L', 1911, 209–210

Inutile Sacrifice, L', 1911, 332

Iron Workers' Strike, 1910, 193

Irving, Washington, 157

Isle-Adam, Villiers de l', 496n
   Eve future, L', 1888, 496n

Isola brothers, 15, 16

Itala Film, 42, 43, 267
   Cretinetti or *Gribouille* series, 35, 237
   Ugolin, 1909, 267

Jack, 1913, 526n

Jack le ramoneur, 1906, 19, 161–162

Jacquinet, 206, 257, 345

Jalousie et folie, 1907, 502n

Jameson, Fredric, xvii

Janin, Géo, 49

Jasset, Victorin, xiii, 20, 37, 38, 39, 41, 51, 109, 165, 181, 183–184, 196, 246, 249, 262, 263, 270, 276, 277, 278, 280, 299, 329, 344, 346, 347, 358–363, 365–367, 387, 388, 517n
   Au pays des ténèbres, 1912, 51, 344
   Balaoo, 1913, 51, 365, 366
   Cercueil de verre, 1912, 51, 363, 364, 365, 366
   Dans les ruines de Carthage, 1910, 517n
   Docteur Phantom series, 38
   Fleur empoisonnée, La, 1909, 270–271, 272, 277
   Hériodiade, 1910, 39, 263
   Meskal le contrebandier series, 354
   Morgan le pirate series, 38
   Nick Carter series, 38, 180, 195–198, 199, 271, 354, 355, 358
   Protéa, 1913, 51, 367, 368
   Redemption, 1912, 361
   Resurrection de Lazare, 1910, 263
   Riffle Bill series, 38, 180, 354
   Tom Butler, 1912, 51, 57, 301, 363, 364
   Zigomar series, 299, 367, 368, 371, 373, 380, 387, 391, 406

Jaurès, Jean, 3, 5
Javault, J., 51
Jeanne d'Arc, 1900, 13, 492n
Jeteuse de sorts, 1907, 108, 109
Jim le glisseur, 1910, 282–283, 390
Joly, Henri Joseph, 14, 17, 37
Joseph vendu par ses frères, 1909, 262–263
Joubé, Romauld, 267, 317, 318
Jourjon, Charles, 38, 53
Journal, Le, 58, 88, 114, 242, 404
Journée de grève, 1909, 192
Joye Collection, National Film Archive, 507n
Joyeuses lavendières, 1905, 109

Kaiser, Gabriel, 16, 30
Kalem, 54
Karl, Roger, 363
Kastor, 42
Katorza, Charles and Schélmo, 24
Keaton, Buster, 116, 228, 406, 487n
    Cops, 1922, 116
Kemm, Jean, 338, 339
Keppens, Emile, 351, 368, 381, 382
Krauss, Charles, 39, 344, 360, 362, 523n
Krauss, Henry, 49, 275, 276, 305, 306,
    321–324, 335, 345
Kron-Lambert, 48

Laboratories
    Debrie: Paris, 47
    Eclair: Epinay-sur-Seine, 38–39, 345
    Eclair: Fort Lee, 53
    Gaumont: Buttes-Chaumont, 20
    Gaumont: Flushing, 52
    Pathé: Belleville, 20, 34
    Pathé: Blair, 45
    Pathé: Bound Brook, 44
    Pathé: Chatou, 14
    Pathé: Joinville-le-pont, 20, 46
    Pathé: Vicennes, 20
    Vitagraph: Paris, 42
Labrély, 472n
Lacassin, Francis, 78, 196, 215, 371
Lacépède, Etienne de, 38
Lacroix, Georges, 50, 331
    Chalands, Les, 1911, 331
Lafitte, Paul, 31, 39–40, 475n
Lagny, Michèle, 431
Lagrenée, Maurice, 381, 383
Lallement, 42
Lambert, Albert, 249, 252, 255
Lamy, Charles, 425

Langage des pieds, 1909, 220
Lange, Gabrielle, 407, 410, 412
Lanterne magique, 1903, 67, 81
Larry, Gaston, 52
Laurent, Jean-Marie, 381, 382
Lavendan, Henri, 39, 248
Lavendières, Les, 1910, 209
Lawyer Enjoys Himself, 1907, 501n
Le Bargy, Charles, 39–40, 249, 251, 253,
    514n
Le Bret, Suzanne, 378
Le Lion, 38, 506n, 508n, 517n
Le Somptier, René, 50
Léar, 16, 476n
Lectures pour tous, 6
Lefragette, Henri, 36
Légende de la fileuse, La, 1908, 521n
Légende de Polichinelle, La, 1907, 40, 293–
    294
Lemaître, Jules, 255
Lemoine, 47
Léonce series
    Epingles, Les, 1913, 419–420, 427
    Express matrimonial, L', 1911, 418–419,
        427
    Homard, Le, 1912, 419
    Léonce à la campagne, 1913, 421–423, 427
    Léonce cinématographiste, 1913, 423–424,
        427
    Léonce et Toto, 1913, 421, 427
    Léonce flirte, 1913, 420, 423
    Léonce pot au feu, 1913, 420–421, 423
Lepanto, Vittoria, 265
Lépine, Charles, 35, 43, 505n
    Effets du melon, Les, 1906, 23
    Fils du diable à Paris, 1906, 175, 176
    Grève des bonnes, 1906, 113
    J'ai perdu mon l'orgnon, 1906, 113, 116
    Un Jour de paye, 1906, 113
    Un Tour du monde d'un policier, 1906, 107–
        108, 109, 119
Leprince, René, 35, 49, 295, 300, 334, 335,
    410
    Coupable, La, 1912, 335–336, 337, 354,
        527n
    Miracle des fleurs, 1912, 295–296
    Pipe d'opium, 1912, 334–335, 336
    Scènes de la vie cruelle series, 49, 53, 326,
        334, 354, 361
Lerida, Mlle, 385
Leroux, Gaston, 365
Leubas, Louis, 381, 385
Levesque, Marcel, 425

Levesques, 260
Lèvres collées, 1906, 137
Leyda, Jay, 43, 430
Leygues, Georges, 183
Liabel, André, 51, 344, 358, 366
Library of Congress, 94
Lighting effects, 36, 165, 166, 170, 175,
    202, 210, 256, 259, 273–274, 276, 283,
    304, 308, 313, 319, 320–321, 328,
    329, 335, 343, 345, 350, 352, 358, 365,
    382, 385–386, 418, 422–423, 516n
Ligue d'enseignement, 3, 29, 42
Linder, Maud, 236
Linder, Max, 35, 49, 53, 137, 140, 141,
    151, 216, 217, 218–219, 220–221,
    226, 236–245, 278, 279, 293, 393,
    409–417, 421, 511n, 513n
    Max series, 35, 49, 180, 240–245, 301,
    388, 409–417, 424, 427
Linn, K. W., 52
Literary adaptations, 28–29, 39–41, 43,
    49, 50–51, 181–183, 246, 253–255,
    258, 261–262, 264–267, 268–269,
    302–325, 358–361, 365–367, 370–
    380, 425–427
Little Chimney Sweep, 1908, 185
Little Cripple, 1908, 187–188, 195
Little Moritz series
    Little Moritz aime Rosalie, 1911, 394–395
    Little Moritz chasse les grands fauves, 1911,
    391
    Little Moritz demande Rosalie en mariage,
    1911, 395
    Little Moritz enlève Rosalie, 1911, 531n
Little Mother, A, 1908, 506n
Little Tich, 88
Lo Savio, Gerolamo, 43
Löbel, Léopold, 37
Lorant-Heilbronn, 82, 125
    Regne de Louis XIV, 1905, 162
Lorde, André de, 51, 150, 193, 199
    Au Téléphone, 1902, 150, 193
Lordier, Georges, 48, 58
Lorsy, Paulette, 410, 412
Lubin, 14, 54, 109
    Meet Me at the Fountain, 1904, 109
Luguet, André, 376
Luguet, Maurice, 384–385
Luitz-Morat, 376, 378
Lumière, Louis, 10
Lumière et fils, 1, 9, 10–11, 13, 14, 15, 17,
    19, 21, 45, 46, 59, 87, 90, 91–92, 95,
    121, 216, 246, 248, 389, 429, 465n

Arroseur et arrosé, 1895, 87, 90, 216, 389
Repas de bébé, 1895, 91
Sortie des usines, 1895, 11
Lune à un mètre, 1898, 68, 70, 71
Lutetia-Wagram cinema, 55
Lutte pour la vie, 1907, 153
Lutte pour la vie, 1914, 526n
Lux, xvii, 37–38, 45, 51, 179, 180, 184,
    193, 209, 212, 216, 232, 294, 301, 341,
    354, 388, 392, 430, 431, 517n
Lyceum Theater, Chicago, 315

Ma Tante, 1903, 88, 89, 119
Machin, Alfred, 43, 49, 204, 338, 391,
    526n
    Ame des moulins, L', 1912, 49, 338
    Maudite soit la guerre, 1914, 49
    Moulin maudit, 1909, 204–205, 211, 212,
    338
    Nuit de Noël, 1908, 202–204, 338
    Or qui brule, L', 1912, 526n
Madame Tussaud's, 99
Maestro Do-Mi-Sol-Do, 1906, 161
Magicien, Le, 1898, 62
Magnier, Pierre, 336
Main de fer series
    Evasion de Forçat de Croze, L', 1913,
    369–370
    Main de fer, 1912, 302, 350, 364, 368–
    369, 381
    Main de fer contre la Bande aux 'Gents
    Blancs', 1912, 369
Maître, Maurice-André, 43, 320
    Vie et la Passion de N. S. J. C., 1914,
    319–320
Majestic cinema, 57
Malthête, Jacques, 63, 160, 487n
Man Who Walked on Water, 1908, 220
Manoir du diable, 1896–1897, 62
Manoussi, Jean, 50
Manson, Paul, 340
Marey, Etienne-Jules, 11
Mariage de raison, 1900, 96
Mariage enfantine, 1906, 138
Mariaud, Maurice, 50
Marie Antoinette, 1904, 94
Mariée du château maudit, 1910, 211–212
Marks, Martin, 505n
Martial, 378
Martyrs chrétiens, 1905, 162–163
Marx Brothers, 405
Mary, Charles, 49
Massard, Armand, 410, 412

Massart, Léontine, 308, 335, 337, 347, 348
Massenet, Jules, 70, 261, 263
Mater Dolorosa, 1910, 510n
Mathieu, Julienne, 284, 504n, 520n
Matin, Le, 358, 365
Matisse, Henri, 207
Mattress, The, 1908, 218
Maugras, E., 28
Maurice, Clément, 15, 17
Maurice, Georges, 37, 38
Maurras, Charles, 4
Mauvaise Mère, 1907, 151
Max, Edouard de, 48
Max series
    Ane jaloux, L', 1912, 412
    Débuts de Max Linder au cinématograph,
        1910, 244–245, 416, 423
    Joy of Tight Boots, 1910, 513n
    Mari jaloux, 1914, 416–417, 423, 427
    Max a un duel, 1911, 410–411
    Max en convalescence, 1911, 410
    Max et la doctoresse, 1914, 414–415,
        428
    Max et sa belle-mère, 1911, 532n
    Max et son chien Dick, 1912, 412
    Max hypnotise, 1910, 242–243
    Max Jockey par amour, 1912, 533n
    Max Linder contre Nick Winter, 1912, 412
    Max Maîtresse de piano, 1910, 513n
    Max n'aime pas le chats, 1913, 413–414,
        421, 428
    Max pédicure, 1914, 415–416, 427
    Max prend son bain, 1910, 243–244, 245
    Max reprend sa liberté, 1912, 411–412
    Max se trompe d'étage, 1910, 240–241
    Max veut grandir, 1912, 413
    Peintre par amour, 1912, 412–413
    Qui est l'assassin?, 1910, 241–242, 244
    Victime du quinquina, 1911, 411, 427
Maxudian, 315
May, Ernest, 37
Mayeur, Jean-Marie, 1, 3, 4
Mayne, Judith, 121, 494n
McCoy, Joseph, 44
Médor au téléphone, 1907, 139, 152, 175
Meisel, Martin, 96
Melchior, Georges, 372
Méliès, Gaston, xvii, 14, 19, 36–37, 473n
Méliès, Georges, xvii, 9, 10, 13–14, 15,
    16, 19, 20, 23, 24, 29, 35, 36–37, 39,
    44, 46, 61–78, 79, 81, 82, 84, 85,
    86–87, 90–91, 92–93, 97, 104, 156–
    162, 169, 170, 171, 179, 183, 184–

185, 216, 218, 228, 264, 278, 283, 286,
    296–297, 358, 359, 361, 473n, 488n
Mélomane, Le, 1903, 64
Menchen, Joseph, 48
Mendel, Georges, 16, 25
Ménessier, Henri, 20, 516n, 519n
Mercanton, Louis, 51, 317
Merchant of Venice, The, 317
Mérode, Cléo de, 13
Merry Wives of Windsor, The, 315
Merveilleux Eventeil vivant, 1904, 66
Mésaventures d'un artiste, 1903, 79–80
Mésaventures d'une mission nègre, 1907, 113–
    114, 116
Mesguisch, Felix, 11, 15, 37
Mesnery, 378
Messter, Oskar, 36
Metempsychose, 1907, 520n
Metz, Christian, 60
Mévisto, 211, 303, 345
Meyer, Arthur, 15, 93
Meyerbeer, Giacomo, 271
Michel, Louise, 121
    Strike, The, 1890, 121
Migé, Clément, 50, 216, 229, 402
Milano-Film, 41
    Enfer, L' or *Dante's Inferno*, 1910, 41,
        299, 308, 522n
Millet, Jean-François, 85, 341
Millions de la bonne, 1913, 425
Milo, 214–215, 321
Minerva Films, 48
Miracle de Noël, 1905, 164
Mireille, 1909, 508n, 515n
Mischances of a Photographer, 1908, 216
Mistinguett, 40, 49, 53, 184, 210, 214–
    215, 235, 321, 334, 532n
Mitron, Le, 1904, 26, 88
Mitry, Jean, 237
Mix, Tom, 54
Mix Up at Court, A, 1909, 511n
Modot, Gaston, 528n, 532n
Moïse sauvé des eaux, 1911, 256, 257, 319
Molière, 175, 416
    Malade imaginaire, 274
Monca, Georges, 35, 40, 49, 184, 235, 244,
    336, 354, 407, 510n
    Epouvante, L', 1911, 49, 214–215, 334,
        335, 336
    Petit Chose, 1912, 49, 336
    Rigadin series, 35, 49, 53, 180, 216, 235–
        236, 245, 301, 388, 407–409, 427
Monofilm, 41, 54

Monstre, Le, 1903, 66
Montanaro, Carlo, 279
Monteaux, Roger, 254
Moreau, Emile, 303, 315
Moreau, Gaston, 211
Moreau, Léon, 57
Moreau, R., 39
Morlhon, Camille de, 35, 40, 49, 184, 198,
    206, 211, 260, 274, 300, 311, 318, 326,
    336–338, 347–350, 354, 513n, 519n,
    522n
    Bon Patron, 1910, 40, 211
    Britannicus, 1912, 318–319, 320, 325
    Broyeuse de coeurs, 1913, 49, 336–338,
        347, 348, 350
    Cagliostro, 1910, 274–275, 276, 277
    Fleuriste de Toneso, 1913, 49, 347–348
    Madame Tallien, 1911, 519n
    Petite Policière, 1909, 198
    Roman de l'écuyère, 1909, 206–207
    Sacrifice surhumain, 1914, 348–350, 354
    Sémiramis, 1910, 260, 277, 311
    Une Conspiration sous Henri III, 1911,
        522n
    Une Intrigue à la cour d'Henry VIII, 1912,
        311
Mort de Saül, 1912, 319
Mort du Jules César, 1907, 264
Motion Picture Patents Company, 36,
    44–45, 430, 478n
Mottershaw, F. S., 109
    Daring Daylight Burglary, 1903, 109
Moulin Rouge, 31
Mounchaski, 271
Mounet, Paul, 254, 255, 264
Moving Picture World, 24, 36, 52, 54, 180,
    253, 264, 288, 305, 320, 342
Mozart, Wolfgang Amadeus, 271
Mundviller, Joseph, 43
Musée des Soverains, 1910, 520n
Musée Grévin, 15, 19, 30, 97, 158
Museum of Modern Art, 430
Musical accompaniment, 15, 17, 55, 57,
    70, 75, 78, 180, 233, 253–254, 261,
    263, 271, 325, 359, 371, 488n, 503n,
    505n, 525n
Musser, Charles, 22, 48, 61, 103, 109, 430,
    431, 467n, 494n
Mutual Films, 54
Mystères de Paris, 1912, 325

Nalpas, Louis, 50
Napierkowska, Stacia, 258, 259, 275, 276,
    296, 305, 307, 334, 335, 410, 412,
    533n
Narrative construction, 103–104, 148,
    149–150, 153–155, 181, 184, 186,
    195, 196, 201–202, 206–210, 213–
    215, 221–222, 226–227, 241–242,
    244, 248, 260–262, 271–272, 275–
    276, 299–300, 302–325, 332, 336,
    339, 346, 350–354, 356, 358–360,
    363, 366, 373, 377, 383–385, 387,
    427, 505n
Narrative voice, 105, 156, 180, 195, 201,
    204–205, 206, 207, 211, 213–214,
    246, 253, 255, 256–257, 260–262,
    277, 328, 329, 339, 340–341, 351–
    353, 385–386, 494n
Narrow Escape, A, 1908, 193–195, 198,
    207, 221
Nat Pinkerton series
    Cheveu d'or, 1912, 357–358
National Assembly, 27, 29
National Board of Censorship, 45, 204
National Film Archive, 376
Nationalist Revival movement, 4, 183,
    253, 277, 282, 289, 302, 401
Nau, Eugènie, 201, 303, 318, 321
Naudier, 372
Navarre, René, 50, 333, 350, 368, 371,
    372, 373, 380
Néron et Aggripine, 1914, 325, 525n
Nettoyeur de devantures, 1907, 138
New York Clipper, 22
New York Motion Picture Company, 48
Neyret, Jean, 14
Nick Carter series
    Club des suicides, 1909, 198
    Guet-Apens, 1908, 196
Nick Winter series, 301, 354, 355–357, 391
    Nick Winter et le rapt de Mlle Werner,
        1911, 356–357
    Nick Winter et le vol de "La Jocande,"
        1911, 357
    Nick Winter, la voleuse, et la somnambule,
        1911, 528n
    Pickpocket mystifié, 1911, 355–356
    Why Nick Winter Went to the Races, 1910,
        528n
Nielsen, Asta, 522n, 526n
Nihiliste, Le, 1906, 43, 145–146, 248
Noisy Neighbors, 1908, 512n
Nonguet, Lucien, 21, 35, 145, 244, 490n,
    501n, 506n
    Affaire Dreyfus, L', 1908, 193, 277

Nonguet, Lucien (*continued*)
  Assassinat du Grand-Duc Serge, 1905,
    145
  Chat botté, Le, 1903, 85–86, 94, 99
  Don Quichotte, 1903, 84–85, 94, 99
  Epopée napoléonienne, L', 1903, 21, 26,
    93–95, 99, 299, 325, 492n
  Inquisition, L', 1905, 163
  Révolution en Russie, 1905, 21, 119–120
Nordisk Films, 42
Not Guilty, 1908, 184–185
Nuit de carnaval, 1906, 499n
Numès, 39

Oberammergau passion play, 95
Obsession d'or, L', 1906, 174
Offenbach, Jacques, 70
Old Fool, 1908, 512n
Old Woodcutter, 1909, 185–186, 294
Olympia music hall, 16, 19, 31, 37. 70, 78,
    160
Omnia-Pathé cinema, 30, 31, 33, 34, 55,
    56, 334
Oncle Burton, 1909, 225, 227
Onésime series
  Disaparition d'Onésime, 1913, 532n
  Onésime a un duel à l'américaine, 1912,
    404–405
  Onésime aux enfers, 1912, 532n
  Onésime contre Onésime, 1912, 532n
  Onésime début au théâtre, 1913, 532n
  Onésime et le chien bienfaisant, 1912, 405
  Onésime et son âne, 1913, 405
  Onésime gentleman détective, 1912, 405–
    406, 427
  Onésime horloger, 1912, 406–407, 427
Opera, 75–76, 160, 182, 253, 254, 261,
    263, 264, 271
Opération chirugicale, 1905, 109, 288
Orbel, Lucy d', 410, 413, 414, 415

Pacitti, Mlle, 254
Palais de l'Art Nouveau, 59
Palais des mille et une nuits, 1905, 19, 157–
    158, 160
Papillon, Mlle Zizi, 67
Par le trou de la serrure, 1905, 118, 119
Parabol de l'enfant prodigue, 1911, 263–264
Parapluie fantastique, 1903, 66
Paris Exposition, 1889, 10
Paris Exposition, 1990, 1, 3, 11, 12, 17,
    54–55, 91, 93, 121
Paris Opéra, 78, 82

Parisiana cinema, 55
Parisiana music hall, 161
Parnaland, A.-F., 27, 38, 466n
Pascal, Andrée, 303, 336
Pascal, Yvonne, 345
Pasquali et cie, 42
Pathé, Charles, xvii, 9, 10, 14–15, 17, 20,
    25, 29, 33, 34, 41, 44, 45, 46, 47, 49,
    57, 58, 205, 244
Pathé, Emile, 10, 14, 20
Pathé, Théophile, 37, 218, 466n, 474n
Pathé-Eclectic, 367
Pathé-Exchange, 52
Pathé-Frères, xiii, xv, xvii, xviii, xix, 7, 9,
    10, 14–15, 16, 19, 20–27, 29–31,
    33–35, 36, 37, 39–41, 42–49, 52, 53,
    54, 55, 58, 59–61, 78–89, 90, 91–92,
    93–101, 102, 104–141, 144, 145–156,
    160, 161, 162–178, 179, 180, 182,
    183–211, 215–229, 234–245, 246–
    248, 249, 255, 257–258, 260, 262,
    265, 272, 274, 277, 278–280, 289–
    296, 298–302, 304, 305, 308–311,
    318–320, 325, 326–328, 334–336,
    338–339, 344, 345, 354–357, 358,
    361, 364–365, 371, 380, 387, 388–
    390, 391, 400, 407–417, 426, 429,
    430, 431, 477n, 478n, 479n, 480n,
    482n, 500n
  early intertitles, 85, 94, 95, 99, 104
  early letter inserts, 108, 115, 144, 154
  early title cards, 96, 117
  trademarks, 20, 34, 76, 99, 118, 125,
    137, 171, 501n, 533n
Pathé-Frères catalog, 1907, 20, 94, 171
Pathé-Frères catalog KOK, 1913, 94, 96
Pathé-Frères russe, 43, 53
  Lekhaim, 1911, 43
  Peter the Great, 1909, 43, 477n
  Princess Tarakanova, 1910, 43, 518n
Pathé-Journal, 35, 49
Pathé-Journal cinema, 55
Pathé-Palace, 55, 334
Pathé-Weekly, 52
Patouillard or *Bill* series, 38, 216, 232–233,
    245
  Bill as a Boxer, 1910, 232–233
  Bill Pays His Debts, 1911, 233
  Patouillard amoureux, 1910, 233
  That Horse Did Run, 1911, 233
Paul, R. W., 59
Paulin, Gaston, 15
Pearson, Roberta, 264

Pêche miraculeuse, 1902, 79
Pêcheur des perles, 1907, 291–292
Peeping Tom, 1901, 118
Peerless Pictures, 53
Peintre et modèle, 1902, 117
Peinture animée, 1903, 78, 80
People's Institute, 45
Periodization schema, xv, xviii–xix, 7, 9
Perret, Léonce, 36, 50, 55, 57, 213, 258,
    274, 300, 301, 326, 328, 339–342,
    351–354, 368–370, 380–388, 395–
    396, 417–424, 432, 508n, 527n
    Amour qui tue, L', 1911, 328
    Coeur et l'argent, 1912, 340–341, 354
    Comment on les garde, 1911, 417–418,
        420
    Comment on les prend, 1911, 417, 418
    Enfant de Paris, L', 1913, 50, 57, 380,
        381–384, 530n
    Eugène amoureux, 1911, 395–396, 423
    Leçon d'amour, 1912, 396
    Léonce series, 50, 301, 388, 417–424, 428
    Main de fer series, 368–370, 371, 380,
        387
    Mystère des Roches de Kador, 1912, 50, 57,
        351–353, 354, 364, 365, 369, 384
    Obsession du souvenir, 1913, 527n
    Roman d'un mousse, 1914, 50, 55, 380,
        384–387
    Sur les rails, 1912, 341–342, 354
    Vertige, Le, 1910, 213–214, 340, 510n
    Vie de Molière, 1910, 274, 277
Perret "style," 340–342, 381–383, 385–
    387, 388, 419–423, 527n
Perrier, Jean, 340, 381, 533n
Perruque, La, 1905, 112–113, 114
Petit Echo de la mode, 333
Petit Français Illustré, 87
Petit Journal, 6, 16, 18, 91, 129, 150
Petit Parisien, 6, 24, 129, 150
Petit Poucet, 1909, 291
Petit, Adrien, 385
Petit, Valentin, 50, 369, 418, 421–423
Petite Aveugle, 1907, 152–153
Petite Rosse, La, 237–238, 240
Petits Vagabonds, 1905, 110, 115, 116
Petronille series, 51, 390
    Petronille gagne le Grand Steeple, 1912,
        391
Phono-Ciné-Gazette, xiii, 20, 23, 25, 29, 33,
    108, 246, 280, 467n
Phono-Cinéma-Théâtre, 12, 17
Phonography, 10, 12, 14, 20, 391–392

Photography, 10, 17, 91, 92, 94, 207–210,
    332, 336
Pied du mouton, 1907, 521n
Pierre, Emile, 37
Pilules du diable, 64
Pinel, Vicent, 46
Pinto, Edouard, 393
Pirates, The, 1907, 188–190, 195
Pirou, Eugène, 16
Pitou amoureux, 1906, 138
Pixerécourt, 157
Plaissetty, René, 48
Planche, La, 1907, 218
Poirier, Léon, 50
Polycarpe series
    Trouvaille de Polycarpe, 1913, 393
Polyte series, 390
    Polyte escalve de la consigne, 1912, 390
Poor Pig, 1907, 110–111, 112, 116
Populaire cinema, 24
Pordenone Silent Film Festival, xiv, 429
Porter, Edwin S., 280, 494n
Portrait mystérieux, 1899, 62
Possession de l'enfant, 1909, 509n
Pouctal, Henri, 40, 50, 57, 261, 302, 523n
    Alibi, L', 1914, 50
    Camille Desmoulins, 1911, 40, 54, 523n
    Maître de forges, 1913, 50
    Trois Mousquetaires, 1913, 50, 54, 57,
        302, 325, 380
    Werther, 1910, 40, 261–262, 277, 516n
Poudre de valse, 1911, 234
Pour un collier!, 1907, 150–151, 156, 180
Poyen, René, 50, 399
Pradier, Pierre, 336
Pré, Renée, 206
Premier Cigare du collegien, 1903, 26, 88,
    220
Première Sortie, 1905, 220, 236, 511n
Presse, La, 393
Prévat, Suzanne, 381, 382
Prince, Charles, 35, 40, 184, 216, 235–
    236, 407, 411
Promio, Alexandre, 11, 37, 474n
Puccini, Giacomo, 253
Puvis de Chavannes, 260

Quatre Cent Coups du diable, 158
Quatre Cent Farces du diable, 1906, 19, 158–
    159

Racine, 318
Radios Films, 37, 38

Raid Paris-Monte Carlo en deux heures, 1905,
    19, 157, 502n
Raleigh & Robert, 29, 38, 41
Ramoneur et patissier, 1903, 26, 89
Ravel, Gaston, 50
Ravet, 303
Raynal, Maurice, 378
Reade, Charles, 201, 508n
Rearick, Charles, 1, 7
Rebérioux, Madeleine, 1, 3, 4
Reception of films, xviii, 60–61, 78, 99,
    101, 107, 108, 118, 120, 136, 148, 156,
    301–302, 514n, 525n, 534n
Reine Elisabeth, La, 315
Réjane, Gabrielle, 13, 36, 312–313
Rembrandt de la rue Lepic, 1911, 223–224
Renoir, Jean, 236
Renouard, Jane, 411–412, 413
Repos impossible, 1909, 512n
Retour de Colombine, 1909, 294–295
Reuver, Germaine, 407, 408
Revanche de l'enfant, 1906, 130–131, 147
Rêves d'agent, 1908, 282, 283
Rêve de Dranem, 1904, 88
Rêve de l'horloger, 1904, 488n
Rêve de Noël, 1900, 68–69, 70, 71
Rêve du maître de ballet, 1903, 66
Rêve d'une féministe, 1909, 224
Rêve et réalité, 1901, 88
Reynaud, Emile, 15, 466n, 491n
    Autour d'une cabine, 15
    Pauvre Pierrot, 15
Riblet, Doug, 112
Ricardi, Re, 43
Riche, Daniel, 35, 338
Richébé family, 24
Richesse d'un jour, 1906, 120–121
Rigadin series
    Docteresse, La, 1911, 532n
    Negre blanc, 1910, 236, 513n
    Nex de Rigadin, 1911, 407–408
    Rigadin avale son ocarina, 1912, 408
    Rigadin, défenseur de la vertu, 1912, 409,
        427
    Rigadin et la baguette magique, 1912, 408
    Timidités de Rigadin, 1910, 235
Rip Van Winkle, 1905, 157
Robert-Houdin Théâtre, 10, 13, 15, 62, 70
Robinne, Gabrielle, 49, 249, 252, 275, 334,
    336
Robinson, David, 228, 388
Roch, Madeleine, 257, 258, 259, 260, 311
Roi du maquillage, 1904, 64

Rollini, G., 21, 35, 394, 412, 506n
Romain, Mlle, 315
Roman d'amour, 1904, 99
    Roman d'un malheureux, 1908, 186, 187,
        195
Rosalie series
    Rosalie et sa phono, 1911, 391–392
    Rosalie et ses meubles fidèles, 1911, 531n
Rostand, Edmond, 5, 525n
    Aiglon, L', 1900, 5
Roudès, Gaston, 37, 50
    Arizona Bill series, 50, 354, 528n
    Nat Pinkerton series, 50, 301, 357–358
Roussel, Arthur, 47, 52
Roussel, Henry, 39, 345, 427
    Ame du bronze, L', 1918, 345
Royaume des fées, 1903, 73–75, 157, 158
Ruse de mari, 1907, 140, 141, 224

Sacre de Napoléon, Le, 94, 96
Sadoul, Georges, 9, 23, 87, 99, 101, 228,
    240, 333, 344, 381
Saint-Denis cinema, 33
Saint-Saëns, Camille, 490n, 514n
Sales Company, 45, 53, 54
Salle à manger fantastique, 1898, 62
Salle Charras, 39
Salle des Capucines, 15
Salt, Barry, xiv, 102, 116, 489n
Sanders, Willy, 39, 301, 398
Sardou, Victorin, 181, 253, 258, 312, 519n
Sartre, Jean-Paul, xviii, 7, 298, 301
Satan en prison, 1907, 296–297
Satyre de bois-joli, 1909, 512n
Saucisse mystèrieuse, 1913, 389–390
Savada, Elias, 279
Sazie, Léon, 51, 358, 365, 367
SCAGL, xvii, 40–41, 45, 46, 49, 53, 96,
    179, 182, 183, 184, 199–202, 214,
    235, 246, 267–270, 272, 277, 298,
    299, 302–308, 321, 322, 336, 344
Scala music hall, 31
Scenarios, 48, 262, 300, 331, 329, 354, 381,
    384, 407, 431, 463n
Scènes de la vie telle qu'elle est series
    Destin des mères, 1912, 333–334, 354
    Nain, Le, 1912, 335
    Roi Lear au village, 1911, 330–331
    Tare, La, 1911, 41, 331–333, 336, 351,
        354, 358, 359, 373
    Vipères, Les, 1911, 329–330, 332, 354
Schiller, Friedrich von, 254
Schlupmann, Heidi, 156

Schwartz, Maurice, 216, 301, 391, 394
Scientia series, 51
Sckramson, Charles, 59
Secret Incident in Life of Marie Antoinette,
    1910, 274
Select Cinéma Saint-Denis, 15
Selig, 54, 367
    Adventures of Dolly, 1913–1914, 367
Sentimental Wife, 1909, 507n
Sentinelle endormie, 94
Sept Péchès capitaux, 1910, 516n
Série d'Art (Eclipse), 41
Séries d'Art Pathé-Frères, xvii, 40, 184,
    258
Servaes, Ernest, 37, 51, 216, 301, 390
    Arthème series, 37, 51, 216, 301, 390
    Polycarpe series, 51, 393
Sévérin, 295, 521n
Séverine, Mme, 93
Shakespeare, William, 183, 237, 258, 264–
    267, 315, 317–318, 330, 517n
Shelley, Mary, 365
Short-Sighted Cyclist, 1907, 113
Signalement, Le, 1912, 338–339
Signoret, Gabriel, 254, 318
Sirène, La, 1904, 66–67
Smalley, Phillip, 215
    Suspense, 1913, 215
Société de cinématographe automobile, 34
Société des Amis de Fantômas, 371
Société des auteurs et compositeurs, 57
Société des Films Azur, 48
Société des gens de lettres, 40
Société du film négatif, 38
Société Establissements L. Aubert, 41–42,
    48, 54, 55, 179, 298, 388, 425–426,
    430
Société française de photographie, 13
Société française des auteurs dramatiques,
    40
Société populaire des beaux-arts, 29, 42
Soirées de Paris, Les, 371
Solax, 52
Soleillade, Albert, 206
Sontag, Susan, 208
Sorel, Cecile, 253
Sorgius, Albert, 516n, 519n, 524n
Soubrette ingénieuse, 1903, 79
Sound cues, 131, 135, 147, 185, 214
Souvestre, Pierre, 370, 371
Specht, Georges, 340, 368, 381, 424, 533n
Staging-in-depth, 164, 182–183, 249, 254,
    256, 257, 259, 260, 263, 264, 265, 268,

271–273, 275–276, 300, 304, 306–
    307, 309–310, 312, 314, 316, 318,
    320–321, 323, 325, 328, 329–334,
    335–336, 344–349, 350–353, 374–
    376, 381–382, 385–386, 418, 506n
Staiger, Janet, xiv, 22, 48, 430, 431, 467n
Star system, 35, 182, 210–211, 227, 236,
    240, 249–250, 264–265, 277, 300–
    301, 305, 308, 312, 322, 334, 371, 373,
    410, 484n
Star-Film, 13–14, 19, 216, 217
Starace, Gino, 370
Steinheil, Marguerite, 206
Stepmother, The, 1907, 502n
Strong Arm of the Law, 1905, 110, 111
Studios
    Aubert: Joinville (rue des Réservoirs), 48
    Eclair: Epinay-sur-Seine, 38–39
    Eclair: Fort Lee, 52, 53
    Eclair: Tucson, 53
    Eclipse: Courbevoie, 37
    Film d'Art: Neuilly, 39
    Gaumont: Buttes-Chaumont, 20, 35, 38
    Gaumont: Victorine, Nice, 49
    Lux: Gentilly, 38, 48
    Méliès: Montreuil, 13–14, 36, 37, 93,
        160, 216
    Menchen: Epinay-sur-Seine, 48
    Pathé: Edendale, 52
    Pathé: Jersey City, 45, 52, 53
    Pathé: Joinville-le-pont, 20, 34
    Pathé: Montreuil, 20, 34, 125
    Pathé: Nice, 34, 35
    Pathé: Vincennes, 14–15, 21, 34, 49
    Radios: Boulogne-sur-Seine, 37, 51
    SCAGL: Vincennes, 40, 49
Surrealists, 289, 291
Sylvie, Mlle, 318, 345
Syndicat française des directeurs de ciné-
    matographes, 58

Talbot, Frederick, 280, 518n, 521n
Tallandier, Jules, 49
Talmeyr, Maurice, 1
Taming of the Shrew, 1911, 266, 420
Taxil, Léo, 371
Tellegen, Lou, 314, 315
Temps, Le, 400
Tentation de Saint Antoine, 1898, 65
Terrible Angoisse, 1906, 150, 193
Théâtre Ambigu, 21, 22
Théâtre Châtelet, 19, 21, 64, 158, 160,
    167, 228

Théâtre de la Renaissance, 51
Théâtre de la République, 35
Théâtre des Variétés, 29, 30, 39, 167, 235
Théâtre du Grand Guignol, 51, 150, 199, 206
Théâtre du Gymnase, 19
Théâtre Libre, 150, 518n
Théâtre Odéon, 37, 39, 51
Théâtre Réjane, 312
Théâtre Saint-Denis, 15
Théâtre Trianon, 29
Théâtro-Films, 41, 518n
Thiberville, Anatole, 11, 280
Third Republic
    class, 20–21, 85, 97–98, 99, 106–107,
        120, 121–123, 125, 127, 132–133,
        141, 143, 145, 151, 152, 153, 178, 185,
        186, 191–192, 193–194, 196–197,
        199, 201, 206–207, 209, 211–215,
        218–219, 222, 228, 229, 234, 235,
        236–237, 240, 242–243, 270–271,
        275–276, 326–327, 332–334, 344–
        347, 365, 370, 380–381, 384–385,
        389–390, 392–394, 400–401, 404,
        405, 410–424
    colonialism, xiii, 1, 2, 4, 23, 25, 46, 50,
        72, 82, 91, 107–108, 113–114, 116,
        158, 232–233, 247, 256, 273–274,
        283, 334–335, 381
    economy, 1–3, 23, 27, 120, 470n
    education, 3–4, 42, 57, 96
    gender, 65–70, 81, 82, 88, 90, 99, 118,
        129–130, 133, 134–135, 141, 151,
        154–156, 163, 166, 169–170, 186–
        187, 193, 202, 204, 209–210, 212–
        215, 219–220, 224–225, 234, 235,
        238, 240, 247–248, 255–260, 270–
        271, 275–276, 283–286, 288, 290–
        291, 294–295, 329, 332–338, 340–341,
        347–354, 363, 365, 367, 381–387,
        388, 396, 410–424, 427, 464n, 507n,
        521n
    generation, 83–84, 86, 89, 114, 139–
        140, 153–154, 185–188, 193, 208–
        210, 216–217, 221, 225, 231–232,
        333–335, 336, 338–339, 340, 380–
        387, 388, 389, 396–400
    imperialism, xiii, 1, 2, 4, 23, 25, 43–46,
        106, 107–108, 120, 188, 256, 258,
        263, 369, 381, 385
    mass culture, 6–7, 15–17, 25, 30–31,
        59, 70, 91, 95, 105, 195–196, 333,
        358, 364–365, 370

politics, 2–3, 91, 92–93, 107–108, 119–
    120, 127, 183, 193, 216, 270, 311
race/ethnicity, 65, 88, 106–107, 108,
    113–114, 149, 197–198, 232–233,
    236, 266, 283, 285
region, 89, 131, 188, 202–205, 213–214,
    232, 384–385
social relations, xvi, 3–7, 64–65, 87,
    92–93, 101, 105, 129–130, 136, 206,
    207, 210, 217, 227, 245, 277, 294, 297,
    301–302, 305, 308, 313, 314–315,
    329, 353–354, 358, 361, 364–365,
    376, 387–388, 407, 427–428, 497n
Thompson, Kristin, xiv, 52, 102, 431, 505n
Thousand and One Nights, 81, 175
Three Neighbors, 1909, 509n
Tie That Binds, 1911, 327
Tissot, James, 165, 264, 503n, 517n
Tivoli cinema, 55, 334
Tom Pouce suite une femme, 1910, 234–235
Tom Tight et Dum Dum, 1903, 90
Tommy series, 216, 233–234
    Tommy étrenne son cor de chasse, 1911,
        233–234
Tonnerre de Jupiter, 1903, 488n
Tommy in Society, 1907, 139–140, 144
Tormented by His Mother-in-law, 1908, 278,
    279
Toto fait de la peinture, 1907, 114, 115, 116
Toulet, Emmanuelle, 17, 215, 431
Tour de Nesle, 1909, 267
Tourneur, Maurice, 51, 53, 382, 426–427,
    432, 527n
    Corso rouge, 1914, 527n
    Dame de Monsoreau, 1913, 51
    Figures de cire, 1912, 51
    Gaîtés de l'escadron, 1913, 51, 388, 426–
        427
    Wishing Ring, 1914, 53
Tout est bien qui finit bien, 238, 239
Trans-Oceanic Films, 54
Traveling on the Cheap, 1907, 278–279
Trésors de Satan, 1902, 65
Tréville, Georges, 303
Trimbach, Pierre, 49, 324
Tripot clandestin, Le, 1905–1906, 160–161
Trocadéro Théâtre, 29
Trois Mannequins, 1909, 217
Troubles of a Grass Widower, 533n
Tunnel sous la manche, 1907, 36, 297

Umès, Arlette d', 238
Un Attentat sur la voie ferrée, 1906, 500n

Un Coup d'oeil par étage, 1904, 26, 119, 121
Un Drame dans les airs, 1904, 26, 106, 119, 121
Un Drame en express, 1906, 133–134, 207
Un Homme de tête, 1898, 62
Un Maleur n'arrive pas jamais seule, 1903, 90–91
Un Match enragé, 1909, 226–227
Un Monsieur qui a mangé du taureau, 1909, 222–223
Une Belle-mère collante, 1910, 234
Une Bonne Histoire, 1903, 88
Une Dispute, 1900, 88
Une Maison bien lavée, 1912, 389
Une Nuit agitée, 1907, 512n
Unik, Pierre, 24
Universal, 48, 53, 54, 215, 300
   Traffic in Souls, 1913, 300
Urban, Charles, 14, 93
Urban Trading, 27, 37
Uricchio, William, 264

Valse excentrique, 1903, 78
Van Langendonck, 59
Vandal, Marcel, 38
Velle, Gaston, 21, 35, 43, 167, 168, 169, 278, 293, 295, 504n
   Album merveilleuse, L', 1905, 168
   Amour de page, 1910, 278
   Amoureux ensorcelé, 1905, 26, 167
   Barbe-bleue, 1910, 293
   Cartes lumineuses, 1905, 118–119
   Cascades de feu, 1905, 168
   Cauchemar de Pierrot, 1911, 295
   Dénicheurs d'oiseaux, 1904, 26, 122, 124, 128, 129
   D'Ou vient-il?, 1905, 167
   Effet de l'orage, L', 1906, 127–128, 129
   Fée aux fleurs, 1905, 26, 167–168
   Metamorphose du papillon, 1904, 80–81
   Metamorphoses du roi de pique, 1903–1904, 80
   Paravent mystérieux, 1904, 80
   Peine du talon, 1905, 168–169
   Petite Bergère, 1910, 293
   Petite Blanche-Neige, 1910, 293
   Poule aux oeufs d'or, 1905, 21, 171–174, 175, 244, 504n
   Poule phenomène, 1905, 167
   Rêve à la lune, 1905, 21, 26, 171, 288
   Rose d'or, 1910, 278
   Ruche merveilleuse, 1905, 26, 168
   Voyage autour d'une étoile, 1906, 174–175

Vengéance de concierge, 1912, 389
Vengéance de nègre, 1906, 113
Vengéance du forgeron, 1907, 188
Ventura, Marie, 321, 322
Vercingétorix, 1909, 267
Verdi, Giuseppe, 254
Verhylle, Armand, 35
Verne, Jules, 70, 77, 529n
Vernet, Horace, 96
Veyre, Gabriel, 11
Vibert, Marcel, 344
Vie de Moïse, 1905, 163
Vie drole series, 388, 425
Vie d'un joueur, 1903, 99
Vie et Passion du Christ, 1900, 95
Vigo, Jean, 331
   Atalante, L', 1933, 331
Vinot, Marthe, 399
Violet, Emile, 50
Visite sous-marine du 'Maine,' 1898, 92
Vitagraph, 24, 29, 42, 44, 54, 104, 179, 183, 184, 246, 264, 267, 280, 281, 327, 329, 359, 484n, 500n, 514n
   Antony and Cleopatra, 1908, 264
   Francesca de Ramini, 1908, 514n
   Haunted Hotel, 1907, 42, 280
   Julius Caesar, 1908, 264
   King Lear, 1909, 264
   Macbeth, 1908, 264
   Merchant of Venice, 1908, 264
   Richard III, 1908, 264
   Romeo and Juliet, 1908, 264
   Scènes muettes de la vie réele, 42, 328
   Washington, 1909, 267
Vlaminck, Maurice de, 353
Volbert, 372
Voleur de bicyclettes, 1906, 111
Voleur invisible, 1909, 520n
Volny, Auguste, 311
Volny, Jacques, 312, 313
Vot' permis? Viens l'chercher! 1905, 110, 115
Voyage à travers l'impossible, 1904, 19, 77–78, 157, 489n
Voyage dans la lune, 1902, 14, 70, 71–73, 74, 77, 292
Voyage irréalisable, 1906, 113
Voyages de Gulliver, 1902, 283
Vues d'espagne en cartes postales, 1907, 207

Wagenknecht, Edward, 24, 179
Waif, The, 1908, 185
Waldeck, Rousseau, René, 10
Warwick Trading Company, 14, 93

Weber, Eugen, 236
Wells, H. G., 70, 520n
Western Imports/Jacques Haik, 54, 484n
White, Pearl, 52
White Heather, 1987, 97
Why That Actor Was Late, 1908, 218
Williams, Alan, 10
Williams, Linda, 62, 67, 488n
Williams, Raymond, xviii
Willy series
    Trois Willys, 1913, 398
    Willy et le prestidigitateur, 1912, 398
    Willy et les Parisiens, 1913, 398–399
Winter, Georges, 355
Wizard of Oz, 1939, 235
Wonderful Hair Restorer, 1903, 79, 121
Wonderful Mirror, 1908, 284–285
World Pictures, 53
World Special, 53
Would-Be-Juggler, 1908, 226, 237

Young Aviator's Dream, A, 1910, 521n
Young Deer, James, 52

Zecca, Ferdinand, 14–15, 21, 22, 23, 35,
    41, 47, 81–82, 88, 97–98, 171, 490n,
    504n
    Ali-Baba, 1901–1902, 81–82, 83, 87
    Au bagne, 1905, 1906, 125, 127, 152,
        163, 185
    Au pays noir, 1905, 21, 125–127, 163,
        346
    Automobile et le cul-de-jatte, 1905, 112
    Brigandage moderne, 1905, 123, 124, 128,
        134
    Créations renversantes, 1905, 167
    Fée des roches noires, 1902–1903, 82–83

Fée printemps, 1902–1903, 26, 82, 83–
    84, 87, 164
Grève, La, 1904, 26, 121–122, 123, 192,
    497n
Histoire d'un crime, 1901, 14, 27, 97–99,
    121, 125, 150, 493n
Honneur d'un père, L', 1905, 21, 127,
    128–129, 130
Incendiaire, L', 1905, 106–107, 108
Remords, Le, 1905, 123, 136
Samson et Delila, 1903, 82, 83
Sept Chateaux du diable, 1902–1903, 82,
    83
Un Drame au fond de la mer, 1901, 96–97,
    150
Vendetta, 1905, 123
Victimes de l'alcoolisme, 1902, 14, 15, 99–
    101, 121
Vie et la Passion de Jésus-Christ, 1903, 95,
    99, 299
Vie et la Passion de N. S. J. C., 1907,
    164–166, 175
Zigomar series
    Zigomar, 1911, 41, 358–359, 366
    Zigomar, contre Nick Carter, 1912, 51,
        359–362, 366, 482n, 528n
    Zigomar, peau d'anguille, 1913, 51, 366–
        367, 369
Zigoto series, 50, 391
    Zigoto toreador, 1912, 391
Zola, Emile, 3, 10, 99, 201, 212, 326, 344,
    345, 346, 347
    Assomoir, L', 99
    Bête humaine, La, 212
    Germinal, 344
Zukor, Adolphe, 51, 315

Designer: Sandy Drooker
Compositor: G&S Typesetters, Inc.
Text: Bembo
Display: Bembo, Egyptienne Bold Condensed
Printer: Malloy Lithographing, Inc.
Binder: John H. Dekker & Sons